Computers and Their Applications

FOURTH EDITION

COMPUTERS AND THEIR APPLICATIONS

FOURTH EDITION

CHARLES S. PARKER

The College of Santa Fe, New Mexico

The Dryden Press
Harcourt Brace College Publishers

Fort Worth Philadelphia San Diego New York Orlando Austin San Antonio
Toronto Montreal London Sydney Tokyo

To Mom and Dad

Publisher	Elizabeth Widdicombe
Executive Editor	Richard J. Bonacci
Developmental Editor	Elizabeth Hayes
Project Editor	Michele Tomiak
Art Director	Beverly Baker
Senior Production Manager	Erin Gregg
Photo Editor	Steven Lunetta
Marketing Manager	Scott Timian
Director of Editing, Design, and Production	Diane Southworth
Project Management	Elm Street Publishing Services, Inc.
Compositor	Monotype Composition Company, Inc.
Text Type	11/12 Bodoni Book
Cover Image	Jack Zeman

Address for Editorial Correspondence
The Dryden Press, 301 Commerce Street, Suite 3700, Fort Worth, TX 76102

Address for Orders
The Dryden Press, 6277 Sea Harbor Drive, Orlando, FL 32887
1-800-782-4479, or 1-800-433-0001 (in Florida)

ISBN: 0-03-007533-5

Library of Congress Catalog Number: 94-071560

Printed in the United States of America

4 5 6 7 8 9 0 1 2 3 032 9 8 7 6 5 4 3 2 1

The Dryden Press
Harcourt Brace College Publishers

THE DRYDEN PRESS SERIES IN INFORMATION SYSTEMS

Arthur Andersen & Co./Flaatten, McCubbrey, O'Riordan, and Burgess
Foundations of Business Systems
Second Edition

Arthur Andersen & Co./Boynton and Shank
Foundations of Business Systems: Projects and Cases

Anderson
Structured Programming Using Turbo Pascal: A Brief Introduction
Second Edition

Brown and McKeown
Structured Programming with Microsoft BASIC

Coburn
Beginning Structured COBOL

Coburn
Advanced Structured COBOL

Dean and Effinger
Commonsense BASIC: Structured Programming with Microsoft QuickBASIC

Federico
WordPerfect 5.1 Primer

Forcht
Management Information Systems: A Casebook

Goldstein Software, Inc.
Joe Spreadsheet, Macintosh Version

Goldstein Software, Inc.
Joe Spreadsheet, Statistical

Gray, King, McLean, and Watson
Management of Information Systems
Second Edition

Harrington
Database Management for Microcomputers: Design and Implementation
Second Edition

Harris
Systems Analysis and Design: A Project Approach

Head
Introduction to Programming with QuickBASIC

Janossy
COBOL: An Introduction to Software Engineering

Laudon and Laudon
Information Systems: A Problem-Solving Approach
Third Edition

Laudon and Laudon
Information Systems: A Problem-Solving Approach
(A CD-ROM interactive version)

Laudon, Laudon, and Weill
The Integrated Solution

Lawlor
Computer Information Systems
Third Edition

Liebowitz
The Dynamics of Decision Support Systems and Expert Systems

McKeown
Living with Computers
Fifth Edition

McKeown
Working with Computers
Second Edition

McKeown
Working with Computers with Software Tutorials
Second Edition

McKeown and Badarinathi
Applications Software Tutorials: A Computer Lab Manual Using WordPerfect 5.1, Lotus 1-2-3, dBASE III PLUS and dBASE IV

McKeown and Leitch
Management Information Systems: Managing with Computers

McLeod
Systems Analysis and Design: An Organizational Approach

Martin
QBASIC: A Short Course in Structured Programming

Martin and Burstein
Computer Systems Fundamentals

Mason
Using IBM Microcomputers in Business: Decision Making with Lotus 1-2-3 and dBASE III Plus/dBASE IV

Millspaugh
Business Programming in C for DOS-Based Systems

O'Brien
The Nature of Computers
Second Edition

Parker
Computers and Their Applications
Fourth Edition

Parker
Understanding Computers & Information Processing: Today and Tomorrow
Fifth Edition

Parker
Understanding Computers & Information Processing: Today and Tomorrow with BASIC
Fifth Edition

Robertson and Robertson
Microcomputer Applications and Programming: A Complete Computer Course with DOS, WordPerfect 5.1, Lotus 1-2-3, dBASE III PLUS (or dBASE IV) and BASIC

Robertson and Robertson
Using Microcomputer Applications (A Series of Computer Lab Manuals)

Simpson and Tesch
Introductory COBOL: A Transaction-Oriented Approach

Sullivan
The New Computer User

Swafford and Haff
dBASE III PLUS

Thommes and Carey
An Introduction to CASE Tools with Visible Analyst (DOS)
Using CASE Tools with Visible Analyst (Windows)

Electronic Learning Facilitators, Inc.
- The DOS Book
- The Lotus 1-2-3 Book
- Stepping Through Excel 4.0 for Windows
- Stepping Through Windows 3.1
- Stepping Through Word 2.0 for Windows
- Up and Running with Harvard Graphics 1.03 for Windows
- Up and Running with PageMaker 5.0 for Windows
- Up and Running with WordPerfect 5.2 for Windows
- Up and Running with Quattro Pro 1.0 for Windows
- Up and Running with Microsoft Works 2.0 for Windows
- Up and Running with Lotus 1-2-3 Release 4 for Windows
- Up and Running with Paradox 4.5 for Windows
- Up and Running with DOS 6.0
- Up and Running with Paradox 4.0 for DOS

Up and Running with Microsoft Works 3.0 for DOS
Up and Running with Excel 4.0 for the Macintosh
Up and Running with Word 5.1 for the Macintosh
Up and Running with PageMaker 5.0 for the Macintosh
Up and Running with Windows 4.0
Up and Running with WordPerfect 6.0 for Windows
Up and Running with Access 2.0 for Windows
Up and Running with Microsoft Works 3.0 for Windows
Up and Running with Excel 5.0 for Windows
Working Smarter with DOS 5.0
Working with WordPerfect 5.0
Working with WordPerfect 5.1

Martin and Parker
Mastering Today's Software Series
Texts available in any combination of the following:
Microcomputer Concepts
Extended Microcomputer Concepts
Disk Operating System 5.0 (DOS 5.0)
Disk Operating System 6.0 (DOS 6.0)
Windows 3.1
Word Processing with WordPerfect 5.1
Word Processing with WordPerfect 5.2 for Windows
Word Processing with WordPerfect 6.0 for DOS
Word Processing with WordPerfect 6.0 for Windows
Spreadsheets with Lotus 1-2-3 (2.2/2.3)
Spreadsheets with Lotus 1-2-3 (2.4)
Spreadsheets with Lotus 1-2-3 for Windows (4.01)
Spreadsheets with Quattro Pro 4.0
Spreadsheets with Quattro Pro 6.0 for Windows
Database Management with dBASE III Plus
Database Management with dBASE IV (1.5/2.0)
Database Management with Paradox 4.0
Database Management with Paradox 5.0 for Windows

Martin, Series Editor
Productivity Software Guide Lab Manual Series
Disk Operating System (DOS)
Windows 3.1
Word Processing with WordPerfect 5.1
Word Processing with WordPerfect 5.2 for Windows
Word Processing with WordPerfect 6.0 for Windows
Spreadsheets with Lotus 1-2-3
Spreadsheets with Lotus 1-2-3 for Windows (4.0)
Spreadsheets with Quattro Pro 4.0
Spreadsheets with Quattro Pro 6.0 for Windows
Database Management with dBASE III PLUS
Database Management with dBASE IV
Database Management with Paradox 4.0
Database Management with Paradox 5.0 for Windows
A Beginner's Guide to BASIC

The Harcourt Brace College Outline Series

Kreitzberg
Introduction to BASIC

Kreitzberg
Introduction to Fortran

Pierson
Introduction to Business Information Systems

Veklerov and Pekelny
Computer Language C

PREFACE

We are living at a time when the key to success in virtually every profession or career depends on the skillful use of information. Whether one is a teacher, lawyer, doctor, politician, manager, or corporate president, the main ingredient in the work involved is information—knowing how to get it, how to use it, where to keep it, and how to disseminate it to others.

At the root of all of these information-based work activities are computers and the applications that are supported by them. Currently there are millions of computer systems in the world, and collectively, they are capable of being used in thousands of different ways. Some of the applications that computer systems can now handle—such as making movies and creating art, or "speaking," "seeing," and "listening"—were thought impossible not too long ago. Few professions remain untouched by computers today or will remain so in tomorrow's world. No matter who you are or what you do for a living, it is highly likely that computers somehow affect the way you work.

The importance of computers in virtually every profession brings us to the purpose of this book. *Computers and Their Applications,* fourth edition, has been written with the end user of computers in mind. This nontechnical, introductory text explains in straightforward terms the importance of learning about computers, the types of computer systems and their components, the principles by which computer systems work, and practical applications of computers and related technologies. The goal of the text is both to provide knowledge of computer basics and to impart a perspective for using this knowledge effectively in the workplace.

The textbook is but one component of a complete and flexible instructional package—one that can easily be adapted to virtually any course format. With The Dryden Press's EXACT program, instructors can combine with the text any number of software lab manuals for a truly customized approach. Supplementing the textbook and lab manuals are a comprehensive set of student and teacher support materials.

The Textbook

Computers and Their Applications, fourth edition, is designed for students taking a first course in computers and information processing. The text meets the requirements proposed for the first course in computing by both the Data Processing Management Association (DPMA) and the Association for Computing Machinery (ACM). Although it provides a comprehensive introduction to the world of computers, the text is not overly technical. Coverage is given to both commercial and personal applications of computers and large and small computer systems.

Key Features

Like previous editions, the fourth edition of *Computers and Their Applications* is current and comprehensive. It offers a flexible teaching organization and a readable and engaging presentation. Learning tools in each chapter help students master important concepts. Tomorrow boxes and Feature boxes provide insight on current issues of interest. The eight thematic "Windows," each of which highlights a major aspect of information processing, bring the world of computers to life. A glossary at the end of the book gives concise definitions of important terms. The materials on productivity software, for those who adopt a version of the text that contains them, provide a comprehensive introduction to commercial software packages in a style students will find easy to use.

Currency. Perhaps more than texbooks in any other field, computer texts must reflect current technologies, trends, and classroom needs. The state-of-the-art content of this book and its support package reflects these considerations. Before the fourth edition was started, reviews were commissioned and meetings were held to identify key areas of change for the text and support package. Also, throughout the writing and production stages, enhancements and new developments were continually being made to ensure that the final product would be as state-of-the-art as possible throughout its life. A glance at the Windows, Tomorrow boxes, Feature boxes, User Solution boxes, and chapter outlines should illustrate why this text has been and will continue to remain among the most current in the marketplace.

Comprehensiveness and Depth. In planning for the fourth edition of this book, the publisher conducted an extensive research study to determine the selection of topics, degree of depth, and other features that instructors of introductory information processing courses most want to see in their texts. As the manuscript evolved, instructors at a variety of institutions around the country were asked for their comments. The resulting textbook accommodates a wide range of teaching preferences. It not only covers traditional topics thoroughly but also includes the facts every student should know about today's "hot" topics, such as multimedia, wireless communications, microcomputers, global computing issues, desktop publishing, decision support and expert systems, object-oriented-language products, image processing, virtual reality, client-server networks, user and programmer productivity tools, computer graphics, and nontraditional approaches to systems development.

Flexible Organization. A textbook locked into a rigid organization, no matter how thorough, will inevitably find its uses limited. To appeal to a wide audience, this book is designed to be flexible. Its 14 chapters are grouped into six modules: Introduction (Chapters 1–2), Hardware (Chapters 3–5), Support Systems (Chapters 6–7), Productivity Software (Chapters 8–10), Information Systems (Chapters 11–13), and Computers in Society (Chapter 14). Every effort was made to have each chapter as self-contained as possible, making it easy for one to skip chapters or learn them in a sequence other than the one in the book. Each chapter is organized into well-defined sections, so you can assign parts of a chapter if the whole provides more depth than you need.

Readability. We remember more about a subject if it is presented in a straightforward way and made interesting and exciting. This book is written in a conversational, down-to-earth style—one designed to be accurate without being intimidating. Concepts are explained clearly and simply, without use of overly technical terminology. Where technical points are presented, they are made understandable with realistic examples from everyday life.

Chapter Learning Tools. Each chapter contains a number of learning tools to help students master the materials.

1. **Outline** An outline of the headings in the chapter shows the major topics to be covered.
2. **Learning Objectives** A list of learning objectives is provided to serve as a guide while students read the chapter.
3. **Overview** Each chapter starts with an overview that puts the subject matter of the chapter in perspective and lets students know what they will be reading about.
4. **Boldfaced Key Terms and Marginal Glossary** Important terms appear in boldface type as they are introduced in the chapter. These terms are also defined in the margin of the page on which they appear and in the end-of-text glossary.
5. **Tomorrow Boxes** These special elements, one in each chapter, provide students with a look at possible future developments in the world of computers and serve as a focus for class discussion.
6. **Feature Boxes** Each chapter contains one or more Feature boxes designed to stimulate interest and discussion about today's uses of information processing technology.
7. **User Solution Boxes** User Solution boxes describe how real-world organizations are using technology to solve business-related problems. Each chapter contains at least one of these features.
8. **Photographs and Diagrams** Instructive, full-color photographs and diagrams appear throughout the book to help illustrate important concepts. The use of color in the diagrams is a functional part of the book.
9. **Summary and Key Terms** This is a concise, section-by-section summary of the main points in the chapter. Every boldfaced key term in the chapter also appears in boldface type in the summary. Students will find the summary a valuable tool for study and review.
10. **Review Exercises** Every chapter ends with a set of fill-in, matching, discussion, and critical thinking questions.

Windows. The book contains eight spectacular photo essays. Each of these "Windows" on the world of computers is organized around a major text theme and vividly illustrates state-of-the-art uses of computer technology.

End-of-Text Glossary. The glossary at the end of the book defines over 450 important computer terms mentioned in the text, including all boldfaced key terms. Each glossary item has a page reference indicating where it is boldfaced or where it first appears in the text.

Appendix A: Numbering Systems. At the end of the book is an appendix that covers numbering systems. Contained in it are explanations of the binary, decimal, and hexadecimal numbering systems, as well as rules both for converting numbers from one system into another and for doing simple arithmetic.

EXACT Custom Versions. With the EXACT custom publishing program, instructors can choose any combination from The Dryden Press's wide variety of applications manuals to go with *Computers and Their Applications,* as well as from a variety of binding options. The manuals provide a comprehensive introduction to one or more commercial productivity software packages—including DOS, Windows, WordPerfect, Lotus 1-2-3, Quattro, Paradox, dBASE, and a number of others. The end result is a customized text tailored to meet specific classroom needs.

More than a list of rules and procedures, the manuals are a set of engaging, easy-to-read tutorials that encourage students to begin creating applications immediately. Systematic application development techniques and the honing of problem-solving skills are also an integral part of the presentation. A separately bound *Instructor's Manual and Test Bank* is available free to adopters of any version of *Computers and Their Applications* that has a productivity software supplement.

Changes from the Third Edition

Although the third edition of this text was highly successful, the pace of technological advances has necessitated a number of key changes. Among the noteworthy differences between the third and fourth editions of *Computers and Their Applications* are the following:

1. New to this edition is Chapter 14, which covers in depth such topics as health and social dangers introduced by computers, computer crime, ethical issues, and matters of privacy.
2. Window 8, also a new item, illustrates with 28 photographs the history of computers, from early mechanical devices to the present.
3. A large number of business and problem-solving examples have been added to the text, giving the text a much more applications-oriented flavor. Some of these examples are highlighted in User Solution boxes throughout each chapter. Each of these boxes shows how a real-world organization is using state-of-the-art technology to creatively solve business problems.
4. Each chapter in the last two modules of the text—Module E (Information Systems) and Module F (Computers in Society)—contains a boxed feature and a Critical Thinking Question that address some international aspect of computers and/or communciations. (Each such feature or question is identified with a small globe icon.) This coverage reflects the increasing role of global issues in the technology field, as they relate to business, economic development, and the workplace.
5. Most of the line illustrations and photos are new, reflecting the most recent advances in technology and applications.
6. There is increased emphasis on microcomputer-based processing in this edition of the text. This shift reflects the trend in business toward downsizing computing operations from larger machines as well as the social trend of more and more people getting involved with microcomputers—both on the job and at home.
7. A number of topics have emerged in importance since the text was last published and have received greater attention in this edition. Among these

topics are personal digital assistants (PDAs), virtual reality, flash memory, RAID and parallel processing systems, client-server systems, pen-based computing, object-oriented languages, global and international issues, beta testing of software, multimedia applications, graphical user interfaces (GUIs), wireless networks, global positioning systems, 32-bit operating systems for microcomputers, and optical-disk applications.
8. Coverage of presentation graphics and communicating with information utilities has been increased substantially.

Student and Teacher Support Materials

Computers and Their Applications is available with a complete package of support materials for instructors and students. Included in the package are an *Instructor's Manual* with transparency masters, *Transparency Acetates,* a *Test Bank* in hard-copy and computerized form, videotapes from Dryden's Information Processing Video Library, and a variety of productivity software manuals and supporting documentation to meet lab needs.

Instructor's Manual

In the *Instructor's Manual* I draw on my own teaching experience to provide instructors with practical suggestions for enhancing classroom presentation. The *Instructor's Manual* contains suggestions for adapting this textbook to various course schedules, including one-quarter, two-quarter, one-semester, two-semester, and night courses. For each of the fourteen chapters of the text, the *Instructor's Manual* provides

1. A list of **Learning Objectives.**
2. A **Summary,** oriented to the instructor, with teaching suggestions.
3. A list of the **Key Terms** in the chapter and their definitions.
4. A **Teaching Outline** that gives a detailed breakdown of the chapter, with all major headings and subheadings, as well as points to cover under each. References to the Transparency Acetates and Transparency Masters are keyed in to this outline.
5. **Teaching Tips,** with recommended topics for class discussion, important points to cover on the transparency acetates, and mention of additional instructor resources.
6. **Lecture Anecdotes** providing additional stories, news items, and information specific to chapter content to liven up lectures.
7. **Transparency Scripts** for each transparency acetate and transparency master in the instructional package.
8. **Answers to Discussion Questions** that appear at the end of the chapter.
9. **Additional Discussion Questions,** for in-class discussion or testing, and their answers.
10. **Answers to Critical Thinking Questions** that appear at the end of the chapter.
11. **Transparency Masters** covering the chapter objectives and other key topics for classroom discussion.

Transparency Acetates

A set of over 100 *Transparency Acetates* for use with an overhead projector is available to help explain key points. Included among the acetates are outlines for every chapter, figures derived from selected text diagrams, and new pieces of art. The Teaching Outlines in the *Instructor's Manual* indicate when to show each of the acetates (as well as the Transparency Masters), and the Transparency Scripts in the *Instructor's Manual* list points to make about each.

Test Bank

The *Test Bank*—covering all 14 chapters of the text and the numbering-systems appendix—contains over 2,400 test items in various formats, including true/false, multiple-choice, matching, fill-in, and short-answer questions. Answers are provided for all but the short-answer questions. The *Test Bank* is available in both hard-copy and computerized forms. The electronic versions—available for use with IBM and Macintosh microcomputers—allow instructors to preview, edit, or delete questions as well as to add their own questions, print scrambled forms of tests, and print answer keys.

A key indicating the chapter section from which each question was taken is also provided as part of the *Test Bank*. Keys are included with each question, except for the matching questions. Also provided is a ten-question, ready-to-copy-and-distribute multiple-choice quiz for every chapter, which tests students on a representative sample of important topics.

Information Systems Interactive Tutorial

This tutorial software, available for IBM-compatible microcomputers on 3½-inch diskettes, helps students review important concepts presented in classroom lectures. The program addresses four major aspects of computers: hardware, software, systems, and computers in society. Each learning module has three parts: a content section, a practice section that includes a brief review of the concepts followed by multiple-choice questions, and a Flash Card Review that allows the student to make a "flash card" of any particular content screen for easy review. The flash card section lets the student review all the flash cards created for the module.

Other features include a notepad function allowing the student to take notes that can be printed as hard copy, "hot" words that when double-clicked give a definition, and a pretest and final test that can be used by the instructor for tracking purposes.

LectureActive Software with Laserdisc

This package, featuring a laserdisc and software, is notable for its ease of use and time savings in creating vivid classroom presentations. The laserdisc includes video segments from CBS News and CSTV, hundreds of full-color electronic transparencies, and bulleted lecture outlines of the text for display in the classroom.

The laserdisc is driven by LectureActive, a user-friendly software program that lets the instructor create custom lectures swiftly and simply. A browse function helps the instructor search through the hundreds of stills and nearly 58 minutes of motion video entries on the laserdisc. Once any video segment or still has been selected, the instructor has the opportunity to attach the visual material to a lecture notecard on the computer screen. Instructors can use existing notecard prompts, editing or revising as needed, or they can create their own. Lecture notes from other sources can be brought over to the notecard lectures, so previous work is not lost. LectureActive is available for Microsoft Windows and Macintosh platforms.

Videotapes

Videotapes from Dryden's Information Processing Video Library will be available to adopters of *Computers and Their Applications*, fourth edition. Videos focus on applications and cutting-edge technology involving computers, and illustrate concepts such as hardware, software, and systems; database management; graphics; and telecommunications. Adopters will have immediate access to professional-quality videotapes that explore such landmarks of technology as the electrical digital computer, the laser, and communications satellites; information theory; and the role of computers at Florida's Sea World theme park. Also available are "The New Literacy" series from the Annenberg foundation and the series "The Machine That Changed the World."

Acknowledgments

I could never have completed a project of this scope alone. I owe a special word of thanks to the many people who reviewed the text—those whose extensive suggestions on the first three editions helped define the fourth, those whose comments on drafts of the fourth helped mold it into its final form, and those who reviewed the instructional package.

James Ambroise, Jr., *Southern University, Louisiana;* Virginia T. Anderson, *University of North Dakota;* Robert Andree, *Indiana University Northwest;* Linda Armbruster, *Rancho Santiago College:* Gary E. Baker, *Marshalltown Community College;* Phillip Barnhart, *Mt. San Antonio College;* Dick Barton, *El Camino College;* Richard Batt, *Saint Louis Community College at Meremec;* Bert Bernreuter, *Jones College;* Jerry Booher, *Scottsdale Community College;* James Bradley, *University of Calgary;* Curtis Bring, *Moorhead State University;* Cath Brotherton, *Riverside Community College;* James Buxton, *Tidewater Community College, Virginia;* Dick Callahan, *Mississippi State University;* Becky Calliham, *Northeast State Technical Community College;* Gena Casas, *Florida Community College, Jacksonville;* Thomas L. Case, *Georgia Southern University;* John E. Castek, *University of Wisconsin-La Crosse;* Mario E. Cecchetti, *Westmoreland County Community College;* Carl Clavadetscher, *California State Polytechnic University;* Vernon Clodfelter, *Rowan Technical College, North Carolina;* Laura Cooper, *College of the Mainland, Texas;* Cynthia Corritore, *University of Nebraska at Omaha;* Mary B. Cottier, *St. Philips College;* Marvin Daugherty, *Indiana Vocational Technical College;* Donald L. Davis, *University of Mississippi;* Robert H. Dependahl, Jr., *Santa Barbara City College, California;* John DiElsi, *Mercy College, New York;* Mark Dishaw, *Boston University;* Eugene Dolan, *University of the District of Columbia,* William Dorin, *Indiana University Northwest;* Hyun B. Eom, *Middle Tennessee State University;* Ray Fanselau, *American River College;* Hilda Federico, *Jacksonville University;* Michael Feiler, *Merritt College;* J. Patrick Fenton, *West Valley Community College, California;* James H. Finger, *University of South Carolina at Columbia;* William C. Fink, *Lewis and Clark Community College, Illinois;* Gene Garza, *University of Montevallo,* Timothy Gottleber, *North Lake College;* Kay H. Gray, *Jacksonville State University;* David W. Green, *Nashville State Technical Institute, Tennessee;* George P. Grill, *University of North Carolina, Greensboro,* John R. Groh, *San Joaquin Delta College;* Rosemary C. Gross, *Creighton University;* Dennis Guster, *Saint Louis Community College at Meremec;* Donald Hall, *Manatee Community College;* Susan Hansen, *University of Nebraska;* L. D. Harber, *Volunteer State Community College, Tennessee;* Hank Hartman, *Iowa State University;* Richard Hatch, *San Diego State University;* Mary Lou Hawkins, *Del Mar College;* William Hightower, *Elon College, North Carolina;* Sharon A. Hill, *Prince George's Community College, Maryland;* Stanley P. Honacki, *Moraine Valley Community College;* L. Wayne Horn, *Pensacola Junior College;* J. William Howorth, *Seneca College, Ontario, Canada;* Peter L. Irwin, *Richland College, Texas;* Elizabeth Swoope Johnston, *Louisiana State University;* Bruce W. Judkins, *Southwest Virginia Community College;* Orlando E. Katter, Jr., *Wingate College;* Richard Kerns, *East Carolina University, North Carolina;* Glenn Kersnick, *Sinclair Community College, Ohio;* Gordon C. Kimbell, *Everett Community College, Washington,* Robert Kirklin, *Los Angeles Harbor Community College;* Judith A. Knapp, *Indiana University Northwest;* James G. Kriz, *Cuyahoga Community College, Ohio;* Joan Krone, *Ohio State University;* Fran Kubicek, *Kalamazoo Valley Community College;* Robert Landrum, *Jones Junior College;* Shelly Langman, *Bellevue Community College;* Liang Chee Wee, *University of Arizona;* Alden Lorents, *Northern Arizona University;* James McMahon, *Community College of Rhode Island;* Wayne Madison, *Clemson University, South Carolina;* LaVonne Manning, *University of the District of Columbia;* Richard Manthei, *Joliet Junior College;* Gary Marks, *Austin Community College, Texas;* Ed Martin, *Kingsborough Community College;* Don B. Medley, *California State Polytechnic University;* Mary Meredith, *University of Southwestern Louisiana;* Marilyn Meyer, *Fresno City College;* Marilyn Moore, *Purdue University;* Donavan J. Nielsen, *Golden West College;* George Novotny, *Ferris State University;* Bob Palank, *Florissant Community College;* James Payne, *Kellogg Community College;* Robert Ralph, *Fayetteville Technical Institute, North Carolina;* Laura Rao, *Central Missouri State University;* Nicholas John Robak, *Saint Joseph's University;* Ronald D. Robison, *Arkansas Tech University;* Elaine Russell, *Angelina College;* Alfred C. St. Onge, *Springfield Technical Community College, Massachusetts;* Larry Schwartzman, *Trident Technical College;* Benito R. Serenil, *South Seattle Community College;* John J. Shuler, *San Antonio College, Texas;* Susan Silvera, *Los Angeles Trade-Technical College;* Harold Smith, *Brigham Young University;* Willard A. Smith, *Tennessee State University;* Sandra Stalker, *North Shore Community College;* Michael L. Stratford, *Charles County Community College, Maryland;* Karen Studniarz, *Kishwaukee College;* Sandra Swanson, *Lewis and Clark Community College, Illinois;* Jane M. Thompson, *Solano Community College;* Sue Traynor, *Clarion University of Pennsylvania;* James R. Walters, *Pikes Peak Community College;* Joyce V. Walton, *Seneca College, Ontario, Canada;* Joseph Waters, *Santa Rosa Junior*

College, California; Fred J. Wilke, *Saint Louis Community College;* Roseanne Witkowski, *Orange County Community College;* Charles M. Williams, *Georgia State University;* James D. Woolever, *Cerritos College;* A. James Wynne, *Virginia Commonwealth University;* Robert D. Yearout, *University of North Carolina at Asheville.*

I am indebted to scores of people at dozens of organizations for the photographs they provided for this text. I would especially like to thank Jessie O. Kempter at IBM, Candice Clemens at Lotus Development, Kayla Wilhelm at Intergraph, Kim Sudhalter of Time Warner Interactive Media, Bruce Fox of Evans and Sutherland, Carol Parcels of Hewlett-Packard, and computer artists Clifford Pickover, Karl Sims, and James Dowlen for the particularly outstanding contributions they made. Also, I extend heart-felt thanks to Jeff Glickman at The College of Santa Fe (CSF) for the help he provided in preparing the computer programs that are contained in this text. Additionally, I deeply appreciate the continuing help and support on this textbook from my departmental colleagues and good friends at CSF, Dan Breheny and Pat Donahoe.

At The Dryden Press, a special word of thanks to my publisher, Liz Widdicombe, to my acquisitions editor, Richard Bonacci, to Elizabeth Hayes, developmental editor, and to Michele Tomiak, project editor, for the suggestions and accommodations they made to produce a better manuscript. Also I would like to thank Beverly Baker, Erin Gregg, Steven Lunetta, Sheryl Nelson, Scott Timian, and the many others who worked hard on behalf of this book. At Elm Street Publishing Services—the company that collaborated in producing the text for me—I am especially grateful to Karen Hill, Jane Perkins, Cate Rzasa, Barb Lange, and Martha Beyerlein.

Charles S. Parker

BRIEF CONTENTS

Module A	**Introduction**	**1**
Chapter 1	*Introduction to the World of Computers*	*3*
Chapter 2	*Computer Systems and Information Processing*	*39*
Module B	**Hardware**	**63**
Chapter 3	*The Central Processing Unit and Memory*	*65*
Chapter 4	*Secondary Storage*	*93*
Chapter 5	*Input and Output Equipment*	*129*
Module C	**Support Systems**	**175**
Chapter 6	*Telecommunications*	*177*
Chapter 7	*Systems Software*	*217*
Module D	**Productivity Software**	**257**
Chapter 8	*Word Processing and Desktop Publishing*	*259*
Chapter 9	*Spreadsheets and Presentation Graphics*	*295*
Chapter 10	*Database Management*	*331*
Module E	**Information Systems**	**365**
Chapter 11	*Developing Business Systems*	*367*
Chapter 12	*Program Development and Programming Languages*	*413*
Chapter 13	*Becoming a Microcomputer Owner or User*	*449*
Module F	**Computers in Society**	**479**
Chapter 14	*Computers in Our Lives: The Costs and the Benefits*	*481*
Appendix A	**Numbering Systems**	**A-1**
Glossary		*G-1*
Answers to Fill-in and Matching Review Questions		*Ans-1*
Credits		*C-1*
Index		*I-1*

W I N D O W S

Window 1
Computers in Our World *31*
A Visual Portfolio of the Widespread Use of Computers

Window 2
The Electronic Canvas *167*
A Peek at the Leading Edge in Computer Output

Window 3
Inside Prodigy *213*
A Closer Look at an Information Utility

Window 4
Graphical User Interfaces *251*
Tools of the Electronic Desktop

Window 5
Desktop Publishing *289*
A Step-by-Step Look at What's Involved

Window 6
Multimedia Computing *357*
It May Revolutionize the Way We Deal with Information

Window 7
The World of Computer Graphics *403*
Techniques and Applications

Window 8
The History of Computers *515*
A Picture Essay of the People and Devices That Pioneered the Computer Revolution

C O N T E N T S

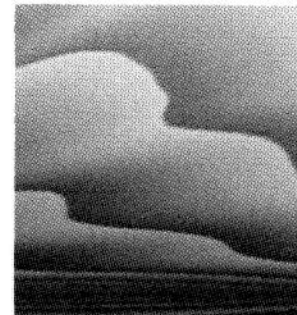

MODULE A

Introduction 1

Chapter 1 ***Introduction to the World of Computers*** **3**

Overview 4

Computers in the 1990s Workplace 4

What's a Computer and What Does It Do? 7

Computer Systems 8

Data and Programs 8

A Look at Computer Storage 10

Hardware and Software 12

Users and the Experts 12

Benefits Computers Provide 14

Computer Systems to Fit Every Need and Pocketbook 15

Microcomputers 15

Minicomputers 17

Mainframes 19

Supercomputers 20

Using Computers: Some Examples 20

Computers and Society 25

Computers in Action 27

User Solution 1–1: *Selling Smart with Laptops* 6

Feature 1-1: *Self-Service Computing* 10

User Solution 1–2: *Computers Tackle California Droughts* 14

Tomorrow: *The PDAs Are Coming! The PDAs Are Coming!* 18

Feature 1–2: *Teledemocracy* 26

Chapter 2 ***Computer Systems and Information Processing*** **39**

Overview 40

Computer Hardware 40

Peripheral Equipment 40

Input, Output, or Storage? 42

Input/Output Media 45

Online and Offline 46

Organizing Data for Computer Systems 46

A Brief Introduction to Software 48

Information Processing 49

Getting It All Together: Combining Elements into a Complete Computer System 55

Feature 2–1: *Debunking the Billy the Kid Legend* 41
User Solution 2–1: *Online Processing for Fresher Information and Better Control* 46
Tomorrow: *Virtual Reality* 54
User Solution 2–2: *Updating the Wireless Way* 56

MODULE B
Hardware 63

Chapter 3 *The Central Processing Unit and Memory* **65**
Overview 66
How the CPU Works 67
The CPU and Its Memory 67
Registers 68
Machine Cycles 70
Data and Program Representation 71
ASCII and EBCDIC 74
Machine Language 77
The System Unit 77
CPU Chip 77
Specialized Processor Chips 80
RAM 80
ROM 81
Add-in Boards 81
Ports 81
I/O Bus 82
Making Computers Speedier 84
User Solution 3–1: *Honey, Phone Home* 67
Feature 3–1: *Flash Memory* 69
Tomorrow: *The Coming Chip Technologies* 84
Feature 3–2: *Massively Parallel Processors* 87

Chapter 4 *Secondary Storage* **93**
Overview 94
Properties of Secondary Storage Systems 94
Magnetic Disk 96
Diskettes 97
Hard Disks for Small Computers 101
Other Types of Magnetic Disks for Small Computers 107

RAM Disk and Cache Disk	*108*
Disk Systems for Large Computers	*109*
Magnetic Tape	111
Processing Tapes	*113*
Storing Data on Tape	*114*
Optical Disk	115
Data Organization	116
User Solution 4–1: *CD-Type Programming for Record Lovers*	*96*
Feature 4–1: *RAID*	*110*
User Solution 4–2: *Optical Disks for Customer Support*	*118*
Tomorrow: *Photo CDs*	*119*

Chapter 5 ***Input and Output Equipment***	***129***
Overview	130
Input and Output	130
Keyboards	131
Display Devices	132
Monochrome and Color Display Devices	*134*
CRT and Flat-Panel Display Devices	*134*
Text versus Graphics	*135*
Printers	138
Impact Printing	*138*
Nonimpact Printing	*141*
Printers for Microcomputers	*143*
Printers for Large Computers	*145*
Source Data Automation	146
Optical Character Recognition (OCR)	*146*
Image Scanners	*150*
Magnetic Ink Character Recognition (MICR)	*151*
Digitizers	*153*
Voice-Input Devices	*157*
Handwriting Recognition Devices	*158*
Smart Cards	*158*
Special-Purpose Output Equipment	159
Plotters	*159*
Voice-Output Devices	*159*
Film Recorders	*161*
Computer Output Microfilm (COM)	*161*
User Solution 5–1: *High-Tech Services for Air Travelers*	*135*
Tomorrow: *Retailing in the 21st Century*	*148*

Feature 5–1: *It's Showtime for Pen Computing* 154
User Solution 5–2: *Zipping the Mail Along with Voice Recognition* 157

MODULE C
Support Systems 175

Chapter 6 *Telecommunications* ***177***
Overview 178
Telecommunications Applications 179
Communcations Media 185
Types of Media *185*
Media Speed *190*
Media Mode *190*
Media Signal *190*
Parallel versus Serial Transmission *193*
Asynchronous versus Synchronous Transmission *194*
Wide Area Networks and Local Networks 195
Wide Area Networks *195*
Local Networks *198*
Network Topologies 203
Communications Among Devices 205
Protocols *205*
Hardware for Managing Communications Traffic *206*
User Solution 6–1: *Speeding Products to Market with Networks* *179*
Tomorrow: *Global Positioning Systems* *189*
Feature 6–1: *Modem Software* *196*
User Solution 6–2: *A Contractor Turns to LANs* *200*
Feature 6–2: *Wireless LANs* *202*

Chapter 7 *Systems Software* ***217***
Overview 218
The Operating System 218
Differences among Operating Systems *220*
Functions of the Operating System *221*
Interleaved Processing Techniques *225*
A Closer Look at Several Operating Systems 228
MS-DOS and PC-DOS *229*
DOS with Windows *229*

Macintosh System Software 231
UNIX 232
OS/2 233
Windows NT 235
NetWare 236
Language Translators 238
Utility Programs 240
Tomorrow: *The Battle of the 32-bit Operating Systems* 222
User Solution 7–1: *Fault Tolerance Spells Uninterrupted Service* 228
Feature 7–1: *Bill Gates: Microsoft's "Boy Billionaire"* 230
User Solution 7–2: *A Windows Solution at Fidelity* 232
Feature 7–2: *Document-Management Utilities* 244

MODULE D
Productivity Software 257

Chapter 8 *Word Processing and Desktop Publishing* ***259***
Overview 260
Word Processing 260
Learning to Use a Word Processor: The Basics 260
Learning to Use a Word Processor: Advanced Operations 269
Add-On Packages 275
Desktop Publishing 276
What Is Desktop Publishing? 277
Components of a Desktop Publishing System 278
Tomorrow: *Graphical Word Processors* 270
User Solution 8–1: *Saving a Million Bucks through Desktop Publishing* 279
Feature 8–1: *A Crash Course in Typography* 280

Chapter 9 *Spreadsheets and Presentation Graphics* ***295***
Overview 296
Spreadsheets 297
How Spreadsheets Work 297
Basic Entering and Editing Operations 308
Advanced Features 314
Presentation Graphics 317
Forms of Presentation Graphics 317

Types of Packages 323
Feature 9–1: *The Complete Desktop Solution* 298
User Solution 9–1: *Selling Homes With What-If Analysis* 303
User Solution 9–2: *Models That Motivate Motorcycle Merchants* 307
Tomorrow: *Intelligent Spreadsheets and Graphics* 324

Chapter 10 *Database Management* **331**
Overview 332
Database Management Systems 332
Database Management on Microcomputers 332
Database Management on Large Computer Systems 342
Advantages and Disadvantages of Database Management 347
Multimedia Data Management 348
Feature 10–1: *Geographic Information Systems (GISs)* 342
Tomorrow: *Managing Unstructured Data* 349
User Solution 10–1: *Wooing Execs With Multimedia* 353

MODULE E
Information Systems 365

Chapter 11 *Developing Business Systems* **367**
Overview 368
On Systems 368
Business Systems 369
Transaction Processing Systems 370
Information Systems 371
Information Reporting Systems 372
Office Systems 374
Design and Manufacturing Systems 378
Artificial Intelligence 381
Responsibility for Systems Development 381
The Information Systems Department 384
Outsourcing 387
The Systems Development Life Cycle 388
The Preliminary Investigation 389
Systems Analysis 389
System Design 390
System Acquisition 394
System Implementation 395

Approaches to Systems Development 396
The Traditional Approach *396*
Prototyping *397*
End-User Development *398*
Tomorrow: *Re-Engineering* *369*
User Solution 11–1: *A GDSS Helps Insurers* *375*
Feature 11–1: *Neural-Net Computing* *384*
Feature 11–2: *Developing International Systems* *390*
User Solution 11–2: *An Automated Help Desk That Really Helps* *397*

Chapter 12 ***Program Development and Programming Languages*** ***413***
Overview 414
Program Development Activities 414
The Make-or-Buy Decision 415
Program Design 415
Program Design Tools *416*
Program Flowcharts *416*
Pseudocode *421*
Structure Charts *424*
Programming Languages 425
Low-Level Languages *425*
High-Level Languages *425*
Fourth-Generation Languages (4GLs) *434*
Natural Languages *435*
Program Coding 437
Debugging and Testing Programs 438
Program Maintenance 439
Program Documentation 439
Quality Assurance 440
Computer-Aided Software Engineering (CASE) 441
Tomorrow: *The Coming Threat to U.S. Software Dominance* *416*
Feature 12–1: *Visual Programming* *432*
Feature 12–2: *Beta Testing* *440*
User Solution 12–1: *Developing A Small System in Record Time* *442*

Chapter 13 ***Becoming A Microcomputer Owner or User*** ***449***
Overview 450
The Microcomputer Marketplace 450

Microcomputer Products 450
Sales and Distribution 452
Selecting a Computer System 455
Analyzing Needs 455
Listing Alternatives 456
Evaluating Alternatives 458
Choosing a System 460
Operating a Computer System 461
Backup 462
Proper Maintenance of Resources 467
Troubleshooting and Repairs 469
Upgrading 471
Functional versus Technological Obsolescence 473
Learning More about Microcomputers 473
User Solution 13–1: *Docking Stations* 451
Feature 13–1: *Selling Technology to Japan* 453
Tomorrow: *Software Support* 460
Feature 13–2: *Buying Software* 462
Feature 13–3: *Buying Hardware* 464

MODULE F

Computers in Society 479

Chapter 14 *Computers in Our Lives: The Costs and the Benefits* ***481***

Overview 482
Computers, Work, and Health 482
Stress-related Concerns 482
Ergonomics-related Concerns 483
Environment-related Concerns 486
Other Areas of Concern 487
Computer Crime 488
Types of Computer Crime 488
Preventing Computer Crime 492
Computers and Privacy 494
Privacy Legislation 495
Privacy and Electronic Mail 495
Caller Identification 496
Ethical Issues Regarding Computers 497
Computers in Our Lives: Today and Tomorrow 500
Computers for Home and Personal Use 500

Computers in Education 503
Computers in Entertainment and Leisure Activities 504
Computers in Science and Medicine 507
Feature 14–1: *Toward a National Technology Policy* 484
Feature 14–2: *Virus Protection* 490
Feature 14–3: *How Do They Know I Ski?* 496
User Solution 14–1: *Was It Wrong?* 499
Tomorrow: *Interactive Television* 501

Appendix A *Numbering Systems* **A-1**
Numbering Systems A-2
The Decimal Numbering System A-2
The Binary Numbering System A-3
The Hexadecimal Numbering System A-4
Computer Arithmetic A-8

Glossary **G-1**

Answers to Fill-in and Matching Review Exercises **Ans-1**

Credits **C-1**

Index **I-1**

COMPUTERS AND THEIR APPLICATIONS

FOURTH EDITION

MODULE A

INTRODUCTION

We are living in an age of computers. Businesses, government agencies, and other organizations use computers and related technologies to handle tedious paperwork, provide better service to customers, and assist managers in making better decisions. As the benefits to using computers continue to mount, and as the costs of computing resources continue to decrease relative to the price of everything else, computer technology will become even more widespread in our society. It is therefore essential to know something about it.

The chapters in this module introduce you to computers and some of their uses. Chapters 1 and 2 orient you to what computer systems are, how they work, and how they're used. These chapters also present some key terminology that you will see repeatedly throughout the text.

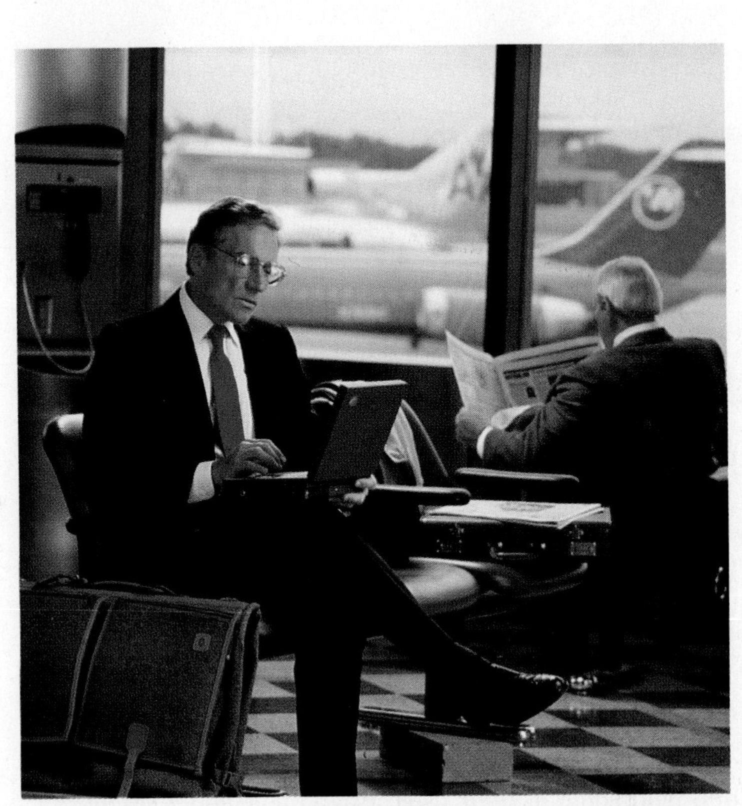

Introduction to the World of Computers

1

Why are managers increasingly hitting the road with their computers? As you'll learn in this chapter, computers that can be toted about can be used to make presentations to clients, enter and check the status of orders, prepare field reports . . . and so much more.

OUTLINE

Overview
Computers in the 1990s Workplace
What's a Computer and What Does It Do?
  Computer Systems
  Data and Programs
  A Look at Computer Storage
  Hardware and Software
  Users and the Experts
  Benefits Computers Provide
Computers Systems to Fit Every Need and Pocketbook
  Microcomputers
  Minicomputers
  Mainframes
  Supercomputers
Using Computers: Some Examples
Computers and Society
Computers in Action

LEARNING OBJECTIVES

After completing this chapter, you will be able to:

1. Understand why it's especially important to learn about computers today.
2. Identify some of the major components in a computing environment and their relationships to one another.
3. Describe several applications in business and other areas of society in which computers play an important role.
4. Define several terms that are useful to know when reading about or discussing computers.
5. Appreciate the social impact of computers.

Overview

Unless you plan to spend your life living off the land in the upper reaches of the Yukon, computers and other forms of high technology will probably have an important impact on your life.

Computer systems keep track of our bank accounts and credit card purchases. They, along with sophisticated communications systems, are the cornerstones of the airlines' massive reservations systems. Computers perform the millions upon millions of computations needed to send astronauts into outer space and bring them back safely. Computers also direct production in our factories and provide executives with the up-to-date information they need to make decisions. Computers are embedded in watches, microwave ovens, television sets, phones, fax machines, automobiles, and probably even the stationary workout bike at your local gym. The applications are almost endless. Fifty short years ago, computers were part of an obscure technology of interest to only a handful of scientists. Today they are part of almost everyone's daily life.

Computers are very much like cars in that you don't need to know everything about them to use them effectively. You can learn to drive a car without knowing about internal combustion engines, and you can learn to use a computer without knowing about technical details such as logic circuits. Still, with both cars and computers, a little knowledge can give you a big advantage. Knowing something about cars can help you make wise purchases and save money on repairs. Likewise, knowing something about computers can help you use them for maximum benefit.

This book is about computers—what they are, how they work, and what they do. It is intended to give you the knowledge you need to use them effectively today and, through the Tomorrow boxes, give you a look into the future. Other boxed features throughout the text provide additional insights into the dynamic world of computers.

This book is not designed to make you a computer expert. It's a beginner's guide. If you're considering a career as a computer professional in business, this book will give you a comprehensive introduction to the field. If you're not, it will give you the basic knowledge you need to understand and use computers in school and on the job.

In this chapter, we'll first take a look at how computers are reshaping the workplace in the 1990s. From there, we turn to what computers are and how they work. Then we'll look at the various sizes in which computers come. Finally, we'll examine several examples of computer systems in action. Window 1, which follows Chapter 1, gives you a glimpse of the myriad applications of computers in today's world.

Computers in the 1990s Workplace

Prior to 1980, it was not critical for an ordinary person to know how to use a computer in his or her job. Computers were expensive, and few people had access to them. Furthermore, the use of computers generally required a lot of technical knowledge. Worse yet, most business computers were equipped to do little but carry out high-volume paperwork processing, such as issuing bills and keeping track of customer-account and inventory balances. Not only were most

FIGURE 1-1

Computers shaping the 1990s workplace. (a) Personal desktop workstations are rapidly becoming a necessity for office work. (b) Portable computers enable data to be electronically gathered out in the field. (c) People are increasingly buying computers for personal use, making it easier than ever before to run home-based businesses.

(a)

(b)

(c)

ordinary working people afraid of computers, but also there were few good reasons for getting familiar with them.

Then, suddenly, things began to change. Microcomputers—small, inexpensive computers that you will read about later in this chapter—were created. Consequently, today there are thousands of times more computers and hundreds of times more people involved with computers than just a couple of decades or so ago. This has resulted in a flood of high-quality, high-technology products in the marketplace. It has also changed the way many companies do business and the type of skills they seek in the people they hire.

Today, we are living in an era when most skill-based jobs heavily depend

User Solution 1-1

Selling Smart with Laptops

Champion Products sportswear is a familiar item in the locker rooms of schools and professional sports teams. These days, when Champion salespeople go calling on customers—such as retail stores, college bookstores, and athletic departments—they go equipped with a laptop computer. In pre-laptop times, it used to take as long as two weeks to get a handwritten order from the field entered into the sales system. Now the salesperson can key in the order on the spot, as the customer is giving it, and automatically transmit it to headquarters for confirmation and immediate processing. This way, the customer has a guaranteed delivery date before the salesperson ever leaves the premises. The laptop can also be used to check on the status of any previously placed orders and the amount of stock on hand. Champion says that not only have the laptops provided better service, but they have also reduced errors, labor costs, and returned goods.

on the collection, use, creation, and dissemination of information. Whether you become a teacher, lawyer, doctor, professional athlete, executive, or blue-collar worker, your performance will largely depend on information and your use of it. Because computer systems can process facts at dizzying speeds, their availability may be equivalent to having an army of clerks at your disposal.

Following are several examples of how computers are being used in the workplace to enhance personal productivity (see also Figure 1-1):

- Virtually everyone who needs to type in a job uses a computer system or electronic typewriter to do word processing. *Word processing*—which enables keystrokes to be stored and edited electronically—produces documents such as letters and books faster and better than an ordinary typewriter.
- Managers and professionals at all levels of the business world use computing products called electronic *spreadsheets*—which in essence are powerful calculators—to perform analytical tasks in minutes that once took hours or days to do by hand. Not only can these people assemble information faster than they did before, they also can do tasks that once were impossible to perform manually. By being able to study "all the angles" of strategies or propositions, these individuals often find that they make better decisions.
- Executives are relying increasingly on *database management systems*—tools that provide instant access to local or remote banks of information—to learn about business conditions. Many of these systems are so easy to use that even the most computer-shy executives are being won over to their use, knowing that failure to keep up will give competitors an edge. Worker groups such as lawyers, doctors, and stockbrokers, who need to search through mounds of data to draw conclusions, have also found that database technology has improved their performance.

- Many companies have given thousands of *laptop computers*—computers the size of a notebook—to their field sales forces. These devices often give salespeople an advantage when dealing with clients, because the salesperson can analyze a client proposal on the spot, while he or she is in a receptive mood (see User Solution 1-1). The laptop can also be used to access remote data—possibly supplying information that will help close the sale. And, at the end of a day, it can be used to quickly prepare sales reports to send to headquarters.
- At all levels of business, computers are helping workers put *presentation materials* together by creating stunning charts and slides to help sway a live audience and by enhancing the look of handout materials. Researchers have found that people who use computers in this manner often are considered by others to be more "professional."
- In fields such as design and publishing, computers have completely revolutionized the way people work. Products such as cars, packages, buildings, shoes, and fabrics are often designed today with *computer-aided design (CAD)* systems. The rise of powerful *desktop publishing systems*—computer systems that fit on a desktop and enable ordinary people to produce work that looks as if it came from a professional printing press—has altered the structure of the entire publishing industry.
- Many businesses are now using some form of modern *communications system* to get faster and better information. For instance, facsimile (fax) machines are today widely used to transmit documents between sites almost instantaneously. This allows people to complete within a few hours a task that could stretch out over days or even weeks with just a physical delivery system at hand. Also, electronic mailbox and messaging systems enable people to work in groups more easily, even though they may be at different locations.

These applications only scratch the surface in demonstrating how computers are affecting the workplace in the 1990s. As you read further in this text, you will learn about dozens of others.

What's a Computer and What Does It Do?

Four words sum up the operation of a computer system: **input, processing, output,** and **storage.** To see what these words mean, let's look at something you probably have in your own home—a stereo system.

A simple stereo system often consists of a compact disk (CD) player and/or turntable, an amplifier, and a pair of speakers. To use the system, you place a CD or record on the CD player or turntable and turn the system on. The CD player or turntable converts the patterns in the tracks or grooves into sounds and transmits them to the amplifier as electronic signals. The amplifier takes the signals, strengthens them, and transmits them to the speakers. The result is music. In computer terms, the CD player or turntable sends signals as *input* to the amplifier. The amplifier *processes* the signals and sends them to the speakers, which produce a musical *output.* The CD player and turntable are **input devices,** the amplifier is a *processing unit,* and the speakers are **output devices.** The amplifier is the heart of the system, whereas the CD player, turntable, and speakers are examples of **peripheral equipment.**

Input.
What is supplied to a computer process.

Processing.
The conversion of input to output.

Output.
The results of a computer process.

Storage.
An area that holds materials going to or coming from the computer.

Input device.
A machine used to supply materials going to the computer.

Output device.
A machine used to accept materials coming from the computer.

Peripheral equipment.
The machines that work with the computer.

Input/output (I/O) media. Objects used to store computer-processed materials.

Machine-readable. Any form in which data are represented so that they can be read by a machine.

Most stereo systems have a variety of other peripheral equipment. An antenna, for example, is another kind of input device. Headphones are another type of output device. A tape recorder is both an input and output device—you can use it to send signals to the amplifier or to receive signals from it. The tapes, compact disks, and records in your collection are, in computer terms, **input/output (I/O) media.** They *store* music in a **machine-readable** form—a form that the associated input device (tape recorder, CD player, or record turntable) can recognize (that is, "read") and convert into signals for the amplifier to process.

Computer Systems

Computer system. A collection of elements that includes the computer as well as all the components that contribute to making it a useful tool.

Computer. The piece of hardware, also known as the **central processing unit (CPU),** that interprets and executes program instructions and communicates with support devices.

All the elements in a stereo system have their counterparts in a computer system. A **computer system** consists of the computer itself, all the peripheral equipment, and the machine-readable instructions and facts it processes, as well as operating manuals, procedures, and the people who use the system. In other words, all the components that contribute to making the computer a useful tool can be said to be parts of a computer system.

At the heart of any computer system is the **computer** itself, or **central processing unit (CPU).** The CPU is the equivalent of the stereo amplifier. Like its counterpart, the CPU can't do anything useful without peripheral equipment for input and output and I/O media for storage. Computer input and output devices include, to name just a few, keyboards, display devices, disk units, tape units, and printers. I/O media include disks, tapes, and paper. We will discuss these and many other items in Chapters 2, 4, and 5.

A computer system, of course, is not a stereo system, and a computer is much more versatile than a stereo amplifier. For example, a computer system can perform an enormous variety of processing tasks and a stereo system only a few. Also, a computer can support a much greater variety of input and output devices than can a stereo amplifier.

What gives a computer its flexibility? The answer, in a word, is *memory.* A computer has access to a memory, or "workspace," that allows it to retain whatever inputs it receives and the results it produces from these inputs. An ordinary home stereo system has no such memory; what's playing on the compact disk player, tape recorder, or turntable passes directly through the amplifier to the speakers. Because computers can hold materials in such a workspace, they can be directed by *programs* to rearrange or recombine those materials in an amazing variety of ways before sending them along as output.

Data and Programs

Data. A collection of raw, unorganized facts.

Program. A set of instructions that causes the computer system to perform specific actions.

The material that a computer receives as input is of two kinds: data and programs. **Data** are essentially raw, unorganized facts. **Programs** are instructions that tell the computer how to process those facts to produce the results that you, the computer system user, want. Let's discuss these important terms in a little more detail.

Data Almost any kind of fact can become computer data—facts about a company's employees, facts about airline flight schedules, or facts about baseball batting averages. Even pictures and sounds can become data. When we input data into a computer system, we usually aren't interested in getting them back just as we entered them. We want the system to process the data and give us new, useful *information.* **Information,** in the language of computers, refers to data that have been processed into a *meaningful* form.

Information. Data that have been processed into a meaningful form.

We might want to know, for example, how many employees earn over $15,000, how many seats are available on Flight 495 from Los Angeles to San Francisco, or what Dave Justice's batting average was during last year's regular baseball season. The difference between data and information lies in the word "meaningful." Dave Justice's batting average may be meaningful to you because it will enable you to make a prediction about an upcoming game or merely because it will make watching the game more interesting. To a friend who doesn't follow baseball, however, Dave Justice's batting average may be meaningless—just ordinary data, not information. Thus, information is a *relative* term; it is something that has meaning for a specific person in a specific situation. Like beauty, the difference between data and information is strictly in the eye of the beholder.

Of course, you don't necessarily need a computer system to get information from a set of facts. For example, anyone can go through an employee file and make a list of people earning a certain salary. But to do so would take a lot of time, especially for a company with thousands of employees. In contrast, with their electronically fast speeds, computers can do such jobs almost instantly. Computer processing of data into information is called by a variety of terms, one of which is **information processing.**

Information processing. Computer operations that transform data into meaningful information.

Information processing has become an especially important activity in recent years because most jobs depend heavily on the wise use of information. Because better information often means better decisions, many companies today regard information as one of their most important assets.

Feature 1-1 describes the use of multimedia kiosks in providing information to an increasingly computer-literate and information-hungry public.

Programs Like many other machines, the amplifier in your home stereo system is a *special-purpose* device. It is designed to support only a few specific tasks—interact with a CD player and a record turntable, play music into speakers or headphones, and so forth. These functions are built into its circuitry. To put it another way, it is "hardwired" to perform a very limited number of specific tasks.

Most computers, in contrast, are *general-purpose* devices. They are able to perform an enormous variety of tasks—for instance, preparing letters to clients, analyzing sales figures, and creating slide presentations, to name just a few. Because most computers must be flexible, they can't be hardwired to do all the tasks they may be required to do. Instead, they rely on program instructions for guidance. As each program is read into the computer system, it is provided data by the user to process. The program then directs the circuits in the computer to open and close in the manner needed to do whatever task needs to be done with these data.

Programs cannot yet be written in ordinary English. They must be written in a **programming language**—a code the computer system can read and translate into the electronic pulses that make it work. Programming languages

Programming language. A set of rules used to write computer programs.

Feature 1-1

Self-Service Computing

Multimedia kiosks are making their move

It's a trend that actually began over 25 years ago, when the first automatic teller machines (ATMs) from the banking industry hit the scene.

Now that people are comfortable with ATMs, and technology has advanced by leaps and bounds in a number of related areas, a new breed of product has evolved—the multimedia kiosk. A *kiosk* is a self-service station, equipped with its own computer and storage bank, that users can go to for specific information or to make specific transactions. *Multimedia* means that the kiosk can handle a variety of data types—text, still pictures, animated images, and/or sound. Often, kiosks are housed in plastic consoles or in glass-and-wood enclosures and equipped with easy-to-work touch-screen menus.

Increasingly, kiosks are popping up in airports, stores and supermarkets, auto showrooms, schools, museums and exhibitions, government

Kiosk. Information dissemination 1990s style.

come in many varieties—BASIC, Pascal, and C are three with which you may be familiar. In the early days of computers, programming languages consisted of strings of numbers that only experts could comprehend. Over the years, they have become easier for ordinary mortals to understand and use. We will discuss programs and programming languages in detail in Module E.

A Look at Computer Storage

So far we've seen that if you want to get something done on a computer system, you must supply it with both facts (data) and instructions (a program) specifying how to process those facts. For example, if you want the system to write payroll checks, you must supply such data as employees' names, social security numbers, and salaries. The program instructions must "tell" the system how to compute taxes, how to take deductions, where and how to print the checks, and so forth. Also, the computer relies on a memory (storage) to remember all these details as it is doing the work.

Primary (internal) storage.
Also known as **memory,** this section of the computer system temporarily holds data and program instructions awaiting processing, intermediate results, and processed output.

Actually, computer systems contain two types of storage. A **primary (internal) storage**—often called **memory**—holds the data and programs that the computer is currently processing. When data are "captured" in the computer's offices, malls, restaurants, and even offices. In a word, everywhere.

In California, state and local governments are using kiosks for a variety of purposes. In San Diego and Sacramento, for instance, kiosks help local residents find employment and get health-care information. In South Central Los Angeles, where rioting occurred in 1992, a kiosk was installed to help residents hook up with community-assistance programs. Kiosks are also widely used in California and other states to assist with quizzing in the driver-licensing process.

A large Connecticut company decided to go the kiosk route when it searched for a convenient way to provide its employees with up-to-date information about health benefits. A multimedia kiosk was chosen over other computerbased alternatives because many people in the company were intimidated by conventional computer systems and did not know how to use them. Moreover, not everyone had access to a networked, desktop computer readily available.

Hotels are also beginning to seriously consider kiosks in a big way. Professionals in the hotel industry have avoided such technologies in the past because they felt machines violated the warm, friendly feeling that they wanted to project. However, a number of hotels are now pilot-testing self-service checkout stations to cut down lines at the front desk. Hotel kiosks are likely to prove most useful to the frequent business traveler who is in a rush.

One firm has even developed a kiosk that sells sheet music in music stores. A customer uses a touch screen to select from hundreds of titles. After a selection is made, the kiosk plays a few bars while the score is displayed on a screen. Once the score is purchased, the kiosk can also print the score in any key.

Many computer-industry experts feel that the multimedia kiosk business is poised to take off. Some even go so far as to say that these high-tech self-service stations will be more numerous than gasoline pumps within a few years. Businesses like kiosks because they cut down on labor costs and can be used as powerful selling tools, by providing information to which a clerk does not have access. They can even help businesses get a leg up on low-tech competitors. Customers like kiosks because they often provide better service than humans. Not only that, but many people are discovering that kiosks can be fun to use.

memory or "workspace," they can be rearranged or recombined by the instructions in the program. Memory is contained in the unit that houses the computer.

Data and programs the computer doesn't need for the job at hand are stored in **secondary (external) storage.** In large computer systems, secondary storage is usually located in a device separate from the computer itself. In smaller computer systems, secondary storage is usually implemented by a device that is fitted into the unit containing the computer. Whatever the case, this piece of equipment is called a *secondary storage device.* It enables us to conveniently save large quantities of data and programs in machine-readable form so that we need not rekey them into the system every time we use them. Some secondary storage devices are capable of storing thousands of programs and billions of pieces of data.

Secondary storage. Storage on media such as disk and tape that supplements memory. Also called **external storage.**

When the CPU needs a certain program or set of data, it requests it from the secondary storage device—much as you might request a particular song from a jukebox—and reads them into its memory for processing. Unlike the jukebox turntable, however, which puts the original record in play, the CPU puts only a copy of the original program or data into memory for use. It is often useful to think of secondary storage as a large "library" of programs and data resources on full-time call to the CPU.

FIGURE 1-2

Input, processing, output, and storage. Often, the computer fetches most of the programs and data it needs from secondary storage and from instructions given to it by a user at an input device. While it is working on specific programs and data, the computer uses primary storage as a "scratchpad" area. When finished, results are transferred from primary storage to an output device.

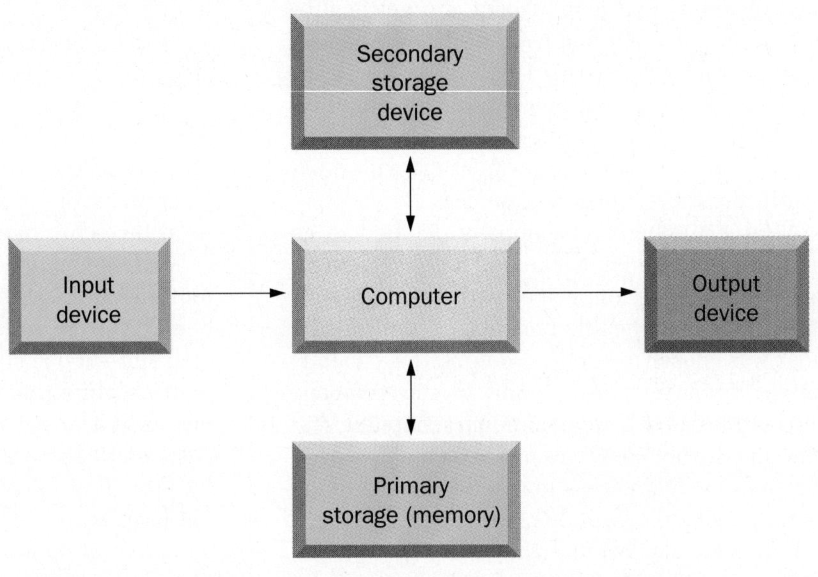

Figure 1-2 illustrates the relationships among input, processing, output, memory, and secondary storage.

Hardware and Software

Hardware.
Physical equipment in a computing environment, such as the computer and its peripheral devices.

Software.
Computer programs.

In the world of computers, it is common to distinguish between hardware and software. The word **hardware** refers to the actual machinery that makes up a computer system—for example, the CPU, I/O devices, and storage devices. The word **software** refers to computer programs.

Virtually all of the software you buy today in a computer store or through the mail is in "package" form (see Figure 1-3). Typically, such a *software package* consists of program disks, operating instructions, training tutorials, a warranty, and reference manuals inside of a shrink-wrapped box. All of the program disks have been written in some programming language, such as C or assembly language.

Users and the Experts

In the early days of computing, there was a clear distinction between the people who made computers work and those who used the results computers produced. This distinction still exists, but as computers become more available and easier to use, it is breaking down.

End users, or *users,* are the people who need the output computer systems produce. They include the accountant who needs a report on a client's taxes, the secretary who is word processing a letter, the engineer who needs to know whether a bridge will be structurally sound, the shop-floor supervisor who needs to know whether the day's quotas were met, and the company president who needs a report on the firm's profitability over the last ten years.

End user.
A person who needs the results computers produce in order to perform his or her job.

Programmers, on the other hand, are the people who write the programs that produce such outputs. Programming is their primary job responsibility. Thus, although end users may do modest amounts of programming with the packaged software on their desktop computer systems, the distinction between an ordinary end user and a professional programmer is based on what the person has actually been hired to do.

Programmer.
A person whose job is to write, maintain, and test computer programs.

Organizations employ many other types of computer professionals. For instance, *systems analysts* are hired to build large computer systems within a company. *Computer operations personnel,* in contrast, are responsible for the day-to-day operation of large computer systems.

FIGURE 1-3

Software package. A software package normally consists of program disks, operating instructions, training tutorials, a warranty, and reference manuals inside of a shrink-wrapped box.

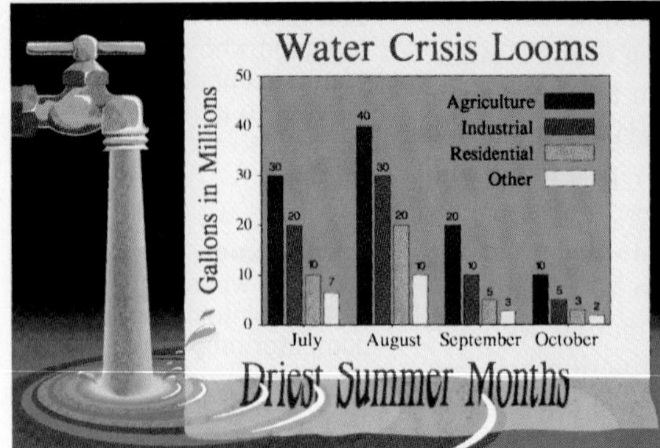

User Solution 1-2

Computers Tackle California Droughts

On the west coast of the Golden State, water has always been a major problem. Typically, for long periods there is no rain. When it finally does arrive, the rain often comes down so hard and so fast that much of it washes into the Pacific Ocean. In Los Angeles County, where more than eight million people consume about a half trillion gallons of water annually, a computer-based system has been installed to trap the precious liquid. While the system can't make it rain, it closely monitors water conditions in drainage channels during storms so that runoff can be diverted into special basin areas where it can seep back into the earth and restock underground water supplies. Sensors in the drainage channels and the seepage areas collect data on water flows and levels and feed these data into the computers. The computers then figure out the best and safest way to route the water through the drainage channels.

Benefits Computers Provide

Virtually every benefit provided by computers boils down to helping organizations or individuals do work either more efficiently or more effectively.

Efficiency *Efficiency* relates to how well a given job is done. Because computers can do certain types of work faster than humans and with fewer errors, many organizations acquire computers for the efficiency they provide. Also, because human labor is expensive, replacing humans with computers often results in less money spent in the long run. The fact that many organizations are operating with fewer employees today than in years past is due in large part to the efficiency computers provide.

Computers contribute to work efficiency by performing such tasks as issuing payroll checks, keeping track of customer purchases and payments, and managing reservations and cancellations. In most cases, greater efficiency means doing work faster, more accurately, or cheaper.

Effectiveness Whereas efficiency relates to doing something the right way, *effectiveness* relates to doing the right thing. And while efficient uses for the computer generally affect the costs of an organization (that is, the money going out), effective uses for the computer have an impact on the revenue (that is, the money coming in).

One good example of computers being used to increase effectiveness is their ability to enhance customer service. For instance, a brokerage business that allows investors to trade securities and get security prices from home computers is using computer technology to improve the level of service it provides. Computers can also increase effectiveness by helping handicapped workers, monitoring the environment for potential dangers (see User Solution 1-2), and creating products that would otherwise be impossible—such as movie special effects.

Computer Systems to Fit Every Need and Pocketbook

A great variety of computer systems are available commercially to serve computer users' needs. Here we'll consider one important way in which computers differ from one another—size.

Computers are generally classified in one of four size categories: small, or microcomputers; medium-sized, or minicomputers; large, or mainframe computers; and super-large, or supercomputers. In practice, the distinction among these different sizes is not always clear-cut. Large minicomputers, for example, often are bigger than small mainframes.

In general, the larger the computer, the greater its processing power. For example, big computers can process data at faster speeds than small computers. Big computers can also accommodate larger and more powerful peripheral devices. Naturally, the larger the computer and its peripheral equipment, the higher the price. A computer system can cost anywhere from a few hundred dollars to many millions.

Microcomputers

A technological breakthrough in the early 1970s made it possible to produce an entire CPU on a single silicon chip smaller than a dime. These "computers-on-a-chip," or *microprocessors,* could be mass produced at very low cost. Microprocessors were quickly integrated into all types of products, making possible powerful hand-held calculators, digital watches, a variety of electronic toys, and sophisticated controls for household appliances such as microwave ovens and automatic coffee makers. Microprocessors also made it possible to build inexpensive computer systems, such as those in Figure 1-4, small enough to fit on a desktop or even in a shirt pocket. These small computer systems have informally come to be called **microcomputers** (or *micros*). Because they are inexpensive and small enough for one person to use at home or work for personal needs, they are also commonly called **personal computers** *(PCs)* or *personal computer systems.*

As illustrated in Figure 1-4, most **microcomputer systems** currently available for business and home use can be classified as desktop, portable (including laptop), or hand-held units.

Microcomputer system. The smallest and least expensive type of computer system. Also known as a **microcomputer** *(micro),* **personal computer** *(PC),* or *personal computer system.*

Desktop Units *Desktop computers* (see Figure 1-4a) are those found most often in schools, homes, and businesses. These are the computer systems that have become household names—IBM PC and PS/2; Apple Macintosh; Compaq Deskpro; and so forth. Desktop units fall into one of two categories: single-user systems and multiuser systems. *Single-user systems,* as their name implies, can be operated by only one user at a time, while *multiuser systems* can accommodate several users concurrently.

Portable and Laptop Units *Portable computers* are designed for users who would like to use the same microcomputer at several sites. These computers are characterized by being lightweight (1 to 18 pounds) and compact (able to

FIGURE 1-4

Three microcomputer systems. (a) IBM Value Point P60/D Pentium computer. (b) Compaq Lite 4/33C laptop computer. (c) Sharp Travel Organizer hand-held computer.

(a)

(b)

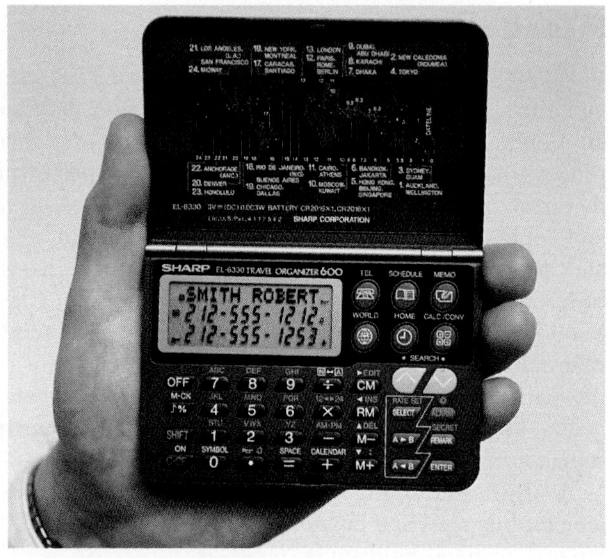

(c)

fit into a carrying case). Technically speaking, the most lightweight portable computers—which can be used on a person's lap, if desired—are called *laptop computers* or *notebook computers* (see Figure 1-4b). Although many portables are just as powerful as their larger desktop cousins, they tend to be more expensive, have small and hard-to-read screens, and have a dense arrangement of keys. These disadvantages notwithstanding, portability is "in" these days, and laptop computers currently are one of the fastest-growing segments of the microcomputer industry.

Hand-held Units *Hand-held computers*—or *palmtop computers*—look and behave a lot like standard pocket calculators. You can generally hold the entire computer system in your hand while operating it. Today, most hand-held computers are relegated to specialized tasks—keeping track of golf or bowling scores, translating words into foreign languages, checking the spelling of words, providing synonyms and antonyms for words, and organizing appointments (see Figure 1-4c). In the next several years, the market for hand-held computers is expected to grow explosively. Hand-held devices called *personal digital assistants,* or *PDAs,* which can be used to carry out such tasks as computing, messaging, form-filling, and faxing are becoming increasingly available (see Tomorrow box).

Micros are widely used in both small and large businesses. Small businesses use them to keep track of merchandise, prepare correspondence, bill customers, and do routine accounting. Large businesses use them as productivity tools for secretaries and as analysis tools for decision makers, to name just two important applications. Also, laptops are popular with salespeople making presentations at client sites and with managers who need a computer as they travel about. Microcomputers are increasingly being networked into large communications systems where they are used as data-entry devices or as general-purpose workstations.

Minicomputers

Minicomputers, or *minis,* generally are regarded as medium-sized computers (see Figure 1-5). Most of them fall between microcomputers and mainframes in their processing power. The very smallest minicomputers, however, are virtually

Minicomputer.
An intermediate-sized and medium-priced type of computer.

FIGURE 1-5

Minicomputers. Minicomputers are particularly useful where several people need to share a common system, such as in small companies or in departments of larger companies.

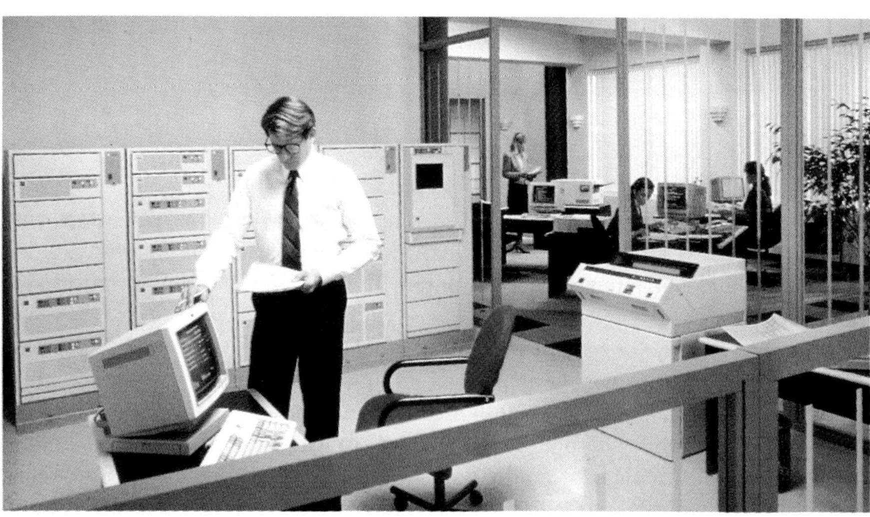

TOMORROW

The PDAs Are Coming! The PDAs Are Coming!

Is a New Major Industry on Its Way?

Some very credible people are saying it could produce one of the biggest revolutions in technology since the personal computer. In fact, Apple Computer has formed a new spinoff company to develop products that hardly anybody's ever used in practice. Bullish computer-industry analysts predict a trillion-dollar industry by the end of the decade.

What we're talking about here is the *personal digital assistant,* or *PDA.*

PDAs are hand-held computers that are specially designed for people who don't like to interact with computers all that much. Newton, Apple's initial product, is a 6-by-8-inch device targeted to business users. It does calculations, keeps track of phone numbers, and manages personal schedules and to-do lists. Not only that, but it is also a communications device that can send and receive faxes and tap into data in larger computers at remote locations.

One of Newton's most compelling advantages is its ease of use. There are no keyboards to confuse you or complicated syntax to remember. You just write your commands onto the PDA or choose from menus with a penlike stylus. So if you want to send a message to Bob, you just write it out, along with the instruction "Fax to Bob." The PDA will then look up Bob's fax number and send the message automatically.

One of the most successful PDAs to date has been Sharp's Wizzard. At Brooklyn Union Gas Company, the Wizzard assists with customer service operations by guiding service representatives through the maze of regulatory data they need to have on hand when helping customers set up accounts. PDAs were chosen because they were the least costly way to conveniently provide every service representative with the tools needed to do his or her job. At Merck & Company, the Wizzard is used as a personal organizer for office managers and to help sales managers easily gain access to the information needed to run territories. Merck reports that the approachable, toylike appearance of the PDA generates interest and use among people who find conventional computers frightening.

At Northern Telecom, the PDA of choice has been Sony's Data Discman. When a repair technician makes a call, he or she brings along a hand-held electronic service manual the size of a paperback book—one that includes the equivalent of 18,000 printed pages of data. By typing keywords on a compressed keypad, the technician can quickly access the required repair procedure on a small display. A PDA of this sort that can also communicate with the home office could conceivably access scores of electronic manuals, all with the latest updates, within seconds.

indistinguishable from the largest microcomputers, and the largest (sometimes called *superminis*) closely resemble small mainframes. Minicomputers usually are far more expensive than microcomputers and are unaffordable for most individuals.

Any of several factors might lead an organization to choose a minicomputer over a micro or mainframe. A small or medium-sized company may simply find microcomputer systems too slow to handle its current volume of processing. Or a company may need a computer system that can do several jobs at once and interact with multiple users at the same time. Many microcomputer systems lack sufficient power for handling such complex applications. Mainframes, of course, can handle these applications, but they are much larger and more expensive than minis.

Wallet power. PDAs and the mobile user (left, Apple Newton; right, SkyTel Message Card).

At Xerox's Palo Alto Research Center (PARC), a PDA developed in the form of an electronic badge can be used for several purposes. For instance, if Judy Smith is away from her office and someone is trying to call her, the phone nearest to Judy will ring with a personalized jingle. Also, the badge can be used to automatically record Judy's daily whereabouts.

SkyTel's credit-card-sized Message Card is ideal if you travel a lot. When callers access a toll-free station with your personal identification number, they can leave their phone number or a complete voice message. Within seconds, the number to call is routed to your card.

The PDA is predicted to go well beyond business, into consumer electronics, as well. PDAs will come in the form of electronic books and entertainment gadgets, and devices that help us better manage the devices we now have. People may even have electronic art in their homes—flat-screen wall hangings that can be programmed to display almost anything you want, if, say, you press the right buttons.

The big unknown with PDAs at this point is whether consumers and businesses will buy them in droves. So far, acceptance has been slow, leaving some industry skeptics to caution that PDA may come to stand for "probably disappointed again." But people are typically cautious about accepting technology and changing the way they do things. Eventually, if a product is useful and exciting enough, and if the price is right, it's sure to be a winner.

Mainframes

The **mainframe** (see Figure 1-6) is the standard for almost all large organizations. It often operates 24 hours a day, serving hundreds of users on display devices during regular business hours and processing large jobs such as payroll and billing late at night. Many large organizations need several mainframes to complete their computing work loads. Typically these organizations own or lease a variety of computer types—say, mainframes, minis, and micros—to meet all their processing needs.

Mainframe. A large, transaction-processing-oriented computer.

Most mainframes are employed to handle high-volume processing of business transactions and routine paperwork. For most businesses, this includes tasks such as keeping track of customer purchases and payments, sending out bills

FIGURE 1-6

IBM ES/9000 mainframe. IBM's ES/9000 series sets the standard for today's mainframes. IBM accounts for close to 75 percent of all mainframes sold.

and reminder notices, paying employees, and maintaining detailed tax records. These operations were some of the earliest applications of computers in business and have been the responsibility of mainframes from day one.

Supercomputers

Supercomputer. The fastest and most expensive type of computer.

Some organizations, such as large scientific and research laboratories, have extraordinary information processing needs. Applications such as sending astronauts into outer space and weather forecasting, for example, require extreme degrees of accuracy and a wealth of computations. High-quality animation, which produces the special effects you see in computer-generated movies and commercials, also demands enormous amounts of high-speed computation. To meet such needs, a few vendors offer very large, sophisticated machines called **supercomputers** (see Figure 1-7). These machines are very expensive, often costing several millions of dollars.

Using Computers: Some Examples

Now that we've briefly seen how a computer system works, let's "walk through" a few applications within a typical organization to put many of the concepts you've just read about into sharper focus.

Large System Paradise Beach Resort is a large hotel on the Florida coast. It uses a *mainframe* computer system to keep track of such matters as guest reservations, bills, and employees. Without the mainframe, the hotel would never be able to accommodate the number of guests it handles with its current staff, nor would it be able to provide the high level of service its guests expect.

In the precomputer days, operations were far less sophisticated. For instance, it was common for bills to be incorrect, misplaced, or mismanaged. Frequently, if a reservation was improperly recorded, the guest was detained in the lobby. In fact, often two desk clerks would be in the process of booking different guests for the same room—an embarrassing mishap for the hotel and one that sometimes resulted in lost business.

Today, with a computer keeping track of guests, these types of problems occur very infrequently. The mainframe also handles various other types of accounting tasks—paying employees and preparing comprehensive reports for management and taxing agencies, for instance. It does these tasks much more quickly and accurately—that is, more efficiently—than was possible in the precomputer days. Some of the information that management now routinely receives was impossible to obtain before the computer arrived. Consequently, managers now can be more effective at doing their jobs.

FIGURE 1-7

Cray supercomputer. Supercomputers are faster than conventional computers because they pack circuits much more tightly. Cray produces more than half of the supercomputers sold worldwide.

The hotel's computer needs are tended to by a staff of just four people. A *director* of computing oversees all planning in computer-related areas. A *systems analyst* decides which software packages and hardware must be bought and which programs must be custom written to meet the evolving needs of the hotel. A resident *programmer* attends to the latter need, coding programs from specific guidelines provided by the systems analyst. An *operations person* ensures that hotel computer systems run smoothly on a daily basis and troubleshoots potential technical problems when any computer system malfunctions.

Profile of an End User Lydia Maxwell is the catering manager at Paradise Beach Resort. She finds a desktop *microcomputer system* a useful tool in her work. The hardware in Lydia's microcomputer system consists of five basic pieces of equipment: a keyboard, a display device, a printer, a system unit, and a mouse (see Figure 1-8). Within the *system unit* are the CPU chip or microprocessor, memory, and secondary storage devices—two diskette drives and a hard-disk drive—as well as a lot of circuitry that we'll talk about later in the book.

The *keyboard,* which resembles that of an ordinary typewriter, enables Lydia to direct the microcomputer system to do what she wants. Everything she inputs at the keyboard and the computer system's responses to these inputs are shown on the *display device* or *monitor,* which resembles a television screen. When Lydia wants something printed out, she directs the computer system to send the output to her *printer*.

The *diskette unit* on Lydia's microcomputer system consists of two *drives*. On the drives, Lydia can mount *diskettes,* or *floppy disks*—small platters capable of storing, say, 100 or more pages worth of data or programs. The diskettes

FIGURE 1-8

The catering manager's microcomputer system. The system unit contains the microprocessor, memory, and secondary storage devices—two diskette drives and a hard-disk drive.

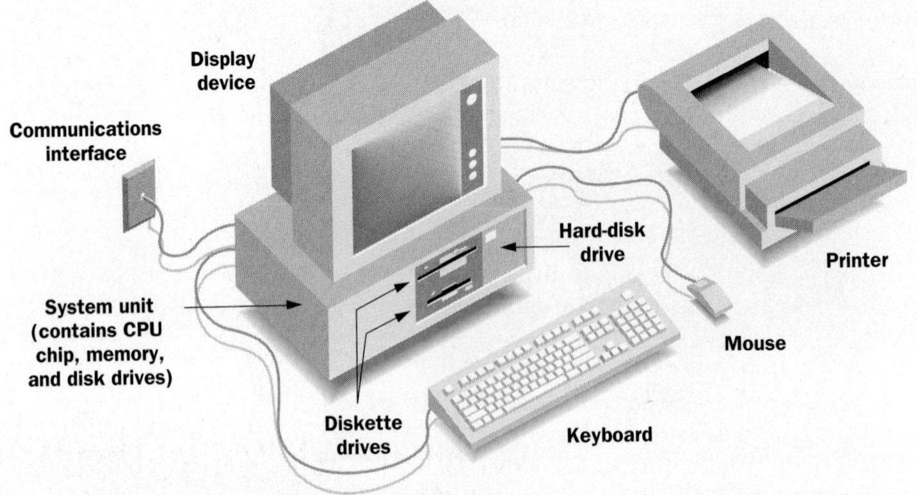

FIGURE 1-9

Meal-planning data stored on disk. Lydia's meal-planning data consists of several filled-in electronic forms. Several thousand such forms can easily be stored on a hard disk.

DISH: TEXAS-STYLE CHILI

DISH: TURKEY FLORENTINE

DISH: BEEF STROGANOFF
INGREDIENTS: BEEF, MUSHROOMS, MUSTARD, ONION, SOUR CREAM, CONSOMME, BUTTER, FLOUR, SALT, PEPPER
REMARKS: MEAT, DINNER, HEAVY, RUSSIAN

must be properly inserted into the computer system's disk drives if the system is to access the programs and data on them. Diskettes make it convenient to transport data and programs to and from the computer system in machine-readable form.

The *hard-disk unit* on Lydia's system, on the other hand, has almost 100 times the capacity of a single diskette and permits much quicker accessing of both programs and data. Three years ago, Lydia acquired a computer system with a hard-disk unit because her collection of programs and data was expanding rapidly and she was getting tired of mounting and dismounting diskettes every time she wanted to use a particular program or set of data.

Once a program and its data are loaded into memory from any of the disk devices, the computer is transformed into a powerful calculating tool.

One application for which Lydia finds her computer system useful is *word processing.* For instance, when a letter must be sent to a client to confirm a booking date, Lydia uses a word processing software package and a "canned" form letter stored on her hard disk. When she finishes customizing the letter, Lydia has it output on her printer.

Lydia also frequently uses her microcomputer system to prepare budgets, a task that requires a *spreadsheet* software package. The spreadsheet enables Lydia to quickly rework her budgets with different assumptions. For instance, she might need to know what would happen if her office expenses increased by five percent or if her budget was slashed by ten percent. Having a computer around to supply fast answers to questions like these makes Lydia better prepared for meetings with her superiors.

To plan meals, Lydia uses a *database management system.* The database program is especially useful in assisting Lydia with searching through descriptions of food dishes to find ones that will fit a particular client's needs. A file of hundreds of filled-in "forms," or records, one for each food dish she can offer to guests, is stored on her hard disk (see Figure 1-9). Each form contains

FIGURE 1-10

A screen menu. Screen menus beckon a user to choose a specific course of action. Using them effectively requires neither typing skills nor an extensive knowledge of computers.

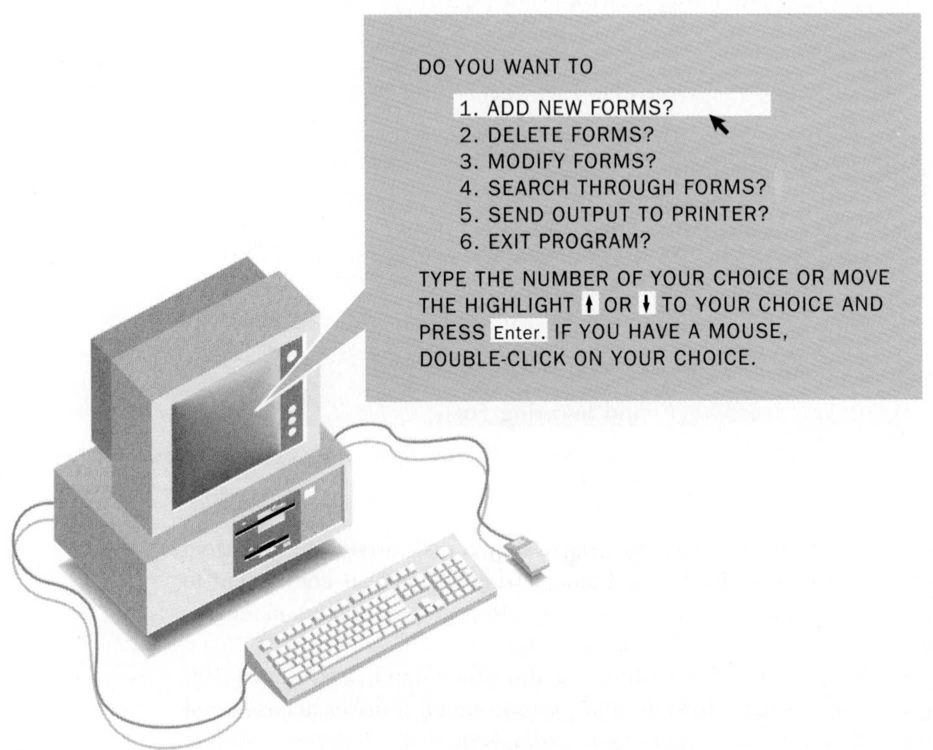

three separate types, or fields, of data—the name of the dish, its ingredients, and a few remarks.

DO YOU WANT TO
1. ADD NEW FORMS?
2. DELETE FORMS?
3. MODIFY FORMS?
4. SEARCH THROUGH FORMS?
5. SEND OUTPUT TO PRINTER?
6. EXIT PROGRAM?
TYPE THE NUMBER OF YOUR CHOICE OR MOVE THE HIGHLIGHT ↑ OR ↓ TO YOUR CHOICE AND PRESS Enter. IF YOU HAVE A MOUSE, DOUBLE-CLICK ON YOUR CHOICE.

If Lydia is helping a client plan a Saturday night banquet over the phone, she can summon the database program to search for all forms on her entrees disk file in which "ingredients" contains "beef" and "remarks" contains "dinner." Then she can have the names of these dishes directed to her display screen.

Of course, Lydia can rely on recall, but having the computer system make the search for her often turns up good alternatives that didn't cross her mind. Also, she can save a lot of phone time by having her computer system do the searching while she attends to other matters with the client. Lydia's database manager lets her add new forms to the file when she wants them, delete forms, and modify forms. She does this with a *screen menu* of processing alternatives (not to be confused with a food menu) that the database manager sends to her display screen, asking her what she wants to do (see Figure 1-10).

To make a screen menu selection, Lydia can use her keyboard or *mouse*, according to the instructions on the screen. Typically, she uses her mouse for this type of selection operation. As she moves the mouse along her desktop, the onscreen arrow—called a *pointer*—moves accordingly. When she activates a button on the mouse, the computer system will execute, or select, that choice.

Lydia also has a *communications interface,* which enables her computer to interact with other computers located miles away. For instance, Lydia uses her computer to automatically place food and beverage orders with a distributor located across town. The communications interface is made up of hardware and software elements that enable Lydia's computer to call up the distributor's computer and transfer a food and beverage order, electronically, over regular telephone lines. The distributor's computer will even relay back a confirmation of the order.

One reason for Lydia's success at her job is her skill at quickly pulling together key information when dealing with clients, managers, and suppliers. The database management system and word processor allow Lydia to give clients first-class service. Hotel management appreciates the value of this; a $50,000 booking can easily be won or lost on the quality of service. The spreadsheet allows her to quickly prepare important financial information for management, and to analyze that information in ways that would not be feasible if she had to do it by hand. Also, the communications interface enables Lydia to place orders more efficiently, saving time and lowering costs.

Computers and Society

The example we've just presented should give you some idea of why computer systems have become such an important part of modern life. Their ability to sort through massive amounts of data and quickly produce useful information for almost any kind of user—from payroll clerk to president—makes them indispensable in a society like ours. Without a computer, the catering manager in our example could not possibly provide the level of service she now extends to clients. The government would be unable to tabulate all the data it collects for the census every ten years. Banks would be overwhelmed by the job of tracking all the transactions they must process. The efficient airline and telephone service we are used to would be impossible. Moon exploration and the space shuttle would still belong to science fiction. The list is virtually endless.

But along with the benefits computers bring to society have come some troubling problems, ranging from health to personal security and privacy to ethics. The catering manager in our example, for instance, spends many hours in front of a display screen. Do the radiation and glare emanating from the screen impair her health? Banks keep data on customers' accounts on external storage devices. Can they prevent clever "computer criminals" from using their computer systems to steal from those accounts? The Internal Revenue Service has confidential information about every American taxpayer. Can it protect that information from unauthorized use? Because commercial software exists in electronic form, it can be easily copied. What restrictions should be placed on who can copy and use this software?

These are serious issues, but we can only mention them briefly in this chapter. In Chapter 14, we will discuss the costs and benefits of computers at length. Feature 1-2 discusses a relatively new use of computers that could change the way we interact socially—teledemocracy. A Critical Thinking question at the end of the chapter asks you to consider ways to keep such technology free from abuse.

Feature 1 – 2

Teledemocracy

A high-tech way to reflect your opinion

It's an old idea waiting for new ways to happen.

Teledemocracy refers to using computer keyboards and other types of data-entry devices to do such things as voice opinions and cast votes. Perhaps the ultimate teledemocratic society is one in which there is a computer in every human hand. Everyone would then have the ability to tap into a common point that provides some reliable way of collecting or passing out survey or voting information.

We are still quite far away from such a scenario. But we are making progress.

Today, perhaps as many as a few million people participate in a limited form of teledemocracy through subscription-based information services, such as Prodigy and CompuServe, on home computers. A subscriber to one of these services might be able to access an *electronic bulletin board* and express an opinion on issues like taxing the rich or ways to cut the budget deficit. Subscribers can often also post notes and read what other subscribers have to say. Other available forms of teledemocracy include taking part in debates and asking questions to political candidates.

But subscriber information services currently have their limitations. First, many people find such services too expensive or not useful enough to buy into, even though they own a computer. Second, not everyone who has the ability to express an opinion is computer literate. Third, the subscriber-based information services often avoid involvement in unpopular and politically incorrect matters. Recently, one person who advocated overthrowing the federal government was allegedly barred from promoting a discussion of this subject on an electronic bulletin board.

Today, only about one percent of Americans subscribe to computerized information services. However, teledemocracy can be implemented in other ways, like interactive cable television. For instance, it's possible to have an "issues channel," where viewers are regularly asked to cast votes with a hand-held keypad. About a decade ago, such a system was tested in Columbus, Ohio, as an alternative for conventional political meetings. The company running the test discovered that citizens participated about ten times more than they did through conventional, face-to-face town meetings. Unfortunately, many of the problems that plague interactive cable TV as a vehicle for teledemocracy—such as viewer expense and issue censorship—are the same as those that affect the computer-based information services.

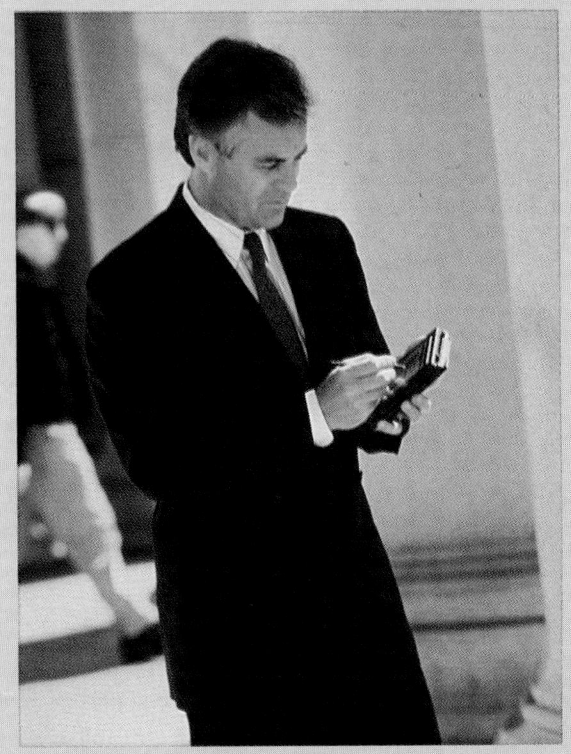

Palmtop voting. Another application for hand-held computers.

While the benefits of teledemocracy are enormous, many questions remain unanswered. Would instant audience feedback make it harder than ever for politicians to stand up for what's right rather than for what's popular? Would it become more difficult for any types of sweeping change or progress to take place? And consider this: Who would ultimately decide whether a vote held opposite *Monday Night Football* was biased?

Computers in Action

Where would you expect to find computers? In our discussion so far, we've seen some of the amazing variety of ways in which computers have become part of our lives. As you read through this book, you should get a good idea of what computer systems can and cannot do and where they do and do not belong. Window 1 presents an extensive picture essay of computers in just a few of the many settings in which you are likely to encounter them.

Summary and Key Terms

Computers appear almost everywhere in today's world. They're embedded in consumer products, used to run businesses, and employed to direct production in our factories, to name just a few applications.

Computers in the 1990s Workplace Computers abound in today's workplace largely because we are living in an era when most jobs heavily depend on the collection, use, creation, and dissemination of information.

What's a Computer and What Does It Do? Four words summarize the operation of a **computer system: input, processing, output,** and **storage.**

The processing function is performed by the **computer** itself, which is sometimes called the **central processing unit,** or **CPU.**

The input and output functions are performed by **peripheral equipment,** such as **input devices** and **output devices.** Just as your stereo amplifier would be useless if it had no speakers, headphones, tape deck, or turntable to supplement it, the computer would be helpless without these peripheral devices.

Mounted on some of the peripheral equipment are **input/output (I/O) media.** Many of these media *store* materials in **machine-readable** form, which the computer system can recognize and process.

The material that a computer receives as input is of two kinds: data and programs. **Data** are facts the computer has at its disposal; **programs** are instructions that explain to the computer what to do with these facts. Programs must be written in a **programming language** that the computer can understand.

Data that have been processed into a useful form are called **information.** The processing of data into information on computers is called **information processing.**

Computer systems have two types of storage. **Primary storage** (sometimes called **memory** or **internal storage**) is often built into the unit housing the computer itself; it holds the programs and data that the system is currently processing. **Secondary (external) storage** holds other programs and data. In many systems, secondary storage is located in a separate hardware device.

In the world of computers, it is common to distinguish between hardware and software. **Hardware** refers to the actual machinery that makes up the computer system, such as the CPU, input and output devices, and secondary storage devices. **Software** refers to computer programs.

End users are the people who need the output that computer systems produce. In a computing environment, there are many types of experts who help users meet their computing needs; for example, **programmers** are responsible for writing programs.

Virtually every benefit provided by computers boils down to making people do work either more efficiently or more effectively.

Computer Systems to Fit Every Need and Pocketbook Small computers are often called **microcomputers (microcomputer systems)** or **personal computers** *(personal computer systems),* medium-sized computers are called **minicomputers,** and large computers are called **mainframes.** The very largest computers, which are used for applications that demand the most in terms of speed and power, are called **supercomputers.** Although categorizing computers by size can be helpful, in practice it is sometimes difficult to classify computers that fall on the borders of these categories.

Using Computers: Some Examples The hotel industry is but one example of an environment where computers—from mainframes to microcomputers—serve a variety of uses.

Computers and Society Although computer systems have become an indispensable part of modern life, their growing use has created troubling problems, ranging from health to personal security and privacy to ethics.

Computers in Action As you read through this book, you should get a good idea of what computer systems can and cannot do and where they do and do not belong. Window 1 presents an extensive picture essay of computers in just a few of the many settings in which you are likely to encounter them.

Review Exercises

Fill-in Questions

1. Four words sum up the operation of a computer system: input, output, __________, and storage.
2. When programs and data are being processed, they are stored in __________ storage.
3. Processed data that are in a useful form are called __________.
4. Another name for computer programs is __________.
5. When programs and data are not being processed but need to be "at the fingertips" of the computer, they are stored in __________ storage.
6. A term used for the equipment in a computing environment is __________.
7. A series of instructions that direct a computer system is known as a(n) __________.
8. The hardware, software, data, procedures, and personnel needed to process data successfully are called a(n) __________.

Matching Questions

Match each term with the description that fits best.

a. minicomputer
b. input device
c. mainframe
d. supercomputer
e. hardware
f. microcomputer

___ 1. The equipment that makes up a computer system.

___ 2. Another name for personal computer.

___ 3. A medium-sized computer.

___ 4. A large computer used to process business transactions in high volume.

___ 5. Any piece of equipment that supplies programs and data to a computer.

___ 6. The most powerful type of electronic computer.

Discussion Questions

1. Name several ways in which computers are used in today's workplace.
2. Provide some examples of input devices, output devices, processing devices, and input/output media that are found in the average household and are not necessarily computer related.

3. What is the difference between a computer and a computer system?
4. Name as many peripheral devices as you can. What is the purpose of each?
5. What are the major differences between primary storage and secondary storage?
6. What is the difference between programs and data?
7. Define and give some examples of end users of a computer system.
8. Identify some social problems created by the existence of computer systems.

Critical Thinking Questions

1. Should everyone getting a degree from a college or university today be required to take an introductory computer course? Defend your response.
2. The section on the workplace of the 1990s provides several examples describing how computers are changing the way ordinary people work. Can you think of any additional examples not mentioned in this section?
3. The term "computer literacy"—knowing something about computers—is widely used today. In your opinion, what types of computer knowledge should people such as yourself be literate about?
4. Feature 1–2 discusses ways in which teledemocracy can be implemented. What problems need to be worked out in this technology to make it possible for people to elect a president over the phone?

WINDOW 1

Computers in Our World

A Visual Portfolio of the Widespread Use of Computers

Computers rapidly have become an important force in almost every segment of our society. This first "window to the world of computers" presents a small sample of the many tasks to which computers may be applied. Included are examples from the fields of business, entertainment, design, advertising, art, education, the environment, health care, and science.

1. Computers are frequently used to alter images in fantastic ways. Here, four faces of Elvis have been read into the computer system and "chiseled" into a high-tech monument.

Business

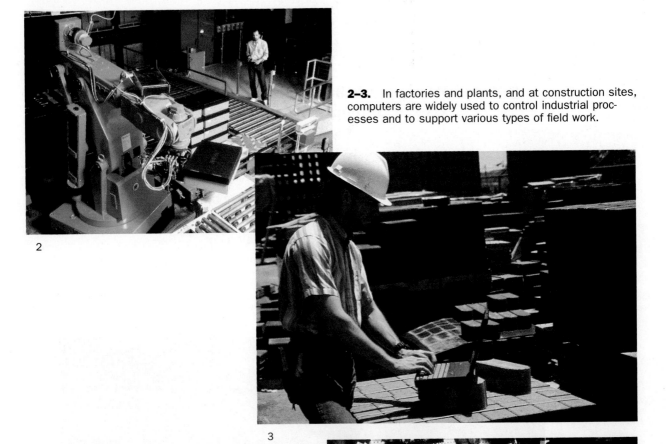

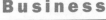

2–3. In factories and plants, and at construction sites, computers are widely used to control industrial processes and to support various types of field work.

2

3

4–5. The computer has become a commonplace fixture in retailing, both for interacting with customers and for performing back-office accounting functions.

4

5

Entertainment

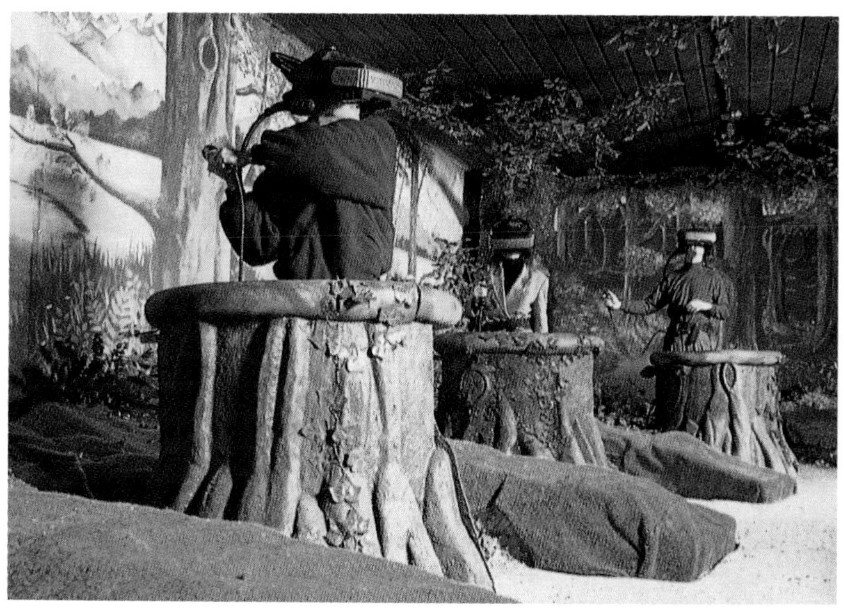

6. Virtual-reality games enable players wearing special goggles to enter their own computer-generated environments. In the game shown here, participants assume active roles in a medieval fantasy game.

6

7

7–9. Through the use of computers, the villain in *Indiana Jones and the Last Crusade* is spectacularly metamorphosized into a mummy before the moviegoer's eyes.

8

9

Design

10–11. Today, computers are widely used to design structures of all types, from homes to industrial facilities. In many cases, the designs are rendered in three dimensions, thereby making it possible to "walk through them" on the computer's display screen.

10

11

12. By using computers to create package designs electronically, both the designer and client can see on a computer screen how the packages look filled with food contents, standing in front of other food (as shown here), or sitting on the store shelf with other products.

12

13. Today, both cars and highways are "built" and "tested" by computer—often before physical building and testing ever take place.

13

Advertising and Art

14–15. Computers are commonly used to create advertising images that appear on film and in print. Many of the ads you see on television are either completely computer created or enhanced by the computer in some way.

14

15

16

16. The field of computer art is rapidly emerging as a serious art medium, with its own contests and shows.

Education and Training

17–18. Computers are often used as in-classroom tools to teach courses and as out-of-classroom tools to complete homework assignments.

18

17

19

19. At many museums and exhibitions, and even on business sites, computer-controlled booths called "kiosks" disseminate information.

20

21

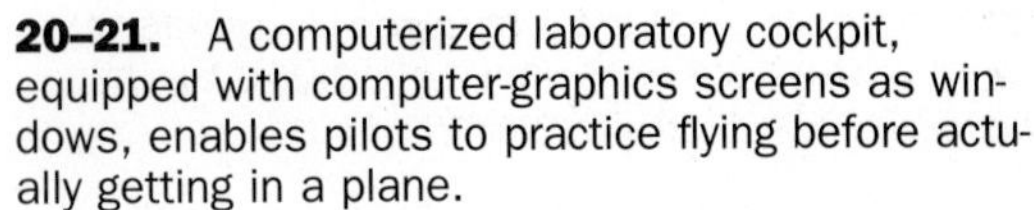

20–21. A computerized laboratory cockpit, equipped with computer-graphics screens as windows, enables pilots to practice flying before actually getting in a plane.

Society and Government

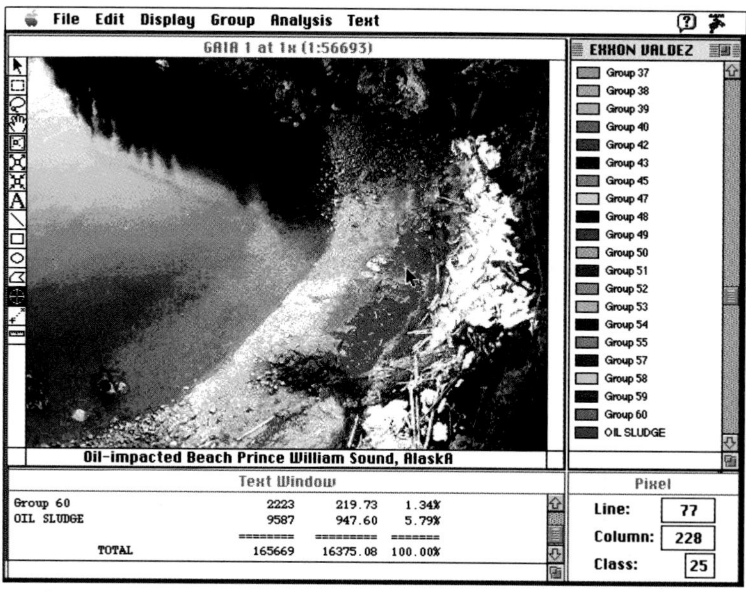

22

22. Technology regularly assists scientists as they study the environment. Here, a computer-enhanced photo of Alaska's Prince William Sound shows in pink the oil sludge left by the Exxon *Valdez* spill.

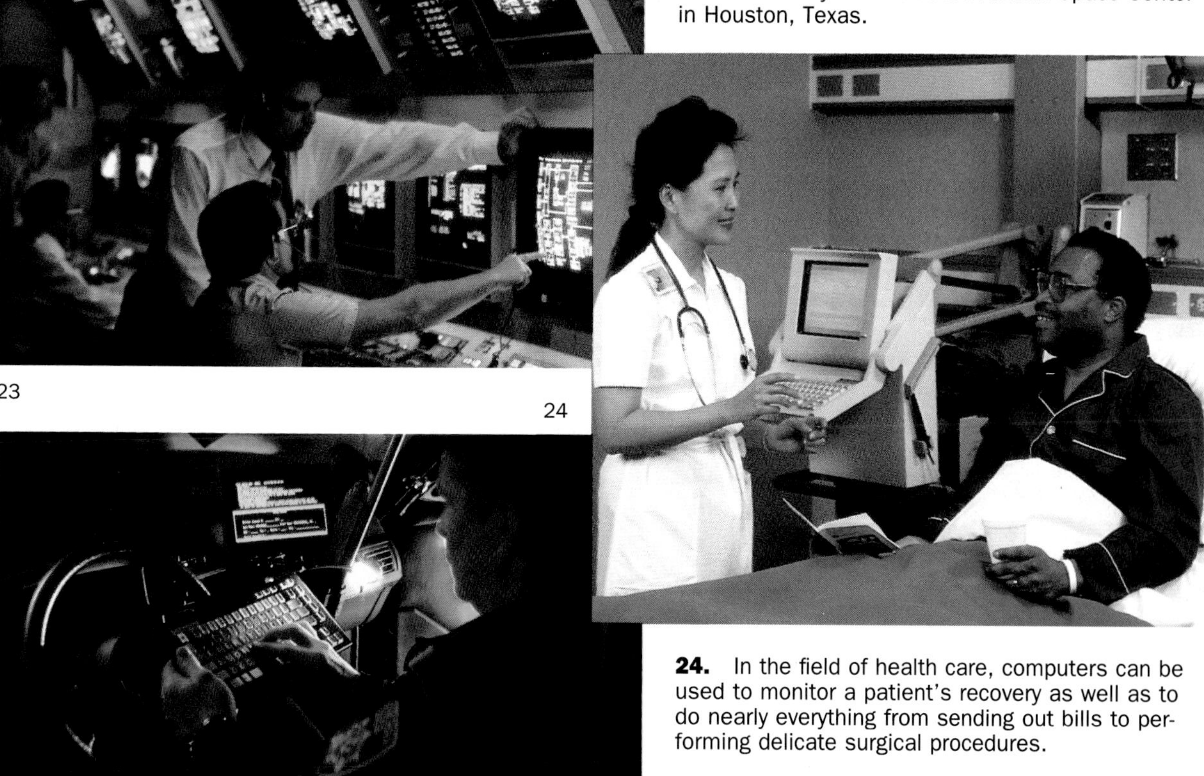

23

24

25

23. Controllers review computer-controlled communications systems at the Johnson Space Center in Houston, Texas.

24. In the field of health care, computers can be used to monitor a patient's recovery as well as to do nearly everything from sending out bills to performing delicate surgical procedures.

25. Technology is employed at virtually all levels today in the fight against crime.

Irish Spring
NEW
CLASSIC
Irish Spring
ROLL-ON
ANTI-PERSPIRANT & DEODORANT
NET WT. 1.50 FL. OZ
Irish Spring

COMPUTER SYSTEMS AND INFORMATION PROCESSING

2

How do computers process data into useful outputs? In this chapter we'll look at some of the ways, and, also, examine types of hardware and software found in a typical computer system.

OUTLINE

Overview

Computer Hardware

  Peripheral Equipment

  Input, Output, or Storage?

  Input/Output Media

  Online and Offline

Organizing Data for Computer Systems

A Brief Introduction to Software

Information Processing

Getting It All Together: Combining Elements into a Complete Computer System

LEARNING OBJECTIVES

After completing this chapter, you will be able to:

1. Identify several major classes of input, output, processing, and storage hardware.
2. Explain how data are organized in a computing environment.
3. Distinguish between applications and systems software.
4. Describe some of the ways in which computer systems process data into useful information.
5. Define several more key terms that are useful to know when reading about or discussing computers.

Overview

As you learned in Chapter 1, input, processing, and output, together with storage, are the major components of any computer system. In this chapter, you will see how they work together in more detail.

First, we'll take a look at computer system hardware. We'll cover some basic hardware concepts and discuss some of the most important kinds of input, output, and storage equipment. Then we'll see how this equipment can be linked, first in a small computer system and then in a large one. This section will prepare you for the detailed discussion of hardware in Module B.

From there, we'll take up the subject of data, specifically how data must be organized for processing on a computer system. Study the terms introduced in this section carefully, because you will encounter them frequently throughout the rest of the book.

Then we'll go on to a discussion of program software to introduce you to a subject we cover extensively later in the text.

Following this, we'll discuss information processing on computer systems. We'll examine representative examples of some of the most common types of processing to see how hardware, data, software, procedures, and users interact to do useful work.

Finally, to integrate many of the chapter materials, we'll look at how the hardware, software, data, and information-processing procedures you read about in earlier sections combine with people to form a sophisticated computer system.

The ways in which computers can provide useful information are too numerous to catalog in any textbook. While the bulk of the chapter covers some of the most widespread uses of computers, Feature 2-1 touches on a more exotic application—helping historians unravel the century-old mystery of Billy the Kid.

Computer Hardware

Computer.
A device that can perform arithmetic, make comparisons, and store and retrieve facts. Also called the **central processing unit (CPU).**

System unit.
The hardware unit that houses the computer and its memory, as well as a number of other devices.

Peripheral equipment.
The machines that work with the computer.

All computer systems consist of some combination of computers and peripheral equipment. The main **computer,** often called the *central processing unit,* or *CPU,* is the heart of the system; it controls the actual processing of data and programs. Closely tied to the CPU is its *memory,* which is almost always housed in the same hardware device, called the **system unit.** Many people, in fact, refer to the system unit as the computer, but strictly speaking it is merely the "box" that contains the computer. **Peripheral equipment** consists of all the machines that make it possible to get data and programs into the CPU, retrieve processed information, and store data and programs for ready access to the CPU.

Peripheral Equipment

Peripheral equipment for computer systems can be classified in a number of ways. One of the most basic classifications is by function: Is the device predominantly for input, output, or storage? Another is by medium: Does it use tapes or disks? A third is by its relation to the CPU: Is it online or offline? Let's consider each of these in turn.

Feature 2–1

Debunking the Billy the Kid Legend

Have computers put to rest an unsolved mystery?

One of the most famous symbols of the Old West is Billy the Kid. History books tell us that this notorious outlaw was shot and killed by Sheriff Pat Garrett—in Fort Sumner, New Mexico Territory—on the night of July 14, 1881. But many people insist that the shooting was a hoax and that the real Billy actually left Fort Sumner alive, managing to live out a long life elsewhere.

One of the most famous of these claims centers around a character named Brushy Bill Roberts, who passed away in Texas in 1950. Prior to his death, Brushy Bill insisted that he was the real Billy the Kid. He even asked the governor of New Mexico to pardon him for his alleged seventy-year-old crimes. Was Roberts the real Kid, or just a misguided publicity hound?

The latter, say some highly reputable computer-imaging reseachers at the University of Chicago.

A few years back, computer experts developed a way to create updated pictures of missing children by electronically altering old photographs. Using many of the same computational techniques, the researchers compared photos of the real Billy the Kid to those of Brushy Bill Roberts and other claimants to the legend. The computer software works on the principle that certain facial structures of a person remain the same throughout time, despite the effects of aging. Consequently, by comparing distances, angles, and ratios between certain facial points—about 15 such measurements, say the researchers—it can be reasonably determined whether the person in one photograph is the same as the person in another.

The photographs to be compared are first "read" into the computer system with a scanning device and are then stored. When the images are later sent to the display screen, a skilled operator marks with a mouse the 15 predetermined facial points on each image. Then, the images are fed to a program that calculates a single statistic, reflecting the result of the comparisons. A 1.0 is a perfect match. Anything below a 0.8 essentially rules out the likelihood of the two people being the same individual.

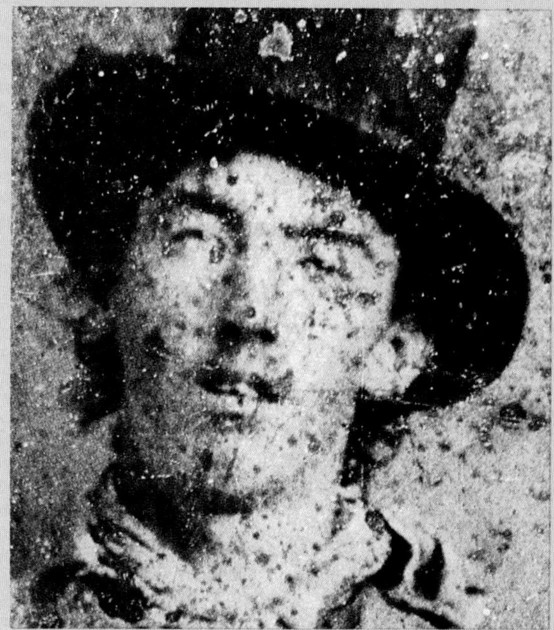

The Kid. Computer technology is proving the history books right.

The highest that any of the wannabe Billys scored was 0.57—far below the range that certifies authenticity. During the time it was being built, the program was tested on hundreds of people and is widely felt to be reliable.

Today, the same types of computer-imaging principles developed in the Billy-the-Kid project are being applied for another purpose—detecting matches from criminal mug-shot files. So, who knows? Maybe the hoodlum whom many feel was not worth much during his lifetime will wind up contributing some good after all.

Input, Output, or Storage?

Input device.
A machine used to supply materials going to the computer.

Output device.
A machine used to accept materials coming from the computer.

Secondary storage device.
A machine, such as a tape or disk unit, that supplements memory.

Input devices are machines that convert data and programs into a form that the CPU can understand and process. **Output devices** are machines that convert processed data into a form that users can understand. **Secondary storage devices** are machines that make frequently used data and programs readily available to the CPU. These functions often overlap in a single machine. Some machines, for example, work as both input and output devices, and all secondary storage devices also function as both input and output devices. Now let's discuss some of the most common kinds of support equipment in terms of these three functions.

Computer *keyboards* (see Figure 2-1) are input devices that closely resemble typewriter keyboards. They are used to type in programs and data and to interactively issue instructions to the computer system. Figure 2-1 also shows a *mouse*, a screen-pointing device that people are increasingly using to supplement

FIGURE 2-1

Input devices. The keyboard (top) is the most widely used input device for entering instructions and data into a computer system. The mouse (bottom) is useful for rapidly moving a pointer around the display screen, for making menu selections, and for moving and resizing objects on the screen.

FIGURE 2-2

Output devices (a) Display devices show both the input users type at the keyboard and the resulting output the computer produces. (b) Printers provide output in a form that can be carried around and later discarded.

(a)

(b)

keyboard operations. While mice aren't absolutely essential for most business uses, they are easier to use than keyboards for certain types of work. The current trend is for display-screen images to mimic office desktops, with several documents onscreen concurrently. Mice are especially handy to have in this type of applications environment because they make it easy to arrange and resize screen documents.

Display devices (see Figure 2-2a), which appear in almost all computer systems, are used for output. The operator enters commands to the computer system through a keyboard or mouse; then both the input the operator enters and the output the CPU produces appear on the screen. A *display terminal* is a display device and a keyboard that are packaged together and used as a communications workstation to a large computer. The local display devices commonly found with microcomputers are generally referred to as *monitors.*

Printers also produce output (see Figure 2-2b). Printers come in a variety of different sizes and capabilities. The printers found in microcomputer systems might cost only a few hundred dollars, print very limited graphics, and output only a page or two a minute. Printers used with large computers, on the other hand, may cost several hundred thousand dollars or more and output several hundred pages per minute.

Secondary storage devices hold frequently used data and programs for ready access to the CPU. They also function as both input and output devices; that

FIGURE 2-3

Microcomputer secondary storage devices. (a) A system unit with two diskette units. (b) A hard-disk unit designed for a notebook or hand-held computer. (c) An optical disk unit with an optical disk cartridge. (d) A tape unit.

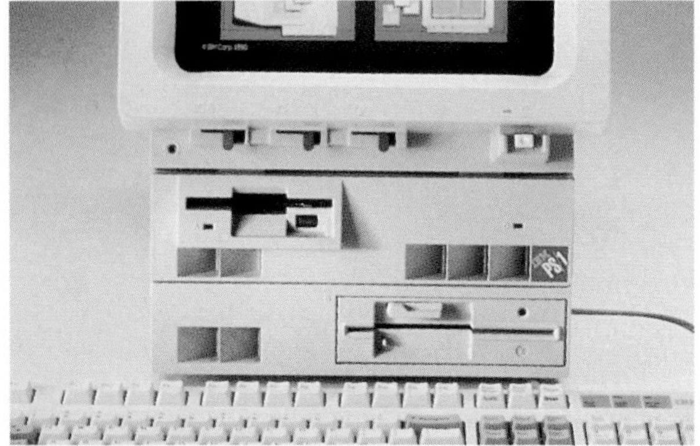

(a)

(b)

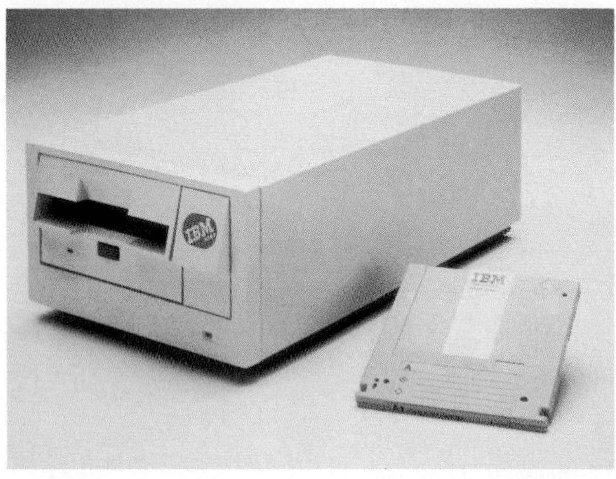

(c)

(d)

is, they contain stored data and programs that are sent to the CPU as input, and the CPU transmits new data and programs to them as output. The most common types of secondary storage devices are disk units and tape units. Figure 2-3 shows several secondary storage devices designed for microcomputers.

Disk units read and write data and programs to or from disks. Most disk units work by either magnetic or optical means. The most common types of *magnetic disk units* are *diskette units* (Figure 2-3a) and *hard-disk units* (Figure 2-3b). *Optical disk units,* which permit much greater amounts of storage than magnetic disks, are also becoming popular in office and home use (Figure 2-3c).

Tape units are designed to read from or write to tapes—either those in detachable-reel form or those packaged in cartridges (see Figure 2-3d). On microcomputers, tapes are commonly used to "back up" a hard disk; that is, to make a duplicate copy of the hard disk's contents as a measure of security. The tape unit shown in Figure 2-3d can accept tape cartridges that store 250 million characters of data, which is more than the capacity of many hard disks.

Disk and tape units can be built directly into the system unit or can exist as separate, "external" devices that you plug into the system unit like you do a keyboard or printer. On most microcomputer systems the diskette and hard-disk units are built in.

Input/Output Media

Input and output devices are, respectively, machines used to get data and programs into a computer and machines used to get the results out in a usable form. Often, however, data and programs are not permanently stored in a particular device. Instead they are recorded on **input/output (I/O) media** in a form the associated device can read and transmit to the CPU. In other words, just as the tape deck on your home stereo system works with tape cassettes, input/output devices work with specific input/ output media. Five of the most common input/output media in use today are *hard magnetic disks, diskettes, optical disks, detachable-reel magnetic tapes,* and *magnetic tape cartridges.* The magnetic media are illustrated in Figure 2-4; an optical disk is shown in Figure 2-3c. All of these media will be discussed in detail in Chapter 4.

Input/output (I/O) media. Objects used to store computer-processed materials.

FIGURE 2-4

Disks and tapes. (left) Hard disks. (right) Magnetic tape cartridge (left background), detachable-reel tape (right background), and diskettes (foreground).

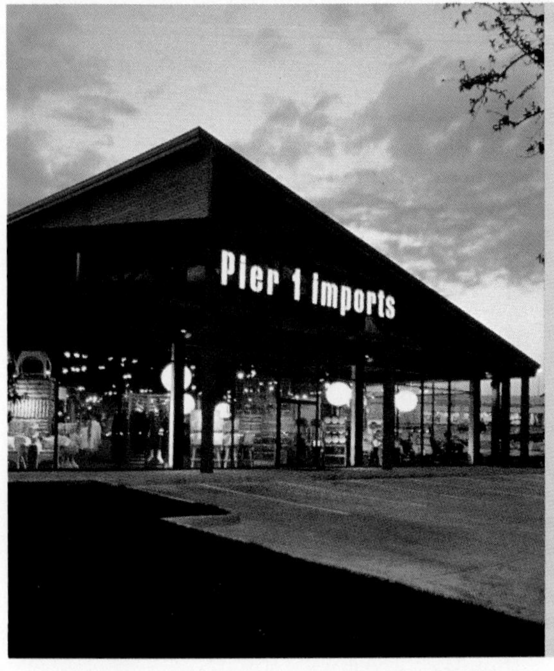

User Solution 2-1

Online Processing for Fresher Information and Better Control

Because the products that Pier 1 Imports sells come from exotic locations, it may take months of bargaining and string pulling to get certain stock to the stores. To have greater control over sales and inventories, Pier 1 is installing a system that will enable its more than 600 stores and distribution centers to hook up online, by means of PCs, to an IBM mainframe at headquarters. The mainframe keeps track of current store sales, forecasts product demand, alerts distribution centers when to send more stock to stores, and tells buyers when to replenish inventory. When a clerk punches in the code of an item being sold, the remote mainframe even supplies the price.

Online and Offline

Online.
Refers to any device ready to communicate with the CPU.

Offline.
Refers to any device not ready to communicate with the CPU.

Peripheral equipment is either online or offline. Any device that is ready to communicate with the computer is said to be **online.** User Solution 2-1, for example, describes how Pier 1 Imports keeps member stores online to a headquarters mainframe so as to have the freshest sales information possible and better control over store pricing. If a device isn't online, it's **offline.** So, for instance, if a PC in the Pier 1 system were to become disconnected in some way from the mainframe, it would be offline to the mainframe.

Organizing Data for Computer Systems

Data, as we said before, are essentially facts. But you can't just randomly input a collection of facts into a computer system and expect to get results. Data to be processed in a computer system must be organized in a systematic way. A common procedure is to organize data into fields, records, files, and databases. Each of these words has a precise meaning in a computing environment, and you should use them with care.

Field.
A collection of related characters.

Record.
A collection of related fields.

File.
A collection of related records.

A **field** is a collection of characters (such as a single digit, letter of the alphabet, or special symbol like a decimal point) that represents a single type of data. A **record** is a collection of related fields. A **file** is a collection of related records. Files, records, and fields normally are stored on an input/output medium such as a disk or a tape. Your school, for example, probably has a *file,* perhaps stored on disk, of all students currently enrolled (see Figure 2-5). The file contains a *record* for each student. Each record has several *fields* containing various types of data about a particular student: ID number, name, street, city and state of residence, major subject area, and the like.

FIGURE 2-5

Differences between a file, record, and field. The file shown contains name and address data on students enrolled at a college. If there were 2,000 active students at the college, this file would contain 2,000 records. Each record in the file has six data fields—the student's number, name, street, city, state, and major.

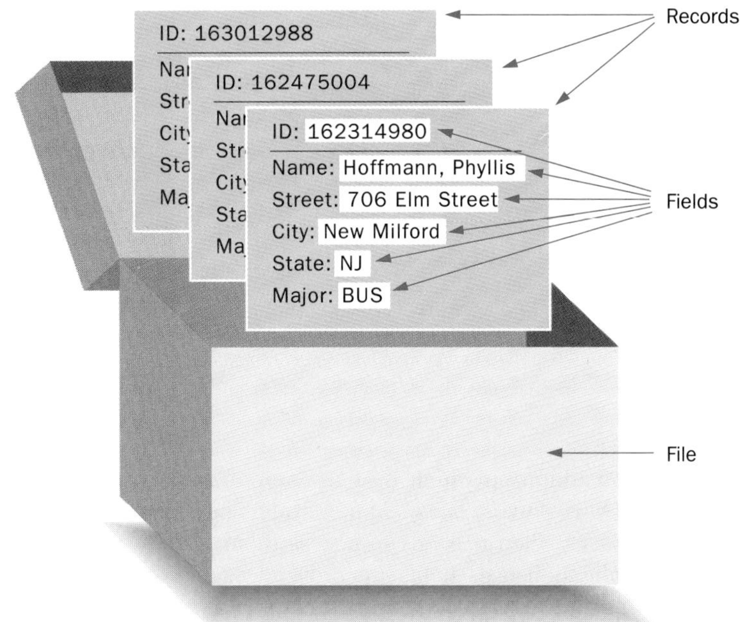

The concept of a **database** is a bit more complicated to explain at this point, but you can safely consider it a collection of data that contains the contents of several files. For example, a student database may contain the contents of a student address file (such as the one in Figure 2-5), a student grade file (containing courses completed and grades earned by each student), and a student medical file (containing data that might help in medical emergencies), as illustrated in Figure 2-6. In other words, most of the information about students would be found in the student database.

Database.
An integrated collection of data that contains the contents of several files.

In most computer systems, data files are kept on disk for rapid access. These files often contain operational data. For example, businesses (such as a department store) have files storing data such as the following:

- Key customer data, such as names, addresses, and credit standings (called a *customer master file*). A **master file** is a file containing relatively permanent data.
- Daily customer transactions, such as purchases and payments (called a *customer transaction file*). A **transaction file** is a file containing data that are used to update or modify data in a master file.

Master file.
A file containing relatively permanent data, such as customer names and addresses.

Transaction file.
A file of occurrences, such as customer payments and purchases, that have taken place over a period of time.

As mentioned previously, data from related files often are stored in databases. For example, data that normally would appear in the customer transaction file and customer master file might be collectively stored in a customer database.

FIGURE 2-6

A student database. Databases, such as the one shown here, enable data that might otherwise exist in several separate files to be easily interrelated. Database technology has made it possible for users to ask the computer system complex questions—questions that require data to be drawn from multiple sources within the database.

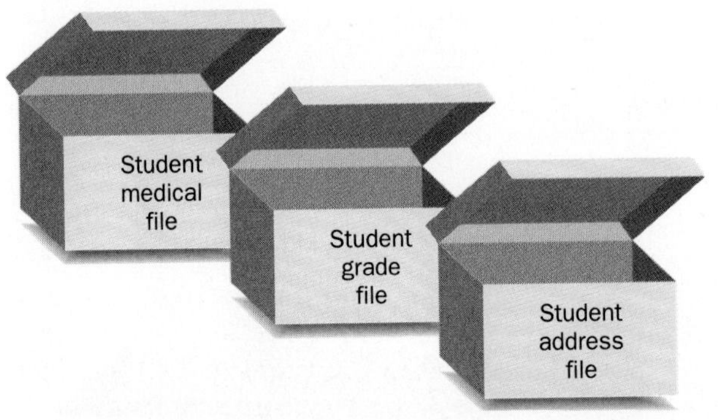

Whatever the medium on which they are stored, entities such as files and databases always have names. The computer system uses these names to identify the files or databases when it needs to access them.

Not every application uses fields, records, files, and/or databases. For instance, most word-processed document files (i.e., simple letters) do not name fields and records, nor are such files stored in a database. Also, some database programs do not store data in conventional record form.

A Brief Introduction to Software

As mentioned earlier, the word *software* refers to computer programs. Programs direct the computer system to do specific tasks, just as your thoughts direct your body to speak or move in certain ways. Software comes in two varieties: applications software and systems software.

Applications software. Programs that do the type of work that people acquire a computer system to do.

Applications Software **Applications software** is designed to perform tasks such as computing the interest on or balance in bank accounts, preparing bills, creating documents, preparing and analyzing budgets, managing files and databases, playing games, scheduling airline flights, or diagnosing hospital patients' illnesses. In other words, applications software makes possible the types of "computer work" end users have in mind when they acquire a computer system. You can buy applications software prewritten or write it yourself. If you write it yourself, you must be familiar with a specific programming language.

Productivity software, which we will discuss in detail in Module D, is the class of easy-to-learn, easy-to-use applications software designed to make workers more productive at their jobs. Some important types of productivity software are described in Figure 2-7.

Systems software. Computer programs, such as the operating system, that enable application programs to run on a computer system's hardware.

Systems Software **Systems software** consists of "background" programs that enable applications software to run on a computer system's hardware devices. One of the most important pieces of systems software is the *operating system,* a set of control programs that supervise the computer system's work. Many recent Hollywood movies have portrayed the role of the operating system in an overly exaggerated manner—for example, as a demon master-control program that tries to take over the world. Fortunately, operating systems don't control people; rather, people control operating systems. We'll address operating systems and other types of systems software in more depth in Chapter 7.

Information Processing

Computer systems process data into information. When we talk about information processing, however, what kinds of processing do we have in mind?

The number of ways in which a full-fledged computer system can turn data into useful information is truly staggering and defies a simple, systematic enumeration at this early stage in the book. So rather than trying to look at all of them, let's focus on just a few commonly encountered information-processing tasks. This will help you appreciate the types of work you will likely need a computer system to do.

FIGURE 2-7

Types of productivity software. Productivity software packages are designed to make both ordinary users and computer professionals more productive at their jobs.

Package Type	Description
Word processor	Turns the computer system into a powerful typewriting tool
Spreadsheet	Turns the computer system into a sophisticated electronic calculator and analysis tool
Presentation graphics	Turns the computer into a tool that can be used to prepare overheads, slides, and presentation materials for meetings
File manager and database management system	Turns the computer system into an electronic research assistant, capable of searching through mounds of data to prepare reports or answer queries for information
Communications software	Enables users to call up remote computers for such things as financial information, marketing information, and news
Desktop publishing	Turns the computer system into a tool that can produce documents that look as if they were produced at a professional print shop
Desk accessory	Provides the electronic equivalent of tools commonly found on an office desktop—calendars, address files, and calculators, for instance
CASE (computer-assisted software engineering)	Automates and integrates many of the tasks performed by computer professionals, thus enabling them to develop systems and software far more effectively
Expert system	Enables workers to tap into expert knowledge to support their work
CAD (computer-aided design)	Gives people like architects and product designers the ability to bring products to market faster.

FIGURE 2-8

Information processing. Depicted are six fundamental ways in which computers are capable of processing data into useful information.

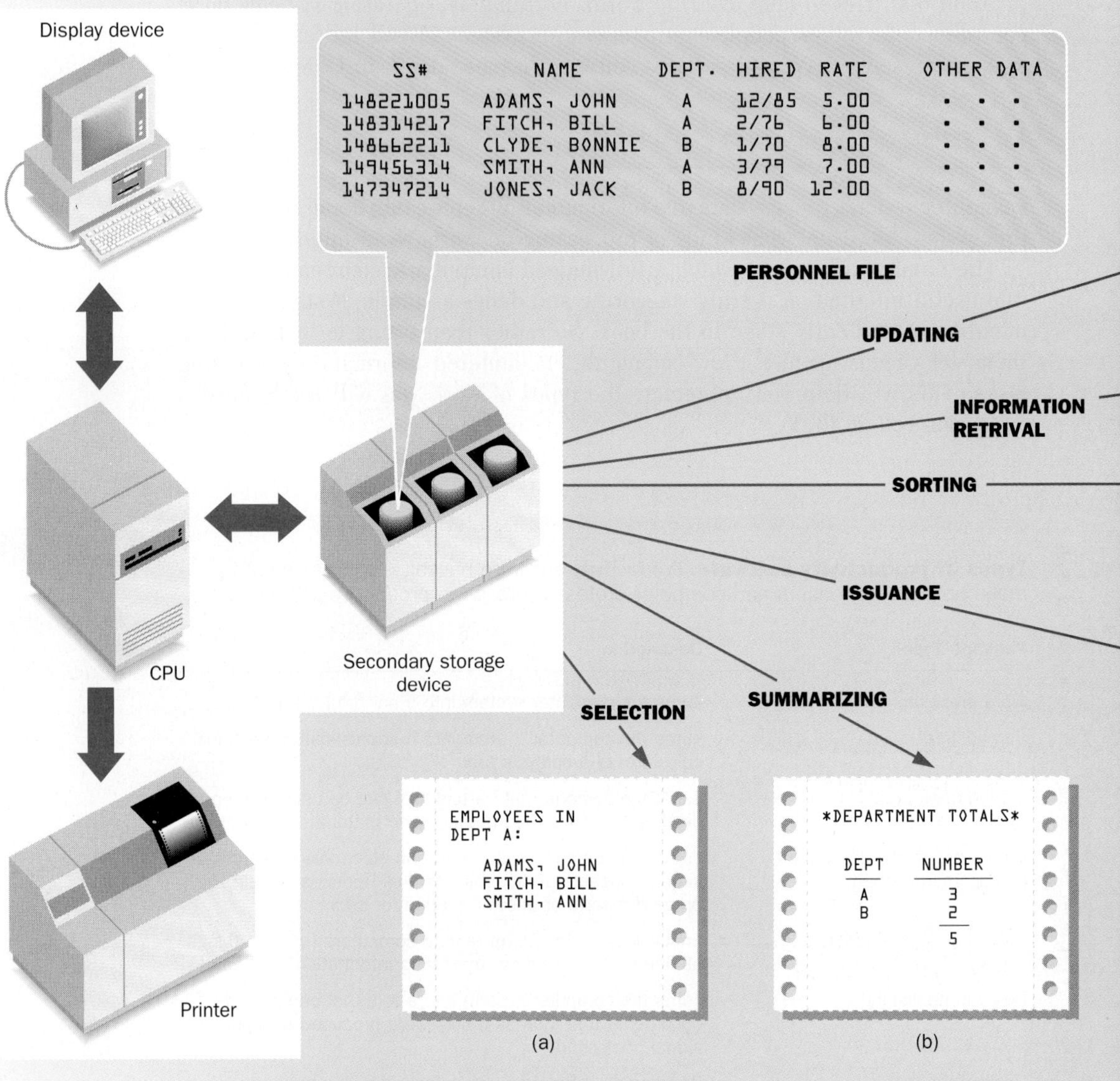

Some common information-processing tasks are

- Selection
- Summarizing
- Issuance
- Sorting
- Information retrieval
- Updating

We will discuss each of these in turn and illustrate each with an example. All of our examples will use the personnel file in Figure 2-8. This file is housed in a secondary storage device, such as the hard-disk unit shown in the figure. We've used a small, five-record file here to simplify the examples (in reality,

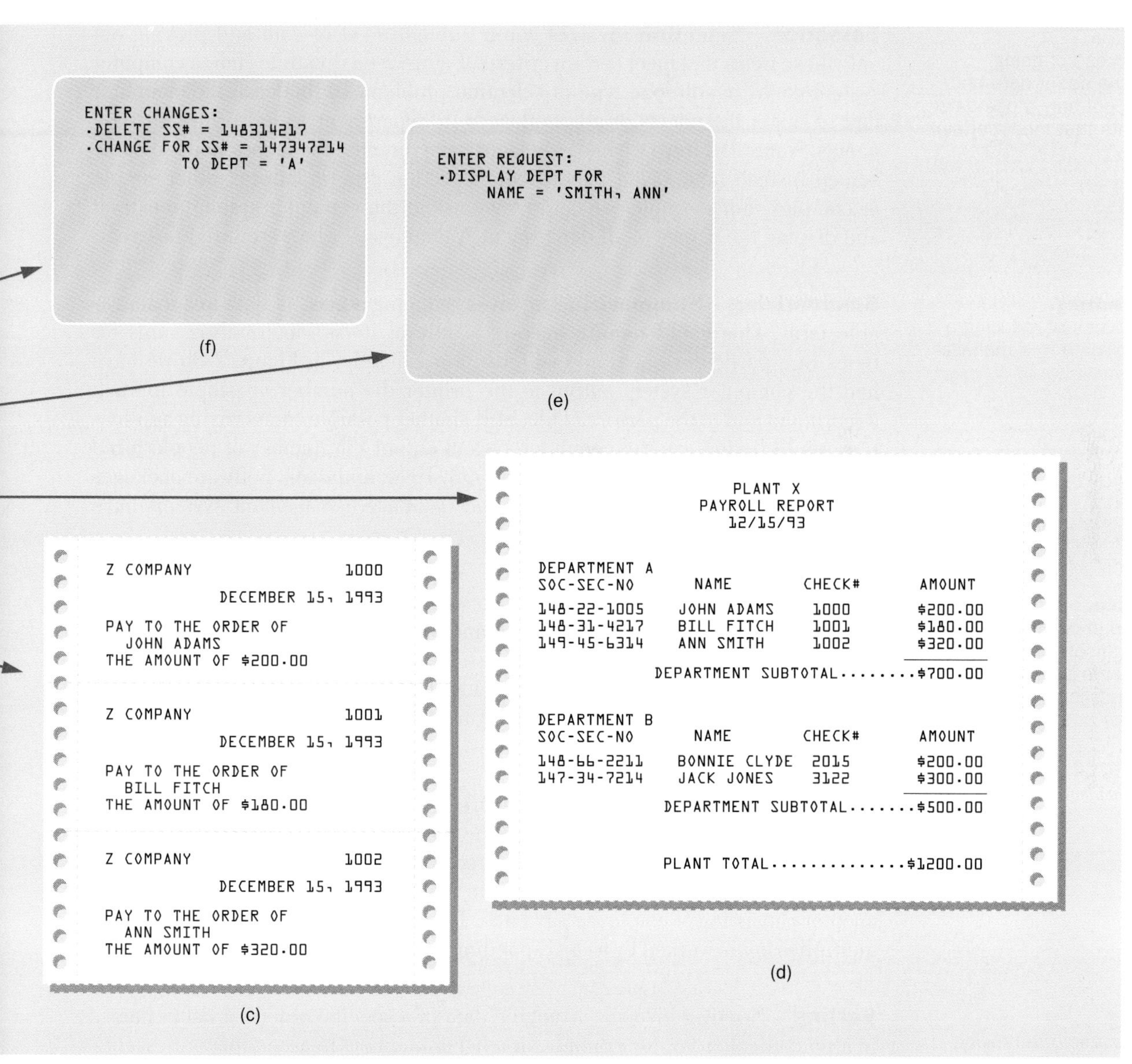
ENTER CHANGES:
.DELETE SS# = 148314217
.CHANGE FOR SS# = 147347214
TO DEPT = 'A'
ENTER REQUEST:
.DISPLAY DEPT FOR
NAME = 'SMITH, ANN'
Z COMPANY 1000
DECEMBER 15, 1993
PAY TO THE ORDER OF
JOHN ADAMS
THE AMOUNT OF $200.00
Z COMPANY 1001
DECEMBER 15, 1993
PAY TO THE ORDER OF
BILL FITCH
THE AMOUNT OF $180.00
Z COMPANY 1002
DECEMBER 15, 1993
PAY TO THE ORDER OF
ANN SMITH
THE AMOUNT OF $320.00
PLANT X
PAYROLL REPORT
12/15/93
DEPARTMENT A
SOC-SEC-NO NAME CHECK# AMOUNT
148-22-1005 JOHN ADAMS 1000 $200.00
148-31-4217 BILL FITCH 1001 $180.00
149-45-6314 ANN SMITH 1002 $320.00
DEPARTMENT SUBTOTAL........$700.00
DEPARTMENT B
SOC-SEC-NO NAME CHECK# AMOUNT
148-66-2211 BONNIE CLYDE 2015 $200.00
147-34-7214 JACK JONES 3122 $300.00
DEPARTMENT SUBTOTAL.......$500.00
PLANT TOTAL..............$1200.00

(f)

(e)

(d)

(c)

many personnel files contain thousands of such records). Also, each record shown contains only five fields. The sixth column, "Other Data," indicates that we could have added many more fields had we wanted to.

Each of the information-processing operations we'll describe should be located in a program somewhere in secondary storage. For example, if we want to sort our data file, we will need a program that will enable us to sort data records.

In each of our examples, output can be directed to one or more output devices in the system—the display, the printer, or secondary storage. Again, to make things straightforward, we've shown output directed to only one device in each of the six example applications in Figure 2-8.

Selection.
The process of going through a set of data and picking out only those data elements that meet certain criteria.

Selection **Selection** involves going through a set of data and picking out only those items that meet certain criteria. Figure 2-8a illustrates how a computer system could handle one type of selection problem. In this case the computer had to select the names of all employees in department A and print out those names. Naturally, if we wished, we could have directed the names to the display screen instead (and saved paper, too). Selection criteria can be either simple or complex. For example, we could have asked the computer system to extract and display the names of all department A employees who were hired last year.

Summarizing.
The process of reducing a mass of data to a manageable form.

Summarizing **Summarizing** involves reducing a mass of data to a manageable form. This could require making a tally of items, determining sums for items in a particular class, and so forth. For example, in Figure 2-8b we have had the computer system output to the printer the number of people in each department and in the personnel file. Still another possible summarizing application would be to have the computer system output the number of people hired in each of several years, such as 1992, 1993, 1994, and so on. Software packages such as spreadsheets, file managers, and database management systems have strong facilities for summarizing data.

Issuance.
The use of computers to produce transaction-oriented documents such as paychecks, bills, and customer reminder notices.

Issuance Computer systems are also widely used to input records, perform a series of calculations on each record, and prepare a document for each record based on these computations. This process is sometimes called **issuance,** since the end result is the issuing of documents. In billing operations, for example, the computer system reads a record of payments and purchases for each customer, computes the amount due, and prepares a bill. Payroll processing, illustrated in Figure 2-8c, is another example.

Checks such as those shown in figure 2-8c cannot be generated from the personnel file alone. After all, how is the computer system to know how much to pay each employee? Therefore, to produce paychecks, the payroll program may consult two other files, one with the hours worked by each employee and another consisting of employee pay rates. Then, for each employee, the computer multiplies hours worked by a corresponding pay rate to produce the earnings due.

Sorting.
The process of arranging data in a specified order.

Sorting **Sorting** involves arranging data in a specific order—a list of names in alphabetical order, for example, or a list of numbers in ascending or descending order. Figure 2-8d shows a computer report in which payroll data are sorted first by department and then by name within each department. The report in Figure 2-8d is also an example of *control-break reporting.* As illustrated, the computer breaks after processing each department to print a subtotal and breaks again at the end of the report to print a final total.

Information retrieval.
Online inquiry to computer files or databases.

Information Retrieval Programs created for **information retrieval,** or *query,* enables users to enter a series of questions at the keyboard for the purpose of extracting information from a database or from many different data files. For example, a bank manager may want to check a customer's credit rating. The checking, savings, trust, and loan data needed to determine credit ratings are contained in a customer database. An information-retrieval program that responds to the manager's request for a credit check could extract all the needed information from the database and calculate the customer's credit rating automatically. Figure 2-8e illustrates a query to the personnel file, in which the operator is trying to determine the department in which Ann Smith works.

Updating **Updating** involves changing the data in a file to reflect new information. Credit card companies, for example, update their customer files regularly to reflect customers' payments and purchases. Updating is done on either a batch or a realtime basis.

Updating.
The process of bringing something up to date by making corrections, adding new data, and so forth.

Batch processing.
Processing transactions or other data in groups, at periodic intervals.

- BATCH PROCESSING **Batch processing** involves accumulating (batching) transactions over time in a separate transaction file and processing them all at once against a master file. For example, if you update your checkbook at the end of the month using data from the checking transactions made throughout that month, you are updating on a batch basis.

  Many issuance tasks, such as payroll, are done by processing work in a batch. For example, many companies pay employees at the end of the month. Billing is another operation that is often done in the batch mode. A company may maintain a file of customer transactions, which include purchases and payments. At a certain time of the month, this transaction file is processed against a master file of all customer balances. The computer system updates

FIGURE 2-9

Realtime processing. Instantaneous updating of master files is absolutely critical for such applications as (left) managing passenger reservations for the airlines and (right) keeping track of customer withdrawals at banks.

TOMORROW

Virtual Reality

Hanging Out in Cyberspace

You're lazing away on a warm beach in Mexico when the sun begins to nudge toward the horizon. The hills to your left take on an orange glow, gulls are diving for fish, and each harmless cloud in the sky looks wildly three-dimensional and painted with its own special color. "If only this could go on for another hour," you think. It does . . . and not because it's actually happening. You've used a computer system to create a virtual reality.

Virtual reality refers to the use of computers to create special, customized environments that seem, to the computer operator, as if they were real. Although we are still far from the virtual reality that science fiction writers tell us about, there are many who believe that computer technology will someday make it possible to create such illusions. Several pioneering virtual-reality applications are visible in the marketplace today.

In architecture, for instance, it is now possible to take "tours" of buildings whose foundations are yet to be poured. How? A computer model of the building is made in three dimensions. Once the building is mathematically specified, what a person can see if standing at any specific point in the building, looking in any specific direction, can be mathematically determined.

Let's say the client taking the tour wants to look at the top floor first and see the lounge before the offices. The tour can be taken in real time, which enables the client to move as he or she so chooses, deciding which facilities to view before

Steven King's CyberJobe. Virtual reality gone awry.

the balance in each account and issues statements that are sent to the customers.

Realtime processing. Updating data immediately in a master file as transactions take place.

- REALTIME PROCESSING **Realtime processing** involves entering transaction data into a computer system as they take place and updating master files immediately (see Figure 2-9). All realtime processing is performed online.

  A prime example of realtime processing occurs in banking. Tellers with terminals can update an account as soon as a customer makes a withdrawal. If the customer makes a withdrawal at an automatic teller machine, the machine updates the account immediately. The ability to check and update accounts on the spot protects the bank from overwithdrawals. Deposits, however, usually are not recorded in a customer's balance until the end of the day, when all deposits made by all customers that day are processed together. In other words, deposits typically are processed in the batch mode.

Figure 2-8f illustrates an update to the personnel file to show that Bill Fitch has left the company and Jack Jones has moved to department A. If changes such as these are immediately reflected in the computer system, realtime processing is others, how much time to spend at each facility, and what to see there. Lighting routines are available that can show how natural light falls in the building on a sunny or rainy day and how artificial light changes a room. Does the client hate the look and size of the lounge? No problem. With a remodeling software package, it can be reshaped, repainted, relighted, refurnished, and ready for reinspection—in just a few minutes.

In the field of business, virtual reality techniques are now being applied to the analysis of securities. One of the problems inherent in conventional analysis is that it's often difficult to tell when a group of securities is moving relative to the market as a whole. With virtual reality, stocks belonging to a certain group—say, technology stocks—can each be given a characteristic color. When general stock movements are viewed in three dimensions over time, which is simulated by animation techniques, the analyst can more clearly visualize how the technology group, or any other group, is behaving.

In addition to benefitting fields such as architecture and business, virtual reality may someday enable the exploration of planets without actually going there, make possible educational and therapeutic experiences in which human confrontation is realistically simulated, help to recreate crime scenes, and allow people to take virtual vacations.

Expect virtual reality applications to arrive in full force in the entertainment industry, where illusion is the principal product. In some cities, shops have already sprouted up that feature virtual reality games in which players can battle demons on a realistic, computer-generated landscape. In many cases, the virtual-reality participant must don special goggles, which project computer-generated images directly toward the eye, and wear gloves with built-in sensors, which change the goggle images when the hands are moved. A golf game has also been developed in which budding Jack Nicklauses can swing away at the best holes on some of the world's greatest courses without ever leaving the local spa.

Perhaps it was the public's increasing curiosity about virtual reality that led to a major film using the topic as its centerpiece. *Lawnmower Man,* based on a Stephen King short story, is about a doctor who conducts virtual-reality experiments on chimps and, later, on a young man named Jobe. But the doctor has the same type of luck Dr. Frankenstein did with his own monstrous creation—science goes awry and CyberJobe (see photo), a being who exists entirely within the computer and who threatens to produce chaos, evolves. The film's creators argue that much of what moviegoers see will soon be available. Coming next to your town: virtual-reality theatres.

in effect; if they are done at the end of a day or week, batch processing is taking place.

The Tomorrow box features *virtual reality,* perhaps the ultimate in realtime processing. User Solution 2-2 describes the use of wireless technology to update computer databases in real time. Wireless terminals can also be used to retrieve database data.

Getting It All Together: Combining Elements into a Complete Computer System

Now that you understand a few concepts about hardware, software, and data, it's time to learn how these elements interact with people and procedures to form a complete computer-based information processing system. Along the way, you'll be introduced to a few new concepts, ones that you will read about in detail in the text.

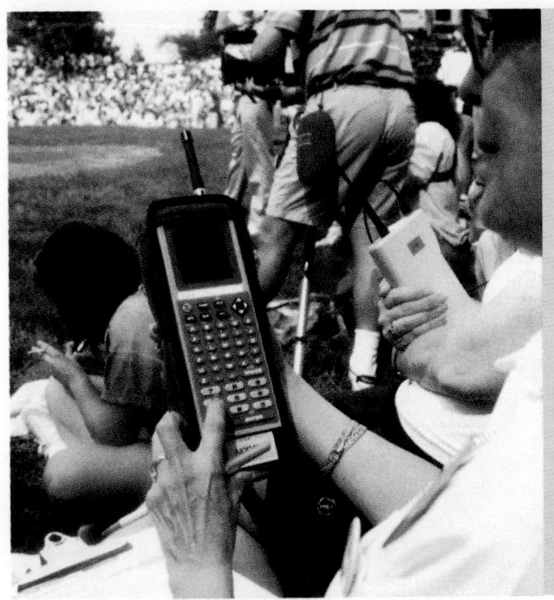

User Solution 2-2

Updating the Wireless Way

Question: What's getting to be the best way to collect and maintain current information on geographically dispersed sporting events such as golf tournaments and Olympics competitions? *Answer:* Using a wireless network. At a golf tournament, say, scorers with hand-held terminals are assigned to track specific golfers and record their strokes. As the scorers enter data into their terminals, these data are transmitted by radio waves to a local computer, where they are stored in a database. Sportscasters tapping into the database can then obtain the latest information about how a tournament is progressing and how specific golfers are doing.

The example that follows describes the sales information system in a hypothetical firm called The Casual Look (see Figure 2-10). The Casual Look is a national chain of 316 retail stores throughout the United States and Canada that sells casual and recreational clothing.

Input Each store owner has a microcomputer system, containing a hard disk, that is used to record sales. When a customer makes a purchase, data such as the current date and the identification number, quantity, and price of each item bought are electronically recorded. Many of these data are entered by keyboard and, when the item being sold has a bar-coded tag, by a hand-held scanner (see Figure 2-11). The scanner—an input device—reads the bar code into the computer system, where the product and its current price are identified. According to a strictly followed procedure at each store, every sale is recorded by computer.

All of the purchase data a store gathers are automatically stored on its local computer's hard disk. Every evening, Casual Look's mainframe system in Dallas calls each store computer and automatically has that day's sales data transferred (or "uploaded") over the phone lines from the store's hard disk to a much larger hard disk on the mainframe system.

Processing The raw data coming into Dallas from 316 sites are coordinated automatically by the mainframe system and processed in various ways.

One important element in processing relates to store performance. Stores are sorted on the basis of their sales from high to low so that executives at headquarters can quickly spot which stores are doing well and which aren't. Stores are also evaluated in terms of how well they are performing compared with previous sales periods (such as the same month last year) and compared with the sales projections that sales executives at headquarters have made for each store. The applications software that assesses performance evaluates stores daily, weekly, seasonally, and yearly so that executives can easily tell which stores consistently

FIGURE 2-10

The Casual Look's sales information system. Each store has a microcomputer system that sends daily sales data to the mainframe at headquarters and receives daily performance reports from it. Sales executives at headquarters can access reports and other relevant sales information through their own desktop workstations.

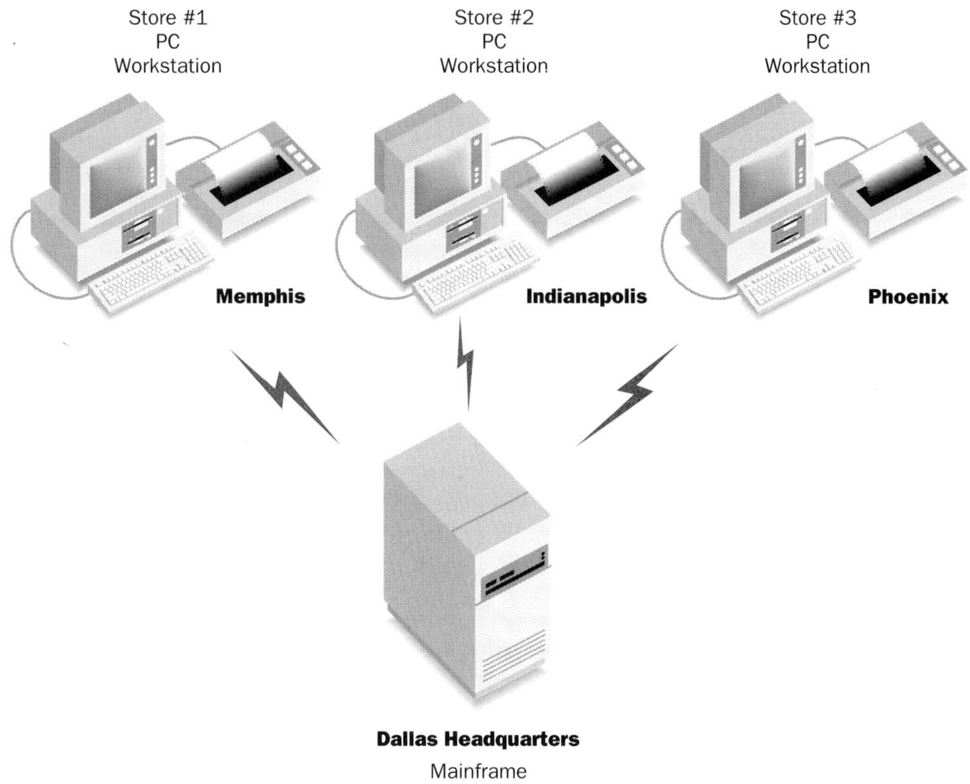

perform well, when a store is having an unusually good or bad day, and when a trend seems to be taking place.

Product performance is another key concern of information processing. Management needs to know which products are moving most quickly and which most slowly. Also important is how well product lines are doing relative to projections, whether projections need to be updated, if inventory is too large or too small relative to consumer demand, and if any trends are evident. Because all the data are up-to-date, headquarters can quickly take advantage of opportunities and avoid potential problems.

The sales data collected at the stores represent only one component of a large sales database. Other data in the database include, among other things, facts on each building (such as square footage and location) and facts on each product (such as type of product and current price). This enables managers at headquarters to have the computer system answer some very sophisticated queries; for example, "Are some products selling better than others in specific areas of the country?" "How sensitive are sales of each product to price changes?" Five years ago, when the data used to answer these questions were

FIGURE 2-11

Recording transactions. When the label attached to each purchased item is read with a hand scanner connected to the computer system, valuable sales data are collected quickly and virtually without error. These data can be used to prepare customer receipts and arc sent daily to headquarters for rapid management analysis.

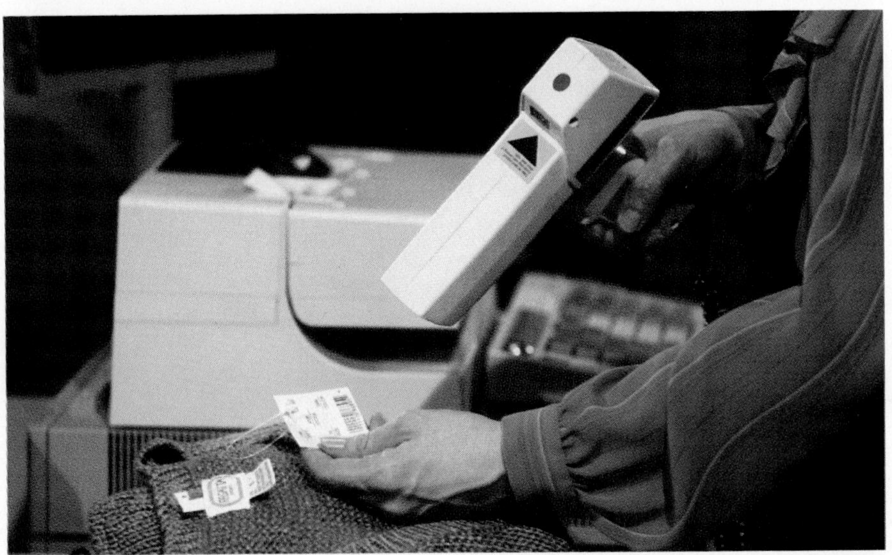

in separate files that couldn't be interrelated and the Dallas mainframe couldn't communicate daily with each of the stores, it took two or three weeks of intensive research to get answers. Most of the time, managers didn't bother.

Output Computer output occurs at several levels in this sales information system.

At headquarters, sales executives are most concerned with how the stores and product lines are performing on the whole and in relation to competitive products. Every evening, computer data reflecting the day's activity are summarized into graphs and reports that sales executives can summon on display screens as soon as they arrive for work in the morning. Executives can also electronically browse through any other facts in the sales database to answer questions that go beyond the information available in the graphs and reports.

An *electronic mail* system enables sales executives and store owners to communicate over ordinary phone lines. If, for instance, an executive has important news to announce to store owners, it is typed as a memo and routed, in seconds, to the hard disks of individual store computers. At each store, a small symbol called a "message icon" shows up on the display screen, indicating a message has been sent. Store owners can also send memos to headquarters over the electronic mail system.

At the store level, details of each purchase are output in the form of a receipt given the customer and in the form of a transaction entry that is written to the hard disk.

Sales reports are sent daily to individual store managers. These reports are automatically routed by headquarters through the electronic mail system and are available to each store owner when stores open for business. These reports show owners how well their store has performed relative to expectations, show goods that will be delivered during the next few weeks, make suggestions for purchasing, and provide interesting news items about other stores in the chain and about trends in the industry. The reports are intended to be both informational and motivational, and store owners are free to make their own decisions. Store owners do not have access to the full sales database at headquarters, however.

Storage Casual Look uses two types of electronic storage in its sales information system: disk and tape.

Both locally and at headquarters, sales data are stored and processed on hard disk. Today, magnetic disk is the most popular means of online secondary storage because it is relatively fast, capacious, and inexpensive. Hard disk, however, is not so capacious that it doesn't get filled over time. Rather than add more hard-disk capacity online, many organizations, including Casual Look, store hard-disk data they no longer need on tape and then store these tapes offline. For instance, because few managers are interested in looking at raw, detailed sales data from two or three years past, such data are put on tape.

Summary and Key Terms

Chapter 2 explains how input, processing, output, and storage work together to produce useful information.

Computer Hardware All computer systems consist of some combination of **computers,** their memories, and **peripheral equipment.** The computer and its memory often are housed in the same hardware device, called the **system unit.** The most common types of support equipment are **input devices, output devices,** and **secondary storage devices.**

Input and output devices include keyboards, display devices such as display terminals and monitors, and printers.

Secondary storage devices include hard-disk units, diskette units, optical disk units, detachable-reel tape units, and cartridge tape units. These devices use, respectively, hard disks, diskettes, optical disks, detachable tape reels, and cartridge tapes as their **input/output (I/O) media.**

Support equipment may be either **online** or **offline** to the CPU at any point in time.

Organizing Data for Computer Systems Data are commonly organized into fields, records, files, and databases. A **field** is a collection of individual characters, such as digits and letters of the alphabet. A **record** is a collection of related fields. A **file** is a collection of related records. As transaction data are generated, they are stored as records in a **transaction file;** a **master file** contains more permanent types of data. A **database** contains the contents of several files.

A Brief Introduction to Software Software falls into one of two categories: applications software and systems software. **Applications software** does the "computer work" most end users have in mind when they buy a computer system. **Systems software** consists of support programs that enable applications software to run on a given set of hardware devices.

Information Processing Six common information-processing tasks are selection, summarizing, issuance, sorting, information retrieval, and updating. **Selection** involves extracting from files only those fields or records that meet certain criteria. **Summarizing** consists of reducing a mass of data to a manageable form. **Issuance** involves inputting records, performing a series of calculations on each record, and preparing a document for each record based on the computations. **Sorting** means arranging data in some specified sequence, such as alphabetical order or numeric order. Summarizing, sorting, and issuance often are combined to do *control-break reporting.* **Information retrieval,** or *query,* enables users to extract information from data files. **Updating,** which involves changing data in a file to reflect new information, can be done on a periodic or immediate basis. These types of updating are called **batch processing** and **realtime processing,** respectively.

Getting It All Together: Combining Elements into a Complete Computer System The case study featuring The Casual Look shows how the hardware, software, data, and information-processing procedures you read about in earlier sections combine with people to form a sophisticated computer system.

Review Exercises

Fill-in Questions

1. To be read by a computer system, data must be recorded in machine-readable form on some type of ____________.

2. A file containing relatively permanent data is called a ____________ file.

3. Any device that is set up to communicate with the CPU is said to be ____________.

4. ____________ software is written by users or programmers to perform tasks such as computing the interest or balance in bank accounts.

5. ____________ software consists of programs that enable applications software to run smoothly on a given set of hardware.

6. A(n) ____________ is a collection of characters that represents a single type of data.

7. ____________ processing refers to collecting transactions until the end of the day or week and processing them all at once.

8. The method of updating that the airline industry uses for passenger reservations is called ____________ processing.

Matching Questions

Match each term with the description that fits best.

a. information retrieval
b. issuance
c. batch processing
d. realtime processing
e. control-break reporting
f. sorting

___ 1. A company prepares a reminder notice for a customer whose payment deadline has passed.

___ 2. A company produces an employee phone book with names in alphabetical order.

___ 3. A bank records all deposits made to customer accounts at the end of each day.

___ 4. A report shows information on the sales of a single product, with three subtotals and a grand total.

___ 5. A librarian keys in the title of a book on a display terminal to see whether it has been checked out.

___ 6. Jane Williams withdraws $100 from her checking account, and that amount is immediately subtracted from her account balance.

Discussion Questions

1. Name some common types of peripheral equipment, and state whether each is used for input, output, storage, or some combination of these functions.
2. Name some common types of secondary storage devices and the I/O media each uses.
3. Create a small file of data. Can you identify the records and fields?
4. What is the difference between applications software and systems software?
5. What is the difference between a master file and a transaction file?
6. Identify and define the types of information processing discussed in this chapter. Can you think of any other examples of information processing?

Critical Thinking Questions

1. At a recent campus computer club meeting, you agreed to conduct a survey on how members feel about tours the club may make of local businesses next semester. You've designed a questionnaire that consists of seven to eight questions. Answers to most questions will be in the form of ideas or opinions that will likely run about two or three sentences. The thought has crossed your mind that the computer might be of some help in tabulating the results. Will it?
2. In the Casual Look example, it is mentioned that store owners do not have unlimited access to mainframe data. Do you think this is a mistake?
3. Virtual reality, covered in the Tomorrow box, is expected to help eliminate unnecessary animal experimentation in medical research. How do you see virtual reality techniques assisting in this area?

M O D U L E **B**

Hardware

When most people think of computers or computer systems today, hardware most readily comes to mind. Hardware comprises the exciting pieces of equipment delivered in crates or boxes when you buy a computer system. As you'll learn in this module, a rich variety of computer hardware is available in today's marketplace. But as you'll see later in this book, hardware needs a guiding force—namely, software—to be of any use. Hardware without software is like a human without the ability to reason and manipulate thoughts.

The hardware discussed in this module is divided into three areas. Chapter 3 describes the use of the CPU—the computer itself. Chapter 4 discusses the class of hardware that provides an indispensable library of resources for the CPU—secondary storage devices. Chapter 5 delves into input and output equipment.

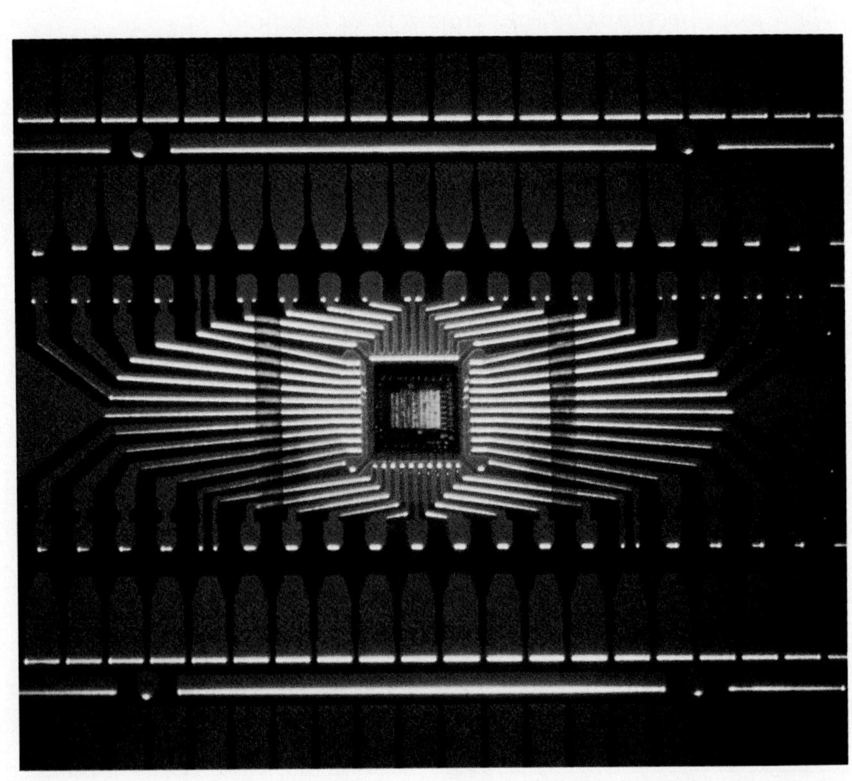

The Central Processing Unit and Memory

3

How sophisticated can a fingernail-sized CPU chip be? Very, as you'll learn in Chapter 3. Hard as it is to believe, the most powerful CPU chips made today contain millions of microscopic circuits and are capable of executing over 100 million instructions every second.

OUTLINE

Overview
How the CPU Works
- The CPU and Its Memory
- Registers
- Machine Cycles

Data and Program Representation
- ASCII and EBCDIC
- Machine Language

The System Unit
- CPU Chip
- Specialized Processor Chips
- RAM
- ROM
- Add-in Boards
- Ports
- I/O Bus

Making Computers Speedier

LEARNING OBJECTIVES

After completing this chapter, you will be able to:

1. Describe how the CPU and its memory process instructions and data.
2. Identify several binary-based codes used in a computing environment.
3. Explain the function of the various pieces of hardware commonly found under the cover of the system unit.
4. Name several strategies for making computers speedier.

Overview

So far we've considered the system unit, which houses the CPU and its memory, to be a mysterious "black box." In this chapter, we'll demystify that notion by flipping the lid off the box and closely examining the functions of the parts inside. In doing so, we'll try to get a feel for how the CPU, memory, and other devices commonly found in the system unit work together.

To start, we'll examine how a CPU is organized and how it interacts with memory to carry out processing tasks. Next, we'll discuss how data and programs must be represented in the computer system. Here we'll talk about the codes developed for translating back and forth from symbols the CPU can understand to symbols people find meaningful. These topics lead us into a discussion of how the CPU and its memory are packaged with other computing and storage devices inside the system unit. Finally, we look at strategies used to speed up the work of the CPU.

Since the first, room-sized electronic computers were sold to businesses almost 50 years ago, computers have been getting cheaper, faster, smaller (see User Solution 3-1), and able to support more storage. If the cost of other things had decreased as fast as that of computers has, you'd be able to pay for both an around-the-world trip and a Rolls Royce with a $5 bill . . . and receive change!

FIGURE 3-1

The CPU and its memory. Memory temporarily stores the program on which the computer is currently working, as well as input data, intermediate computations, and output. Each location in memory has an address, and often a single address can store a single character. Although only 20 locations are shown, memories typically contain from a few thousand addresses to several billion. All "figuring" done by the computer is accomplished in the arithmetic/logic unit (ALU). Data are transferred between memory and the ALU under supervision of the control unit.

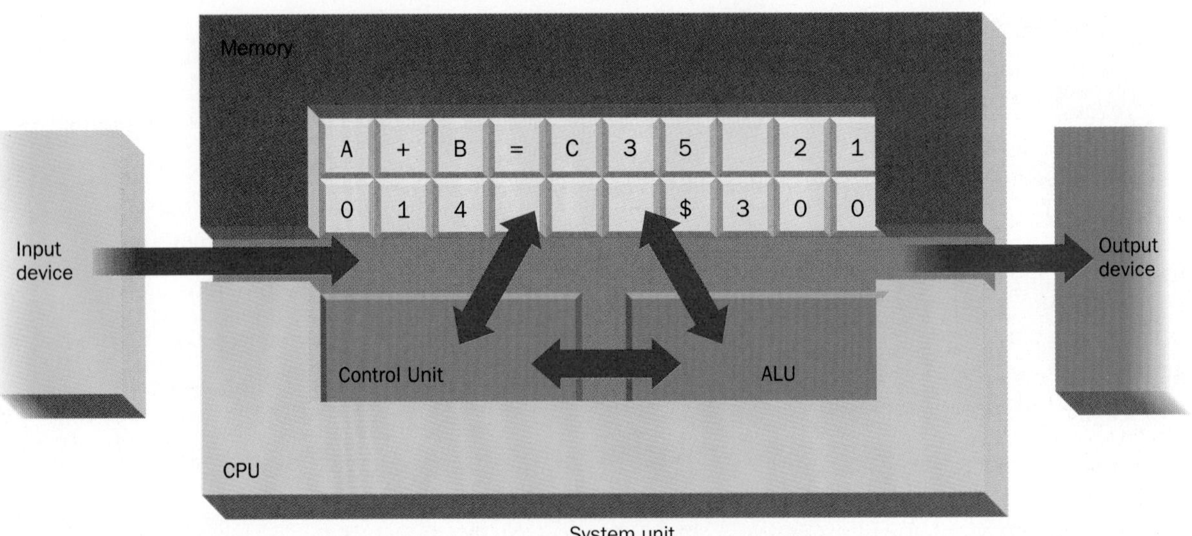

User Solution 3-1

Honey, Phone Home

One of the worst fears of any parent is losing a child in a playground or shopping center. Now, a tiny technology product called Phone Home has taken a step toward preventing such a scenario. The device is about the size of a deck of cards and has a special chip that contains a phone number and the ability to dial it. In other words, storage and processor. A lost child, or any other user, has only to hold the device to a phone mouthpiece and press its "smart button." Phone Home will automatically call the preset number, collect. If the caller is too young to understand or follow detailed directions, the recipient of the call can ask the operator for the phone number and have the police track down the location.

How the CPU Works

Every CPU is basically a collection of electronic circuits. Electronic impulses enter the CPU from an input device. Within the CPU, these impulses are sent under program control through circuits to create a series of new impulses. Eventually a set of impulses leaves the CPU, headed for an output device. What happens in those circuits? To begin to understand this process, we need to know first how the CPU is organized—what its parts are—and then how electronic impulses move from one part to another to process data.

The CPU and Its Memory

The CPU works closely with its memory to carry out processing inside the system unit. This relationship is described in the next sections and illustrated in Figure 3-1.

The CPU The CPU has two principal sections: an arithmetic/logic unit and a control unit.

The **arithmetic/logic unit (ALU)** is the section of the CPU that performs arithmetic and logical operations on data. In other words, it is the part of the computer that does the computing. *Arithmetic* operations include tasks such as addition, subtraction, multiplication, and division. *Logical* operations involve comparing two items of data to determine whether they are equal and, if not, which is larger. As we'll see, all data coming into the CPU, including nonnumeric data such as letters of the alphabet, are coded in digital (numeric) form. As a result, the ALU can perform logical operations on letters and words as well as on numbers.

Arithmetic/logic unit (ALU).
The part of the computer that contains the circuitry to perform arithmetic and logical operations.

The basic arithmetic and logical operations just described are the only ones the computer can perform. That might not seem very impressive. But when combined in various ways at great speeds, these operations enable the computer to perform immensely complex and data-intensive tasks.

Control unit.
The part of the CPU that coordinates the operation of the computer.

The **control unit** is the section of the CPU that directs the flow of electronic traffic between memory and the ALU and between the CPU and input and output devices. In other words, it is the mechanism that coordinates or manages the computer's operation.

Memory.
The section of the computer system that holds data and program instructions awaiting processing, intermediate results, and processed output. Also called **internal (primary) storage.**

Memory **Memory**—also called **primary (internal) storage**—holds the following:

- The programs and data that have been passed to the computer for processing
- Intermediate processing results
- Output that is ready to be transmitted to secondary storage or to an output device

Once programs, data, intermediate results, and output are stored in memory, the CPU must be able to find them again. Thus, each location in memory has an *address*. In many computer systems, a table is automatically set up and maintained that provides the address where the first character of each stored program or data block can be found. Whenever a block of data, an instruction, a program, or the result of a calculation is stored in memory, it is assigned an address so that the CPU can find it again when it is needed.

The size of memory varies among computer systems. The smallest computers can accomodate a memory of only a few thousand characters and the largest a few billion. Because memory is relatively expensive, it is usually limited in size and used only temporarily. Once the computer has finished processing one program and set of data, another program and data set are written over them in the storage space they occupy. Thus, the contents of each storage location are constantly changing. The address of each location, however, never changes. This process can be compared with what happens to the mailboxes in a post office: The number on each box remains the same, but the contents change as patrons remove their mail and new mail arrives.

Sometimes the term *main memory* is used to distinguish conventional memory from products that merely have memory characteristics—such as *read-only memory (ROM),* covered later in the chapter, and flash memory. *Flash memory,* discussed in Feature 3-1, is a recent development that combines the advantages of main memory and disk in a single product (see Feature 3-1).

Registers

Register.
A high-speed staging area within the computer that temporarily stores data during processing.

To enhance the computer's performance, the control unit and ALU contain special storage locations that act as high-speed staging areas. These areas are called **registers.** Since registers are actually a part of the CPU, their contents can be handled much more rapidly than can those of memory. Program instructions and data are normally loaded (that is, staged) into the registers from memory just before processing. Registers play a crucial role in making computer speeds extremely fast.

Feature 3 – 1

Flash Memory

A new storage solution for PCs

Memory has some hefty advantages over disks. Data can be written and retrieved more quickly. And unlike spinning disks—with their comparatively bulky and power-comsumptive disk units—memory contains no moving parts, is extremely lightweight and compact, and has low power requirements.

But one of the major problems with conventional memory is that it loses its contents when the computer is shut off. That's where *flash memory*—a new type of solid-state, credit-card-sized brand of memory technology—comes in handy.

Flash memory is packaged in cartridges that you insert into a computer system just as you would insert a diskette. A cartridge may hold 20 or 40 million characters or more of data, giving it the capacity of a low-end hard disk. But unlike conventional memory, data held in flash memory are retained when power is zapped. This property makes it an ideal storage medium for notebook and hand-held computers and in situations for which disk technology is too fragile—such as use in cars and out in the field. Flash memory is also expected to see widespread use in laser printers, photocopiers, and fax machines.

But along with its advantages, flash memory still has a couple of drawbacks, the most important of which is cost. Although prices are dropping rapidly, flash memory is roughly two or three times the cost of a hard disk, per character stored. Other disadvantages include its lower capacity and limited software support.

Nonetheless, many industry observers feel that the trend toward flash memory is unstoppable. It is likely we'll be seeing a lot of this product by the end of this decade.

Flash memory. Hard-disk capacity in a removable, solid-state cartridge.

Registers are available in several types, including the following:

- **Instruction Register and Address Register** Before each instruction in a program is processed, the control unit breaks it into two parts. The part that indicates what the ALU is to do next (for example, add, multiply, compare) is placed in the **instruction register.** The part that gives the address of the data to be used in the operation is placed in the **address register.**
- **Storage Register** The **storage register** temporarily stores data that have been retrieved from memory prior to processing.
- **Accumulator** The **accumulator** temporarily stores the results of ongoing arithmetic and logic operations.

Instruction register. The register that holds the part of the instruction indicating what the computer is to do next.

Address register. A register containing the memory location of data to be used.

Storage register.
A register that, prior to processing, temporarily stores data that have been retrieved from memory.

Accumulator.
A register that stores the result of an arithmetic or logical operation.

The instruction and address registers are often located in the control unit, whereas the storage register and accumulator are frequently found in the ALU.

Machine Cycles

Now that we've described the CPU, memory, and registers, let's see how these elements work together to process an instruction.

Microcode.
Instructions that are built into the CPU to control the operation of its circuitry.

System clock.
The timing mechanism within the computer system that governs the transmission of instructions and data through the circuitry.

Machine cycle.
The series of operations involved in the execution of a single machine-level instruction.

I-cycle.
The part of the machine cycle in which the control unit fetches an instruction from memory and prepares it for subsequent processing.

E-cycle.
The part of the machine cycle in which data are located, an instruction is executed, and results are stored.

Every instruction that you issue to the computer, whether it is in the form of a command that you type or an icon that you point to with a mouse, is broken down by your computer system into several smaller machine-level instructions called **microcode.** Each piece of microcode corresponds directly to a set of the computer's circuits.

The computer system has a built-in **system clock** that synchronizes its operations, just as a metronome can synchronize work for an orchestra. During each clock tick, a single piece of microcode can be executed, a single piece of data can be moved from one part of the computer system to another, and so on. Microcode instructions are coded in *machine language,* which will be covered later in the chapter.

The processing of a single, machine-level instruction is called a **machine cycle.** A machine cycle has two parts: an *instruction* cycle (I-cycle) and an *execution* cycle (E-cycle). During the **I-cycle,** the control unit fetches a program instruction from memory and prepares for subsequent processing. During the **E-cycle,** the data are located and the instruction is executed. Let's see how this works in a little more detail, using simple addition as an example.

I-cycle

1. The control unit fetches from memory the next instruction to be executed.
2. The control unit decodes the instruction.
3. The control unit puts the part of the instruction that shows what to do into the instruction register.
4. The control unit puts the part of the instruction that shows where the associated data are located into the address register.

E-cycle

5. Using the information in the address register, the control unit retrieves data from memory and places them into the storage register.
6. Using the information in the instruction register, the control unit commands the ALU to perform the required operation.
7. The ALU performs the specified operation, adding together the values found in the storage register and in the accumulator.
8. The result of the operation is placed back into the accumulator, destroying the value that was there previously.

Figure 3-2 depicts how the machine cycle works.

Millisecond.
One thousandth of a second.

Microsecond.
One millionth of a second.

All this may seem like an extremely tedious process, especially when a computer must go through thousands, millions, or even billions of machine cycles to process a single program fully. But computers are *very* fast. In the slowest of them, cycle times are measured in **milliseconds** (thousandths of a second). In others, they are measured in **microseconds** (millionths of a second).

FIGURE 3-2

The machine cycle. Each command that you give to the computer system must be broken down into several machine instructions, or cycles.

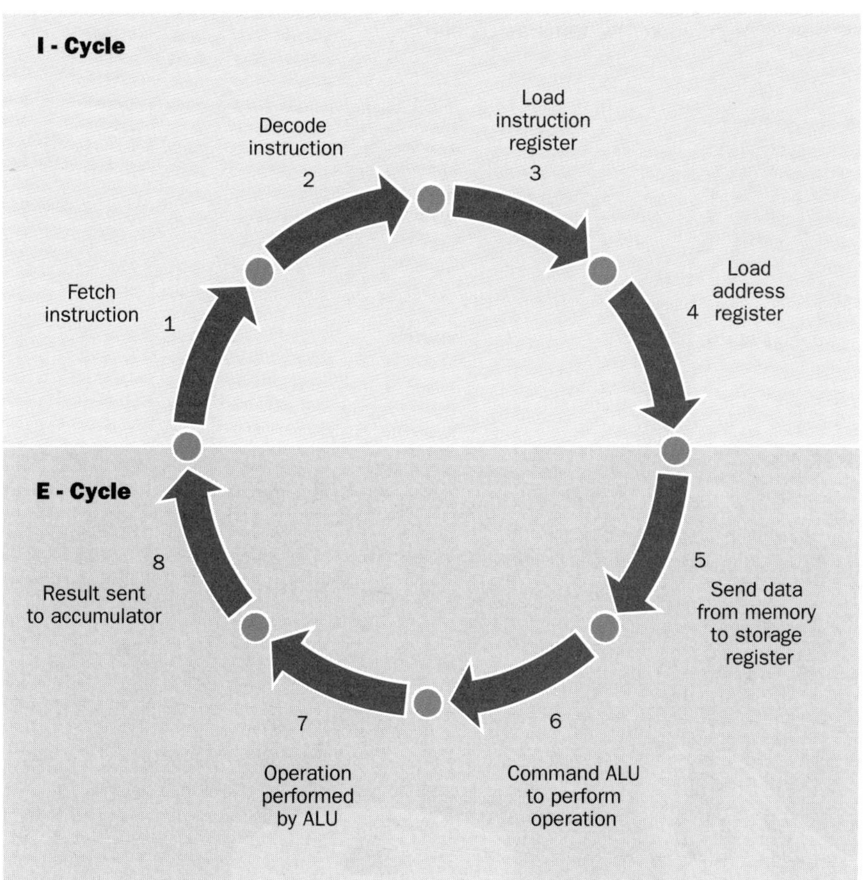

In the fastest computers, they are measured in **nanoseconds** (billionths of a second) or in **picoseconds** (trillionths of a second).

Nanosecond.
One billionth of a second.

Picosecond.
One trillionth of a second.

Different terms are used to rate speeds in different types of computers. In the microcomputer world, speeds are rated in *megahertz (MHz).* Each MHz represents a million clock ticks per second. While the original IBM PC ran at 4.77 MHz, today's desktop microcomputers often push 100 MHz or more. In the mainframe world, speeds are rated in *mips* (each mips represents a million instructions per second); in the supercomputer world, it's *mflops* (each mflops represents a million floating-point operations per second).

Data and Program Representation

The electronic components of most computer systems work in two states. For example, a circuit is either open or closed; a magnetic spot is either present or absent; and so on. This two-state, or **binary,** nature of electronics is illustrated

Binary.
The number system with two possible states.

FIGURE 3-3

The binary nature of electronics. Circuits are either open or closed, a current runs one way or the opposite way, a charge is either present or absent, and so forth. The two possible states of an electronic component are referred to as *bits* and are represented by computer systems as 0s and 1s.

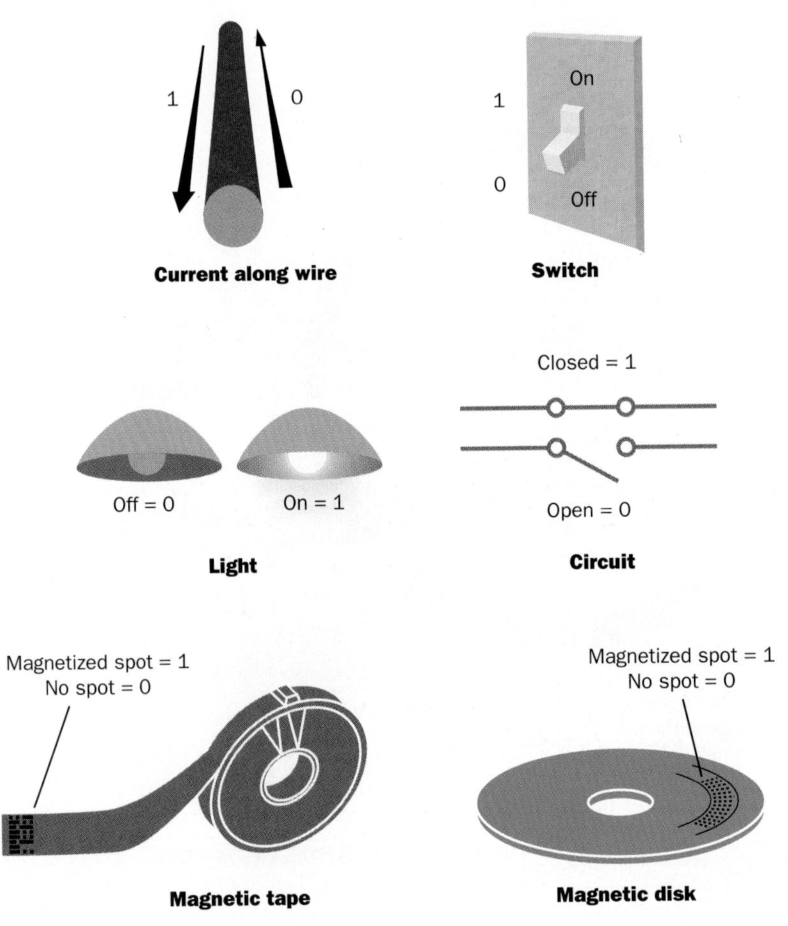

Bit.
A binary digit, such as 0 or 1.

in Figure 3-3. It is convenient to think of these binary states as the *0-state* and the *1-state.* Computer people refer to such zeros and ones as **bits,** which is a contraction of the words *BInary digiTS.* Being primarily electronic, computers do all their processing and communicating by representing programs and data in bit form. Binary, then, is the symbol set that forms the computer's "native tongue."

People, of course, don't speak binary. You're not likely to go up to a friend and say,

"0100100001001001"

which in one binary-based coding system translates as "HI." People communicate with one another in *natural languages,* such as English, Chinese, and Spanish. In our part of the world, we speak mostly English. Also, we write with a 26-character alphabet, and we use a number system with 10 rather than just

2 digits. Computers, however, understand only 0 and 1. So in order for us to interact with a computer, our messages to it must be translated into binary form and its messages to us must be translated from binary into a natural language.

The languages most people use to interact with computer systems consist of a wide variety of natural-language symbols. When we type a message such as

DISPLAY NAMES

at a keyboard, the computer system must translate all the natural-language symbols in the message into 0s and 1s. After processing is finished, the computer system must translate the 0s and 1s it has used to represent the program's results into natural language. This conversion process is illustrated in Figure 3-4. (If, incidentally, a mouse rather than a keyboard is being used for input, the conversion process remains unchanged. That is, any selections made by the user are automatically translated into 0s and 1s by the computer system.)

FIGURE 3-4

Conversion to and from binary-based form. (1) The user types in a message in natural-language symbols. (2) The computer system translates the message into binary-based form (this conversion often takes place in the input device). (3) The CPU does all the required processing in binary-based form. (4) The computer system translates the output back into natural-language symbols (this conversion usually takes place in the output device). (5) The user is able to read the output.

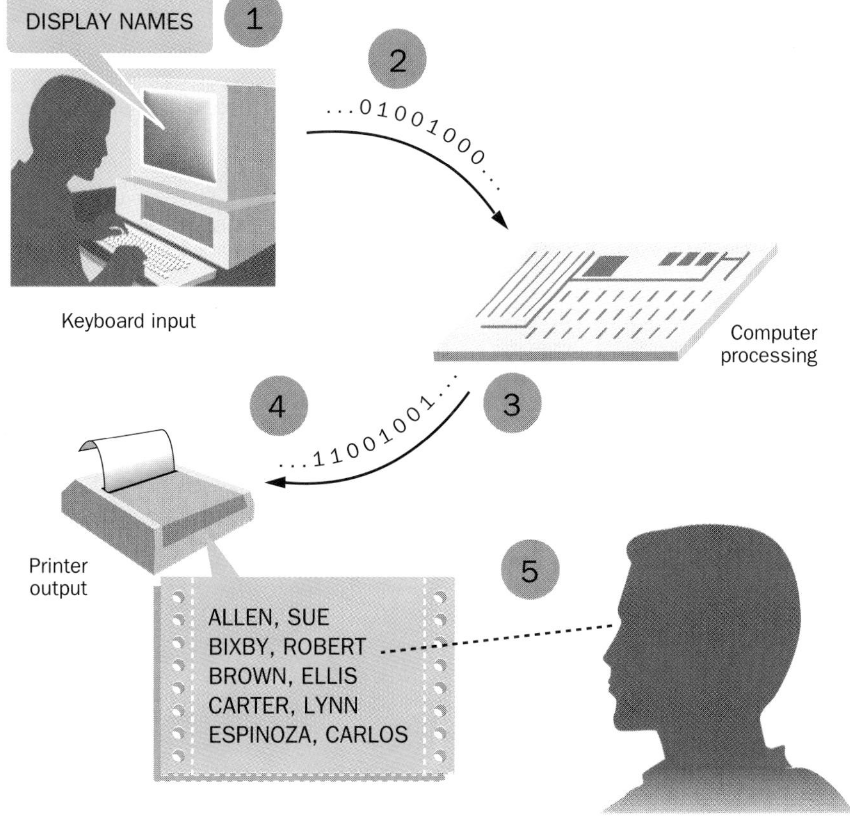

Computer systems use a variety of binary-based codes to represent programs and data. For example, when data and programs are being sent to or from the CPU (steps 2 and 4 in Figure 3-4), a fixed-length, binary-based code such as ASCII or EBCDIC is often used to represent each character transmitted. We will cover these two codes shortly.

Once data and programs are inside the CPU (step 3 of Figure 3-4), other types of binary-based codes typically handle them. For example, when a program is about to be executed, it is represented by a binary code known as machine language. Data, in contrast, may be represented by several different binary-based codes when being manipulated by the computer. One such code, which everyone learning how computers store numbers should know, is *true binary representation.* This code, as well as some fundamentals of number systems, is covered in Appendix A.

ASCII.
A fixed-length, binary-based code widely used to represent data for processing and communications.

EBCDIC.
A fixed-length, binary-based code widely used to represent data on IBM mainframes.

ASCII and EBCDIC

As mentioned earlier, when data or programs are being sent between the computer and its peripheral equipment, a *fixed-length,* binary-based code is commonly used. With a fixed-length code, the machines that are in communication can easily tell where one character ends and another begins. Such codes can be used to represent digits, alphabet characters, and other symbols.

Among the most popular of these codes are **ASCII** (American Standard Code for Information Interchange) and **EBCDIC** (Extended Binary-Coded Decimal

FIGURE 3-5

ASCII and EBCDIC. These two common fixed-length codes represent characters as unique strings of bits.

Character	Standard ASCII-8 Bit Representation	EBCDIC Bit Representation	Character	Standard ASCII-8 Bit Representation	EBCDIC Bit Representation
0	00110000	11110000	I	01001001	11001001
1	00110001	11110001	J	01001010	11010001
2	00110010	11110010	K	01001011	11010010
3	00110011	11110011	L	01001100	11010011
4	00110100	11110100	M	01001101	11010100
5	00110101	11110101	N	01001110	11010101
6	00110110	11110110	O	01001111	11010110
7	00110111	11110111	P	01010000	11010111
8	00111000	11111000	Q	01010001	11011000
9	00111001	11111001	R	01010010	11011001
A	01000001	11000001	S	01010011	11100010
B	01000010	11000010	T	01010100	11100011
C	01000011	11000011	U	01010101	11100100
D	01000100	11000100	V	01010110	11100101
E	01000101	11000101	W	01010111	11100110
F	01000110	11000110	X	01011000	11100111
G	01000111	11000111	Y	01011001	11101000
H	01001000	11001000	Z	01011010	11101001

Interchange Code). ASCII, developed largely through the efforts of the American National Standards Institute, is used on virtually all microcomputers. It is also widely adopted as the standard for data communications systems. EBCDIC, developed by IBM, is used primarily on IBM mainframes.

Both ASCII and EBCDIC represent each printable character as a unique combination of a fixed number of bits (see Figure 3-5). EBCDIC uses 8 bits to represent a character. A group of 8 bits has 256 (2^8) different combinations; therefore, EBCDIC can represent up to 256 characters. This is more than enough to account for the 26 uppercase and 26 lowercase characters, the 10 decimal digits, and several special characters.

ASCII originally was designed as a 7-bit code that could represent 128 (2^7) characters. Several 8-bit versions of ASCII (called ASCII-8 codes) have also been developed because computers are designed to handle data in chunks of 8 bits. Many computer systems can accept data in either coding system—ASCII or EBCDIC—and perform the conversion to their native code. The 8 (7) bits used to represent a character in ASCII or EBCDIC are collectively referred to as a *byte.*

A **byte** represents a single character of data. For this reason, many computer manufacturers use the byte measure to define their machines' storage capacity. As you may have noticed, computer advertisements are filled with references to kilobytes, megabytes, gigabytes, and terabytes. One **kilobyte** (**K-byte** or **KB**) is equal to a little over 1,000 bytes (1,024, to be precise), one **megabyte** (**M-byte** or **MB**) equals about 1 million bytes, one **gigabyte** (**G-byte** or **GB**) equals about 1 billion bytes, and one **terabyte** (**T-byte** or **TB**) equals about 1 trillion bytes.

Byte.
A configuration of seven or eight bits used to represent a single character of data.

Kilobyte (K-byte or **KB).**
Approximately 1,000 (1,024, to be exact) bytes.

Megabyte (M-byte or **MB).**
Approximately 1 million bytes.

Gigabyte (G-byte or **GB).**
Approximately 1 billion bytes.

Terabyte (T-byte or **TB).**
Approximately 1 trillion bytes.

The conversion from natural-language words and numbers to their ASCII (or EBCDIC) equivalents and back again usually takes place on an input/output device. For example, when a user types in a message such as

```
RUN
```

at a keyboard, an encoder chip inside the keyboard usually translates it into ASCII and sends it as a series of bytes to the CPU. The output that the CPU sends back to the display or to some other output device is also in ASCII, which the output device—with the aid of another encoder chip—translates into understandable words and numbers. Therefore, if the CPU sent the ASCII message

```
0100100001001001
```

to your display device, the word 'HI" would appear on your screen.

Computers usually handle data in byte multiples. For instance, a 16-bit computer is built to process data in chunks of two bytes; a (faster) 32-bit computer processes data in chunks of four bytes. These byte multiples are commonly called *words.* We'll look at words in more detail later in the chapter.

The Parity Bit Suppose you are at a keyboard and press the *B* key. If the keyboard encoder supports ASCII coding, it will transmit the byte "01000010" to the CPU. Sometimes, however, something happens during transmission and the CPU receives a garbled message. Interference on the line, for example,

FIGURE 3-6

The parity bit. If the system used supports even parity, as shown here, the 1-bits in every byte must always add up to an even number. The parity bit is set to either 0 or 1 in each byte to force an even number of 1-bits in the byte.

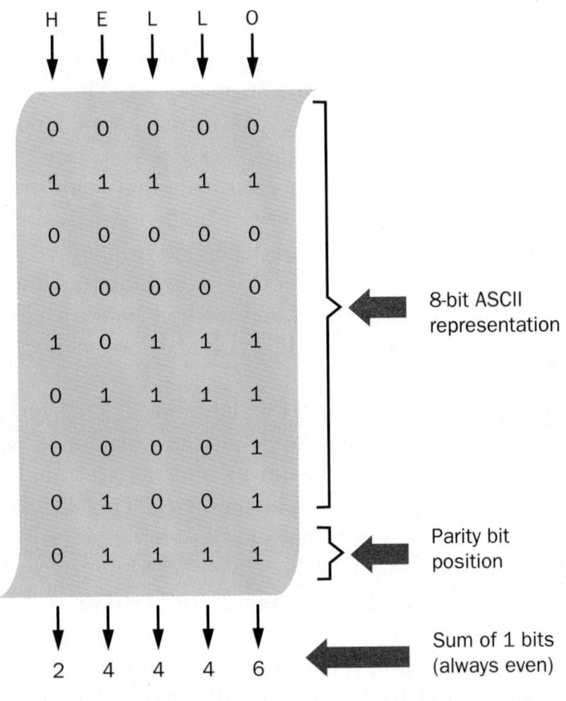

might cause the sixth bit to change from 0 to 1 so that the CPU receives the message "01000110." Unless the CPU had some way of knowing that a mistake was made, it would wrongly interpret this byte as the letter *F*.

Parity bit.
An extra bit added to the byte representation of a character to ensure that there is always either an odd or an even number of 1-bits transmitted with every character.

To enable the CPU to detect such transmission errors, EBCDIC and ASCII have an additional bit position. This bit, called the **parity bit,** is automatically set to either 0 or 1 to make all the bits in a byte add up to either an even or an odd number. Computer systems support either an even or an odd parity. In *odd-parity* systems, the parity bit makes all the 1-bits in a byte add up to an odd number. In *even-parity* systems, it makes them add up to an even number. Figure 3-6 shows how the parity bit works for the ASCII representation of the word "HELLO" on an even-parity system.

The parity bit is automatically generated by the keyboard's processor. Thus, if you typed the *B* character on an even-parity system, "010000100" would be sent up the line to the CPU. If the message were garbled so that the even-parity computer received "010001100" (an odd number of 1-bits), the CPU would sense the error immediately.

The parity check is not foolproof. For example, if two bits are incorrectly transmitted in a byte, they will self-cancel. A two-bit error, however, will rarely occur.

Machine Language

Before any program instruction can be executed by your computer, it must be converted into a binary-based code known as **machine language.** An example of a typical machine-language instruction appears below:

Machine language.
A binary-based programming language that the computer can execute directly.

```
0101100001110000000000000100000010
```

A machine-language instruction may look like a meaningless string of 0s and 1s, but it actually consists of groups of bits that represent specific storage locations and operations. The instruction shown here for an IBM mainframe, for instance, transfers data between two specific memory locations.

In the earliest computers, including even the first microcomputers, all programs were written in machine language. Today, although it is still possible to write in machine language, hardly anybody does. Instead, most people rely on *language translators,* special systems programs that convert instructions automatically into machine language. The translation is so transparent that most users aren't even aware that it is taking place.

Each computer has its own machine language. A code used on an IBM PS/2 computer will be totally foreign to an Apple Macintosh. Incidentally, this is why when you buy a program package, such as a word processor or spreadsheet, you must get the version intended for your specific type of computer system. You don't want the program package translating all of your commands to Macintosh machine language if you have an IBM PS/2 computer that understands only PS/2 machine language.

The System Unit

Now that we've talked conceptually about how the CPU and memory work, let's consider how they're realized in hardware and how they relate to other devices inside a system unit of, say, a typical microcomputer.

Almost all computers sold today use a modular hardware approach; for example, related circuitry is etched onto memory or processor chips, the chips are mounted onto carrier packages that are plugged into boards, and the boards are fitted into slots inside the system unit.

The **system unit** often consists of at least one CPU chip, specialized processor chips, memory (RAM and ROM) chips, boards on which these and other chips are mounted, ports that provide connections for external devices, a power supply, and internal circuitry to hook everything together (see Figure 3-7). Here we'll be discussing these devices. System units also often have built-in diskette and hard-disk units and sometimes even a tape drive. Disks and tapes will be covered in detail in Chapter 4.

System unit.
The hardware unit that houses the computer and its memory, as well as a number of other devices.

CPU Chip

Every microcomputer system unit contains a specific microprocessor chip as its CPU. This chip is put into a carrier package, as shown in Figure 3-8, and the carrier package is mounted onto a special board—called the **system board,**

System board.
The board that contains the computer.

FIGURE 3-7

The inside of a system unit. With the cover of the system unit removed, you can see the parts inside. Generally, the system board is located on the floor. Most system units also contain a fan to keep the parts from overheating.

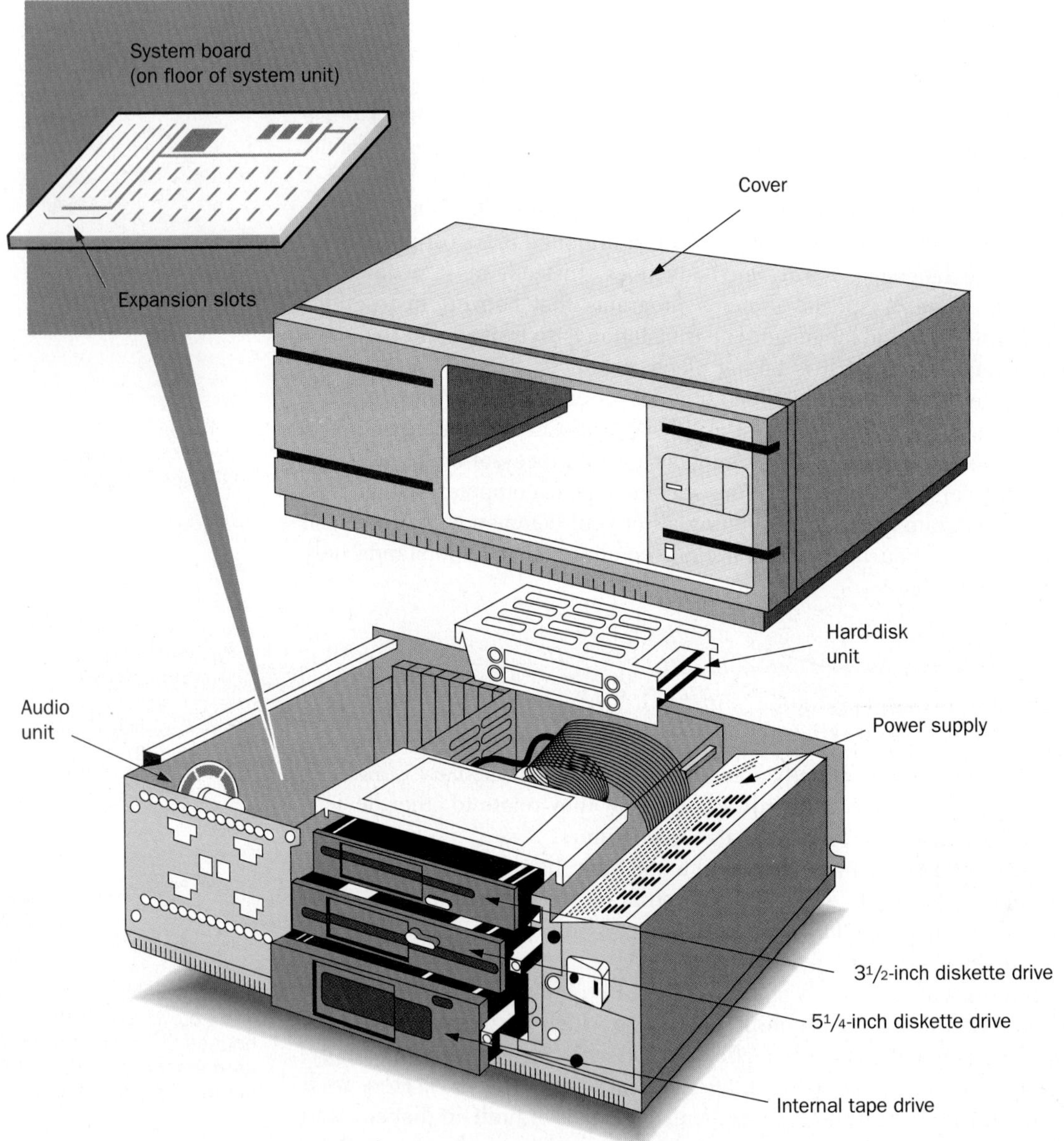

or *motherboard*—that fits inside the system unit (see Figure 3-9). This board is located on the floor of the system unit shown in Figure 3-7.

Most microcomputer systems made today use CPU chips that are manufactured by either Intel or Motorola. The Intel line of chips—such as the 8086, 8088, 80286, 80386, 80486, and Pentium chip—is used on the microcomputer systems made by IBM as well as by Compaq, Dell, and scores of other companies

FIGURE 3-8

CPU chip. (left) A chip itself, alongside a ruler. (right) The Intel Pentium chip mounted in a carrier package, which is plugged into a system board. The Pentium chip packs over three million circuits into a fingernail-sized area.

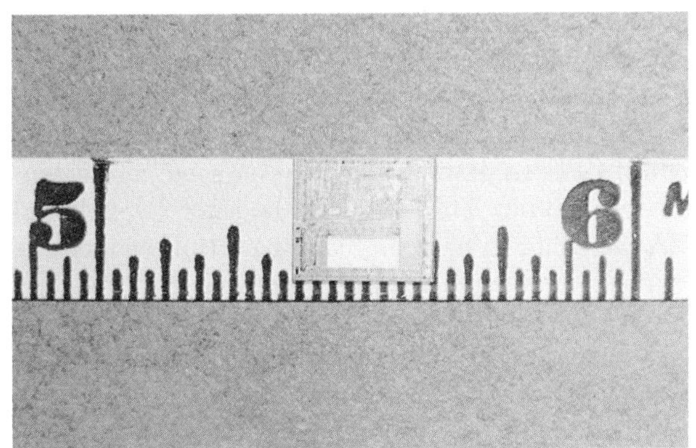

FIGURE 3-9

System board. The system board contains the CPU chip, RAM, ROM, and circuitry for a number of other functions.

that make "IBM-compatible" microcomputer systems. Many Intel chips are commonly referred to by their last three digits—for example, a '486 refers to an 80486 chip. Sometimes the chip numbers come with special suffixes—for instance, "DX" (or no suffix) is the standard chip, whereas "DX2" and "DX4" are faster versions of the chip, "SX" is an economy version, and "SL" is a low-power-consumptive version used on laptop computers.

The Motorola line of chips—including the 68000, 68020, 68030, and 68040—is found primarily on Apple Macintosh computers made before 1994. Recently, Apple, Motorola, and IBM have teamed up on the PowerPC chip, which has become the standard CPU on Macintoshes and on some microcomputers made by IBM and others. The new chip employs the same RISC-based architecture (covered later in the chapter) used on many powerful engineering workstations and is smaller in size and generally less expensive than the Intel Pentium. Some CPU chips in the PowerPC line are the 601, 603, 604, and 620.

The type of CPU chip in a computer's system unit greatly affects what you can do with the computer system. Software is written to work on a specific chip, and a program that works on one chip may not function on another unless modified. For instance, software is not very portable between Intel and Motorola chips, as these chips employ a somewhat dissimilar design philosophy. Also, a program designed for an Intel 80486 chip may not work on the earlier 80286 chip, which is less capable. And, even though a program designed for an 80286 chip may work on an 80486 chip, much of the 80486's power will be wasted.

Word.
A group of bits or characters that are treated by the computer system as a unit.

CPU chips differ in many respects, one of the most important of which is word size. A computer **word** is a group of bits or bytes that may be manipulated and stored as a unit. It is a critical concept, because the internal circuitry of virtually every computer system is designed around a certain word size. The Apple Macintosh Quadra series and IBM PS/2 95 computers, for example, use the Motorola 68040 and Intel 80486 chips, respectively. Both the 68040 and 80486 chips have a 32-bit-word internal architecture, which means that data are transferred within each CPU chip itself in 32-bit chunks. Both chips also have a 32-bit-word I/O bus, meaning that there is a 32-bit-wide data path from each CPU to external devices. Often, the greater the word size, the faster the computer system.

Specialized Processor Chips

Working alongside the CPU chip in many system units are *specialized processor chips,* such as numeric coprocessors and graphic coprocessors. The role of these "slave chips" is to perform specialized tasks for the CPU, thereby enhancing overall system performance. For instance, a *numeric (math) coprocessor* chip helps the CPU perform arithmetic; a *graphic coprocessor* chip helps the CPU with the computationally intensive chore of creating complex screen displays. It is not unusual to boost the speed of a computer system several times over by using specialized chips such as these.

RAM

Random access memory (RAM).
The computer system's main memory.

RAM (for **random access memory**)—the computer system's *main memory*—is used to store the programs and data on which the computer is currently working. Like the microprocessor, the RAM of a microcomputer system consists of circuits etched onto silicon-backed chips. These chips are mounted in carrier packages, just as the CPU is, and the packages are arranged onto boards (called *single in-line memory modules,* or *SIMMs,* which are then plugged into the system board. Most desktop microcomputer systems in use today have enough RAM to store 256 thousand to several billion bytes of data. Many computer systems allow memory expansion (within limits) through add-in boards (which we will discuss shortly) when RAM is insufficient. RAM is *volatile,* meaning that the contents of memory are lost when the computer is shut off.

ROM

ROM, which stands for **read-only memory,** consists of nonerasable hardware modules that contain programs. Like RAM, these software-in-hardware modules are mounted into carrier packages that, in turn, are plugged into one or more boards inside the system unit. You can neither write over these ROM programs (that's why they're called read-only) nor destroy their contents when you shut off the computer's power (that is, they're nonvolatile). A program stored in ROM can be fetched more quickly by the CPU than if it were stored on disk, where it would have to be loaded into memory before the computer could work on it. Key pieces of systems software are often stored in ROM.

Read-only memory (ROM).
A software-in-hardware module that can be read but not written on.

ROM is an example of **firmware,** software-in-hardware modules that are available in several other forms. For instance, *programmable read-only memory (PROM)* is identical to ROM except that the module is blank and the buyer writes the program. Special equipment is needed to write a program onto a PROM module, and once the program is on, it can't be erased. *Erasable programmable read-only memory (EPROM),* on the other hand, is like PROM except that its contents can be erased and a new program written. Firmware is usually supplied when a computer system is purchased, but it can also be bought separately.

Firmware.
Software instructions that are written onto a hardware module.

Add-in Boards

Many microcomputer-system vendors enable you to customize your system by choosing your own **add-in boards.** These boards are cardlike pieces of hardware that contain the circuitry for performing one or more specific functions. They plug into *expansion slots* within the computer's system unit, thereby enabling you to either interface with specific types of peripheral devices or add new capabilities. For example, if you want a certain model of display unit attached to your computer, you may need a special *display adapter board* that contains the proper software routine for establishing the connection. Similarly, you can get your computer system to communicate with fascimile (fax) machines by getting a *fax board.*

Add-in-board.
A board that may be inserted into the computer's system unit to perform one or more functions.

Many types of add-in boards currently are available in the markeplace. Most of these boards provide either a basic function that is unavailable with the system unit or a "value-added" capability that enhances an existing function. With new machines and new capabilities being announced regularly, the number of types of add-in boards is increasing rapidly. Figure 3-10 lists several types of these boards and the functions they perform.

Ports

Most system units contain built-in sockets that enable you to plug in external hardware devices. These sockets, which often are found on the exterior of the

Port.
An outlet on the computer's system unit through which a peripheral device may communicate.

FIGURE 3-10

Add-in boards for microcomputer systems. Add-in boards can provide a microcomputer system with either brand new capabilities or enhancements to existing features.

Board Type	Purpose
Cache card	Provides the microcomputer system with logic to improve disk performance
Concurrent-processor board	Contains a CPU that can be run concurrently with the CPU on the system board
Coprocessor board	Uses specialized processor chips that speed up overall processing in the microcomputer system
Disk controller card	Enables a certain type of disk unit to interface with the microcomputer system
Display adapter board	Enables a certain type of display device to interface with the microcomputer system
Emulator board	Allows the microcomputer system to function as a communications terminal to a large computer system
Fax board	Provides facsimile capabilities for the microcomputer system
Graphics adapter board	Enables the computer system to conform to a particular graphics standard
Memory expansion board	Allows additional RAM to be put into the microcomputer system
Modem board	Provides communications circuitry on a board
Multifunction board	Provides several independent functions on a single board
Sound board	Enables users to attach stereo speakers to a microcomputer system
Upgrade board*	Contains a CPU that can be used in lieu of the CPU on the system board
Video board	Enables the microcomputer to display full-motion, TV-quality video images

*Also known as an accelerator board or a turbo board.

system unit, are known as **ports.** Printers, for instance, generally hook up to microcomputers through either *parallel* ports or *serial* ports. IBM microcomputers and similar devices typically connect printers with parallel ports, whereas Apple computers connect printers with serial ports. Most computers also use serial ports to permit connection to remote devices over phone lines. The technical differences between serial and parallel transmission are explained in Chapter 6.

When an I/O device needs to be plugged into the system unit and there is not a built-in port for it, you normally must buy a special add-in board that has a port on it. When you install the board, the port will extend through a hole in the back of the system unit so that you can plug the I/O device into it.

There is a practical limit to the number of peripheral devices a CPU can handle. Generally, each new device interfaced through an add-in board or port adds to the burden the CPU must manage, thereby possibly degrading system performance.

Bus.
A set of wires that acts as a data highway between the CPU and other devices.

I/O Bus

The CPU connects to RAM, ROM, boards, and ports through circuitry called an I/O (for input/output) **bus,** as shown in Figure 3-11. The bus links the

CPU to every hardware device in the system, enabling data to be exchanged and processed.

Today, there are a number of bus standards in existence. The three most state-of-the-art standards are IBM's *Micro Channel Architecture* (used on the high end of the IBM PS/2 line of computers), Apple's *NuBus* (used on the most recent Macintoshes), and *EISA*, or *Enhanced Industry Standard Architecture* (used on computers made by Compaq and several other vendors). Each of these bus architectures is based on a 32-bit word size. An older and less powerful standard, *ISA* (for *Industry Standard Architecture*), which is based upon the IBM PC AT architecture and its 16-bit word size, is also very widely seen in practice.

Micro Channel Architecture, NuBus, and EISA enable you to configure your computer system with several CPUs, including the native CPU and alternate CPUs on add-in boards. Thus, the native CPU can be working on a spreadsheet application while a CPU on an add-in board is performing a background database search. Such an arrangement will, of course, make the work go much faster than it would if the native CPU alone had to do everything.

The choice of a bus is critical because boards are generally not interchangeable between different types of buses. During the next several years, as more desktop software and hardware products evolve to the 32-bit standard, the ISA standard is expected to gradually lose its appeal.

FIGURE 3-11

How devices are linked. A set of wires or circuits called a *bus* allows the CPU to communicate with RAM, with ROM, and with peripheral devices connected through either boards or ports.

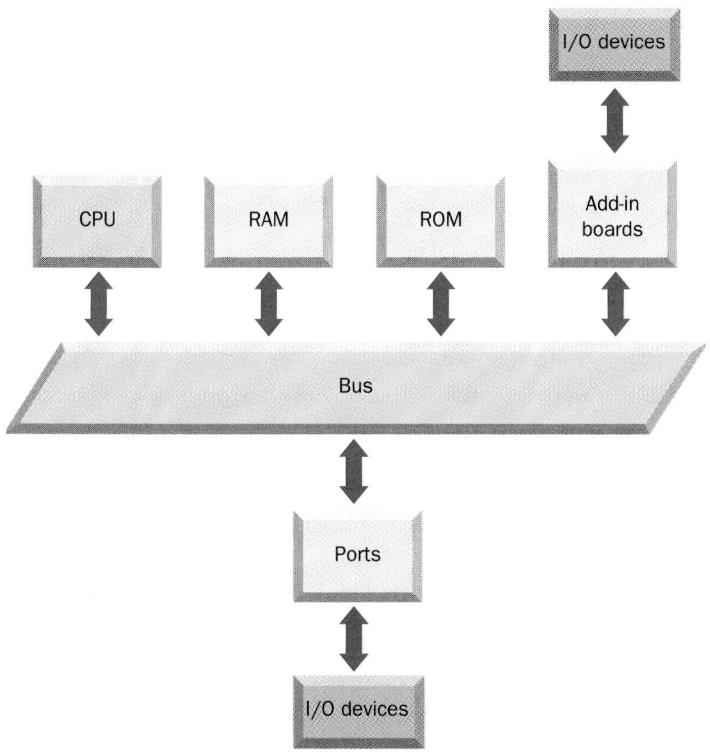

TOMORROW

The Coming Chip Technologies

What Will Be the Next Major Challenger to Silicon?

Since the beginning of modern computing, researchers have constantly searched for new types of circuit technologies to hold data and to manipulate them faster. The earliest computers used hardware such as vacuum tubes, magnetic drums, and core planes as their principal circuit components. In the 1970s, when it was possible to etch circuitry into an area the size of the head of a pin, another major medium evolved: silicon-backed chips. Silicon became popular because it is an unusually pure substance and will not interfere with the metal circuitry etched onto its surface.

Today, although it is possible to place more than a million microminiaturized circuit elements onto a silicon chip, that may not be enough. So researchers are pressing forward with other approaches. Five of the leading challengers to silicon are the following:

Gallium Arsenide Probably the most promising new computer chip technology involves gallium arsenide (GaAs). GaAs chips are superior to those made of silicon because:

GaAs chip. Enough power to transmit 40 encyclopedia volumes every second.

- They move electronic impulses around several times faster (see photo).
- They enable optical transmission, something silicon can't do.
- They can operate at much higher temperatures and emit less heat, enabling circuits to be packed closer together.

Gallium arsenide products are already moving into the marketplace. Some of the more critical components of large computers now consist of GaAs chips, and GaAs is rapidly taking hold in areas such as high-speed communications.

Making Computers Speedier

Over the years, a number of strategies have been used to make computers faster. Four of these are moving circuits closer together, finding new materials with which to make computers, developing reduced instruction set computers (RISC), and using parallel processing.

Moving Circuits Closer Together As complex as computers seem sometimes, all must follow one intuitive natural law: the shorter the length of the circuit paths, the shorter the time it takes to move programs and data along them. During the last several decades, computer manufacturers have been able to pack circuitry ever closer together. Today, it is now possible to fit more than a million circuits on a single fingernail-sized chip.

Unfortunately, when the circuits are in use, they generate heat. And, when circuits are placed too close together, they melt. To circumvent this problem,

But gallium arsenide has some drawbacks. GaAs chips are still often several times more expensive than those made of silicon. And because the newer technology is still in its infancy, GaAs designers can currently squeeze far fewer circuits onto a single chip.

Superconductors One of the problems with conventional circuitry is that it heats up. When circuits get hot, their electrical resistance increases, impeding the flow of message-bearing electrons. If circuits are placed too close together, they can melt. Superconductive materials are those that can transfer electrons without the worry of electrical resistance or heat buildup.

Every year new materials are being discovered that more closely approach the ideal of superconductivity. While most of the superconductors of today must be cooled in order to lose resistance and avoid a meltdown, the search continues for materials that are superconductive at room temperature. If and when naturally superconductive materials emerge from the laboratories and are successfully implemented in products, they may result in circuitry that's 100 times faster than today's silicon-backed chips.

Optical Processing Optical processing uses light waves to do the work of the silicon-backed chip's electrons. Optical chips currently available in the marketplace can move data around about ten times faster than silicon-backed chips. Theoretically, an optical processor would be capable of speeds hundreds of times faster than silicon—if data could be gotten into and out of it fast enough. Optical chips are today surfacing in such applications as collision-avoidance systems for cars, artificial vision systems for robots, and sensors for image processing.

Biotechnology Biotechnology offers yet another compelling alternative to today's silicon chip. Scientists have shown that tiny molecules can be grown and shaped to act as circuits. With such a technology, electrons are passed from molecule to molecule. Some scientists believe that if such a technology is ever perfected, it could possibly result in circuits 500 times smaller than those on today's silicon chips.

Tubes on a Chip Just when everyone thought that it was dead and buried, vacuum electronics—popular in the 1940s and 1950s—is making a comeback. Scientists are now talking about the very real possibility of putting up to ten billion microscopic tubes on a five-inch wafer. Why vacuum tubes? Electrons can travel much faster when placed in a vacuum. Unlike their predecessors, which needed heat to work, these new tubes work by an entirely different set of principles. Some researchers believe that tubes on a chip are capable of packing 1,000 times the power of today's silicon chips.

researchers have used such strategies as immersing circuits in helium "baths" to cool them. Helium baths are found in some supercomputers.

New Materials Most CPU chips today consist of metallic circuitry that is etched onto a silicon backing. Silicon-backed chips have been popular since the 1970s, when manufacturing techniques to microminiaturize circuitry became widely available.

Today, because limits are quickly being reached on the number of circuits that can be packed onto a chip without heat damage, several other alternatives are getting considerable attention. Among these are gallium arsenide chips, superconductors, optical processing, biotechnology, and vacuum electronics (see the Tomorrow box).

Reduced Instruction Set Computers (RISC) To process data effectively, computers must be equipped with a variety of instructions, called the computer's *instruction set.* Each instruction in the set corresponds to a microcode instruction.

Studies have shown that computers are actually faster if they are given only a fraction of the instructions with which computers have traditonally been provided. (The old adage "too many cooks spoil the broth" applies in the world of computers, too.) The instructions that the computer doesn't need just get in the way of efficient and speedy processing.

Reduced instruction set computing (RISC). A term referring to a computer system that gets by with fewer instructions than conventional computer systems.

In the mid-1970s, CPUs with limited instruction sets became available. These machines have aptly been named **reduced instruction set computers (RISC).** In certain test studies, RISC-based computers have been shown to be several times faster than conventional computers with larger instruction sets. Today, RISC devices are rapidly becoming the standard in engineering applications environments and in communications systems. RISC is also the resident architecture in the PowerPC chip. The downside to RISC-based computers is that conventional software needs to be modified to work on them.

Parallel Processing Despite the astounding evolution of computer systems over the past 50 years, most are still driven by a single CPU. A single CPU can perform instructions only in serial, or one step at a time, whether working exclusively on one program or juggling several concurrently.

Parallel processing. Refers to computing in which two or more CPUs share work and process pieces of this work simultaneously.

In the race to develop ever-faster computer systems for tomorrow, scientists are experimenting with ways to have two or more CPUs and memories perform tasks in parallel. For example, instead of relying on one processor to solve a lengthy calculation, a computer system using **parallel processing** assigns portions of the problem to several CPUs operating simultaneously. But just as it is difficult to coordinate two or more workers who are dedicated to completing a single job, so too is it difficult to integrate the parallel efforts of several processors working together at superhuman speeds. Nonetheless, many industry insiders see parallel processing as an unstoppable future reality. As it becomes harder and harder to make computers themselves faster—by, say, packing circuits closer together—parallel processing will become an increasingly important strategy for reducing the time it takes to do work.

Today, several approaches to parallel-processing computer systems are observable in the marketplace. One popular approach is represented by the Cray-2, a supercomputer that carries a price tag of several million dollars. The Cray, like most other supercomputers, employs a common parallel design philosophy—namely, hooking up a small number of expensive, state-of-the-art CPUs. The Cray-2 uses four such processors, which carry out both parallel and serial processing. Another common tack is to design parallel machines with hundreds or thousands of relatively inexpensive, off-the-shelf microprocessors (see Feature 3-2). Although devices built this way are less versatile than conventional supercomputers, they can pack a respectable amount of power at the fraction of the cost.

Summary and Key Terms

In Chapter 3 we flip the lid off of a typical system unit and examine the function of the parts inside.

How the CPU Works The CPU has two major sections. The **arithmetic/logic unit (ALU)** performs arithmetic and logical operations on data. The **control unit** directs the flow of electronic traffic between memory and the ALU

Feature 3-2

Massively Parallel Processors

Supercomputing the microcomputing way

Today a lot of researchers are discovering that the best way to build extremely powerful computers is to buy microcomputers—a lot of them—and connect them all together in order to attack work in parallel.

The approach is called *massively parallel processing (MPP)*. Some computer-industry forecasters believe that MPP will eventually become the standard way to do supercomputing. The idea is to coordinate hundreds, thousands, or maybe even tens of thousands of powerful microprocessors into a single unit. Just as a dozen people can polish off a pizza faster than a single person, so, too, is it possible that a machine with scores of processors could knock off a problem faster than could just a single processor.

Not that it will be easy. A major problem is how to get the processors to do work efficiently without wasting a lot of time passing data back and forth between each other. In addition, complicated synchronizing techniques must be established to get the machines to share data. If, say, one processor is supposed to compute a result and supply it to another processor, you don't want the second processor trying to fetch anything from memory before the first processor has put it there. Nor do you want it to have to wait around too long for the first processor to complete its part of the job.

Because of such complexities, software for parallel processing machines has to be specially written. So far, only a narrow class of problems has been identified that can be handily split into independent pieces and run efficiently on a parallel processing machine. But progress is being made, and the rewards are gigantic.

Consider, for instance, modeling the global climate; that is, simulating the long-term effects of pollutants on the ozone layer, global-warming patterns, and acid-rain levels. Today's supercomputers can only accurately forecast about ten years into the future, which, because pollutants normally take decades to wreak their havoc, is hardly enough. But massively parallel processors may provide the quantum leap in computing power needed to predict environmental conditions a century or more into the future. Because the earth's atmosphere is logically divisible into many pieces, climate modeling falls into the category of problem that MPP handles best.

Intel Touchtone Delta MPP Supercomputer. Hundreds of microcomputers under a single roof.

Massively parallel processors can also help out in the business world. Already, giant retailers such as Wal-Mart, Kmart, and Mervyn's use MPP machines to identify sales patterns. Such supercomputing makes information on sales trends available within hours, instead of the days it would take a conventional mainframe. In retailing, faster information means staying competitive.

Today, the "holy grail" of MPP is the teraflops computer. Roughly described, the teraflops is a machine that can compute a trillion arithmetic operations per second. How fast is that? It's about 50 times more power than today's faster computer. Or, put another way, in one second a teraflops computer will be able to do a job that it would take a person 32,000 years to complete, working on a hand calculator every single second.

and, also, between the CPU and input and output devices. Both of these units work closely with memory to carry out processing tasks inside the system unit.

Memory—also called **primary (internal) storage**—holds the programs and data that have been passed to the computer, the results of intermediate processing, and output that is ready to be transmitted to secondary storage or an output device.

Registers are high-speed staging areas within the CPU that hold program instructions and data immediately before they are processed. The part of a program instruction that indicates what the ALU is to do next is placed in the **instruction register;** the part showing the address of the data to be used in the operation is placed in the **address register.** Before data are processed, they are taken from memory and placed in the **storage register.** The **accumulator** is a register that temporarily stores the results of ongoing operations.

The processing of a single, machine-level instruction is called a **machine cycle.** Each such instruction is broken down further into subinstructions called **microcode,** and each piece of microcode corresponds directly to a set of the computer's circuits. The computer system has a built-in **system clock** that synchronizes the processing of microcode.

A machine cycle has two parts: an **I-cycle** (instruction cycle), in which the control unit fetches and examines an instruction, and an **E-cycle** (execution cycle), in which the instruction is actually executed by the ALU under control unit supervision. A computer may need to go through thousands, millions, or even billions of machine cycles to fully process a single program. Computer cycle times generally are measured in **milliseconds** (thousandths of a second), **microseconds** (millionths of a second), **nanoseconds** (billionths of a second), or **picoseconds** (trillionths of a second).

Data and Program Representation The electronic components of digital computers work in a two-state, or **binary,** fashion. It is convenient to think of these binary states as the 0-state and the 1-state. Computer people refer to such 0s and 1s as **bits.**

The computer uses several binary-based codes to process data. Two popular codes are **ASCII** and **EBCDIC.** These fixed-length codes can represent any single character of data—a digit, alphabet character, or special symbol—as a string of seven or eight bits. This string of bits is called a **byte.** ASCII and EBCDIC allow for an additional bit position, called a **parity bit,** to enable computer systems to check for transmission errors.

The storage capacity of computers often is expressed in **kilobytes** (**K-bytes** or **KB**), or thousands of bytes; **megabytes** (**M-bytes** or **MB**), or millions of bytes; **gigabytes** (**G-bytes** or **GB**), or billions of bytes; and **terabytes** (**T-bytes** or **TB**), or trillions of bytes.

Machine language is the binary-based code used to represent programs. A program must be translated into machine language before the computer can execute it.

The System Unit Almost all computer systems sold today use a modular hardware approach; that is, related circuitry is etched onto *processor chips* or *memory chips,* the chips are mounted onto carrier packages that are later fitted into boards, and the boards are positioned into slots inside the **system unit.**

Every microcomputer system unit contains a specific microprocessor chip as its CPU. This chip is put into a carrier package that is mounted onto a special board, called the **system board,** that fits inside the system unit. CPU chips differ in many respects; one difference is word size. A computer **word** is a group of bits or bytes that can be manipulated as a unit. Often the larger the word size, the more powerful the processor.

Working alongside the CPU chip in many system units are specialized processor chips, such as *numeric coprocessors* and *graphic coprocessors.*

The regular memory chips on microcomputer systems are commonly referred to as **RAM,** for **random access memory.** Memory chips that contain nonerasable programs are referred to as **ROM,** for **read-only memory.** ROM is an example of **firmware.** Other types of firmware include PROM (programmable read-only memory) and EPROM (erasable programmable read-only memory).

Many system units contain a limited number of internal expansion slots, into which **add-in boards** can be mounted by the user. These boards can be used to customize a computer system by supplying more memory, adding facsimile-machine (fax) capability, and so on. Also, many system units have external I/O **ports** into which peripheral devices may be plugged.

The CPU connects to RAM, ROM, and peripherals (interfaced by add-in boards and ports) through circuitry called an I/O **bus.** Some widely used bus architectures include *Micro Channel Architecture,* used on the high end of the IBM PS/2 line of computers; *NuBus,* used on the recent Apple Macintosh line of computers; *EISA,* used extensively on Compaq computers and those of many other vendors; and *ISA,* which is often used on 16-bit computers.

Making Computers Speedier Over the years, a number of strategies have been used to make computers faster. Four of these are moving circuits closer together, finding new materials with which to make computers, developing **reduced instruction set computers (RISC),** and using **parallel processing.**

Review Exercises

Fill-in Questions

1. The register that temporarily stores the results of ongoing arithmetic and logic operations is called the ____________.
2. A millisecond is one ____________ of a second.
3. One trillion bytes are referred to as a(n) ____________.
4. ROM is an acronym for ____________.
5. A(n) ____________ bit is added to a character's byte representation to make all the bits add up to an odd or even number.
6. RISC is an acronym for ____________.
7. The operation of two or more computers working together is known as ____________ processing.

Matching Questions

Match each term with the description that fits best.

a. ALU
b. binary
c. bit
d. EBCDIC
e. ASCII
f. word
g. EPROM
h. parity bit

____ 1. The base-2 numbering system.
____ 2. The fixed-length code most associated with IBM mainframes.
____ 3. A type of firmware that is erasable.
____ 4. A fixed-length code developed by the American National Standards Institute.
____ 5. Used to check for transmission errors.
____ 6. The section of the CPU in which computations are peformed.
____ 7. A group of bits or bytes that may be manipulated and stored as a unit.
____ 8. A binary digit.

Discussion Questions

1. Describe the various sections of the CPU and their roles.
2. Explain how a program instruction is executed.
3. Why is the binary system used to represent data and programs?
4. What is the purpose of the parity bit, and how does it work?

5. What are the differences between a bit, a byte, a kilobyte, a megabyte, and a word?
6. How does RAM differ from ROM?
7. What devices are located under the cover of the system unit? What functions do these devices perform?
8. What is the principle advantage of a reduced instruction set computer (RISC)?

Critical Thinking Questions

1. The chapter mentions the continuing quest for faster computers. What difference could it make to have mainframe computing power on the desk of ordinary end users or computers that are, say, hundreds or thousands of times faster than those we have today?
2. The earliest computers were decimal rather than binary machines. In other words, they broke down each piece of data into ten states instead of just two. Why, would you guess, were decimal computers slower than binary computers?
3. Comment on this statement: "Computers are now so easy to work with that it's no longer necessary for the average user to know any of the technical details about how they work." In making your comments, be sure to state how much technical knowledge you think the average business student should have about computers.

SECONDARY STORAGE

4

Why are hard disks so popular today? Compared with other forms of secondary storage, they are relatively fast and capacious—and reasonably inexpensive per character stored. But as Chapter 4 explains, newer forms of storage are chipping away at the hard disk's dominance.

OUTLINE

Overview
Properties of Secondary Storage Systems
Magnetic Disk
- Diskettes
- Hard Disks for Small Computers
- Other Types of Magnetic Disks for Small Computers
- RAM Disk and Cache Disk
- Disk Systems for Large Computers

Magnetic Tape
- Processing Tapes
- Storing Data on Tape

Optical Disk
Data Organization

LEARNING OBJECTIVES

After completing this chapter, you will be able to:

1. Name several general properties of secondary storage systems.
2. Identify a number of disk storage systems as well as describe how they work and where they are particularly useful.
3. Describe the roles of other secondary storage media and equipment.
4. Explain several types of data access and organization strategies, and identify situations in which each is appropriate.

Overview

In Chapter 3, we discussed the role of memory. Memory is designed to provide immediate access to stored items. It is here that programs, data, intermediate results, and output are temporarily stored. However, as soon as a program has been executed, new data and programs are written over the existing ones. Thus, if data, programs, and processing results are to be preserved for repeated use, additional storage capacity must be made available. Secondary (external) storage serves this purpose. Although slower than memory, secondary storage is less expensive and consequently provides far greater storage capacity for each dollar spent.

We will begin this chapter with a discussion of certain common characteristics of secondary storage systems. One of the most important is data access—the way in which data are retrieved from secondary storage. Then we'll cover the two most important kinds of secondary storage systems in use today: those that use magnetic disk and those that use magnetic tape. Next we'll look at optical disk. Finally, we'll cover data organization—methods of storing data on a medium for efficient access.

Properties of Secondary Storage Systems

In this section, we'll look at several important properties and characteristics of secondary storage systems. We will consider in turn (1) the two physical parts of a secondary storage system, (2) the nonvolatility property of secondary storage, (3) the removability of media from the secondary storage unit, and (4) sequential versus direct access.

Physical Parts Any secondary storage system involves two physical parts: a *peripheral device* and an *input/output medium.* A disk unit and a tape unit are examples of peripheral devices; magnetic disk platters and magnetic tape cartridges are types of media. Data and programs are written onto and read from some type of medium. The medium must be situated on a peripheral device for the CPU to process its contents.

Read/write head. A magnetic station on a disk access mechanism or tape unit that reads or writes data.

In most secondary storage systems, media must pass by a **read/write head** in the peripheral device to be read from or written to. For instance, when you play or record to a music tape on your home stereo system, the tape passes by a head on the tape recorder, which will either play or record music. Magnetic tapes on computer systems work by an identical principle. Magnetic disks also use read/write heads that perform similar types of reading and writing tasks.

Nonvolatile storage. Storage that retains its contents when the power is shut off.

Volatile storage. Storage that loses its contents when the power is shut off.

Nonvolatility Property Secondary storage media are **nonvolatile.** This means that when the power on the peripheral device is shut off, the data stored on the medium remain there. This is in contrast to most types of memory, which are **volatile.** With volatile storage, the data on the medium disappear once the power is shut off.

Removable versus Nonremovable Media In many secondary storage systems, although the peripheral device is online to the computer, the associated medium must be loaded into the device before the computer can read from it or write to it. These are called *removable-media* secondary storage systems. Diskettes, some types of hard disks, magnetic tape cartridges, magnetic tape reels, and optical disks are examples of removable media used on such systems. Other secondary storage systems, such as those that use Winchester disks (discussed later in this chapter), are *fixed-media* secondary storage systems. In Winchester disk systems, the disk is encased in a sealed unit within the peripheral device, and it cannot be conveniently removed.

Removability of media provides virtually unlimited storage capacity, because the medium can be replaced when it is full. Removability also facilitates backup (covered extensively in Chapter 13). *Backup* occurs when a duplicate set of data or programs are written onto a disk or tape and are stored offline, for use if the originals are lost or destroyed. *Security* is also enhanced by removability, because programs or data do not have to stay on the disk unit. Finally, removability makes it possible to assign a specific application to a specific medium—say, assigning all customer accounts to one disk and all vendor accounts to another. Fixed media, in contrast, generally offer the advantages of higher speed, greater online storage capacity, and better reliability.

Sequential versus Direct Access When the computer system is instructed to use data or programs residing in secondary storage, it first must be able to find the materials. The process of retrieving data and programs in storage is called *access.*

Two basic access methods are available: sequential and direct. With **sequential access,** the records in a file can be retrieved only in the same order in which they are physically stored. With **direct access,** also called **random access,** records can be retrieved in any order.

Sequential access. Fetching records in storage in the same order in which they are physically arranged.

Direct access. Reading or writing data in storage so that the access time involved is relatively independent of the location of the data. Also known as **random access.**

The distinction between sequential and direct access can be seen on a typical home stereo system. Suppose you have both a cassette tape and a compact disk (CD) of the same music. You want to hear the fifth song on the CD and this song is also the fifth selection on the tape. With the tape, you must pass sequentially through the first four songs to hear the fifth one. With the CD, however, you can go directly to the fifth song and listen to it immediately.

Music CDs are also effective for sequential access. You can start at the beginning and play tunes in sequence. Thus, the CD is really both a sequential- and direct-access medium because you can play a series of songs sequentially or pick individual ones in random order.

Now let's apply this distinction to computer systems. Computer tape has the sequential properties of music tape, and computer disk has both the sequential and direct properties of the music CD.

Some information processing applications are essentially sequential in nature, while others are direct. For example, the preparation of mailing labels is often a sequential operation. If you want to send Christmas cards to all employees in a company, you can process the computerized employee file sequentially—that is, from the beginning of the file to the end. As names and addresses are extracted from the file, they are printed on the mailing labels. Obtaining the latest inventory information about products, on the other hand, often involves direct processing, because requests are made to the inventory file in random order. For example, suppose a salesperson wants to find out how many units of item number 6402 are on hand. A minute later, a customer calls to get the price of item number 36. Then a question comes up regarding deliveries of

User Solution 4-1

CD-Type Programming for Record Lovers

Problem: You have a large record collection and would like to have the ability to automatically listen to song tracks in any order, as you can on a compact disk (CD). *Solution:* Not to worry. A new high-tech record turntable will let you specify the sequence in which you wish to hear tracks on a particular side of a record. For example, if you want to listen to the third song followed by the fifth song, you just press the "3" button on the front panel, then the "5" button, and then "Play." The turntable, called Song Stalker, works with a laser mechanism in the tone arm that detects the position of an album's song tracks. The device can accommodate up to eight song tracks and 15 entries, enabling you to play songs more than once.

item number 988. In this case, you move back and forth randomly through the records to obtain information from this file.

User Solution 4-1 describes how CD-like access is now possible on turntables that play vinyl records.

Magnetic Disk

Magnetic disk. A secondary storage medium consisting of platters made of rigid metal (hard disk) or flexible plastic (diskette).

Hard disk. A rigid platter coated with a magnetizable substance.

Diskette. A small, removable disk made of a tough, flexible plastic and coated with a magnetizable substance.

Today **magnetic disks** are undoubtedly the most widely used secondary storage medium for information processing. Because they allow direct access to data, disks permit much faster retrieval of information than do tapes, and at a reasonable cost as well. Without disk storage, many of the computer applications we see around us would not be possible. Banking with automatic teller machines and making airline reservations are just two of the many activities that depend on the rapid access to data that magnetic disks provide.

Two common types of magnetic disks are hard disks and diskettes. **Hard disks** are round, rigid platters. Because of their large storage capacities and fast data-retrieval capabilities, hard disks are indispensible for most types of commercial applications. Many types of hard-disk systems are in use today; the most common are those that use either a removable-pack or sealed-pack design.

The advantages of hard disks notwithstanding, inexpensive **diskettes,** which are packaged in small plastic cases, are still widely used—because of their low cost and removability—on many microcomputer systems today. Diskettes are ideal for transferring small amounts of data from one system to another and for storing small amounts of backup.

Every disk system is *addressable.* This means that each data record or program may be stored and later accessed at a unique *disk address,* which can be automatically determined by the computer system. Procedures for locating records on disk are discussed later in the chapter in the section entitled "Data Organization."

In this section, we'll discuss disk systems for small computers first, focusing primarily on diskettes and hard-disk systems and, secondarily, on some alternative products. Next, we'll look at some methods for optimizing disk processing. Finally, we'll turn to disk systems on large computers.

Diskettes

Diskettes, or *floppy disks,* are small, round platters encased in a plastic jacket. The platters are made of a tough Mylar plastic coated with a magnetizable substance. Each side of the diskette contains concentric **tracks,** which are encoded with 0- and 1-bits when data and programs are written to them (see Figure 4-1). The jacket is lined with a soft material that wipes the disk clean as it spins.

Track.
A path on an input/output medium on which data are recorded.

Types of Diskettes Dozens of types of diskettes are commercially available. If one were to cite a single property that most distinguishes one of these products from another, however, that property would probably be *size.*

Diskettes are widely available in two sizes (diameters)—3½ inches and 5¼ inches—as shown in Figure 4-2. Historically, the 5¼-inch diskettes came along before their 3½-inch counterparts. The 5¼-inch diskettes are encased in flexible, plastic-coated cardboard jackets, whereas the 3½-inch diskettes are contained in rugged plastic cases that can fit into a shirt pocket. Strange as it may seem, 3½-inch diskettes can store more data than 5¼-inch ones.

FIGURE 4-1

Surface of a disk. Unlike a phonograph record, which bears a single spiral groove, a disk is composed of concentric tracks. The number of tracks per surface varies among manufacturers. The disk shown here has 80 tracks. Hard disks commonly have hundreds of tracks.

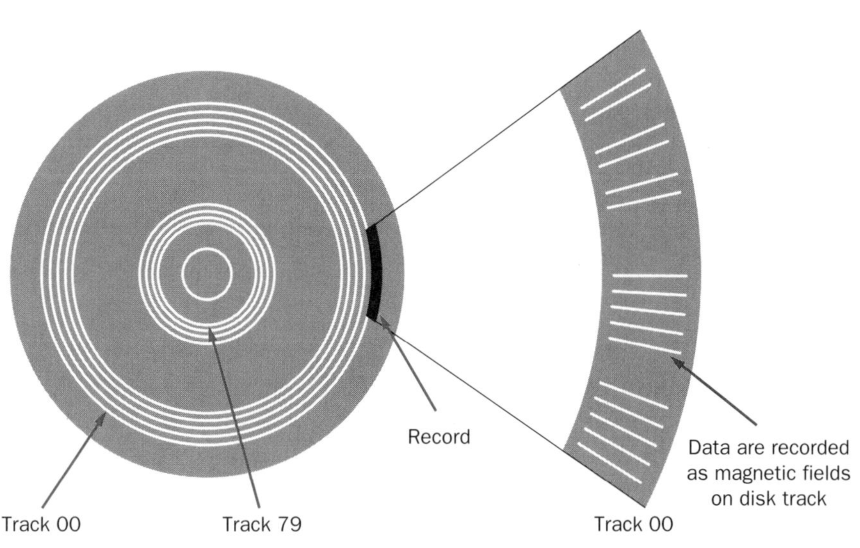

FIGURE 4-2

Diskettes. Despite the fact $3\frac{1}{2}$-inch diskettes (left) have become today's preferred standard on microcomputer systems, $5\frac{1}{4}$-inch diskettes (right) continue to enjoy wide use.

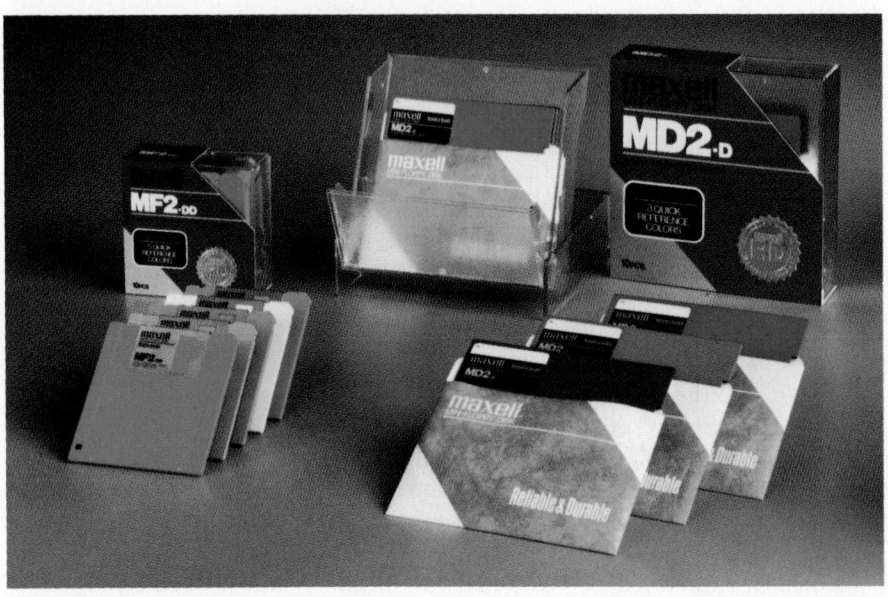

Despite their small size, diskettes can store a respectable amount of data. Common capacities are 360 kilobytes and 1.2 megabytes for $5\frac{1}{4}$-inch diskettes, and 720 kilobytes, 1.44 megabytes, and 2.88 megabytes for $3\frac{1}{2}$-inch diskettes. A 360-kilobyte diskette can store over 100 typewritten pages of information; thus, 1.44-megabyte diskettes can store up to 400 pages and 2.88-megabyte diskettes can store up to 800 pages. The 1.2- and 1.44-megabyte diskettes are often called *high-density* diskettes; the 360- and 720-kilobyte diskettes are called *double-density* or *low-density* diskettes. The 2.88-megabyte diskettes, which began being installed on some microcomputer systems in 1992, are sometimes referred to as *extra-density* diskettes. (Density refers to how tightly bits of data are packed on the diskette.)

To protect data, diskettes also contain a write-protect notch or square (see Figure 4-3). This prevents the user from accidentally writing on the disk. Covering the notch on $5\frac{1}{4}$-inch diskettes makes it impossible to write on the surface. The convention on $3\frac{1}{2}$-inch diskettes is the opposite: Exposing the notch or square makes writing impossible.

Sector.
An addressable pie-shaped area on a disk.

Sectoring on Diskettes Computer systems differ in the number of **sectors** into which they divide, or *format,* a disk. Sectors divide a diskette into addressable, pie-shaped pieces. For example, $5\frac{1}{4}$-inch diskettes formatted with IBM and similar computer systems commonly are divided into 8, 9, 15, 18, or more sectors, depending on the type of diskette and operating system used. Typically there are 512 bytes per sector (see Figure 4-4).

FIGURE 4-3

5¼-inch and 3½-inch diskettes compared. (a) In a 5¼-inch diskette, the recording window is always open, meaning that the disk surface is constantly exposed. (b) In a 3½-inch diskette, the recording window exposes the disk surface only when the shutter mechanism is slid to the left, which happens during reading and writing operations. In addition to offering this improved design feature, having a more rugged cover, and being more compact, 3½-inch diskettes can store more data than can 5¼-inch diskettes.

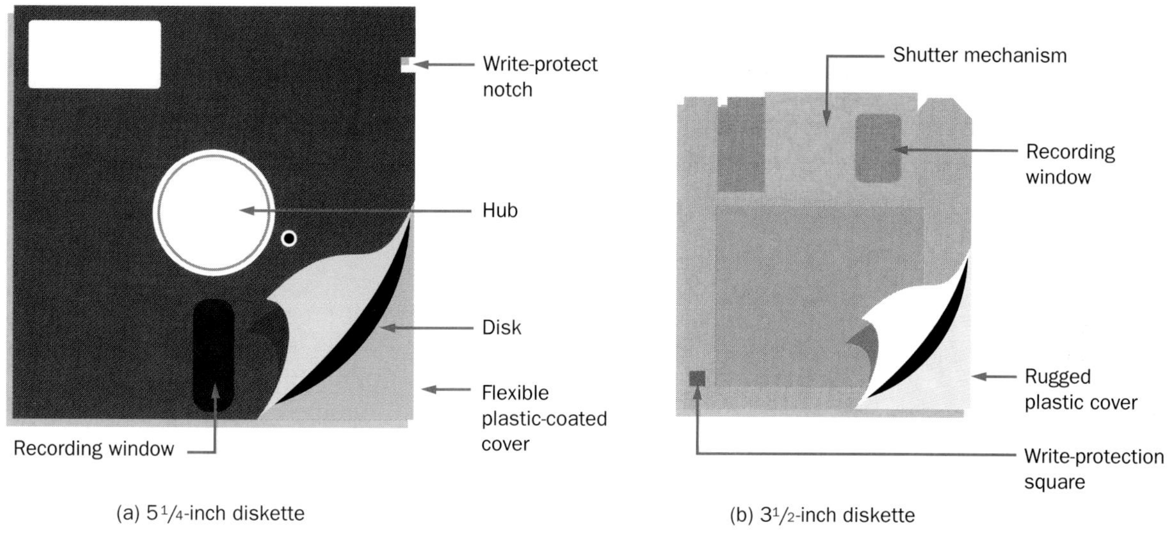

FIGURE 4-4

Formatting a diskette. Formatting a diskette enables it to be divided into addressable, pie-shaped sectors. A diskette is not usable until it is formatted.

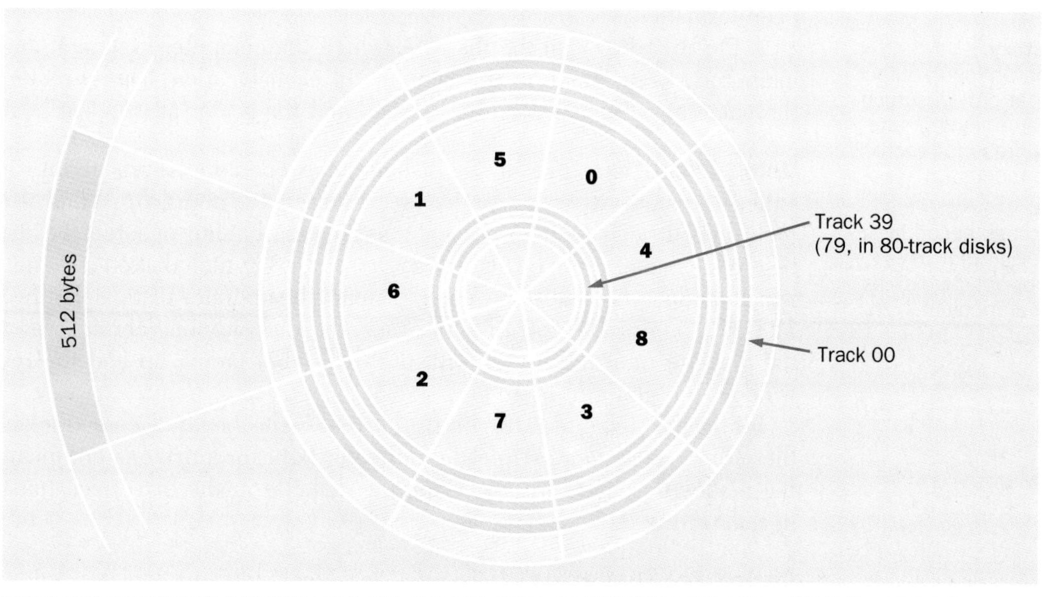

FIGURE 4-5

Inserting a diskette into a drive. Diskettes correctly fit into the drive only one way—with the label up and the recording window toward the drive door, as illustrated. Drive doors come in a variety of styles, as shown in Figure 4-6.

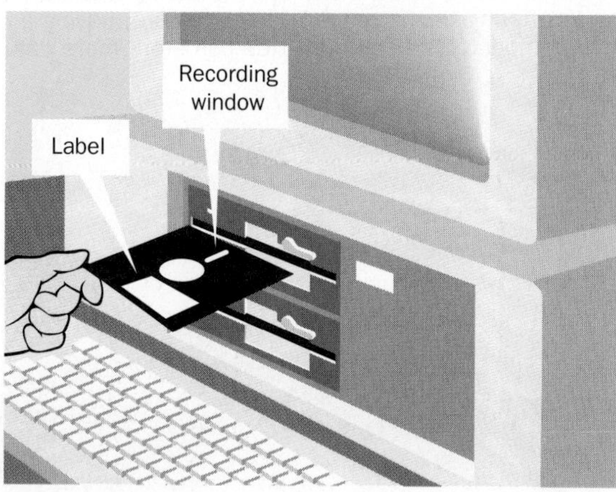

Formatting a diskette organizes it into addressable storage locations, as Figure 4-4 illustrates. For instance, let's assume that the diskette in Figure 4-4 has 40 tracks. Also, let's assume that the computer system divides the diskette into 9 sectors, as shown. Formatting the diskette causes it to be arranged into 9 pie-shaped sectors, 0 through 8. Because the diskette has 40 tracks, this results in $9 \times 40 = 360$ addressable storage locations per side. On many microcomputer systems, a FORMAT command is used by the operating system to format the diskette, and a diskette is not usable for storage unless it has been formatted.

A **file directory** on the diskette, which the computer system automatically maintains, keeps track of the contents of each location. This directory shows the name of each diskette file, its size, and the sector at which it begins.

File directory.
A listing on an input/output medium that provides such data as name, length, and starting address for each file on the medium.

Disk unit.
A direct-access secondary storage device that uses magnetic or optical disk as the principal medium.

Using Diskettes To use a diskette, the operator inserts it into a device called a **disk unit,** or *disk drive* (see Figures 4-5 and 4-6). When using 5¼-inch diskette drives, the operator must manually shut or latch the drive door before the diskette can be accessed. Drives for 3½-inch diskettes do not contain a manual door mechanism as such; instead, the operator just inserts the diskette into the appropriate slot. In both cases, there is only one correct way to insert the diskette into the drive—with the disk label facing up and the recording-window end going in first.

While the diskette is rotating, the read/write heads access tracks through the *recording window.* While the indicator light for a drive is on, meaning that the read/write heads are accessing the diskette in the drive, you must not try to remove the diskette.

Caring for Diskettes Diskettes may look like unsophisticated pieces of plastic, but they are extremely sensitive items and must be cared for accordingly. Care of diskettes is covered in detail in Chapter 13.

Hard Disks for Small Computers

Small computers—such as microcomputers and low-end minicomputers—often employ nonremovable, sealed-pack Winchester disks. *Winchester* hard-disk systems consist of rigid metal platters that are tiered on a mounting shaft (see Figure 4-7, which shows a cutaway view). The term **disk pack,** or *pack,* is commonly used to describe the set of hard disks that are aggregated into such a modular unit. In the Winchester design, the pack is hermetically sealed in the storage unit along with the access mechanism containing the read/write heads. Because the pack is completely sealed and free from the air contamination that plagues removable-pack hard-disk systems, there are usually fewer operational problems.

Disk pack.
A group of tiered hard disks that are mounted on a shaft and treated as a unit.

FIGURE 4-6

Disk-drive doors. Drive doors for diskette units come in several varieties, the three most common of which are shown here. 5¼-inch drive doors have a latch mechanism that you push down to lock in an inserted disk, while 3½-inch doors have no such latch. To remove a disk from a 5¼-inch drive, you simply push up on the latch and remove the disk, while on a 3½-inch drive you must press the eject button.

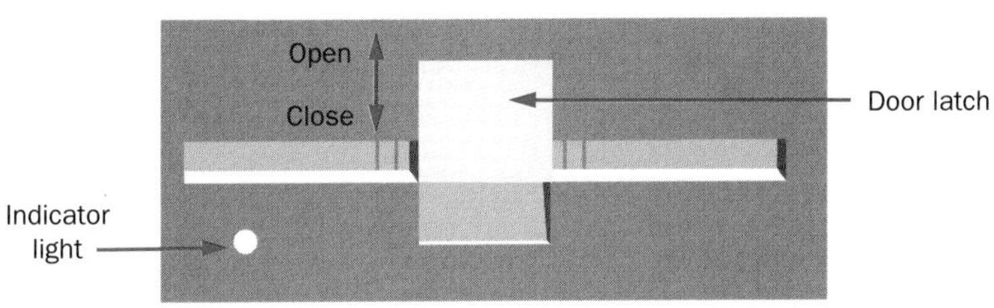

(a) 5¼-inch-drive door used on original IBM PC

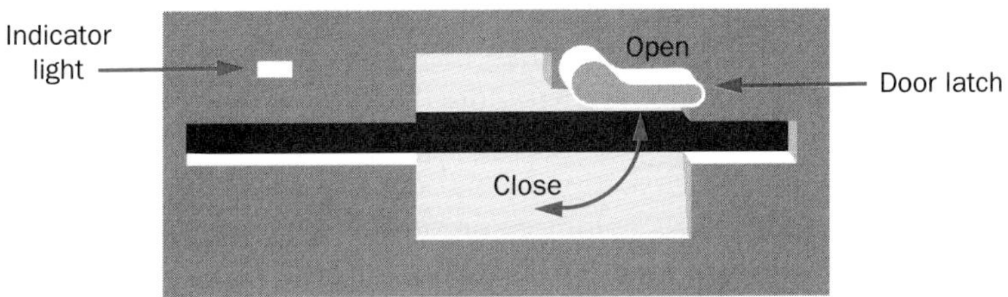

(b) 5¼-inch-drive door sold most widely today

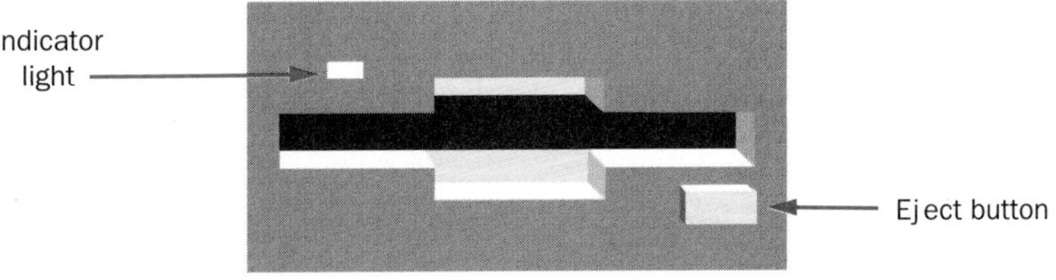

(c) 3½-inch-drive door

FIGURE 4-7

A hard-disk unit. Hard-disk systems for microcomputers are found in capacities of up to several hundred megabytes. Featured here is an *internal* hard-disk system.

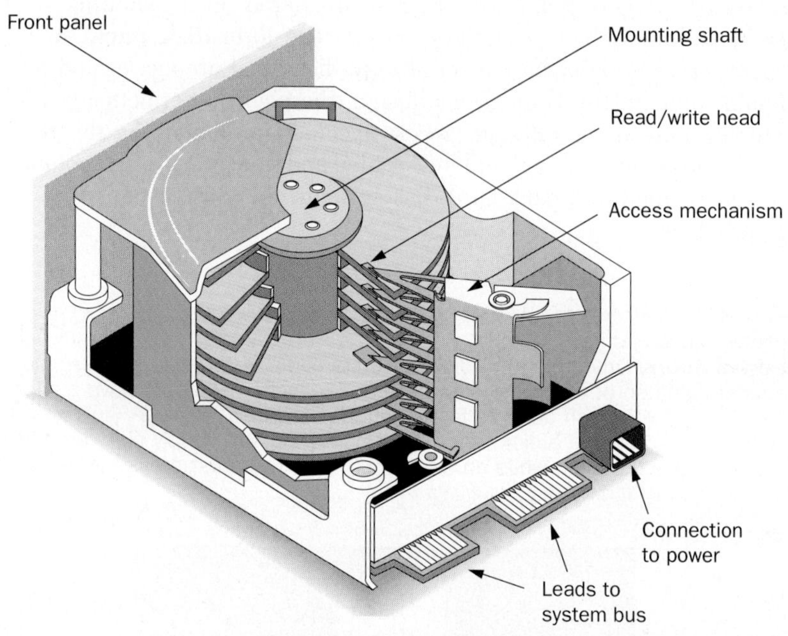

Although many microcomputer systems still use diskettes heavily, hard-disk systems are now a standard feature on virtually all computer systems sold for business purposes. Hard disks provide greater amounts of online storage and faster access to programs and data than diskettes. If you have a 320-megabyte hard-disk unit, you have the storage equivalent of about 800 double-density 5¼-inch diskettes online the minute you turn on the power. Also, you don't have to constantly shuffle diskettes in and out of disk drives.

Hard-disk units for microcomputers are most commonly found in capacities ranging from 20 to several hundred megabytes. For desktop micros, hard disks are most widely available in 3½-inch diameters. The Gateway 2000 P5-66 computer, to cite just one example, comes with a 540 MB 3½-inch disk drive.

Hard-disk units on microcomputer systems can be internal or external. An *internal* hard-disk system, such as the one in Figure 4-7, is fitted into your computer's system unit in the space, or bay, normally occupied by one of the diskette drives. An *external* system is a detached hardware unit that has its own power supply. On large computer systems, hard-disk units are always external.

Access mechanism. A mechanical device in the disk pack or disk unit that positions the read/write heads on the proper tracks.

Reading and Writing Data Most disk systems have at least one read/write head for each recording surface. These heads are mounted on a device called an **access mechanism.** Figure 4-7 shows how access is accomplished with a *movable* access mechanism. The rotating mounting shaft spins at high speeds, and the access mechanism moves the heads in and out *together* between the disk surfaces to access the required data. Movable devices are by far the most popular type of access mechanism.

A head never touches the surface of a disk at any time, even during reading and writing. Head and disk are very close, however—often millionths of an inch above the recording surfaces. A human hair or even a smoke particle (about 2,500 and 100 millionths of an inch, respectively), if present on a surface, will damage the disks and heads—an event known as a *head crash.* As Figure 4-8 shows, the results are like placing a pebble on your favorite phonograph album while playing it.

Disk Cylinders In disk systems that use disk packs, an important principle for understanding disk storage and access strategies is the concept of **disk cylinders.** Consider the two-platter pack in Figure 4-9. There are 4 possible recording surfaces with 400 tracks per surface. One might envision the disk pack as being composed of 400 imaginary concentric cylinders, each consisting of 4 tracks, as illustrated in the figure. Outer cylinders fit over the inner ones like sleeves. Each cylinder is equivalent to a track position to which the heads on the access mechanism can move. With a movable access mechanism, all the read/write heads are positioned on the same cylinder when data are read from or written to one of the tracks on that cylinder.

Disk cylinder. All tracks on a disk pack that are accessible with a single movement of the access mechanism.

Disk Access Time In a removable-pack disk system with a movable access mechanism, three events must occur in order to access data.

First, the read/write head must move to the cylinder on which the data are stored. Suppose, for example, that the read/write head is on cylinder 5 and we wish to retrieve data from cylinder 36. For us to do this, the mechanism must

FIGURE 4-8

The space between a disk and a read/write head compared with a smoke particle and a human hair. A human hair or even a smoke particle, if present on a fast-spinning hard-disk surface, can damage both the surface and the read/write head.

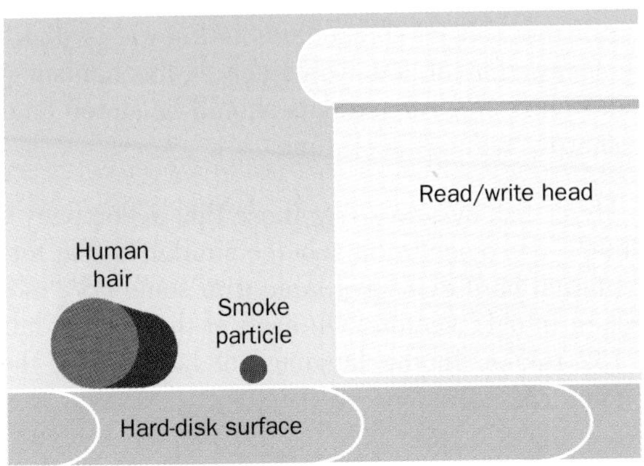

FIGURE 4-9

The cylinder concept. To imagine any particular cylinder, think of pushing an actual cylinder such as a tin can downward through the same track in each disk in the pack. In this example, cylinder 357 is made up of track 357 on surfaces 1 through 4.

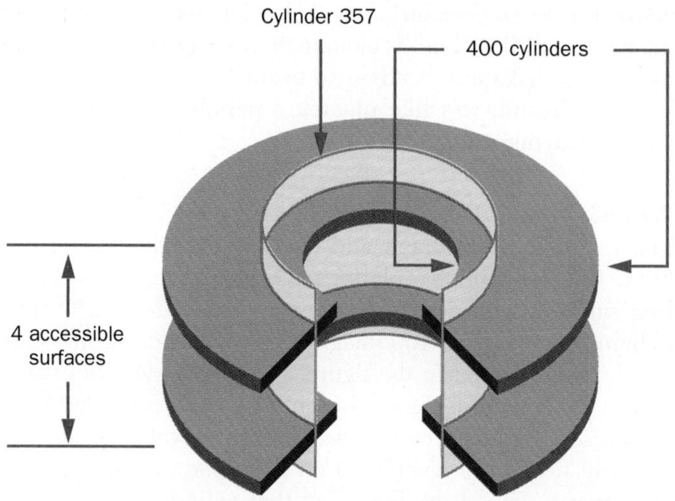

move inward to cylinder 36. The time required for this task is referred to as *seek time.*

Second, when a read or write order is issued, the heads usually are not aligned over the position on the track on which the desired data are stored. So some delay occurs while the mounting shaft rotates the disks into the proper position. (The disks are always spinning whether or not reading or writing is taking place.) The time needed for completing this alignment is called *rotational delay.*

Third, once the read/write head is positioned over the correct data, the data must be read from disk and transferred to the computer (or transferred from the computer and written onto disk). This last step is known as *data movement time.* The sum of these three components is known as **disk access time.** To minimize disk access time on a movable-access-mechanism system such as the one depicted in Figure 4-7, related data should be stored on the same cylinder. This strategy sharply reduces seek time.

Disk access time. The time taken to locate and read (or position and write) data on a disk device.

Sectoring Hard-disk systems, like those that accompany the IBM PS/2 and similar computers, use a sectoring scheme similar to that for diskettes to store data. On the internal hard disks available with some PS/2 models, for instance, tracks are broken into 17 sectors. On each of the 4 recordable surfaces, there is a total of 732 tracks. In the language of hard disks, the tracks on these surfaces trace out 732 cylinders.

Subdirectories Because hard disks have large storage capacities, files commonly are organized hierarchically into *subdirectories.* As Figure 4-10 shows, at the top of the hierarchy is a “master” directory called the root directory. The *root directory,* among other things, contains a list of subdirectories on the hard disk. You can store all of your operating-system programs in one subdirectory, word-processed documents in another subdirectory, and so forth. Moreover, you can further divide these subdirectories. As shown in Figure 4-10, you can organize your word processing subdirectory by putting letters and school papers into two lower subdirectories. If you so wish, you can add several additional levels of subdirectories.

Later, when you want to access a file in any subdirectory, you must specify the *path* through the subdirectories to get to the file; for example,

```
C:\WORD\LETTER\MARY
```

Here the hard disk is the *C* drive and WORD and LETTER are the names of the two subdirectories on the path to a subdirectory of letters named MARY. On most microcomputer systems, the *A* and *B* drive designations are reserved for floppy drives.

Partitioning *Partitioning* a hard disk enables you to divide a hard disk into separate disk drives, such as *D, E, F,* and so forth. You can change the number and size of the partitions at any time, although doing so will destroy any data

FIGURE 4-10

Organizing files into subdirectories. Shown here is a root directory and three levels of subdirectories. The subdirectory MARY, for instance, would contain all letters (files) written to Mary.

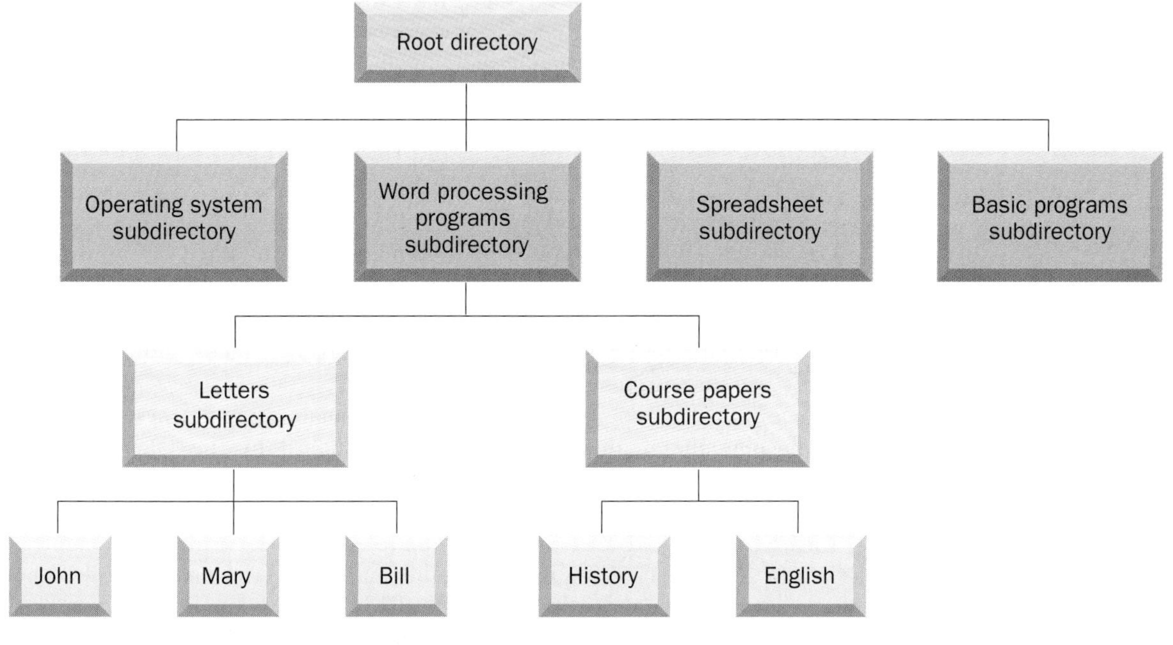

FIGURE 4-11

Microcomputer cartridge disk. Cartridge disk provides a storage alternative with the capacity and performance of a conventional hard disk and the removability of a diskette.

in the partitions. Thus, you have to download any affected data onto diskettes or tape first and then load the data back onto the repartitioned hard disk.

Partitioning a hard disk enables you to use different operating systems on it—say, MS-DOS, OS/2, and UNIX. Each operating system has its own method of formatting and managing disk space. By assigning each operating system to a different partition, you avoid the problem of having an operating system deal with a partition that works in a manner foreign to it.

Disk Standards When buying a hard disk for a microcomputer system, it is easy to become confused when vendors throw around such acronyms as RLL, ESDI, IDE, and SCSI. These acronyms generally refer to the density with which data can be packed onto the disk, the speed of the disk, and the way the disk interfaces with the board (sometimes called the *disk controller*) that runs it.

The oldest standard of those just mentioned is *RLL* (run length limited). This standard is commonly found on disks with a capacity of 40 or fewer megabytes. *ESDI* (enhanced small device interface) and *IDE* (integrated drive electronics) are widely used today by IBM and IBM-compatible computers with a hard-disk capacity of 60 or more megabytes. They both pack data more tightly than the RLL format and are faster. RLL, ESDI, and IDE interfaces allow users access to only two disk drives at one time.

Some industry experts predict that *SCSI* (small computer system interface) will become the main peripheral-device standard by the late 1990s. SCSI (pronounced "scuzzy") provides faster access speeds than both ESDI and IDE. It is now the prevailing standard for Apple Macintosh computers and is found on many high-end IBM and IBM-compatible systems. SCSI allows connection of up to seven devices—disks and other hardware—on one intelligent board that operates independently of the CPU. This independence allows you, say, to back up the contents of a hard disk onto tape while using the CPU for other tasks. SCSI, like ESDI and IDE, is widely used on disks with a capacity of 60 or more megabytes.

FIGURE 4-12

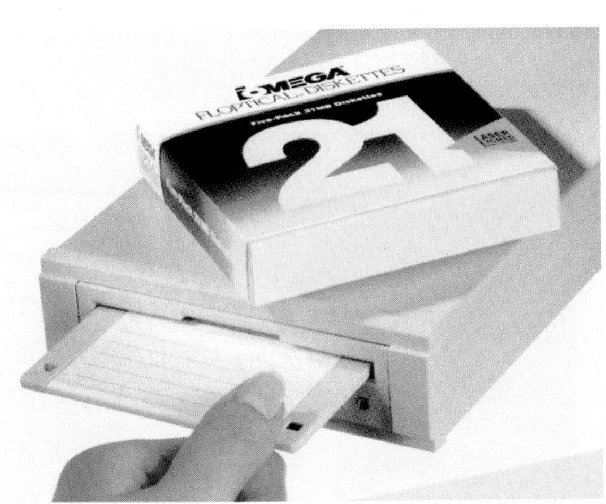

Microcomputer floptical disk. Floptical disks—a disk solution midway between diskettes and hard disks—rely on a combination of magnetic and optical technologies. Shown here is a floptical drive and a 21-megabyte floptical cartridge.

Other Types of Magnetic Disks for Small Computers

Although diskettes and Winchester-type disks dominate the disk scene for small computers, there are alternatives. Two of these are the cartridge disk and floptical disk.

Cartridge Disk Cartridge disk devices are commonly found on microcomputer and minicomputer systems. **Cartridge disk** devices used on microcomputer systems are external hardware units that accept small, removable high-capacity disk cartridges (see Figure 4-11). The high-capacity disk is packaged into a square case (i.e., the cartridge) to protect the disk's contents. The operator inserts a cartridge into a cartridge drive in a manner similar to inserting a diskette into a diskette drive. Cartridge disks commonly have a capacity of about 20 to over 100 megabytes. Their biggest pluses are large storage capacity and, because of their removability, backup and security. The biggest drawback is cost—the disk unit can cost $2,000 to $3,000 and the cartridges about $100 apiece. The drive shown in Figure 4-11 can accept 150 MB cartridges as well as less expensive, lower-capacity cartridges.

Cartridge disk. A magnetic disk in which a single disk platter is contained in a sealed plastic case.

Floptical Disk **Floptical disks** are cartridge disks that offer a secondary storage solution that is midway between a diskette (floppy disk) and hard disk (see Figure 4-12). "Floptical" disks—a contraction of "floppy" and "optical" disks—are so called because they rely on a combination of magnetic and optical technologies. Concentric tracks on the disk store data magnetically, while the drive's read/write heads optically locate tracks. Because the optical heads can be positioned much more precisely than conventional magnetic heads, floptical disks can achieve much greater data densities than conventional diskettes. Floptical drives can also read conventional diskettes.

Floptical disk. A cartridge disk that relies on a combination of magnetic and optical technology.

Floptical technology is still too new and relatively expensive to tell whether it will be lasting. Floptical disks are *not* the same as optical disks, discussed later in the chapter.

FIGURE 4-13

Removable-pack disks. Many larger computers use removable-pack disk units, onto which packs are manually mounted and removed by a computer operator. (a) A removable pack. (b) A disk unit that accepts removable packs.

(a)

(b)

RAM Disk and Cache Disk

RAM disk and cache disk are two strategies for creatively using RAM to compensate for the access-speed differences between memory and secondary storage. Both methods overcome the slow speeds involved with fetching instructions or data from disk, and both can be implemented inexpensively under certain conditions. On many computer systems sold today, RAM disk and cache disk are built-in features.

RAM disk.
A disk management system in which a portion of RAM is set up to function as a disk.

RAM Disk **RAM disk,** sometimes referred to as *electronic disk, E-disk,* or *disk emulation,* is a storage alternative in which the computer's operating system is "tricked" into thinking it is dealing with secondary storage when in fact it is dealing with memory.

When computer systems process programs or data files, typically only a limited number of program instructions or data records are in memory at any given time. When more instructions or data are needed, the operating system must fetch them from disk. However, if your system has enough RAM to store the entire program or data file, you can use an emulation package to load it into RAM and point the system to this part of RAM every time it would go to the disk to fetch additional program commands or data. Thus, the emulation software essentially tricks the system into thinking it's dealing with the disk drive when it actually is dealing with RAM. Such a technique can boost the speed of applications processing considerably.

Cache disk.
A disk management scheme whereby more data than are necessary are read from disk during each time-consuming disk fetch and are stored in RAM to minimize the number of fetches.

Cache Disk **Cache disk** refers to a strategy whereby, during any disk access, program or data contents in neighboring disk areas are also fetched and transported to RAM. For instance, if only a single data record needs to be read, a cache-disk feature may read the entire track on which the record is located. The theory behind cache disk is that neighboring program commands and data will likely have to be read later anyway, so one can save disk accesses by bringing those commands or data into RAM early so that they can be accessed more quickly. Thus, caching saves time as well as wear and tear on the disk unit. In portable computers, it can alse extend battery life. Cache disk is frequently implemented through the board that contains the disk controller.

Disk Systems for Large Computers

Disk systems on larger computers work by many of the same principles as microcomputer-based hard disks. However, some important differences do exist.

First, disk systems on larger computers sometimes have bigger-diameter platters, with many more tracks. It is not uncommon for the size of these platters to be as much as 14 inches in diameter, although the trend today is decidely toward smaller disks.

Second, not all disk systems on larger computers use a sealed-pack design, in which both disks and heads are permanently sealed as a unit. Many larger computers use instead removable-pack disk units, onto which packs are manually mounted or removed by a computer operator (see Figure 4-13). Because removable packs are not permanently sealed—the plastic disk covers are automatically separated from the packs when they are mounted so the heads can access the platters—removable-pack systems require an air-filtration system to keep disk surfaces free of dust. Despite this precaution, removable-pack disks are still vulnerable to dust and are therefore more prone to head crashes than sealed-pack disks. They are also slower and less reliable. However, removable-pack systems have one notable advantage: because packs can be removed from a unit, fewer drives are required.

The trend today in disk systems for larger computers and large networks of smaller computers is definitely toward sealed-pack disks (see Figure 4-14).

FIGURE 4-14

A sealed-pack disk unit. The IBM Direct Access Storage Subsystem featured here, targeted to business minicomputers, has a rack that can contain up to four disk units, each with its own pack. Sealed-pack disk systems are faster and more reliable than those that use removable packs.

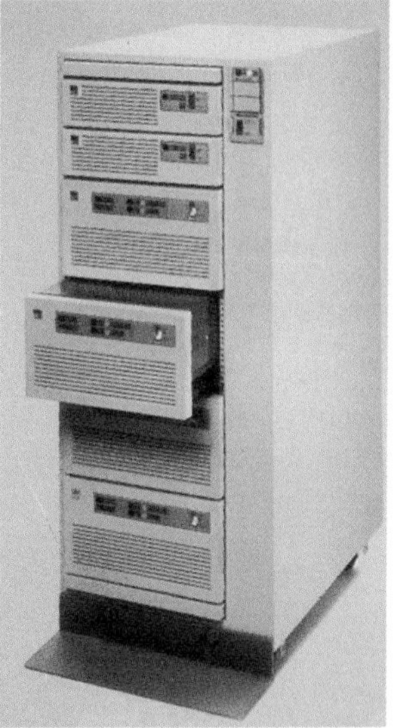

FIGURE 4-15

RAID storage unit. StorageTek's Iceberg 9200 Disk Array Subsystem, which uses arrays of $5^1/_4$-inch disks, can store over 150 gigabytes of data when fully configured.

Feature 4–1

RAID

How a gang of small disks can team up to outperform a larger disk

It's a new and radical idea but one that experts say signals an important trend for disk technology in the near future. It's called RAID—for *r*edundant *a*rrays of *i*nexpensive *d*isks. It refers to a set of several small disks that work together as a unit.

Preliminary findings have shown that disk arrays made up of 5¼-inch hard disks can outperform a single 14-inch disk of the same capacity. Performance increases of several orders of magnitude have been observed in five critical areas: cutting access times, increasing reliability, reducing power consumption, slicing the cost of storing each byte, and reducing the physical size of storage hardware.

Several reasons account for the initial success of disk arrays. First, small disks theoretically can spin faster than larger ones. The larger a disk gets, the greater the potential for wobble at the outer edge of the disk, which causes reading and writing problems. (The more the wobble, the farther away from the disk surface the read/write heads must be positioned to prevent a head crash.) Second, data retrieved from a single disk is read from a track serially, one character after another. When several disks work together, they can be hooked up so that data are drawn off simultaneously—that is, in parallel—speeding up processing considerably.

One of the most-talked-about RAID products in recent years in StorageTek's Iceberg 9200 Disk Array Subsystem (see Figure 4-15). The minimum configuration of this system is 100 gigabytes, spread over 32 disks. If a disk in any array fails, the system has the ability to reconstruct data on a spare disk so that operations can continue uninterrupted.

The switch to disk arrays is likely to cause the greatest upheaval in the mainframe disk marketplace. Currently, more than $12 billion is spent annually on mainframe disk products.

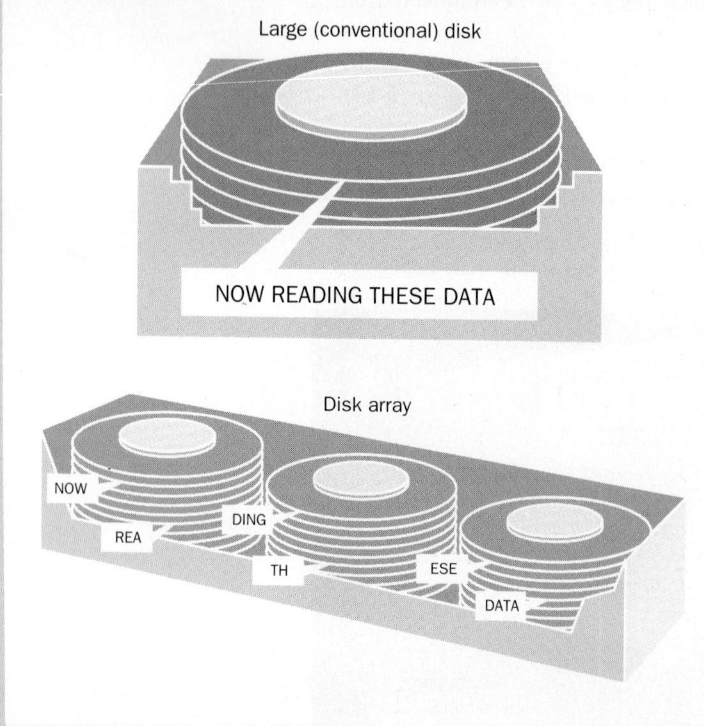

Disk arrays. By reading and writing track data in parallel rather than serially, access times can be sharply reduced.

RAID The use of disk arrays—or *RAID* (for *redundant arrays of inexpensive disks*)—is a relatively new, sealed-pack disk-storage strategy that may signal a new trend in disk technology. RAID, which involves using several smaller disks hooked up in parallel to do the job of a larger disk, is discussed in detail in Feature 4-1. An example of RAID, StorageTek's Iceberg system, is shown in Figure 4-15.

Magnetic Tape

For years, **magnetic tape** has been one of the most prominent secondary storage alternatives. Although less popular than disk, it is still widely used on all sizes of computer systems. The tapes often are stored either on detachable reels or in cartridges. Figure 4-16 shows a tape cartridge compared with a conventional, detachable-reel tape.

Magnetic tape. A plastic tape with a magnetic surface for storing data as a series of magnetic spots.

Detachable-reel tapes are commonly ½-inch wide and are made of plastic Mylar coated with a magnetizable substance. A standard reel diameter is 10½ inches, although smaller "minireels" are also quite common. A typical 2,400-foot reel can pack data at densities as high as 6,250 bytes per inch. When such a tape is read, it can transfer more data in one second than many secretaries could type in a month—and error free.

Detachable-reel tape. Magnetic tape that is wound onto a single reel, which in turn is mounted onto a tape unit with an empty take-up reel.

FIGURE 4-16

Magnetic tape. Shown here are two tape cartridges and, underneath, a conventional tape reel.

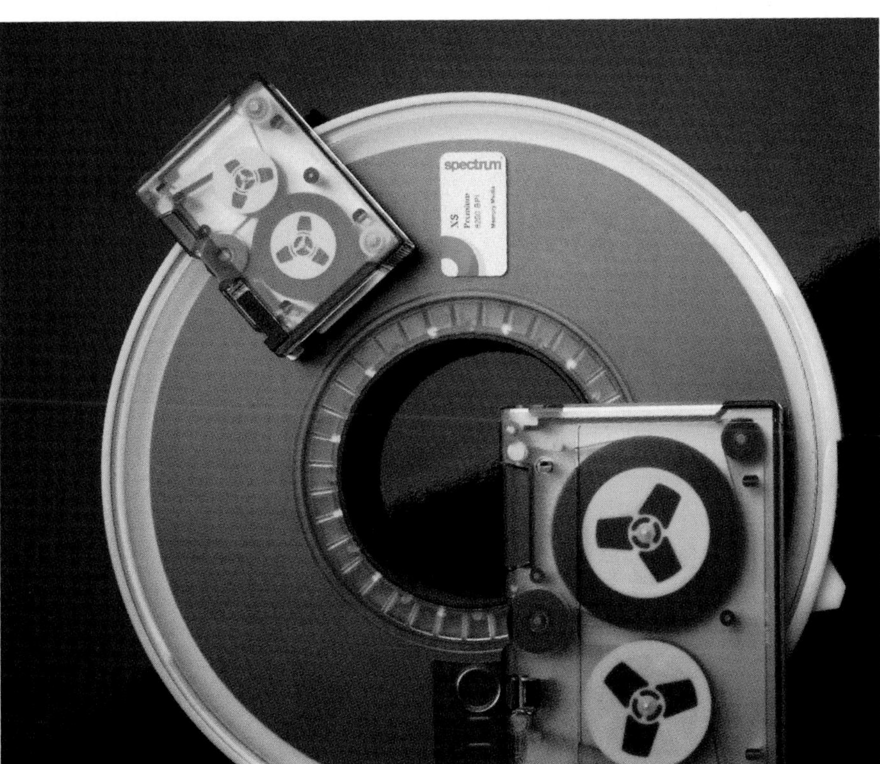

Cartridge tape. Magnetic tape in which the supply and take-up reels are contained in a small plastic case.

Cartridge tapes are housed in a small plastic casing. On microcomputer systems, cartridges are commonly used to back up the contents of a hard disk (see Figure 4-17). These tapes can have huge capacities and work very fast. A ¼-inch tape up to 1,000 feet long can often hold 100 or more megabytes of data and copy the contents of a disk in a matter of minutes. Recently cartridges using *helical-scan* recording methods, which store data at an angle to the edge of the tape rather than perpendicular to it, have permitted storage capacities in the gigabyte range. Cartridge tapes designed specifically for disk backup are sometimes referred to as *streaming tapes.*

The IBM 3480 and 3490 tape storage systems, which are used with IBM mainframe computers, also use cartridge tapes. These tapes have twice the number of tracks as traditional detachable-reel tapes and a storage capacity of hundreds of megabytes. In contrast to streaming tapes, which are intended solely for backup, the IBM 3480 and IBM 3490 cartridges are designed for general use, including both regular input/output processing operations and backup.

The discussion that follows in this section is based principally on the nine-track, detachable-reel tapes that have been used with mainframes and mini-computers for years. These tape systems are still the most prevalent in the marketplace. Nonetheless, many of the principles described here apply to cartridge tapes as well.

FIGURE 4-17

Microcomputer cartridge tape. On microcomputer systems, cartridge tapes are commonly used to back up the contents of a hard disk. Featured here are two *internal* tape units (left), which fit into the computer's system unit, and an *external* tape unit (right).

FIGURE 4-18

Magnetic tape units for large computers. On large computers, magnetic tape is often used for backup and for many types of batch processing. (Background) In conventional detachable-reel systems, any reels of programs or data to be run must be selected manually from an offline tape library and mounted on the tape unit. (Foreground) In cartridge systems, several high-capacity cartridges can be loaded into hoppers for automatic processing.

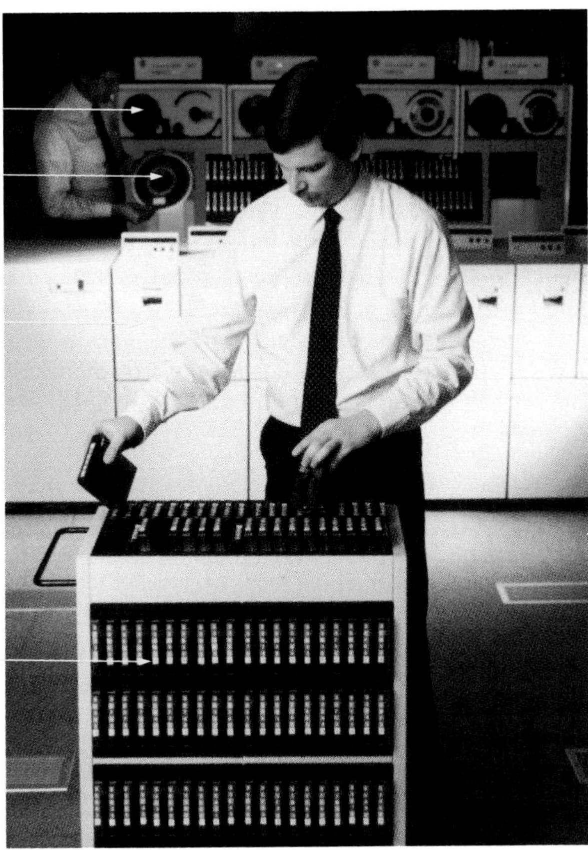

Processing Tapes

Tape unit. A secondary storage device on which magnetic tapes are mounted for processing.

A tape must be mounted onto an online **tape unit** (see Figure 4-18) to be processed. *Detachable-reel tape units* are often the size of a common household refrigerator. The *supply reel* on the unit contains the tape that is to be read from or written to by the computer system. The *take-up reel* collects the tape as it unwinds from the supply reel. As it is processed, the tape passes by a read/write head, which reads data from the tape or records data on it. On many devices, the tape is allowed to droop in a vacuum chamber so that it will not break if the two reels move at different speeds. After processing, the tape is rewound onto the supply reel and removed from the unit. The take-up reel never leaves the unit. On *cartridge tape units*, because both reels are contained in the cartridge, the handling of supply and takeup reels is eliminated. Better yet, it may be possible to stack several cartridges into an input hopper for automatic processing. The trend today is clearly toward cartridge tapes, although detachable-reel tapes are still widely used.

Storing Data on Tape

Figure 4-19 shows how data are stored on nine-track magnetic tape. Data may be coded using the eight-bit byte of either EBCDIC or ASCII-8, depending on the equipment used. Magnetized spots of iron oxide represent 1s; nonmagnetized spots represent 0s. The tape contains a track for each bit of information in a character, plus an additional parity track to allow the computer system to check for transmission errors. The tape unit reads across the nine tracks to identify the character represented in each column. Recall from Chapter 3 that in odd-parity machines, all 1-bits add up to an odd number and in even-parity machines to an even number. An incorrect sum indicates an error. The parity bit is included with the byte representation of each character when it is placed onto tape.

Key field.
A field used to identify a record.

A magnetic tape is basically a long, narrow strip. Thus, when the records in a data file are stored on it, they must be alongside one another in sequence. The sequence often is determined by a **key field,** such as customer ID number,

FIGURE 4-19

Storing data on nine-track magnetic tape. Shown here is the number 6 represented in EBCDIC (11110110, or 111110110 with the odd-parity track). In the shaded cross section of the tape, the magnetized spot representing the 1-bit is shown by a vertical mark in the appropriate track. The 0-bit is characterized by the absence of a mark.

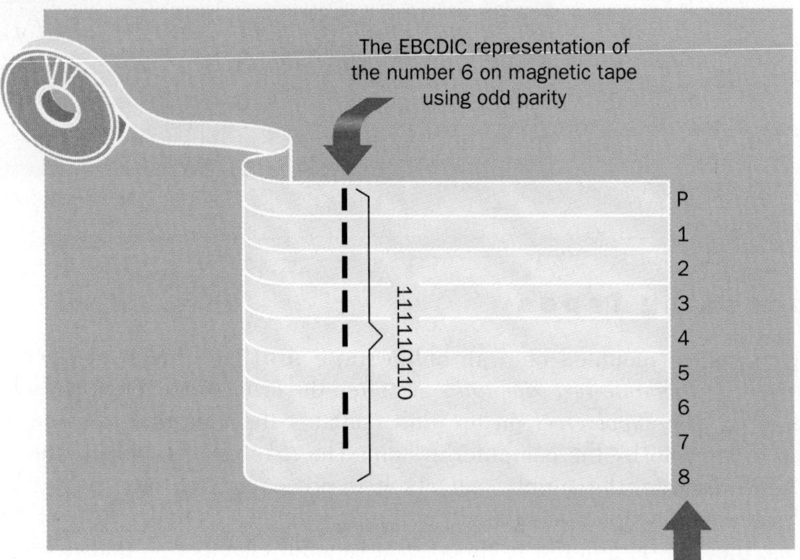

which can be ordered numerically. Every record's key field generally has a different value.

If you want to read a particular record from a tape, you can't go directly to it. Instead, you must pass through all the records that precede it. In a sense, this is similar to the fast forwarding you do on a music tape when the tune you want to hear is in the middle of it. Retrieving records in the order in which they are stored is called *sequential access,* and organizing data in sequence by a key field is called *sequential organization.* We will talk more about data access and organization later in the chapter.

Optical Disk

An emerging technology that is having a profound impact on storage strategies in the 1990s is the **optical disk.** With this technology, laser beams write and read data at incredible densities, hundreds of times finer than the density of a typical magnetic disk. Data—which can consist of text, graphics, voice, or video images—are placed onto optical disks with high-intensity laser beams that burn tiny holes into the disk's surface. Then a lower-intensity laser beam reads the data inscribed.

Optical disk.
A disk read by laser beams rather than by magnetic means.

Today 3½-inch optical disks can store data in the gigabyte range. Roughly translated, one gigabyte is close to 1 million pages of text or, alternatively, the contents of approximately 2,500 low-density, 5¼-inch diskettes. So-called *optical jukeboxes,* which offer online access to scores of optical disks, also have become available. These devices can store 300 or more billion bytes of data (see Figure 4-20).

Optical disk systems are used on computer systems of all sizes—and most of all, on microcomputers. Most optical disk units are of the *CD-ROM* (Compact Disk/Read-Only Memory) type; that is, you buy a prerecorded disk and "play" (read) it on the optical disk unit attached to your computer. You cannot write new data to the disk in any way. Internal CD-ROM optical disk units costing under $500 are available for microcomputers.

Systems also are available that will let you write once to the disk; once written, the data cannot be erased. These are called *WORM* (Write Once, Read Many) disk systems. Since optical disks have very large storage capacities, most users can write to the disk for a year or more before using it up. Optical disk systems that allow you to erase unwanted data—called *fully erasable systems*—have also recently become available. Fully erasable optical systems use a combination of magnetic and optical technology to read and write data, consequently, fully erasable disks are sometimes referred to as *magneto-optical (MO) disks*. MO disks are not the same as floptical disks, which are far less capacious and use optical technology only to better position disk heads.

Uses of optical disk technology abound, and there are far too many applications to name here. One major applications area is learning. IBM's *Illuminated Books and Manuscripts,* for instance, is an optical-disk-based educational product that contains text, pictures, and video clips from several historical events and book classics (see Figure 4-21a). Another major applications area is reference. DeLorme Mapping's *Street Atlas USA,* which contains more than a million detailed maps on a single CD-ROM, is an excellent example (see

FIGURE 4-20

Optical disk units and their optical disks. (a) Optical disk units targeted to ordinary microcomputer users often accept only a single disk at a time. (b) Optical jukeboxes targeted to commercial users often chain several disk units together. Each disk unit accepts a cartridge (magazine) of several disks. The jukebox shown here has online access of up to 42 optical disks.

(a)

(b)

Figure 4-21b). Users of this package can view the whole United States or zoom down to a state, region, neighborhood, or street anywhere in the country. Optical disks are also used in a variety of other environments, as illustrated in User Solution 4-2 and the Tomorrow box.

Despite the excitement over optical disks, hard magnetic disks still have two important advantages. First, hard disks are much faster; 10 to 20 times faster is not unusual. Second, there's a great deal of software written for hard disks that will have to be modified to work on optical disks.

Data Organization

Data access.
Fetching data from a device either sequentially or directly.

Data organization.
The process of setting up a data file so that it may subsequently be accessed in some desired way.

When a computer system is instructed to use data or programs residing in secondary storage, it first must be able to find the materials. The process of retrieving data and programs in storage is called **data access.** Arranging data for efficient retrieval is called **data organization.**

As we have seen, a major difference between, say, tape and disk is that data on tape can be *accessed* only sequentially, whereas data on disk can be retrieved both sequentially and in a direct (random) fashion. With sequential access, the records in a file can be retrieved only in the same sequence in which they are

FIGURE 4-21

Optical disk applications. Optical disks enable microcomputer users to have online access to close to a billion bytes of secondary storage. (a) IBM's *Illuminated Books and Manuscripts* is an interactive educational product. (b) DeLorme Mapping's *Street Atlas USA* provides maps showing U.S. states, regions, neighborhoods, and streets.

(a)

(b)

User Solution 4-2

Optical Disks for Customer Support

When home-appliance manufacturer Whirlpool looked around for a more efficient way to handle the 1.6 million service calls it gets from customers annually, it opted for an optical-disk-based imaging system. Mounted on a centralized optical-disk system are page images of 20 years worth of service and product manuals, which can be accessed by about 100 service agents from desktop workstations. In the past, agents had to browse by hand through printed materials and microfiched records to get information. That same information is now available to them in less than two seconds. Whirlpool also has a software-based "expert system" integrated into this service application that helps agents diagnose the cause of equipment failure and recommend a solution.

physically stored. With direct, or random, access, the time needed to fetch a record is relatively independent of its location in secondary storage.

The need for certain data access methods necessarily dictates the choice of ways to *organize* data files. Let's consider a practical example. Most book libraries are organized with card indexes ordered by title, author, and subject, so you can retrieve books directly. To locate a particular book, you simply look under the book's title in the index, find its call number, and go directly to the appropriate shelf.

However, suppose there were no card indexes and books were organized alphabetically by title on shelves from the first shelf to the last (say, the 758th shelf). With this sequential organization of books, it would take you much longer to retrieve the title you wanted—although you would get a lot of exercise. As you can see, sequential organization does not permit straightforward access to a specific book.

Data organization on computers works in a similar fashion. First, you decide on the type of access you need—direct, sequential, or both. Then you organize the data in a way that will minimize the time needed to retrieve them with the access method selected.

There are many ways to organize data. Here we will describe three—sequential, indexed-sequential, and direct organization.

Sequential organization. Arranging data on a physical medium either ascendingly or descendingly by some key field.

Sequential Organization In a file having a **sequential organization,** records follow one another in a predetermined sequence. Sequentially organized files generally are ordered by a key field or fields, such as ID number. Thus, if a four-digit ID number is the key field being used to order the file, the record belonging to, say ID number 0612 will be stored after number 0611 but before number 0613 (see Figure 4-22).

TOMORROW

Photo CDs

Will They Become a Hot Item?

Photo CDs are a relatively new technology in which ordinary photographs are stored on compact (optical) disks, where they can be viewed and edited. The disks can be played in special photo-CD players that connect to TV sets like a VCR and in CD-ROM drives that connect to computer systems.

How does the technology work in practice?

One way is to have film that was shot with a conventional camera processed onto a photo CD instead of prints or slides. Today's photo CD is capable of holding about 100 images–the output from four boxes of 24-exposures film. Currently, the processing cost per image is more expensive than processing by conventional means, but the cost could drop sharply as more people use the technology.

Photo CDs can also be used to make prepackaged optical-disk products. Recently, Kodak—the most bullish advocate of photo CD technology—has been working with outdoor-apparel maker L.L. Bean to place apparel catalogs onto disk. A person receiving a photo CD catalog reads it on a TV or computer screen, where it is accompanied by a sound track. Computer users would be able to find items quickly by typing in key words, such as "green" and "sweater" to pull up all green sweaters.

Another possible application for photo CDs is to have users access remote CDs with their home or office computers. As computer networks become more popular and readily available, it's a good bet that a lot of people will be doing their shopping electronically. But how far out in the future this will be is anyone's guess.

Depending on the equipment they have available, users of photo CD technology have a wealth of high-tech options available to them. Once photos are in a high-resolution digital form, they can be blown up and cropped, manipulated with computer tools such as airbrushes and paintboxes, and combined with sound effects and narration. If you thought your parents' carousel projector was neat, you'll be dazzled by what you can do with this new technology.

Photo CDs. The potential market is enormous.

When you think about it, the potential market for photo CD products is enormous. Just consider the photography market. By Kodak's estimate, about 50 billion snapshots are taken annually by 250 million cameras. The U.S. alone can account for 15 billion snapshots and 100 million cameras.

But while design professionals are generally excited about photo CDs, severe hurdles face the new technology at the consumer level. Are average consumers, many of whom cannot program their VCRs, sophisticated enough to use such a product? Will people be willing to let go of the slide and print media they've grown accustomed to for images they can only see through a TV or computer screen? Does the average home entertainment cabinet have room for another electronic gadget?

Over the next few years, we will find out.

FIGURE 4-22

Sequential organization of records on tape.

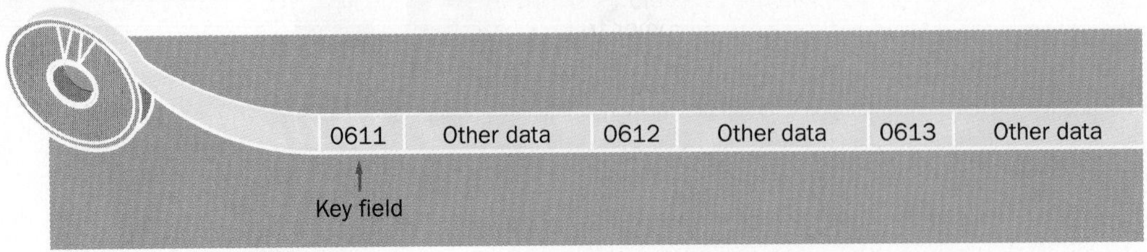

Now that you have an idea of what sequential organization is, let's see how it is used in information processing. Many companies update customer balances and prepare bills at the end of the month. Such an operation is known as a *sequential update.* Two data files are used. The *master file* normally contains the customer's ID number, the amount owed at the beginning of the month, and additional information about the customer. This file is sorted by the key field, customer ID number, and records are arranged in ascending sequence—from the lowest ID number to the highest. The *transaction file* contains all the transactions made during the month by old customers, who appear in the master file, and by new customers, who do not. Transactions might include purchases and payments. Like the master file, the transaction file is ordered in ascending sequence by customer ID number.

In a sequential update, the two files are processed together in the manner shown in Figure 4-23. The sequential-update program reads a record from each file. If the key fields match, the operation specified in the transaction file is performed. Note that in Figure 4-23, the key fields of the first records in each file match. Thus, record 101 is updated to the updated customer master file. For example, if the transaction file shows that customer 101 bought a toaster, data on this purchase are added to the master file. Next, both files are "rolled forward" to the next records. Here the program observes that customer 102 is not in the master file, since the next master file record after 101 is 103. Therefore, this must be a new customer, and the program will create a new record for customer 102 in the updated master file. At this point, only the transaction file will be rolled forward, to customer 103. The program now observes that this record matches the one to which it is currently pointing in the master file. However, the transaction file indicates that 103 is a new customer. Hence, there appears to be an inconsistency, since the master file contains only old customers. The program makes no entry in the updated master file but sends information about this transaction to the error report.

The processing continues in this manner until both files are exhausted. The processing is sequential because the computer processes the records in both files in the order in which they physically appear.

Indexed-sequential organization.
A method of organizing data on a direct-access medium so that they can be accessed directly (through an index) or sequentially.

Indexed-Sequential Organization **Indexed-sequential organization** is a way of organizing data for both sequential and direct access. This type of

FIGURE 4-23

A sequential update of a master file. Each customer record in the original master file might contain the customer's ID number (the key field), name, address, amount owed, and credit limit. For simplicity, only the key field is shown in the illustration. The transaction file contains a record of each customer transaction. Each record in this file might contain the customer's ID number (the key field), the amount of the purchase or payment, and the type of transaction involved (update, add, or delete). Only the key field and type of transaction are shown in the illustration. As both files are processed together, an updated master file is produced, as well as a printed listing of records that couldn't be processed because of some discrepancy.

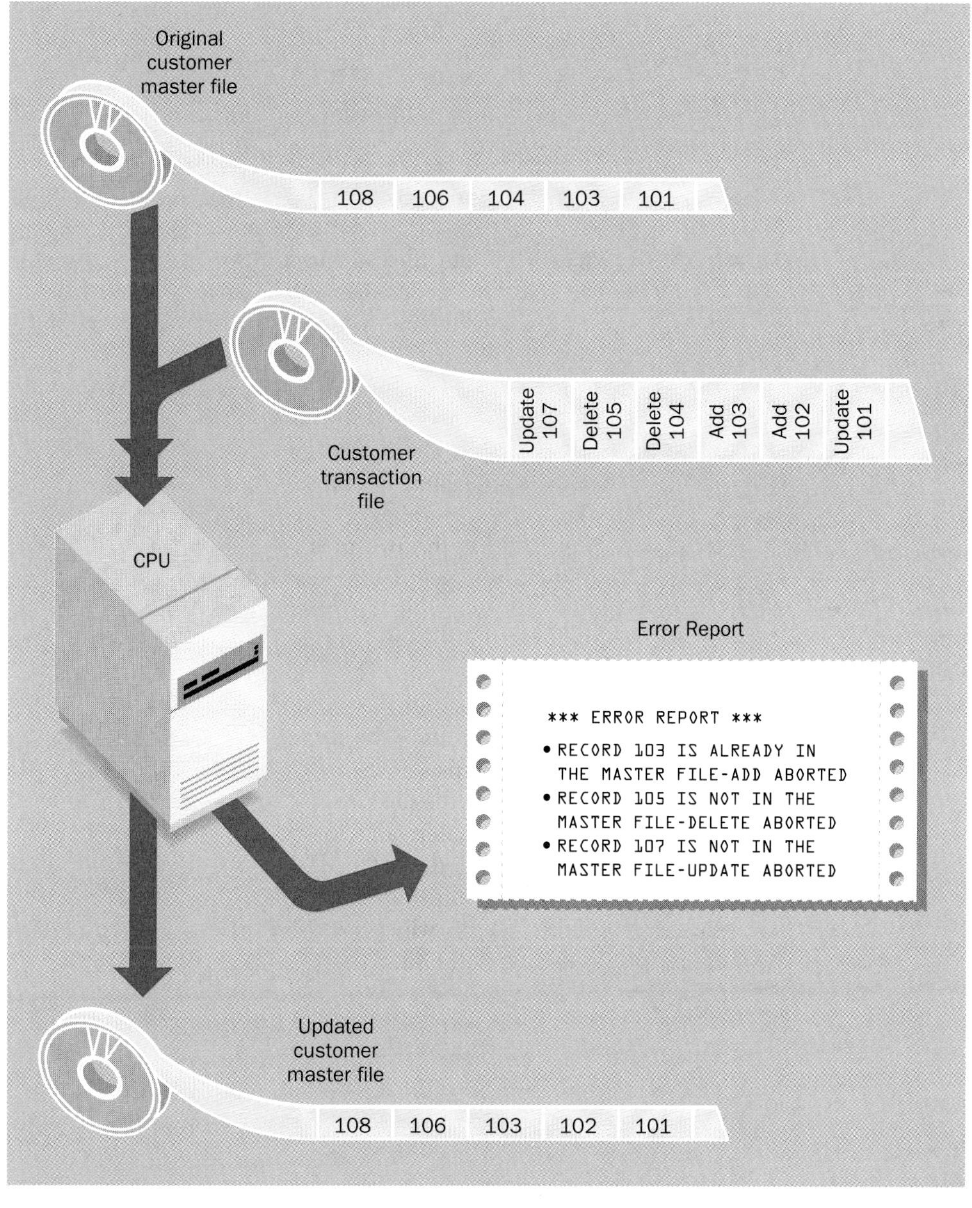

FIGURE 4-24

Indexed-sequential organization. Records are ordered on disk by key, and all record addresses are entered in an index. To process a request to find a record—say, record 200—the computer system first searches a cylinder index and then a track index for the record's address. In the cylinder index, it learns that the record is on cylinder 009. The computer system then consults the track index for cylinder 009, where it observes that the record is on track 2 of that cylinder. The access mechanism then proceeds to this track to locate the record.

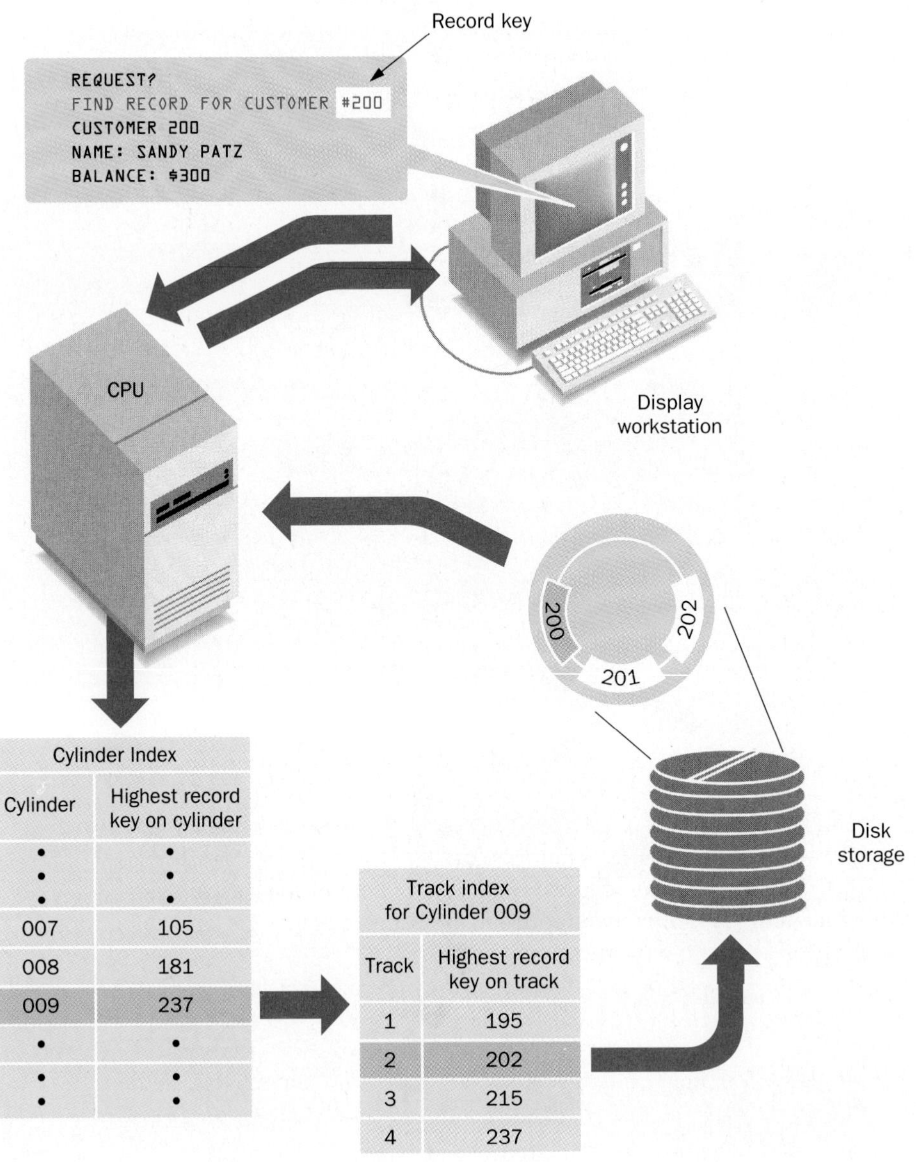

Cylinder Index	
Cylinder	Highest record key on cylinder
•	•
•	•
•	•
007	105
008	181
009	237
•	•
•	•
•	•

Track index for Cylinder 009	
Track	Highest record key on track
1	195
2	202
3	215
4	237

organization requires disk, since tapes can't provide direct access. Records are ordered on the disk by key field. Also, several indexes are created to locate these records later. These indexes work similarly to those in a phone book. For example, if the top of a phone book page reads "Alexander—Ashton," you'll know to look for the phone number of Amazon Sewer Service on that page. When implemented on a computer, as Figure 4-24 shows, such indexes permit rapid access to records.

Many computer systems have systems programs that help programmers set up indexes and indexed-sequential-organized files painlessly. As records are added to or deleted from a file, the systems software automatically adds them or deletes them from the disk and updates the index. Because the records remain organized sequentially on the disk, the file can be processed sequentially at any time.

Direct Organization Although indexed files are suitable for many applications, the process of finding disk addresses through index searches can be time consuming. Direct-organization schemes have been developed to provide faster direct access.

Direct organization eliminates the need for an index by translating the record's key field directly into a disk address. This is done with the use of mathematical formulas called *hashing algorithms.* Several hashing procedures have been developed. One of the simplest involves dividing the key field by the prime number closest to, but not greater than, the number of records to be stored. A prime number can be divided evenly by itself and 1 but not by any other number. The remainder of the division by the prime number (not the quotient) becomes the address of the relative location in which the record will be stored.

Direct organization. A method of organizing data on a device so they can be accessed directly (randomly).

Let's consider an example. Suppose that a company has 1,000 employees and therefore 1,000 active employee numbers. Also suppose that all employee identification numbers (the key field) are four digits long. Therefore, the possible range of ID numbers is from 0000 to 9999.

Assume that this company wants to place the record of employee number 8742 onto disk. The hashing procedure will be as follows. The prime number closest to 1,000, the number of records to be stored, is 997. Figure 4-25 shows that the hashed disk address computes to 766. After the record has been placed at an address corresponding to this number, the computer can retrieve it as needed by applying the hashing procedure to the key field of the record again. Calculation of an address in this manner usually consumes much less time than would a search through one or more indexes.

Hashing procedures are difficult to develop and pose certain problems. For example, it is possible for two or more records to be hashed to the same relative disk location. This, of course, means they will "collide" at their common disk address. When this happens, one record is placed in the computed location and assigned a "pointer" that chains it to the other, which often goes in the closest-available location to the hashed address. Good hashing procedures result in few collisions.

The disadvantage of direct organization is that, since records are not stored sequentially by key, it is usually impractical to process the records sequentially.

FIGURE 4-25

Hashing illustrated. The CPU follows a hashing procedure to assign a record to a disk address. In this case, the hashing procedure involves dividing the key field by the prime number closest to 1,000—997. The remainder corresponds to an actual disk address.

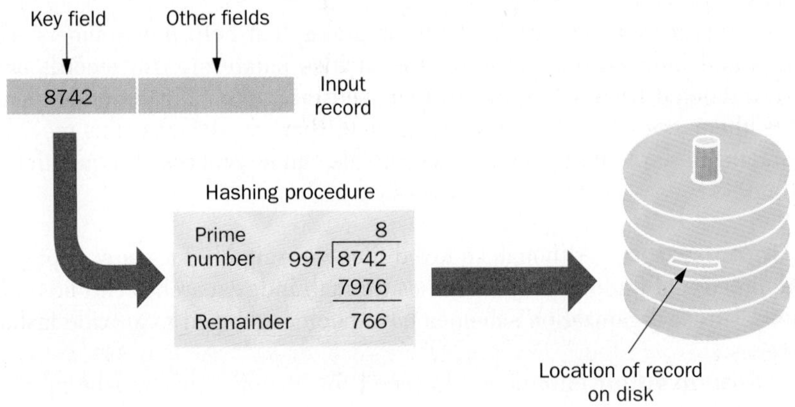

Summary and Key Terms

Secondary storage technologies make it economically feasible to keep several programs and sets of data online to the CPU. The most common types of secondary storage media are magnetic disk and magnetic tape.

Properties of Secondary Storage Systems Any secondary storage system involves two physical parts: a peripheral device and an input/output medium. In most systems, media must pass by a **read/write head** in the peripheral device to be read from or written to.

Secondary storage media are **nonvolatile**—that is, when the power to the peripheral device is shut off, the data stored on the medium remain intact. This contrasts with most types of memory, which are **volatile.** Also, media on secondary storage devices can be either *removable,* meaning they must be mounted onto the peripheral device every time they are used, or *fixed,* meaning they are permanently mounted, or nonremovable.

Two basic access methods are used on secondary storage systems: sequential and direct. With **sequential access,** the records in a file can be retrieved only in the same order in which they are physically stored. With **direct access** (or **random access**), records can be retrieved in any order.

Magnetic Disk **Magnetic disk** is most commonly available in the form of hard disks and diskettes. **Hard disks** are rigid platters. **Diskettes,** or *floppy disks,* in contrast, are flexible platters.

Diskettes are commonly used with microcomputers and small minicomputers. Each side of a diskette contains concentric **tracks,** which are encoded with 0- and 1-bits when data and programs are written to them. Diskettes are available in a number of sizes (diameters) and densities. **Sectors** divide a diskette into addressable, pie-shaped pieces. The disk's **file directory,** which the computer system maintains automatically, keeps track of the contents at each disk address. To use a diskette, the operator inserts it into a **disk unit,** or *drive.* A disk drive works only when the appropriate type of diskette is inserted correctly.

Sealed-pack hard-disk units are today a standard item on microcomputer systems. Hard disks are faster and have greater data-carrying capacity than diskettes.

In a hard-disk system, disks are tiered into units called **disk packs.** A read/write head is assigned to each recordable disk surface. The heads are mounted onto an **access mechanism,** which can move them in and out among the concentric tracks to fetch data. All tracks in the same position on the tiered platters of a disk pack form a **disk cylinder.**

Three events determine the time needed to read from or write to most disks. *Seek time* is the time required for the access mechanism to reach a particular track. The time needed for the disk to spin to a specific area of a track is known as *rotational delay.* Once located, data must be transferred to or from the disk, a process known as *data movement time.* The sum of these three time components is called **disk access time.**

Cartridge disk and **floptical disk** devices are two other disk alternatives for microcomputer systems.

Two strategies for reducing the number of time-consuming disk accesses are RAM disk and cache disk. **RAM disk** is a storage strategy whereby the computer's operating system is "tricked" into thinking it is dealing with secondary storage when in fact it is dealing with memory. **Cache disk** refers to a strategy whereby during any disk access, program or data contents in neighboring disk areas are also fetched and transported to RAM.

Disk systems on larger computers work by many of the same principles as microcomputer-based hard disks. Most disk systems for larger computers use either a sealed-pack or removable-pack design. Recently, *RAID* (for *redundant arrays of inexpensive disks*) technology has infiltrated the disk market for larger computers.

Magnetic Tape **Magnetic tape** consists of plastic Mylar coated with a magnetizable substance and wound on a reel. Each character of data is represented in byte form across the tracks in the tape. Many **detachable-reel tapes** contain nine tracks—eight corresponding to the eight bits in a byte and an additional parity track to check for transmission errors. **Cartridge tapes,** in which both supply and take-up reels are enclosed in a plastic case, are also widely available.

To be processed by the CPU, the tape must be mounted on a hardware device called a **tape unit.** The drives on the tape unit spin the tape past a read/write head, which either reads from or writes to the tape. Often records are systematically organized on a tape by means of a **key field,** such as customer ID numbers.

Optical Disk **Optical disks,** which work with laser read/write devices, are a relatively recent secondary storage technology. Most optical disk systems available today are *CD-ROM, WORM,* or *fully erasable* systems.

Data Organization The process of retrieving data and programs in storage is called **data access.** Systematically arranging data for efficient retrieval is called **data organization.**

There are three major methods of storing files in secondary storage: sequential, indexed-sequential, and direct organization. With **sequential organization,** records are arranged with respect to a key field. With **indexed-sequential organization,** records are arranged sequentially by key field on the disk to facilitate sequential access. In addition, one or more indexes are available to permit direct access to the records. **Direct organization** facilitates even faster direct access to data. It uses a process called *hashing* to transform the key field of each record into a disk address.

Review Exercises

Fill-in Questions

1. A storage medium is __________ if it loses its contents when the power is shut off.
2. A tiered assembly of disk platters enclosed in a protective cover is known as a(n) __________.
3. For rapid access, related data often are stored on the same __________, a collection of disk tracks that are in the same relative position on different disk surfaces of a pack.
4. RDO and CD-ROM refer to types of __________ disk.
5. SCSI is an acronym for __________.
6. Each character of data on magnetic tape is represented in byte form across parallel __________ of the tape.
7. Direct access relies on mathematical formulas called __________ algorithms.
8. WORM is an acronym that stands for __________.

Matching Questions

Match each term with the description that fits best.

a. diskette
b. cache disk
c. removable-pack disk unit
d. hard disk
e. optical disk
f. RAM disk

____ 1. Used when one needs a lot of fast, random access to run a business on a microcomputer system.

____ 2. A storage alternative, often under one or two megabytes in capacity, that is available in low-density or high-density format.

____ 3. A common storage alternative for minicomputers and mainframes.

____ 4. Used to "trick" the operating system into thinking it is dealing with secondary storage when it is really dealing with memory.

____ 5. Used by organizations needing extremely large amounts of data online.

____ 6. Used to fetch more data from disk on each access than the amount of data needed immediately.

Discussion Questions

1. What is the difference between volatile and nonvolatile storage?
2. Describe the advantages and disadvantages of removable media.
3. Identify several types of magnetic disk, and for each type describe a situation in which it may be useful.
4. Provide examples of sequential access and direct access to data.
5. What physical differences exist among diskettes?
6. What advantages do 3½-inch disks have over 5¼-inch disks?
7. What potential do optical disks offer?
8. Name several standards for hard disks and explain in what way these standards differ.
9. Explain how data are stored on magnetic tape.
10. How does indexed-sequential organization work?

Critical Thinking Questions

1. Does the user of a microcomputer with a hard-disk drive really need diskette drives, too?
2. Some people believe that magnetic tape will completely disappear early in the 21st century. What argument(s) do you think support this contention? Do you think that there are any types of applications for which magnetic tape will continue to hold a strong competitive edge?
3. In comparing computers to humans, observers have noted the similarities of computer memory to human memory and of the CPU chip to the human mind. Extending this analogy, what would secondary storage resemble?

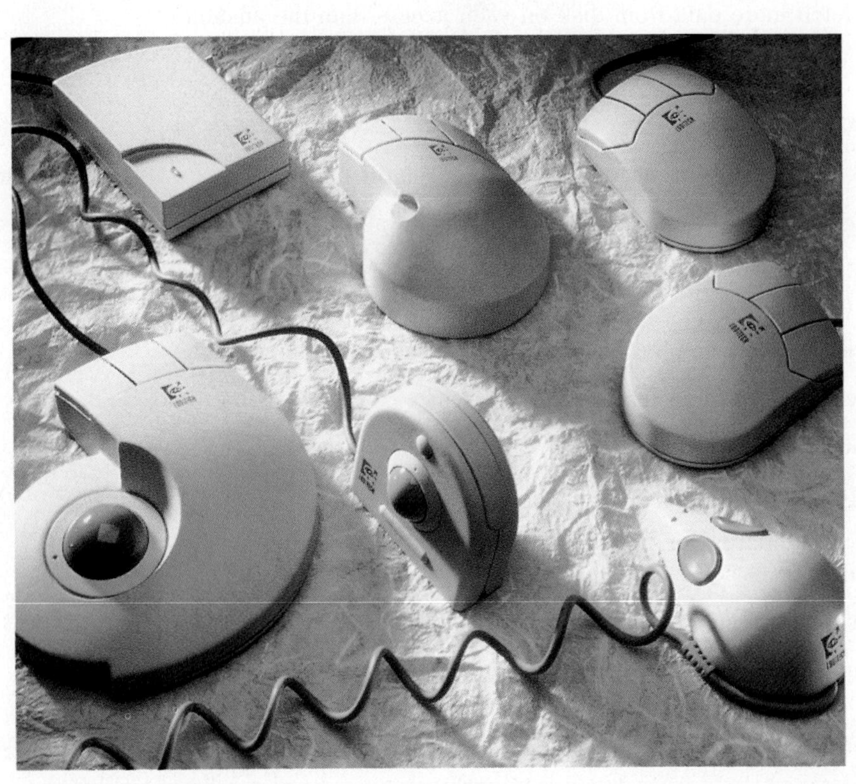

Input and Output Equipment

5

How many varieties of input and output devices are there? Perhaps so many that no one can say. As Chapter 5 suggests, the increasing popularity of desktop computers has led to an explosive number of product options, catering to a wide range of needs and tastes.

OUTLINE

Overview
Input and Output
Keyboards
Display Devices
- Monochrome and Color Display Devices
- CRT and Flat-Panel Display Devices
- Text versus Graphics

Printers
- Impact Printing
- Nonimpact Printing
- Printers for Microcomputers
- Printers for Large Computers

Source Data Automation
- Optical Character Recognition (OCR)
- Image Scanners
- Magnetic Ink Character Recognition (MICR)
- Digitizers
- Voice-Input Devices
- Handwriting Recognition Devices
- Smart Cards

Special-Purpose Output Equipment
- Plotters
- Voice-Output Devices
- Film Recorders
- Computer Output Microfilm (COM)

LEARNING OBJECTIVES

After completing this chapter, you will be able to:

1. Identify several types of input and output devices and explain their functions.
2. Describe some of the differences that exist among keyboards, among display devices, and among printers.
3. Explain what source data automation means and discuss several ways to accomplish it.
4. Discuss several types of special-purpose output equipment.
5. Appreciate the large variety of input and output equipment available in the marketplace.

Overview

In Chapter 4, we covered secondary storage devices. Although most of those devices perform both input and output operations for the computer, storage is their main role. In this chapter, we turn to equipment designed primarily for input of programs and data into the computer, for output, or for both. Many of these devices possess a limited amount of storage capacity as well.

We'll begin the chapter with a look at keyboards, which most users turn to for entering commands, programs, or data into the computer system.

Following that, we'll explore display devices. These hardware units are ideal for applications that require considerable interaction between the operator and the computer. We'll also highlight some of the qualities that distinguish one display device from another.

Next, we will turn to printers. Printers place the results of computer processing onto paper, sometimes at incredible speeds.

From there, we'll cover hardware designed for source data automation. This hardware equipment provides fast, relatively error-free input for certain kinds of applications.

Finally, we'll describe some special-purpose output equipment. Included among these devices are machines that can record output onto microfilm, machines that can speak, plotters, and film recorders.

Keep in mind that the hardware described in this chapter is only a small sample of the kinds of input/output equipment available today. There are, in fact, thousands of products in the marketplace, and these can be put together in so many ways that it is possible to create a computer system to fit almost any conceivable need.

Input and Output

Input device.
A machine used to supply programs and data to the computer.

Output device.
A machine used to output computer-processed results.

Input and output equipment allows people and computers to communicate. **Input devices** convert data and programs that humans can understand into a form the computer can comprehend. These devices translate the letters, numbers, and other natural-language symbols that humans conventionally use in reading and writing into the configurations of 0- and 1-bits that the computer uses to process data. **Output devices,** on the other hand, convert the strings of bits the computer uses back into natural-language form to make them understandable to humans. These devices produce output for screen display, output onto paper or film, and so forth.

Equipment is often discussed in terms of its input or output functions. Display terminals, for example, are capable of both input and output. Keyboards and optical character recognition devices are designed primarily for input. Printers, monitors, and most computer microfilm devices specialize in output. Most input and output devices contain limited storage capacity as well.

Hard copy.
A permanent form of usable output—for example, output on paper or film.

Soft copy.
A nonpermanent form of usable output—for example, display output.

Output devices produce results in either hard-copy or soft-copy form. The term **hard copy** generally refers to output that has been recorded onto a medium such as paper or microfilm—in other words, output that is in a permanent and highly portable form. Printed reports and program listings are among the most common examples. The term **soft copy** generally refers to display output—output that is temporary and of limited portability.

Keyboards

Keyboard.
An input device composed of numerous typewriterlike keys, arranged in a configuration similar to that of a typewriter.

For most people, a computer system would be useless without a **keyboard,** which often is the main vehicle for input. Keyboards vary tremendously in number of keys, key arrangement, types of special keys, and touch. Figure 5-1 shows the Enhanced Keyboard developed for the IBM PS/2 line of computers and describes the purpose of several of these keys. Potential buyers should carefully evaluate keyboards, considering several factors.

First, the keyboards on most computer systems have several special keys that involve specific software routines. A Delete key, for example, removes characters from the screen, and an Insert key enables characters to be added onto the screen. Also, there are several *function keys* (see the top of Figure 5-1). These keys are often labeled F1, F2, F3, and so on and are located in a cluster on the left-hand side or at the top of the keyboard. When depressed by the operator, these keys initiate a command or even an entire computer

FIGURE 5-1

Keyboard. This 102-key Enhanced Keyboard is sold with many IBM PS/2 computers. For operator convenience, this keyboard features two Ctrl, Alt, Insert, and Delete keys, as well as an extra set of arrow keys.

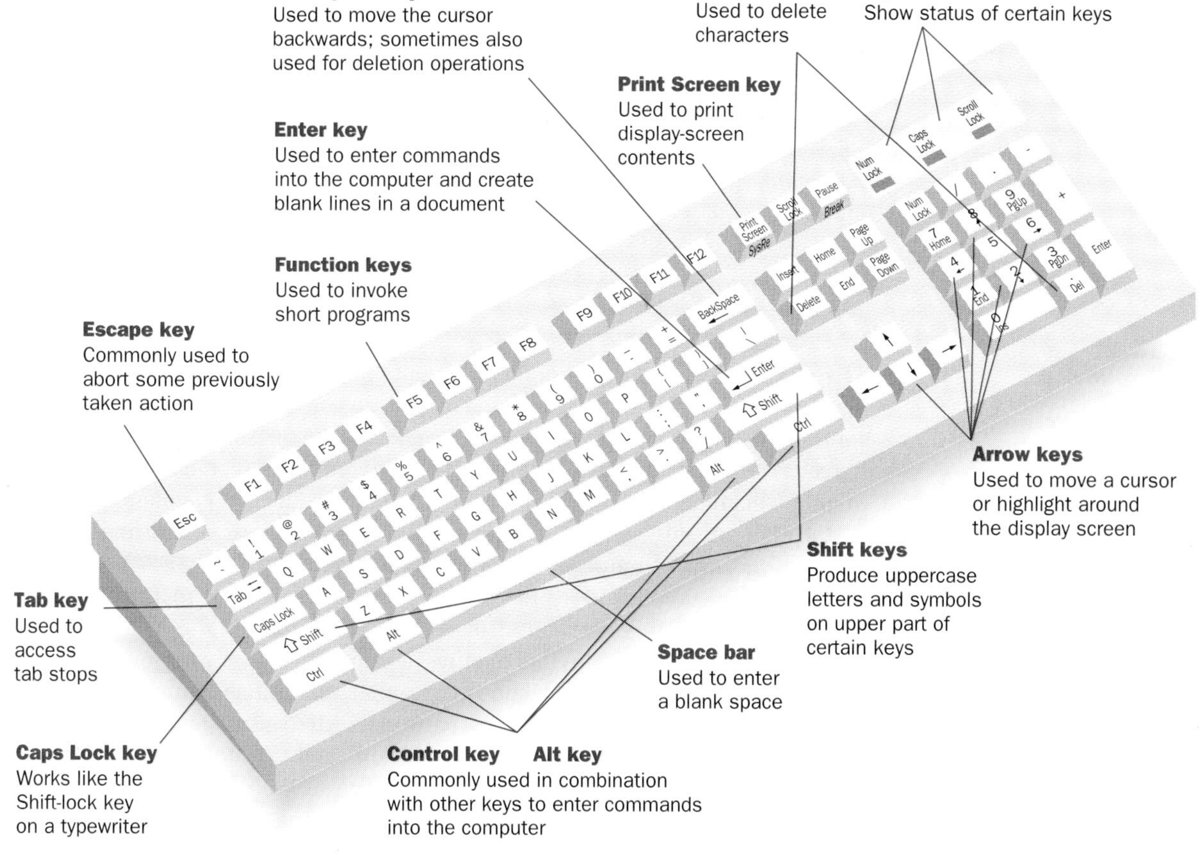

program. Generally speaking, each software package you work with will define the function keys differently. For example, depressing the F2 key may enable you to block-indent text with your word processor but edit cells with your spreadsheet package. Most keyboards also have a *numeric keypad* (see rightmost part of Figure 5-1), which is activated by the NumLock key and makes it easy to enter numbers quickly. The number of special keys, as well as their capabilities and placement, varies widely among manufacturers.

Second, not all keyboards have the same key arrangement as that on a standard typewriter. For example, the QWERTY keyboard uses the conventional typewriter format, whereas the newer and more sensibly designed Dvorak keyboard uses another arrangement, placing the five vowels under the fingertips of the left hand and the five most-used consonants under the fingertips of the right. One interesting story has it that the QWERTY keyboard, which became a standard a century or so ago, was actually created to slow down typists, so that they wouldn't get their fingers stuck in the keyboard. Despite the QWERTY keyboard's somewhat awkward design, most typists have been trained on it and wouldn't think about switching.

Third, keyboards differ with respect to touch. Some are sculpted to match the contours of the fingertips, for instance, whereas others have either flat, calculator-style keys or a flat membrane panel with touch-sensitive keys. Also, manufacturers space keys differently, so keys that feel just right to one person may seem too far apart to another. Key spacing can be a real problem for word processing users who need a laptop computer, because the keyboards on these units are designed to be as compact as possible. Still another difference regarding touch is that some keyboards make a faint clicking sound each time you depress a key, while others are completely silent.

Finally, most keyboards are detached hardware units that you can place wherever convenient. Others are built into the display or system unit. Although the standard today is clearly detachable keyboards, this design feature is not always feasible.

Display Devices

Display device.
A peripheral device that contains a viewing screen.

Monitor.
A display device without a keyboard.

Display terminal.
A communications workstation that consists of a display device and a keyboard.

Display devices are peripheral equipment that contain a televisionlike viewing screen. Most display devices fall into one of two categories: monitors and display terminals. A **monitor** is an *output* device that consists of only the viewing screen. A **display terminal** is typically an *input/output* "communications workstation" that includes the screen (for output) and an attached keyboard (for input).

In practice, one commonly finds monitors plugged into and sitting on top of the system units of microcomputers. The keyboard is usually a separate input device that also connects to the system unit. Although the monitor is strictly an output device, the user can also see keyboard input on the display because the computer routes it to the monitor as output. Display terminals, on the other hand, are generally hooked up to either mainframes, minicomputers, or supercomputers in communications networks. After all, communication is the primary function of these display devices. The keyboard unit is cabled directly to the display unit, which in turn is hooked up to the computer.

As each key on the keyboard is depressed, the corresponding character representation of the key appears on the display screen at the cursor position.

The **cursor** is a highlighted symbol on the screen indicating where the next character to be typed in will be placed. Alternatively, the cursor may point to the option the operator can select next. To have even greater flexibility in manipulating the screen cursor, many people supplement keyboard operations with a mouse, light pen, or other such cursor-movement device. These devices are examples of *digitizers,* which we'll discuss at length later in the chapter.

Cursor.
A highlighting symbol that appears on a display screen to indicate the position where the next character typed in will appear.

Display devices are handy when the user requires only small amounts of output and has to see what is being sent as input to the computer system. A student word processing a paper for a class, an airline clerk making inquiries to a flight information database, a stockbroker analyzing a security, and a bank teller checking the status of a customer account would each employ a display device. However, the display is useful only up to a point. If, for example, the student writing the paper wanted to take a copy of it home, he or she would have to direct the output to a printer.

Many features differentiate the hundreds of display devices currently in the market (see Figure 5-2). A discussion of the more noteworthy features follows.

FIGURE 5-2

Display devices. (a) Monochrome CRT-type displays are commonly used in manufacturing settings. (b) Color CRT-type displays are the standard for desktop workstations in offices. (c) Monochrome, flat-panel displays are the norm for laptop computing.

(a)

(b)

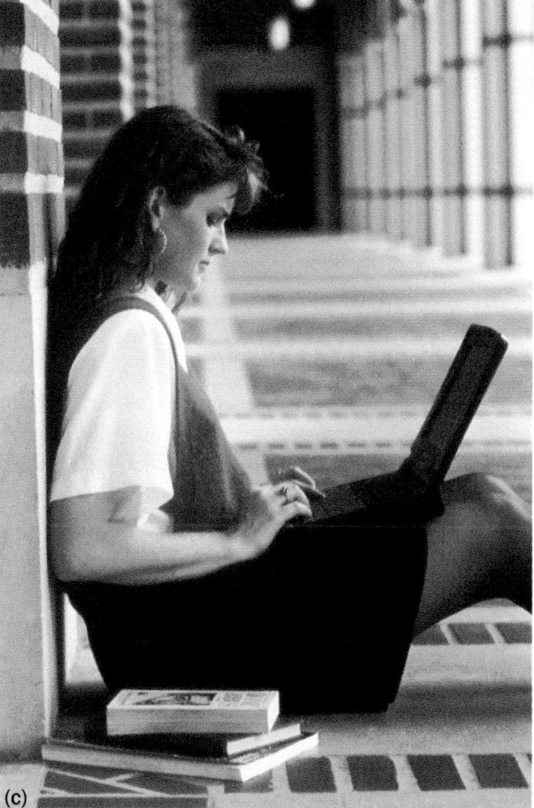

(c)

Monochrome and Color Display Devices

Most display devices in use today are classifiable as monochrome or color.

Monochrome *Monochrome displays* output images using a single foreground color (see Figure 5-2a). Many of the earliest monochrome devices were of the black-and-white variety, providing white text on a black background. Through a technique known as *reverse video,* black text on a white background also became possible. Over the years, studies have shown that people become less fatigued when working with amber or green on a black background. Although such studies have produced conflicting results, many of the monochrome display devices now available in the markeplace are of the amber or green type.

Color Most *color displays* (see Figure 5-2b) are of the *red-green-blue (RGB)* type. That is, all colors available on the screen are formed by intermixing light beams of only these three colors. Depending on such factors as the sophistication of the display unit itself and the amount of RAM available with the computer, users may be able to display from a few colors to millions. Business users often need only a few colors, but people such as artists and product designers need many more.

Monochrome display devices have advantages over color ones because they are cheaper, generally provide better resolution for text display (an important consideration if the display will be used extensively for simple text processing), and emit less radiation. But if you need more than a single color and want flexibility, only a color monitor will suffice. Today, color displays have become the standard for desktop computers, while monochrome displays dominate the laptop-computing market.

CRT and Flat-Panel Display Devices

Cathode-ray tube (CRT). A display device that contains a long-necked display tube similar to that used in television sets.

Flat-panel display. A slim-profile display device.

Traditionally, most display devices have used a large picture-tube element similar to the one inside a standard TV set. This type of display device (see Figures 5-2a and 5-2b) is commonly called a **CRT (cathode-ray tube).** CRT technology is relatively mature. Over the years, CRTs have become very inexpensive and capable of providing excellent color output. These features notwithstanding, CRTs are bulky, fragile, and consume a great deal of power.

Recently monitors and display terminals that use charged chemicals or gases sandwiched between panes of glass have become popular alternatives to CRTs. These slim-profile devices are called **flat-panel displays.** Although they can be relatively expensive and have only recently become commercially viable for color output, flat-panel displays are compact, are lightweight, and require little power. Because of these features, they are commonly found on laptop and notebook computers and in portable handwriting recognition devices. Also, as described in User Solution 5-1, flat-panel displays are today helping to create new technology products that virtually nobody imagined a decade or so ago.

Figure 5-2c features a flat-panel display that uses a *liquid crystal display (LCD)* technology. LCDs are by far the most common type of flat-panel display devices in use. Among the major advantages of LCD technology over CRTs are low cost, low power consumption, portability, and compactness. However, LCDs provide less contrast, produce more glare, and have poorer screen resolution than CRTs. To overcome the contrast problem, many LCDs are back-lit.

User Solution 5-1

High-Tech Services for Air Travelers

One of the nice things about flat-panel displays is that they can be squeezed in almost anywhere. Like on the back of a plane seat, hard as that may be to imagine. Recently, with the appearance of a product called FlightLink, commercial airlines have moved another step closer to providing air travelers with an all-digital communications system. Now being used on a trial basis, FlightLink enables laptop users to communicate with computers on the ground. It also offers passengers without their own machines the services of an on-board computer system. The system consists of a combination keypad/phone that is positioned on the back of the seat in front of the user-passenger. He or she can make calls or use the LCD panel to summon computer games, airport and gate information, stock quotes, reservations services, city and travel guides, headline news, and weather and sports information.

Text versus Graphics

Many of the display devices sold today are capable of providing both text and graphics output. *Text* output consists of only letters, digits, and special characters. Two examples are program listings and letters to friends. *Graphics* output includes complex picture images, such as maps and drawings.

Resolution A key characteristic of any display device is *resolution,* or sharpness of the screen image. On many displays, images are formed by lighting up tiny dots on the screen. On such devices, resolution is measured by the density of these dots, or **pixels** (a contraction of the phrase *picture elements*). The more pixels per square inch of screen, the higher the resolution (i.e., the clearer the picture). A display resolution of, say, 640 by 480 means that the screen consists of 640 columns by 480 rows of dots—that is, 640 × 480 = 307,200 pixels.

Text characters are formed on the screen in a dot-matrix configuration, as shown in Figure 5-3. Generally, several specific matrix sizes—say, 5 by 7 (= 35 pixels) or 7 by 12 (= 84 pixels)—are available for users to display text. For instance, a user may be able to display 25 rows of 65-character lines for one application and 50 rows of 132-character lines for another. The more pixels used to form characters, the more pixels packed per square inch of screen, and the higher the text resolution.

Pixels are electronically maintained and manipulated at lightning-fast speeds. For instance, the pixels on a typical desktop display screen are *refreshed*—that is, recharged with a built-in electron gun so they will remain bright—at a rate of dozens of times each second.

FIGURE 5-3

The letter *C* formed by a 5-by-7 dot matrix.
Generally, the more dots available in the matrix, the better the character resolution.

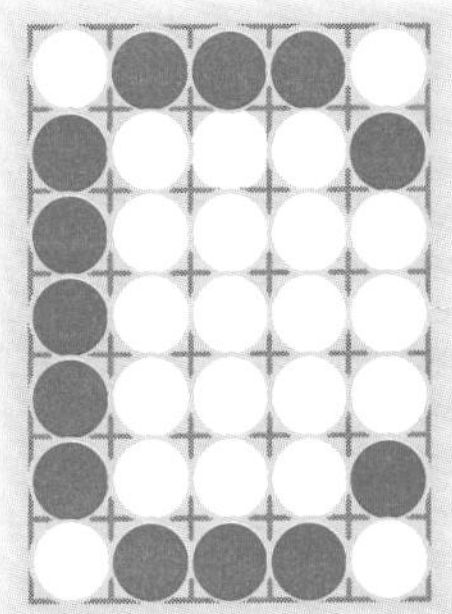

Pixel.
A single dot on a display screen that is used to compose images.

Bit mapping The earliest display devices were strictly *character addressable;* that is, only text could be output. Every character sent to the screen was the same size and was fitted into a specific block of pixels in a predesignated grid. As demand for graphics devices grew, manufacturers developed techniques to make displays multipurpose—that is, capable of both graphics and standard text output.

Bit mapping.
A graphical output technique in which each of the dots in the output image may be individually operator controlled.

Display devices that produce graphics output often use a technique called **bit mapping.** With bit-mapped graphics, each pixel on the screen (rather than simply a block of pixels) can be individually controlled by the computer operator or the software package in use. Bit mapping enables the operator or software to create virtually any type of image on the screen. Figure 5-4 features a variety of graphics applications.

One of the largest markets for graphics display devices today are in the engineering, science, and art fields. Powerful devices called *technical workstations* are used for mapping, circuit design, mechanical and engineering design (see Figure 5-4a), drafting, art, advertising, and other graphics-intensive tasks. Such applications collectively fall under the heading of *computer-aided design (CAD).* We will discuss CAD in greater detail in Chapter 11.

Another large market for computer graphics is in the business sector. Managers can easily become overwhelmed as they try to make decisions from piles of raw data. A possible solution lies in the old adage "A picture is worth a thousand words." Using a graphics image, a decision maker can more easily spot problems, opportunities, and trends. Many business applications of computer graphics fall into the general category of *presentation graphics,* which we'll cover in Chapter 9. With presentation graphics, computer images are used to increase the effectiveness of presenting data to others (Figure 5-4b).

Recently, computer graphics techniques have brought many businesses squarely into the age of *electronic document handling,* in which digital images of

FIGURE 5-4

Common graphics applications. (a) Engineering design. (b) Business presentation graphics. (c) Electronic document handling.

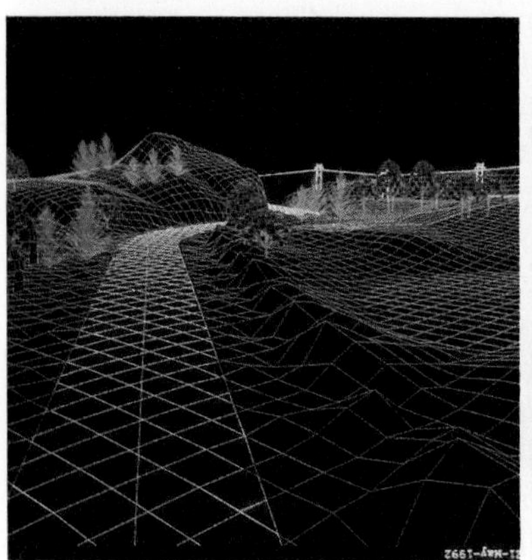

(a)

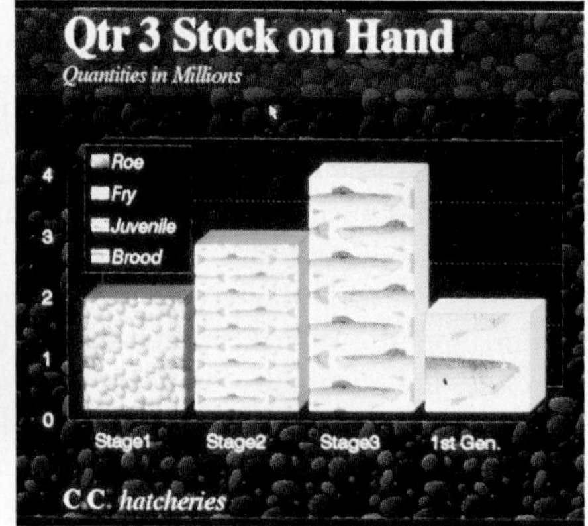

(b)

(c)

FIGURE 5-5

VGA versus Super VGA (SVGA). Because an SVGA screen (right) contains over twice the number of pixels as a VGA screen (left) of the same size, it can contain over twice the amount of information. SVGA is ideal for applications in which users wish to squeeze more information onto a single screen.

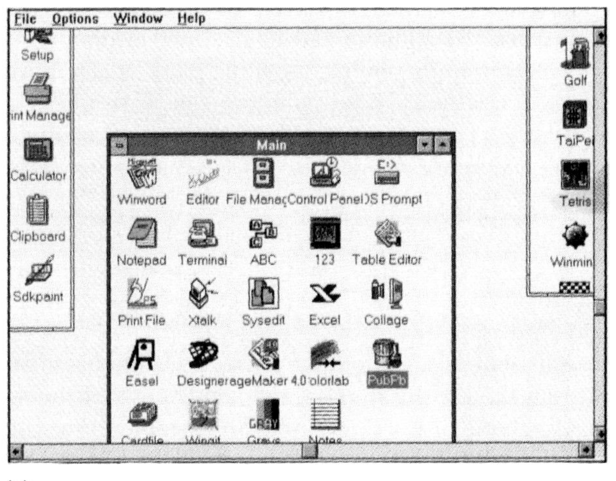

(a)

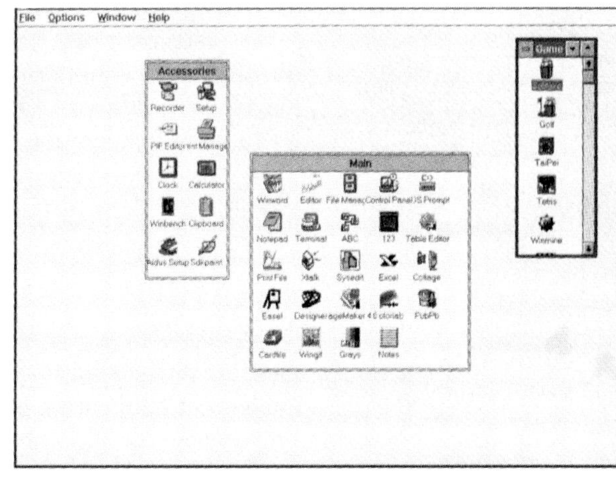

(b)

paper documents and photographs are electronically maintained by organizations and processed by workers at their display workstations (see Figure 5-4c). The paper documents and photographs are initially read into the computer system with a scanner. Once in electronic form, the images are stored on a high-capacity optical disk system. Workers having access to the system can summon documents to their workstations, where they can cull, sort, summarize, or repackage the information to their heart's content. Workers may also be authorized to annotate certain documents with comments or approvals and send them to other workers who are hooked into the system.

Graphics Standards A number of standards for display devices are currently in effect. In the IBM microcomputing world, standards such as Hercules monochrome, Monochrome Display Adapter (MDA), Color Graphics Adapter (CGA), Multi-color Graphics Array (MCGA), Enhanced Graphics Adapter (EGA), are widely found on display devices made before 1987. Video Graphics Array (VGA), the current standard, has been dominant over the last several years. VGA is available in three principal variants—in order of finer screen-resolution they are the original VGA standard (VGA), Super VGA (SVGA), and Extended VGA (XVGA). The Apple Macintosh line has a similar set of graphics standards.

Graphics standards specify "modes" in which the display device can run. For example, VGA can run in 17 different modes. One mode, for instance, divides the screen into a matrix of 320 by 200 pixels and allows 256 colors to be displayed simultaneously; another divides the screen into a matrix of 720 by 400 pixels and permits monochrome display only. SVGA and XVGA allow even larger pixel matrices than these. An SVGA display, for instance, shows

FIGURE 5-6

Solid-font and dot-matrix characters. (a) Printer-produced solid-font characters are like typewritten characters. (b) Dot-matrix characters are formed as a series of dots that blend together when viewed from a distance.

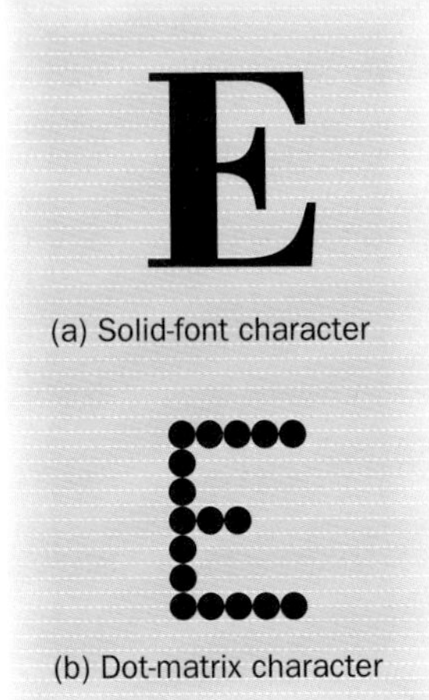

FIGURE 5-7

Daisywheel print element. Daisywheel printers have superb output quality, but their lack of speed, text-only orientation, and noise level have caused them to lose out to laser printers in many applications environments.

about two-and-a-half times the amount of information as a VGA display of the same size (see Figure 5-5). A major drawback to SVGA when compared to VGA is that its characters are minimally readable on a 14- or 15-inch display—and generally unreadable on a laptop screen. Another drawback is speed; because there is more information showing on an SVGA screen, the screen takes longer to rewrite every time it is changed.

In response to the large number of standards and modes now available for display, many monitor manufacturers in the microcomputing marketplace have developed *multiscan (multisync) monitors.* These monitors can work under a wide variety of graphics standards. Thus, for instance, such a monitor might be able to support software designed to work under either VGA and Super VGA.

Printers

Display devices have two major limitations as output devices: (1) only a small amount of data can be shown on the screen at one time, and (2) output, being in soft copy form, is not very portable. To obtain output in portable form, you must either take notes or use a device that captures output onto paper or film.

Printers overcome these limitations by producing hard copy—a permanent record of output. Hard copy is created when digital electronic signals from the computer are converted into printed material in a natural language that people can easily read and understand. A great deal of output can be placed onto computer printouts, although hard copy can become difficult to handle and store as it accumulates. In fact, many executives now complain that they are literally drowning in a sea of computer-generated paperwork.

Printers differ in a number of important respects. One involves the printing technology used—namely, whether it is *impact* or *nonimpact.* Another concerns speed of operation. *Low-speed printers* are capable of outputting only one character at a time, whereas *high-speed printers* can output either a full line or a full page at a time.

Impact Printing

Impact printing is the method used by conventionl typewriters. In some types of impact printing, a metal "hammer" embossed with a character strikes a print ribbon, which presses the character's image onto paper. In other types, the hammer strikes the paper and presses it into the ribbon. Characters created through impact printing can be formed by either a solid-font or dot-matrix printing mechanism (see Figure 5-6).

Solid-Font Mechanisms A **solid-font mechanism** produces fully formed characters similar to those on conventional typewriters.

A popular device for producing fully formed characters on low-speed printers is the daisywheel print element, shown in Figure 5-7. *Daisywheel printers* operate at very slow speeds—often in the neighborhood of 30 to 80 characters per second—but their output quality is very high. Thus, daisywheel printers are sometimes called *letter-quality* printers, because they are often used to produce attractive correspondence to be sent outside the user's organization. *Print-*

thimble printers, popularized by NEC, are another example of low-speed, solid-font, letter-quality printers. A print thimble looks like a daisywheel with its spokes bent upward in the shape of a sewing thimble.

The recent popularity of low-priced laser printers has greatly diminished the demand for daisywheel and print-thimble devices. Many high-speed printers—such as chain printers and band printers—also employ a solid-font mechanism to produce fully formed characters.

Dot-Matrix Mechanisms Most low-speed printers in use today employ a print head that's an impact dot-matrix mechanism. Typically, an **impact dot-matrix mechanism** constructs printed characters by repeatedly activating one or more vertical rows of pins, as illustrated in Figure 5-8. Impact dot-matrix printers are usually much faster than solid-font printers; a speed of 100 to several hundred characters per second is common.

The quality of output on impact dot-matrix devices is often lower than that on solid-font devices. Nonetheless, many relatively inexpensive impact dot-matrix printers are capable of printing very respectable-looking output. These printers use techniques such as packing as many pins as possible on the print

Printer.
A device that places computer output onto paper.

Impact printing.
The formation of characters by causing a metal hammer to strike a ribbon into paper or paper into a ribbon.

Solid-font mechanism.
A printing element that produces solid characters.

Impact dot-matrix mechanism.
A print head that forms dot-matrix characters through impact printing.

FIGURE 5-8

Impact dot-matrix printing. This character-formation technique is similar to the one used to light up electronic scoreboards at sports stadiums. The printing mechanism contains a vertical line of pins that form the characters on the paper. Depending on the character to be represented, different pins in the mechanism are activated. The characters shown are formed from a 5-by-7 dot matrix. The more dots in the matrix, naturally, the higher the quality of the printed character.

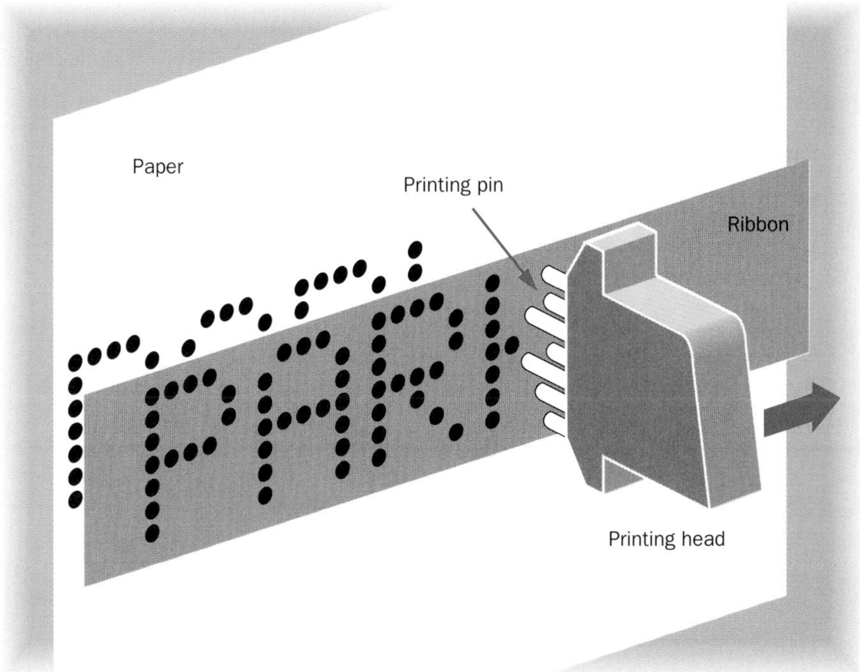

FIGURE 5-9

Overstriking on a dot-matrix printer. (a) Single striking. (b) Overstriking with multiple passes produces denser characters.

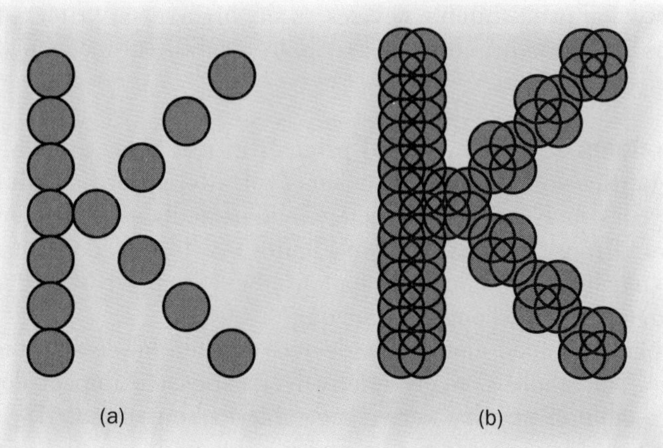

head, overstriking by making multiple passes on a line, and blending overstrike dots into previous dots by shifting the paper very slightly (see Figure 5-9). Top-of-the-line impact dot-matrix printers have 24 pins on their print heads, configured in two 12-pin rows. Generally, these printers can create characters that are virtually indistinguishable from those produced by solid-font printers. In the world of impact dot-matrix printing, low-quality output is often referred

FIGURE 5-10

Impact dot-matrix printer. Often costing only a few hundred dollars, impact dot-matrix printers are popular in microcomputing environments where draft-quality output is acceptable.

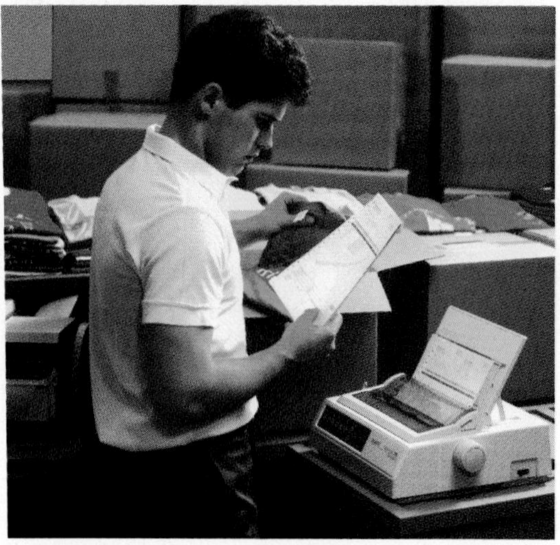

FIGURE 5-11

Thermal-transfer printers. Thermal-transfer technology is used for both (a) small portable printers and (b) situations where high-quality color output is required.

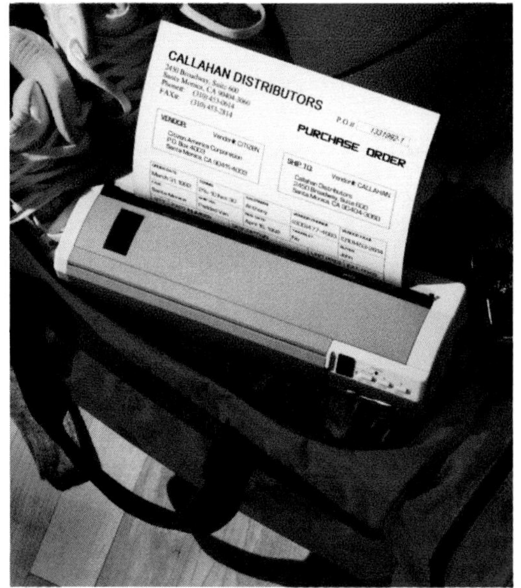

(a)

(b)

to as *draft-quality* printing and presentation-quality output as *near-letter-quality (NLQ)* printing. Many impact dot-matrix printers can also be used to produce graphical or color output.

An impact dot-matrix printer is featured in Figure 5-10.

Nonimpact Printing

Nonimpact printing, which most often employs dot-matrix characters, does not depend on the impact of metal on paper. In fact, no physical contact at all occurs between the printing mechanism and the paper. The most popular nonimpact methods today utilize electrothermal, thermal-transfer, ink-jet, and laser technologies.

Nonimpact printing. The formation of characters on a surface by means of heat, lasers, photography, or ink jets.

In *electrothermal printing,* characters are burned onto a special paper by heated rods on a print head. Electrothermal printers are available at a very low cost, but they have the disadvantages of poor output quality, requiring special paper (which some people find unpleasant to touch), and being unable to produce color output. Electrothermal printing is the technology most used by fax machines, which are covered in Chapter 6.

Thermal-transfer printers, which represent a relatively new technology, thermally transfer ink from a wax-based ribbon or transfer dye onto plain paper (see Figure 5-11). The wax-based printers can produce text output that rivals a daisywheel's and, because they use a dot-matrix print head, can support high-quality graphics as well (see Figure 5-11a). The more-expensive dye-based printers, which have just recently become available, can produce images of near-photographic quality (see Figure 5-11b).

FIGURE 5-12

Laser printer. Laser printers are most useful for producing high-resolution, black-and-white text and graphics—all at a reasonable speed and price, They work on a principle similar to that of copying machines.

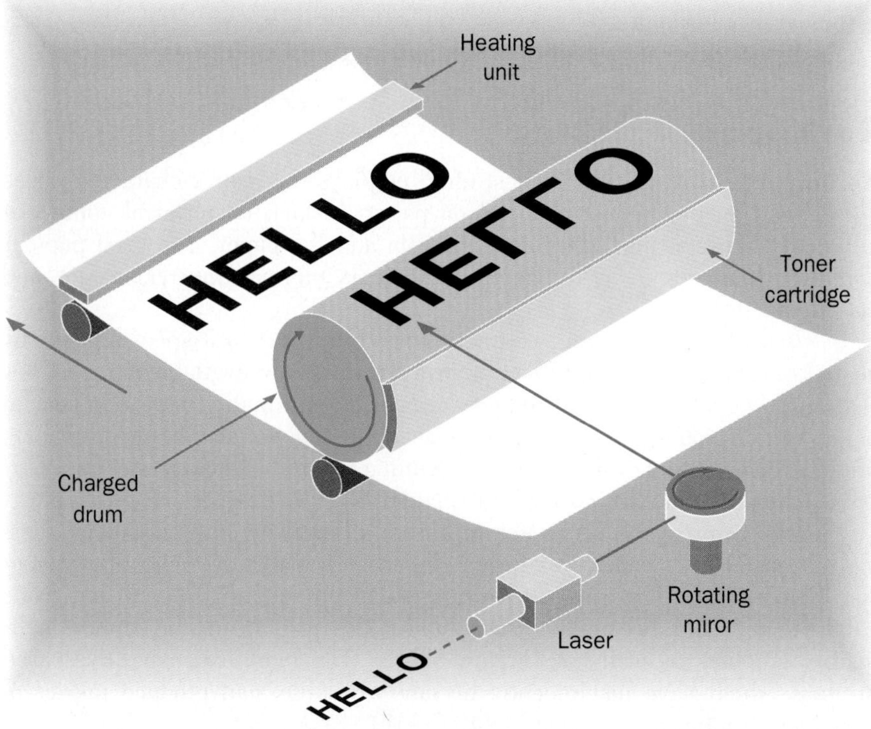

Ink-jet printers typically work by spraying small dots of electrically charged ink onto a page to form images. Some models can hold several color cartridges simultaneously, so they are excellent for producing color output. Many ink-jet printers are flexible enough to be used as plotters, an output device we'll discuss later in the chapter, and as transparency-making machines. Ink-jet technology is also used in some portable printers; Canon calls its line of personal ink-jet products *bubble-jet printers.*

Laser printers form images like copying machines—by charging thousands of dots on a drum with a very-high-intensity laser beam. Toner from a cartridge is affixed to the charged positions and, when paper is pressed against the drum, an image is formed. A heating unit fuses the image permanently onto the paper. Laser printers quickly produce high-resolution text and graphics (see Figure 5-12), but they are usually more expensive than other types of printers.

Impact versus Nonimpact Printers Impact and nonimpact printers have many important practical differences. For one, because nonimpact printers contain fewer moving parts, they generally are much faster and subject to fewer breakdowns. In addition, because they don't use hammers, nonimpact printers are quiet. But unless you need high speeds, graphics, or high-quality color, these printers are often an expensive alternative. Figure 5-13 highlights some other differences between the most common types of impact and nonimpact printers.

Printers for Microcomputers

A rich assortment of printers is available today for microcomputers. Most of these printers are of the low-speed variety and output a single character at a time. By far the most common low-speed printers are of the impact dot-matrix type. Daisywheel, print-thimble, thermal-transfer, and ink-jet printers are also used with microcomputers.

Low-speed printers typically operate in the range of 30 to several hundred characters per second. The slower units print in a single direction, like a

FIGURE 5-13

Comparison of printing technologies.

	Device					
Criterion	**Impact Dot Matrix**	**Daisywheel and Print Thimble**	**Ink Jet**	**Electrothermal**	**Thermal Transfer**	**Laser**
Type	Impact	Impact	Nonimpact	Nonimpact	Nonimpact	Nonimpact
Speed	Fast	Slow	Medium to very fast	Medium to fast	Medium to fast	Very fast
Print quality	Fair to very good	Excellent	Good to excellent	Fair to very good	Excellent	Excellent
Cost	Low	Medium	Medium to high	Low	Medium to high	High
Graphics capabilities	Fair	Very limited	Fair to excellent	Good	Good to excellent	Excellent
Color	Fair	Very limited	Excellent	Not available	Excellent	Limited

FIGURE 5-14

A line printer. Line printers are targeted to larger computers—most notably minicomputers and mainframes—and produce output at speeds ranging from 300 to 3,000 lines per minute (lpm).

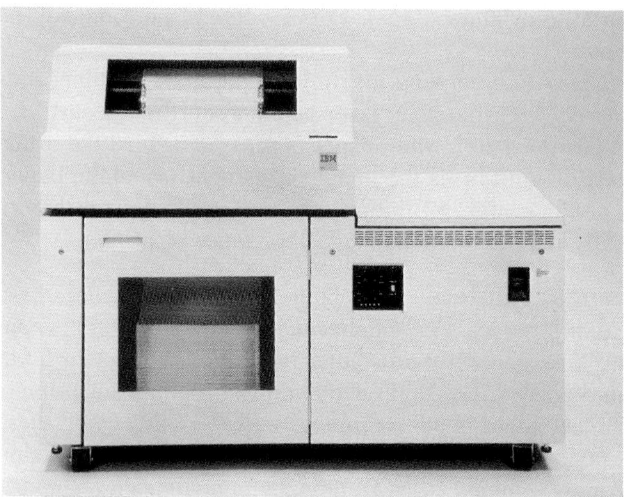

conventional typewriter. The faster ones print in two directions (i.e., *bidirectionally*) to save a time-consuming carriage return. Usually the latter devices are also *logic-seeking* in that they are always "peeking" at the next line to decide how to print it the fastest way. Many low-speed printers can output subscripts, superscripts, color, graphic material, and multilingual and scientific text.

Many low-speed printers offer adjustable character widths, enabling the operator to change the number of characters per line or lines per inch. On dot-matrix units, the operator can make these adjustments by setting a switch or through the use of software. With solid-font devices, however, the operator must usually change the printing element by hand.

Changing *fonts*, or typefaces, is also usually easily achievable. On dot-matrix printers, fonts are usually changed by switching font cartridges, which contain character descriptions. On solid-font printers, fonts are changed by replacing the printing element.

Perhaps the greatest potential for high-speed printing on microcomputer systems exists with laser printing. Only since the mid-1980s have relatively inexpensive laser devices—costing about $1,000 and printing about four to eight pages per minute—become available for microcomputers. Many of these print at a resolution of either 300 or 600 dots per inch (dpi). At 600 dpi, every square inch of the output image is broken down into a 600-by-600 matrix of dots. That's 360,000 dots packed into every inch! Laser devices have become especially popular in business in the last few years, because they can produce letter-quality output that rivals that of solid-font printers, can quickly create presentation graphics for reports and meetings, and permit performance of certain publishing functions on a desktop. Laser printing is a special case of page printing, which we shall cover shortly.

FIGURE 5-15

A page printer. Operating at peak capacity over a weekend, some page printers produce well over a million pages of output.

Printers for Large Computers

Most printing on large computer systems is accomplished with high-speed printers. Whereas low-speed printers top out at speeds of several hundred *characters per second,* the slowest high-speed printers operate at several hundred *lines per minute* (roughly twice the speed of the fastest low-speed printer). In many commercial settings that use both kinds of printers, you will often find the high-speed printers operating at speeds of from 10 to 30 times higher than the low-speed printers.

High-speed printers fall into two major categories: line printers and page printers.

Line Printers **Line printers** (see Figure 5-14) are so called because they print whole lines at a time rather than just characters. Most line printers use impact printing technologies. For instance, many line printers use the solid-font, impact chain mechanism, which IBM introduced in 1959 on its 1403 printer. This device has proved to be the most popular printer of all time and is still used today. Band printers, which use a character-embossed print band instead of a chain, are currently the most common type of line printer. Other forms of line printers use mechanical devices such as print trains, drums, wheels, and belts. Impact line printing typically occurs at speeds ranging from 300 to 3,000 lines per minute.

Line printer.
A high-speed printer that produces output a line at a time.

Page Printers As the term suggests, **page printers** (see Figure 5-15) can produce a page of output at a time. These devices, which can print up to a few hundred pages of output per minute, all employ nonimpact technology. Many

Page printer.
A high-speed printer that delivers output one page at a time.

of them utilize an electrophotographic process similar to that used by the copying machines found in many offices. The printing commonly occurs on 8-by-11-inch paper, which is cheaper than the larger, sprocket-fed paper line printers typically use. The smaller-size paper is cheaper to file and mail as well. Some page printers can print in color and on both sides of the page.

A useful feature of page printers is their ability to output digital images of forms and letterheads. Forms can be filled out by users at display devices and automatically printed. Thus, page printers offer considerable savings over line printers, which require changing of paper and printing elements when output dictates a new form or format.

Page printers generally cost considerably more than line printers. Line printers range from $3,000 to $50,000, whereas page printers for large computers may cost between $50,000 and $300,000. In general, an organization that produces over a million lines of output per month should investigate the feasibility of acquiring one of these machines.

Source Data Automation

Often data must be translated from handwritten form into machine-readable form so that they can be processed, a procedure that sometimes consumes thousands of hours of duplicated effort and that can result in many mistakes and delays. Data must be hand-entered on documents or forms, keyed into machine-readable form on a data preparation device, verified, and read into the computer. Usually, several people will be involved in this process, complicating matters further.

Source data automation. The process of making data available in machine-readable form at the time they are collected.

Source data automation eliminates much of this duplicated effort, delay, extra handling, and potential for error by making data available in machine-readable form at the time they are collected. Because ready-to-process transaction data are collected by the people who know most about them, source data automation is rapidly becoming the dominant form of data entry today.

Source data automation has been applied to a number of tasks. For example, many orders taken over the phone today are entered directly into display workstations, so they don't have to be recorded twice. Source data automation has also been used to speed up checkout lines and inventory taking at supermarkets, quality control operations in factories, and processing of checks by banks.

In the next few pages, we will discuss several technologies that can be used to achieve source data automation: optical character recognition (OCR), magnetic ink character recognition (MICR), digitizing, image scanning, voice input, handwriting recognition, and smart cards.

Optical Character Recognition (OCR)

Optical character recognition (OCR). The use of light reflectivity to identify marks, characters, or codes.

Optical character recognition (OCR) refers to a wide range of optical-scanning procedures and equipment designed for machine recognition of marks, characters, and codes. These symbols are transformed into digital form for storage in the computer. Most symbols designed for OCR can be read by humans as well as by machines. Optical recognition of hand-printed characters is also technically possible but is still in its infancy. OCR equipment is among the

FIGURE 5-16

A selection of characters from an optical character set.

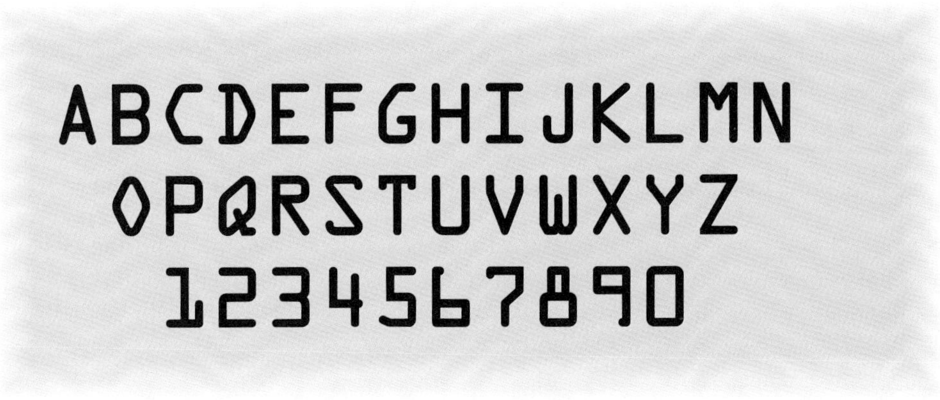

ABCDEFGHIJKLMN
OPQRSTUVWXYZ
1234567890

most varied and highly specialized in the information processing industry. A scanner that can read one type of document may be totally unable to read another.

Optical Marks One of the oldest applications of OCR is the processing of tests and questionnaires completed on special forms using *optical marks.* Take the case of grading a test in which the student darkens the bubbles on the answer sheet to indicate the answers to multiple-choice questions. An optical document reader scans the answer sheets offline. This machine passes a light beam across the spaces corresponding to the set of possible responses to each question. The light is reflected where a response is penciled in, and the machine tallies that choice.

Optical Characters *Optical characters* are characters specially designed to be identifiable by humans as well as by some type of OCR reader. Optical characters conform to a certain font, such as that shown in Figure 5-16. The optical reader reflects light off the characters and converts them into electronic patterns for recognition. The reader can identify a character only if it is familiar with the font used.

In the early days of optical character reading, fonts differed widely among OCR manufacturers. As the years passed, however, a few fonts became industry standards. Today many machines are designed to read several fonts even when these fonts are mixed in a single document.

Probably the best-known use of optical characters is in **point-of-sale (POS) systems,** which are employed widely in retail stores. POS systems allow a store to record a purchase at the time and place it occurs. A sale is often automatically recorded from machine-readable information on a price tag attached to the product. The information on the tag is input to a special cash register. Today many cash registers are equipped with local, direct-access memories containing descriptions of stocked items, so they can print what each item is along with its price on the customer receipt (see Figure 5-17 and the Tomorrow box).

FIGURE 5-17

An informative cash register receipt made possible by a local memory.

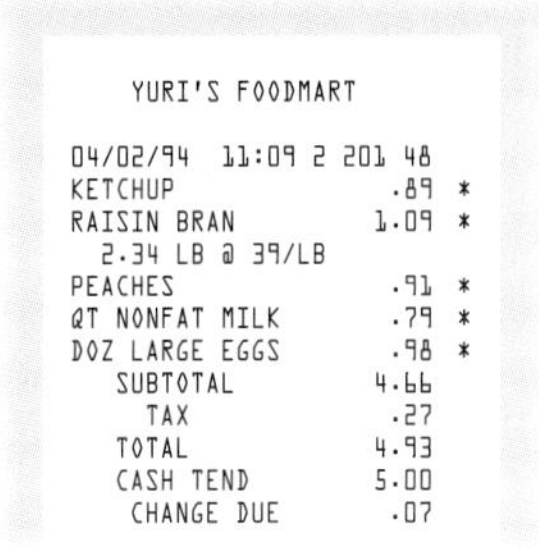

```
      YURI'S FOODMART

04/02/94  11:09 2 201 48
KETCHUP               .89  *
RAISIN BRAN          1.09  *
  2.34 LB @ 39/LB
PEACHES               .91  *
QT NONFAT MILK        .79  *
DOZ LARGE EGGS        .98  *
   SUBTOTAL          4.66
     TAX              .27
   TOTAL             4.93
   CASH TEND         5.00
    CHANGE DUE        .07
```

Point-of-sale (POS) system.
A computer system, commonly found in department stores and supermarkets, that uses electronic cash register terminals to process sales transactions.

TOMORROW

Retailing in the 21st Century

How Much Will Technology Change the Way We Shop?

Like a lot of other industries, retailing has turned into a dog-eat-dog affair. If a supermarket or a department store doesn't have price, quality, convenience, or some type of curiosity factor going for it these days, it probably doesn't have much of a future.

Retailing has undergone many changes in the recent past. Warehouse stores and factory outlets have sprouted up to appeal to the price conscious. More and more companies are selling by catalog to professionals who don't have time to shop. And for customers who have both time and money but savor convenience, the competition among retailers to provide the best-quality service has reached heights that probably few dreamed of just a couple of decades ago. In all cases, the bottom line in the retailing business has come down to maintaining a competitive advantage in some key area.

Many companies are turning to technology for new ways to provide such an advantage. Some ideas are now getting a serious look:

- **Self-service checkout aisles.** This service would allow grocery shoppers to scan their own bar codes at the checkout counter. "Smart" hardware and software products will be available to make sure no one cheats. For instance, each product scanned must be put on an intelligent scale before it's sent to the section where it can be packaged. That would prevent a $12.45 rump roast from being declared a 59-cent head of lettuce.
- **Shopping by computer network.** Some futurists say that as computer networks become ever more popular people will begin doing more of their shopping by remote computer. Someday you might be able to call your local supermarket on your home or office computer, electronically select the items you want to buy, and show up at a distribution center where the items are all bagged and ready to take home.
- **Signature systems.** The cost of handling signed paper receipts amounts to a large expense for any retail firm. Recently, pen-based handwriting systems have come to the fore that eliminate the need to file hard copies of signatures. The customer signs a digitizing pad that has a paper receipt on it; the customer then receives the paper copy, while the store logs the electronic copy into its record system.
- **Information kiosks.** In supermarkets, you would be able to go up to a kiosk—a booth that looks like an automatic-teller machine at a bank—and get recipe information. Not only that, you would also be able to find the aisles where the ingredients for the recipe can be found and check to see if the items you want are in stock. In department stores, you could also use a kiosk to see how sweaters or shirts look on photorealistic models—in any color or style available.
- **Tracking systems.** While many stores know what's selling and what's not, they desperately need information on *how* people shop. Some companies are now using computer-based sensor systems to count the number of shoppers visiting various areas of their stores. Kiosks can also be used to monitor the number of times requests of a certain type are made.
- **Multifunction cash registers.** The first generation of cash registers merely rang up each sale. Then, in the 1960s, point-of-sale (POS) terminals came along to process sales electronically. The most recent crop of cash registers are multifunctional workstations that also make it possible for store personnel to check inventory at member stores, if a demanded item is not in stock (see photo).
- **Video information.** Now in the test stage at several stores are videocarts—weather-

Technology and retailing. Multifunction terminals and flat-panel displays add speed, convenience, and fun to shopping.

proof, flat-panel displays that attach onto the backs of supermarket carts (see photo). When the cart enters a particular aisle, the screen picks up data from a transmitter and displays information about nearby products. At the checkout counter, the video cart also provides information on news and sports to keep shoppers from getting bored. Electronic, flat-panel shelf tags are now also being tried out in a number of stores to keep prices up to date and, at the push of a button, provide such data as cost per serving and coupon discounts.

- **Virtual reality.** Perhaps the ultimate in shopping—though still many years away—is the virtual-reality store. The customer will don a special pair of goggles and gloves and will then be sent through a magical-mystery tour of a shopping experience without ever leaving home. Virtual reality was covered in the Chapter 2 Tomorrow box.

FIGURE 5-18

A UPC code. The digit to the left denotes the product category; the numbers below identify the manufacturer and product.

Another common application of optical characters is in billing operations, such as the processing of insurance and utility bills.

Optical Codes The most widely used type of *optical code* is the **bar code,** and the most familiar bar code is the *universal product code (UPC)* commonly found on packaged goods in supermarkets (see Figure 5-18). Because they enable immediate recording of purchases, bar codes also fall into the category of POS systems.

Bar codes such as the UPC often consist of several vertical bars of varying widths. Information in the code describes the product and identifies the manufacturer. Bar codes can be read either by passing a wand or gun containing a scanner over the coded label or by sending the item past a fixed scanning station (see Figure 5-19). Using the data from the code, the terminal/cash register in a retailing application can identify the item, look up its latest price, and print the information on a receipt such as the one in Figure 5-17. The UPC has been in use since 1973, and currently more than 80 percent of the products sold in supermarkets carry it.

Image Scanners

Image scanners, such as those in Figure 5-20, are used to digitize images of photographs, drawings, and documents into computer storage. Many image scanners sold for PCs scan at a resolution of 300 dpi. As you might expect, the more dots the computer uses to store the image, the better the resolution will be when the image is finally output. Typeset-quality imaging, available

FIGURE 5-19

Bar code applications. Bar codes are useful in environments in which products need to be quickly and accurately identified. (a) Supermarket scanning station with scanning bed. (b) Red Cross worker using a scanning wand to identify a blood sample. (c) Librarian using a scanning gun to input book information.

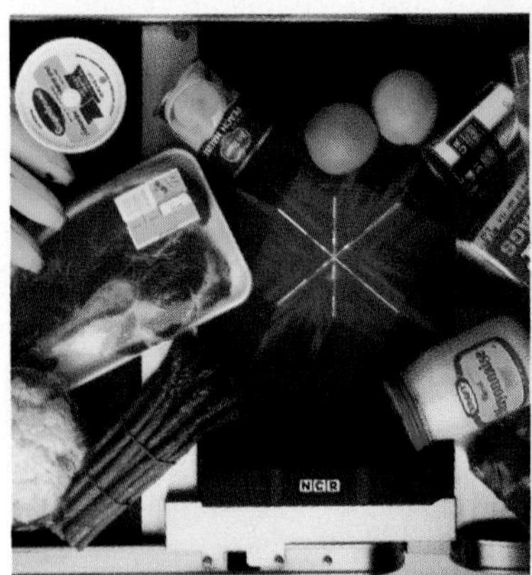

(a)

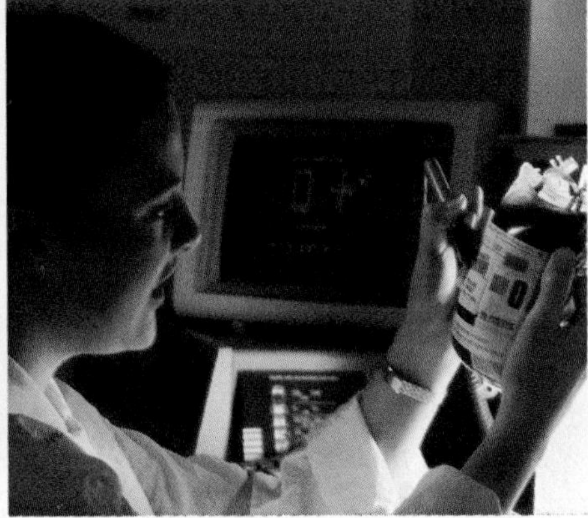

(b)

(c)

FIGURE 5-20

Image scanners. Image scanners are used to digitize images of photographs, drawings, and documents into computer memory. (a) Page scanner. (b) Hand-held scanner.

(a)

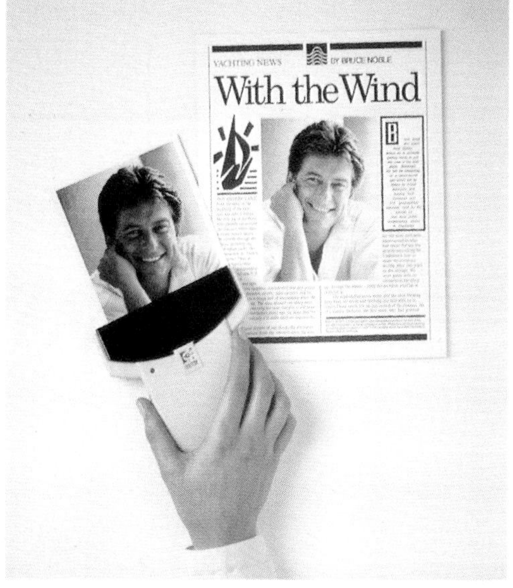

(b)

through professional print shops, generally starts at a resolution of about 1,000 dpi.

Many image scanners are "dumb," meaning that they can't recognize any of the text they read. "Intelligent" image scanners, on the other hand, are accompanied by optical character recognition (OCR) software, which enables them to recognize as well as read characters. Thus, a person with an OCR-capable image scanner can later edit any text on a standard word processor once it is read in. Although such software packages allow only a limited number of fonts to be read, many of them contain routines that enable the scanners to learn new fonts.

Bar code.
A machine-readable code consisting of sets of bars of varying widths.

Image scanner.
A device that can "read" into memory a hard-copy image such as a text page, photograph, map, or drawing.

Magnetic Ink Character Recognition (MICR)

Magnetic ink character recognition (MICR) is a technology confined almost exclusively to the banking industry, where it is used for processing checks in high volume (see Figure 5-21). Figure 5-21a illustrates a check that has been encoded with MICR characters. The MICR characters are contained on the bottom line of the check. The characters at the bottom left of the check are preprinted and contain identifying information, including the issuing bank and the customer's account number. The characters at the bottom right show the amount of the check and are imprinted by an operator after the check has been cashed. The standard font adopted by the industry contains only 14 characters—the ten decimal digits (0 through 9) and four special symbols.

Magnetic ink character recognition (MICR).
A technology that involves the processing of checks inscribed with special characters set in a special magnetic ink.

FIGURE 5-21

Magnetic ink character recognition (MICR). MICR is a technology confined almost exclusively to the banking industry, where it is used for processing checks in high volume. (a) A MICR-encoded check. (b) An electronic sorter capable of processing 2,400 checks a minute.

(a)

(b)

The characters are written on the check with a special magnetic ink. As with OCR readers, a machine called a MICR reader/sorter senses the identity of a MICR-encoded character on the check by recognizing its shape. But in contrast to OCR, the characters must be magnetized in order to be sensed by the reading device; no optical recognition is used. With MICR, checks can be quickly sorted, processed, and routed to the proper banks (see Figure 5-21b).

Digitizers

A **digitizer** is a device that converts a measurement into a digital value. By being moved along a surface or, alternatively, staying stationary and having another device move along them, digitizers determine position, distance, or speed and move the cursor on the display screen accordingly. Digitizers aid source data automation because they directly collect data on events in machine-readable form. Six common types of digitizers are the mouse, light pen, joystick, trackball, crosshair cursor, and digitizing tablet.

Digitizer.
An input device that converts a measurement into a digital value.

Mouse Many people supplement keyboard operations with a **mouse,** the most widely used digitizing device (see Figure 5-22). When the mouse is moved along a flat surface, the cursor on the display screen moves correspondingly. Mice are very useful for moving the cursor rapidly from one location to another on a display screen, and for dragging images from one part of the screen to another. Using a mouse often is much faster than pressing combinations of cursor-movement keys on keyboard. Mice are especially handy when pointing to **icons** on the screen—small graphics symbols that represent commands or program options. When you use the mouse, say, to move to an icon on the display screen, you select or activate that icon by clicking a button on the mouse once or twice.

Mouse.
A device used to rapidly move a cursor around a display screen.

Icon.
A graphical image on a display screen that invokes a particular program action when activated by the operator.

Light Pen A **light pen** contains a light-sensitive cell in its tip. When the tip of the pen is placed close to the screen, the display device can identify its

Light pen.
An electrical device, resembling an ordinary pen, used to enter input.

FIGURE 5-22

Mouse input. When the mouse is moved along a flat surface, the cursor on the display screen moves correspondingly.

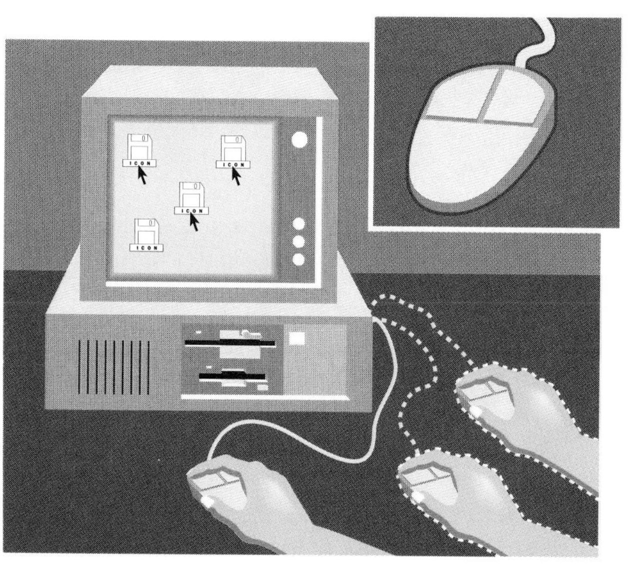

Feature 5-1

It's Showtime for Pen Computing

Applications target the "lapless" worker

In chemistry, when you add two distinct elements together, they often combine to form a third distinct element. That pretty much sums up how many new technology products see the light of day.

Take the pen computer. It essentially marries the light pen and the laptop computer. But unlike laptops, which are generally targeted to white-collar workers who need a keyboard-based unit to port from one office to the next, pen-based computers are rugged devices pitched to people on the go—those who have no use for a word processor or spreadsheet when they are "on their feet." Potential users include sales representatives, real-estate agents, police officers, doctors and nurses, insurance adjusters, store clerks, truck drivers, and inspectors—in other words, anybody that now regularly carries around a clipboard and has forms to fill out.

And the benefits don't stop there. In this age of widespread literacy problems, pen computers can also help workers who can't read English do their jobs. Even if workers can't understand what words on the screen mean, they can, with the help of co-workers, memorize collections of symbols and where they appear on the display.

Sound farfetched? Ford Motor Company's Dearborn plant doesn't think so. The facility has used pen-based computers since 1988 to record defects and repairs on newly assembled vehicles. Ford estimates that between five and ten percent of its inspectors and repairpeople cannot read. It doesn't know the number exactly because many people hide their handicap. A spokesman for the company reports that it only takes 30 minutes to train workers to use its pen-based devices.

Pen computers at work. High-tech clipboards make inroads.

Pen input comes in several possible varieties. The most straightforward is *menu selection.* Here, the user simply activates the pen every time a "selection" is to be made from a menu of choices. Next on the scale of difficulty is *signature capture.* One application for this type of pen computing occurs when an invoice is on the display and needs to be finished off with the purchaser's electronic signature. The most complicated type of pen-based computing features *handwriting recognition.* To date, the most commercially successful handwriting-recognition devices can only identify *printed* characters in a reliable fashion. And, still, it's common for a *2* and a *Z* or a *U* and *V* to be confused.

Back in the early 1980s, the introduction of the electronic spreadsheet made the personal computer a fixture in corporations. Word processing helped out considerably, too. At this point in time, it's too early in the game to predict whether a similar "killer application" will arise to make pen-based computing a fixture in corporate life or if it will become another flash in the pan of experimental technology.

position. Some pens are even equipped with a remote-control press-button feature so that when the button is clicked, the computer system flips forward or backward to successive-page-length images on the display screen. Recently, as discussed in Feature 5-1, pen-based computing has become a very hot area. Display devices that are designed to allow a finger rather than a light pen to

FIGURE 5-23

Touch screen devices. Touch screens are ideal for (a) manufacturing applications, where workers aren't touch typists and may at times be wearing gloves and (b) information kiosks, where people can't be assumed to be computer literate.

(a)

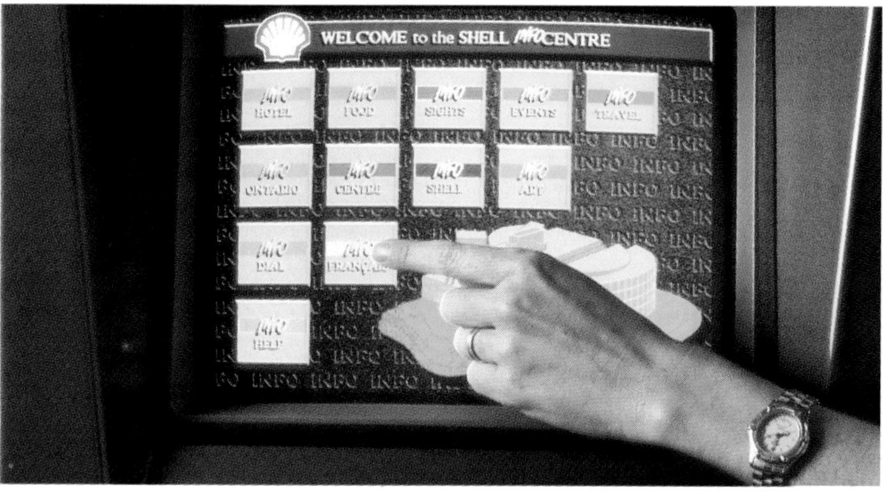

(b)

activate the screen are commonly called **touch-screen devices** (see Figure 5-23).

Touch-screen device. A display device that can be activated by touching a finger to the screen.

Joystick A **joystick** (see Figure 5-24a), which looks like a car's stick shift, is often used for computer games and for computer-aided design (CAD) work. With many joysticks, the speed at which they move and the distance they travel determine the speed and distance traveled by the screen cursor. Today, some electronic games are using gloves with built-in sensors in place of joysticks, enabling the computer to directly detect hand movements.

Joystick. An input device that resembles a car's stick shift.

Trackball.
A cursor-movement device that consists of a sphere, with only the top of the sphere exposed outside its case.

Trackball A **trackball** (see Figure 5-24b) consists of a sphere in a case, with only the top of the sphere exposed. The screen cursor travels in whatever direction the operator spins the sphere. A trackball is merely a mouse turned upside down.

Crosshair cursor.
A digitizing device that is often moved over hard-copy images of maps and drawings to enter them.

Crosshair Cursor A **crosshair cursor** (Figure 5-24c) can be moved over hard-copy images of maps, survey photos, and even large drawings. The image is digitized into the computer system's memory as the cursor passes over it. Using a keypad on the cursor, the operator can enter supplementary information into the memory. With maps, for example, features such as rivers, roads, and buildings may be scanned with the crosshair and any identifying labels keyed in from the pad. Once the maps are in digital form, the operator can call them up for display on the screen and modify them.

Digitizing tablet.
A digitizer that consists of a flat board and a device that traces over the board, storing the traced pattern in computer memory.

Digitizing Tablet A **digitizing tablet** usually employs either a crosshair cursor or a penlike stylus. The operator uses one or the other of these devices to trace over the flat tablet (Figure 5-24c). You can think of the tablet as a matrix of thousands of tiny dots. Each dot has a machine address. When you trace a line on the tablet, the stylus or cursor passes over some of the dots, causing their status in computer memory to change from a 0-state to a 1-state. When the drawing is complete, it is stored in digital form as a large matrix of 0s and 1s and may be recalled at any time.

FIGURE 5-24

Digitizers. The wide variety of digitizing devices on the market today powerfully illustrates the large number of ways it is possible for ordinary users to input data at their desk tops. (a) Joystick. (b) Trackball. (c) Digitizing tablet with crosshair cursor.

(a)

(b)

(c)

User Solution 5-2

Zipping the Mail Along with Voice Recognition

The U.S. Postal Service is benefiting in big ways from the introduction of voice technology in several of its branches. Most addresses within the United States fall into distribution zones. When letters or packages arrive at a post office, they have to be manually sorted into the right zone so they can be given to the proper truck or postal-delivery person for distribution. Sorting has traditionally been handled by postal operators who have memorized addresses and the zones they fall into. Memorizing often requires several weeks of training, and addresses that are forgotten have to be keyed into a computer system for the zone. With voice-recognition equipment, training and keying are unnecessary. The operator merely speaks the address into the headset and the computer supplies the zone. Also, both hands are always free for manipulating mail.

Voice-Input Devices

Machines that can convert spoken words into digital form for computer storage and processing are known as **voice-input devices.** If you stop to think about how complicated the interpretation of a spoken word can be for humans, you can realize how tricky it is to design a voice-input device to do essentially the same thing. Two people may pronounce the same word differently because of accents, personal styles of speech, and the unique quality of each person's voice. Even the same person can pronounce words differently at various times—when eating, for instance, or when under the influence of a cold. Moreover, in listening to others, we not only ignore irrelevant background noises but decode sentence fragments.

Voice-input device. A device capable of recognizing the human voice.

Equipment designers have tried to overcome these obstacles in a number of ways. Some voice-input devices are designed to be "trained" by users, who repeat words until the machines know their voices. These devices can also screen out background noise. Unfortunately, most voice-input devices can recognize only a limited number of isolated words and not whole sentences composed of continous speech. Thus, the complexity of the messages to which they can respond is quite limited.

Still, the possible applications of this technology are exciting. Imagine yourself speaking into a microphone while a printer automatically types your words. Such a system is, in fact, commercially available today; however, the number of words the computer can "understand" is extremely limited, typically under 1,000. Experts say that voice-actuated word processing will require recognition of at least 10,000 words.

The use of a voice-input system to help the post office sort mail is the subject of User Solution 5-2.

FIGURE 5-25

Smart card. The VISA SuperSmart Card shown here contains a keyboard and tiny display to complement its CPU and memory.

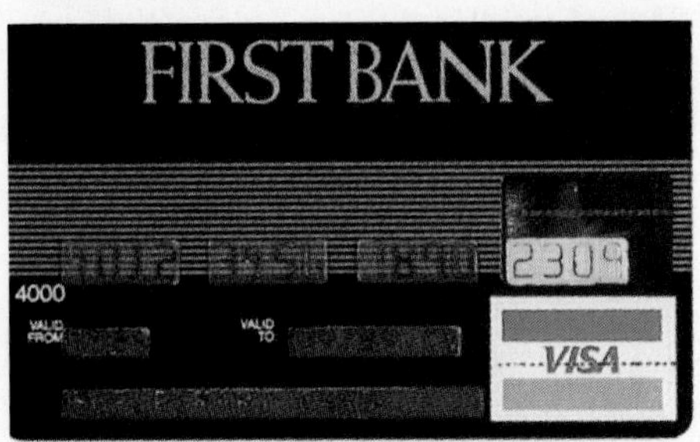

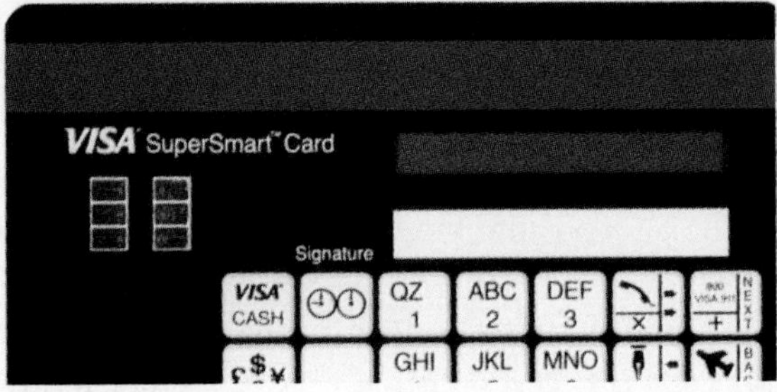

Handwriting Recognition Devices

Handwriting recognition device.
A device that can identify handwritten characters.

Handwriting recognition devices generally consist of a flat-screen display tablet and a penlike stylus (see Feature 5-1). Theoretically, as users write words and numbers on the tablet, they are machine recognized. Practically speaking, however, handwriting recognition devices are still in the pioneering stage, and virtually all systems commercially available today can recognize only hand-printed characters. That computer systems have difficulty recognizing characters should not strike you as surprising. After all, if humans have difficulty reading each others' handwriting, how can computers be programmed to fare much better?

Closely related to handwriting recognition devices are devices that electronically capture signatures. While this latter class of hardware can input and store handwritten characters, it cannot identify the characters.

Smart Cards

Smart card.
A credit-card-sized plastic card with storage and a microprocessor.

Smart cards are credit-card-sized pieces of plastic that contain, at a minimum, a microprocessor chip and a memory (see Figure 5-25). The memory capacity may be as small as a few thousand characters or as large as a few million. Still in the pioneering stage, smart cards are most often used to make electronic purchases or to transfer funds between accounts—say, between the cardholder's account and the account at a bank or credit card company.

The uses for smart cards abound. A university issuing such cards could use them to allow students access to grade or financial data. Smart cards also could be useful for making phone calls; a cardholder would have an electronic record of all phone calls made—useful for tax and billing purposes—right on the card. In security applications, such a card could carry a digitized version of a fingerprint or voice and thereby serve as an electronic passkey, allowing an authorized user into restricted areas or access to a sensitive computer network. In some areas, smart cards are now being tried out at toll booths. The card is mounted in a specific place in the front window area of the car and scanned electronically by a transmitter as the cardholder cruises by. Then the cardholder's account is debited for the toll.

Special-Purpose Output Equipment

In this section, we will consider output devices that are appropriate for specialized uses. The technologies we will describe are plotters, voice-output devices, film recorders, and computer-output microfilm (COM).

Plotters

A **plotter** is an output device that is primarily used to produce charts, drawings, maps, three-dimensional illustrations, and other forms of hard copy. The two most common types of plotters are pen plotters and electrostatic plotters.

Plotter.
An output device used for printing graphs and diagrams.

A *pen plotter* (see Figure 5-26a) is an output device that employs pens, which create images by moving across the paper surface. Watching these machines draw is an experience and always attracts interest among people who are seeing them for the first time. The plotter looks like a mechanical artist working in fast motion. As the machine switches colors and begins new patterns, the audience is hard put to guess what the plotter will do next. Many pen plotters can accept either standard fiber-tipped pens or, if the highest possible output quality is desired, high-precision, technical drafting pens.

Electrostatic plotters (see Figure 5-26b) are also very popular for graphics output. These devices work with a toner bed similar to that of a copying machine, but instead of light they use a matrix of tiny wires to charge the paper with electricity. When the charged paper passes over the toner, the toner adheres to it and produces an image. Electrostatic plotters are relatively fast, but their output quality is lower than that of pen plotters. Nonetheless, the output quality of electrostatic devices is improving, and many industry experts expect them to eventually replace the slower, mechanically intensive pen plotters.

Whether they employ pens or electrostatic printing, plotters are of either the flatbed or drum type. A *flatbed plotter,* such as the one in Figure 5-26a, resembles a flat drafting board. By contrast, *drum plotters,* such as the one in Figure 5-26b, draw on paper that is rolled onto a drumlike mechanism.

Voice-Output Devices

For a number of years, computers have been able to communicate with users, after a fashion, by "speaking" to them. How often have you dialed a phone number only to hear, "We're sorry, the number you are trying to reach,

FIGURE 5-26

Plotters. Plotters are designed to produce charts, drawings, maps, and other forms of graphical hard copy. (a) Flatbed pen plotter. (b) Electrostatic drum plotter.

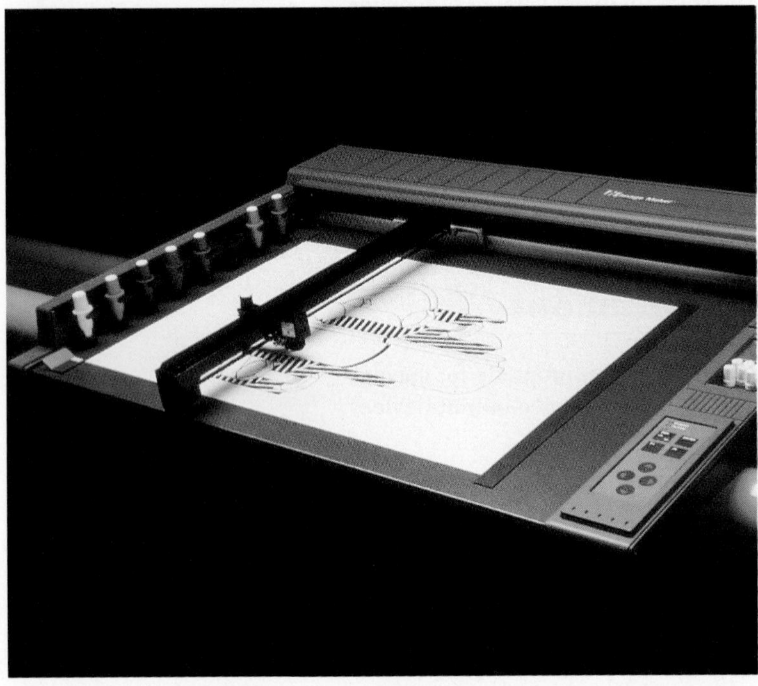

(a)

(b)

Voice-output device. A device that enables the computer system to produce spoken output.

774-0202, is no longer in service," or "The time is 6:15 . . . the downtown temperature is 75 degrees"? **Voice-output devices,** the machines responsible for such messages, convert digital data in storage into spoken messages. These messages may be constructed as needed from a file of prerecorded words, or they may be synthesized using other techniques.

Computerized voice output is also used extensively at airline terminals to broadcast information about flight departures and arrivals, in the securities business to quote the prices of stocks and bonds, and in the supermarket industry to announce descriptions and prices of items as they are scanned. Voice output has great potential in any company with employees who do little else all day but, say, give out balances and status reports.

Currently one of the main shortcomings of this technology is that the number of potential messages is limited if the system must create them extemporaneously. Most voice-output devices have a vocabulary on the order of a few hundred words and a limited ability to combine words dynamically to form intelligible sentences. As a result, these devices are most useful when short messages are required—a telephone number, a bank balance, a price, and so on.

Film Recorders

Film recorders are cameralike devices that capture high-resolution, computer-generated images directly onto 35mm slides, transparencies, and other film media. Just a few years ago, film recorders served only large computers, with which they were used for applications such as art, medical imaging, and scientific CAD work. Today they are increasingly being used with PCs for applications such as spicing up corporate business meetings or client presentations with slide shows. Some experts predict that such computer-generated slides will soon account for a large percentage of all business slides made. Because film recorders, like cameras, are "dumb" and need not recognize an image in order to record it, they can easily transfer onto film virtually any image that can be captured on a display screen. Most of the images in Window 2 were produced on film recorders, which by far provide the highest resolution of any of the output devices discussed in this chapter.

Film recorder.
A cameralike device that captures computer output onto film.

Computer Output Microfilm (COM)

Computer output microfilm (COM) is a way of placing computer output on microfilm media, typically either a *microfilm reel* or *microfiche card.* Microfilming can result in tremendous savings in paper costs, storage space, the mailing of document images, and handling. For example, a 4-by-6-inch microfiche card can contain the equivalent of 270 printed pages. COM is particulary useful for organizations that must keep massive files of information that do not need to be updated. It's also useful for organizations that need to manipulate large amounts of data but find fast methods of online access too costly. In recent years, the near monopoly once held by COM for efficient document storage and retrieval has been seriously challenged by optical disks.

Computer output microfilm (COM).
A term that refers to reducing computer output to microscopic form and putting it on photosensitive film.

Summary and Key Terms

A wide variety of input and output devices is available in today's marketplace.

Input and Output Input and output devices enable people and computers to communicate. **Input devices** convert data and programs into a form that the CPU will understand. **Output devices** convert computer-processed information into a form that people will comprehend.

Output devices produce results in either hard copy or soft copy form. The term **hard copy** generally refers to output that has been recorded into a *permanent* form onto a medium such as paper or microfilm. The term **soft copy,** in contrast, generally refers to display output, which is *temporary.*

Keyboards For most people, a computer system would be useless without a **keyboard,** which is often the main vehicle for input. Keyboards vary tremendously in terms of such factors as number of keys, key arrangement, types of special keys, and touch. Most computer keyboards offer several *function keys*—labeled F1, F2, and so on—that can be used to activate single commands or entire computer programs. Usually a *numeric keypad* is also present that allows numbers to be keyed in faster.

Display Devices **Display devices** are peripheral devices that contain a televisionlike viewing screen. Most display devices fall into one of two categories: monitors and display terminals. A **monitor** is an output device that consists of only the viewing screen. A **display terminal** is an input/output communications workstation that consists of a screen for output and a keyboard for input. As each key on the keyboard is depressed, the corresponding character representation of the key appears on the display screen at the **cursor** position.

One common way to classify display devices is according to whether they are monochrome or color. *Monochrome* display devices output using a single foreground color, whereas *color* display devices often are capable of outputting in eight or more colors.

Most display devices on the market today use a large picture-tube element similar to those found inside standard TV sets. These devices are called **CRTs (cathode-ray tubes).** Recently, slim-profile devices called **flat-panel displays** have also become available.

A key characteristic of any display device is *resolution,* or the sharpness of the screen image. On many display devices, resolution is measured by the number of dots, or **pixels,** on the screen. With **bit mapping,** the operator can control each pixel on the screen.

Printers Unlike display devices, **printers** produce hard-copy output. *Low-speed printers* output one character at a time. Because of their relatively low cost, they are popular units for small computer systems. *High-speed printers,* which can output either a line or a page at a time, are popular for larger computer systems.

All printers use either an impact or a nonimpact printing technology. In **impact printing,** a hammer strikes the paper or ribbon to form characters. A **solid-font mechanism** is an impact device that produces fully formed characters like those a typewriter creates. Most low-speed printers in use today employ a print head that's an **impact dot-matrix mechanism,** which constructs printed characters out of a series of closely packed dots. **Nonimpact printing,** which outputs dot-matrix characters, uses a variety of techniques to form printed images. The most popular nonimpact printing methods today use *electro-thermal, thermal-transfer, ink-jet,* and *laser* technologies.

The printers most commonly found on microcomputer systems are low-speed devices. Although impact dot-matrix printers are still the most widely used devices, relatively high-speed laser printers have become especially popular in the last few years. Laser printers produce letter-quality output that rivals that of solid-font printers, quickly generate presentation graphics for reports and meetings, and enable certain publishing functions to be performed on a desktop.

Most of the printing done on large computer systems is accomplished by high-speed printers. High-speed printers fall into one of two major categories; **line printers,** which produce a line of output at a time, and **page printers,** which produce a page of output at a time.

Source Data Automation **Source data automation** refers to technologies for collecting data in machine-readable form at their point of origin. Among these technologies are optical character recognition (OCR), magnetic ink character recognition (MICR), digitizing, image scanning, voice input, handwriting recognition, and smart cards.

Optical character recognition (OCR) refers to a wide range of optical-scanning procedures and equipment designed for machine recognition of marks, characters, and codes. *Optical marks* are most frequently used in test-taking situations in which students darken bubbles on special forms to show responses. Probably the best-known use of *optical characters* is in the **point-of-sale (POS) systems** widely used at checkout stations in stores. In many of these systems, the characters on the price tag are coded in a special font readable by both machines and humans. Some POS systems use *optical codes,* such as **bar codes.** The most widely used bar code is the *universal product code (UPC),* which appears on the labels of most packaged supermarket goods.

An **image scanner** is used to input images such as photographs, drawings, and documents into computer storage. In the case of text documents, some image scanners are accompanied by software that enables the scanners to recognize the inputted characters.

Magnetic ink character recognition (MICR) is a technology confined almost exclusively to the banking industry. MICR characters, preprinted on bank checks, enable the checks to be rapidly sorted, processed, and routed to the proper banks.

A **digitizer** is an input device that converts a measurement into a digital value. One of the most widely used digitizers is the **mouse,** which, when rolled along a flat surface, moves the screen cursor accordingly. Mice are especially handy when pointing to **icons** on the screen. Some other widely used digitizing devices are the **light pen, joystick, trackball, crosshair cursor,** and **digitizing tablet.** Display devices that are designed to allow a finger rather than a light pen to activate the screen are commonly called **touch-screen devices.**

Voice-input devices enable computer systems to recognize the spoken word. Voice-input technologies have tremendous work-saving potential but have been slow to mature because of their relative complexity.

Handwriting recognition devices generally consist of a flat-screen display tablet and a penlike stylus. Practically speaking, handwriting recognition devices are still in the pioneering stage, and virtually all systems commercially available today can recognize only hand-printed characters.

Smart cards are credit-card sized pieces of plastic that contain a microprocessor chip and a memory.

Special-Purpose Output Equipment A number of special-purpose output devices exist for a variety of information processing applications. Among these are plotters, voice-output devices, film recorders and computer output microfilm (COM) equipment.

A **plotter** is an output device that is used primarily to produce graphic output such as charts, maps, and engineering drawings. The two most common types of plotters are *pen plotters,* which use drawing pens to create images, and *electrostatic plotters,* which create images through electrostatic charges. Whether they employ pens or electrostatic charges, plotters are of either the flatbed or the drum type. A *flatbed plotter* uses a drawing surface that resembles a drafting table. A *drum plotter* draws on a cylindrically backed surface.

Voice-output devices enable computer systems to compose intelligible spoken messages from digitally stored words and phrases.

Film recorders are cameralike devices that are used to capture computer-generated images directly onto 35mm slides, transparencies, and other film media. Virtually any image that can be captured on a display screen can be output onto film.

Computer output microfilm (COM) is a way of placing computer output on microfilm media such as microfilm reels or microfiche cards. COM can result in savings in paper costs, storage space, and handling.

Review Exercises

Fill-in Questions

1. The term ______________ generally refers to output that has been recorded onto a medium such as paper or film.
2. Resolution on a display screen is measured by the number of dots, or ______________.
3. A highlighted position on a display screen indicating where the next character the operator types in will be placed is called a(n) ______________.
4. A display device that outputs images in a single foreground color is known as a(n) ______________ display.
5. High-quality dot-matrix printing is sometimes called ______________ (NLQ) printing.
6. A(n) ______________ printer heats ink from a wax-based ribbon onto paper.
7. A(n) ______________ printer sprays small droplets of electrically charged ink onto paper to form images.
8. Two types of pen plotters are ______________ and ______________ plotters.
9. A display device in which all screen pixels can be controlled by the operator is called ______________.
10. A(n) ______________ is a cameralike device used to capture computer-generated images directly onto 35mm slides.

Matching Questions

Match each term with the description that fits best.

a. crosshair cursor	d. UPC	g. plotter
b. OCR	e. MICR	h. mouse
c. POS	f. COM	

___ 1. Used almost exclusively by the banking industry.

___ 2. Refers to microfilmed output.

____ 3. A type of output device used to produce graphical images on paper with pens.

____ 4. Refers to a collection of different technologies used for optical recognition of marks, characters, and codes.

____ 5. A code that is prominent on the packaging of most supermarket goods.

____ 6. A device that would be useful for digitizing a map into computer storage.

____ 7. A device used to move the cursor rapidly around the display screen.

____ 8. Refers to the use of electronic cash registers, optical scanning devices, and so forth in retail establishments.

Discussion Questions

1. List several types of input and output devices. State whether each device is used for input, output, or both.
2. Identify several ways in which display devices differ.
3. Name some hardware devices that are used in conjunction with display devices for entering data into the computer system.
4. In what major respects do printers differ?
5. What is source data automation, and why is it significant?
6. How does MICR differ from OCR?
7. What are the limitations of voice-input and voice-output devices?
8. What is the difference between VGA and Super VGA?

Critical Thinking Questions

1. A page of typed text that is created and saved with a word processor takes up a different amount of storage than a copy of that same page read by a scanner. Why do you think this is so? Which would take up more space?
2. Some people predicted years ago that there would never be a significant market for color CRTs among office workers. This prediction proved dead wrong. What do you think motivated this prediction and why would you guess it proved wrong?
3. The president of J.C. Penney has stated that the leading retailers in the future will be those who make the best use of information processing technologies. Do you agree with this point of view? Explain why or why not.

The Electronic Canvas

A Peek at the Leading Edge in Computer Output

Probably nothing exemplifies the rapid advances made in computer output over the last decade better than the field of computer art. Early computer artists were scientists with a keen knowledge of both computers and mathematical modeling, and they worked on large, general-purpose computers. As the potential and demand for computer-generated art in business-related fields such as advertising, publishing, and movie production evolved, specialized hardware and software for noncomputer professionals began to emerge. The field of computer art is still in the pioneering stage, and one can only guess what the leading edge will look like ten years from now.

1. An image created with a painting package. The computer can be used as a tool for rendering art from scratch or for reading images into storage with a scanner and treating them with special effects at a display.

2

2–3. Two watercolors produced with a painting package.

3

Special Effects

Many art packages have an assortment of drawing and/or painting tools that enable artists to imitate traditional art forms, creating images that look as if they were produced with pastels or watercolors, were sketched, or were painted with oils.

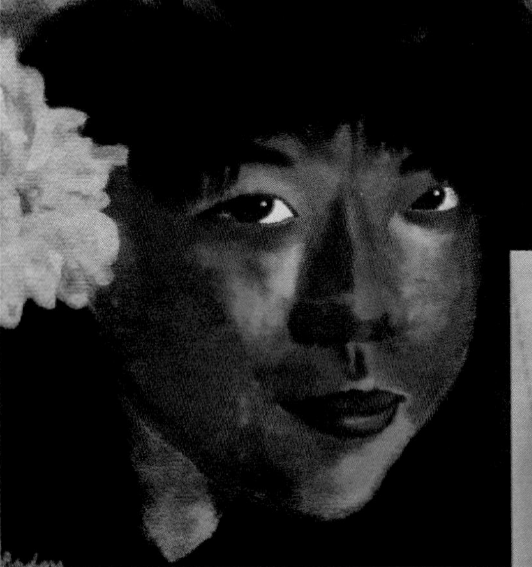

4. Using a painting package to impart an oil-painting effect.

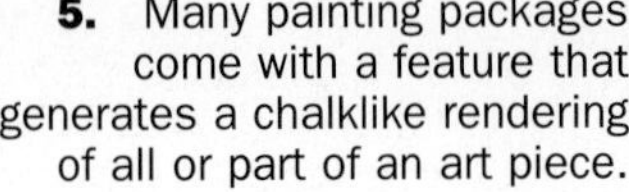

5. Many painting packages come with a feature that generates a chalklike rendering of all or part of an art piece.

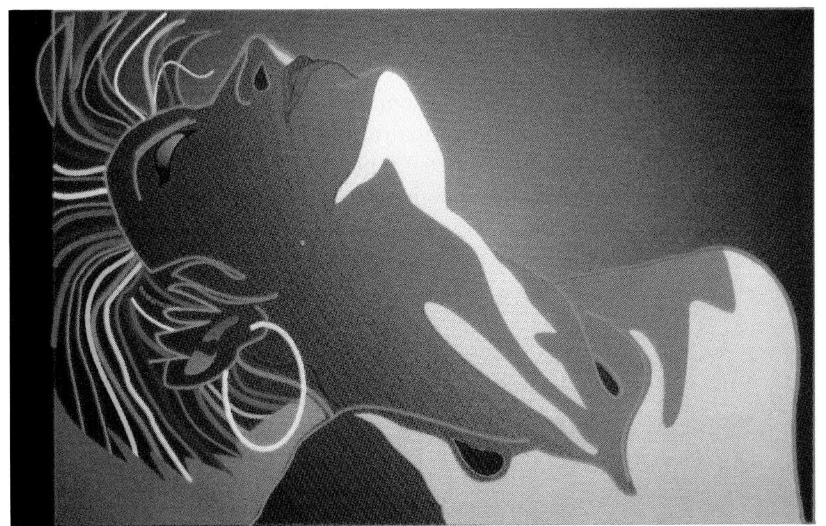

6

7

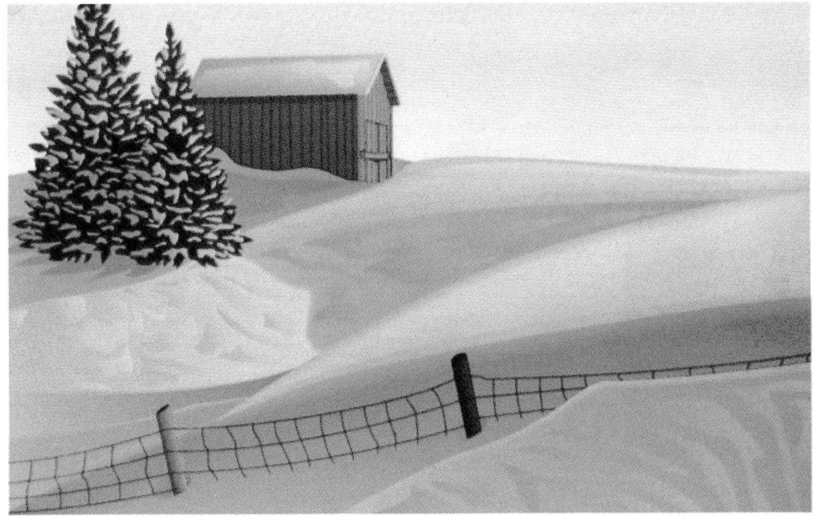

8

6–8. Airbrushing is a special effect commonly found in art packages. It allows a color gradient to be applied to a defined surface—like a background, sky, or snow bank—making it look more natural.

Algorithmic Art

Many forms of computer art are based upon complex mathematical algorithms. These algorithms allow the artist to specify formulas that create sophisticated geometric shapes and curious random patterns. Art pieces produced in this way are often somewhat "accidental," in that the artist has partly left the computer in charge of generating images.

9

10

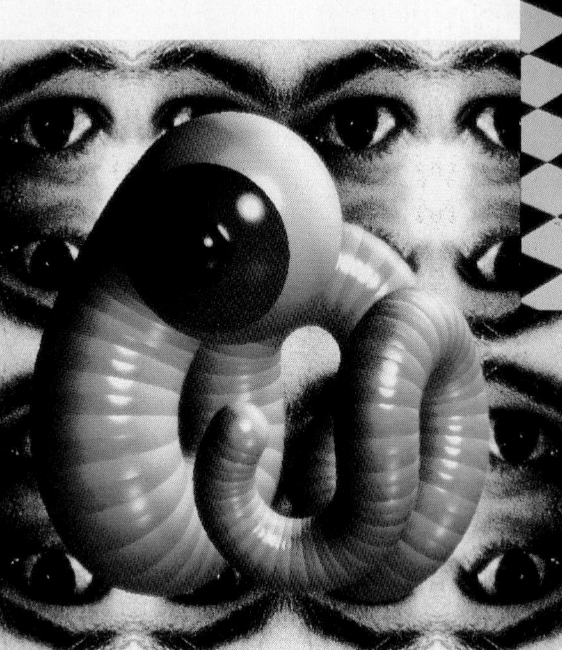

11

9–11. The art of Clifford Pickover—of IBM's Thomas J. Watson Research Center—often mimics patterns and forms found in nature.

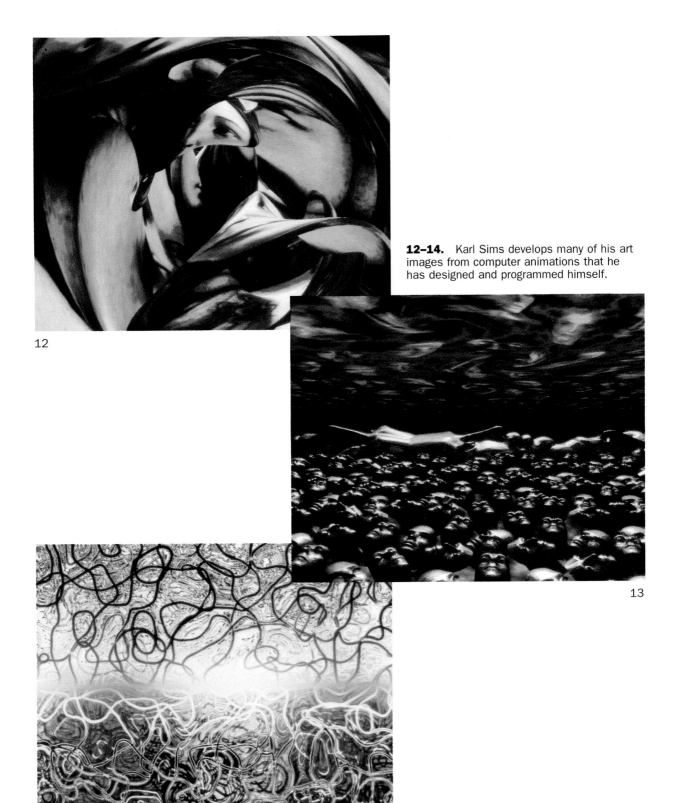

12

12–14. Karl Sims develops many of his art images from computer animations that he has designed and programmed himself.

13

14

15

16

15–17. Photorealistic images are often produced using special art packages that work in three dimensions and have natural-lighting tools.

17

18. The computer is often used as a tool to enhance and size photographs.

18

Photorealism

Computers today are capable of creating very high-resolution images that look as though they were captured with a camera.

Commercial Art

Today, usually the most cost-effective way to produce art for commercial purposes is by computer. Shown here is just a small sampling of applications employed in the commercial art field.

19

19–20. Holiday cards and posters are natural outlets for computer-produced art.

21. Covers for games, book jackets, and CD-album jackets are often designed by computer.

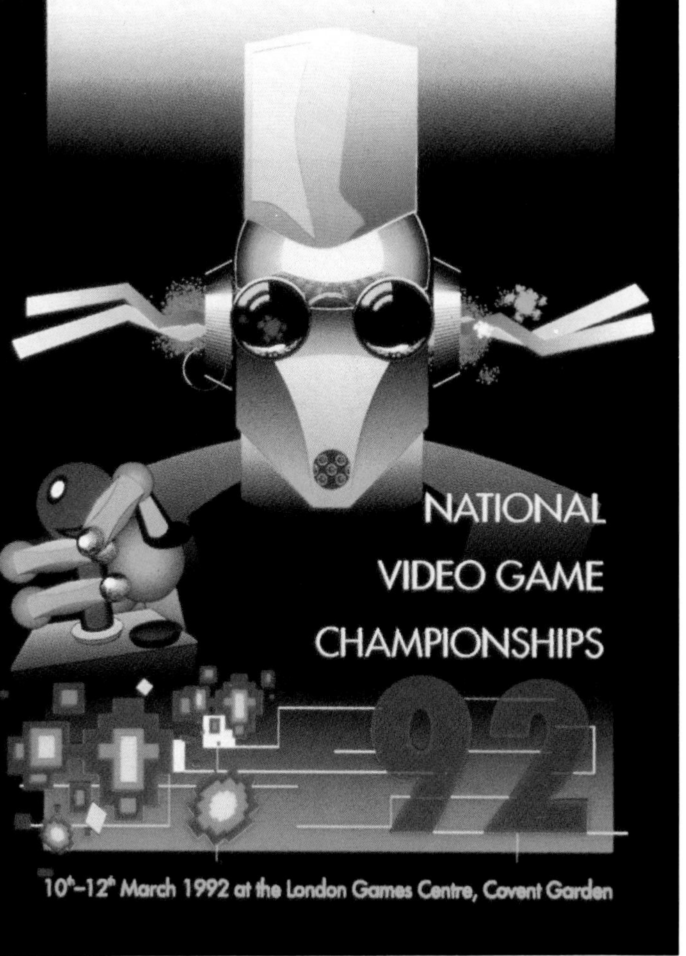

20

22

23

22–23. A set of stamps can be quickly developed and redesigned by computer technology.

M O D U L E C

SUPPORT SYSTEMS

In this module we examine two areas that play support roles in a computer system—telecommunications and systems software.

Telecommunications, covered in Chapter 6, refers to applications that involve data traveling over distances, as well as the hardware and software that enable this to be done. For instance, special hardware devices send data over ordinary phone lines, and software is required to ensure that the receiving devices understand exactly what the sending devices are communicating. Because companies need to transmit and receive up-to-date information to operate successfully in today's highly competitive world, telecommunications is a top priority on managers' agendas.

Systems software, the topic of Chapter 7, refers to the programs that enable applications software to run on hardware devices. Systems software allows you to start up your computer system, summon applications programs so that you can work on them, recover lost files, reorganize disk storage, and translate applications software into the machine language native to your computer. Everybody who uses a computer system must in some way interact with systems software.

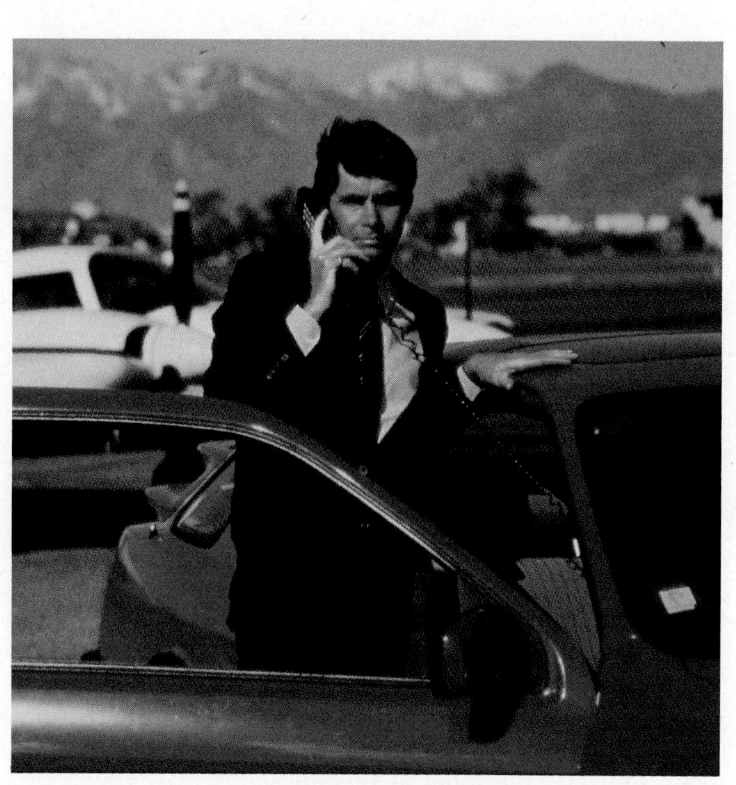

TELECOMMUNICATIONS

6

What's hot in the world of telecommunications? As discussed in Chapter 6, wireless technology, which enables electronic data to be sent from and received virtually anywhere. Wireless technology has changed the way many companies do business and made it possible for developing countries to compete economically.

OUTLINE

Overview

Telecommunications Applications

Communications Media
- Types of Media
- Media Speed
- Media Mode
- Media Signal
- Parallel versus Serial Transmission
- Asynchronous versus Synchronous Transmission

Wide Area Networks and Local Networks
- Wide Area Networks
- Local Networks

Network Topologies

Communications among Devices
- Protocols
- Hardware for Managing Communications Traffic

LEARNING OBJECTIVES

After completing this chapter, you will be able to:

1. Describe several uses of telecommunications technology.
2. Identify the hardware and software components of a telecommunications system.
3. Describe various types of communications media and explain how messages can be sent over them.
4. Identify some types of communications services and network facilities that organizations may acquire.
5. Explain the conventions that devices use to communicate with one another.
6. Describe some of the strategies used to manage networks.

Overview

Telecommunications. A term that refers to transmitting data over a distance.

Telecommunications, or *telecom,* refers to communication over a distance—over phone lines, via privately owned cable, or by satellite, for instance. Today, telecommunications technologies are integrated in a variety of ways into many organizations' routine operations. Through telecommunications, for example, a marketing manager at company headquarters can instantly receive information on inventories from a warehouse at another location and then transmit that information to a division office across the country or even across the globe. Or a purchasing agent on the 25th floor of an office building can use a personal computer workstation to call up the status of a purchase order stored on the mainframe system located in the building's basement. Later, the agent can use

FIGURE 6-1

Distributed processing: trailing a VISA transaction. (a) In Chicago, a VISA card is used to pay for a $1,295 computer. (b) The transaction data travel by satellite or by ground to a processing center in New Jersey. (c) Because the transaction tops $50, it is routed to a computer in Atlanta for closer scrutiny. (d) The computer in Atlanta sends the transaction to California for processing. (e) The California computer finds that the card was issued by a Portland bank and checks that bank's computer system to see if the transaction request should be approved or denied. The answer retraces the same path back to the store. The total elapsed time of the transaction is 15 seconds.

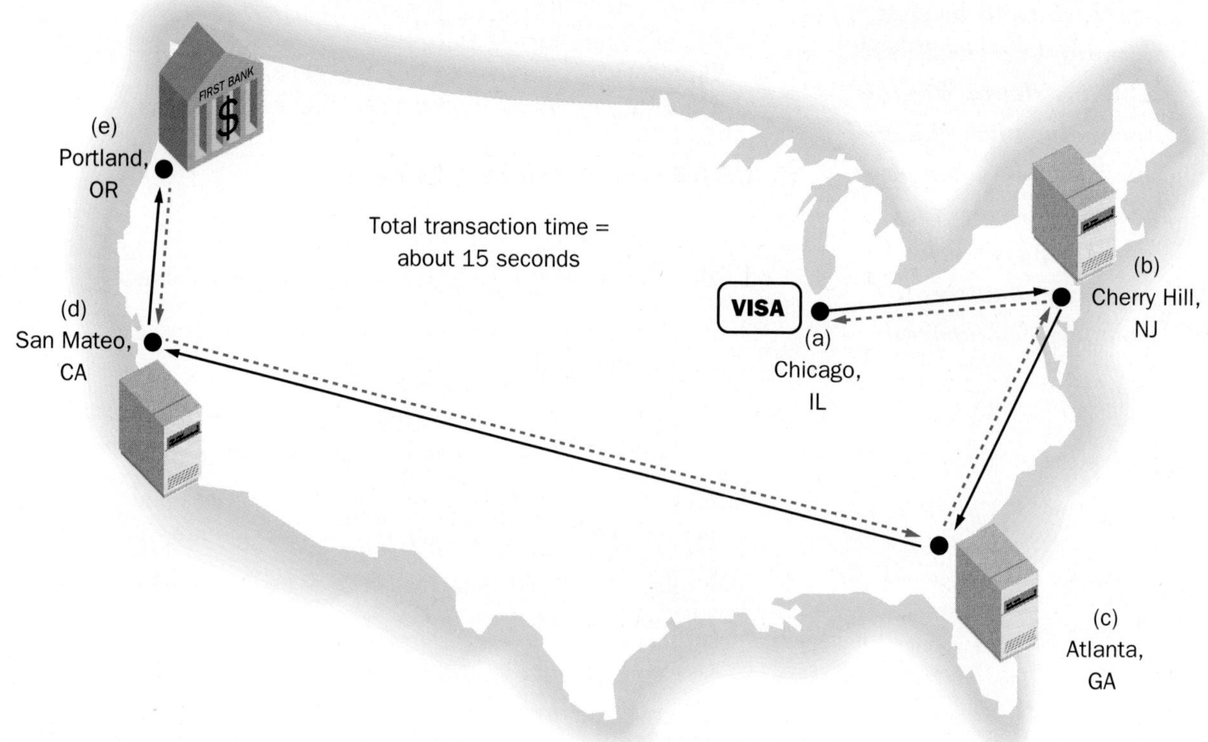

User Solution 6-1

Speeding Products to Market with Networks

At TRW's Ross Gear Division, gears, linkages, and related components for trucks are designed and manufactured. A computer network enables professionals to electronically collaborate on engineering drawings, thereby getting work done faster and reducing the time between a product's conception and the day it goes on the market. Such speed often translates into a competitive advantage for TRW. The network now in place stores product designs on a mainframe-based system. Engineers can download the designs onto their local PC workstations. There, new drawings can be quickly cut and pasted out of old ones, sent back to the mainframe, and electronically accessed locally or remotely by coworkers and clients.

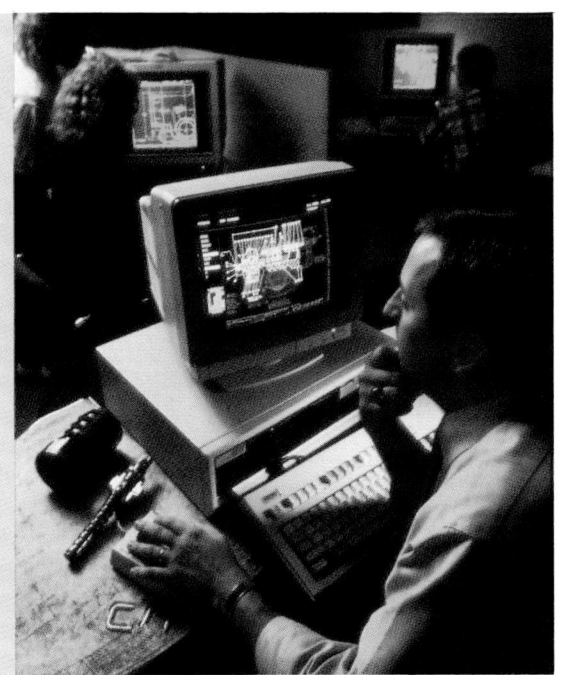

the same workstation to dial up a computer owned by a supplier, 1,000 miles away, and get a list of prices. User Solution 6-1 provides a good example of how companies are increasingly relying on telecommunications to keep competitive.

In this chapter, we'll look first at several business applications of telecommunications. Then we'll consider how data are sent over distances. We'll begin by describing the media that carry data, such as phone lines and microwaves, as well as the types of signals that encode the data. Next, we'll discuss the various ways in which people or organizations can get the resources they need to transmit data. Finally, we'll examine several issues concerning the management of telecommunications traffic.

Telecommunications Applications

Today a wide variety of important business applications involve telecommunications. Here we'll briefly discuss several.

Distributed Transaction Processing At one time, transaction processing operations such as accounts receivable and order entry were totally centralized. As communications systems made it possible to *distribute* workloads to multiple sites, many organizations modified their systems accordingly. The airlines' passenger reservation system is one noteworthy example; thousands of agents located across the globe use display terminals or microcomputer workstations to tap into computerized databases located elsewhere that contain flight, hotel, and rental-car information. While a computer in, say, Chicago is processing a Cerritos, California, agent's request for flight information, that same agent may be processing a ticket for another client locally. Credit-card systems, such as the one for VISA shown in Figure 6-1, are also good examples of distributed

FIGURE 6-2

Electronic data interchange. Electronic data interchange enables companies to electronically exchange documents such as purchase orders and bills.

transaction processing. Once a store clerk inserts your credit card into a verification terminal, computers hundreds or thousands of miles away approve or deny the purchase.

Virtually every large organization today has several types of distributed transaction processing systems in place. For instance, chain stores often collect and process data locally, then transmit these data to a headquarters site for timely analysis. Mail-order firms frequently process orders at one site and then transmit transaction data to a warehouse site to initiate packing and delivery. The applications are virtually endless.

Strategic Alliances Recently, many companies have gone a step further with their distributed transaction processing systems by creating *inter-organizational systems (IOSs),* in which their computers are strategically linked to the computers of key customers and/or suppliers. For instance, many of the major automakers use their own computer systems to constantly monitor their suppliers' computer systems to ensure that proper inventory levels for critical parts are kept. They also may use the IOSs to shop electronically for the best prices.

Another widely used type of interorganizational information system used now by many companies is **electronic data interchange (EDI).** EDI enables standard business documents such as purchase orders and invoices to be exchanged from one company's computer system to the computer system of another company (see Figure 6-2). The company doing the purchasing often is able to electronically track its order's progress on the seller's computer system. Many large companies today order a sizable percentage of their supplies and raw materials through computer-to-computer order processing.

Electronic data interchange (EDI). A computer procedure that enables standard business documents—such as purchase orders and invoices—to be exchanged electronically between companies.

Some firms use modern communications technology to further tighten strategic alliances. At General Motors and Dupont, large suppliers of key items no longer have to wait for purchase orders. When General Motors' or Dupont's computers show raw materials getting low, the suppliers automatically ship the goods and send the invoices electronically.

Electronic Mailboxes and Voice Mail **Electronic mailboxes** are the computer-age equivalents of traditional mailboxes. They consist of files on hard disk, belonging to specific individuals or accounts, authorized to receive electronic messages. In one common application, a manager types a memo and electronically routes it to the electronic mailboxes of selected company employees (see Figure 6-3).

Electronic mailbox. A storage area used to hold messages, memos, and other documents sent to a person.

Voice mail, which involves voice data, is a telecommunications technology that takes electronic mailboxes one step further. In a voice-mail system, the sender's spoken messages are digitized by voice tone and stored in bit form on an answering device at the receiver's location. When the receiver presses a "listen" key, the digitized message is reconverted to voice data.

Voice mail. An electronic mail system in which spoken phone messages are digitally recorded and stored in an electronic mailbox.

Bulletin Boards Whereas electronic mailboxes usually consist of several individual files, each accessible by one specific person, an **electronic bulletin board** is a file that is shared by many people. Each person with access to the

Electronic bulletin board. A computer file that is shared by several people, enabling them to post or broadcast messages.

FIGURE 6-3

Electronic mailboxes. With an electronic mail package, users can create or summon electronic documents and route them to the electronic mailboxes of selected individuals.

FIGURE 6-4

Fax transmission. A three-page memo can be sent from Kansas City to New York in less than a minute. In Kansas City, pages are placed in an input hopper in the back of the fax machine. As they are read, they exit out the front. The images are sent over the phone lines in electronic form, and when they reach New York, they are converted into natural-language form—identical to the originals—and output on continuous-roll fax paper.

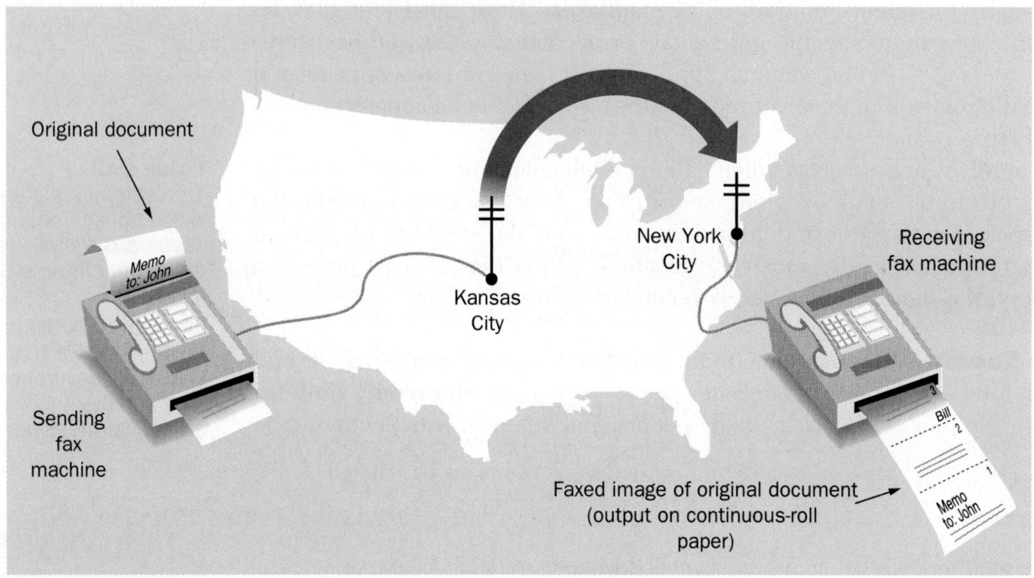

bulletin board can see the information "posted" on it, add information, and delete information.

Many organizations use in-house bulletin boards to carry out a high-tech phenomenon known as *computer conferencing.* Computer conferencing allows a meeting to take place by computer—even when the participants aren't all using their computer workstations at the same time. For instance, computer conferencing might be available to a group of executives who are investigating the feasibility of a big merger during a hectic two-week period. At any time, participants can broadcast messages to all other participants and can retrieve all or any part of the proceedings of the "conference." Computer conferencing will be covered more fully in Chapter 11, in the section on office automation.

Facsimile (fax) machine. A device that can transmit or receive hard-copy images of text, pictures, maps, diagrams, and the like over the phone lines.

Facsimile Machines **Facsimile (fax) machines** enable hard-copy images of documents to be sent from one location to another over ordinary phone lines. For example, a secretary in Kansas City may place a short document containing both text and pictures into a fax machine, such as the one in Figure 6-4. The fax machine will digitize the page images and transmit them over ordinary phone lines to New York. In New York another fax machine will receive the electronic page images and reproduce them in hard-copy form. All of this may take place in less than a minute. Also, microcomputer systems can be equipped with *fax boards* that enable them to communicate with fax machines.

Facsimile machines have been in use for a long time. If you're an old-movie buff, you may remember the 1948 film *Call Northside 777,* in which a young Jimmy Stewart proves that a key trial witness has lied by summoning from across the country a timely fax image contradicting her testimony. It has only been since the recent development of both the microprocessor and improved manufacturing techniques, however, that inexpensive faxing—and the ensuing boom in personal fax machines—has occurred.

Information Retrieval The assortment of information you can get over the phone lines today is, in a word, amazing. Thousands of public databases are currently available for online *information retrieval.* Among these are services for recreational users, shoppers, businesses, researchers, travelers, and other microcomputer users with specialized information needs.

Businesspeople can summon a variety of corporate financial reports, such as those available from Moody's, Standard & Poor's, and Dun & Bradstreet. Also available is a never-ending stream of information from news wires such as those of Dow Jones and Reuters.

For researchers and others who read a lot, virtually every major general-interest or trade magazine, newspaper, and journal published worldwide is now online. Also, many regional newspapers in dozens of U.S. cities are available in electronic versions that can be "delivered" to your monitor screen. There are even clipping services that will scan publications for you and save articles in an electronic mailbox on subjects you designate.

Professionals such as lawyers and doctors also have databases targeted to their specialized needs. Mead Corporation, one of the largest electronic publishers, has been extremely successful with Lexis, a legal database. For the medical professional, there's Medis.

Most people get their online information through a particular services company, which works similarly to a pay-television network. When you subscribe to the services company, you gain access to the variety of participating databases to which it, in turn, subscribes. Prodigy, CompuServe, GEnie, and America Online, for instance, are targeted to information useful to the average person and they include news and weather, personal investing and money management, travel, and shopping (see Figure 6-5 and Window 3, which take an in-depth look at Prodigy). Such companies also link to Internet, a worldwide web of some 50,000 networks connecting over 15 million users and hundreds of universities and government agencies. Services companies often have a one-time fee and, sometimes, an hourly hookup charge. They may also impose special charges for some types of services—say, Internet access.

Cellular Phones **Cellular phones** are mobile phones that do not need to be hooked up to a phone outlet in order to work. They can put two people into contact with each other anywhere, even if they are in motion.

Cellular phone. A mobile phone that uses special stations called cells to communicate with the regular phone system.

Currently those who most benefit from the cellular phone boom are people who need to be in constant contact with the office or clients but must be on the move as well—such as a busy executive, salesperson, field worker, or real estate agent. Such a user might, for instance, take a cellular phone out of a

FIGURE 6-5

Using Prodigy to fetch a stock quote. Shown here are the steps a user follows to make connections with Prodigy and request a quote.

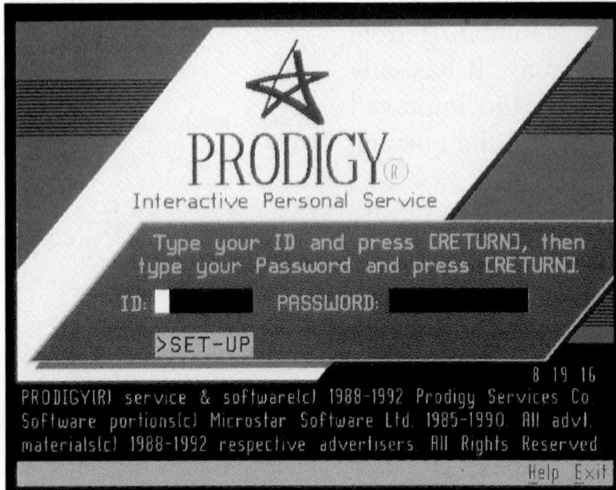

(a) The opening Prodigy screen.

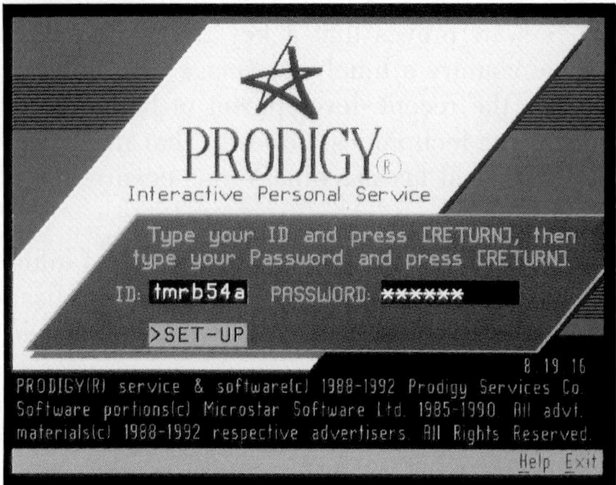

(b) User enters ID and password, with the password hidden. Prodigy is then automatically dialed.

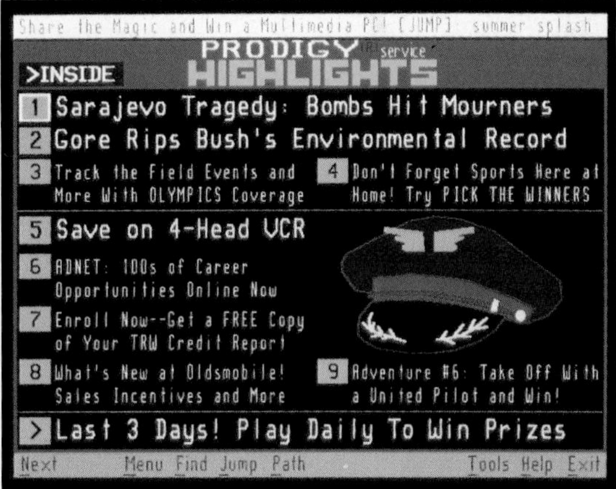

(c) The opening menu. User selects "Jump" (see bottom line) to access stock quotes.

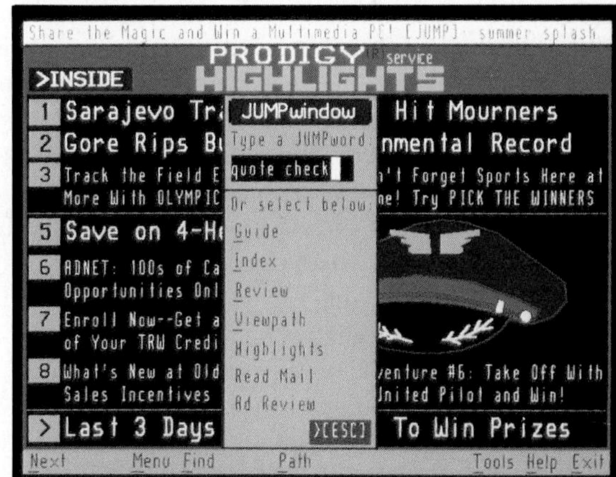

(d) When the JUMP window box appears, the keyword "quote check" is entered at the cursor position.

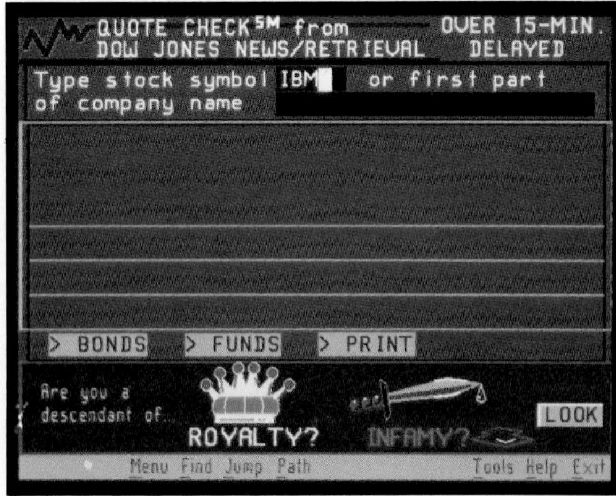

(e) When the Quote Check screen appears, the ticker symbol of a stock (e.g., IBM) is entered.

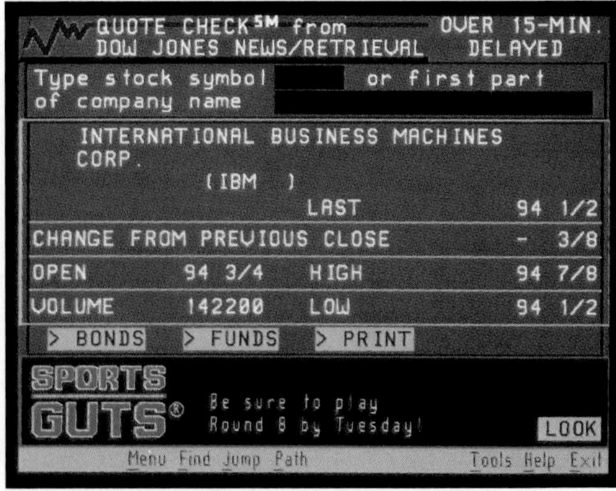

(f) A screen showing IBM's latest price appears. Other quotes can be retrieved similarly.

briefcase and use it while waiting in line, sitting at a traffic light, or taxiing down a runway. People who work outdoors, such as farmers and refinery workers (see Figure 6-6), who may need to be in contact with others but can't afford the time it takes to get to a regular phone, are also reaping the benefits of cellular phone technology. You can even hook up a laptop computer with a cellular phone and gain access to huge databases of information while you are far from an office or a regular phone.

Cellular phones are also becoming a big hit internationally, especially in less developed countries such as Poland and China. In places as these, communication systems are crude by North American standards; it is much easier to build new, cellular networks than to fix current facilities or to put in wired systems.

Cellular phones operate by keeping in contact with transmitter stations called *cell stations,* or *cells.* These stations, which resemble tall metal telephone poles, are strategically placed throughout a calling area. Cells perform two essential functions: (1) They provide an interface with the regular public phone network, and (2) they enable a moving vehicle with a phone to receive uninterrupted transmitting power by passing signals off to contiguous cells located in the zone into which the vehicle is moving.

Recently, allegations have been made that cellular-phone use—or overuse—may lead to brain cancer. To date, however, there is no proof that cellular phones are harmful.

FIGURE 6-6

Cellular phones. Cellular phones are useful for people who are on the go, need to keep in contact with an office, or don't have access to a conventional phone.

Communications Media

Figure 6-7 shows a simple telecommunications system. Two hardware units that are distant from each other transfer messages over some type of **communications medium.** The hardware units may be a terminal and a computer, two computers, or some other combination of two devices. The medium may be privately operated, or it may use public phone lines, microwave, or some other alternative. When a message is transmitted, one of the hardware units is designated as the *sender* and the other as the *receiver.* There are several ways to send the message over the medium, as this section will demonstrate.

Communications medium. The intervening substance, such as a telephone wire or cable, that connects two physically distant hardware devices.

Types of Media

Communications media fall into one of two classes: physical lines and microwaves.

Physical Lines Three types of physical lines are used in telecommunications systems today: twisted-pair wires, coaxial cable, and fiber optic cable.

FIGURE 6-7

A simple telecommunications system. As complicated as telecommunications systems may seem, they reduce to simply one device being able to communicate effectively with another.

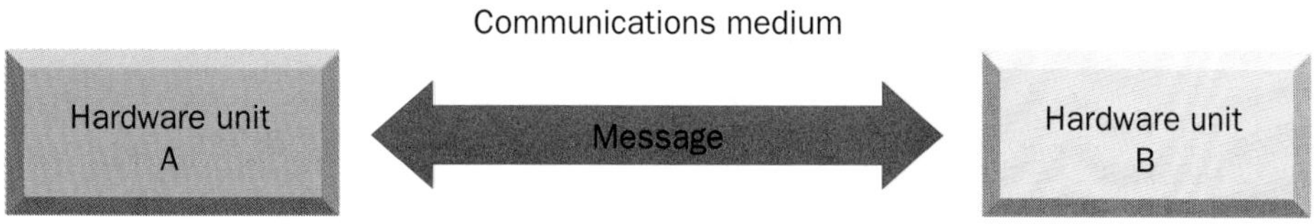

Communications medium

Hardware unit A

Message

Hardware unit B

Twisted-pair wires.
A communications medium consisting of pairs of wires twisted together and bound into a cable.

Twisted-pair wires, in which strands of wire are twisted in twos, is the communications technology that has been in use the longest. The telephone system, which carries most of the data transmitted in this country and abroad, still consists heavily of twisted-pair wires. In some cases, several thousand pairs may be placed into single cables, which might connect switching stations within a city. In contrast, only a few pairs are needed to connect a home phone to the closest telephone pole. Twisted-pair wires can be manufactured and installed at a very low cost, but when used over long distances, they are appropriate only for relatively unsophisticated applications such as text and voice transmission.

Coaxial cable.
A transmission line developed for transmitting text and video data at high speeds.

Coaxial cable, the medium pioneered by the cable television industry, was developed primarily to provide high-speed, interference-free video transmission. Coaxial cable is now also widely used in other types of communication systems. And it is employed extensively by the phone companies, typically as a replacement for twisted-pair wires in large "trunk" lines.

Fiber optic cable.
A cable composed of hundreds of hair-thin, transparent fibers along which data are passed from lasers as light waves.

One of the most promising developments in cable technology is fiber optics. An innovation whose potential is just beginning to be realized, **fiber optic cable** (see Figure 6-8) consists of as many as hundreds of clear glass fiber strands, each approximately the thickness of a human hair. Transmission is made possible by the transformation of data into light beams, which are sent through the cable by a laser device at speeds on the order of billions of bits per second. Each hairlike fiber has the capacity to carry a few television stations or a few thousand two-way voice conversations.

The principal advantages of fiber optics over wire media include speed, size, weight, resistance to tapping, and longevity. The speed differences between

FIGURE 6-8

Fiber optic cable. Fiber optic cable is commonly used in cities today to connect major communications arteries. A fiber optic cable the width of a pencil may contain hundreds of optical fibers, each capable of carrying more than 1,000 telephone conversations simultaneously.

FIGURE 6-9

Terrestrial microwave station. Stations normally are placed on mountaintops and tall buildings.

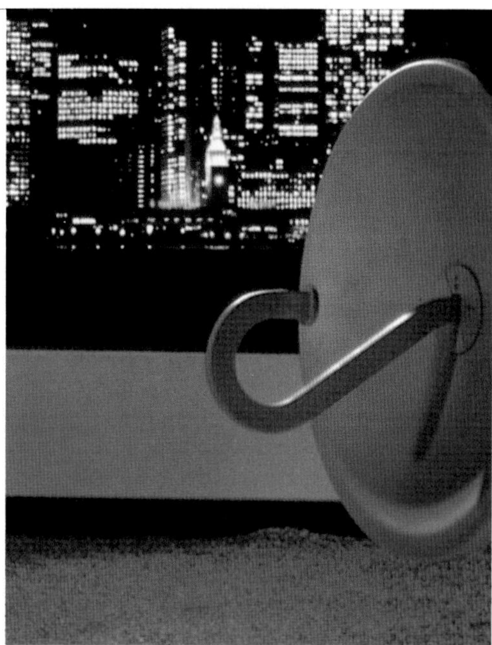

wire and fiber optic cable can be enormous; in the six seconds it takes to transmit a page of Webster's *Unabridged Dictionary* over wire, the entire 2,000-plus pages of the work can be transmitted over a single fiber strand. Fiber optic cable is especially suitable in situations involving heavy point-to-point transmission between two stations.

Microwaves **Microwaves** are high-frequency radio signals. Text, graphics, voice, and video data can all be converted to microwave impulses. Microwave transmission stations need not be within sight of each other; however, they should have a relatively unobstructed path along which to communicate. When one microwave station receives a message from another, it amplifies it and passes it on. Because of mountains and the curvature of the earth, microwave stations often are placed on tall buildings and mountaintops to ensure an obstacle-free transmission path.

Microwave.
An electomagnetic wave in the high-frequency range.

Microwave signals can be sent in two ways: via terrestrial stations or by way of satellite. Both technologies can transmit data in large quantities and at much higher speeds than can twisted-pair wires.

Terrestrial microwave stations, illustrated in Figure 6-9, must be no more than 25 to 30 miles apart to communicate with each other directly. This limitation arises because the moisture at the earth's surface causes interference, which impedes communication between stations. As you can imagine, it is quite impractical to build all the repeater stations needed to connect distant locations.

Terrestrial microwave station.
A ground station that receives microwave signals, amplifies them, and passes them on.

FIGURE 6-10

Communications satellites. Satellites move in correspondence to the earth's rotation, so they appear stationary to an observer on earth. Because each satellite can communicate effectively over slightly less than half the circumference of the earth, it takes a minimum of three satellites to provide worldwide service.

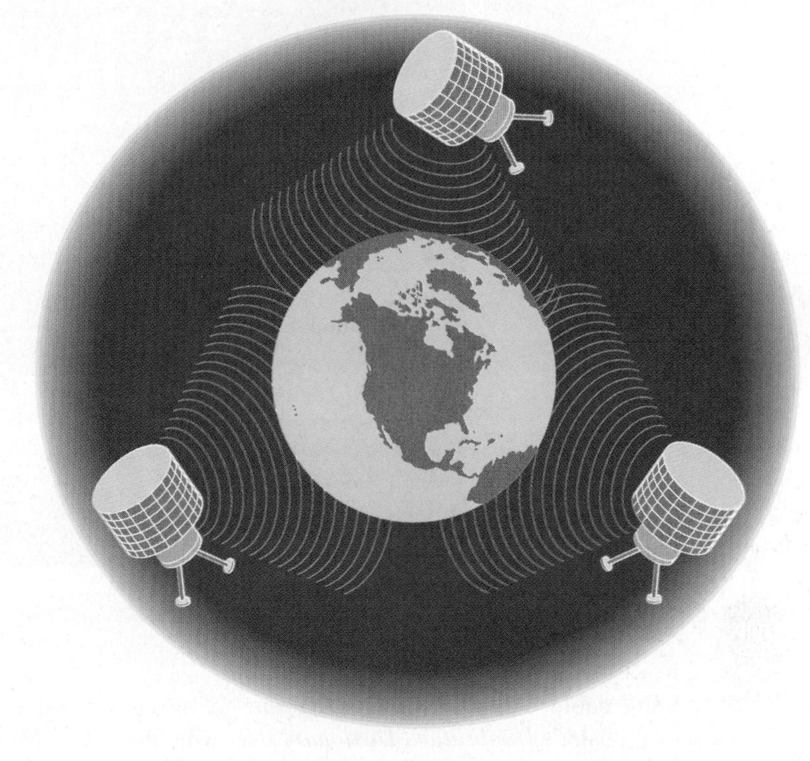

Communications satellite. An earth-orbiting device that relays communications signals over long distances.

Communications satellites were developed to reduce the cost of long-distance transmission via terrestrial repeater stations as well as to provide a cheaper and better overseas communications medium than underseas cable. Communications satellites, such as the one shown in Figure 6-10, are placed into *geosynchronous orbit* thousands of miles above the earth. "Geosynchronous" means that, because they travel at a speed to keep pace with the earth's rotation, they appear to remain stationary over a given spot. During the 1991 Gulf War, satellites were deployed to pinpoint the positions of soldiers in the desert who carried small signaling devices about the size of paperbacks. This technology—called *global positioning*—is now being used in a variety of civilian applications, as the Tomorrow box explains.

Both communications satellites and terrestrial microwave stations are most appropriate for transmitting large amounts of data one way at a time. Thus, they are ideal for applications such as television and radio broadcasting. Because of the long transmission distances involved, they are often not feasible for rapid-response, interactive communications.

TOMORROW

Global Positioning Systems

Do You Know Where Your Truck Drivers Are?

Combine a technology that's been around for a couple of decades with a high-tech war and what do you get? A brand new technology and a better way of getting work done.

Global positioning systems (GPSs) were originally developed in the United States for military operations during the Persian Gulf War to pinpoint the position of troops. This new technology currently uses a squad of Department of Defense satellites that circle the earth, each in a different plane. When special hand-held devices, about the size of a paperback book, send signals to these satellites from earth, the exact latitude and longitude of the devices can be established within 45 feet. Not bad, considering satellites hover thousands of feet above the earth's surface.

Now that the Gulf War is history, GPS technology is enjoying a variety of civilian applications.

Take trucking—or any business that relies heavily on a vehicle fleet, such as the taxi trade or the overnight package business. In the past, it was often difficult for companies to tell exactly where a vehicle was at any given moment. Now, with the aid of GPSs, the home office can determine the location of all vehicles without requiring the driver to constantly call in. That means when an unanticipated passenger or package has to be picked up, the driver closest to the pickup location can be called. If the driver isn't available, a message can be left. Thus, companies can not only improve service, but they can manage their fleets in a more cost-effective manner.

In agriculture, GPSs are beginning to help with aerial crop spraying and—strange as it may seem—cutting down on pollution. Instead of relying on manual methods to determine where to take the next spray pass, pilots can use a GPS to pinpoint exactly where they are at all times. Consequently, planes can take the minimum number of passes and avoid overspraying. Eventually, say some advocates, GPSs will make it possible to speed up takeoffs and landings at commercial airports with increased reliability.

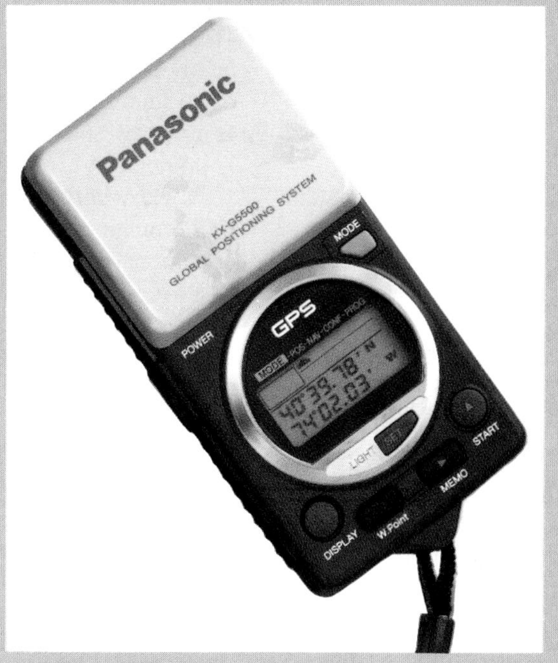

GPS unit. Small enough to be carried by back-country skiers and hikers.

Scientists are also starting to benefit from GPSs. For instance, geologists can use global positioning to identify subtle changes in the earth's surface, thereby getting better advance warnings of earthquakes. It may someday also be possible to use satellites and computers to monitor the entire surface of the earth on a round-the-clock basis, thereby detecting even the tiniest environmental changes and their potential impact.

Affordable GPS devices would also be an ideal safety item for backpackers and backcountry skiers to carry with them on treacherous journeys. Additionally, the boating and automobile industries are anticipating the day when each boat or car comes equipped with a built-in GPS chip. Boats lost at sea would be a thing of the past. And just imagine how much more difficult it would be for anyone to steal your car.

Media Speed

Bits per second (bps). A measure of the speed of a communications device.

The capacity of a communications medium, generally measured in terms of the number of bits that can be transmitted per second (**bits per second,** or **bps**), partly determines the uses to which the medium can be put. Media can be grouped by speed into three grades, or bandwidths. The speed of transmission is proportional to the width of the frequency band.

Narrowband transmission. Low-speed transmission characterized by telegraph transmission.

Voice-grade transmission. Medium-speed transmission characterized by the rates of speed available over ordinary telephone lines.

Wideband transmission. High-speed transmission characterized by the rates of speed available over coaxial cable, fiber optic cable, and microwave.

Narrowband transmission refers to a medium with a data-carrying capacity in the range of 45 to 150 bps. These rates are suitable only for very-low-speed operations, such as telegraph and teletype communication.

Voice-grade transmission (300 to 9,600 bps) represents a medium level of speed. This kind of transmission is so called because spoken messages can be transmitted in this speed range. On regular telephone lines, the most common voice-grade lines, speeds of 4,800 and 9,600 bps are common for reliably transmitting data.

Wideband transmission rates (19,200 to 500,000 or more bps) are generally possible only with coaxial and fiber optic cable and with microwave media.

Media Mode

Communications media also can be classified in terms of whether or not they can send messages in two directions. In the terminology of communications, transmission mode is said to be simplex, half-duplex, or full-duplex.

Simplex transmission. Any type of transmission in which a message can be sent along a path in only a single prespecified direction.

In **simplex transmission,** data can be transmitted only in a single, prespecified direction. An example from everyday life is a doorbell—the signal can go only from the button to the chime. Another example is television broadcasting. Although simplex lines are cheap, they are uncommon for many types of computer-based telecommunications applications, which generally involve two-way communication. Even devices that are designed primarily to receive information, such as printers, communicate an acknowledgment back to the sender device.

Half-duplex transmission. Any type of transmission in which messages may be sent in two directions—but only one way at a time—along a communications path.

Full-duplex transmission. A type of transmission in which messages may be sent in two directions simultaneously along a communications path.

In **half-duplex transmission,** messages can be carried in either direction, but only one way at a time. The press-to-talk radio phones used in police cars employ this mode of transmission; only one person can talk at a time. Often the line between a display terminal and its host CPU is half-duplex. If the computer is transmitting to the terminal, the operator cannot send new messages until the computer is finished.

Full-duplex transmission is like traffic on a busy two-way street: The flow moves in two directions at the same time. Full-duplexing is ideal for hardware units that need to pass large amounts of data between each other, as in computer-to-computer communication. Full-duplex channels generally are not needed for terminal-to-host links, because the terminal operator's response usually depends on the results sent back from the computer.

Media Signal

Analog transmission. The transmission of data as continuous-wave patterns.

Digital transmission. The transmission of data as discrete impulses.

Signals sent along a medium can be analog or digital.

The phone system, established many years ago to handle voice traffic, carries signals in an **analog** fashion—that is, by a *continuous* wave over a certain frequency range. The continuous wave reflects the myriad variations in the pitch of the human voice. Unfortunately, most business computing equipment is **digital;** it is built to handle data coded into two *discrete* states—that is, as

FIGURE 6-11

Analog and digital transmission.

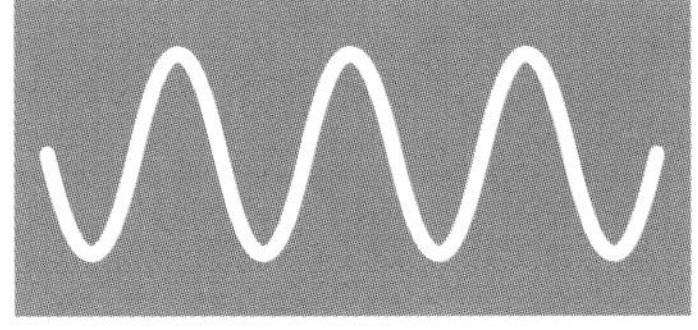

Analog mode

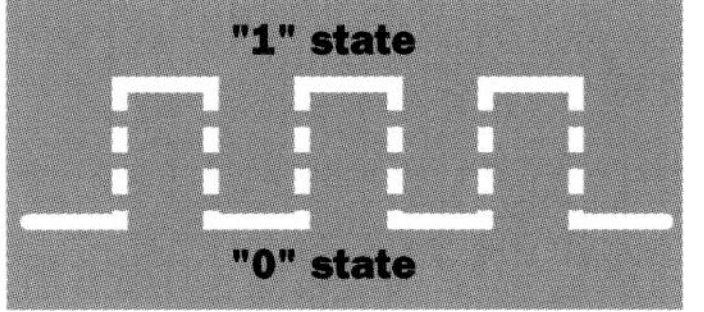

Digital mode

0- and 1-bits. This difference between analog and digital states is illustrated in Figure 6-11.

Modems Because digital impulses can't be sent over analog phone lines, some means of translating each kind of signal into the other had to be developed. Conversion of signals from digital to continuous-wave form is called *modulation,* and translation from continuous waves back to digital impulses is termed *demodulation.* A single device called a **modem** (coined from the words *MOdulation* and *DEModulation*) takes care of both operations. As Figure 6-12 shows, when a workstation sends a remote CPU a message that must be carried over an analog line, a modem is needed at both the sending end (to convert from digital to analog) and the receiving end (to convert from analog to digital).

Modem.
A communications device that enables computers and their support devices to communicate over ordinary telephone lines.

Modems are available as add-in boards, which can be inserted into an expansion slot within the computer's system unit, and as standalone hardware

FIGURE 6-12

How modems work. An operator at a display workstation types in data that are encoded digitally and sent to modem A. Modem A converts the data to analog form and sends them over the phone lines to modem B. Modem B reconverts the data to digital form and delivers them to the CPU. When the CPU transmits back to the workstation, these steps are reversed.

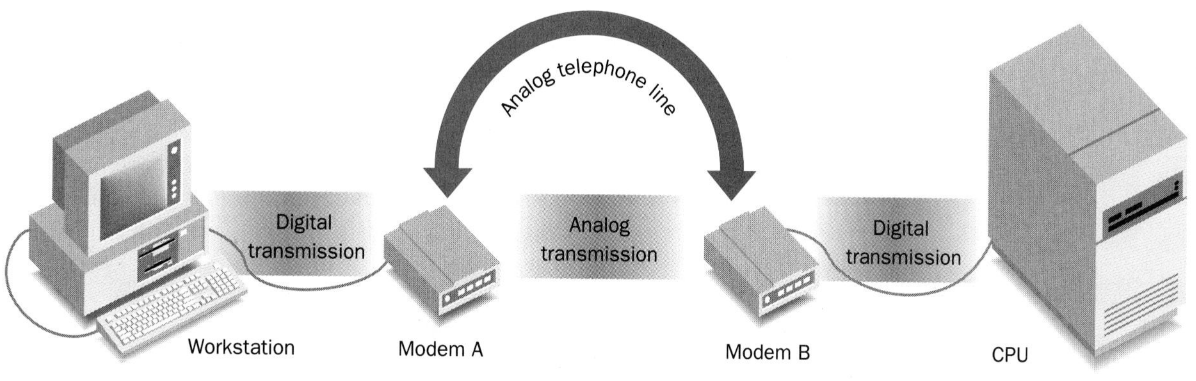

FIGURE 6-13

Modems. (a) An external modem is detached from the system unit. (b) A board (internal) modem fits in an expansion slot within the system unit.

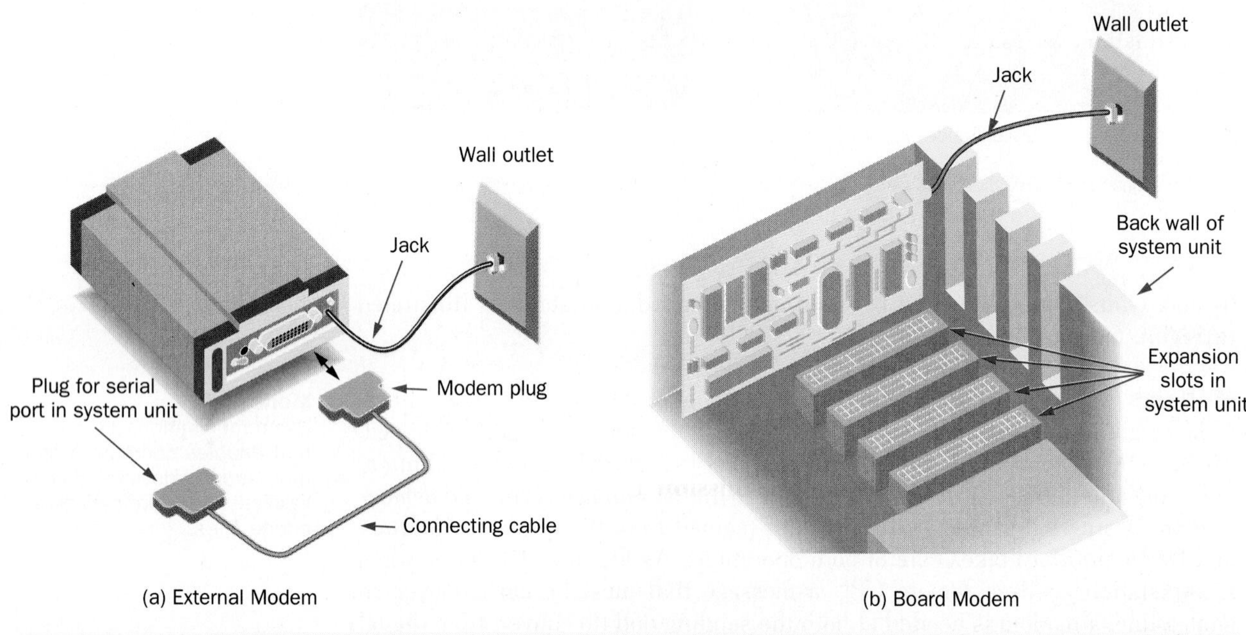

devices (see Figure 6-13), which are physically detached from the system unit. Cellular modems, which do not require wires, are also now available and are expected to play an increasing role in the laptop computer market. Common bps rates on modems targeted to microcomputer users are 300, 1,200, 2,400, 4,800, 9,600, 14,400, and 28,800 bps. Often modems capable of higher speeds can function at the lower rates as well.

Digital Lines Although physical lines traditionally have been analog, *digital lines* are also available. These lines can transmit data considerably faster and more accurately than their analog counterparts. Also, with digital lines, several types of data (say, text, voice, and video) can be sent along the same circuit. And, of course, no modem is necessary. The public phone network is still far from being all digital, but urban areas are rapidly moving in that direction.

During the last several years, digital communications networks have started to appear throughout the world. For example, ISDN (for *integrated services digital network*) is an international effort to make totally digital telephone service possible. ISDNs are designed to simultaneously carry several different types of data—text, graphics, voice, and video, for instance—at greater speeds than those realizable with conventional voice-grade lines. ISDN will someday make it possible for you to send data instantaneously from your microcomputer workstation screen to someone else's as you talk to them on the phone. An ISDN user will be able to connect a phone, computer, fax machine, or another communications device to any other ISDN-supported equipment.

Another digital-communications effort taking place in many countries is the development of a national fiber-optic backbone. The Japanese industrial community would like its country to be fully fiber optic by the year 2015, with even direct fiber-optic feeds to homes. In the United States, the current plan is to build the backbone and to make the first direct feed available to schools, hospitals, and businesses. Where an all-fiber-optic path is available from source to destination, access to all types of data can be had at lightning-fast speeds. Where a path is broken by another medium—such as coaxial cable going from a fiber-optic trunk into a home—communications capability will be limited by the slower medium. The cost of a fiber-optic "information superhighway" in the United States is expected to exceed $200 billion.

Parallel versus Serial Transmission

Transmission devices differ in the number of channels, or tracks, that they use to transmit data. The bits used to represent characters may be transmitted in parallel or in serial. If, for example, all the 8-bits needed to convey the letter *A* are sent out at once in eight separate channels, **parallel transmission** is being used. On the other hand, if the bits representing *A* are sent out one at a time over a single channel, **serial transmission** is occurring. Figure 6-14 illustrates the difference between the two.

Parallel transmission. Data transmission in which each bit in a byte has its own path and all of the bits in a byte are transmitted simultaneously.

Serial transmission. Data transmission in which every bit in a byte must travel down the same path in succession.

FIGURE 6-14

Serial and parallel transmission. In serial transmission, all of the bits of a byte follow one another over a single path. In parallel transmission, the bits of a byte are split into nine channels (for each of the eight bits and a parity bit) and transmitted. Parallel transmission is faster but more expensive per foot of cable used. Shown in the figure is transmission of the ASCII representation of the letter *A*.

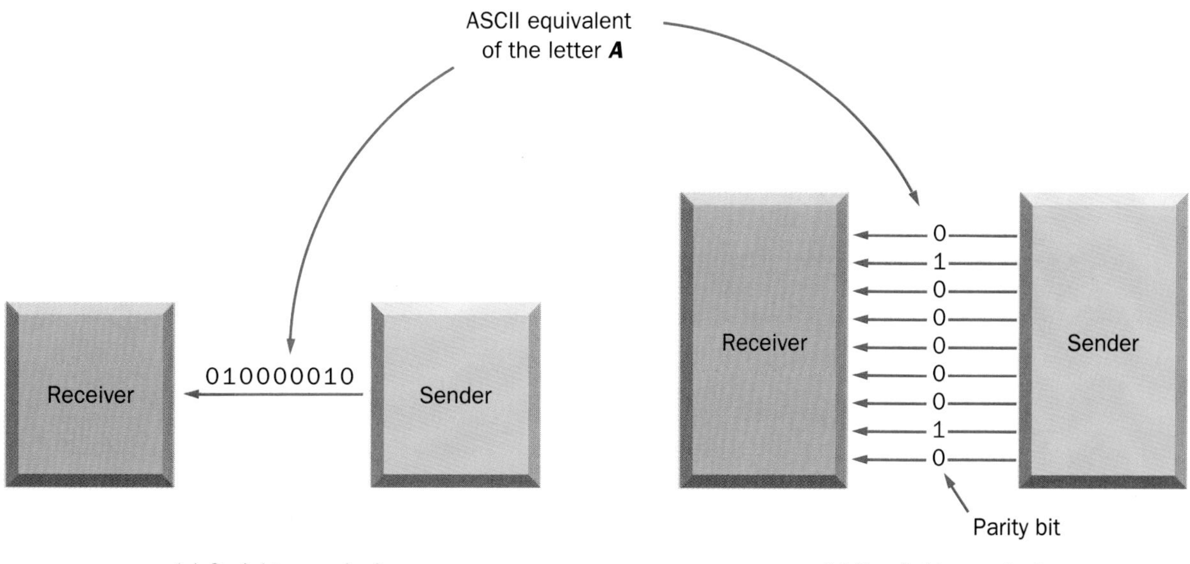

As Figure 6-14 suggests, parallel transmission is much faster than serial transmission. However, because it requires many more channels, parallel transmission is also more expensive. Thus, parallel transmission usually is limited to short distances, such as computer-to-computer communications. Serial transmission is used to connect workstations to remote computer systems.

A common serial interface, the RS-232C, was developed to standardize remote computer-to-terminal connections. Modems, for instance, use this particular interface on many computer systems. An enhanced form of this interface, the RS-422, is widely used on the Apple Macintosh line of computers to connect modems, printers, and electronic musical instruments. These ports will also accept most RS-232C devices, which operate at higher voltages, without damage to the ports.

Of course, computers must communicate at high speeds with other nearby peripherals, such as disk and tape units. Since the distance involved is short, parallel transmission is feasible for this purpose. In many IBM microcomputer systems, nearby printers are connected in parallel to the computer's system unit with a popular standard known as the *Centronics* interface.

Asynchronous versus Synchronous Transmission

Asynchronous transmission. The transmission of data over a line one character at a time.

Serial transmission can be further classified in terms of whether it's asynchronous or synchronous.

In **asynchronous transmission,** one character at a time is transmitted over a line. When the operator strikes a key on the terminal, the character's byte

FIGURE 6-15

Asynchronous and synchronous transmission. In asynchronous transmission, each byte is sent up the line as soon as it is generated. In synchronous transmission, bytes are collected in a buffer and sent in blocks.

(a) Asynchronous transmission

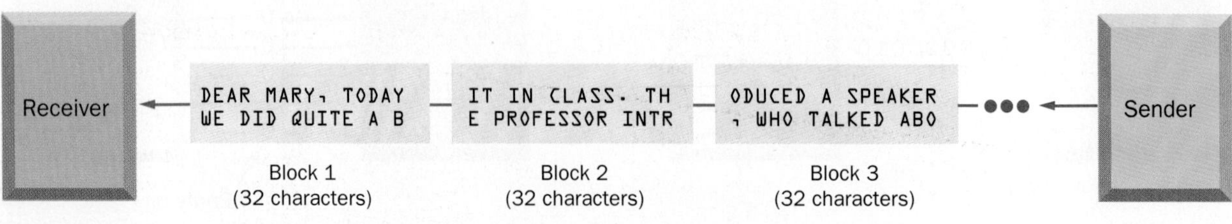

(b) Synchronous transmission

representation is sent up the line to the computer; striking a second key sends a second character; and so forth. But because even the fastest typist can generate only a very small amount of data relative to what the line can accept, a lot of idle time occurs on the line. Furthermore, each character sent must be packaged with a "start bit" and "stop bit," resulting in substantial transmission overhead.

Synchronous transmission corrects for this deficiency by dispatching data in blocks of characters rather than one at a time. Each block can consist of thousands of characters. Because no idle time occurs between transmission of individual characters in the block and less transmission overhead is required, the utilization of the line is much more efficient. Synchronous transmission is made possible by a *buffer* in the terminal—a storage area large enough to hold a block of characters. As soon as the buffer is filled, all the characters in it are sent up the line to the computer.

Synchronous transmission.
The transmission of data over a line one block of characters at a time.

Figure 6-15 illustrates the differences between asynchronous and synchronous transmission. Synchronous transmission is commonly used for data speeds greater than 2,400 bps.

Wide Area Networks and Local Networks

An organization generally has two choices for transmitting data: wide area networks and local networks.

Wide Area Networks

Wide area networks (WANs) are communications networks that encompass a relatively wide geographic area. Three common types of wide area networks are public-access networks, value-added networks, and private wide area networks.

Wide area network (WAN).
A network that covers a wide geographic area.

Public-Access Networks **Public-access networks** are those maintained by phone companies, or common carriers. **Common carriers** are companies licensed by the government to provide wide area communications services to the general public. Although there are dozens of phone companies in the United States alone, virtually all are interconnected so that they appear to be a single, seamless network.

Public-access network.
A network—such as the phone system—that is designed to be used by the general public.

Common carrier.
A government-regulated private organization that provides communications services to the public.

Among the most familiar common carriers are the Bell-system phone companies and firms such as US Sprint, MCI, and AT&T Communications. The Bell-system companies provide in-state and nearby-state communications services, and the other firms serve a wider area. Among the less familiar common carriers are the *specialized carrier companies*, such as those that provide satellite transmission facilities.

Value-Added Networks (VANs) **Value-added network (VAN)** vendors are firms that use the facilities of a common carrier to offer the general subscribing public additional services using those facilities. These services include information processing, information retrieval, electronic mail, and the like. Individuals and organizations that use the services are billed by both the common carrier (if toll charges are involved) and the VAN company.

Value-added network (VAN).
Use of the phone network by a firm other than the phone company to offer communications-related services over the network.

One of the most popular types of VAN service is information retrieval, which we discussed earlier. Examples of firms that offer such services are Prodigy, CompuServe, GEnie, and America Online. Once users make phone contact with

Feature 6-1

Modem Software

Interacting With the Programs That Enable Communications

Here, we tie together a number of the concepts in this chapter, explaining how terms such as *modems, parity, duplexing,* and several others figure into using the communications software that comes with your computer system.

Modems, like computers, are hardware devices that use software to work. The programs used with modems—which enable you to communicate with remote databases and bulletin boards with your microcomputer system—are commonly referred to in the microcomputing world as *modem software.*

When you buy a modem, you will often get modem software bundled in with it. If not, or if you prefer to buy your own software separately, you can acquire it from an independent vendor. There are a variety of well-tested products to choose from, among which are Procomm, Smartcom, and Crosstalk. The prices of such products typically range from about $25 to $200.

Although products in the modem-software marketplace differ in terms of features, most of them let you

- Access information services such as Prodigy and CompuServe.
- Connect to electronic mail services and bulletin boards.
- Exchange disk files with other microcomputers.
- Access large computers in other cities, states, or countries.
- Turn your modem on and off (to save laptop batteries from drawing down).

In addition, some packages will automatically place and answer calls for you, interface with voice and fax machines, provide security for your files, and simplify a number of routine, phone-related tasks (such as accessing phone directories and keying in passwords to an information service or bulletin board). The accompanying figure shows some of the typical information you must supply when setting up a communications application with modem software.

When you summon the software from your operating system, one of the first tasks you will need to do is set up a file of calling parameters for each phone number you want the software to dial. So, for instance, if you regularly called CompuServe, you could create a file with its phone number, your passwords, and other pertinent calling data (see figure). Then, later, upon supplying the filename associated with CompuServe and declaring your password, your call would be put through automatically. If you declare "Y" to the auto redial prompt, the modem will keep redialing the phone number at periodic intervals if it is getting a busy signal.

Transmission parameters such as the type of parity and duplexing involved, communications speed, code used, and number of stop bits ensure

the VAN company, the firm's software systems generally provide easy-to-use menus of available options. After users make a request from their keyboards, the selected services become available over the phone lines for use at the users' remote workstations. Feature 6-1, "Modem Software," explores the use of modem software to call up a VAN service.

In the United States, phone companies were for years blocked by law from offering information processing and related services over phone lines. That is, regional phone companies such as those that serve your area could not become VANs (ironically, by using the phone lines they lay themselves). In recent years, however—especially with the onslaught of competition from foreign organizations—the federal government has supported a strong deregulation movement regarding communications. Many of the phone companies want to enter the cable TV business; if the courts continue to back recent government rulings, this type of broadened access could eventually result in lower cable TV rates and better cable TV service.

```
CALLING PARAMETERS

      Destination (<Name> or Number)          :     505-555-3101
      Auto sign-on? (Y or N)                  :     N
      Password? (<Password> or None)          :     NONE
      Auto redial? (Y or N)                   :     Y

TRANSMISSION PARAMETERS

      Parity (None, Even, Odd)                :     NONE
      Duplexing (Full or Half)                :     FULL
      Speed (in bps)                          :     9600
      Code?                                   :     ASCII
      Stop bits (1 or 2)                      :     1
```

Modem programs. Most programs cost under $100.

that your modem sends data in the form the receiver expects. Generally, when you subscribe to a communications service like CompuServe or Prodigy, you will be told what types of settings for these parameters are acceptable. Virtually all modem software packages allow you to edit any parameter files you create, in the event that settings later need to be changed.

The screen shown in the figure is but one of many a modem package may use. As soon as you dial up a communications service or an electronic bulletin board, the software of these companies controls your computer system. Each of them has its own set of menu screens and retrieval procedures you must follow (see Figure 6-5, which shows some sample Prodigy screens).

Modem software will also turn your microcomputer into a type of answering machine. If you want your computer to receive incoming, electronically encoded messages while you are away from it, you must leave your computer on, with the modem software set to a "receive calls" mode. As calls come into the system, they are answered by your modem, which establishes a connection with the remote device. The modem sets up a path so that the remote device can send data to it over the phone lines onto your system's hard disk.

One controversial type of VAN is the company with the 900-prefix phone number. Today, these firms are often collectively more famous for public abuses than for the useful services they actually do offer. While some companies may wrongfully charge teenagers hundreds of dollars for interacting with an alluring voice at the other end of the line, a number of other, reputable 900-line companies offer the public such useful information as technical support on computer products, legal and tax advice, and news. Considering the appetite of people for instant information, 900 lines seem to be an unstoppable business trend. The issue of what types of regulatory controls you think government should place on operators of 900 lines is the subject of a Critical Thinking question at the end of the chapter.

Private Wide Area Networks Because many organizations today have such massive communications requirements, a number of them have set up their own exclusive **private wide area networks.** These networks are created by building

Private wide area network.
A wide area network that is built by an organization for its own use.

certain facilities, leasing capacity on existing satellites, and generally stitching together a variety of cost-effective land- and air-based communications media dedicated to delivering a certain level of performance to the organization.

One such network has been built by Sears, the large Chicago-based retailer. The Sears network hooks up tens of thousands of workstations nationwide and supports the communications needs of the Sears merchandising group and Sears' member organizations. The network is hosted by an IBM mainframe in Chicago and handles both management information requests and transactions from the millions of users of the Sears Discover card. Sears has also set up a separate organization to sell excess capacity in the network as well as to sell the communications expertise it has acquired in building the network. In recent years, Sears has joined forces with IBM to establish Prodigy Services Company and several other joint communications ventures.

Local Networks

Although wide area networks certainly are useful, many firms need communications facilities that connect local resources—say, computers and terminals located on the same college campus or several microcomputer workstations located in the same office. These types of networks are known as **local networks.**

Local network.
A privately run communications network of several machines located within a mile or so of one another.

Local networks often are acquired from communications media vendors—firms that sell or lease media for private rather than public use. These media may consist of dedicated point-to-point lines, shared lines, switched lines that are unavailable for public use, or perhaps networks composed of a combination of these lines. Three common types of local networks are host-independent local area networks (LANs), private branch exchanges (PBXs), and hierarchical local networks.

Local Area Networks (LANs) For many years, most networks consisted of a remote, central *host computer*—such as a mainframe—that controlled a large number of display terminals. With the arrival of inexpensive microcomputers, which could do their own local processing, local area networks (LANs) became possible.

Local area networks (LANs), such as the one in Figure 6-16, are local networks that do not utilize a host computer as such. Instead, computers within the network itself manage the devices as they demand the shared facilities. LANs are available principally as client-server LANs and peer-to-peer LANs.

Local area network (LAN).
A local network without a host computer that usually consists entirely of microcomputer workstations and shared peripherals.

- CLIENT-SERVER LANs **Client-server LANs,** such as those that run under Novell's NetWare operating system, are the most prevalent type of LAN. Each workstation getting network service is called a **client,** while the computers (not shown in Figure 6-16) managing the network are called **servers.** For example, a *file server* might be used to manage disk-storage activities, enabling workstation users to access any of several available operating systems, applications programs, or data files. Similarly, a *print server* is used to handle printing-related activities, such as managing devices and user outputs. One also sees on LANs such devices as *mail servers* and *fax servers,* which are dedicated to managing electronic mail and facsimile transmissions, respectively. Because servers often need to manage large databases, perform processing chores for clients, and interact with several other computers, powerful microcomputers like those based on the Intel Pentium chip are often chosen as servers.

Client-server LAN.
A LAN that is composed of *client* devices, which receive service, and *server* devices, which provide the service.

Client.
A device designed to receive service in a client-server network.

Server.
A computer that manages shared devices, such as laser printers or high-capacity hard disks, on a local area network (LAN).

FIGURE 6-16

A local area network (LAN). The surge in microcomputer usage has made local area networking a particularly attractive solution for sharing resources.

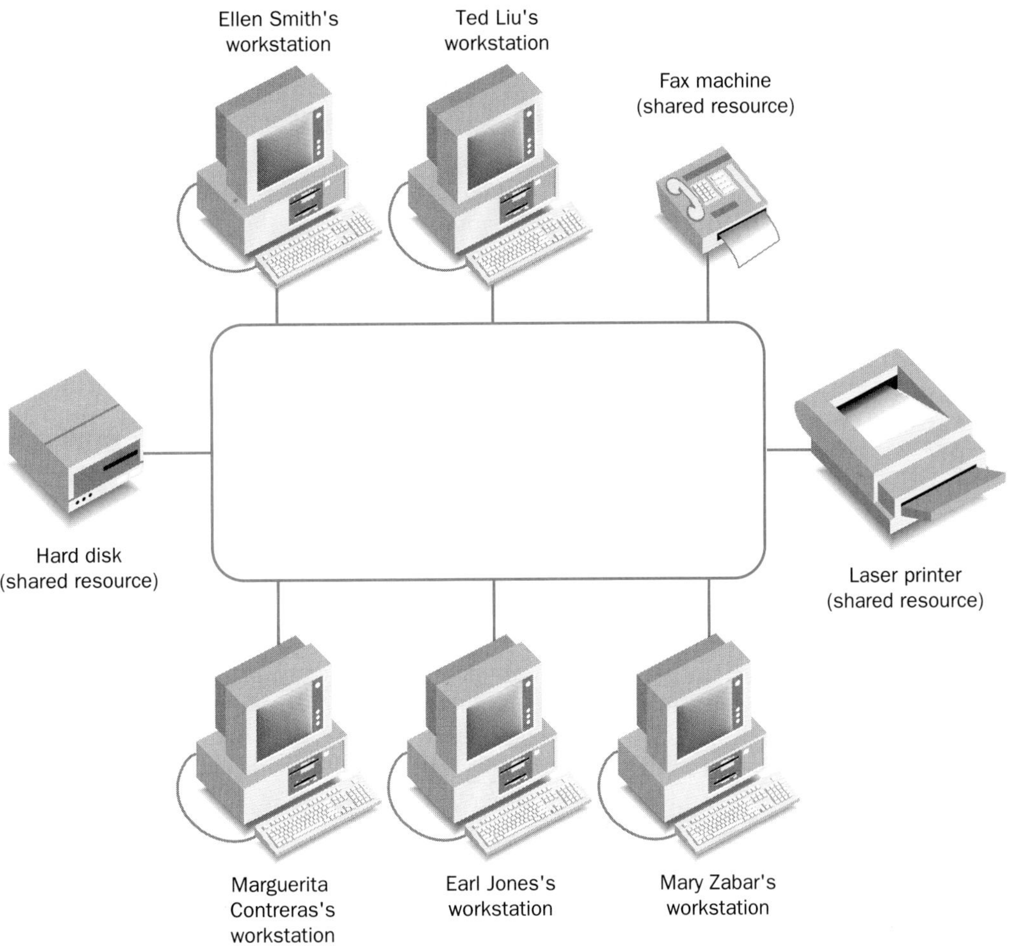

■ PEER-TO-PEER LANS **Peer-to-peer LANs,** the most well known of which run under Artisoft's LANtastic and Novell's NetWare Lite operating systems, are typically selected for small networks. These LANs do not use predesignated clients and servers per se. Instead, all of the user workstations and shared peripherals are on the same level. Any networked computer can act in a client or server role. Peer-to-peer LANs were designed as a way to bring networking to small groups without the complexity and expense that normally accompany client-server systems.

Peer-to-peer LAN. A LAN in which all of the user workstations and shared peripheral devices operate on the same level.

LANs are used today for a variety of applications, the simplest of which involves just sharing expensive hard disks and laser printers. Although these were among the first types of LAN applications, LAN technology has evolved to include numerous other uses (see Figure 6-17). For instance, some firms that once would have centralized their transaction processing on mainframes are now doing the workload on microcomputer-based LANs (see User Solution

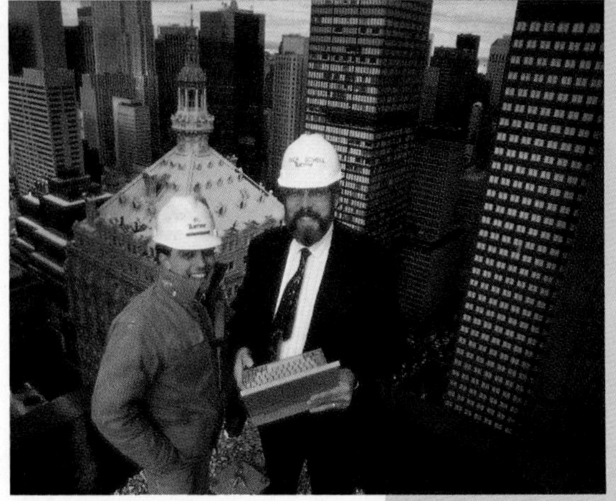

User Solution 6-2

A Contractor Turns to LANs

Turner Construction Company is one organization that decided to run its computer operations the way it runs its business—decentralized. Headquartered in New York, Turner is a general contractor, meaning it bids on construction projects and then buys materials, hires subcontractors to do the work, and manages the projects. Operating out of more than two dozen offices spreading over more than 15 countries, in the 1980s Turner ran its business primarily with a New-York-based mainframe. But with a geographically dispersed work force that has to be paid and managed regularly, remote coordination was difficult and the mainframe was frequently bogged down. Today, the mainframe has been replaced by a couple of thousand PCs and over 45 LANs. Most of the company's offices have LANs as do the major building sites.

6-2). Also, many electronic mailbox systems (see Figure 6-18) and computer conferences are run on LANs. And, *workgroup computing*—computing in which a common job, such as preparing a publication or solving a problem, is performed by people working simultaneously on a networked computer system—primarily uses LANs. Microcomputer-based LANs have a big advantage over systems based on larger computers: Organizations can inexpensively add small increments of extra computing power as their needs grow—say, by adding extra workstations or by adding more servers.

Some LANs—like those used to link soldiers in a battlefield and sports commentators at sporting events—are wireless (see Feature 6-2). Most, however, use coaxial cable or fiber-optic cable technology. Cable-based LANs usually employ either a baseband or broadband technology. *Baseband* products consist of a single, high-speed digital path over which text, graphics, voice, and video data can pass—but only one type of data can pass at a time. *Broadband* networks, in contrast, consist of several paths, thereby allowing transmission of many dissimilar types of data simultaneously. Broadband, which involves analog transmission, can also cover much longer distances than baseband.

FIGURE 6-17

Uses for LANs.

- Sharing expensive devices among several users
- Handling certain types of transaction processing more efficiently than mainframes
- Performing electronic mail and database retrieval operations
- Sharing work among a group of users (called *workgroup computing*)

FIGURE 6-18

LAN-based electronic mail. This store-and-forward mail system connects two local area networks (LANs), each in a separate building. Mary, whose computer is connected to the mail server on network A, sends a memo to Joe and Linda. Server A stores the memo until it can make a delivery. Joe receives his copy as soon as he logs on to his network. Linda's copy is forwarded from the server in building A to the one in building B whenever the two networks are in contact (immediately, if they are always connected). The server on network B stores Linda's copy until she logs on to her network.

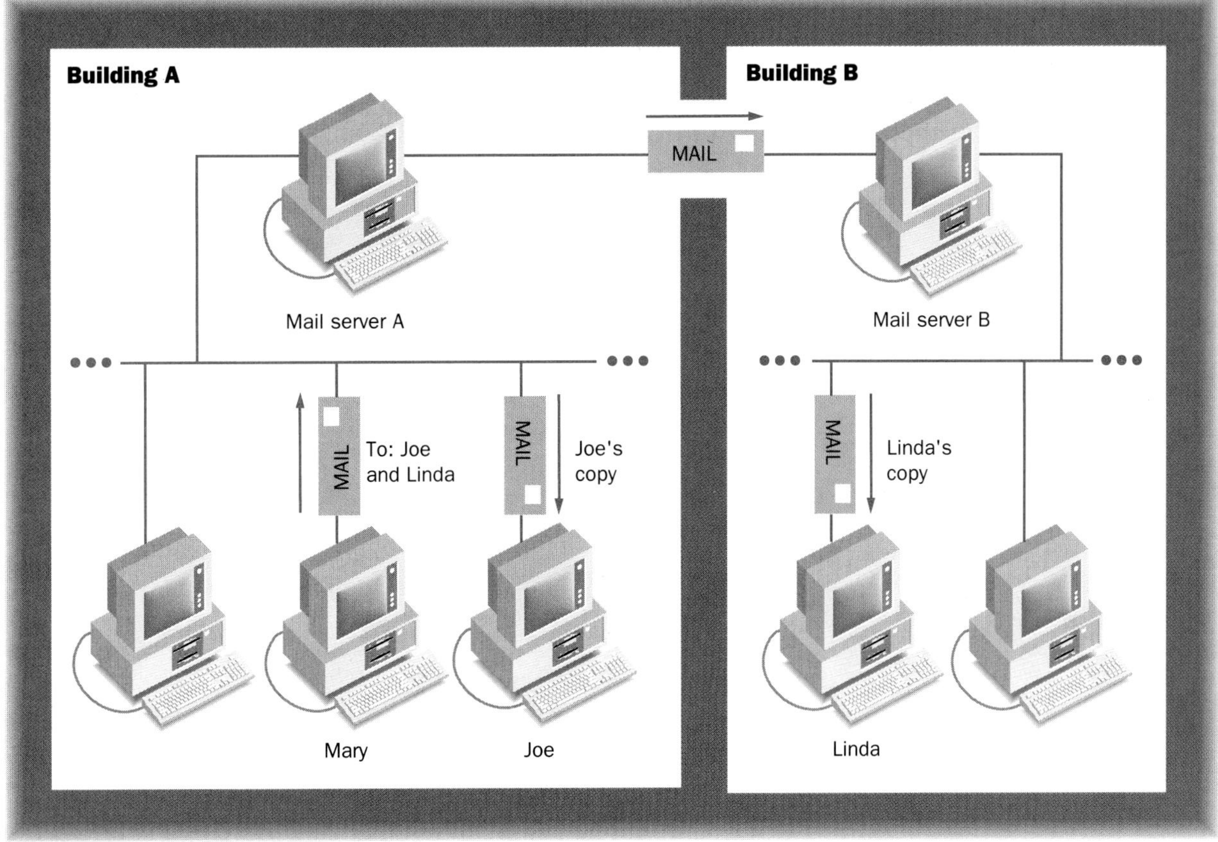

Xerox's Ethernet is one of the most widely used baseband products. Wang's Wangnet is a prominent broadband product. Broadband, being more complex and powerful than baseband, is, as you might expect, more expensive as well.

Private Branch Exchanges (PBXs) The phone system consists of numerous switching stations that essentially are public branch exchanges. When a company leases or purchases a switching station for its own use, such a facility becomes known as a **private branch exchange (PBX).** Most PBXs are commonly referred to as "company switchboards"—you call a company's number and a private (company) operator routes you to the proper extension. In the world of computers, however, many PBXs need to deal with machine-to-machine communication. Thus, such PBXs are controlled by host computers that route

Private branch exchange (PBX).
A call-switching station that an organization acquires for its own use.

Feature 6–2

Wireless LANs

Today's hot item in network computing

At Wright-Patterson Air Force Base in Dayton, Ohio, an all-too-familiar networking problem has surfaced. Thousands of PCs are used by base personnel, and many of the PCs are connected to LANs. However, the LANs keep changing. A thirty-person cabling crew is needed at the base that does nothing but adjust and install networks.

Wright-Patterson is learning something that many large corporations have already discovered—LANs often need to be rewired to meet changing needs. For instance, work units are frequently merged, new managers are hired, or assignments and locations are changed. Also, some LANs are just meant to be temporary, as those servicing retail stores that increase staff during peak selling seasons and insurance companies that need to form groups at emergency locations—such as in Florida after Hurricane Andrew hit.

When a LAN involves lots of wiring, a cabling specialist is often required to make adjustments. However, when the LAN is basically wireless, this step is unnecessary. Wright-Patterson Air Force Base has recently joined the ranks of organizations that are now experimenting with wireless LANs.

Wireless warehousing. Radio communication with a mainframe makes inventory management a realtime affair.

machine-to-machine calls automatically and let the human operator deal with many of the interpersonal communications. Sometimes these computer-based private branch exchanges are referred to as *CBXs* (*computerized branch exchanges*) or *PABXs* (*private automatic branch exchanges*).

Hierarchical local network.
A local network in which a relatively powerful "host" CPU is at the top of the hierarchy and communications terminals or less-powerful CPUs are at the bottom.

Downloading.
The process of transferring data or information from a large computer system to a smaller one.

Uploading.
The process of sending data from a small computer system to a larger computer system for storage or processing purposes.

Hierarchical Local Networks **Hierarchical local networks** are the oldest type of local network. At the top of the hierarchy is often a big host computer such as a mainframe or minicomputer. At the bottom are display terminals. Between the top and bottom are devices such as communications controllers, which manage exchanges between the host and the terminals.

Files in hierarchical local networks can be either downloaded from or uploaded to the host. **Downloading** means that copies of existing files can be sent from the host to the microcomputer workstations. **Uploading** means that new data can be created at the microcomuter workstations and sent to the host. Both downloading and uploading usually require stringent organizational control. Downloading presents the danger that data will be retrieved for unauthorized use, whereas uploading entails the risk of garbage data corrupting other applications.

Gateways and Bridges Local networks often must communicate with outside resources, such as those on wide area networks and on other local networks.

Here's how a wireless LAN might work in an office environment. Each microcomputer workstation in the office is wired to a nearby device called a controller, which collects data from the workstation and later passes data back to it. Each controller, which can service several workstations, communicates by radio or infrared waves to a centrally located transmitter in the office. The transmitter then communicates to other controllers around the office that serve other workstations.

While the type of wireless LAN just described does not completely eliminate physical wiring, it does reduce the amount of it, making alterations relatively easy. This type of wireless LAN is expected to be very prevalent in offices during the next several years.

When a LAN needs to be set up outdoors or in places where wiring is infeasible, another approach is required. The U.S. Open Golf Championship turned to wireless LANs for the first time in 1992 to provide speedy information to television broadcasters and the news media. Operators carrying hand-held terminals, each with their own built-in transmitters, followed golfers around the course. Data on strokes and golfer progress were then beamed from the terminals to a mainframe at the course site where they were stored in a central database for authorized users. One consultant on the 1992 installation reported that hand-held terminals posted results quicker than it would take someone to gather the information by phone.

Warehousing is another application where wireless LANs offer appeal. A driver who is connected to the LAN can use a screen mounted on a mobile forklift truck to pull up the latest inventory information. As pallets of goods are loaded onto the truck and carried away for shipment, inventory records in remote databases can be updated in real time (see photo).

Wireless LANs are a compelling option for networks of the future. But the technology has not yet taken off, and some major problems still need to be worked out. For example, which design standard, or protocol, should be followed? A common standard would enable many distinct wireless LANs to communicate with each other easily. Another problem is health related. Are all of those waves zooming around the air going to be detrimental to people's health over the long term?

Let's look at an example. An executive working at a microcomputer workstation on a LAN may wish to access a financial database such as Dow Jones News/Retrieval. In this particular case, a facility known as a gateway is necessary for linking the two networks—here, the LAN and the WAN. A **gateway** is a collection of hardware and software resources that enables devices on one network to communicate with devices on another, *dissimilar* network.

Gateway.
An interface that enables two dissimilar networks to communicate.

When the two networks being linked—say, a LAN in one campus building and an identical LAN in another nearby campus building—are based on similar technology, a device called a bridge is used to connect them. A **bridge** is a collection of hardware and software resources that enable devices on one network to communicate with devices on another, *similar* network.

Bridge.
An interface that enables two similar networks to communicate.

Network Topologies

Telecommunications networks can be classified in terms of their *topology*, or shape. Three common topologies are the star, bus, and ring.

Star network.
A network consisting of a host device connected directly to several other devices.

Star Networks A **star network** often consists of a host computer that's hierarchically connected to several display terminals in a point-to-point fashion.

This configuration is illustrated in Figure 6-19a. In a common variant of this pattern, several microcomputer systems (the terminals) are connected to a larger host computer that switches data and programs between them. The private branch exchange (PBX), discussed earlier, is another example of a star network. Star networks are also especially suited to an organization with several related plants or divisions, because each plant or division may need access to common centralized files but may also need its own local facilities.

Bus network.
A telecommunications network consisting of a line and several devices that are tapped into the line.

Bus Networks A **bus network** works a lot like ordinary city buses in ground-based transportation systems. Moreover, the hardware devices are like "bus stops" and the data like "passengers." For example, the network in Figure 6-19b contains four terminal stations (bus stops) at which data (passengers) are "picked up" or "let off." Local area networks (LANs), discussed earlier, often use a bus topology. The bus line commonly consists of a high-capacity, high-speed coaxial cable, with inexpensive twisted-pair wires dropped off each terminal station. A bus network contains no host computer.

Ring network.
A telecommunications network in which machines are connected serially in a closed loop.

Ring Networks A less common and more expensive alternative to the star and the bus is the **ring network,** in which a host computer is absent and a number of computers or other devices are connected by a loop. A ring network is shown in Figure 6-19c. One popular form of ring network is the *token-ring* local area network (LAN) pattern, which we'll discuss in the next section.

FIGURE 6-19 **Three network topologies.** (a) Star. (b) Bus. (c) Ring.

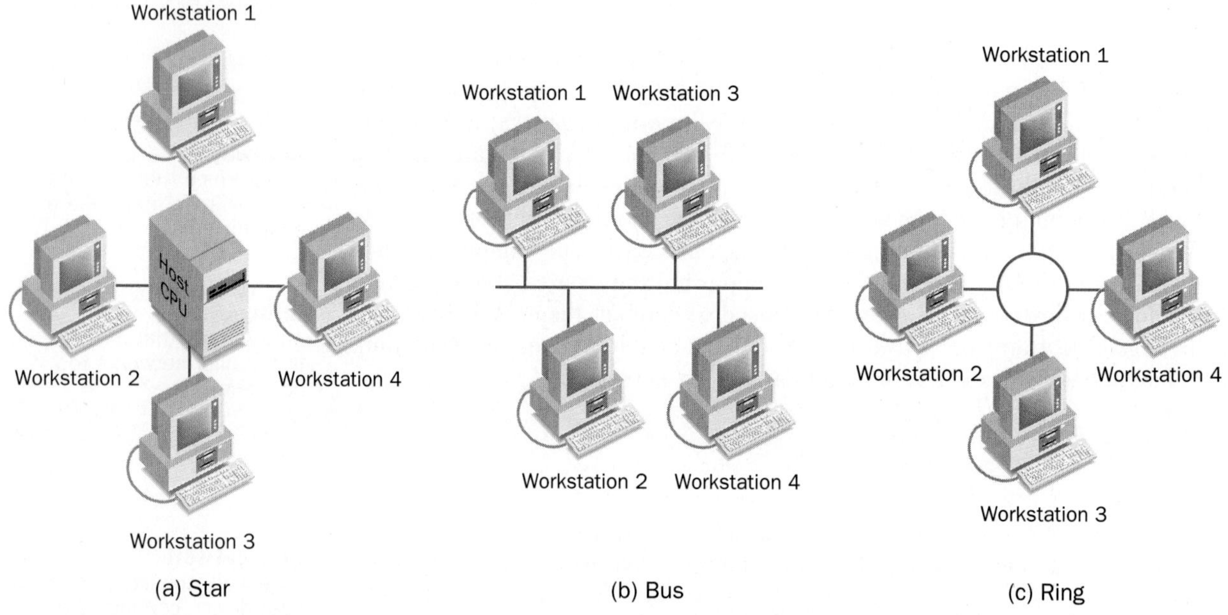

Communications Among Devices

In the last few sections, we covered various types of communications media and networks. In this section, we will discuss communications standards and special communications management techniques designed to optimize the flow of communications traffic.

Protocols

Because manufacturers have long produced devices that use a variety of transmission techniques, communications standards for the industry have been a major problem. Everyone recognizes the need for standardizing transmission methods, but the form such standards should take is still widely debated. What is needed is some common agreement on matters such as communications protocols.

The term *protocol* originates from the areas of diplomacy and etiquette. For instance, at a dinner party in the elegant home of a family on the social register, the protocol in effect may be formal attire, impeccable table manners, and remaining at the table until beckoned to the parlor by the host or hostess. At a backwoods country barbeque, a different protocol will probably exist. In the communications field, protocols have comparable rules.

A communications **protocol** is a collection of procedures used to establish, maintain, and terminate transmission between devices. Protocols specify how devices will physically connect into a network, how data will be packaged during transmission (e.g., asynchronously or synchronously), how receiver devices will acknowledge sender devices (a process called *handshaking*), how errors will be handled, and so on. Just as people need an agreed-upon set of rules to communicate effectively, so do machines need a common set of rules to help them get along with one another. Protocols are found in all types of networks. Two common protocols found in LANs, for instance, are token passing and CSMA/CD.

Protocol. A set of conventions used by machines to establish communication with one another in a telecommunications environment.

Token passing often is used with a ring network topology. Here's how it works: A small packet called a *token* is sent around a loop or ring. The token has room for messages and addresses. As the token is passed around the ring, workstations either check to see if the token is addressed to them or try to seize it so that they can assign messages to it. A token traveling around the ring contains a control area, which specifies whether the token is free or carries a message. When a sender device captures a free token, it changes the status of the token from "free" to "busy," adds a message, and releases it. The message then travels around the ring to the receiver location. The receiver copies the message, puts an acknowledgement on the token, and sends the token back to the sender station. The sender notes the acknowledgement message and changes the status of the token to "free."

CSMA/CD is an acronym for *carrier sense multiple access with collision detection.* With CSMA/CD, which is most commonly used in bus networks, workstations try to seize the network's attention whenever they are ready. The collision detection feature ensures that the devices can't use the line at exactly the same moment and thus interfere with each other. The collision-detection feature merely automates something we humans do almost unconsciously when speaking on the phone—making sure the other person isn't speaking when we begin to talk.

Hardware for Managing Communications Traffic

Now that we've covered some of the basic elements of telecommunications systems, let's see how these systems have been made more efficient. As an example, we'll look at several types of devices that enhance the efficiency of wide area telecommunications networks. The most notable of these *communications management devices* are multiplexers, concentrators, front-end processors, and back-end processors.

Multiplexer.
A communications device that interleaves the messages of several low-speed devices and sends them along a single high-speed path.

Multiplexers Communications lines almost always have far greater capacity than a single terminal can use. Many workstations can work adequately at speeds of 300 bps, and voice-grade lines can transmit up to 9,600 bps. Since communications lines are expensive, it is desirable that several low-speed devices share the same line. A device called a **multiplexer** makes this possible.

Figure 6-20 illustrates the use of two multiplexers servicing several workstations and a host CPU. The first multiplexes, or combines, the data from low-speed lines into a high-speed line. The second demultiplexes the incoming character stream so that the CPU appears to get the messages from the work-

FIGURE 6-20

Multiplexing. Multiplexers enable several low-speed devices to share a high-speed line. Here multiplexer A combines the messages sent from four workstations. Multiplexer B "demultiplexes" the message for the CPU so that they look like standard local input.

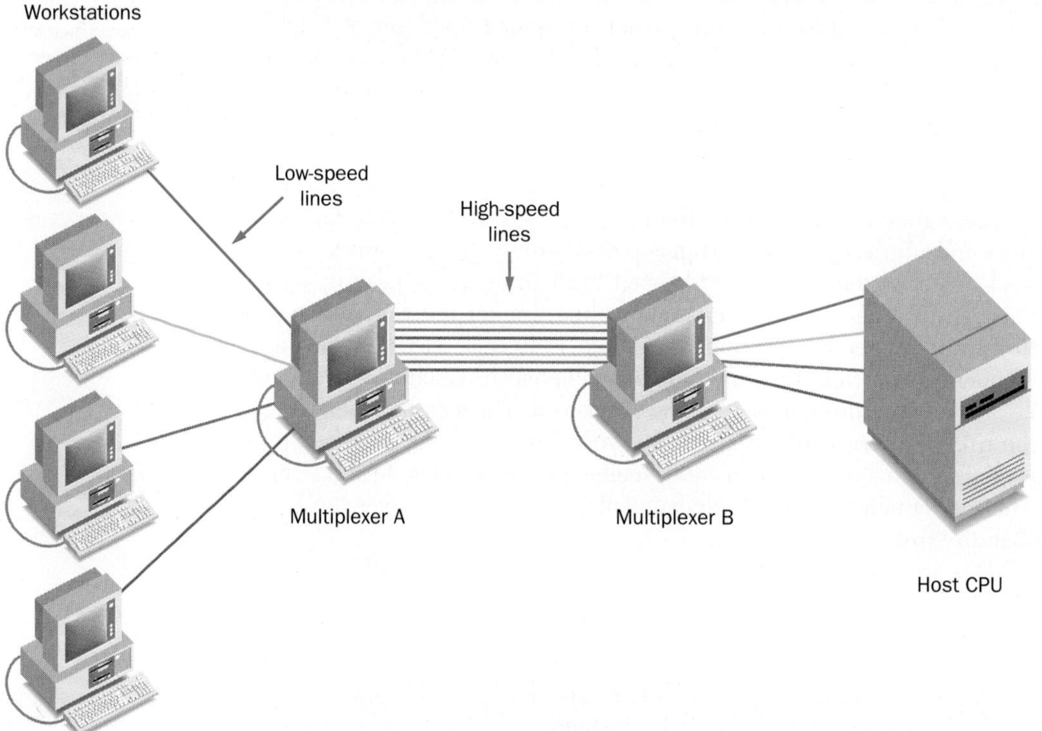

stations individually. Recently, with the appearance of high-speed digital lines, devices called *T1 multiplexers* have arrived on the scene. These multiplexers have the capacity to carry as much voice and data traffic as 24 conventional (analog) phone lines.

Concentrators A **concentrator** is a hardware device that combines control and multiplexing functions, among other things. Commonly it is a minicomputer with a facility that provides a store-and-forward capability. Thus, messages from slow devices such as asynchronous terminals can be stored at the concentrator until enough characters are collected to make forwarding to another device worthwhile.

Concentrator. A communications device that combines terminal control and multiplexing functions.

In airline passenger-reservations systems, concentrators placed at key sites, such as Boston, New York, Los Angeles, and other transportation centers, allow several agents to share communications lines economically. Messages initiated by agents are sent to the concentrator, stored, multiplexed with messages from other agents, and transmitted at very high speeds over long-distance lines to a central processing site. Using the long-distance line in this fashion minimizes communications costs.

Front- and Back-End Processors Large computer systems often use front-end processors and back-end processors to eliminate bottlenecks in networks.

A **front-end processor** is a computer that screens messages sent to the main (host) computer and also relieves it of certain computational chores. Front-end processors are commonly employed for such things as checking the validity of user account numbers, processing protocols, changing the format of incoming data (thereby simplifying processing for the host), and providing access to network servers.

Front-end processor. A computer that screens messages sent to the main computer and also relieves the main computer of certain computational chores.

Large computer systems also often contain **back-end processors** that relieve the host of retrieval, update, and storage-management tasks associated with selected large banks of data. Such data may include corporate databases, electronic-mail messages, and electronic documents.

Back-end processors. A computer that relieves the main computer of processing tasks for selected large banks of data.

Here's an example of how processing takes place in a network in which the processing workload is distributed among front- and back-end processors: At one large national service center, incoming phone calls for customer assistance go to a front-end processor. This computer uses the caller's area code to automatically route the call to the appropriate service agent. At the same time, it also hands the phone number to a back-end processor, which fetches the caller's name and account history from a database and sends it to the agent's display screen—before the agent picks up the phone. During the course of the call, the agent may use the host mainframe to look up prices or check on the availability of field repair personnel.

Summary and Key Terms

Telecommunications refers to communications over a distance, such as over phone lines, via privately owned cable, or by satellite.

Telecommunications Applications A wide variety of important business applications involve telecommunications. Among these are distributed transaction processing, interorganizational systems (IOSs), **electronic data inter-**

change (EDI), electronic mailboxes, voice mail, electronic bulletin boards, computer conferencing, **facsimile (fax) machine, cellular phones,** and information retrieval.

Communications Media Messages transmitted in a telecommunications system are sent over some type of **communications medium.** Physical lines, such as **twisted-pair wires, coaxial cable,** and **fiber optic cable,** constitute one major class of media. Messages also are commonly sent through the air, in the form of **microwave** signals. **Terrestrial microwave stations** accommodate microwave transmission when either the sender or the receiver is on the ground. **Communications satellites** reduce the cost of long-distance transmission via terrestrial microwave stations and provide better overseas communications.

The *speed* of a data-communications medium is measured in **bits per second (bps).** The slowest speeds are referred to as **narrowband transmission.** Medium-speed lines, which are the type commonly found in the public phone network, are capable of **voice-grade transmission.** The highest speeds, referred to as **wideband transmission,** as possible only with coaxial cable, fiber optic cable, and microwaves.

Communications media can be in either the simplex, half-duplex, or full-duplex mode. In **simplex transmission,** messages can be sent only in a single, prespecified direction (such as with a doorbell). In **half-duplex transmission,** messages can be sent both ways but not simultaneously (for example, as with press-to-talk phones). **Full-duplex transmission** permits transmission in two directions simultaneously (as with traffic on a busy two-way street).

Signals sent along a phone line travel in an **analog** fashion—that is, as continuous waves. Computers and their support equipment, however, are **digital** devices that handle data coded into two discrete states—0s and 1s. For two or more digital devices to communicate with each other over analog phone lines, a **modem** must be placed between each piece of equipment and the phone lines. Modems perform digital-to-analog and analog-to-digital conversion. Modems can be bypassed when *digital lines* are used to interconnect devices.

To exchange data along a communications medium, two machines must "agree" on a mode of transmission and on a method of packaging data. Transmission between machines is done either in **parallel,** in which each bit of a byte is sent along a different path, or in **serial,** in which bits of a byte follow one another serially along a single path. Serially transmitted data are packaged either **asynchronously** (one byte to a package) or **synchronously** (several bytes to a package).

Wide Area Networks and Local Networks **Wide area networks (WANs)** are communications networks designed to encompass a relatively wide geographic area. Three types of WANs are public-access networks, value-added networks, and private wide area networks. **Public-access networks** generally are maintained by the phone companies, or **common carriers. Value-added network (VAN)** vendors are firms that use the facilities of a common carrier to offer the general subscribing public additional services using those facilities. These services include information retrieval, information processing, and electronic mail. Because many organizations today have massive communications requirements, some have set up their own **private wide area networks.**

Many organizations take heavy advantage of these and also build their own **local networks**—networks that link devices in a single building or at a single site. Three common types of local networks are local area networks, private branch exchanges, and hierarchical networks.

Local area networks (LANs) typically fall into one of two categories. The first, **client-server LANs,** consist of **server** devices that provide workstations services such as access to peripherals, database lookups, and computing. The second, **peer-to-peer LANs,** have the user workstations and shared peripherals in the network operating at the same level. A **private branch exchange (PBX)** consists of a central, private switchboard that links to devices by switched lines. A **hierarchical local network** typically consists of a powerful host CPU at the top level of the hierarchy and microcomputer workstations and display terminals at lower levels. Data used by the workstations can be either **downloaded** from the host or **uploaded** to it. Devices on two *dissimilar* networks can communicate with each other if they are connected by a **gateway.** Devices on two *similar* networks can communicate with each other if they are connected by a **bridge.**

Network Topologies Telecommunications networks can be classified in terms of their topology, or shape. Three common topologies are the **star network,** the **bus network,** and the **ring network.**

Communications among Devices A communications **protocol** is a collection of procedures used to establish, maintain, and terminate transmission between devices. Because there are so many ways to transmit data, many industry groups have pushed for certain protocols to become industry standards. These efforts notwithstanding, a number of incompatible guidelines remain in effect. Two major LAN protocols are *token passing* and *carrier sense multiple access with collision detection* (*CSMA/CD*).

Communications management devices enhance the efficiency of telecommunications traffic flow. Common devices are multiplexers, concentrators, and front-end processors. **Multiplexers** enable several low-speed devices to share one high-speed line. **Concentrators** perform multiplexing functions and can store and forward data as well. **Front-end processors** screen messages sent to the main (host) computer and also relieve it of certain computational chores. **Back-end processors** relieve the host of processing tasks associated with selected large banks of data.

Review Exercises

Fill-in Questions

1. ____________ (EDI) refers to sending electronic purchase orders and invoices from company to company.
2. A(n)____________ machine enables images of hard-copy documents to be sent over the phone lines.
3. ____________, the communications medium employed by cable television, was developed primarily to provide interference-free video transmission.
4. In contrast to the continuous waves used to represent analog signals over phone lines, computers generate ____________ signals.
5. ____________ is a transmission medium that involves laser-generated light waves sent over transparent, hairlike strands.
6. Conversion from analog to digital and digital to analog is performed by a(n)____________.
7. ____________ transmission involves sending data along a communications line in blocks of several characters at a time.
8. ____________ are companies licensed by the government to provide communications services to the public.
9. ____________ transmission is a type of serial transmission in which characters are sent along a line as they are generated.
10. A hierarchical local network is an example of a(n) ____________ network topology.

Matching Questions

Match each term with the description that fits best.

a. front-end processor
b. modem
c. gateway
d. multiplexer
e. concentrator
f. protocol

___ 1. A device that combines several low-speed lines into a high-speed line.

___ 2. A hardware device that collects messages and forwards them in a transmission-efficient fashion.

___ 3. A device that converts digital data for transmission over the phone lines.

___ 4. A device used to screen data sent to the host computer.

___ 5. A standard used to make communications devices more compatible.

___ 6. A device that enables two dissimilar networks to communicate with each other.

Discussion Questions

1. What is the difference between an electronic mailbox and a computer bulletin board?
2. What is the difference between a local area network (LAN) and a value-added network (VAN)?
3. What is the difference between a client-server LAN and a peer-to-peer LAN?
4. Name some types of communications media and explain how they differ.
5. What is the difference between uploading and downloading?
6. What is the difference between baseband and broadband transmission?
7. How do parallel and serial communications differ?
8. What is a protocol?

Critical Thinking Questions

1. It has been said that advances in communications technology are collapsing the "information float"—the amount of time information spends in transit when being communicated from one point to another. Can you think of three business examples of collapsing information float? What is the benefit to a business in each example?
2. Identify two examples of computer applications that need the type of transmission that broadband cable provides.
3. You are asked by a teacher in your former high school to give a 45-minute presentation to her students on telecommunications. You are to prepare a list of the half-dozen things that every student today should know about telecommunications. What would be on your list?
4. EDI, its benefits notwithstanding, poses some new legal problems. One is that it's not clear who is at fault if transmission problems cause a miscommunicated transaction that results in a loss. Can you think of any ways in which an organization might protect itself from such legal headaches with EDI?
5. Should the government place special controls on operators of 900-prefix phone numbers? Defend your position by preparing a list of uses or practices you feel are not in the public interest and a list of uses or practices you feel are. If you believe there should be some controls, identify them.
6. In the section of VANs, the possibility of allowing phone companies to sell information over the phone lines is raised. What arguments can you present for and against letting the phone companies become VAN operators?

W I N D O W 3

Inside Prodigy

A Closer Look at an Information Utility

Prodigy—created in 1988 as a joint venture between Sears and IBM—is an easy-to-use information-retrieval service that's targeted to the needs of the average person. It contains facilities for online shopping, banking, securities trading, news on a variety of topics, weather reports, mail, educational information, and dozens of other services. This window surveys types of potentially valuable information available through Prodigy and similar services.

1

1. Most Prodigy screens either provide information or, as shown here, ask users to make a selection from a menu of choices. The user highlights the choice and then presses the Enter key. Here, the "Race to Promontory" choice is highlighted; by pressing the Enter key the user will get information screens and further choices regarding this historical event.

3

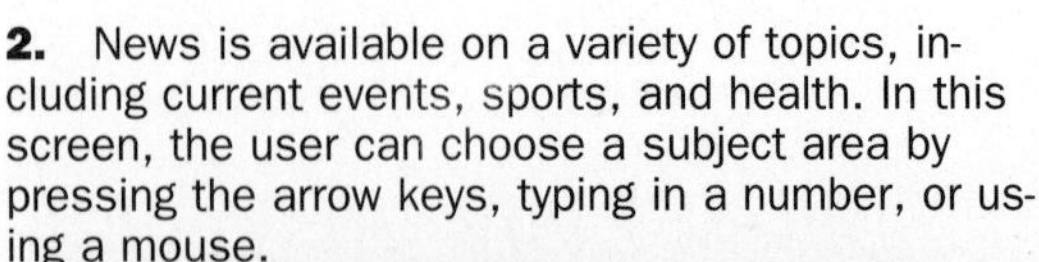

2. News is available on a variety of topics, including current events, sports, and health. In this screen, the user can choose a subject area by pressing the arrow keys, typing in a number, or using a mouse.

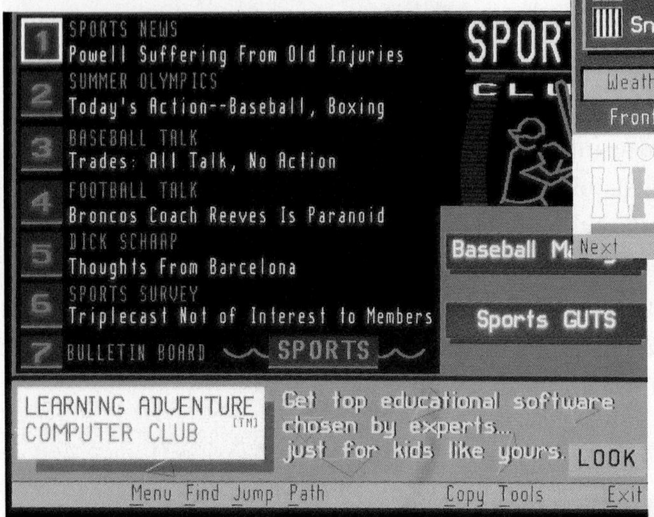

2

3. Both weather and news are updated continuously throughout the day. The weather map here indicates that by highlighting and selecting "Next" in the lower part of the screen, the user can pull up information about weather fronts.

4

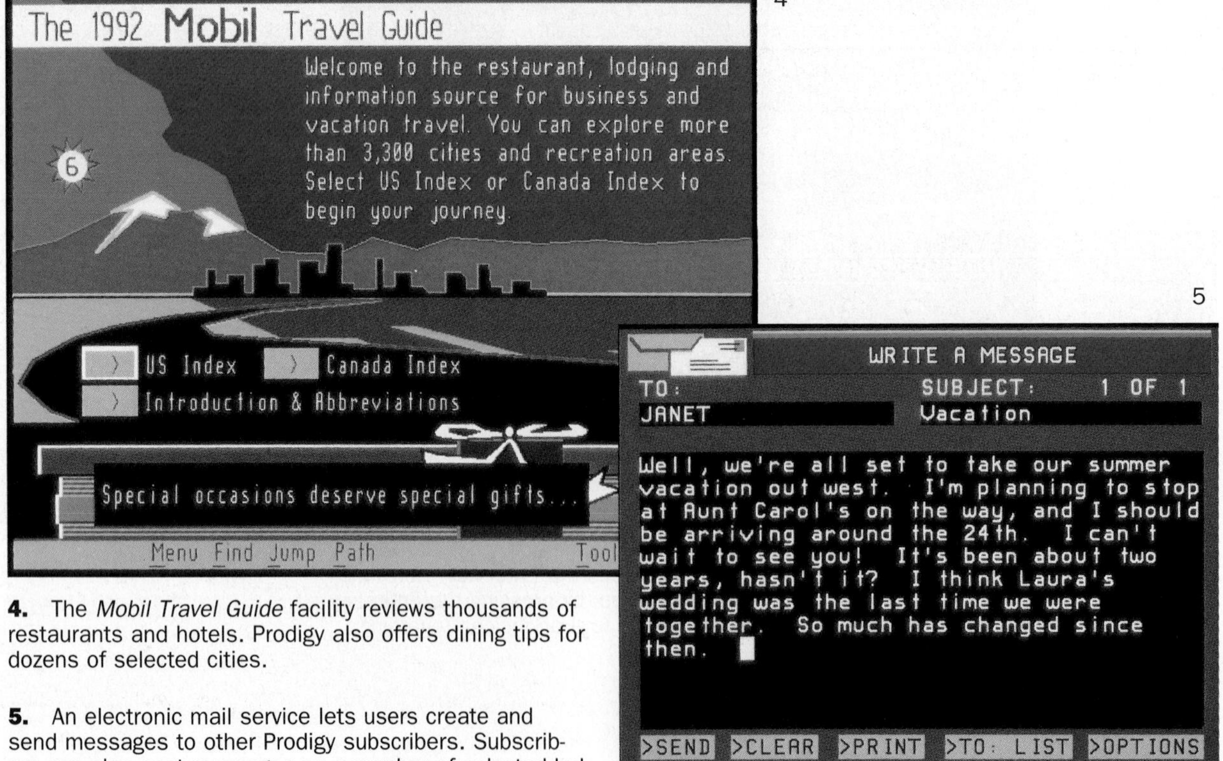

5

4. The *Mobil Travel Guide* facility reviews thousands of restaurants and hotels. Prodigy also offers dining tips for dozens of selected cities.

5. An electronic mail service lets users create and send messages to other Prodigy subscribers. Subscribers can also post messages on a number of selected bulletin boards.

6

6. The EAASY SABRE system books and confirms reservations on all major airlines and reserves hotel rooms and cars worldwide. The system also automatically finds the lowest airfare from a database of about 50 million fares.

7

7. Hundreds of thousands of items are available for sale—occasionally at special discounts to Prodigy subscribers. Subscribers can buy anything from flowers to major catalog items to cruise packages. Payment can also be made online.

8

9

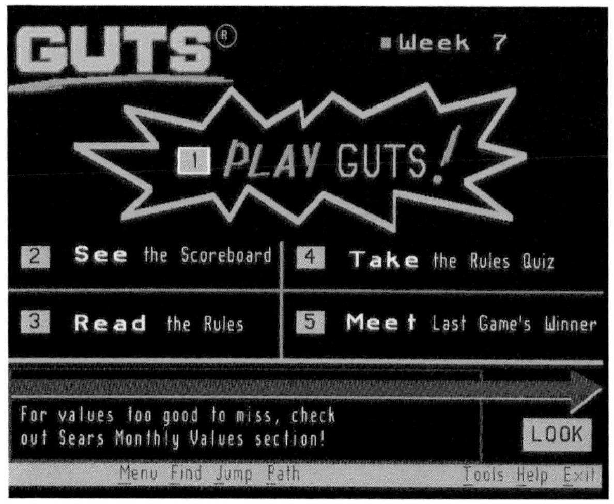

8. Prodigy offers a variety of financial services including automatic and manual price lookups for securities, financial news on specific companies, and market reports.

9. Games are available for subscribers to play alone or with other subscribers.

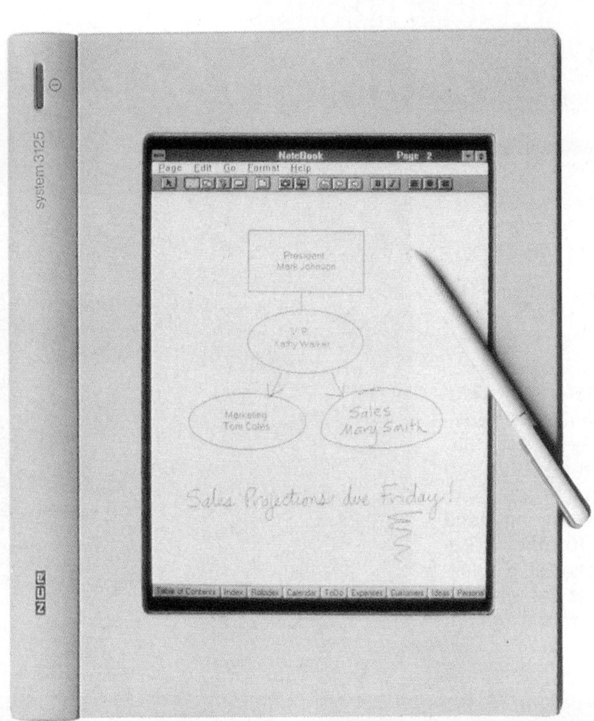
system3125
NCR
NoteBook
Page 2
Page Edit Go Format Help
President
Mark Johnson
V.P.
Kathy Walker
Marketing
Tom Coles
Sales
Mary Smith
Sales Projections due Friday!

Systems Software

7

Do pen computers have operating systems, too? You betcha. Shown here is Pen Windows, an operating system created so that pen computers can understand pen commands from applications software and, also, make selections from the Microsoft Windows interface. Chapter 7 covers the basics of operating systems.

OUTLINE

Overview

The Operating System
- Differences among Operating Systems
- Functions of the Operating System
- Interleaved Processing Techniques

A Closer Look at Several Operating Systems
- MS-DOS and PC-DOS
- DOS with Windows
- Macintosh System Software
- UNIX
- OS/2
- Windows NT
- NetWare

Language Translators

Utility Programs

LEARNING OBJECTIVES

After completing this chapter, you will be able to:

1. Describe the types of systems software.
2. Explain the activities of an operating system and describe some of the differences between operating systems.
3. Describe several ways in which computer systems interleave operations to process data more efficiently.
4. Explain the role of a language translator and describe several types of language translators.
5. Explain the role of a utility program and describe several types of utility programs.

Overview

Systems software. Computer programs that enable application programs to run on a given set of hardware.

Systems software consists of programs that coordinate the various parts of the computer system to make it run rapidly and efficiently. They perform such tasks as formatting disks so that they are suitable for storing budgets or word-processed documents, copying program files or data files from one diskette to another, and enabling your brand of applications software to work on your printer or display device.

Most users aren't aware of what systems software is doing for them. On microcomputer systems, for example, issuing a save command to store a program onto disk requires that systems software look for adequate space on the disk, write the program onto "addresses" of this space, and update the disk's directory (indicating the addresses at which the program has been placed). And when users are having their systems communicate with databases on remote mainframes, they may not realize that systems software goes to work checking the validity of their ID numbers or passwords and, later, translating their database commands into machine language.

Systems software is available in three basic types: operating systems, language translators, and utility programs.

In this chapter, we'll first look closely at the *operating system,* which is the main piece of systems software in any computer system. Here we'll discuss what operating systems do and examine the various differences among them. We'll also take a closer look at a few of today's most talked-about operating systems.

Next, we will look at *language translators.* A language translator is a program that translates a program in BASIC, COBOL, or some other programming language into machine language.

Finally, we will cover *utility programs,* or utilities. Utilities typically perform less-frequent or less-critical types of control functions, such as allowing you to recover inadvertently erased disk files. These packages are often sold by third-party vendors as add-ons to specific operating systems.

The Operating System

Before the 1960s, human operators generally ran computers manually. For each incoming job needing processing, the operator had to reset a number of circuits on the computer by hand. In fact, every function of the computer system—input, output, processing, and storage—required substantial operator supervision and intervention.

On these early computers, jobs could be processed only in a serial fashion—one program at a time. As a result, the computers sat idle for long periods while operators took care of manual procedures between jobs.

Operating system. The main collection of systems software that enables the computer system to manage the resources under its control.

The development of operating systems greatly improved the efficiency of computers. An **operating system** is the main collection of programs that manage the computer system's activities. Operating systems have eliminated much of the manual work formerly required to process programs. Many of today's operating systems enable processing of several jobs concurrently and permit the computer to be left completely unattended by the operator while programs are running.

The primary chores of the operating system are management and control. The operating system ensures that each valid incoming program is processed in an orderly fashion and that the computer system's resources are made available to run the programs optimally. For example, on a large computer system, the operating system checks to see that people trying to gain access to the computer system are authorized users. When a user's identification number is found to be valid, he or she is signed in, or "logged on." Next, the operating system determines which of the computer system's resources will be needed to do the user's job. Then it automatically assigns these resources to the work request if and when they are available.

Generally, the user will need to tap a number of the system's resources. For example, a typical job might need the number-crunching power of the CPU, a language translator that understands the BASIC programming language, primary storage for storing intermediate results, secondary storage for storing data and programs, and a printer for output. The operating system makes all these facilities available. Finally, when the user finishes with the computer system, he or she is logged off. In effect, the operating system is the go-between that meshes the user's applications program with the system's hardware resources.

Figure 7-1 depicts the hierarchical principle by which computer systems work. The operating system serves as the gateway to applications programs,

FIGURE 7-1

The gateway role of the operating system. The operating system makes computer system resources available to the user. Everyone using a computer system must interact with the operating system in some way.

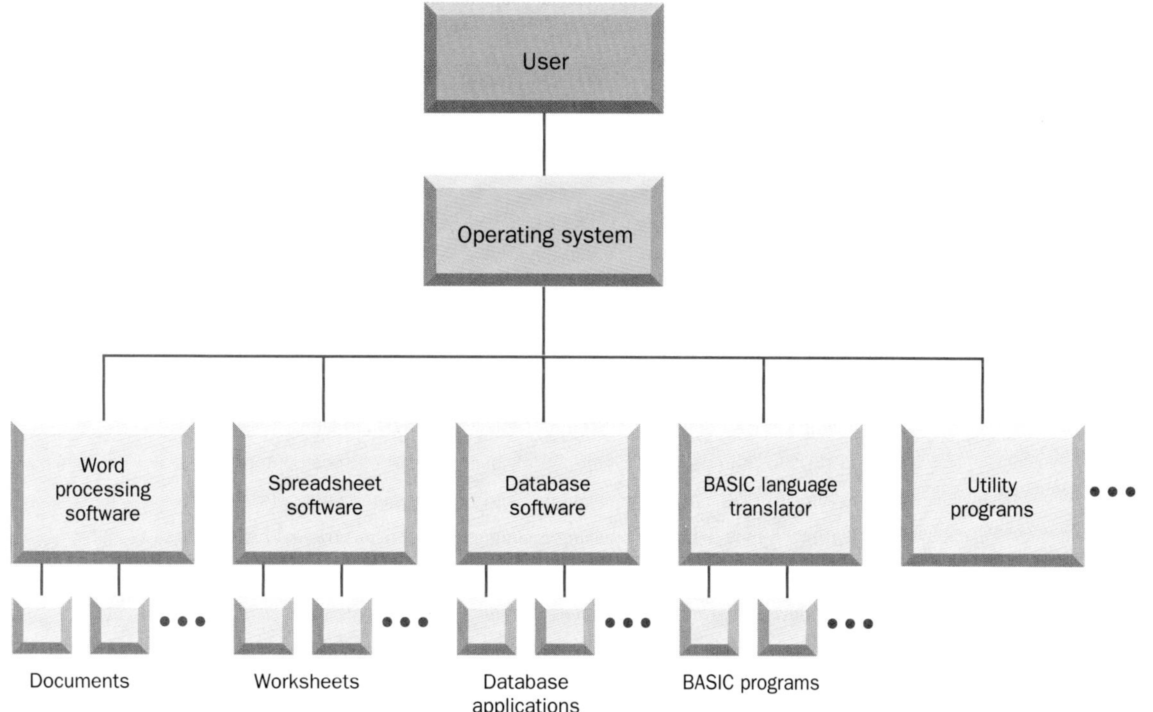

their data, and other system resources. As soon as you turn on your computer system or terminal, you are confronted with the operating system. From there, you choose the program with which you wish to work—say, word processor or spreadsheet—and the operating system retrieves it from disk for you. When finished, you generally must exit back to the operating system before you can invoke another program.

Because of the central role of the operating system in managing the computer system's activities, many consider the operating system to be the most critical piece of software in the computer system. Without an operating system, none of the other programs can run.

Differences among Operating Systems

The marketplace offers a wide selection of operating systems (see Figure 7-2). Like the executives who manage and control large corporations, the various operating systems differ in many important respects. For example, some operating systems are designed for only one "brand" of computer, whereas others are compatible with several. Other important differences concern ease of use, speed, number of features available, portability, and cost. Often these criteria conflict. For example, an operating system that's designed to be either easy to use or

FIGURE 7-2

Some popular operating systems. Operating systems can differ substantially with respect to ease of use, speed, number of features available, portability, and cost. Each operating system is targeted to one or more specific types of computers.

AOS, DG Operating systems used on Data General minicomputers

CPF, SSP Operating systems available on IBM's small business systems

Macintosh System Software The graphically oriented operating system used on Apple Macintosh microcomputers

MCP/AS, OS/1100 Operating systems used on Unisys mainframes

MS-DOS The most widely used operating system on IBM-compatible microcomputers

MVS, VM Operating systems used on IBM mainframes

NetWare The most widely used operating system on local area networks (LANs)

OS/2 The operating system designed for the high end of IBM's PS/2 line of microcomputers

Penpoint An operating system designed for pen-based computers

PC-DOS An operating system widely used on IBM microcomputers

UNICOS, COS Operating systems used by Cray supercomputers

UNIX A multiuser, multitasking operating system used by small computers

VAX/VMS An operating system used by DEC VAX minicomputers

Windows A graphically oriented operating environment.

Windows New Technology (Windows NT) Microsoft's high-end, graphically oriented operating system.

Xenix, Venix, Ultrix, A/UX, AIX, PowerOpen Six UNIX-like operating systems flexible generally isn't fast. In other words, the more overhead the operating system must carry, the slower it will be and the more storage it requires. And, as you might expect, a system that's packaged with an assortment of sophisticated features isn't likely to be inexpensive.

On large computers such as mainframes, operating systems can be quite powerful. Hundreds of users may be seeking access to the mainframe at more or less the same time. Many of those users will be running several programs concurrently. For instance, someone may be working on a set of database retrievals while having a 50-page report printed out. On large computer systems there are sophisticated facilities for interleaving users' work, for keeping the computer safe from unauthorized access, for bookkeeping, and for a number of other complex tasks. Because these systems often have huge memories, their operating systems can afford to be large and sophisticated.

Microcomputers, in contrast, have almost always been hampered by a limited amount of memory. For instance, the original IBM PC of 1981 came with only 128 KB RAM. Thus, PC-DOS, the flagship operating system of the IBM PC, was originally limited to this amount. Although later models of the IBM PC came with more RAM, allowing DOS to grow, 16-bit DOS—which is based on the primitive Intel 8088 chip—has a RAM limit of 640 KB. This situation has forced 16-bit DOS to become essentially just a partial operating system (by mainframe standards).

Now that powerful 32-bit chips such as the Intel Pentium and the PowerPC are available—and powerful operating systems such as OS/2, Windows NT, and UNIX are here to make use of them—we are beginning to see microcomputer operating-system environments that are approaching those of mainframes (see Tomorrow box).

Functions of the Operating System

Now that you have a general idea of what operating systems do and what some of the differences among them are, we can discuss their functions in greater detail. As we examine these functions, keep in mind that not all of them—especially functions that deal with more than one user or one program—will apply to the operating system on your computer.

Assignment of System Resources When most computers are first activated, a major component of the operating system—a program called the **supervisor**—is also activated. On some systems, this program may be referred to as the *monitor*, the *kernel*, or something else. The supervisor will always be in memory when the computer is on. On many computers, other programs in the operating system are brought into memory from secondary storage only as they are needed. The supervisor mobilizes these other programs to perform system tasks for applications programs.

Supervisor. The central program in an operating system.

Once the supervisor activates any other program in the operating system, it relinquishes control to that program until the program has performed its role. At that point, control returns to the supervisor, which may then call up other systems programs that the job requires. The supervisor operates somewhat like a master of ceremonies, repeatedly introducing the next speaker on the program after the previous one has finished his or her talk.

TOMORROW

The Battle of the 32-bit Operating Systems

OS/2, Windows NT, and UNIX Duke It Out

It's shaping up as possibly the biggest software war of all time. The stakes: coronation as the corporate operating system of choice for the new breed of high-end desktop computers—a crown that will probably be worn for at least the next decade. The main participants: OS/2, Windows New Technology (Windows NT), and UNIX—operating systems that are designed specifically for computer systems run by chips with 32-bit architectures.

What's so special about 32-bit chips? They have 4 GB or more of addressable memory on board as well as 32-bit-wide data paths to and from the CPU (see photo). With the ability to access only 640 KB RAM at a time, DOS hardly dents the power of these chips. The new breed of 32-bit operating systems does. Included among the most well-known 32-bit chips are the Intel '386, '486, and Pentium chips, the Motorola 68030 and 68040 chips, and the PowerPC chip found on the new Apple Macintoshes.

OS/2 has in its favor the sheer clout of being backed by the world's largest computer company, IBM. Also noteworthy is the fact that probably many desktop computers in the future will communicate with mainframes in corporate environments, two arenas where IBM has a long track record of experience and success.

Windows NT has a strong position because of the large base of Windows applications now already in use. Also, Microsoft Corporation, which produces Windows, has sold more software for microcomputers than anyone else. Its DOS software is the most widely sold piece of systems software of all time.

UNIX has been around the longest of any of the 32-bit operating systems and users have more experience with it than with any of its challengers.

32-bit chip. DOS hardly dents its power, but the new breed of operating systems does.

UNIX may also be the most flexible of all of the operating systems at sites where a diverse mix of hardware is used. Recently, Novell has made a major commitment to develop UNIX and to integrate it with its NetWare communications environmment.

Currently, most attention has focused on OS/2 and Windows NT, with UNIX running third. Critics observe that UNIX's current strength is in scientific rather than business applications. Also, many versions of UNIX are now in use, which inhibits it from developing into a standard platform for corporate applications.

But the real winner—if there is one—may not be decided for several years. If the past is any indication, companies will probably take a slow, cautious approach to making their decisions—especially with cost, compatibility of choices, and so many other factors riding on the line.

In addition to the supervisor, a number of other operating system programs have a hand in determining which parts of the computer system will be mobilized for any given job. One of these is the **command-language translator.** This program reads instructions to the operating system that the user or programmer initiates. These instructions, which often are coded in a **command language** (sometimes referred to as a *job-control language*, or *JCL*), permit the user and programmer to specify orders for retrieving, saving, deleting, copying, or moving files; which I/O devices are to be used; which language the user or programmer is employing; any customized requests for output format; and any other special processing needs of the applications program. The command language, in effect, gives the user or programmer a channel for communicating directly with the operating system.

Command-language translator.
Systems software that translates instructions written in a command language into machine-language instructions.

Command language.
A programming language used to communicate with the operating system.

Operating systems can differ significantly in how command-language instructions are invoked. Take deleting a file, for example. With operating systems such as MS-DOS and PC-DOS, which are used on many IBM microcomputers and similar machines from other manufacturers, you generally type in a command such as

```
ERASE FRED
```

to delete a file named FRED. Both MS-DOS and PC-DOS employ a *language interface*, meaning that users generally must know the syntax of a particular command language to communicate with these operating systems.

On the Apple Macintosh line of computers, icons representing operating-system commands have traditionally been used in conjunction with a mouse to carry out similar operations. So, to delete FRED, you can use the mouse to point first to a file-folder-shaped icon labeled FRED and then to a wastebasket-shaped icon to activate the delete operation. Operating systems such as Macintosh System Software employ a *graphical interface*—or **graphical user interface (GUI)**—meaning that users need only point to menus and graphical icons to issue commands rather than remember a specific syntax. Figure 7-3 illustrates the difference between a language interface and a graphical interface.

Graphical user interface (GUI).
Refers to the computer graphics screens that make it easier for users to interact with software.

Virtually any operating system that naturally uses a language interface can be complemented with a graphically oriented "shell" program, thereby overlaying it with a graphical interface. These shell programs are commonly called **operating environments.** Probably the most well-known operating environment is Microsoft Windows, created to fit over the MS-DOS operating system. The use of graphical user interfaces in software products is explored more fully in Window 4.

Operating environment.
A term that refers to a graphical interface or to the combination of an operating system and graphical interface.

In the absence of special command-language instructions from the user—regardless of whether these instructions are invoked through written commands or via a graphical interface—the command-language translator makes some standard assumptions about how things are to be done. These assumptions are called **defaults.** However, you can often override the defaults. For instance, you can override the standard default of one printed copy of a document by asking for two, or you can change the way characters are displayed onscreen by asking for a higher or lower screen resolution.

Default.
The assumption a computer program makes when no specific choice is indicated by the user or programmer.

Scheduling Resources and Jobs Closely related to the process of assigning system resources to a job is that of scheduling resources and jobs. The operating

FIGURE 7-3

Language interface versus graphical user interface. (a) A language command must be typed at the system prompt. (b) A graphical user interface lets users issue commands by selecting file and command icons with a mouse; here, the user is deleting a file named FRED.

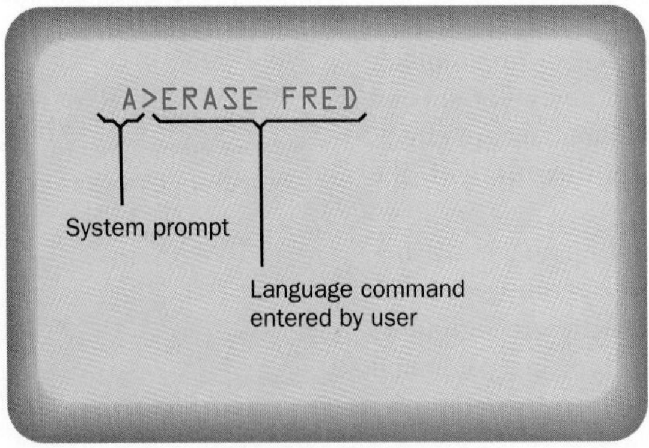

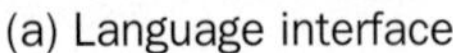

(a) Language interface

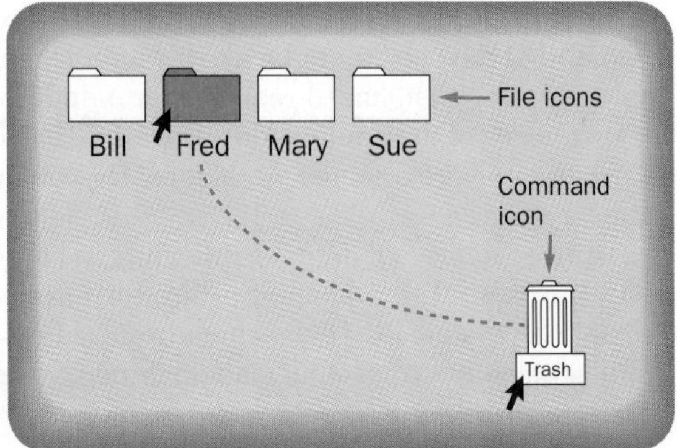

(b) Graphical user interface

system helps decide not only which resources to use (assignment) but when to use them (scheduling). Scheduling can become extremely complicated when the system must handle a number of jobs at once.

Scheduling programs in the operating system determine the order in which jobs are processed. A job's place in line is not necessarily on a first-come, first-served basis. Some users may have higher priority than others, the devices needed to process the next job in line may not be free, or other factors may affect the order of processing.

The operating system also schedules the operation of parts of the computer system so that they work on different portions of various jobs at the same time. Because input and output devices work much more slowly than the CPU itself, millions of calculations may be performed for several programs while the contents of a single program are being printed or displayed. Using a number of techniques, the operating system juggles the various jobs to be done in order to employ system devices as efficiently as possible. Later in this section, we'll discuss some of the methods of processing a number of jobs at more or less the same time. These procedures are known collectively as *interleaved processing techniques.*

Monitoring Activities A third general function of operating systems is monitoring, or keeping track of, activities in the computer system while processing is under way. The operating system terminates programs that contain errors or exceed their maximum storage allocations. It also sends an appropriate message to the user or operator. Similarly, if any abnormalities arise in I/O devices or elsewhere in the system, the operating system sends a message to the user.

Bookkeeping and security are two other monitoring tasks of the operating system. Records may be kept of log-on and log-off times, programs' running times, programs that each user has run, and other information. In some environments, such records enable the organization to bill users. The operating system also can protect the system against unauthorized access by checking the validity of users' ID numbers and reporting attempts to breach system security. Moreover, it must protect memory so that an error in a program will not "crash" the computer system or, worse yet, corrupt vital data in other programs.

Interleaved Processing Techniques

In this section, we will examine some of the assignment and scheduling techniques that computers use to handle a large number of jobs at the same time. Sophisticated computers often take advantage of *interleaved processing techniques* such as multiprogramming, multitasking, time-sharing, virtual memory, and multiprocessing to operate more efficiently. These operating-system features enable computers to process many programs at almost the same time and, consequently, to increase the number of jobs the computer system can handle in any given period.

Multiprogramming **Multiprogramming,** a term that refers to multiuser operating systems, is somewhat similar to the operation of a busy dentist's office. The dentist *concurrently* attends to several patients in different rooms within a given time period. The dentist may pull a tooth in room 1, move to room 2 to prepare a cavity for filling, move back to room 1 to treat the hole created by the pulled tooth, and so forth. As the dentist moves from patient to patient, assistants do minor tasks.

Multiprogramming. The execution of two or more programs *concurrently* on the same computer.

In a computer system with a multiprogrammed operating system, several applications programs may be stored in memory at the same time. The CPU, like the dentist, works on only one program at a time. When it reaches a point in a program at which peripheral devices or other elements of the computer system must take over some of the work, the CPU interrupts processing to move on to another program, returning to the first program when that program is ready to be processed again. While the computer is waiting for data on one program to be accessed on disk, for example, it can perform calculations for another program. The systems software for the disk unit, like the dental assistants, does background work; in this case, it retrieves the data stored on disk.

Multiprogramming is feasible because computers can perform thousands of computations in the time it takes to ask for and receive a single piece of data from disk. Such disk I/O operations are much slower than computation, because the computer must interact with and receive communications from an external device to obtain the data it needs. It must also contend with the slower access speeds of secondary storage.

Multitasking **Multitasking** refers to a multiprogramming capability on single-user operating systems. Thus, it refers to the ability of an operating system to enable two or more programs or program tasks from a single user to execute concurrently on one computer. This feature generally allows a user to do such things as edit one program while another program is executing and have two or more programs displayed on screen at the same time and modify them concurrently (see Figure 7-4). Remember, one computer, like one dentist, can

Multitasking. The ability of a single-user operating system to enable two or more programs or program tasks to execute concurrently.

FIGURE 7-4

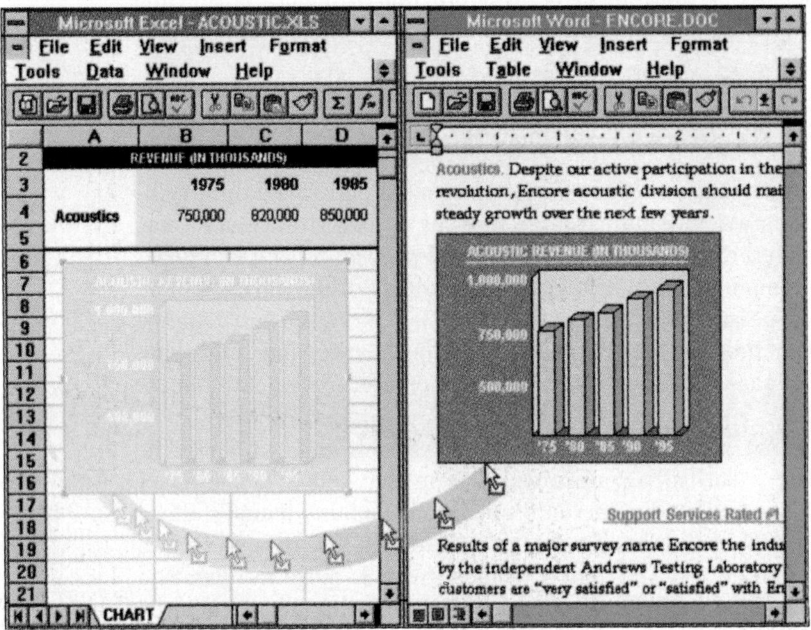

Multitasking. Multitasking enables users to work on two or more programs or tasks concurrently. Here, a mouse is being used to drag and drop a chart from a spreadsheet application into a word-processed document.

attend to only one task at a time. But the computer works so fast that the user often has the illusion that it is doing two things at once.

One situation in which multitasking is very helpful occurs when a program has an exceptionally long processing time and the computer is needed for other work. For example, suppose that you want to search through a large employee file for all people between the ages of 25 and 35 with six years of service and some experience with computers. On a relatively small computer, such a search may take several minutes, during which time you may want to use the computer for other work. With multitasking, you can use your computer to perform another task, on the same or a different program, while the search is taking place in the background.

Time-sharing.
Processing in a multiuser environment in which the computer handles users' jobs in a round-robin fashion.

Time-sharing **Time-sharing** is a very popular technique for computer systems that support numerous terminals. The operating system cycles through all the active programs in the system that need processing and gives each one a small time slice on each cycle.

For example, say there are 20 programs in the system and each program is to be allocated a time slice of 1 second (the time slice usually is much smaller than this, and all slices aren't necessarily equal). The computer will work on program 1 for one second, then on program 2 for one second, and so forth. When it finishes working on program 20 for one second, it will go back to program 1 for another second, program 2 for another second, and so on. Thus, if there is an average of 20 programs on the system, each program will get a total of 3 seconds of processing during each minute of actual clock time, or 1 second in every 20-second period. As you can see, in a time-sharing system it is difficult for a single program to dominate the CPU's attention, thereby holding up the processing of shorter programs.

Both time-sharing and multiprogramming are techniques for working on many programs concurrently by allotting short uninterrupted time periods to each. They differ in the way they allot time, however. In time-sharing, the computer spends a fixed amount of time on each program and then goes on to another. In multiprogramming, the computer works on a program until it encounters a logical stopping point, such as when more data must be read in, before going on to another program. Many computers today combine time-sharing and multiprogramming techniques to expedite processing.

Virtual Memory In the early days of computing, users who had large programs faced numerous problems with loading them into memory. Often they had to manually split such programs into pieces so that only small portions of them resided in the limited memory space at any one time. In the early 1970s, a virtual-memory feature became available on some operating systems. It permitted users the luxury of writing extremely long programs that the operating system would automatically split up and manage.

Virtual memory refers to using disk to extend conventional memory, or RAM. This is the way it usually works: The operating system delivers programs to be processed to the virtual-memory area on disk. Here the programs generally are divided into either fixed-length *pages* or variable-length *segments.* Whether the programs are subdivided into pages or segments depends on the operating system's capabilities.

Virtual memory.
An area on disk in which programs are "cut up" into manageable pieces so that they can be processed.

A virtual memory system using paging breaks a program into pages. If a program is 40 kilobytes long and the system divides programs into 4 kilobyte lengths, the program is divided into 10 pages. As the computer works on the program, it stores only a few pages at a time in RAM. As it requires other pages during program execution, it selects them from virtual memory and writes over the pages in RAM that it no longer needs. All the original pages, or modified ones, remain intact in virtual memory as the computer processes the program. So, if the computer again needs a page that has been written over in RAM, it can readily fetch it. This process continues until the program is finished.

Segmentation works somewhat like paging except that the segments are variable in length. Each segment normally consists of a contiguous block of logically interrelated material from the program. Some systems use a combination of segmentation and paging.

Not all operating systems on large computers use virtual memory. Although this technique permits a computer system to get by with a smaller RAM, it requires extra computer time to swap pages or segments in and out of RAM.

Multiprocessing **Multiprocessing** refers to the use of two or more computers linked together to perform work at the same time. This, of course, requires systems software that will realize that multiple processors are in use and has the ability to assign work to them as efficiently as possible. Whereas multiprogramming involves processing several programs or tasks *concurrently* on a single computer, multiprocessing involves handling multiple programs or tasks *simultaneously* (at precisely the same instant) on several computers. There are many ways to implement multiprocessing; two common ones covered here are coprocessing and parallel processing.

Multiprocessing.
The *simultaneous* execution of two or more program sequences by multiple computers operating under common control.

User Solution 7-1

Fault Tolerance Spells Uninterrupted Service

New York's financial district is one place where it's becoming increasingly popular to do computing the fault-tolerant way. For most companies in the investment industry, the computer is the centerpiece of transaction operations and communications with customers. The data that firms rely on to make decisions constantly change, and even a single transaction can be of mission-critical value to a company. Fault tolerance is a fast-growing trend on Wall Street because losing access to data results in work stoppage, lost opportunities, and a perception among clients of "not being on top of situations."

With *coprocessing,* which we covered briefly in Chapter 3, the native CPU works in conjunction with specialized "slave" processors that perform dedicated chores. For instance, many microcomputer systems today have slave processors that handle tasks such as high-speed mathematical computation, display-screen graphics, and keyboard operations. At any point in time, two or more processors within the system unit may be performing work simultaneously. However, the time taken to perform an entire job will be largely constrained by the main CPU, which is at the top of the hierarchy.

In *parallel processing,* which is the most sophisticated and fastest type of multiprocessing, the multiple processors involved are full-fledged, general-purpose CPUs that operate at roughly the same level. They are tightly integrated so that they can work together on a job by sharing memory. This may sound simple, but there are many practical complications, and special software is often required.

Multiprocessing is closely related to *fault-tolerant computing,* in which computer systems are built with important circuitry duplicated. If a critical component fails, an identical backup component takes over. Even though duplicate processors (or sets of processors) are involved, however, only one processor (or set of processors) will be in operation at any point in time. User Solution 7-1 describes the need for fault-tolerant computing in mission-critical applications.

A Closer Look at Several Operating Systems

Here, we briefly cover several of the most widely used operating systems to give you a feel for their principal characteristics and to help you understand how they differ from each other. The operating systems we discuss in this section include MS-DOS and PC-DOS, Macintosh System Software, UNIX,

OS/2, Windows NT, and NetWare. We also discuss the Microsoft Windows operating environment.

MS-DOS and PC-DOS

During the 1980s, DOS* (for Disk Operating System) was the predominant microcomputer-based operating system for most businesses. Millions of copies of it have been sold to date, making it the most widely used software package ever developed. Even though it has been made technologically obsolete by newer products, well over 50 percent of today's microcomputer systems still use DOS.

DOS is available in two forms: PC-DOS and MS-DOS. Both were originally developed by Microsoft Corporation of Redmond, Washington (see Feature 7-1). Except for a few minor differences, these operating systems are virtually identical. **PC-DOS** was created originally for the IBM PC, whereas **MS-DOS** was devised to operate on computer systems that look and work a lot like the IBM PC. All of these computer systems used the 16-bit Intel 8088 chip or the closely related 16-bit Intel 8086 chip. These chips supported less than a megabyte of RAM.

PC-DOS. The operating system most widely used on IBM microcomputers.

MS-DOS. The operating system most widely used by microcomputer systems similar to those made by IBM.

Both the MS-DOS and PC-DOS operating systems have been revised many times since they were first developed. Each major revision is referred to as a *version.* All versions starting with the number 1 (such as 1.0 and 1.1) were designed for the earliest microcomputer systems, such as the original IBM PC, which used only floppy disk and cassette tapes for secondary storage. Today, DOS is up to Version 6 and has been extended to work with hard disks, networks, and the latest Intel microprocessors. Yet because it was originally designed around 16-bit chips—which supported limited amounts of RAM—16-bit DOS cannot take full advantage of the power of new chips.

Today, it is not clear whether the successor to DOS will be Windows NT, OS/2, UNIX, or some other multitasking operating system. Despite the fact that DOS has become technologically obsolete, it is likely that DOS and DOS-based applications will be prevalent for a good part of this decade. So many DOS-based computers are around today that vendors of new software are still supplying—in force—DOS-based applications to the marketplace. Furthermore, products such as Microsoft Windows have extended the popularity of DOS. A sample of DOS commands is provided in Figure 7-5.

DOS with Windows

Microsoft **Windows** is an interconnected series of programs that supplies a graphical operating environment for microcomputer systems. Most versions of Windows provide a graphical shell for DOS. They turn a display into an electronic desktop. Just as an ordinary desktop may be arranged with a calendar, clock, calculator, and notepads on top of it—along with work papers stacked one on top of another or placed so that each is in full view—so, too, can the Microsoft Windows desktop be arranged. As with the conventional desktop, the electronic desktop gives you the freedom to rearrange projects at will or to make them

Windows. A graphical operating environment created by Microsoft Corporation.

*For simplicity, when used in this text, DOS refers strictly to MS-DOS and PC-DOS. DOS, however, is not a proprietary name, and other, lesser-known operating systems also use the name DOS—Radio Shack TRSDOS and Apple ProDOS, for instance.

Feature 7-1

Bill Gates
Microsoft's "Boy Billionaire"

Twenty years ago, who would have ever thought that a systems-software programmer—a "techie"—would become one of the richest people in the world?

But that's exactly what happened. Today, William H. Gates III, founder and chairman of the board of Microsoft Corporation, the largest software company in the world, has a net worth of several billion dollars. And he's barely 40 years old! Bill Gates has made a lot of other people rich, too. Had you bought $1,000 worth of Microsoft stock when the company went public in 1986, it would have been worth close to $35,000 at the beginning of 1994.

Before he graduated from high school, Bill Gates was already an accomplished programmer. He had written a class-scheduling program for his high school and a traffic logging program for the city of Bellevue, Washington. What's more, he also worked as a programmer for TRW, a large computer-services firm—reportedly the only time he has ever had a boss.

After high school, it was on to Harvard. He never finished, dropping out instead in the mid 1970s to build a BASIC language translator for the Altair 8800 computer, the world's first microcomputer system. While the Altair was a commercial flop—it was available only in kit form and thus would only work if a diligent and talented buyer assembled it correctly—the microcomputer industry was just beginning, and Gates started building language translators for other computers.

Bill Gates. *Forbes* magazine recently ranked him as USA's second-richest.

Bill Gates' biggest break came around 1980, when IBM was looking for a company to deliver an operating system for the IBM PC, its first foray into microcomputers. At that point in time, Microsoft was only a 50-person outfit, writing mostly BASIC, COBOL, and FORTRAN language translators. IBM's first choice had been a California company called Digital Research, which produced CP/M, then the most widely used operating system for personal computers. But, as the legend goes, Digital Research's founder, Gary Kildall, who was already rich beyond most people's wildest dreams, was off flying his plane in the Santa Cruz mountains when the IBM people came calling. Put off, the IBMers left for the state of Washington, to meet with Bill Gates.

The rest, as they say, is history. Microsoft is now the largest software company in the world, employing over 10,000 people.

disappear from view. The basic elements of a Windows desktop are shown in Figure 7-6. User Solution 7-2 describes a Windows application environment at Fidelity Investments.

Windows provides several advantages over "plain," 16-bit DOS, including the following:

Window.
A box of information overlaid on a screen display.

- It replaces the DOS command line with a system of menus, information boxes called **windows,** and icons, thereby eliminating the need to remember a command syntax.
- It lets users perform more than one *task* at a time; for example, you can be typing in one document while printing out another.

FIGURE 7-5

DOS. Even though DOS has been technologically obsolesced by sophisticated graphical environments and newer operating systems, most microcomputers still use DOS. Shown here are some of the most widely used DOS commands.

Command	Description	Example	Explanation
COPY	Copies individual files	COPY BOSS WORKER	Makes a copy of BOSS and stores it in WORKER
		COPY BOSS B:WORKER	Makes a copy of BOSS and stores it, on the B drive, in WORKER
DIR	Displays the names of files on a disk	DIR	Displays names of files on the default drive
		DIR B:	Displays names of files on the B drive
		DIR/W	Displays names of files on the default drive in a table format
ERASE (DEL)	Erases individual files	ERASE DOLLAR	Erases DOLLAR from the default drive
		ERASE B:DOLLAR	Erases DOLLAR from the B drive
REN	Renames individual files	REN SAM BILL	Renames SAM to BILL
DISKCOPY	Copies the contents of one disk to another disk	DISKCOPY A: B:	Copies the contents of the disk in drive A to the disk in drive B
FORMAT	Prepares a disk for use, erasing what was there before	FORMAT	Formats the disk in the default drive
		FORMAT B:	Formats the disk in the B drive

- It lets users easily work on more than one *program* at a time; for example, you can temporarily abandon your word processor to work with a spreadsheet program and then return to the word processor at the same place you left off.
- It has built-in utilities that make it easier for users to share data among applications; that allows you to, say, prepare a graph with your spreadsheet program and store it in seconds in a word-processed document.
- It encourages a consistent user interface; once you learn how to use one Windows program it becomes easier to learn others. To provide such consistency, a variety of Windows **applications programming interfaces (APIs)**—functions that are part of Windows and accessible to any Windows application—are available.
- It provides a variety of desk accessory programs—such as a card file, calendar, and calculator—that support doing work in a business environment.
- It furnishes a cohesive system under which all applications can be managed.

Applications programming interface (API). A set of functions that are part of one software package and available to other packages.

Macintosh System Software

Macintosh System Software is the proprietary, icon-oriented operating system that comes with the Apple Macintosh line of computers. The Apple Macintosh, introduced in 1984, has set the standard for graphical user interfaces. Today, many operating systems are trying to copy what the Mac originally started.

Macintosh System Software. The operating system that's primarily used on Apple's Macintosh line of computer systems.

User Solution 7–2

A Windows Solution at Fidelity

Boston-based Fidelity Investments is one of the world's largest financial-services companies. Account holders can choose among any of dozens of Fidelity mutual funds, scores of mutual funds from other companies, and thousands of stocks and bonds. A customer calling in with a query may first want information about one of his or her retirement accounts, then a balance from a second account, followed by the prices of several mutual funds, and ending with confirmation that paperwork sent two weeks ago was received. To keep up with such multiple transactions, the hundreds of service representatives at Fidelity's investment centers across the country must constantly be able to switch from one application to another while on the phone. To meet this need, Fidelity chose Microsoft Windows. The firm reports that information is better presented now than in the past and more of it is available on each rep's display screen.

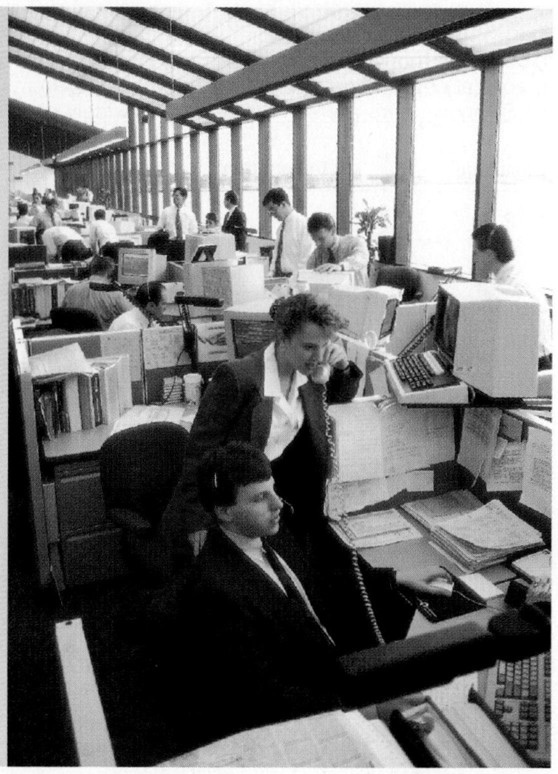

Macintosh System Software has grown with the times, keeping pace with the increases in power made available with each new Motorola CPU chip and each new Macintosh computer system. The latest version of Macintosh System Software, Version 7, can be used on virtually all recent Macintoshes that have at least two megabytes of RAM. Some of the features it provides are typographic capabilities for display devices and printers, and multitasking.

Macintosh System Software is found, almost exclusively, on computers in the Apple Macintosh line. An example of the graphical user interface provided with the Macintosh is shown in Figure 7-7. Macintosh owners also frequently use UNIX, a flexible operating system that is not tied to any particular brand of computer.

UNIX

UNIX.
A multiuser, multitasking operating system.

UNIX was originally developed almost two decades ago at Bell Laboratories as a highly portable operating system for minicomputers. Many properties make UNIX a compelling choice for the new breed of 32-bit microcomputers arriving in the marketplace.

First, UNIX already has a relatively successful track record as a multiuser, multitasking operating system. During the 20 years it has been available, it has attracted a large, loyal following.

Second, UNIX is flexibly built, so it can be used on a wide variety of machines. Unlike other operating systems—such as DOS and OS/2, which are based on Intel chips, or Macintosh System Software, which is based on Motorola chips—UNIX is not built around a single family of processors. Computers from micros

FIGURE 7-6

Microsoft Windows Microsoft Windows provides computers running the MS-DOS and PC-DOS operating systems—and their applications (as shown here)—with a graphical user interface. Annotated in the figure are some of the principal elements of the Windows electronic desktop.

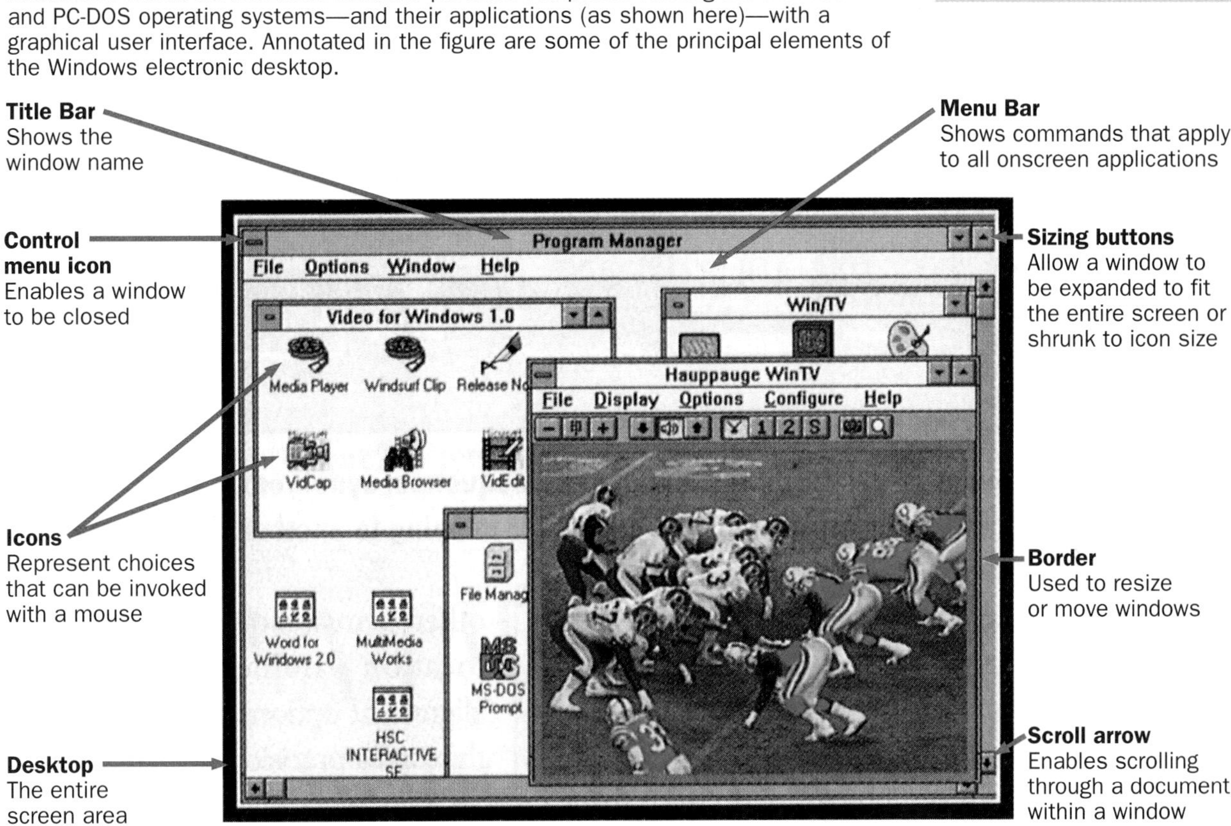

to mainframes can run UNIX, and a variety of devices from different manufacturers can easily run under UNIX while hooked into the same network. This flexibility gives UNIX a big advantage over competing operating systems for many types of applications.

But UNIX also has certain disadvantages. Many people complain that it isn't very easy to use. Also, its flexibility makes UNIX slower than operating systems tailored around a particular family of microprocessors when UNIX is used in an environment dominated by that particular family. Still another disadvantage of UNIX is that several "brands" of it are now available, many of them incompatible with each other.

Figure 7-8 shows a UNIX screen with a graphical user interface.

OS/2

OS/2 is a multiuser, multitasking operating system developed for high-end IBM and IBM-compatible microcomputers. It provides a graphical user interface called *Presentation Manager,* which is similar to the Microsoft Windows interface (see Figure 7-9). In fact, OS/2 can even run Windows. OS/2 is available in two versions. *OS/2 Extended Edition* contains built-in local area network (LAN) and database features, whereas *OS/2 Standard Edition* has no such capabilities.

OS/2.
An operating system designed by IBM for high-end IBM and IBM-compatible microcomputers.

FIGURE 7-7

Macintosh System Software. Macintosh System Software sported the first commercially successful graphical interface for operating systems and it is still one of the most popular. Annotated in the figure are some of the principal elements of the Macintosh electronic desktop. Although the names and appearance of many of the features differ from the Windows desktop, the types of tasks that you can perform are virtually identical to those in Windows.

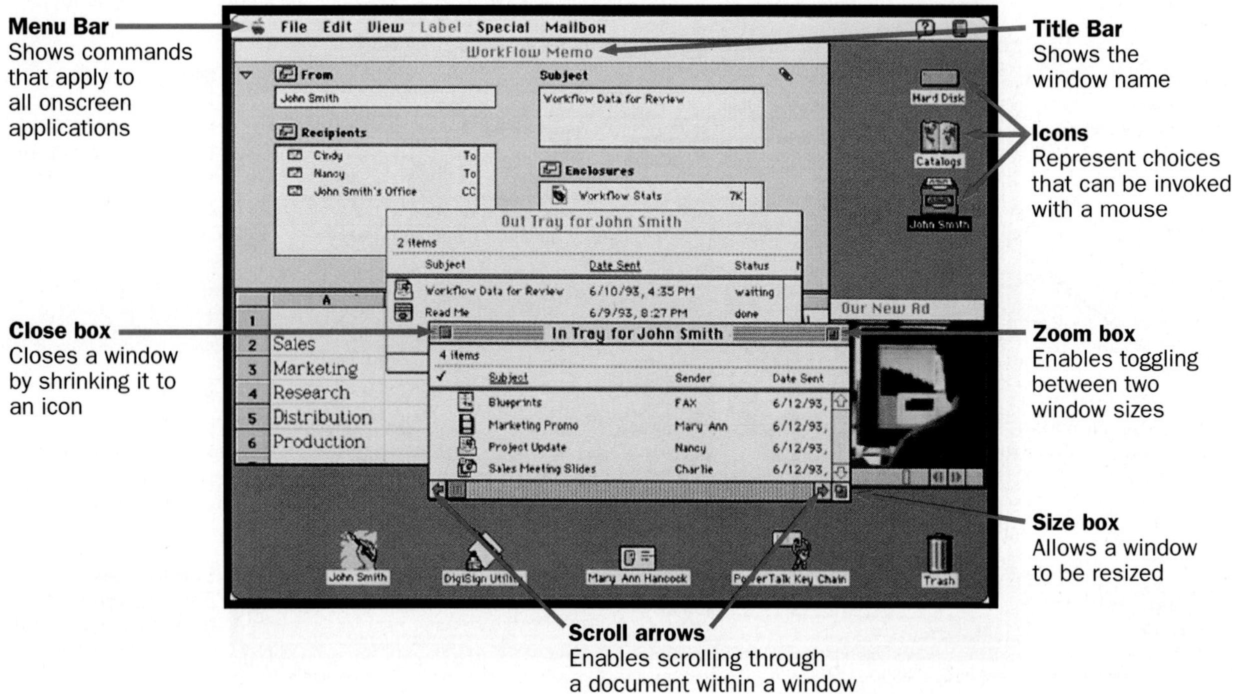

Part of IBM's plan is to have all applications that run under OS/2 have a commonality to them—a concept IBM includes in its *Systems Applications Architecture (SAA).* Introduced in 1987, SAA proposes a consistent framework within which applications can fit together across IBM PS/2 computers, IBM small business systems (such as computers in the AS/400 line), and IBM mainframes. The framework is designed so that applications interfaces will have the same "look" to users and programmers, no matter what type of IBM computer the user or programmer is working on. The user or programmer does not even have to know where the programs or data used on the system are stored. While both OS/2 and SAA are IBM concepts, they will also work with computers compatible with those in the IBM line, such as Compaq computers and scores of others.

The OS/2 operating system makes it possible to address 16 MB RAM. OS/2 can operate in either of two modes. In the *real (compatibility) mode,* OS/2 is capable of running programs that were created to run under 16-bit DOS. Because 16-bit DOS can address only 640 KB RAM, the real mode can address only this amount of space. In the *protected mode,* in contrast, OS/2 is designed to run applications that are created specifically for OS/2 and to take advantage of the fact that it can address 16 MB RAM and can do multitasking. When

FIGURE 7-8

UNIX. The UNIX operating system is available in a variety of versions. Pictured here is Apple's A/UX implementation of UNIX—a product that includes compatibility with Macintosh System Software.

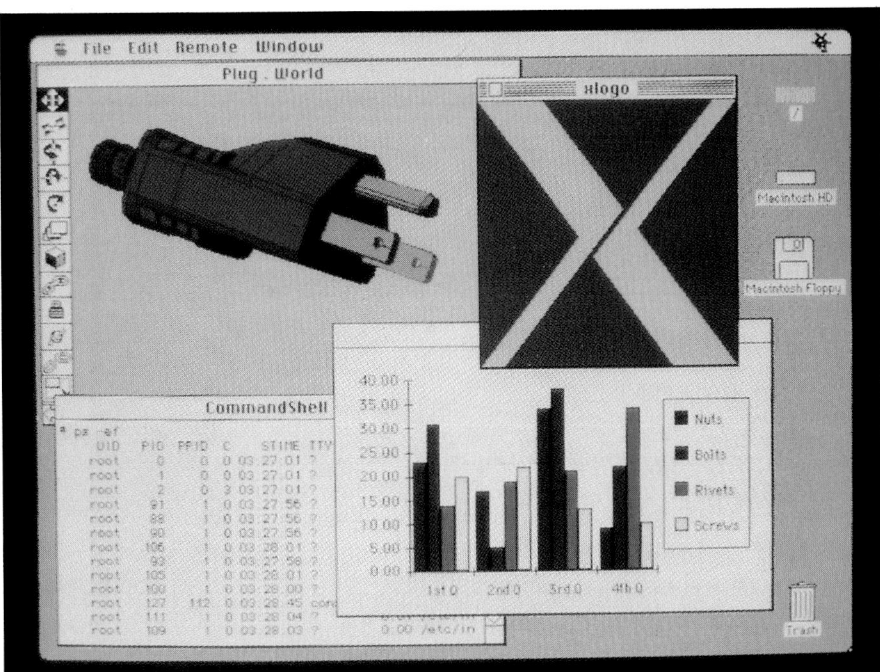

OS/2 runs in the protected mode, a *memory protection* feature ensures that multiple tasks won't collide with each other in RAM.

Windows NT

Windows NT (for New Technology), or NT for short, is a multitasking operating system developed by Microsoft Corporation for high-end, 32-bit computer systems. It has a graphical user interface similar to the one in the Microsoft Windows operating environment.

Windows NT. A multitasking, multiprocessing operating system designed by Microsoft Corporation for 32-bit microcomputers.

One of NT's principal features is its modular design (see Figure 7-10). At the heart of the system is a small kernel program, the *Executive,* that is in charge of the entire operating system. Beyond the Executive are a set of utility modules. When summoned by the Executive, the utilities do such chores as page files in and out of virtual memory, send messages, provide system security, and manage memory and screen windows. In other words, they do the main work of the operating system.

Another important feature of Windows NT is its ability to be run on a variety of computer systems, not just those using conventional Intel chips. Thus, applications written for Windows NT can be developed on a desktop microcomputer system that uses a Pentium chip and run on a workstation that

FIGURE 7-9

OS/2. OS/2 is a multiuser, multitasking operating system developed for high-end IBM microcomputers and compatible machines. The OS/2 graphical user interface is similar-looking to that of Microsoft Windows and Macintosh System Software, and it provides the same type of functionality.

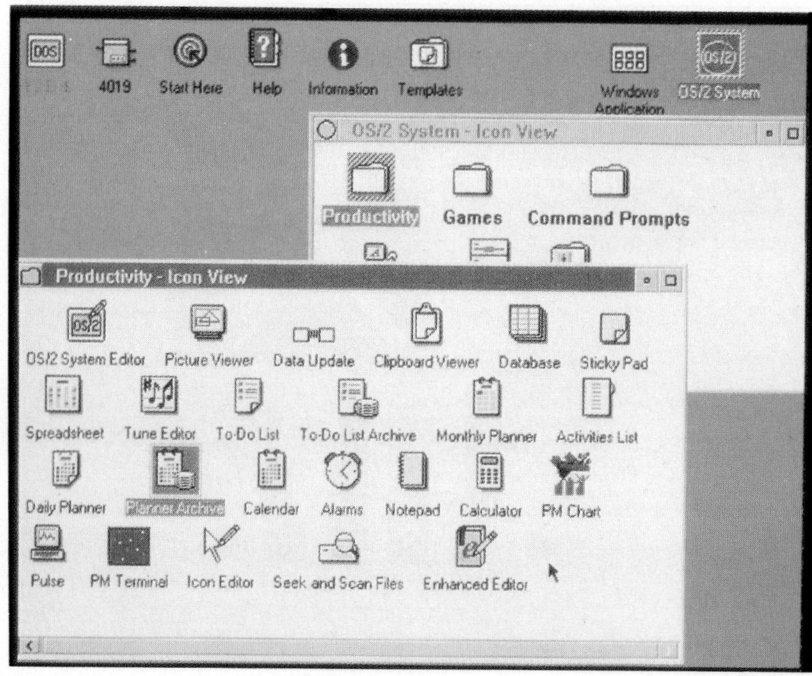

uses a RISC chip such as the PowerPC. Windows NT is also capable of "symmetric" multiprocessing. This means that NT can divide tasks among several CPUs, as long as all of those CPUs are running NT.

Windows NT is available in two principal forms. A *Desktop* edition is targeted to advanced users working at powerful desktop computers, while an *Advanced Server* edition is aimed at network-management tasks. To date, the biggest limitation with Windows NT is its large storage requirements.

NetWare

NetWare. The most widely used operating system on local area networks (LANs).

NetWare—developed by Novell, Inc. during the mid-1980s—is today the most widely used operating system on microcomputer-based local area networks (LANs). Most users of NetWare interact with it when they log in to a network or when they deal with a print server or a file server on a network. NetWare provides a shell around the user's chosen operating system, thereby enabling files to be retrieved or saved on a shared hard disk and also printed on a shared printer (see Figure 7-11). The shell routine enables users to communicate with NetWare, which is located on the shared disk.

Here's how a typical NetWare session works on a network of IBM microcomputers or similar machines: When you turn on a workstation that is hooked into

FIGURE 7-10

Windows NT. The Windows NT operating system has a modular design, with a small kernel at the core and set of support routines. The Windows NT graphical user interface is similar to that of Windows.

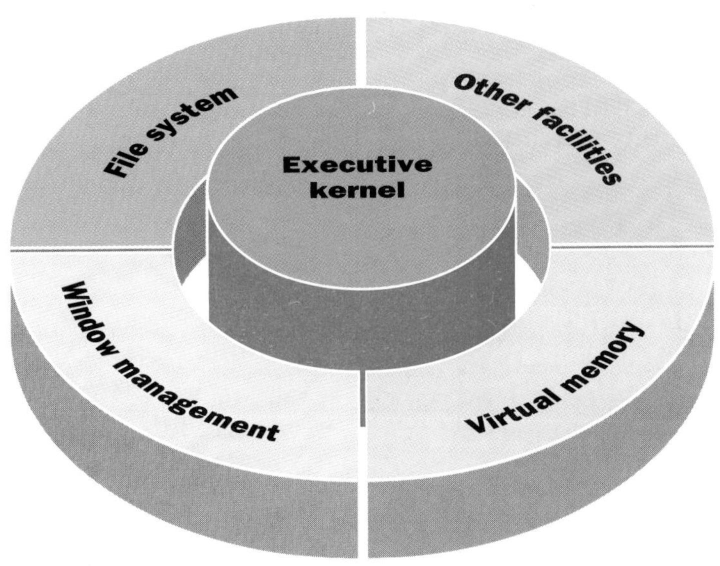

the network, the network will send a prompt to your display. Often, the prompt is

```
F>
```

At this point, you can decide to work on or off the network.

If you wish to work on the network, a log-in message must be typed in next. For instance, if the network recognizes you as KJOHNSON, you might have to type in

```
LOGIN KJOHNSON
```

When the log-in is accepted, you have *access rights* to the network, and you are free to do any network operation within the access rights that have been assigned to you. Access rights, managed by a person called the *network administrator*, will vary from user to user. They include such operations as reading or writing to files, executing programs, and creating or deleting files. When you are working at the F> prompt, which typically corresponds to the shared hard disk on the network, you generally treat it as if it were just another disk drive.

If you choose not to work on the network, you simply respond A:, B:, or C: to the F> prompt, and you are then pointed to your local diskette drives or your local hard drive. You then work just as you would if you were on a non-networked computer system. Keep in mind, however, that if you need to gain access to a program on the shared hard disk, save a program to the shared hard disk, or output to a shared printer, you must first get network access.

FIGURE 7-11

NetWare shell. At the workstation level, NetWare provides a shell around each user's local operating system (such as DOS). The shell routine enables users to communicate with NetWare, which is located on the file server. When the user asks for a job to be printed out, for instance, the user's applications program passes the job on to the local operating system, which sends it to the NetWare shell, which sends it on to NetWare. NetWare then lines the job up in the print queue on the appropriate server device.

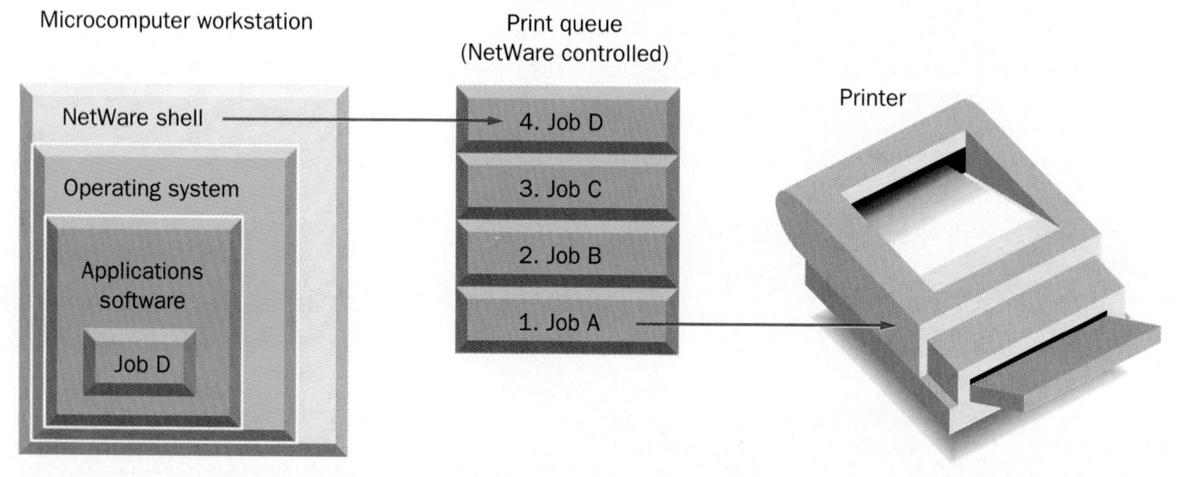

Language Translators

As mentioned earlier, computers can execute programs only after the latter have been translated into machine language. People don't generally write programs in this language for two reasons. First, machine-language instructions consist of complex-looking strings of binary 0s and 1s—for example:

01011000011100000000000100000010

Few people enjoy or are successful at writing long programs consisting of statements like this. Second, machine-language instructions must be written at the most detailed level of exposition, which requires a technical knowledge beyond the grasp of most people.

Language translator. A systems program that converts an applications program into machine language.

A **language translator** is simply a systems program that converts into machine language an applications program written in a higher-level language—for example, in BASIC, in COBOL, or in the programming language available within dBASE. Three common types of language translators are compilers, interpreters, and assemblers.

Compiler. A systems program that translates a program entirely into machine language before the translated program is executed.

Compilers A **compiler** translates a high-level or very-high-level language program entirely into machine language before it is executed. Every compiler-oriented language requires its own special compiler. Thus, a COBOL program needs a COBOL compiler; it cannot run on a BASIC compiler.

The program that you write and enter in the computer is called a **source module,** or *source program.* The machine-level program that the compiler then produces from it is called an **object module,** or *object program.*

Normally, before the object module is actually executed, it is bound together with other object modules that the CPU may need in order to process the program. For example, most computers can't compute square roots directly. To do so, they rely on small "subprograms," which are stored in secondary storage in object module form. Thus if your program calls for calculating a square root, the operating system will bind the object-module version of your program together with this square root routine to form an "executable package" for the computer. The binding process is referred to as *linkage editing,* or the *link-edit stage,* and the executable package that is formed is called a **load module.** A special systems program, called a **linkage editor,** is available on computer systems to do the binding automatically.

It is the load module that the computer actually executes, or runs. When your program is ready to run, it has reached the *Go (execution) stage.* Figure 7-12 shows the complete process from compiling to link-editing to execution. Both object and load modules can be saved on disk for later use so that compilation and linkage editing need not be performed every time the program is executed.

Source module.
The original form in which a program is entered into an input device by a user or programmer.

Object module.
The machine-language program that is the output from a language translator.

Load module.
A complete machine-language program that is ready to be executed by the computer.

Linkage editor.
A systems program that binds together related object-module program segments so that they may be run as a unit.

Interpreters An **interpreter,** unlike a compiler, does not create an object module. Interpreters read, translate, and execute source programs one line at a time. Thus, the translation into machine language is performed while the program is running.

Interpreters have advantages and disadvantages compared with compilers. Two major advantages are that interpreters are easier to use and they enable errors to be discovered in programs more quickly. The interpreter itself requires relatively little storage space, and it does not generate an object module that must be stored. For these reasons, interpreters are ideal for beginning programmers and for people with limited storage space on their systems.

The major disadvantage of interpreters is that they are less efficient than compilers, and, consequently, programs run more slowly on them. Because interpreters translate each program statement into machine language just before executing it, they can chew up a lot of time—especially when the same statements may be executed thousands of times during the course of program execution and must be reinterpreted every time they are encountered. With a compiler, in contrast, each program statement is translated only once—before the program is run. In addition, the object module of a compiled program can be saved on disk, so the source program doesn't have to be retranslated every time the program is executed.

Some programming-language packages are equipped with both an interpreter and compiler, giving the programmer the best of both worlds. This allows the programmer to work with the interpreter while rooting out program errors and, when the program is error-free, to use the compiler to save it in object-module form.

Interpreter.
A systems program that translates a program into machine language on a line-by-line basis, as each statement is executed.

Assemblers The third type of translator, the **assembler,** is used exclusively with assembly languages (discussed in Chapter 12). It works like a compiler, producing a stored object module. Each computer system typically has only one assembly language available to it; thus, only one assembler is required.

Assembler.
A computer program that takes assembly-language instructions and converts them to machine language.

FIGURE 7-12

Compile, link-edit, go. A compiler and a linkage editor convert a source module into a load module, which is processed by the CPU.

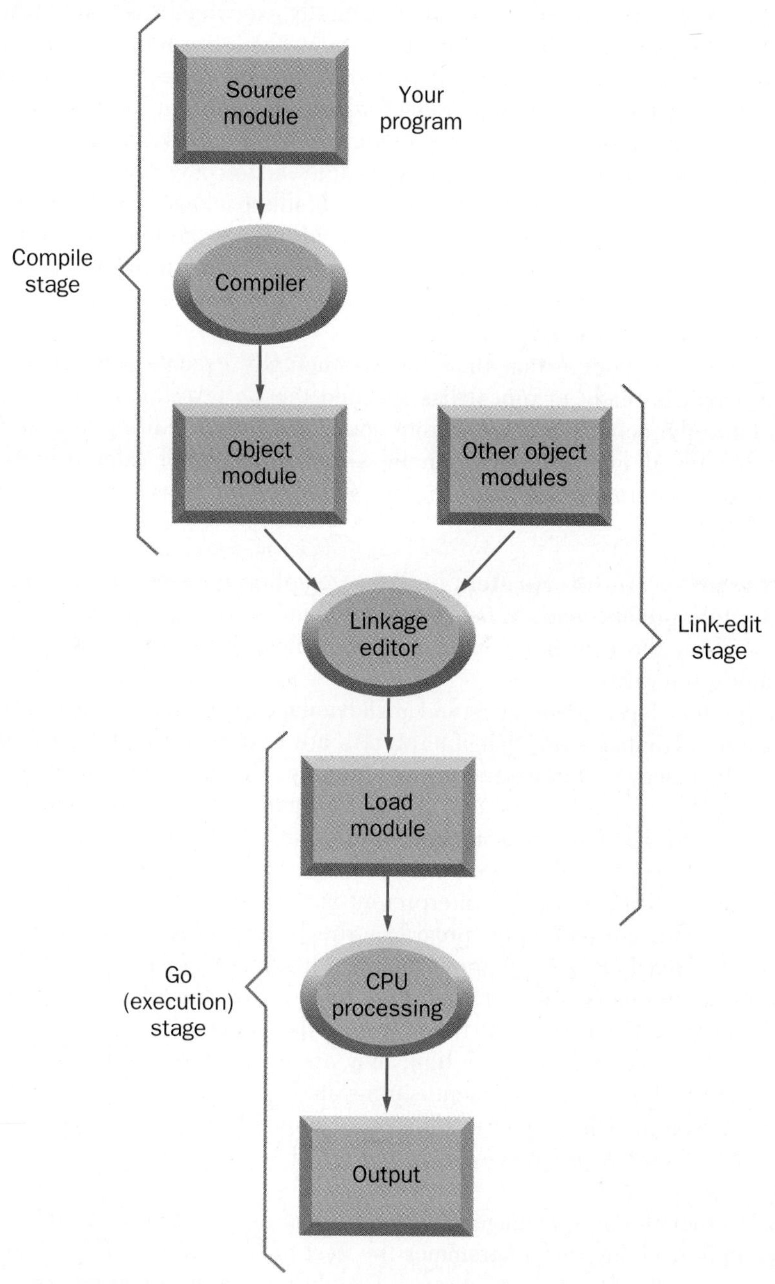

Utility Programs

Some tasks are performed so often in the course of processing that it would be extremely inefficient if every user had to code them into programs over and over again. Sorting records, formatting disks and tapes, and copying programs from one medium to another are examples of such tasks. To eliminate the need for users and programmers to waste time writing such routines, computer systems normally have available a library of **utility programs** to perform these types of functions. Typically, utility programs reside in secondary storage and are summoned by the operating system's supervisor program or by the user when needed.

Utility program.
A program used to perform some frequently encountered operation in a computer system.

Utility programs are packaged in a variety of ways. Sometimes they are bundled into an operating system. For instance, utility programs for formatting disks, copying the contents of disks, and checking the allocation of disk space are built directly into the MS-DOS operating system. In DOS, these utilities are called *external commands.* In other cases, utilities are independent programs that can be acquired from third-party vendors and made to run with a given operating system.

System utilities are of two principal types: those that load automatically into RAM when the computer is started up and those that you must explicitly call every time you need them. In the IBM microcomputing world, the first types are called *TSR*s, for *terminate-and-stay-resident.* These programs are so named because every time you use and finish with (i.e., terminate) them, they remain resident in RAM. In the Apple Macintosh world, TSRs are often referred to as *INIT*s, which stands for "initializing" utilities. The second type of utility program, those that you must load into RAM each time you use them, includes a variety of programs. For instance, DOS's external commands fall into this class, as do Microsoft Window's desk accessory (DA) programs.

Three widely used types of utility programs that we will cover in depth here are disk utilities, spooling software, and device drivers. Figure 7-13 briefly describes these and other types of utilities.

Disk Utilities Many operating systems have built-in disk utility routines that format disks, copy disk files, copy the contents of one disk to another disk or to tape, compare disks, provide disk directories, and so on. A number of third-party, aftermarket companies have created packages of other, less-familiar **disk utility** programs that go well beyond those available with many operating systems. Five such types of utilities are disk toolkits, data compression utilities, disk optimizers, backup utilities, and document-management utilities.

Disk utility.
A program that assists with such disk-related tasks as backup, data compression, space allocation, and the like.

- *Disk toolkits,* the most famous of which is The Norton Utilities, are used to recover from accidental data destruction. They allow you to recover damaged or erased files, repair damaged format markings and directories, and recover from a disk crash (a crippling of the disk itself).
- *Data compression programs* enable files to be stored in a smaller space. This helps free up disk space and enables files to be sent over the phone lines faster. The person at the other end of the line must have the proper decompression program.
- *Disk optimizers* enable programs on disk to be accessed faster. They perform such tasks as allocating certain files to the outer cylinders (where they may be reached more quickly), rewriting fragmented files (that is, rewriting in contiguous sectors files that originally were written into many noncontiguous disk sectors), and sorting file directory names for faster access.
- *Backup utilities* are programs designed to rapidly back up the contents of a hard disk (see Figure 7-14). You can back up the entire disk or merely selected files on the disk.

FIGURE 7-13

Utility programs. Utility programs extend the duties of your computer's operating system.

Utility type	Description
Backup utilities	Quickly and easily back up the contents of a hard disk
Cosmetic utilities	Let you customize the user environment, for example, by changing the colors on your display or by changing the way in which menus are presented
Data compression utilities	Enable files to be compressed
Device drivers	Enable applications software to work on a specific configuration of hardware
Diagnostic software	Enable bugs to be more easily rooted out of your computer system
Disk optimizers	Better utilize space on disk
Disk toolkits	Recover and repair damaged or lost files
Document managers	Enable you to find a lost file on your system by typing in part of its name or by typing in short strings of text known to be contained in the file (see Feature 7-2)
Extenders	Let you add new fonts, commands, or programs to your operating system
File transfer utilities	Make it possible for you to transfer files between two distinct programs or computer systems
Keyboard utilities	Let you construct keyboard macros (small programs that execute when you press a certain key) or let you reconfigure your keyboard
Performance monitors	Tell you how efficiently your computer system is performing its work
Screen capture programs	Enable you to download any screen image onto a hard-copy output device
Screen savers	Turn the display off to prevent the phosphor coating from burning
Spooling programs	Control outputs going to the printer, thereby preventing your computer system from being tied up while the printer is outputting
Text editors	Allow text in a nondocument file to be manipulated
Vaccine programs	Protect your system from virus attacks (see Feature 14-2)
Workgroup utilities	Enable you to interconnect computers so that people working on them can pass messages back and forth

- *Document-management utilities* enable users to search a hard disk for "lost" or misplaced files. These utilities, which have become popular in recent years as hard-disk capacities have swelled in size, are discussed in Feature 7-2.

Spooling Software Some input and output devices are extremely slow. Tape devices and printers, for example, work at a snail's pace compared to the CPU. If the CPU had to wait for these slower devices to finish their work, the

FIGURE 7-14

Backup utility. Backup utilities let you back up all or part of the contents of a disk drive. Symantec's Norton Backup for Windows, featured here, allows you to establish preset backup routines that you can select from a pull-down menu.

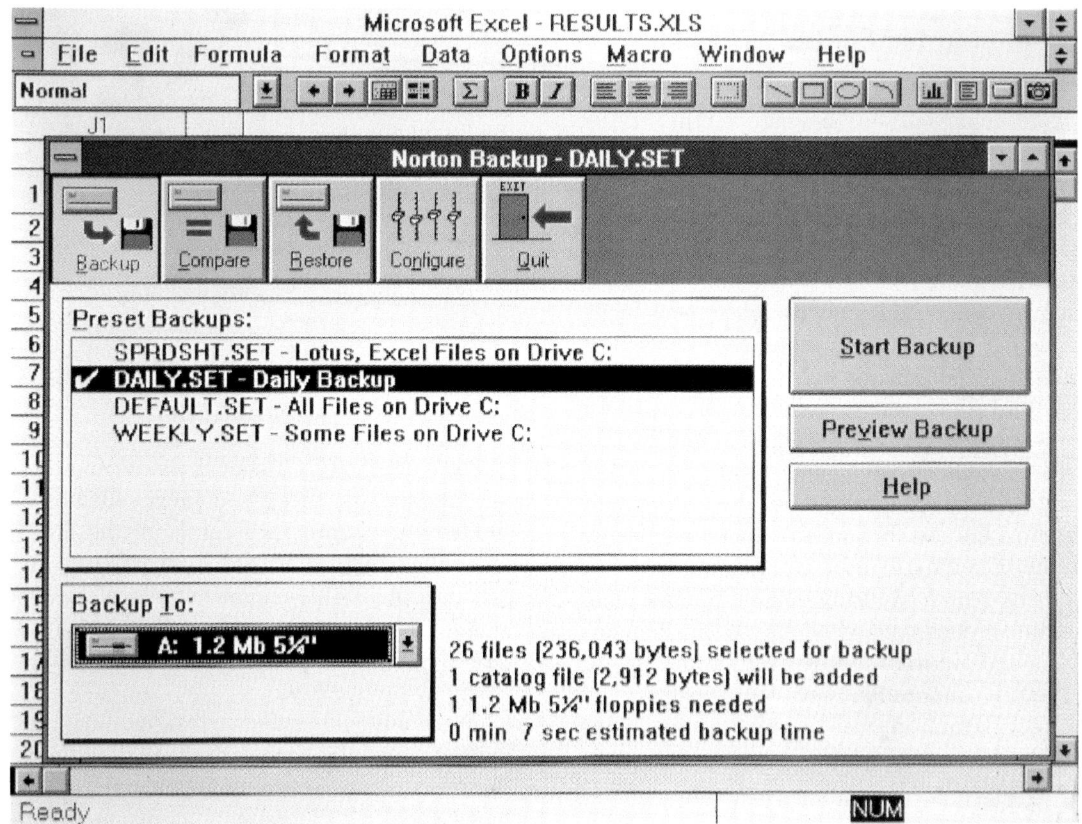

computer system would face a horrendous bottleneck. For example, suppose the computer has just completed a 5-second job that generated 100 pages of hard copy for the printer. On a printer that prints 600 lines per minute, this job would take about 10 minutes to print. If the CPU had to deal directly from the printer, memory would be tied up for 10 minutes waiting for the printer to complete the job. As a result, other programs would have to wait for processing while this output was being transferred from memory to paper.

To avoid such a delay, disks on almost all large systems contain *output spooling areas* to store output destined for the printer (see Figure 7-15). As the computer processes a program, a **spooling program** rapidly transfers, or "spools," the output from memory to the disk spooling area. The computer is then free to process another program, leaving it to the spooling program to transfer the output of the first program from disk to printer.

Spooling program. A program that temporarily stages input or output in secondary storage to expedite processing.

Feature 7-2

Document-Management Utilities

A solution for finding "lost" files

As hard disks increase in capacity, allowing more and more documents to be stored online, trying to find a letter or a worksheet that you created months ago can become a real problem. Questions that may pop up: What did you name it? Did you save it or erase it? What directory might you have put it in?

This is where document-management software—programs that help ordinary users and/or network managers locate hard-disk files created with a word processor, spreadsheet, or any other type of software package—comes in handy.

With document-management software, users can automatically search across directories and even across file servers for "lost" documents using a variety of search tools.

A *string search* would be handy, for instance, for finding a document when all you can remember was that it was addressed to someone at, say, Amgen Corporation. You could instruct the software to search the hard disk(s) until it found the first file—or all files—containing the text string "Amgen".

An *attribute search* is especially useful when all the person doing the search can say about a file is who created it and when it was created. So if a network administrator remembers that a file was created by Susan Smith during the week of January 14, these two facts (attributes) can be used to narrow the search for the file. Other attributes that might aid in the search include the document's file extension or format, the workstation at which the document was created, and the department in which the document's creator works.

Naturally, the more strings or attributes you can specify, the more selective the search will be. Document-management software is available for standalone computer systems as well as for networks. One of the most widely used document-management utilities in Lotus Development's Magellan package.

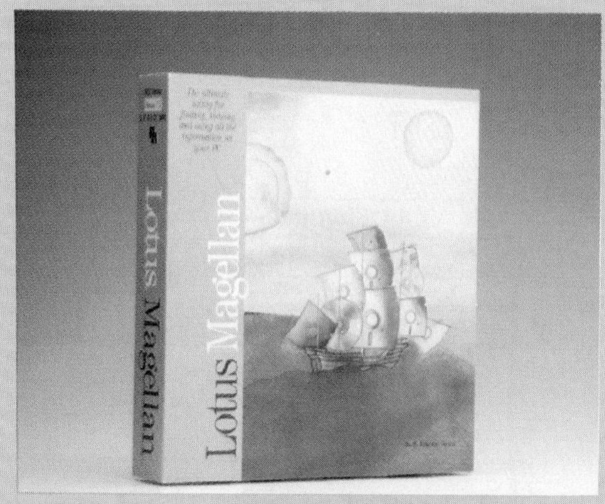

Lotus Magellan. Navigates your hard disk to find files.

At any given time, the spooling area of, say, a large computer system may contain more than 100 completed jobs waiting to be delivered to output devices. As long as space remains in the output spooling area, the CPU can continue to operate without delay. Output spooling is popular on microcomputers, too. For example, if your printer will be tied up for 15 minutes or so typing a long document, a spooling routine will let you use your computer to edit another document while the first one is printing.

As Figure 7-15 shows, spooling is also used to hold, or stage, input on its way to the computer. As programs enter the computer system, they are stored in an *input spooling area,* or *queue.* When the operating system is ready to deliver the next program to the CPU, it checks the queue to see which one to process next. On many computer systems, priorities can be assigned to programs.

FIGURE 7-15

Spooling. On busy computer systems, input is spooled before it is processed and output is spooled before it is sent to the printer.

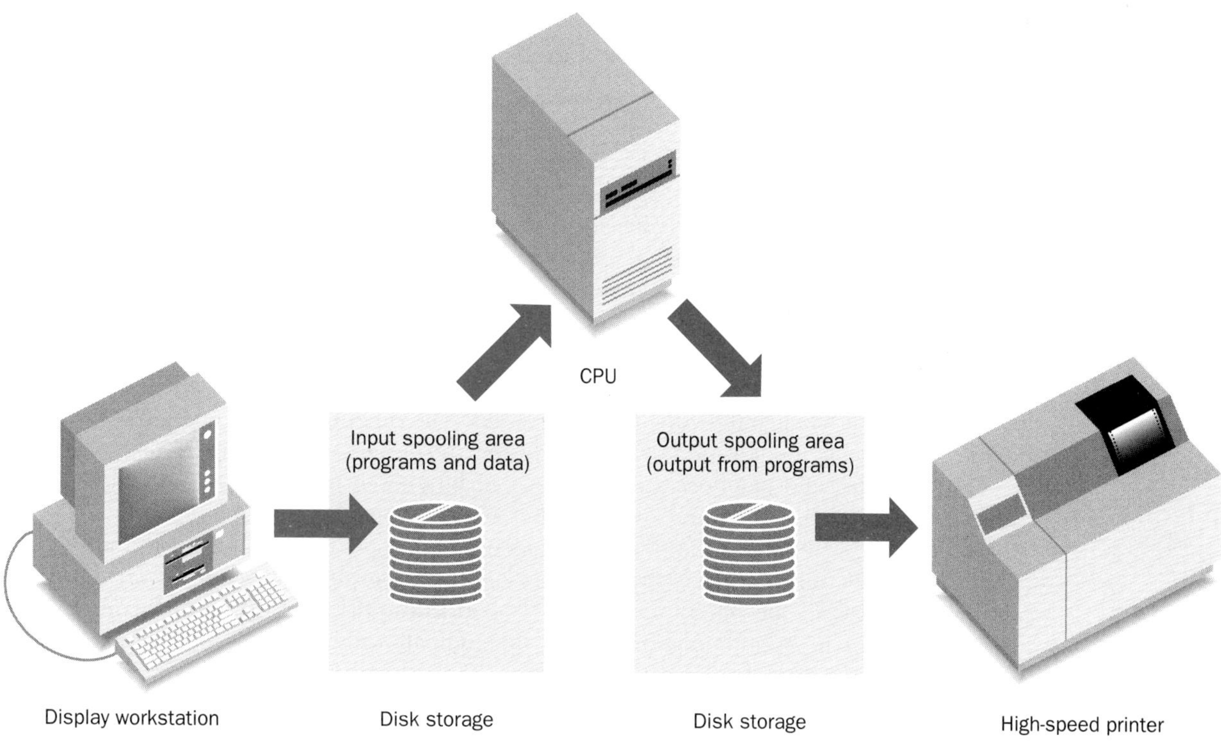

If this is possible, the computer will attend to high-priority jobs before it processes jobs that may have been waiting longer but have a lower priority.

Device Drivers When communicating with output hardware such as display devices and printers, applications software packages commonly rely on utility programs known as device drivers. **Device drivers** act as interfaces between applications programs and specific hardware devices.

Device driver. A utility program that enables an applications program to function with a specific hardware device.

A device driver typically works as follows. A software package that you buy—say, a word processor—will often include both an installation program and a utilities disk that contains several device drivers. You install the word processor to work on a specific set of hardware devices by running the installation program. The installation program will ask you a number of questions—for instance, what type of printer and what type of monitor you are using. You answer these questions by selecting the appropriate devices from a list. As you make selections, the installation program retrieves the drivers corresponding to the selected devices and incorporates them into an "installed version" of the word processor, which it is building as the question-and-answer session is taking place. When this process is finished, the installed version of the program is ready for use on a specific hardware system.

As you later work with the installed version of the word processor, it will defer to the driver routines you have built into it to handle any hardware-specific commands. Generally, you will have to run the installation program only once—at the time you acquire the word processor. If, however, you replace one brand or model of hardware device with another, you will probably have to rerun the installation program to declare the new device.

Summary and Key Terms

Systems software consists of programs that coordinate the various parts of the computer system to make it run rapidly and efficiently. The basic role of systems software is to act as a mediator between applications programs and the computer system's hardware.

The Operating System An **operating system** is a collection of programs that manage the computer's activities. The functions of the operating system—which include assignment of system resources, scheduling of resources and jobs, and monitoring activities—can be viewed as aspects of a single general mission—to control the computer system's operations.

Two of the most prominent programs of the operating system are the supervisor and the command-language translator. The **supervisor** controls all the other parts of the operating system. The **command-language translator** enables both users and programmers to communicate with the operating system by using a **command language.** When interfacing with the operating system, you can use the standard system **defaults,** chosen by the operating system, or can request customized service through command-language instructions.

On some computer systems, the operator uses a *language interface* to carry out command-language instructions. On others, which employ a *graphical interface*—or **graphical user interface (GUI)**—the operator points on the screen to icons to carry out such instructions. An **operating environment** is a shell program that fits over an operating system, giving it a friendlier and more flexible user interface than its native one.

Sophisticated computers often take advantage of interleaved processing techniques, such as multiprogramming, multitasking, time-sharing, virtual memory, and multiprocessing, to operate more efficiently.

Multiprogramming is a term commonly used to describe some *multiuser* computer systems. In a computer system with multiprogramming, the computer works on several programs *concurrently.* For example, while the computer is waiting for data from one user's program to be accessed on disk, it can perform calculations for another user's program.

Multitasking refers to a multiprogramming-like capability on *single-user* operating systems. Thus, multitasking connotes the ability of two or more programs from any single user to execute *concurrently* on one computer or, more commonly, the ability of two or more tasks performed by a single program to execute concurrently.

Time-sharing is a technique in which the operating system cycles through all the active programs that need processing in the system and gives each one a small slice of time on each cycle.

Virtual memory refers to using disk to extend conventional memory. The operating system delivers programs to be processed to the virtual memory area, where they are subdivided into either fixed-length *pages* or variable-length *segments.*

Multiprocessing refers to the use of two or more computers, linked together, to perform work at the *same* time.

A Closer Look at Several Operating Systems Some of today's most widely used operating systems include MS-DOS and PC-DOS, Macintosh System Software, UNIX, OS/2, Windows NT, and NetWare.

MS-DOS and **PC-DOS** are commonly found on IBM microcomputers and similar devices. DOS—as these operating systems are called for short—is the most widely used software package ever developed. Today, many DOS users have gravitated to the Microsoft **Windows** GUI. Windows replaces the DOS command line with a system of menus, icons, and information boxes called **windows**. It also comes packaged with a variety of **applications programming interfaces (APIs)** to ensure consistency among applications. **Macintosh System Software** is the operating system native to the Apple Macintosh line of computers. **OS/2, Windows NT,** and **UNIX** are multitasking operating systems that are targeted to today's most powerful microcomputer systems. **NetWare** is an operating system designed for the operation of local area networks (LANs).

Language Translators A **language translator** is a systems program that converts into machine language an applications program written in a higher-level language. There are three common types of language translators: compilers, interpreters, and assemblers.

A **compiler** translates a high-level- or very-high-level-language program entirely into machine language before the program is executed. The program written by the user or programmer, called a **source module,** is first translated by the compiler into an **object module.** The object-module version of the program is then inputted to a **linkage editor,** which combines it with supplementary object modules needed to run the program to form a **load module.** It is the load module that the computer executes.

Interpreters read, translate, and execute source programs one line at a time. Thus, the translation into machine language occurs while the program is being run.

The third type of translator, the **assembler,** is used exclusively with assembly languages.

Utility Programs A **utility program** is a type of systems program written to perform repetitive processing tasks. There are many types of utility programs. **Disk utility** routines extend the operating system's disk-handling capabilities, enabling users to do such things as recover erased files and reorganize disk data for faster access. **Spooling programs** free the CPU from time-consuming interaction with I/O devices such as printers. **Device drivers** act as interfaces between applications programs and specific hardware devices.

Review Exercises

Fill-in Questions

1. ______________ software consists of programs that act as a mediator between applications software and the computer system's hardware.
2. A(n) ______________ is a collection of programs that manage the computer system's activities.
3. In a computer system with ______________, the computer works on several users' programs concurrently, leaving one at some logical stopping point to begin work on another.
4. ______________ is a technique in which the operating system cycles through active programs in the system that need processing and gives each one a small slice of time on each cycle.
5. ______________ refers to the use of two or more computers, linked together, to perform work on programs at the same time.
6. The most widely used operating system on LANs is ______________.
7. A(n) ______________ is a systems program that converts an applications program written in a high-level language or in an assembly language into machine language.
8. ______________ programs are systems programs written to perform repetitive processing tasks, such as formatting disks and compressing data on disks.

Matching Questions

Match each term with the description that fits best.

a. device driver
b. compiler
c. linkage editor
d. spooling software
e. interpreter
f. operating system

____ 1. A language translator that reads, translates, and executes source programs a line at a time.

____ 2. Enables a user to edit one document on a microcomputer system while printing out another.

____ 3. A program that enables an applications software package to work on a specific hardware device.

____ 4. Binds object modules together.

____ 5. A piece of systems software without which a computer will do nothing.

____ 6. A language translator that creates an object module.

Discussion Questions

1. What is systems software?
2. What is an operating system and what are its major functions?
3. Describe multiprogramming, multitasking, time-sharing, virtual memory, and multiprocessing.
4. Describe the differences between UNIX, OS/2, and Windows NT.
5. What is the principal difference between a language interface and a graphical user interface (GUI)?
6. What is the difference between Windows and Windows NT?
7. What are the differences between a compiler, an interpreter, and an assembler?
8. Identify several types of utility programs and explain what they do.

Critical Thinking Questions

1. UNIX has been available for about two decades, but it has only been during the last few years that it has received much attention. Why do you think this is so?
2. MS-DOS has sold millions of copies, making it the most widely used software package ever written. Now that powerful microcomputer systems are available and powerful operating systems are coming to take advantage of them, do you think a sizeable market will still exist for users who want these new computers but still want to use MS-DOS?
3. Many users of computer systems have argued that graphical interfaces, while potentially useful to some people, are totally undesirable for their needs. Where do you think these users are "coming from"?

W I N D O W 4

Graphical User Interfaces

Tools of the Electronic Desktop

In the decade or so that they've been available, graphical user interfaces (GUIs)—sometimes called electronic desktops because they emulate the look of a real desktop—have become increasingly popular. In the 1980s, most users who wanted a GUI turned to the Apple Macintosh, which represented the biggest line of computers that fully supported graphics applications. In 1990, with the arrival of Microsoft Windows as a shell for DOS, GUIs also became commonplace on IBM and IBM-compatible microcomputers. Today, virtually every new software product arriving in the marketplace sports a graphical interface of some type. In this window, we look at a number of the special features employed by GUIs. A miniglossary of widely used GUI terms appears on the last two pages of this window.

1

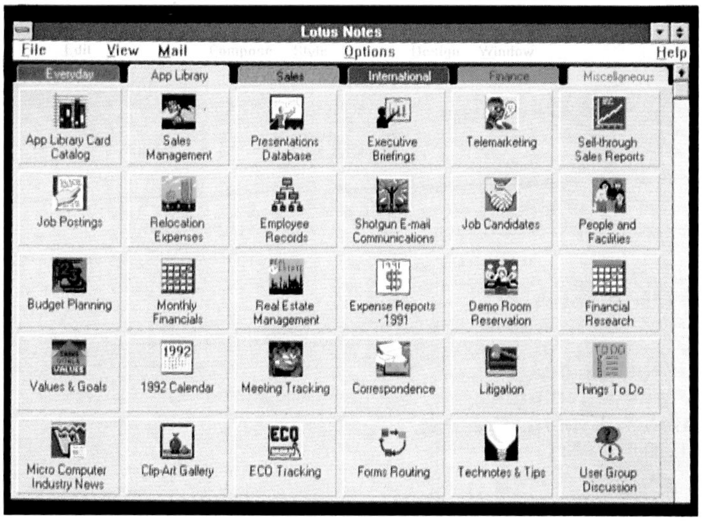

1. A state-of-the-art graphical user interface is illustrated by Lotus Notes, a work-group computing package, which is shown here running under Microsoft Windows. Users can choose any of the 30 applications in the panel by clicking on them with a mouse or by selecting them with a keyboard.

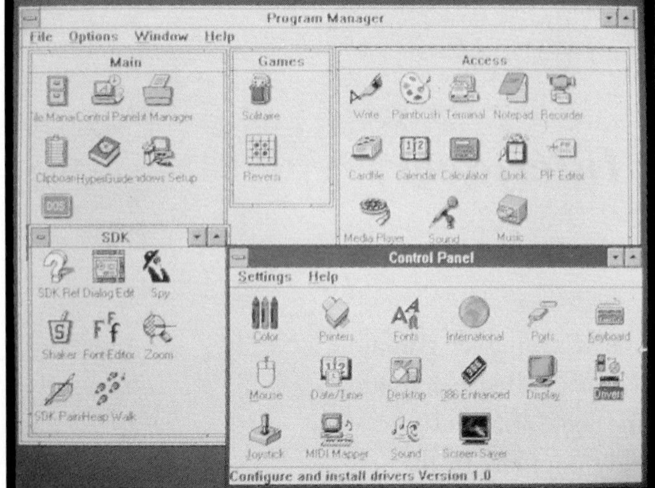

2

2–3. The staple of the GUI is the *window,* a self-contained box of information. Windows can be arranged onscreen in either of two ways: by *tiling* them side by side (image 2) or by *overlapping* them (image 3). The active, or foreground, window often has a darkened title bar and/or a darkened border. The windows shown here contain mostly *program icons.* The programs corresponding to these icons can be run when the icons are selected with a mouse or keyboard.

3

4–5. Selections in GUI screens are often made with *command buttons.* Buttons are chosen by clicking them with a mouse or, alternatively, by pressing Enter on the keyboard. Usually the active choice will be darkened, as in image 5. Image 5 is also an example of a *warning box,* which pops up on the screen when a potential problem situation is unfolding.

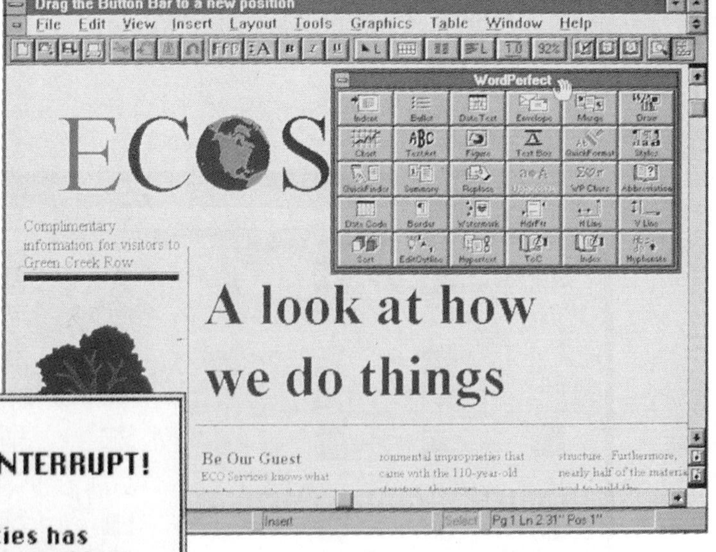

4

SORRY TO INTERRUPT!
Public Utilities has discovered a problem on the disk "HD." The Volume Bitmap is incorrect. We suggest you fix this.
Don't Fix
Fix Now

5

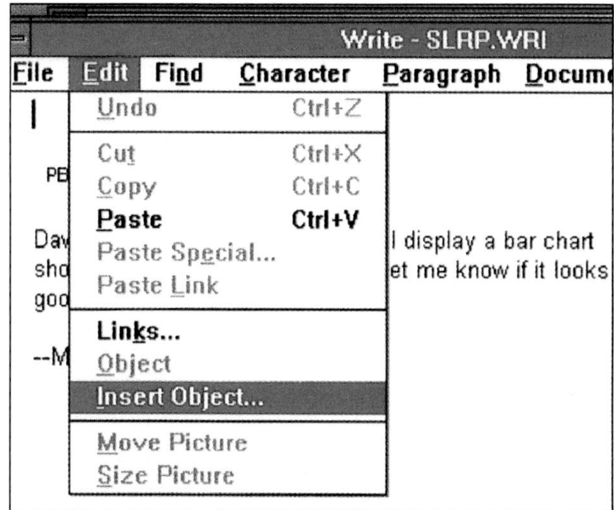

6

6. Many GUIs work with top-of-screen *menu bars* and *pull-down menus.* Here, when Edit is selected on the menu bar, the pull-down menu corresponding to it is unfurled onscreen and any of the choices on it can be accessed—unless they are shown in faded type (such as Undo and Cut). Current command choices are usually highlighted onscreen, such as Edit and Insert Object, here. Pull-down-menu commands shown with an ellipsis (. . .) lead to other pull-down menus if selected. Underlined letters indicate keystrokes that can be used to access commands with a keyboard.

7. *Dialog boxes* prompt the GUI user for information. In the top left box shown here are round *radio buttons;* they work like push buttons on many radios in that only one choice in the panel can be active at a time. Below the radio buttons are square *check boxes;* any number of options in a check-box panel can be made active by placing an "X" in the appropriate box. At the top right are *text boxes;* they require the user to type in data.

7

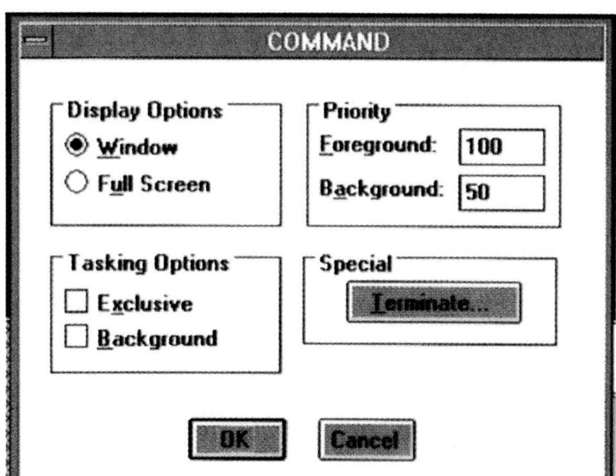

8

8. Many GUIs come with an *online help* feature, enhanced with diagrams. *Scroll bars* shown here in the right of the foreground window indicate that the diagram is larger than can fit in the window. By activating the scroll bar with a mouse or keyboard, the user can see the rest of the diagram. Alternatively, the window can be enlarged, so that the entire diagram or more of it fits onscreen.

A GUI Miniglossary

Defined below are several terms that users often encounter when working in a GUI environment. Most of the terms contained here can be found either in italic type in the image captions for Window 4 or in the annotations that accompany Figures 7-6 and 7-7, which respectively illustrate the Microsoft Windows and Macintosh environments.

Active window The window that represents the foreground application or document. This window is typically the topmost window on the screen and has a darkened title bar and/or darkened border.

Border In the Microsoft Windows environment, a boundary that denotes the outside edge of a window and enables the window to be moved or resized. In the Macintosh environment, windows are resized through a *size box.*

Check box A menu that enables the user to make one or more selections by placing check marks to the left of them.

Click Refers to pressing the mouse button once, to highlight or select a choice.

Clipboard A program feature that provides temporary storage for data you wish to transfer between applications.

Close box In the Macintosh environment, a small box located at the top left of a window that enables the window to be closed. Works similar to the *control-menu icons* in Microsoft Windows.

Command button In the Microsoft Windows environment, an icon representing a choice that can be activated or deactivated by clicking on it. Frequently used command buttons are "OK," "Cancel," and "Help."

Context-sensitive help An online help feature that provides assistance relating to the type of operation the user is currently trying to perform.

Control panel A feature that enables the user to customize the GUI environment.

Control-menu icon In the Microsoft Windows environment, a small box located at the top left of a window that enables the window to be closed. Works similar to the *close box* on the Macintosh.

Corner In the Microsoft Windows environment, the region where two adjoining edges of a border meet. The corner can be activated to shorten or lengthen two border edges simultaneously.

Desk accessory (DA) A program—such as a clock or calendar—that provides a feature commonly found on a conventional office desktop.

Desktop The area of the screen that is available for GUI applications. Usually, the desktop is the entire screen area.

Dialog box A box that requires the user to supply information to the computer system about the task being performed.

Dimmed option A faded-looking icon or command, indicating that the associated operation is not available in the current context.

Double-click Pressing the mouse button twice in rapid succession, to open or activate an application or document.

Drag A technique used to move icons on the screen or to resize windows. Dragging is normally performed by clicking on the desired screen item and moving the mouse while holding down the mouse button.

Drop-down list box A list box through which the user scrolls to see all the choices available.

Font manager A program feature that lets the user select and size typefaces.

Icon A graphic symbol that can represent either a program or program group, a command, a file or file folder, a disk drive, and the like.

Linesize box A box that enables the user to choose the thickness of lines for a drawing.

List box A box that presents a list of choices. Often, the default or current choice is highlighted, and it can be changed using the mouse or keyboard.

Menu bar A horizontal list of choices that appears on a highlighted line, usually below the window title. Often called the *main menu.*

Online help A feature that enables the user to request help while on the computer. Online help is often *context sensitive.*

Paint program A program that enables users to create drawings and to color the drawings.

Palette A toolbox-type menu that enables users to select among various colors.

Pointer The screen symbol showing where the mouse is currently pointing. Usually, the pointer is in the form of a small arrow, but the pointer often changes shape in various ways as the user performs such operations as typing text into a text box and resizing windows.

Pull-down menu A menu of subcommands that drops down vertically from a horizontal menu bar or to the right of another pull-down menu.

Radio buttons A set of choices that represents mutually exclusive options. Sometimes called *option buttons.*

Scroll bar A horizontal or vertical bar along a side of a window indicating that the window is too small to display all the information involved. The user must activate the scroll arrows on the bar to see offscreen information.

Scroll arrows Arrows on a scroll bar that enable users to see additional information.

Size button In the Microsoft Windows environment, one or two small symbols that appear on the right edge of the title bar and enable a window to be maximized to take up the full screen, minimized to icon size, or restored to its previous size. This feature is implemented in the Macintosh environment by a *zoom box.*

Size box In the Macintosh environment, a box in the lower-right corner of the active window that enables the window to be resized. In the Microsoft Windows environment, this feature is implemented by clicking the mouse on the window border and dragging it.

Tear-off menu A pull-down menu that can be kept visible and moved to a new location on the screen so that the user can refer to it while working.

Text box A box that contains a space(s) for the user to type in text, such as a file's name.

Title bar A horizontal bar, usually at the top of a window, that contains the window's name.

Toolbox A menu in which icons are tightly arranged in a horizontal or vertical rectangular grid.

Warning box A box that displays a warning when the user is trying to do something that is disallowed or is doing something that can result in a loss of data. Sometimes called an *alert box.*

Window A box within an application that displays information or that contains an embedded application.

Zoom box In the Macintosh environment, a small symbol that enables the user to toggle between two window sizes. This feature is implemented in Microsoft Windows by *sizing buttons.*

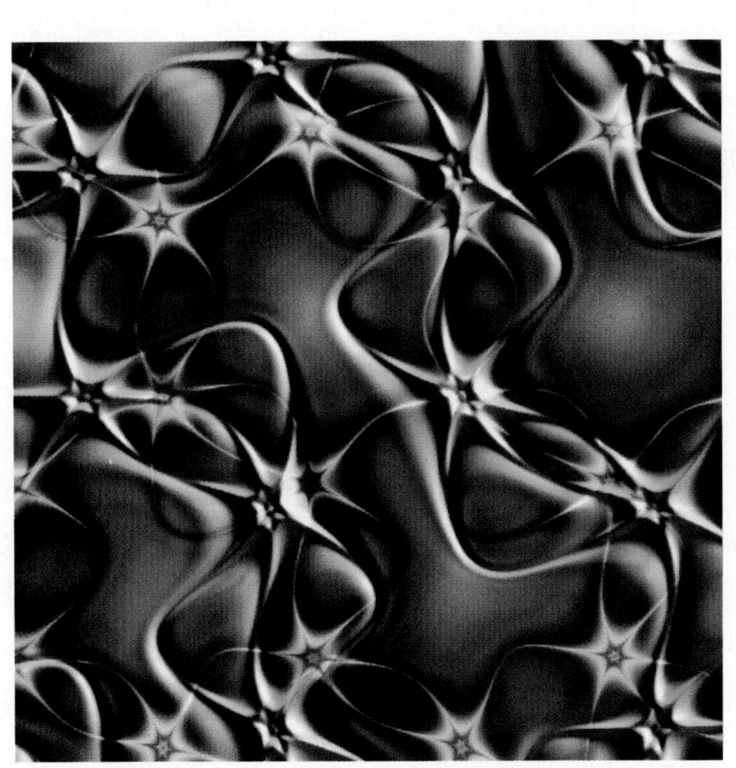

MODULE D

Productivity Software

Over the last decade or so, computers have completely transformed the workplace. Look at the desktops of many managers, analysts, designers, engineers, secretaries, and even corporate presidents today and you will usually see a computer system. Managers and analysts regularly use computers to crunch numbers, send and receive electronic-mail messages, and prepare presentation materials for meetings. Designers and engineers typically employ computers to create products. Secretaries use computers on a daily basis to prepare correspondence and reports. And corporate presidents rely on computers to access important facts about their organizations.

At the heart of this workplace transformation is productivity software. Productivity software refers to applications-software packages that enable end users to better perform their jobs. These packages help users save time, reduce costs, and perform types of work that couldn't possibly be done without the aid of a computer system.

Module D opens, in Chapter 8, with a look at word processors and desktop publishing systems, both of which assist in the development of documents. In Chapter 9 we cover spreadsheets and presentation graphics. Spreadsheets aid in the analysis of numbers, while presentation graphics packages help prepare graphs and charts showing numbers in a pictorial format. The module closes, in Chapter 10, with a discussion of database management systems, which specialize in providing rapid access to electronically stored facts.

Word Processing and Desktop Publishing

8

Have you ever wanted to create and publish your own magazine or book? As you will learn in this chapter, word processing and desktop publishing systems enable you to do just that—at a cost you can probably afford.

OUTLINE

Overview

Word Processing
- Learning to Use a Word Processor: The Basics
- Learning to Use a Word Processor: Advanced Operations
- Add-On Packages

Desktop Publishing
- What Is Desktop Publishing?
- Components of a Desktop Publishing System

LEARNING OBJECTIVES

After completing this chapter, you will be able to:

1. Describe word processing.
2. Identify the operations you must master to effectively use word processing software.
3. Explain the features common to many word processing packages.
4. Identify the software and hardware components found in many desktop publishing systems.

Overview

Word processing and desktop publishing are technologies that deal with the manipulation of words. *Word processing* enables a computer system to serve as a powerful typewriting tool. When using the computer in this way, one can quickly create, edit, and print documents and manage them as no ordinary typewriter can. *Desktop publishing,* available only since high-powered microcomputers entered the marketplace, carries word processing a step further. With desktop publishing hardware and software, one can create documents that look as though they were prepared by a professional print shop.

In this chapter, we'll first discuss word processors. We'll explore in detail some of the types of word processors currently available and many of the features that differentiate one word processor from another. We'll also look at some of the add-on packages that are available to make the word processing environment even more powerful. Then we'll turn to desktop publishing and the hardware and software found on desktop publishing systems.

Word Processing

Word processing. The use of computer technology to create, manipulate, and print text material such as letters, legal contracts, and manuscripts.

When you use your computer to do the kinds of work you normally do on a typewriter, you're doing word processing. **Word processing** is the use of computer technology to create, manipulate, and print text materials such as letters, legal contracts, manuscripts, and other documents. Word processing is such a timesaver, in fact, that most people who learn to do it let their typewriters gather dust.

Most word processing software products in use today are *general-purpose*; that is, they are designed to suit the needs of a variety of users, such as secretaries, authors, and average microcomputer users. Among today's best-selling packages are WordPerfect, Microsoft Word, and Ami Pro. Word and WordPerfect are the undisputed leaders in today's word processing marketplace, with close to a 75 percent combined market share.

Learning to Use a Word Processor: The Basics

Even though many word processing packages have hundreds of features, usually only a handful of them account for 90 percent or more of what you will do during the course of word processing a typical document. This basic set of word processing operations can be divided into three groups: general operations, entering and editing operations, and print-formatting operations.

General Operations To use virtually any type of productivity software package—word processor, spreadsheet, or whatever—you need to know how to carry out a number of general tasks. These are listed in Figure 8-1 and are functionally equivalent to activities like starting and stopping when operating a car.

Entering and Editing Operations Every word processor contains an assortment of entering and editing operations for keying in text and manipulating text on the screen. Among the most common of these operations are moving the cursor, scrolling, making a line return, inserting and deleting, moving and copying, and searching and replacing.

FIGURE 8-1

General operations needed for operating any productivity software package. Depending on the package you use, the file that you work on may contain a word-processed document, a worksheet, a graph, a collection of database records, or something else.

- **Accessing** your package from the operating system
- Informing the package that you either want to **create** a new file or **retrieve** an old one from disk
- Commanding the package to **save** a file onto disk
- Commanding the package to **print** a file
- Commanding the package to **delete** a file that's on disk
- Indicating to the package that you want to **quit** working on your current file and do something on another file
- **Terminating** your work on the package and getting back to the operating system

- **Moving the Cursor** Many word processors offer well over a dozen ways to move the cursor around the screen. Usually you can move the cursor a character, a word, a line, or a screen at a time, as well as to the beginning or the end of a document. You can usually move the cursor either by typing in a short command or by depressing one of several function keys or cursor-movement keys. Many word processing users acquire a mouse to obtain additional cursor-movement capabilities.
- **Scrolling** Scrolling lets you move contiguous lines of text up and down on the screen similarly to the way the roll on a player piano unwinds. When scrolling down, for example, as lines successively disappear from the top of the screen, new ones appear from the bottom. With many word processing packages, you can use the up-arrow and down-arrow keys to scroll a document line by line. By using the PgUp and PgDn keys, you can scroll even faster—page by page instead of line by line.
- **Making a Line Return** With a conventional typewriter, you generally must press the Return key every time you finish typing in a line. Not so with a word processor. Word processors provide an automatic line return when the cursor reaches a certain column position at the right-hand side of the screen. This return is called a **soft return,** and the built-in feature that provides soft returns is called a **wordwrap** feature (see Figure 8-2).

  Word processors also allow you to key in **hard returns** by hitting the Enter key. Normally, you will use hard returns between paragraphs or blocks of text or after typing in titles. You should not hit the Enter key after every line as you would on a normal typewriter. Hitting the Enter key will deny you any chances of reformatting the document later on.
- **Inserting and Deleting** Inserting and deleting are two of the most basic editing operations.

  Virtually all word processors have an *insert mode* that lets you insert characters at the cursor position on the screen. Often, you enter the insert mode by depressing the Insert key on the keyboard. When you are not in

Soft return.
An automatic line return carried out by word-processing software.

Wordwrap.
The word processing feature that automatically produces soft returns.

Hard return.
The use of the Enter key to provide line spacing in a document.

FIGURE 8-2

Wordwrap. Wordwrapping produces a soft return when the cursor reaches a certain position at the right-hand side of the screen.

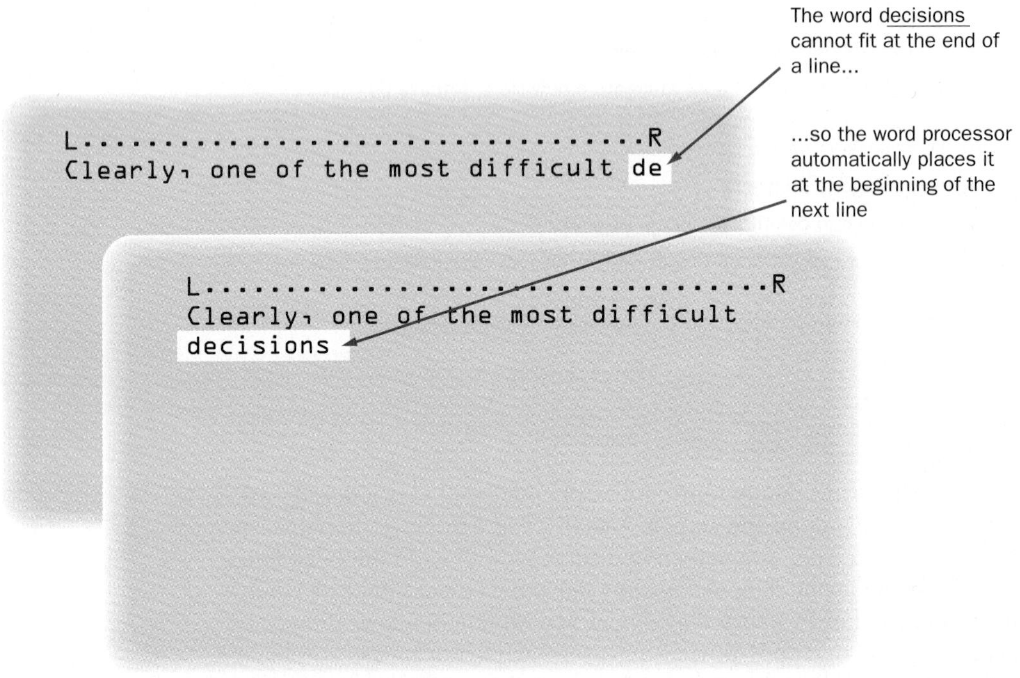
The word decisions cannot fit at the end of a line...
L..................................R
Clearly, one of the most difficult de
...so the word processor automatically places it at the beginning of the next line
L..................................R
Clearly, one of the most difficult
decisions

the insert mode, you are automatically in the *typeover mode,* in which case every character you type into an already existing line replaces the character at the cursor position. On most systems, the Insert key is a *toggle key*—depressing it once activates the insert mode, and depressing it again deactivates the insert mode.

Word processors will generally allow you to delete a character, word, line, or block of characters at a time. Deleting one character at a time is normally done through either the Delete or Backspace key. Deleting one word or line at a time is generally done by positioning the cursor on the word or line to be deleted and depressing one or two keys. When you want to delete a block of characters, you normally must first identify the beginning and end of the block, an operation called *block marking,* and then invoke a delete command. Block marking, illustrated in Figure 8-3, is also necessary when you want to move, copy, boldface, or underline text.

- **Moving and Copying** Moving and copying are operations that allow you to "cut and paste" text with a word processor. *Moving* means identifying a specific block of text and physically relocating it in a new place in the document. *Copying* is similar to moving except that a copy of the block remains in the original place as well.
- **Searching and Replacing** Searching and replacing are extremely useful features. They enable you to search automatically for all occurrences of a

FIGURE 8-3

Marking a block of text. A block is usually marked by highlighting it onscreen (as shown here) or by marking its beginning and end with special characters. Once a block has been marked, it can be moved, copied, formatted, or deleted.

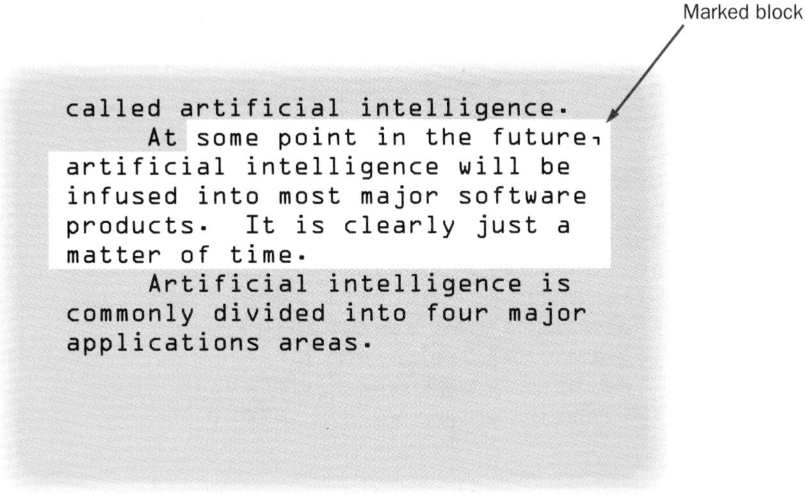

Marked block

```
called artificial intelligence.
     At some point in the future,
artificial intelligence will be
infused into most major software
products.  It is clearly just a
matter of time.
     Artificial intelligence is
commonly divided into four major
applications areas.
```

particular word or phrase and change them to something else. For example, let's say you've typed out a long document that should repeatedly refer to a person named "Snider." If you've misspelled this name as "Schneider," you can instruct the word processor to look up all occurrences of "Schneider" and change them to "Snider."

Some people take dangerous shortcuts in searching and replacing. For example, suppose you ask the word processor to change all occurrences of "chne" to "n." This will change all "Schneider" occurrences to "Snider," but it will also change a name such as "Schneymann" to "Snymann," which you probably did not intend to do.

Figure 8-4 shows a document before and after a searching and replacing operation.

Print-Formatting Operations Print-formatting operations tell the printer how to output the text onto paper. These operations include adjusting line spacing, indenting, justifying, establishing a page format, reformatting, centering, tabbing, paginating, setting up headers and footers, selecting typefaces, WYSIWYG output control, putting text into multiple columns, and footnoting.

- **Adjusting Line Spacing** Adjusting line spacing is an important word processing operation. Suppose that you've single-spaced a paper, but your English 101 instructor wants all the essays you hand in to be double-spaced. Virtually all word processors will enable you to adjust the line spacing to a double space in a few second or minutes. Many packages will also permit triple-spacing, fractional blank lines between text lines, and several other line-spacing options.

FIGURE 8-4

Searching and replacing. In the figure, the operator wishes to search for all occurrences of the date March 27 and replace them with the date April 3. Such an operation is called a global search-and-replace. Many word processors will also stop at each occurrence of the search string, if desired, and provide the operator the option of changing each one individually.

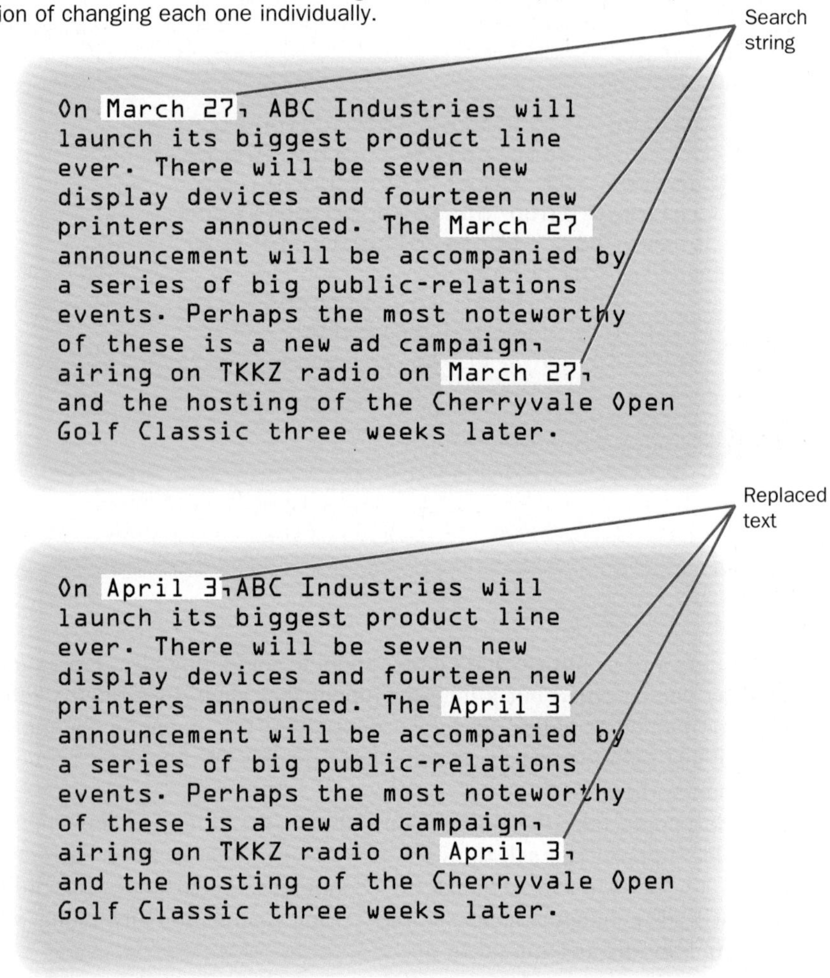

Search string
On March 27, ABC Industries will launch its biggest product line ever. There will be seven new display devices and fourteen new printers announced. The March 27 announcement will be accompanied by a series of big public-relations events. Perhaps the most noteworthy of these is a new ad campaign, airing on TKKZ radio on March 27, and the hosting of the Cherryvale Open Golf Classic three weeks later.
Replaced text
On April 3,ABC Industries will launch its biggest product line ever. There will be seven new display devices and fourteen new printers announced. The April 3 announcement will be accompanied by a series of big public-relations events. Perhaps the most noteworthy of these is a new ad campaign, airing on TKKZ radio on April 3, and the hosting of the Cherryvale Open Golf Classic three weeks later.

- **INDENTING** Indenting, or adjusting margins, is useful when you are typing a paper with many quotations and want to set off these passages from the main text. Many word processors allow you to choose among several types of indenting styles. One of the most widely used of these is the *hanging indent,* which is used to indent text in numbered and bulleted lists (such as this list).
- **JUSTIFYING** Virtually all word processing packages enable a printed document to be formatted with either a ragged or smooth right edge. These style alternatives are respectively referred to as *left justification* and *full justification.* The text that you are reading at this instant has fully justified margins. The text inside the two screens of Figure 8-4, in contrast, has a left-justified or ragged right margin. Users who create business documents

often prefer left justification, as the extra blank spaces between words that often come with full justification can sometimes make documents too visually difficult to read. Full justification can look quite attractive, however, if the word processor and printer in use can handle proportional spacing (to be discussed shortly).

- **Establishing a Page Format** Most word processors let you choose the way in which you would like your pages to be formatted. For instance, you can tell the word processor how many lines to print per page; the maximum number of characters to fit on each line; and the settings of the left, right, top, and bottom margins. A number of word processing packages will also automatically number lines for you—a useful feature if you are preparing legal documents or printer galleys. Having a number attached to each line makes it easy to identify text quickly and with less chance of error.
- **Reformatting** Reformatting normally is necessary when you insert text, delete text, change line spacing, readjust margins in your document, change justification, or change the basic page format. Reformatting places the document in a form suitable for output, for instance, by ensuring that the document is properly fitted within the margins after an insertion or deletion is made. Most packages reformat automatically after each edit.
- **Centering** Centering text is important for most users of word processors. Word processing packages usually require you to have the cursor on the line containing the text to be centered when invoking the centering command.
- **Tabbing** Tabbing is a formatting feature that typists have relied on for years. Like typewriters, most word processors enable you to set your own tab stops. The tab-stop positions on the screen can normally be reached through the Tab key.
- **Paginating** A pagination feature lets you choose whether to number pages in a document. For example, you may want page numbers placed on class reports but not on short letters. Many word processing packages will place page numbers wherever you specify.
- **Setting Up Headers and Footers** *Headers* are titles automatically printed at the top of every page; *footers* are titles automatically printed at the bottom. Some word processors give you a great deal of flexibility with respect to headers and footers. For instance, you can print both headers and footers on the same page and even alternate the title placed in a header or a footer. This textbook, like many other books, alternates headers; module letter and title are on the left-facing pages and chapter number and title are on the right-facing pages. Many word processors also allow page numbers to appear in a header or footer and give you several choices about where to place them.
- **Selecting Typefaces** A **typeface** is a collection of characters that share a common design. Typeface selection features enable you to output characters in a variety of typefaces and typeface sizes (called **point sizes**). A typeface in a particular point size is referred to as a **font;** for instance, 12-point Courier is a font. Figures 8-5 and 8-6 illustrate typefaces, point sizes, and fonts.

  Many word processors will also let you create boldface, italic, underlined, subscript, or superscript characters. Both the word processor and the printer on your system must support a particular styling feature for you to be able to use it.

Typeface.
A collection of characters that share a common design.

Point size.
A measurement used in the scaling of typefaces.

Font.
A typeface in a particular point size—for instance, 12-point Helvetica.

FIGURE 8-5

Typefaces. A typeface is a collection of visually consistent characters. Shown here are the (a) Courier, (b) Helvetica, and (c) Times typefaces.

ABC
DEFGHIJKLMNOPQRS
TUVWXYZØŁ&
abcdefghijklmnopqrst
uvwxyz ıłøß ªº†‡§
1234567890•*¶@#\/⁄
% +|–·= ~<>^_ – – —
ÅÇËÎÑÒŠÚåçëîñòšú
'",‘’„“”.,…:;?¿!¡ «»‹›
$¢£¥ƒ¤{[(`´ˆ˜¯˘˙¨˚¸˝˛ˇ)]}

(a) Courier

ABC
DEFGHIJKLMNOPQR
STUVWXYZÆŒØŁ&
abcdefghijklmnopqrst
uvwxyzæœıłøßfiflªº†‡§
1234567890•*¶@#\/⁄
%‰+|–·=¬~<>^_ – – —
ÅÇËÎÑÒŠÚåçëîñòšú
'",‘’„“”.,…:;?¿!¡®™©«»‹›
$¢£¥ƒ¤{[(`´ˆ˜¯˘˙¨˚¸˝˛ˇ)]}

(b) Helvetica

ABC
DEFGHIJKLMNOPQR
STUVWXYZÆŒØŁ&
abcdefghijklmnopqrst
uvwxyzæœıłøßfiflªº†‡§
1234567890•*¶@#\/⁄
%‰+|–·=¬~<>^_ – – —
ÅÇËÎÑÒŠÚåçëîñòšú
'",‘’„“”.,…:;?¿!¡®™©«»‹›
$¢£¥ƒ¤{[(`´ˆ˜¯˘˙¨˚¸˝˛ˇ)]}

(c) Times

WYSIWYG. An acronym for "What You See Is What You Get," WYSIWYG refers to showing on the display screen an output image identical or very close to the final hard-copy image.

■ WYSIWYG Ideally, the image on the screen and the image on the printed page correspond exactly. This feature is referred to as **WYSIWYG,** for What You See Is What You Get (see Figure 8-7a). WYSIWYG—which is pronounced "wizzy-wig"—is a standard operation in desktop publishing applications, where the design of a page can be critical. There, users frequently employ high-resolution graphics monitors capable of simultaneously displaying a variety of type styles, sometimes scaled to different point sizes. Users can experiment onscreen with different styles and inspect document pages in fine detail before committing anything to print.

Today, many word processors and monitors in use fall short of the full WYSIWYG ideal. In fact, boldface, italic, and underlined characters often do not display conveniently onscreen even though they will be output as

FIGURE 8-6

Point size. Point size refers to the size of type. A typeface in a particular point size is commonly called a font.

This is 10-point Helvetica

This is 12-point Helvetica

This is 18-point Helvetica

This is 24-point Helvetica

FIGURE 8-7

WYSIWYG versus embedded formatting codes. With WYSIWYG, what you see on the screen is exactly what you get in print. Most users of word processors today must, however, rely on some type of embedded formatting codes to tell them if text is to be given special treatment.

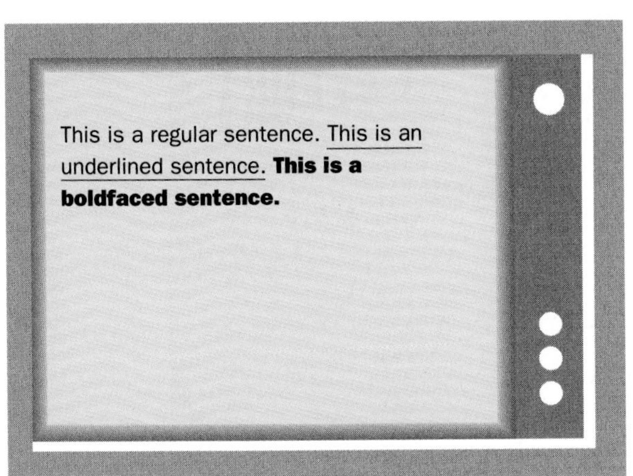

(a) WYSIWYG

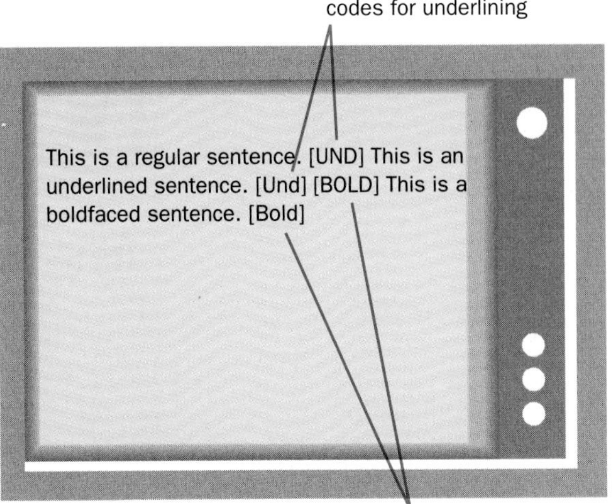

(b) Embedded formatting codes

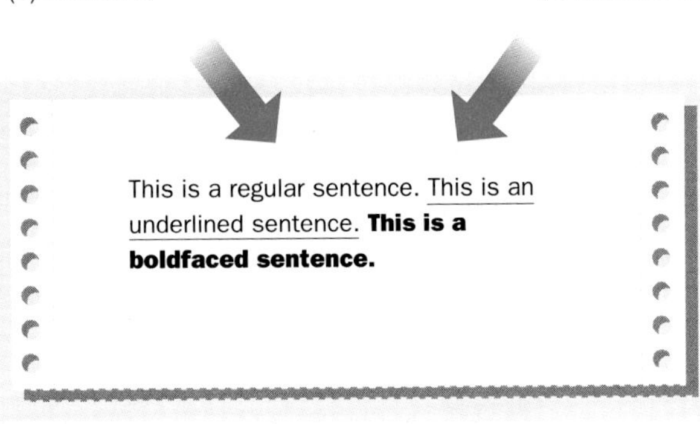

(c) Printed page

such on the printed document. To apprise users of such print-formatting effects, many word processors use *embedded formatting codes.* Typically, the user places these codes before and after a word or phrase that is to be output in a special way (see Figure 8-7b). The code placed before the word or phrase alerts the printer to turn on a formatting feature; the code following the word or phrase alerts it to turn off the feature. Most word processors will reveal the codes on demand.

In recognition of the usefulness of WYSIWYG, many word processors also have a *preview feature* (see Figure 8-8) that enables users to inspect

FIGURE 8-8

Previewing documents. Most word processors let you inspect a document prior to printing by looking onscreen at WYSIWYG full-page images, facing-page images, and close up views. Some also allow you to edit documents in graphical displays like the ones shown here, without having to return to standard text-editing mode.

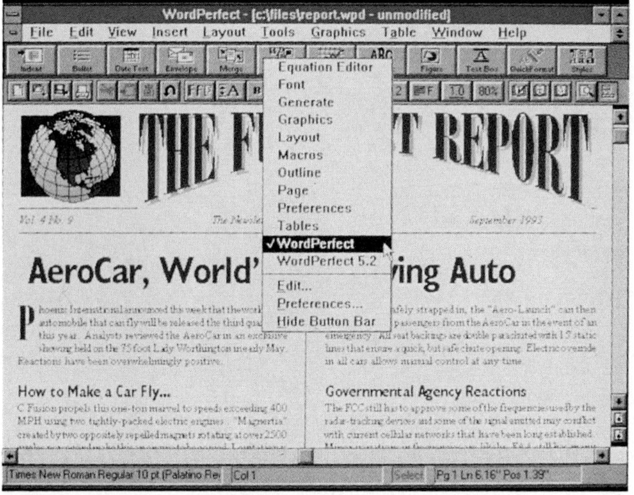

(a) WordPerfect 100% display

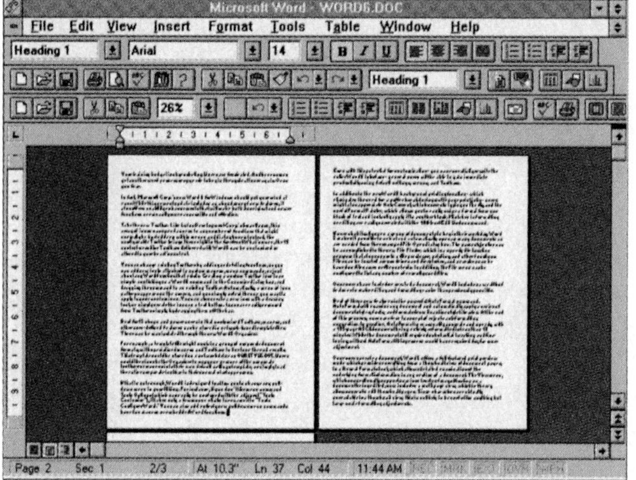

(b) Microsoft Word facing-page display

an onscreen version of what the document will actually look like when printed. Previewing lets users check carefully such things as typeface choices, point sizes, placement of graphics, and overall attractiveness of a page or page spread. WYSIWYG screens are but one example of the strong trend among word processors to sport graphical user interfaces (see the Tomorrow box).

- **Putting Text into Multiple Columns** Multiple-column formatting lets you print text in a columnar format similar to that used in newspapers and magazines. If you are doing multiple-column formatting, it is especially useful to have a feature that eliminates orphans and widows (discussed later in the chapter).

- **Footnoting** A footnoting feature allows you to create, edit, and delete footnotes in a document. Typically, the routine that manages the footnoting is designed to remember footnote references and automatically renumber footnotes if you insert or delete any.

Learning to Use a Word Processor: Advanced Operations

In addition to the basic operations we've just covered, the more sophisticated word processors enable you to do a number of other useful tasks. Some of these may be especially valuable if you are a professional typist or an author, or if your business requires a lot of correspondence. Among such tasks are using proportional spacing, spelling checkers and thesauruses, mailing list and mail merge operations, and a math feature; setting up macros; redlining; preparing an index and table of contents; eliminating orphans and widows; sorting; embedding codes for typesetters; embedding graphics into word processed text; and using style sheets.

Proportional Spacing On many printers, text is **monospaced;** that is, each character takes up the same amount of horizontal space. This textbook, however, like most others, was typeset on a system that proportionally spaces characters. **Proportional spacing** allocates more horizontal space on a line to some characters than to others. For example, a capital *M* takes up more space than a lowercase *i*. A microspacing feature may also be available. With **microspacing,** fractions of a full blank space are inserted within each line in places where they aren't likely to be noticed so that the left- and right-hand margins are flush. Proportional spacing and microspacing are shown in Figure 8-9.

Both your word processor and your printer must support proportional spacing and microspacing for your documents to achieve a typeset look.

Monospacing.
A printing feature that allocates the same amount of space on a line to each character.

Proportional spacing.
A printing feature that allocates more horizonal space on a line to some characters than to others.

Microspacing.
A technique used by some printers and software packages to insert fractional spaces between characters to give text a typeset look.

Spelling Checker Most leading word processing packages today include a routine that reads through a document and searches for misspelled words. This routine and its accompanying dictionary are collectively known as a **spelling checker.**

Spelling checker.
A program or routine that is often used with a word processor to check for misspelled words.

The capabilities of spelling checkers can vary dramatically. Some spelling checkers have dictionaries that contain around 50,000 words, whereas others have 130,000 or more. A particularly important feature is the ability to place additional words into a dictionary. A writer of a computer text or medical article, for example, uses very specialized terms, most of which aren't in the dictionaries of standard spelling checkers.

Many spelling checkers allow you to check for misspelled words either after you've finished typing or while you're typing a document. The latter feature, which is usually practical only if you have a hard disk, assists you as you type by beeping whenever you key in a word that it doesn't recognize. Spelling checkers usually also come with a feature that displays onscreen suggestions

TOMORROW

Graphical Word Processors

How Fast Will They Catch On?

During the last several years there has been a growing trend toward software that sports a graphical user interface (GUI). For a long time, this trend barely touched word processing, an applications area that is predominantly text based. But as computer hardware systems have become more powerful, word processing companies have taken advantage of the additional bytes and faster cycle times available on the new machines. As a result, word processors have leapt into the world of graphics.

In word processing, the graphics features being incorporated are generally of three principal types: a graphical command interface, improved WYSIWYG features, and drawing capabilities.

Graphical command interfaces refer to such features as mouse pointing and moving, onscreen windows and icons, and the ability to make choices from menus. Many of these features were covered in Window 4. Word processors that come with graphical interfaces include such products as WordPerfect 6.0, WordPerfect for Windows, Microsoft Word for Windows, and Ami Pro (see photo). At a minimum, a graphical command interface lets you use a mouse to select screen icons and choices from menu bars and pull-down menus. You may also be able to move text by "dragging and dropping" it with a mouse. And to save extra keystroking, you may even be able to define your own screen icons and have them perform customized functions.

Although most high-end word processors allow you to preview text in some sort of *WYSIWYG* mode, graphically oriented word processors often go a step or two further. For instance, many will let you edit the text you are previewing directly on the WYSIWYG screen rather than making you switch back and forth between WYSIWYG and standard-text modes. Also, some packages are making a greater selection of built-in fonts and automatic-styling features available, so documents can look even more like they were professionally typeset. Consequently, high-end word processors are looking more and more like low-end desktop publishing systems.

Several word processors are now also packing in a greater number of *drawing* features. Among other things, these features allow you to import art from other software packages and size, rotate, and crop it. Some word processors even provide a drawing capability within documents.

In addition to providing features such as those just named, some graphical word processors also integrate such non-word-processing features as spreadsheet and database capabilities and fax and electronic-mail routines.

Reaction to this new breed of graphical products has been mixed. Most heavy users of word

for how to properly spell a word they don't recognize (see Figure 8-10) and a feature that counts words.

Spelling checkers will not catch all spelling errors. For instance, if you misspell the word "their" as "there," which is also a word in the English language, the spelling checker will not flag it. To root out errors of this sort you need a *style/grammar checker* (discussed shortly).

Thesaurus feature. A word processing program or routine that enables electronic lookup of word synonyms.

Thesaurus Feature A **thesaurus feature** allows you to check words for possible synonyms. To use a thesaurus, you first flag a word you wish to replace in your document. If the thesaurus feature recognizes the word, it will provide onscreen replacement suggestions in a form resembling that of a hard-copy thesaurus (see Figure 8-11). Often, when you see a word you like, you need only type in the key corresponding to it to perform the replacement. Many thesaurus routines automatically reformat text after replacing a word. In addition,

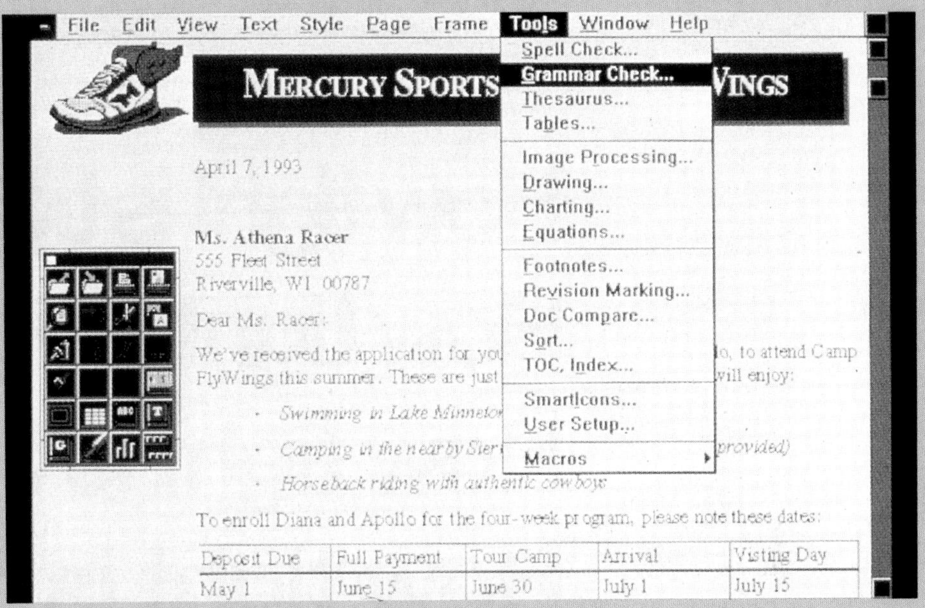

Word processing for the 1990s. Lotus' Ami Pro.

processing packages are touch typists who produce documents consisting of straight text—letters, memos, reports, and the like. Consequently, they don't have much need for WYSIWYG and drawing. Also, many touch typists dislike a graphical command interface because they feel it encourages them to use a mouse—forcing their hands off the keyboard. Moreover, a number of people complain that GUI word processors run slower than their non-GUI counterparts and that the graphical features word processors are now incorporating are best left to specialized support (add-on) packages, which do them better on the whole.

These drawbacks notwithstanding, the new breed of graphical word processors is drawing serious notice and appears to be an unstoppable trend. It's a good bet that as computers get ever more powerful, the word processing companies will be offering an even wider range of products from which to choose, including everything from full-blown desktop publishing with lots of typesetting and imagesetting features to watered-down packages aimed at folks who like to write an occasional letter to Mom and Dad.

several allow you to do word searches within other word searches, and many provide antonyms as well as synonyms. The thesauruses packaged with the leading word processors typically contain anywhere from 10,000 to 70,000 words. Some commercial-level electronic thesauruses used by newspapers and magazines have over a million words.

Mailing List/Mail Merge Programs A **mailing list program** is used to generate mailing labels. With such a feature, you can usually sort records by specific fields (such as zip code) or extract records having special characteristics (such as all alumni from the class of 1992 living in San Francisco) prior to processing the labels.

Mailing list program. A program that is used to generate mailing labels.

Individuals and organizations often have a need to send the same letter—more or less—to dozens or even thousands of people. A word processor's **mail merge program** is specifically designed to produce form letters of this sort.

Mail merge program. A program that is specifically designed to produce form letters.

FIGURE 8-9

Proportionally spaced characters with microspacing. With proportional spacing, more horizontal space on a line is allotted to some characters than to others. Note, for instance, that a capital *H* takes up more space than the lowercase *t* and *i* combined. Microspacing inserts fractional spaces between characters to make a line appear more attractive to the eye.

How tight is tight?

How tight is tight?

How tight is tight?

How tight is tight?

This type of feature is so named because it prints such letters in volume by merging a file containing a list of names and addresses with a file containing the *boilerplate,* or form letter.

Math Feature A *math feature* allows you to perform modest amounts of computation during the course of word processing. Such a feature is useful for

FIGURE 8-10

Using a spelling checker. Many spelling checkers stop to highlight words that they don't recognize when scanning a completed text document. Here the checker can't find "glossery" in its dictionary and, below the dotted line, offers the operator some replacement suggestions. Many spelling checkers automatically make a replacement when the operator depresses the assigned key—the *A* key, in this example.

```
After I finished reading the book, I noticed that the
glossery contained a few slang words. This was not
quite what I expected.

------------------------------------------------------

A. glossary           B. glacier           C. glasser
D. glassier           E. glazer            F. glazier
G. glossier
```

FIGURE 8-11

Using a thesaurus. In many word processors, the user points to a word to be "looked up" by positioning the cursor on it and then invokes the thesaurus feature. Here the operator has pointed to *want,* and the replacement suggestions in the middle of the screen have appeared. Many thesaurus routines automatically make a replacement when the key that corresponds to it is depressed.

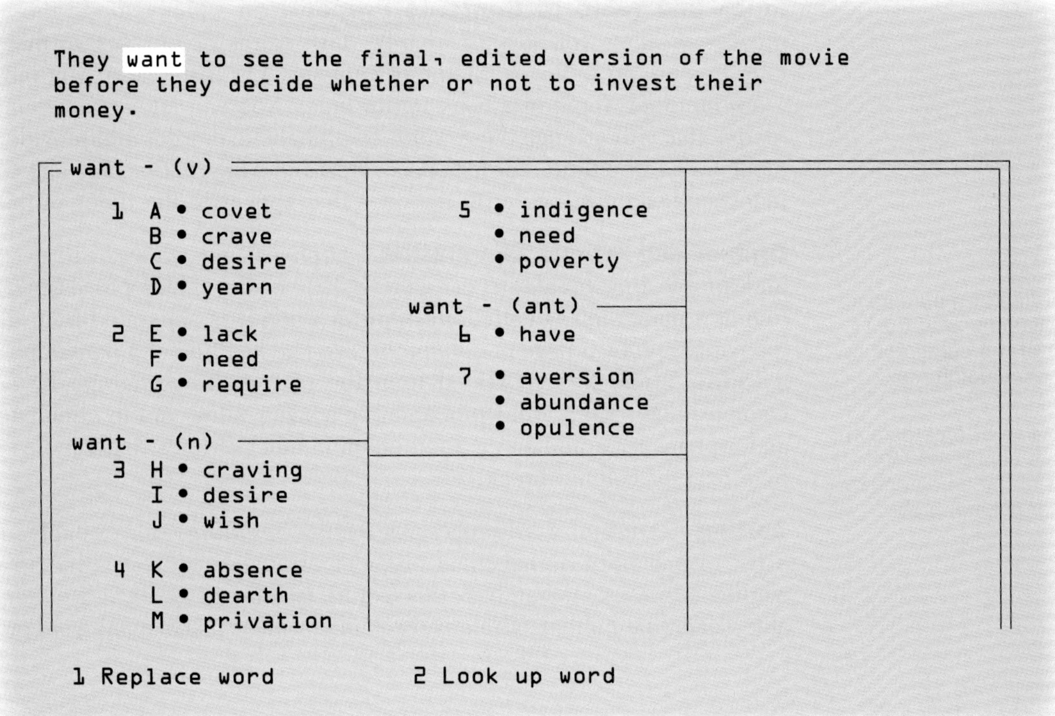

preparing expense reports, simple budgets, and other types of business documents that require little more than summing columns or rows of numbers. If you need to do more sophisticated forms of math, you might do well to acquire instead an integrated software package (with a spreadsheeting capability).

Macros Many word processors allow users to create macros. A **macro** is a sequence of keystrokes that is saved in a special file so that you can use it whenever you wish. For instance, say you are going to be typing several letters containing your home address and a canned, "we-wish-you-were-here" paragraph. You would first invoke a "define macro" command in your word processor. Then you would type the address, saving it in a macro file. Next you would type the canned paragraph and save it in a different macro file. During the course of preparing your letters, you would invoke either of the macros at the point where you wanted the associated text placed in your document. This is normally done by pressing one or two keys followed by the name of the macro.

Macro.
A predetermined series of keystrokes or commands that can be invoked by a single keystroke or command.

Redlining.
A word processing facility that provides the electronic equivalent of the editor's red pen.

Redlining When editing the hard-copy documents of others, many people use a red pen to cross out certain words or phrases and substitute others. This process is called **redlining.** After a document is redlined, the original author can see both what he or she originally wrote and the changes made by the editor. The redlining feature found in many word processors provides the electronic equivalent of the manual redlining process.

Index and Table of Contents Preparation Many top-of-the-line word processors allow you to individually "tag" words or phrases so that you can later prepare an index or a table of contents. For instance, if you have tagged a few hundred words in a book for an index, you can later invoke an *indexing routine* that will arrange these words in alphabetical order and provide the page numbers on which the words appear. Most indexing routines also let you create index subheadings similar to the ones that appear in the index of this book.

Orphan.
The first line of a paragraph when it is separated from the rest of the paragraph by a page or column break.

Widow.
The last line of a paragraph when it is separated from the rest of the paragraph by a page or column break.

Orphan and Widow Elimination Orphans and widows are aesthetically undesirable line breaks (see Figure 8-12). In document processing, the first line of a paragraph is called an **orphan** when it is separated from the rest of the paragraph by a page or column break. The last line of a paragraph is called a **widow** when it is separated from the rest of the paragraph by a page or column break. Many word processing packages allow you to eliminate widows and orphans by establishing a minimum number of lines that can be separated by a page or column break.

Sorting A useful word processing feature is *sorting*—for example, arranging a list of names in alphabetical order or arranging addresses by zip code for mailing purposes. As handy as this feature may be, however, it is either unavailable, somewhat limited, or relatively cumbersome to use in many word processors.

FIGURE 8-12

Orphans and widows. Orphans and widows are aesthetically undesirable line breaks that many word processors can eliminate.

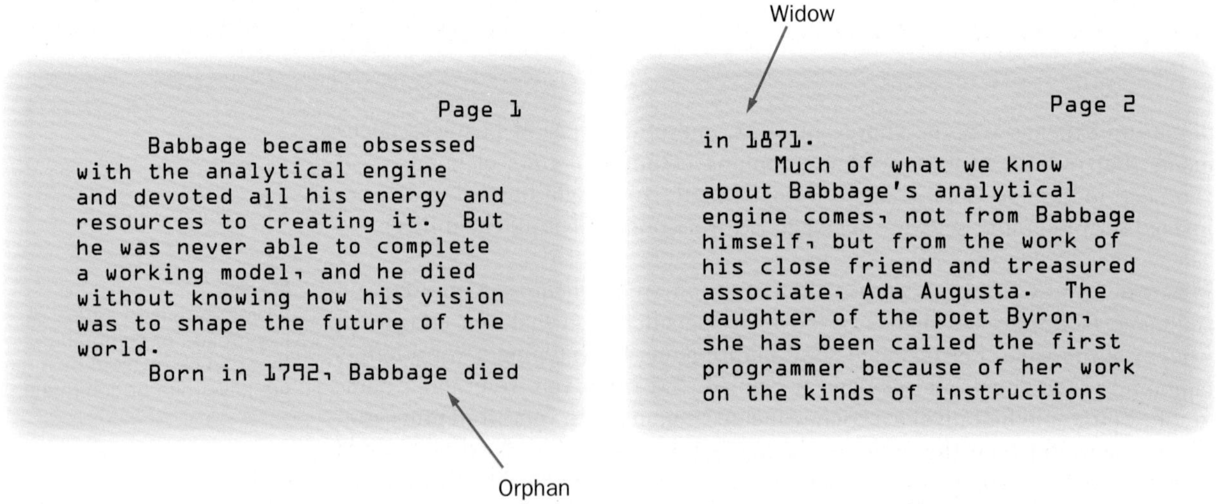

Page 1
Babbage became obsessed
with the analytical engine
and devoted all his energy and
resources to creating it. But
he was never able to complete
a working model, and he died
without knowing how his vision
was to shape the future of the
world.
Born in 1792, Babbage died
Orphan
Widow
Page 2
in 1871.
Much of what we know
about Babbage's analytical
engine comes, not from Babbage
himself, but from the work of
his close friend and treasured
associate, Ada Augusta. The
daughter of the poet Byron,
she has been called the first
programmer because of her work
on the kinds of instructions

(a) Orphan

(b) Widow

Embedded Typesetting Codes Sometimes word-processed text is sent directly to a professional compositor for typesetting. When this is done, considerable savings can result if *typesetting codes,* such as codes for special fonts or complex printing effects, are embedded into the document before it is sent to the typesetter. Many of the more powerful word processing packages targeted for commercial environments offer this feature.

Graphics Many word processors have a *graphics feature* that enables users to create attractive boxes of information within text documents. An example of this feature is the boxed table at the bottom of the image that accompanies the Tomorrow box. A graphics capability usually also lets users import art into a document—from other program files or from a library of art images—as well as do a limited amount of drawing.

Style Sheets A feature that several leading word processors have begun incorporating—and that is standard fare in desktop publishing packages—is the style sheet. A **style sheet** is a collection of font and formatting specifications that is saved as a file and later used to prepare documents in a particular way. For instance, if your letters to clients are to conform to a certain letterhead style and to use a specific typeface and point size, you can declare all of these specifications in a style sheet that you invoke when preparing such letters. Reports, in contrast, would probably use a different style sheet.

Style sheet.
A collection of design specifications that can be saved as a file and later used to format documents in a particular way.

Add-On Packages

When a word processor is missing a critical feature, chances are there's an aftermarket (third-party) vendor that offers such a feature as an add-on. Aftermarket vendors specialize in complementing a product made by another vendor with some type of "value-added" functionality. Four of the most widely used types of **add-on packages** are discussed in the following paragraphs.

Add-on package.
A software package that supplements the activities of a larger software package, either by providing new functions or improving on already existing functions.

Reference Shelves *Reference shelves,* the most prominent of which is Microsoft Bookshelf (see Figure 8-13), provide a number of handy reference books online to the writer. For instance, Bookshelf packs electronic versions of the *American Heritage Dictionary,* a thesaurus, the *Chicago Manual of Style, Bartlett's Familiar Quotations,* an atlas, a zip-code directory, and a world almanac onto a single optical disk. Bookshelf enables any of its works to be summoned by a word processor with a couple of keystrokes. Once the computer system is pointing to a particular reference work on the "shelf," the work can be electronically searched for a particular block of text. When the block is found, it can be "cut and pasted" back into the document being word processed.

Bibliographic Databases *Bibliographic databases* are specifically tailored to writers who prepare long reference lists or bibliographies. The programs use onscreen templates for entering information about references into specific fields and for entering lengthy notes. You can also select a style by which the entire bibliography will be automatically formatted.

Style/Grammar Checkers *Style/grammar checkers* are designed to root out errors in grammar, punctuation, and word usage. They also analyze writing

FIGURE 8-13

Microsoft Bookshelf. Users of this add-on package can summon any of the works shown on the screen with a couple of keystrokes.

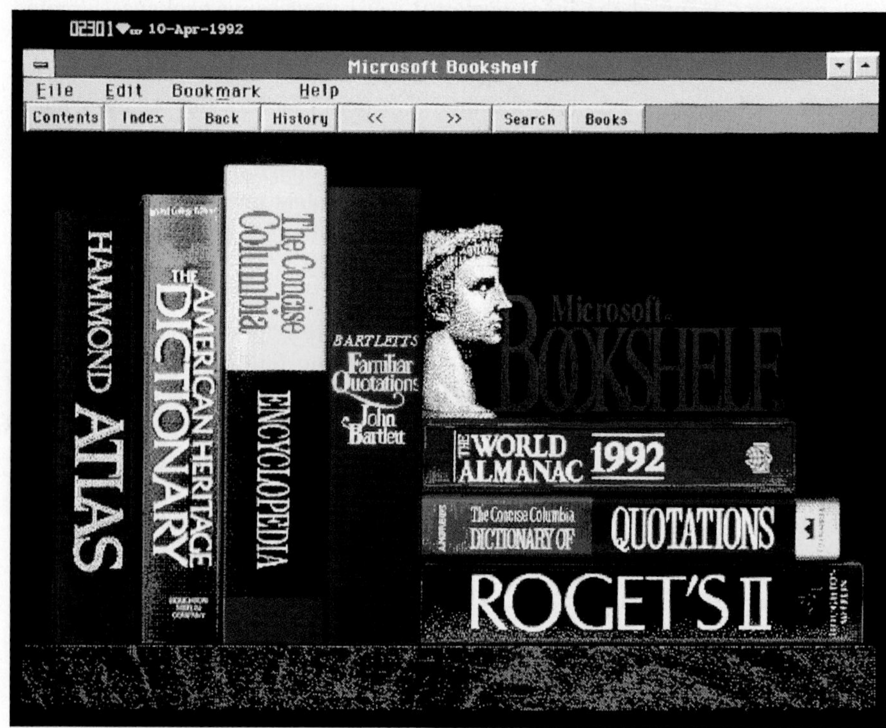

styles for specific weaknesses (such as overused words, overly long sentences, and words that are sexist or out-of-date). In addition, most packages will calculate some type of overall reading-level statistic for your written work. Unfortunately, good writing often depends on bending rules. So, although style/grammar checkers may help people write in an understandable fashion, they cannot turn a wretched writer into an instant Hemingway. Figure 8-14 shows a style/grammar checker at work.

Font Libraries Even though many word processors come packaged with a variety of fonts, you can add others by acquiring a font library. A font library is a collection of fonts that supplements those packaged into your word processor. Font libraries are particularly useful for users who want to give their documents a "desktop publishing" look.

Desktop Publishing

The late 1970s introduced desktop computing—an entire computer system capable of fitting on a desktop. Thanks to other major improvements on the software and hardware fronts, we now have desktop publishing—microcomputer-based publishing systems that fit on a desktop.

FIGURE 8-14

Style/grammar checker. Style/grammar checkers are designed to root out errors in grammar, punctuation, and word usage. They will not, however, turn a wretched writer into an instant Hemingway.

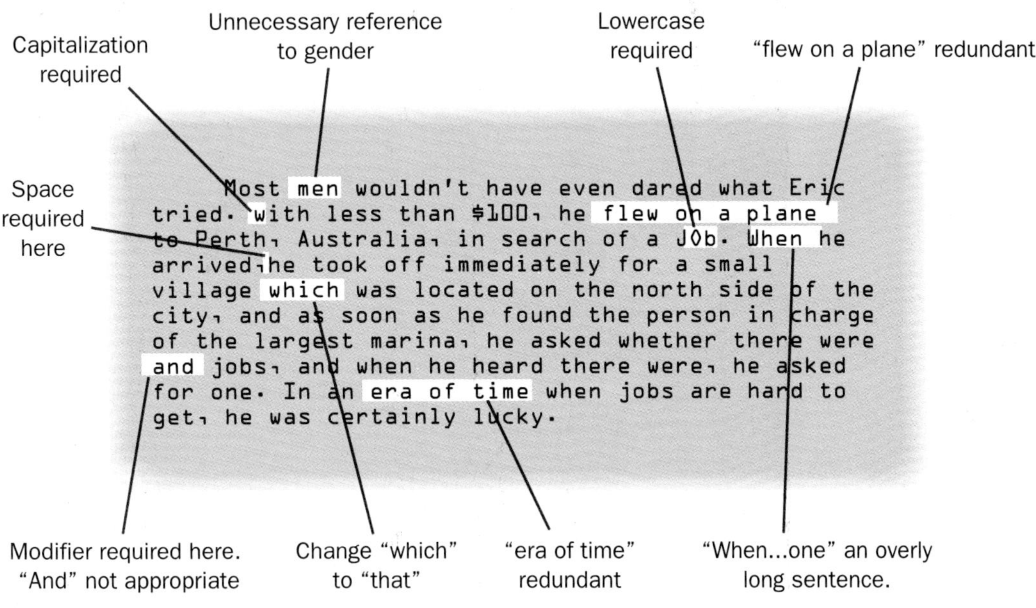

Capitalization required
Unnecessary reference to gender
Lowercase required
"flew on a plane" redundant
Space required here
Most men wouldn't have even dared what Eric tried. with less than $100, he flew on a plane to Perth, Australia, in search of a JOb. When he arrived,he took off immediately for a small village which was located on the north side of the city, and as soon as he found the person in charge of the largest marina, he asked whether there were and jobs, and when he heard there were, he asked for one. In an era of time when jobs are hard to get, he was certainly lucky.
Modifier required here. "And" not appropriate
Change "which" to "that"
"era of time" redundant
"When...one" an overly long sentence.

What Is Desktop Publishing?

Desktop publishing. A microcomputer-based publishing system that can fit on a desktop.

Desktop publishing systems are hardware/software systems that let you combine on a page such elements as text (in a variety of typefaces), art, and photos, thus creating attractive documents that look as if they came off a printer's press (see Figure 8-15). Desktop publishing systems are designed to replace many of the traditionally manual, labor-intensive tasks associated with cutting, arranging, and pasting elements onto a page. Because they make it possible for publishing to be done in-house, they also enable companies to save money, save time, and have more control over the look of finished documents (see User Solution 8-1). In the last decade or so, desktop publishing has rapidly evolved into a major applications area within the field of computers. Figure 8-16 lists several applications for desktop publishing.

As you can see from studying the image in Figure 8-15, the basic difference between word processing and desktop publishing is one of document "look." Whereas word processing deals mainly with straight, nontypeset text—and maybe a few simple fonts for emphasis—desktop publishing involves full-fledged typesetting and imagesetting. *Typesetting* implies full control over type styles and sizes as well as spacing between words, letters, and lines. *Imagesetting* involves combining on a page both type and such artwork elements as drawings, photographs, and color. Although there is a theoretical distinction that separates desktop publishing from word processing, many of the leading word processors are increasingly being packaged with desktop publishing features.

FIGURE 8-15

Desktop publishing. Desktop publishing lets you combine on a page such elements as text, art, and photos, thus creating documents that look professionally prepared.

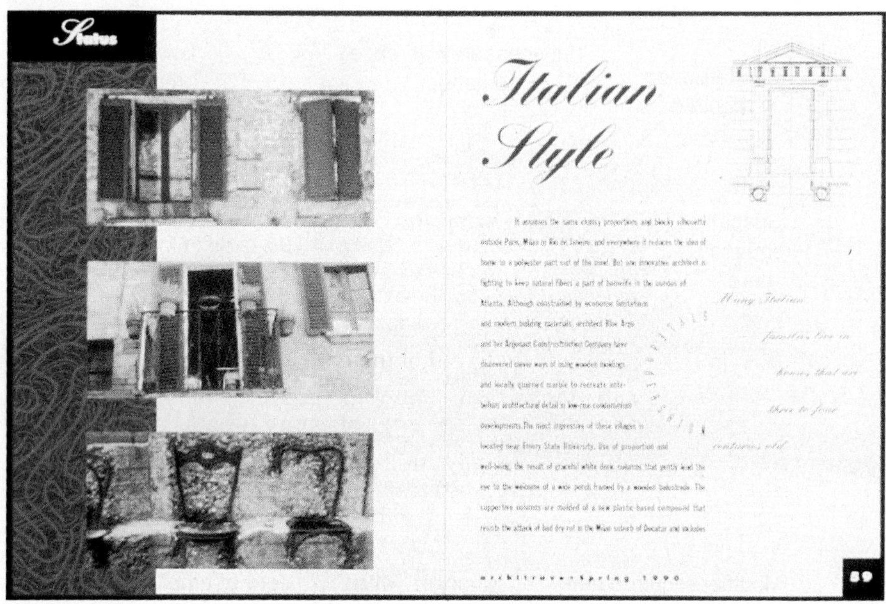

Desktop publishing systems have come a long way in providing individuals with the capability to produce documents that look as if they were professionally prepared, but they are still a far cry from professional-level publishing systems. Systems falling into this latter category are the preferred choice for producing large volumes of high-quality printed materials such as corporate annual reports and four-color books like this one.

Components of a Desktop Publishing System

Naturally, not all desktop publishing systems are the same. You can spend less than a hundred dollars for a system that produces simple newsletters, but you will pay several times that amount for one that creates stunning color artwork. Desktop publishing systems targeted for commercial applications often consist of several hardware and software components. These components are described in this section, and their use is covered in Window 5. Feature 8-1 offers a crash course in typography, covering some of the key terms.

Hardware Hardware used to do high-end desktop publishing usually includes a high-end microcomputer system, a laser printer, a graphics-oriented monitor, and an image scanner. These devices were covered in depth in Chapter 5 of the text and are therefore addressed only briefly here.

- **High-End Microcomputer System** High-quality desktop publishing requires a microprocessor that packs plenty of power, a respectable amount

User Solution 8-1

Saving a Million Bucks through Desktop Publishing

The New Yorker Magazine has joined the ranks of publishers that are moving some of their traditional operations onto the desktop. In the past, all corrections made in the proofing process at the 70-year-old magazine were faxed to Chicago to be printed into galleys. Then, the galleys—which represent how text copy looks typeset before it is put into final page form—were faxed back to New York for final proofing. Copy changes were subsequently made over the phone. Now, all of the typed copy is prepared in-house in New York with Aldus PageMaker and output on a local laser printer and an imagesetter. The magazine reports an initial savings of over a million dollars, and it is now in the process of digitizing its art library and preparing cartoons on the desktop.

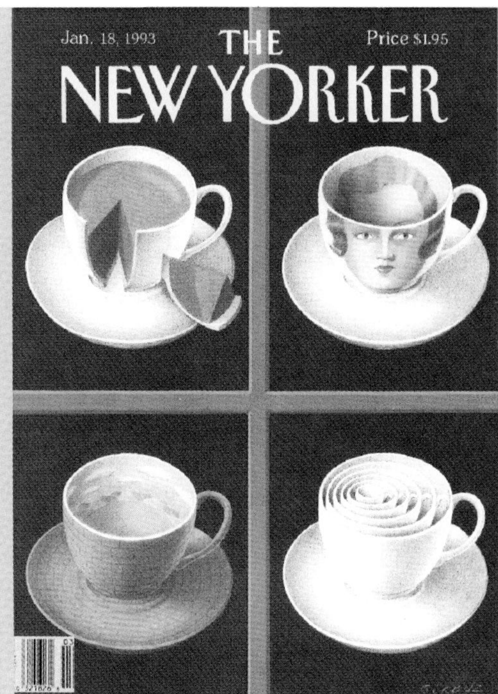

of RAM, and a hard disk with plenty of storage. Manipulation of graphical fonts, photos, and art can be computationally intensive. A mere two-page newsletter, for instance, can require 200 KB of storage, a 30-point character set uses about 150 KB, and a half-page scanned image needs another 500 KB. Such work requires a system unit like those based on high-end Intel or Motorola chips. The systems should have at least 4 to 8 MB of RAM and at least 100 MB of hard-disk storage.

- **Laser Printer** Most laser printers for microcomputer-based desktop publishing applications cost anywhere from about $600 to $10,000. These devices have their own built-in microprocessors, about 1 to 3 MB RAM, and several ROM chips that carry popular fonts. Greater amounts of RAM allow you to output images of greater complexity. Many laser printers output

FIGURE 8-16

Desktop publishing applications. Applications for desktop publishing run the gamut from business résumés and business cards to books and magazines.

- Advertisements
- Annual reports
- Books
- Brochures
- Business reports
- Catalogs
- Business cards
- Résumés
- Restaurant menus
- Magazines
- Newsletters
- Newspapers
- Posters
- Price lists
- Software/system documentation
- Stationery and business forms
- Training manuals
- Signs

Feature 8–1

A Crash Course in Typography

A look at some of the terms of the typographer's trade

At one time, most computer buffs cared little about the somewhat arcane terminology used in the publishing industry. Then, quite suddenly, came desktop publishing. Now, if you are going to wade through a trade book or a reference manual to understand how a particular desktop publishing package works, you'd better know your serifs from your ascenders.

Many professional graphic designers devote years to the study of typography. Fortunately for the part-time desktop publisher, such an immersion into the publishing field is hardly necessary. One can get by just by learning a few terms, most of which apply to type. Following is a miniglossary of some of the most useful terms to know:

Ascender The portion of a lowercase character that falls above the x-height (see Figure 1).

Baseline The imaginary line formed by connecting the bottommost parts of characters on a line, ignoring descenders (see Figure 1).

Body-copy typeface The typeface used for the main text, or "body," of a document. Body-copy typefaces are chosen to guide the eye along comfortably on a page and are often serif.

Descender The portion of a lowercase character that falls below the baseline (see Figure 1).

Display typeface The typeface used in banners, headings, or decorative text on a page. Display typefaces usually are greater than 12 points.

Folio A page number.

Font Traditionally, a term that refers to the complete set of characters in a particular typeface and point size, for instance, 12-point Helvetica. In practice today, many people use the terms *font* and *typeface* interchangeably.

Greeking Nonsense text used in a simulated layout to depict actual size, style, and placement of text.

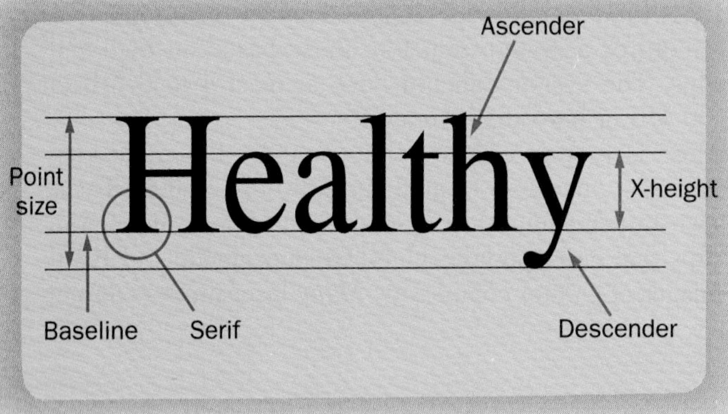

Figure 1.

at a resolution of either 300 dpi (dots per vertical and horizontal inch, or 90,000 dots to the inch) or 600 dpi. If you require higher resolution than this, you'll need professional typesetting equipment (which works at 1,000 dpi or more).

Page description language (PDL). A language used to communicate instructions to a laser printer.

The laser printer in your computer system relies on a specific **page description language (PDL)** to carry out its work. The two most common PDLs are Adobe's *PostScript,* which is widely used in the fastest and most expensive laser printers, and Hewlett-Packard's *Printer Command Language (PCL),* which is more popular on slower and less expensive laser printers.

Halftoning The process of converting a continuous-tone photographic image into a series of dots.

Kerning Adjusting the spacing between certain character combinations to create a more visually consistent image. For instance, the two letters *AW* naturally appear to have more space between them than the two letters *MN*, and a kerning feature can reduce the disparity.

Leading The amount of vertical space between lines of a page; usually expressed in points.

Phototypesetting The process of transferring a page image to film or photosensitive paper so that it can be printed out by a very-high-resolution output device called a *phototypesetting machine* (such as a Linotronic 300).

Pica A unit of type measure commonly used to determine the depth of a set of lines, a paragraph, a photo, or a piece of art on a page. There are six picas to an inch.

Point The smallest unit of type measure, commonly used when referring to the size of type on a page. There are 12 points to a pica and 72 points to an inch (see Figure 1).

Roman Nonslanted type; often contrasted with *italic* type.

Rule A line on a page; for instance, the vertical line that appears to the right of this column of type is an example of a rule.

Sans serif A typeface without serifs, such as Helvetica.

Screen A measure, usually expressed as a percentage, of grayscale or color intensity. For instance, a 90 percent yellow screen translates into a bright yellow and a 10 percent yellow screen into a pale yellow. All of the artwork in this text is colored with screens, which consist of tightly or loosely packed dots. (You can see the dots under a magnifying glass.)

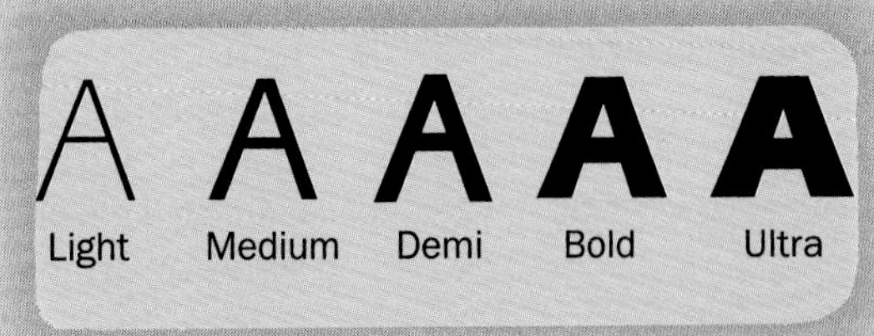

Figure 2.

Script A typeface that looks like handwriting or calligraphy.

Serif Short lines used to finish off the main strokes of a character to give it a distinctive styling (see Figure 1).

Style A variation within a typeface. For instance, a magazine article may be done in four styles of the Times typeface—roman, bold, italic, and bold italic.

Thumbnail A miniature copy of an image, used for referencing or planning purposes.

Vertical justification The ability to insert fractional lines within a page so that the top and bottom margins of all pages are even.

Weight The relative thickness of type (see Figure 2).

X-height The height of the lowercase letter *x* in a particular typeface (see Figure 1).

■ **Graphics-Oriented Monitor** Most monitors used with microcomputer systems contain a relatively small (13-to-15-inch) screen that can comfortably display about a third of a standard printed page at a time. On such screens, the resolution usually is adequate for text and some simple graphics. For desktop publishing applications, however, it generally is preferable to have a bigger screen with SVGA or XVGA resolution, both to fine-tune detailed graphics and to see without eyestrain either a full-page or a two-page layout on the screen at one time. Monitors designed for these purposes often have screens up to 50 percent larger than the typical microcomputer display (see Figure 8-17).

- **Image Scanner** An image scanner (see Figure 5-20) allows you to scan photographs, drawings, or text and digitize them directly into computer memory. Later, you can edit the images with illustration software and hardware. Some image scanners also use optical character recognition (OCR) software, which enables them to recognize certain text characters instead of just digitizing them. Such a feature allows you to later edit any text that you enter with the scanner. Both color and grey-scale scanners are widely available.

Software A variety of software and software-based products are used in desktop publishing environments. These include page-makeup software, word processing software, fonts, clip-art libraries, and art and illustration software.

- **Page-Makeup Software** The programs that allow you to combine text, photos, and art elements into a finished page are collectively referred to as **page-makeup software.** Because page makeup is the central function in desktop publishing, page-makeup programs are often loosely referred to as "desktop publishing packages." Some of the leading page-makeup programs are Aldus Corporation's PageMaker (see Figure 8-18), Xerox Corporation's Ventura Publisher, and Quark Inc.'s Quark Xpress. Your page-makeup software must be compatible with the other desktop publishing products you use, such as fonts, clip-art libraries, and the software used to develop text or illustration files.

Page-makeup software. Programs used to compose page layouts in a desktop publishing system.

- **Word Processing Software** Because most users already have their own word processing software, such as WordPerfect or Word, the vendors of the leading desktop publishing packages have designed their products to accept text prepared with several of the leading word processors. Thus, when acquiring a desktop publishing system, it is always wise to check out which word processors it recognizes. Although most page-makeup programs do contain built-in word processing features, enabling you to modify any text that you import to them, it is important to recognize that their primary function is page makeup. Consequently, they are not as easy to use for word processing as your average word processor.
- **Fonts** A variety of *fonts*—that is, typefaces conforming to a specific style and size—are available for desktop publishing applications. Some fonts are available as ROM chips that are packaged into the laser printer you buy. You can acquire additional fonts in disk form and load them into the laser printer's RAM. When choosing type for desktop-publishing work, most people need both large and small fonts. Large fonts are widely used for banners and titles; small fonts are commonly used for body copy.

  Fonts are of two types: bit-mapped and outline (see Figure 8-19). *Bit-mapped fonts* are described by a fixed configuration of dots. While they are the least expensive kind of font, you cannot scale them to different sizes. *Outline fonts* consist of mathematical curves that describe how characters are shaped. They are more expensive than bit-mapped fonts, but you can scale them to virtually any size you want and also create your own fonts. Two widely used outline fonts are *TrueType,* often bundled with Microsoft and Apple software, and *PostScript Type 1,* commonly found in high-end desktop publishing applications.

FIGURE 8-17

Graphics-oriented monitor. Desktop publishing systems frequently use special monitors with oversized screens and the ability to output crisp images.

FIGURE 8-18

Page-makeup software. Because page makeup is the central function in desktop publishing, page-makeup programs are usually called desktop publishing packages.

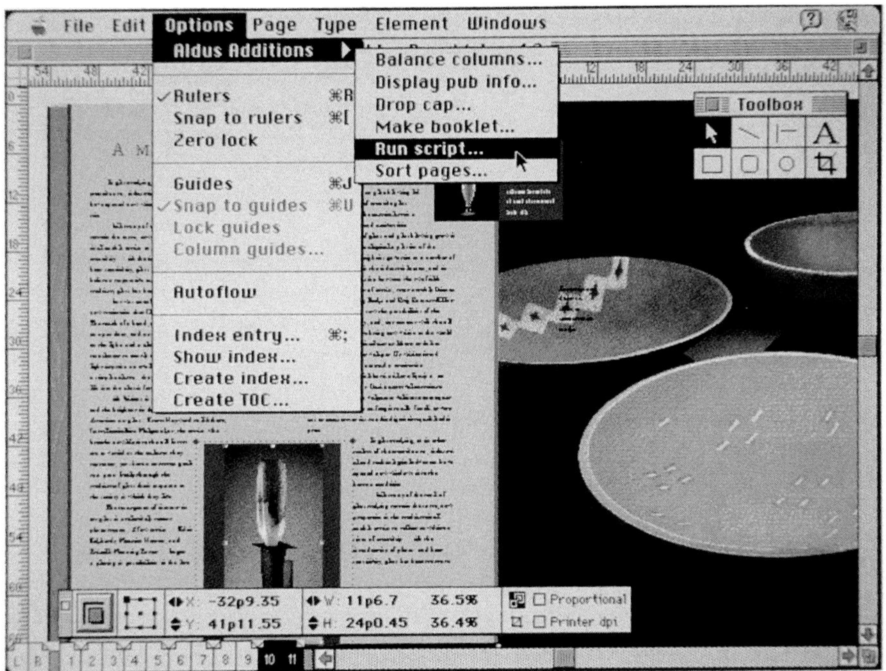

■ **Clip-Art Libraries** A **clip-art** library is a collection of prepared art images. You can use these images on their own or as building blocks to create other images. You can even modify them. A sample of clip-art pieces appears in Figure 8-20.

Clip art.
Prepackaged artwork designed to be imported into text documents or charts, say, by desktop publishing or presentation graphics software.

Clip-art libraries are bundled into many illustration packages and are also sold separately by third-party vendors. Vendors of illustration packages often use a proprietary format for their clip art, usually one that supports their other products, whereas third-party clip-art vendors typically make their clip art available in a variety of standard formats.

■ **Illustration Software** **Illustration software packages** enable artwork to be created from scratch. Also, they accept existing artwork as input and allow it to be modified using the software's image-manipulation facilities.

Illustration software package.
A program package that enables users to paint or draw.

An image can be input to illustration software in several ways. If you have an image scanner, you can read a hard-copy image directly into RAM. If you have a digitizing tablet, you can trace over a hard-copy image with a stylus, thereby transferring the outline of the image to memory. Or, if the image is in a clip-art library, you can transfer the appropriate clip-art file directly to the illustration software if both use the same file formats.

High-quality illustration software enables you to size, rotate, flip, recolor, distort, and edit virtually any digitally stored drawing or photograph to

FIGURE 8-19

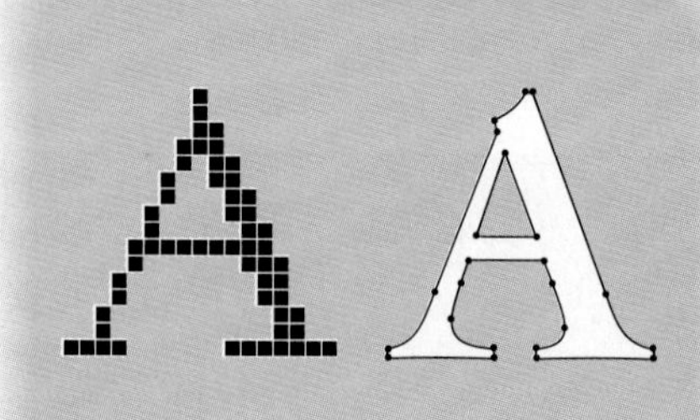

Bit-mapped versus outline fonts. Bit-mapped fonts (left) are made up of a fixed pattern of dots, whereas outline fonts (right) are defined by a series of curves. Outline fonts can be resized to different point sizes; bit-mapped fonts can't.

your heart's content (see Figure 8-21). Because images are manipulated at electronically fast speeds, it is possible to try out dozens of possibilities in the time it would normally take to produce only a single image by manual means. Once an image is satisfactory, it can be imported to a desktop publishing (page-makeup) program.

Sometimes illustration software packages are distinguished by whether they are primarily oriented toward painting or drawing. *Painting packages* enable you to create bit-mapped images and to color them pixel by pixel. Usually, the images you create cannot be resized without loss of resolution. For instance, blowing them up may result in jagged edges, whereas reducing them may result in a blurry mess. In contrast, *drawing packages* enable you to create outlines that can be resized. Once properly sized, these outlines can be filled in with colors.

FIGURE 8-20

Clip art. Clip-art libraries are bundled into many software packages and are also sold separately.

FIGURE 8-21

Illustration software. Illustration packages enable art images to be created and developed. Here, the tools at the right enable the artist to select colors and styling effects.

Many illustration software packages are available today. Among the best-selling packages are Adobe's Illustrator, Aldus's Freehand, Corel's Corel Draw!, Z-Soft's PC Paintbrush, and Claris's McDraw and McPaint.

Summary and Key Terms

Both word processing and desktop publishing are technologies that deal with the manipulation of words.

Word Processing **Word processing** is the use of computer technology to create, manipulate, and print text materials such as letters, legal contracts, manuscripts, and other documents. Most people today use *general-purpose* word processing packages, such as WordPerfect and Microsoft Word.

Using a word processor, or for that matter, any type of productivity software package, requires learning several general operations. These operations include accessing the package from the operating system, informing the package that you want to create a new file or retrieve an old one, commanding the package to save a file, commanding the package to print a file, commanding the package to delete a file, indicating to the package that you want to quit working on your current file and do something on another file, and terminating the package and getting back to the operating system.

Learning to use a word processor at a minimal level involves mastering a number of elementary editing operations as well as several print-formatting commands. Entering and editing operations include moving the cursor, scrolling, making line returns through either a **soft return** (the **wordwrap** feature) or a **hard return,** inserting and deleting, moving and copying, and searching and replacing. Among the print-formatting operations that one must learn are adjusting line spacing; indenting; justifying text; setting up page formats; reformatting body text; centering; tabbing; paginating; setting up headers and footers; selecting **typefaces, point sizes,** and **fonts;** multiple-column formatting; **WYSIWYG** output control; and footnoting.

More sophisticated use of word processing packages often requires software and hardware that provide **proportional spacing** and **microspacing** so that they can produce typeset-quality output. Without these features, text will be **monospaced.** In addition, advanced applications often make use of such features as **spelling checkers, thesauruses, mailing list programs, mail merge programs,** a math feature, **macros, redlining,** index and table of contents preparation, **orphan** and **widow** elimination, sorting, embedded typesetting codes, graphics, and **style sheets.**

A wide variety of **add-on packages** can be acquired to enhance a word processing environment. Among such packages are reference shelves, bibliographic databases, style/grammar checkers, and font libraries.

Desktop Publishing **Desktop publishing** systems go a step further than word processors. They let you combine on a page such elements as text (in a variety of fonts), art, and photos, thus creating attractive documents that look as if they came off a printer's press.

Whereas word processing deals mainly with straight, nontypeset text—perhaps using a few simple fonts for emphasis—desktop publishing involves full-fledged *typesetting* and *imagesetting.* But as much as desktop publishing systems have improved, they are still not capable of the document quality possible with professional composition systems.

Desktop publishing systems are commonly configured with some of the following hardware and software components. Hardware includes a high-end microcomputer system, a laser printer (which is used in concert with a specific **page-description language,** or **PDL**), a graphics-oriented monitor capable of WYSIWYG display, and an image scanner. Software components include **page-makeup software,** word processing software, fonts, a **clip-art** library, and **illustration software packages** such as *painting* and *drawing packages.*

Review Exercises

Fill-in Questions

1. Most word processors have a(n) ____________ feature that automatically produces a soft return.
2. ____________ is a word processing feature that allocates more horizontal space on a line to some characters than to others.
3. A(n) ____________ program is used to generate mailing labels.
4. A(n) ____________ word processing system is a computer system exclusively designed for word processing applications.
5. WYSIWYG is an acronym for ____________.
6. The first line of a paragraph is called a(n) ____________ when it is separated from the rest of the paragraph by a page or column break.
7. PDL is an acronym for ____________.
8. Prestored art images used in a desktop publishing environment are referred to as ____________.

Matching Questions

Match each term with the description that fits best.

a. copying
b. redlining
c. proportional spacing
d. inserting
e. scrolling
f. moving

___ 1. Moving contiguous lines of text up and down on screen similarly to the way the roll on a player piano is unwound.

___ 2. A feature particularly useful when one person must edit another's written work.

___ 3. An operation that involves replication.

___ 4. An operation that entails physically relocating text so that it no longer appears in its original location.

___ 5. A word processing feature that gives text a typeset-quality look.

___ 6. An operation you would use on a word processor to quickly change the string MISSIPPI to MISSISSIPPI.

Discussion Questions

1. What is WYSIWYG and how do many word processors implement it?
2. What is the difference between monospacing and proportional spacing?
3. What are orphans and widows?
4. What is a reference shelf?
5. Identify the components of a desktop publishing system.
6. Why is it getting increasingly more difficult to distinguish word processing from desktop publishing?

Critical Thinking Questions

1. Spelling checkers are said to be of greatest utility to people who can spell reasonably well. Why do you think this is so?
2. Comment on this statement: "Now that desktop publishing is available, the professional typesetting and print shop is doomed."
3. Word processing and desktop publishing present undeniable benefits to organizations that can effectively use them. Can you think of any problems that these technologies pose to the average organizations?

WINDOW 5

Desktop Publishing

A Step-by-Step Look at What's Involved

During the last decade, the desktop publishing industry has evolved from a dream to a highly sophisticated reality—one characterized by powerful art and illustration systems, electronic darkrooms, and a spate of fonts and clip art libraries to satisfy almost every need. In this window, we'll look at some of the steps involved in using a desktop publishing package—laying out pages, handling type, manipulating art and photos, and refining pages so that the finished product looks just right.

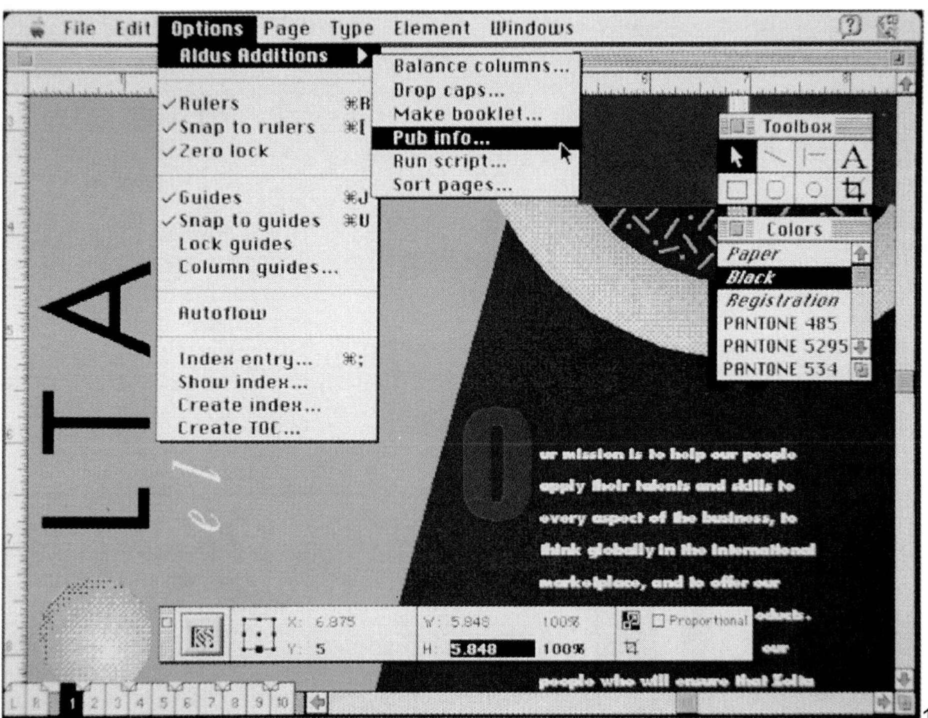

1. Desktop publishing packages enable finished pages consisting of text and art to be composed onscreen. Illustrated here is a zoom feature that enables pages to be previewed in fine detail before they are approved for printing.

Page Layout

Desktop publishing generally begins after word processing ends. The first step in desktop publishing is designing the page layout.

2. Page layout is usually begun by creating or retrieving a page template. The template shows how the columns are to be formed on the page and where elements such as headings, art, and the main body of text are to go. Here, the areas shaded in blue will receive the text imported from a word processor.

2

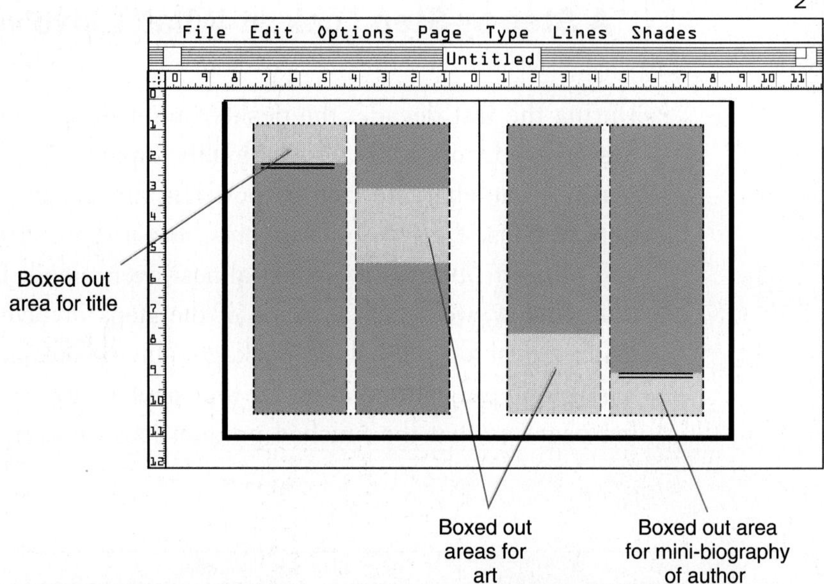

3–4. The layout should be balanced so that it is pleasing to the eye. The piece at the left shows a good balance among the photo, heading, and body-copy text. The piece at the right, which has a "hole" in the middle, is unbalanced. Today, creating balance is largely a manual, judgmental process left to the talents of the user.

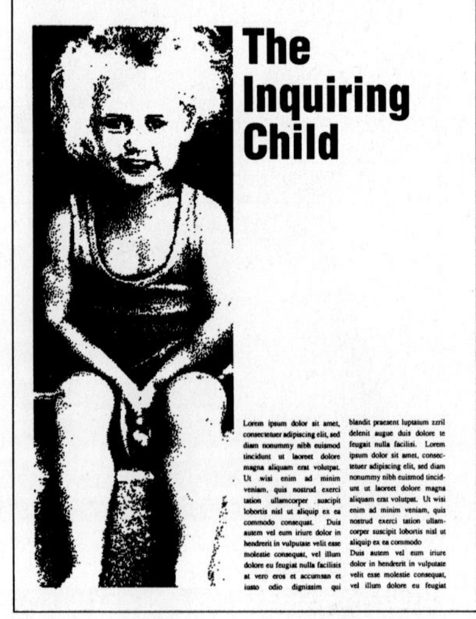

3

4

Type

A major element in any page layout is the typeface or typefaces used. In today's world of desktop publishing, hundreds of typefaces are available.

5

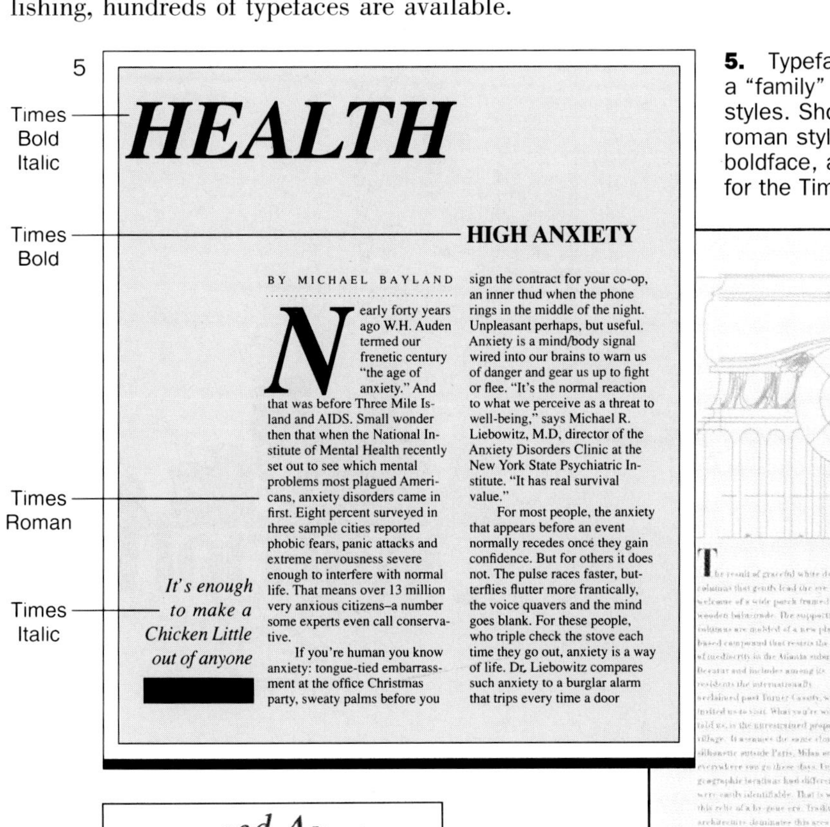

HEALTH

HIGH ANXIETY

BY MICHAEL BAYLAND

Nearly forty years ago W.H. Auden termed our frenetic century "the age of anxiety." And that was before Three Mile Island and AIDS. Small wonder then that when the National Institute of Mental Health recently set out to see which mental problems most plagued Americans, anxiety disorders came in first. Eight percent surveyed in three sample cities reported phobic fears, panic attacks and extreme nervousness severe enough to interfere with normal life. That means over 13 million very anxious citizens–a number some experts even call conservative.

If you're human you know anxiety: tongue-tied embarrassment at the office Christmas party, sweaty palms before you sign the contract for your co-op, an inner thud when the phone rings in the middle of the night. Unpleasant perhaps, but useful. Anxiety is a mind/body signal wired into our brains to warn us of danger and gear us up to fight or flee. "It's the normal reaction to what we perceive as a threat to well-being," says Michael R. Liebowitz, M.D, director of the Anxiety Disorders Clinic at the New York State Psychiatric Institute. "It has real survival value."

For most people, the anxiety that appears before an event normally recedes once they gain confidence. But for others it does not. The pulse races faster, butterflies flutter more frantically, the voice quavers and the mind goes blank. For these people, who triple check the stove each time they go out, anxiety is a way of life. Dr. Liebowitz compares such anxiety to a burglar alarm that trips every time a door

It's enough to make a Chicken Little out of anyone

5. Typefaces are often available as a "family" that sports a variety of styles. Shown here is the standard roman style as well as the italic, boldface, and boldface italic styles for the Times typeface.

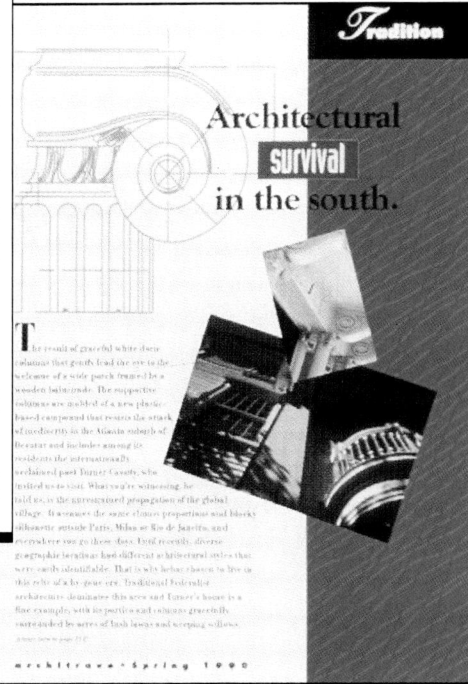

6

6. Type is frequently wrapped around photos and diagrams, as shown here.

Centered Arc Text

Faded

Drop Shadow

7

7. Special effects for typefaces can be created with many illustration software packages.

8

Typeface Sample	Mood Imparted
THE ELEGANT GOURMET	Elegant and formal
The Elegant Gourmet	Elegant and informal
The Elegant Gourmet	Playful
THE ELEGANT GOURMET	Serious
THE ELEGANT GOURMET	Action-oriented

8. Typeface selection, along with color, affect the mood of a document.

Illustration Packages

Illustration packages are of two principal types: drawing and painting. Drawing packages enable users to create outlines that can be easily resized and filled in whereas painting packages enable users to create images pixel by pixel.

9

10

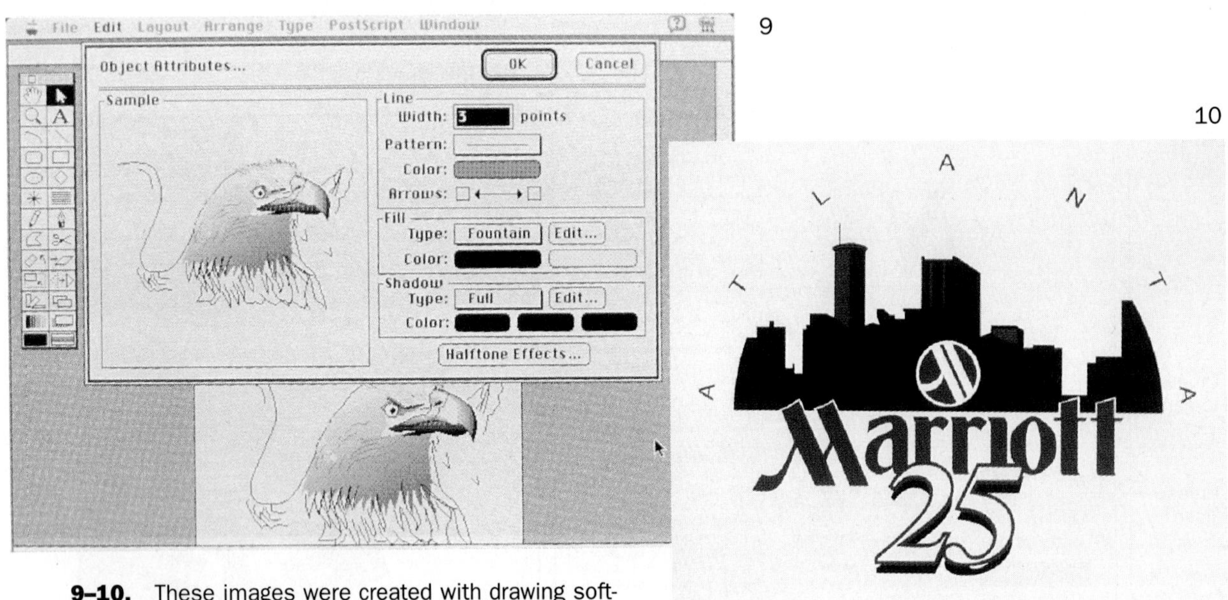

9–10. These images were created with drawing software. The finished art can be stored in independent files and later imported to a desktop publishing package to be merged with text.

11

12

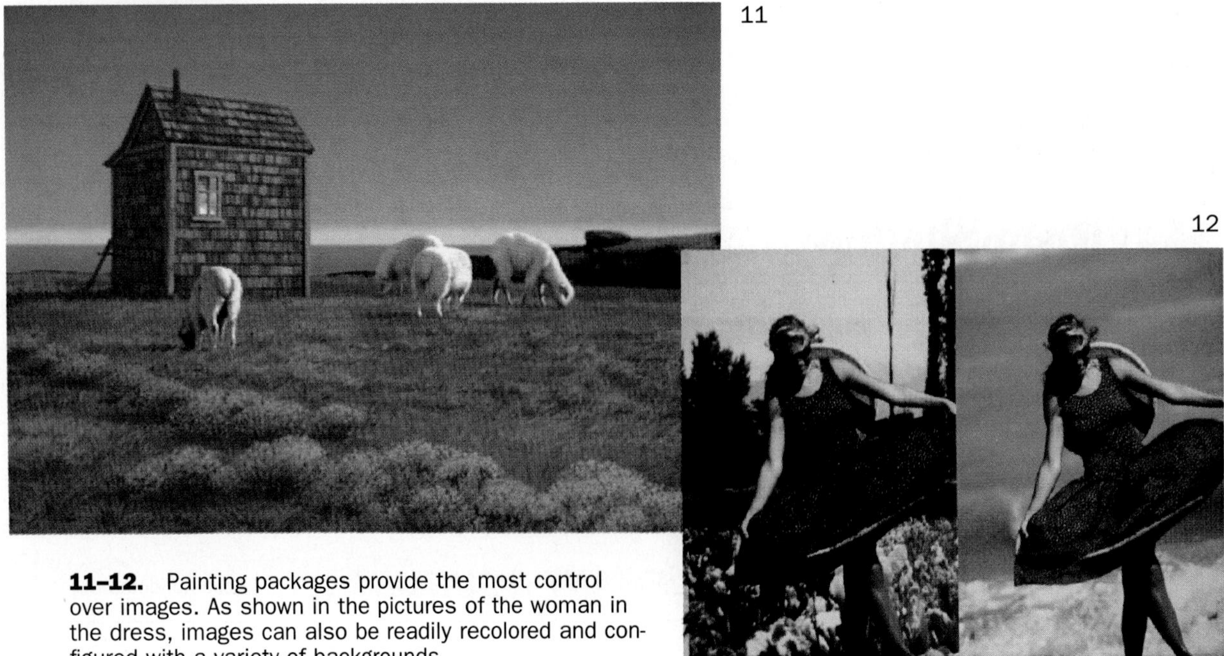

11–12. Painting packages provide the most control over images. As shown in the pictures of the woman in the dress, images can also be readily recolored and configured with a variety of backgrounds.

Photographs

Photographs are either captured electronically or read with an image scanner into the computer system. Once they are digitized, they can be stored, touched up, or even distorted with photo-styling software.

13

13. This photo is being manipulated on a computer screen. With a zooming feature, photos can be inspected close up and color corrected using a palette such as the one at the right.

14

14. Photos stored on disk can be recalled to the screen in miniature or "thumbnail" form. In this form they can be easily organized and cataloged.

15

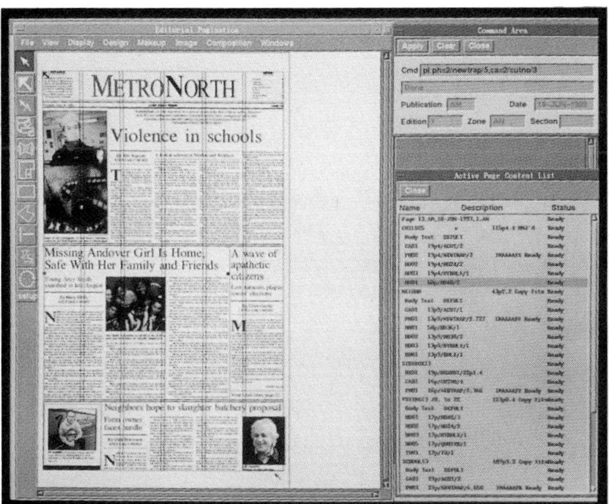

15. Here, photos are imported into a page layout and cropped, so that they conform to the narrow specifications of a newspaper column.

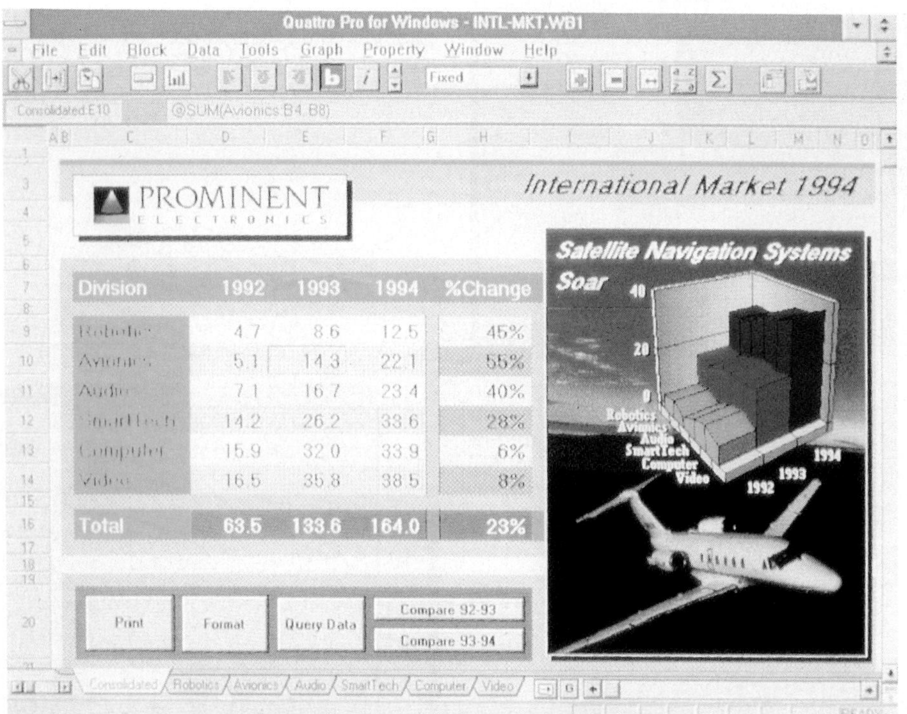
Quattro Pro for Windows - INTL-MKT.WB1
File Edit Block Data Tools Graph Property Window Help
Fixed
Consolidated:E10
@SUM(Avionics:B4..B8)
PROMINENT
ELECTRONICS
International Market 1994
Division 1992 1993 1994 %Change
Robotics 4.7 8.6 12.5 45%
Avionics 5.1 14.3 22.1 55%
Audio 7.1 16.7 23.4 40%
SmartTech 14.2 26.2 33.6 28%
Computer 15.9 32.0 33.9 6%
Video 16.5 35.8 38.5 8%
Total 63.5 133.6 164.0 23%
Print
Format
Query Data
Compare 92-93
Compare 93-94
Satellite Navigation Systems Soar
40
20
0
Robotics
Avionics
Audio
SmartTech
Computer
Video
1992
1993
1994
Consolidated
Robotics
Avionics
Audio
SmartTech
Computer
Video
READY

SPREADSHEETS AND PRESENTATION GRAPHICS

9

How do managers use computers to analyze data? As you will see in Chapter 9, analysis is often done with spreadsheet and presentation graphics software. These products make it easy for users to rapidly process business data into table form and graphs.

OUTLINE

Overview

Spreadsheets
- How Spreadsheets Work
- Basic Entering and Editing Operations
- Advanced Features

Presentation Graphics
- Forms of Presentation Graphics
- Types of Packages

LEARNING OBJECTIVES

After completing this chapter, you will be able to:

1. Describe what spreadsheet packages do and how they work.
2. Identify the basic operations you must master to effectively use spreadsheet software.
3. Explain the use of several advanced spreadsheet features.
4. Describe how presentation graphics packages work, some of the differences among them, and the images they let you create.

Overview

Today, one of the most important software packages that *any* businessperson—whether he or she is a manager, an office worker, or a sales representative—should learn is the *electronic spreadsheet.* Spreadsheet software is to the current generation of end users what the pocket calculator was to previous generations: a convenient means of performing calculations. But while most pocket calculators can compute and display only one result each time you enter new data, electronic spreadsheets can present you with hundreds or even thousands of results each

FIGURE 9-1

Manually prepared and electronic worksheets. An electronic spreadsheet package produces computerized counterparts to the ruled, ledger-style worksheets with which accountants frequently work.

(a) Manually prepared worksheet

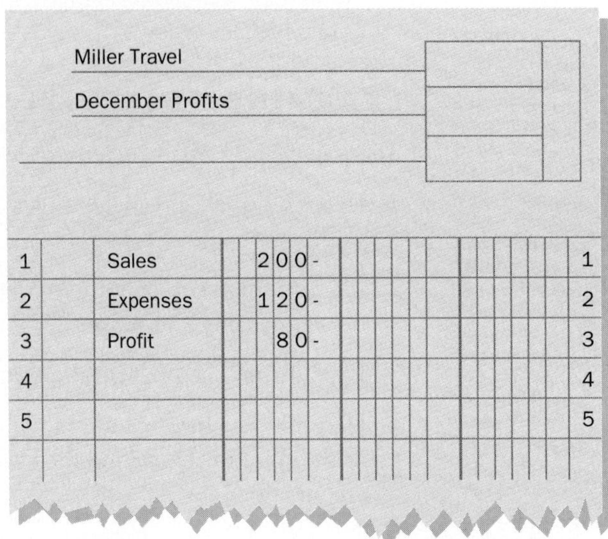

(b) Worksheet prepared by electronic spreadsheet package

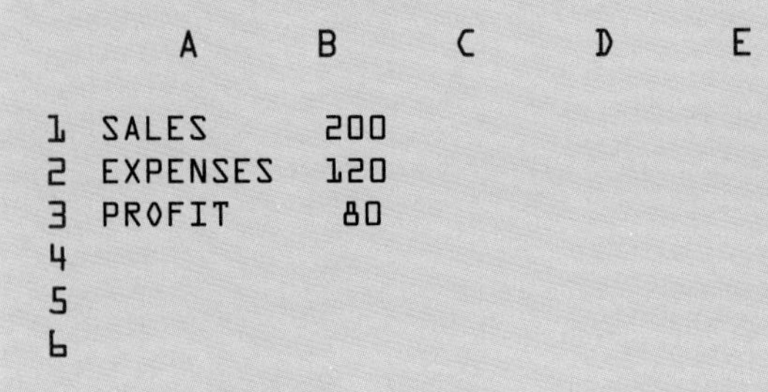

time you enter a single new value or command. What spreadsheets can do and how they work are two of the primary subjects of this chapter.

From our discussion of spreadsheets we'll move on to *presentation graphics software,* which is designed to present the results of business computations in a visually oriented, easily understood way. This class of business software is easy to learn and use. Today most spreadsheet packages are equipped with built-in presentation graphics features and tools. Also, many dedicated presentation graphics packages, which enable you to produce higher-quality presentation images than those possible with spreadsheet packages, are commercially available.

Spreadsheets

An **electronic spreadsheet** package produces computerized counterparts to the ruled, ledger-style worksheets with which accountants frequently work (see Figure 9-1). Electronic spreadsheets first came to public notice in the late 1970s when a Harvard Business School student named Dan Bricklin and a programmer friend produced a microcomputer package called VisiCalc ("The VISIble CALCulator"). Bricklin conceived of the idea while watching his accounting professor erase large chunks of blackboard computations every time a single number changed in an interdependent series of calculations. Awed by the amount of repetitive labor involved, Bricklin quickly saw the potential of computerized worksheets.

Electronic spreadsheet. A productivity software package that enables operators to develop tables and financial schedules quickly.

To call VisiCalc a huge success would be an understatement. It shattered sales records for applications software and made microcomputers valuable decision-making tools in business. It is also widely credited for moving Apple—the company that supported VisiCalc on its Apple II line of microcomputers—into the ranks of the computer-industry heavyweights. Both VisiCalc and the spreadsheet products that followed it have been easy to use and clearly made managers who mastered them more productive.

Today, although VisiCalc is gone from the scene, spreadsheet software for all sizes of computers abounds in the marketplace. Among the leading spreadsheet packages currently available for microcomputers are 1-2-3, Excel, and Quattro, with 1-2-3 and Excel the pacesetters in sales. As explained in Feature 9-1, many spreadsheets are sold as part of *software suites* or are scaled down in order to fit into *integrated software packages.*

How Spreadsheets Work

Here we discuss some of the principles by which spreadsheets work.

The Anatomy of a Worksheet In electronic spreadsheets, the display screen is viewed as a *window* looking in on a big grid, called a **worksheet** (see Figure 9-2). Most major spreadsheet packages allow worksheets that consist of thousands of *rows* and a couple hundred *columns.* In Microsoft Excel, for instance, a maximum of 16,384 rows and 256 columns is available to create worksheets. Each of the 4,194,304 (16,384 × 256) **cells** formed by the intersection of a row and column may contain text, a number, or a formula. Each cell can be accessed through a **cell address,** such as B8 or E223.

Worksheet. The computerized counterpart to the ruled, ledger-style paper used by accountants.

Cell. The part of the worksheet that can hold a single label or value; a cell occurs where a row and column intersect.

Cell address. The column/row combination that uniquely identifies a spreadsheet cell.

Feature 9-1

The Complete Desktop Solution

Software Suites and Integrated Software Packages

For users who wish to tie together several applications under a single roof, either a software suite or an integrated software package may be just the ticket.

Software Suites *Software suites*—such as Microsoft Office, Lotus SmartSuite, and Borland Office—provide a set of compatible, full-featured software products at a reduced price. For instance, Lotus SmartSuite assembles together the full-featured versions of Ami Pro, 1-2-3, Freelance Graphics, Organizer, and cc:Mail at a price lower than it would cost to buy all of the packages individually. Thus, you have all the desktop tools you need to do word processing, spreadsheeting, data management, graphics, communications, and organizing at your complete disposal.

Currently, software suites have become the hottest new way to package software. Microsoft—the leader in suite sales—claims it sells more copies of its popular word processor, Word, in suite form than it does as individual units.

A trend in suites is the development of applications interfaces, so users need know only a single set of commands to operate any package in the suite. Figure 7-4, on page 226, illustrates how easy it is to select any object (like a graph or chart) from one application in the suite and bring it into another.

Integrated Software Packages *Integrated software packages* compress all the types of functions you would normally get in a software suite into a single package. So, for instance, instead of getting a fully featured word processor or spreadsheet, you are getting slightly "watered down" versions with fewer features available. Not that this is a huge limitation. Integrated packages are far cheaper than suites, and most people who buy fully featured software wind up using only a tiny percentage of the features, anyway. Today, one of the most popular integrated software packages is Microsoft Works, which bundles word processing, spreadsheeting, data management, graphics, and communications under a single roof.

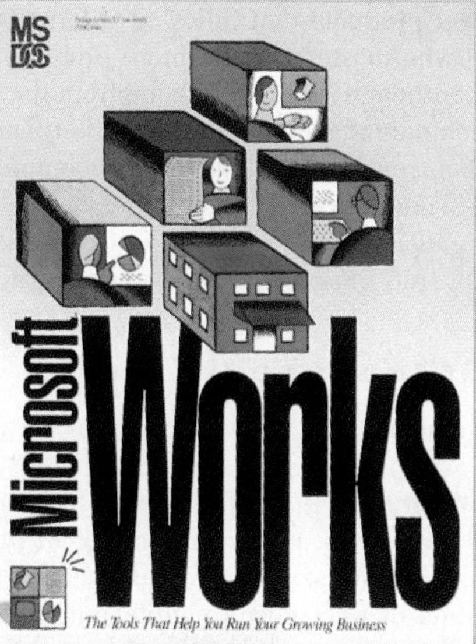

Complete solutions. Suite and integrated software give you lots of functionality at a reduced price.

FIGURE 9-2

A worksheet and a window to the worksheet. Worksheets can be too large to view on the display screen at a single moment. The window allows users to see the worksheet in screen-sized chunks.

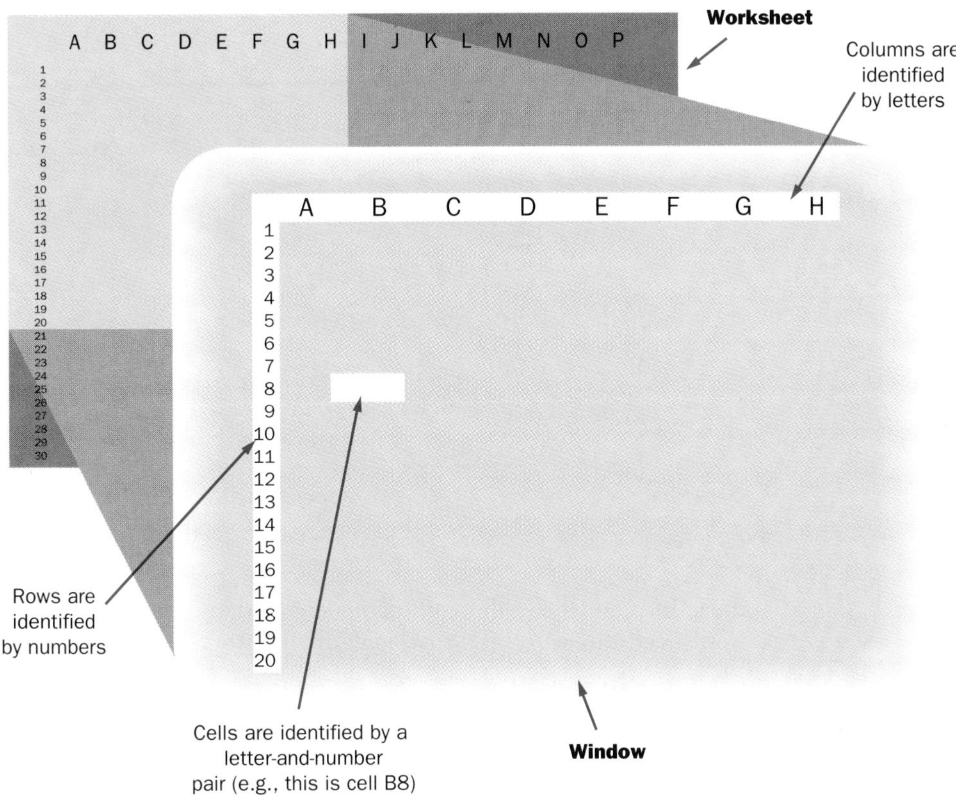

In most commercial spreadsheet packages, columns are identified by letters, rows by numbers, and each cell by a letter-and-number pair. For example, cell B8 is found at the intersection of column B and row 8. Of course, the display screen is too small to permit the viewing of more than a few rows and columns at any give time. However, users can press certain keys on the keyboard that will move the worksheet window around, letting them view other portions of the worksheet through it. After we've covered a couple of other important matters, we'll describe how to do this.

The discussion that immediately follows concerns two-dimensional spreadsheet applications. Later in the chapter, we'll look at the multidimensional capabilities rapidly being infused into most major spreadsheet packages.

The Spreadsheet's Screen The format of a typical-looking screen from a spreadsheet package is shown in Figure 9-3. Each screen, such as the one shown here, is divided into two main areas: a control panel and a worksheet

FIGURE 9-3

Elements of spreadsheet-package screen. Most screens are divided into two areas—a control panel, where cell contents are prepared, and a worksheet area, which holds the finished contents.

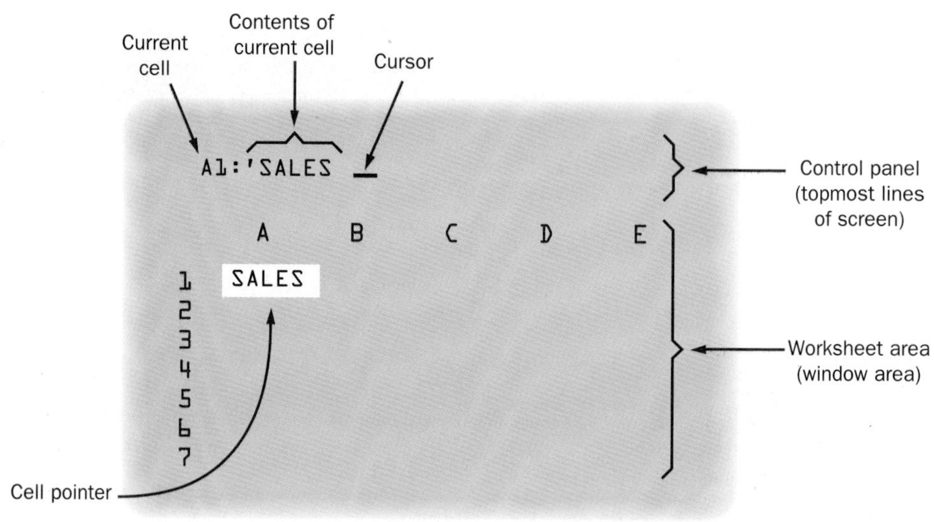

area. In a nutshell, the *control panel* is where you prepare entries for the worksheet; the *worksheet area* contains the worksheet itself.

Control panel. The portion of the screen display that is used for issuing commands and observing what is being typed into the computer system.

Current cell. In spreadsheet software, the worksheet cell at which the highlight is currently positioned.

Cursor. A highlighting symbol in the control panel that appears where the next character to be typed in will be placed.

Worksheet area. The portion of the screen that contains the window onto the worksheet. Also called the **window area.**

- **THE CONTROL PANEL** The **control panel** in many spreadsheet packages consists of approximately three lines and is located in the top portion of the screen. The control panel serves several functions. Most important, it displays the address and contents of the current cell, as well as the spreadsheet's command menu.

  The **current cell** is the cell to which the spreadsheet package is currently pointing. Spreadsheet packages point to one cell at a time; you can always tell which cell is current by looking at the control panel. In Figure 9-3, the current cell is A1.

  To the right of the address of the current cell are its contents. If the cell is empty, nothing will be showing in this portion of the screen. As you type in the contents of the current cell or edit the contents of this cell, each keystroke you hit will appear at the **cursor** position in this part of the control panel. In Figure 9-3, the content of cell A1 is SALES.

  Every spreadsheet package has a set of commands for activities such as inserting or deleting rows or columns, moving and copying cell entries, and saving and printing worksheets. All of these tasks are accomplished by selecting commands off of a menu that is displayed in the control panel. For simplicity, we have not shown this menu in Figure 9-3. Later in the chapter, however, we'll cover a number of operations that can be performed from the command menu.

- **THE WORKSHEET AREA** The worksheet itself is displayed in the part of the screen called the **worksheet area,** or **window area.** One important element in the worksheet area is the **cell pointer,** sometimes referred to as the **highlight** or simply the *pointer.* The cell pointer highlights the current cell. As you can see in Figure 9-3, the current cell (as indicated in the control panel) is cell A1, and this is the cell at which the cell pointer is positioned. As each cell is filled in the control panel, its contents are not entered into the worksheet area until the Enter key is depressed.

Cell pointer.
A cursorlike mechanism used in the worksheet area to point to cells, thereby making them active. Also called the **highlight.**

Remember, the window area may not be large enough to show the whole worksheet at a single glance, but you can scroll the window about to see other parts of the worksheet if you desire. *Scrolling* is similar to moving a magnifying glass over a large map; the movable glass acts like the window, while the underlying map acts like the worksheet. We can scroll the worksheet a row or column at a time when the highlight is at the edge of the screen and we press one of the arrow keys. Keys such as Tab, PgUp, and PgDn let us scroll the worksheet in window-sized blocks.

Creating a Worksheet Now that you are familiar with a few of the basic mechanics of spreadsheet-package use, let's learn how to create a worksheet. Refer to Figure 9-4. In the worksheet shown in the figure, we are computing a business income statement in which expenses are 60 percent of sales and profit is the difference between sales and expenses. Here we will show how to enter the text and numbers in the figure into the computer. We'll also look at some of the details that the spreadsheet software will take care of for you.

Into each worksheet cell the user can type either a label or a value. In the terminology of the spreadsheet world, a **label** is a cell entry that cannot be manipulated mathematically, whereas a **value** is an entry that can.

Label.
A cell entry that cannot be manipulated mathematically.

Value.
A cell entry that can be manipulated mathematically.

FIGURE 9-4

An electronic spreadsheet package at work. It's their *recalculation feature*—the ability to quickly rework thousands of tedious calculations—that makes spreadsheet packages so valuable to users.

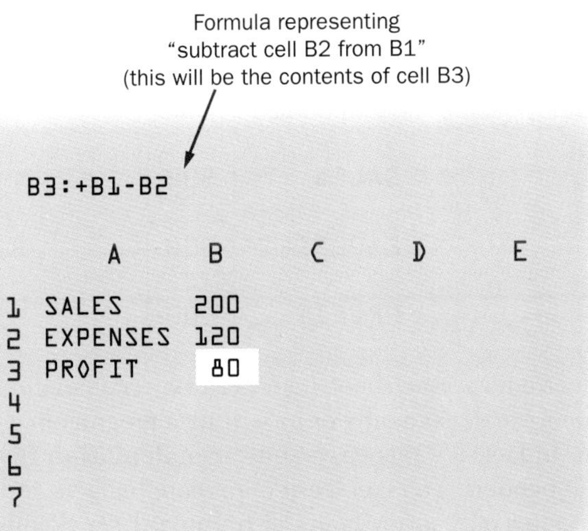

In the figure, we have entered—one at a time—the following six things into the control panel:

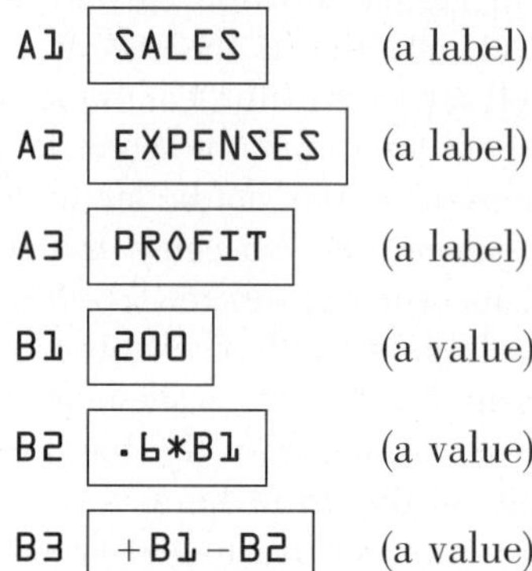

The spreadsheet package automatically assumes that each entry beginning with a letter (or a label-prefix character, which we'll cover shortly) is a label; otherwise, it's a value. (Incidentally, that's why we had to type the formula in cell B3 with a "+" in front of it.)

As we type each label or value into the control panel and enter it, that label or value is processed by the spreadsheet software, and the results are automatically transferred to the worksheet. For cells A1, A2, A3, and B1 in Figure 9-4, notice that a direct transfer occurs. For cells B2 and B3, the computer first makes the computation indicated by the *formulas* and then transfers the result to the corresponding worksheet cells.

What-if analysis. An approach to problem solving in which the decision maker repeatedly commands the computer system to recalculate a set of figures based on alternative inputs.

The Recalculation Feature Electronic spreadsheet packages are particularly useful for **what-if analysis.** For example, suppose we wish to know *what* profit will result in Figure 9-4 *if* sales are changed to $500. If we simply enter into cell B1 the value

```
500
```

the spreadsheet package automatically reworks all the figures according to the prestored formulas. Thus, the computer responds

```
SALES      500
EXPENSES   300
PROFIT     200
```

Recalculation feature. The ability of spreadsheet software to quickly and automatically recalculate the contents of several cells, based on new operator inputs.

In seconds, electronic spreadsheets can perform recalculations that would require several hours to do manually or by writing a program in a regular programming language. In fact, it's this easy-to-use **recalculation feature** that makes spreadsheets so popular. You can learn to prepare budgets and financial schedules with them after only a few hours of training. User Solution 9-1 describes the use of what-if analysis in selling homes.

User Solution 9-1

Selling Homes With What-If Analysis

At Old Town Builders in Visalia, California, 1-2-3 and what-if analysis are now being used as marketing tools. In the past, a home buyer had to wait endlessly for a salesperson to figure out with a calculator the cost of a changing list of customized building options and financing alternatives. Now, a customer can get answers instantaneously. After choosing a financing package, subdivision, lot, and various configuration options, the buyer is supplied with a variety of cash-requirement and monthly-payment information. Because the spreadsheet does all the recalculations, the buyer can easily change options to find the best house within budget. "It creates excitement," reports a member of the firm. "Buyers don't feel they're getting a tract home because they get a chance to make their own choices."

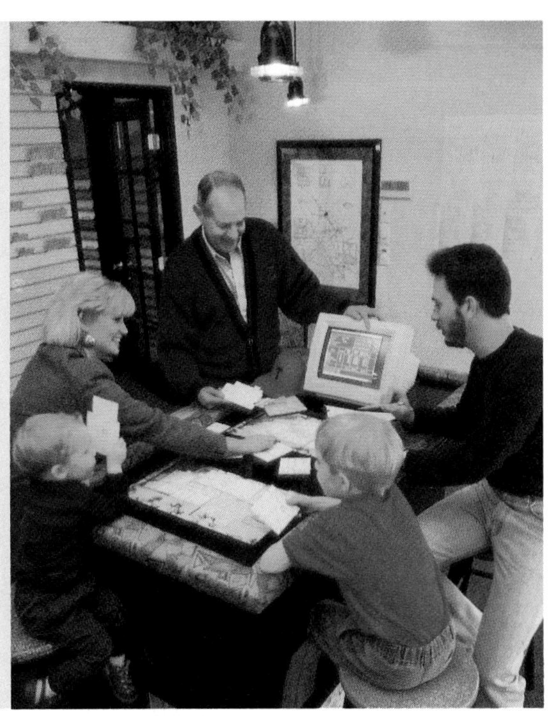

Blocks of Cells: The Range Concept Often, users need to be able to manipulate data in a set of contiguous cells—say, in a row or column of several cells or in a rectangular-shaped block of cells. To enable you to do this, spreadsheet packages have you declare **ranges** of cells. Figure 9-5 shows four examples of valid ranges. You will generally have to declare ranges of cells when you want to print, move, copy, insert, delete, sort, or graph parts of the worksheet.

Range.
A set of contiguous cells arranged in a rectangle.

For instance, telling the spreadsheet package to print the range B4..C6 will result in the 3-by-2 block of cells in the southeast corner of Figure 9-5 being

FIGURE 9-5

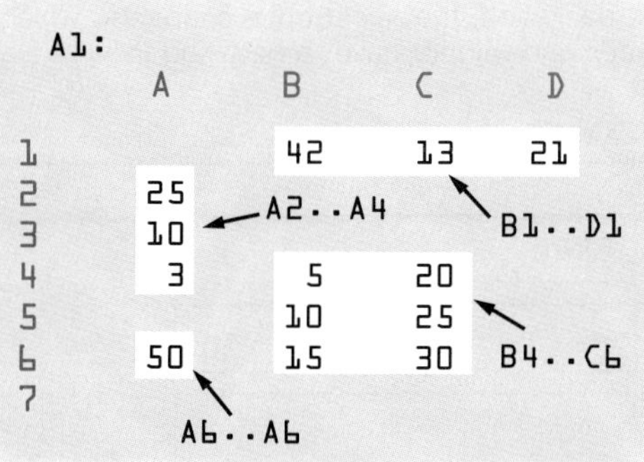

The range concept. A range is defined as any *rectangular* block of cells. It may be as small as a single cell or as large as a grid with several hundred cells on each side.

FIGURE 9-6

Examples of labels and values. Labels cannot be manipulated mathematically, whereas values can.

Example	Description
ABC Company	Label
Costs	Label
1.10	Value (numeric constant)
$300	Value (numeric constant)
.3*A1 − B2	Value (formula)
@AVG(B1..B4)	Value (function)
+A1 − B1	Value (formula)

output. Generally, a range can be declared by explicitly typing it into the control panel—for instance, you would type in all six characters in the string. "B4..C6" to declare it as a range—or by highlighting the range in the worksheet area.

More on Labels and Values As mentioned earlier, a cell can contain either a label or a value. A *label* is an entry that cannot be manipulated mathematically; a *value* is an entry that can. Several examples of labels and values are given in Figure 9-6.

Many spreadsheets automatically assume that an entry that starts with a letter or the ', ^, ", or \ character is a label; otherwise, it's a value. The ', ^, ", and \ characters are examples of *label-prefix characters* used in many packages. When typed as the first character in a label, these characters will, respectively, left justify, center, right justify, and repeat text placed into a cell (see Figure 9-7). When a label-prefix character is not explicitly typed in, the spreadsheet package typically assumes left justification as the default.

FIGURE 9-7

Label prefixes. In many spreadsheet packages, the apostrophe character, which left-justifies labels, is the default label prefix and will not have to be typed in.

Character	Action Taken	Example
'	Left-justifies	FROG
^	Centers	FROG
"	Right-justifies	FROG
\	Repeats	FROG FROG FROG FROG

FIGURE 9-8

Spreadsheet functions. In many spreadsheet packages, functions always start with the @ key. A package may contain over a hundred built-in functions.

Function	Description
@SUM (range)	Calculates the sum of all values in a range
@MAX (range)	Finds the highest value in a range
@MIN (range)	Finds the lowest value in a range
@COUNT (range)	Counts the number of nonempty cells in a range
@AVG (range)	Calculates the average of values in a range
@ABS (cell or expression)	Calculates the absolute value of the argument
@SQRT (cell or expression)	Calculates the square root of the expression
@PV (period payment, rate, number of payments)	Calculates the present value of an annuity at a specified interest rate
@FV (period payment, rate, number of payments)	Calculates the future value of an annuity at a specified interest rate
@PMT (present value, rate, number of payments)	Calculates an annuity (period payment) equivalent to a given present value at a specified interest rate
@IF (conditional expression, value if true, value if false)	Supplies to a cell a value that depends on whether the conditional expression is true or false

A value is generally one of three types: a numeric constant, a formula, or a function.

- **NUMERIC CONSTANTS** *Numeric constants* are values that are in numeric form—for example, 200 or −10.
- **FORMULAS** A *formula* consists of cell references and mathematical operators, such as those for addition (+), subtraction (−), and so on. An example of a formula is +B1−B2, which tells the computer that the value in the current cell is computed as the value in cell B1 minus the value in cell B2.
- **FUNCTIONS** A *function* is a reference to a prestored formula or a preset value (such as today's date). An example is the SUM function; the string @SUM(B1..B3) tells the spreadsheet package that the value in the current cell is computed as the sum of the values in the range B1 through B3. Figure 9-8 provides a listing of useful functions. Several examples of how to use functions are given in Figure 9-9.

When preparing value entries for a cell, you should note that numeric constants, formulas, and functions are often intermixed. By their basic nature, formulas consist of combinations of numeric constants and functions.

Values are used to build mathematical models with spreadsheets. *Models* do such things as calculate final grades for students in a college class, compute commissions due to salespeople based on sales and bonus criteria, and prepare customized reports (see User Solution 9-2).

FIGURE 9-9

Using functions. Most functions represent prestored formulas, such as those that compute an average, count up cells, or find maximum or minimum values. The functions shown here, and others, are described in Figure 9–8.

	A	B	C	D
1	10	5	15	20
2	6	7	3	4
3	8	2	9	4
4	-1	0	3	15

@ SUM (A1..D1) = 50

@ SUM (C1..C4) = 30

@ SUM (A1..D4) = 110

@ MIN (A1..D4) = -1

@ MIN (B2..C3) = 2

@ MAX (A1..D4) = 20

@ MAX (A1..D4, 100) = 100

@ AVG (A1..D1) = 12.5

@ AVG (B1..B4, 2) = 4

@ ABS (A4) = 1

@ SQRT (C3..C3) = 3

@ COUNT (A1..D4) = 16

@ SQRT (@ COUNT (A1..A4)) = 2

@ IF (A4 < 0, 10, 20) = 10

FIGURE 9-10

Spreadsheet commands. In many spreadsheet packages, there are about a dozen or so basic commands. Each of these commands, in turn, corresponds to a hierarchy of options.

Command	Explanation
Worksheet	Allows you to perform a variety of operations that affect either the entire worksheet or parts of it. For example, it allows you to change the width of one or more columns and to insert or delete columns or rows.
Range	Allows you to perform operations on a portion of the worksheet.
Copy	Allows you to reproduce any portion of the worksheet in another place on the worksheet.
Move	Lets you relocate any portion of the worksheet in another place on the worksheet.
File	Enables you to access your disk to save, retrieve, or combine worksheets.
Print	Allows you to print all or any portion of your worksheet.
Graph	Enables you to create graphs from your worksheet.
Data	Enables you to sort data, group data, or retrieve records with specific characteristics.
System	Lets you temporarily leave your spreadsheet package in order to issue operating system commands.
Add-in	Lets you attach add-on routines and packages to the spreadsheet program.
Quit	Ends your spreadsheeting session and enables you to return to the operating system.

User Solution 9-2

Models That Motivate Motorcycle Merchants

Can a spreadsheet package be used as a motivational tool? At Harley-Davidson Inc., the motorcycle company, the answer would be a resounding "yes." Each regional sales manager at Harley has a microcomputer system and access to the company's mainframe at its Milwaukee headquarters. On each computer is a spreadsheet model designed to encourage dealers to sell more motorcycles and parts. The models download regional sales data and compute the dealer's sales ranking among other dealers in the region. The regional sales manager can then prepare a report that shows any dealer's position without revealing the other dealers' names—only their sales. Taking a report along on a sales call to a dealer who's lagging behind the pack can help the local sales representative assigned to the dealership apply peer pressure.

Commands and Menus One of the most powerful features of any spreadsheet package is its command set. Commands enable you to save and print worksheets, copy the contents of one cell into other cells, sort data, erase worksheets, and so forth. Figure 9-10 shows a typical sample of spreadsheet commands. In this subsection, we'll look at a number of general principles governing commands. Later, in the section entitled "Basic Entering and Editing Operations," we'll examine in greater detail some of the types of tasks that can be done through commands.

Spreadsheet packages use a hierarchical series of menus from which users can select commands. The *main menu* (*command menu*)—usually in the form of a top-of-screen menu bar that appears in the control panel when a special key is depressed—shows the principal command set (see Figure 9-11). Subordinate to each command in the main menu are *submenus* that prompt users for finer and finer levels of detail. On either the main menu or submenus, selections are typically made by moving one of the arrow keys to highlight a choice and selecting it with the Enter key. That, or by typing in the first letter in the command name. As each selection is made by the user, successive submenus are presented onscreen until the spreadsheet package collects enough information to take a specific action.

Invoking spreadsheet commands can be thought of as a process of navigating through a *tree* of choices. Since you can point to the choices on the screen, there is no complicated command syntax to remember. Most packages are set up to enable ordinary users to apply their intuition, without constantly having to leaf through a reference manual. If you select the wrong option, you can, in most cases, easily void the choice and backtrack to where you were before.

FIGURE 9-11

Main menu. The main menu, shown here on the second line of the control panel, provides the principal command set. Below the main menu is a description or set of options relating to the command that is active, or highlighted.

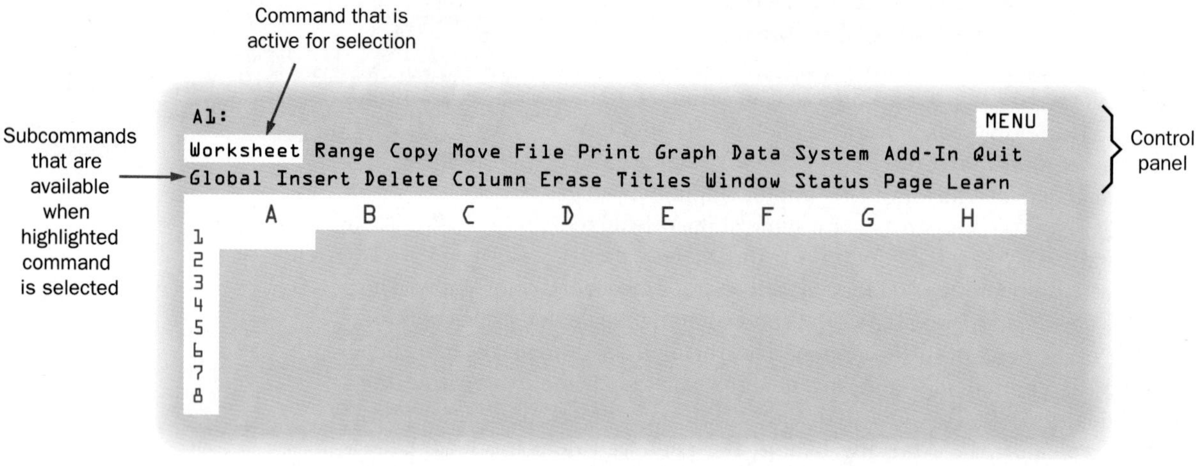

Graphical Interfaces An increasing number of spreadsheet packages are gravitating toward *graphical user interfaces (GUIs)* that sport pull-down menus and pop-up (dialog) boxes for submenus, multitasked windowing environments, mouse pointer control, and simultaneous viewing of spreadsheet and graphical data. Many of these features were pioneered by Microsoft's Excel. With the success of Excel and with better graphics now available on all of the leading microcomputers, such interfaces are rapidly becoming an industry standard (see Figure 9-12).

Basic Entering and Editing Operations

Spreadsheet packages have numerous command options that help you enter and edit data. A sampling of the most important of these features follows.

Inserting and Deleting Virtually all spreadsheet packages allow you to insert a new column or row in a worksheet. Also, you can delete a column or row that you no longer need. Generally, inserting or deleting involves moving the cell pointer to the appropriate position on the worksheet and issuing the proper command. Figure 9-13a illustrates inserting a blank row to make a worksheet more attractive.

Copying Most spreadsheets have a command that enables you to copy the contents of one cell (or several cells) into another cell (or several others). The command usually works by prompting you for a *source range* that contains the data to be copied and a *destination range* that will receive the copied data.

If you are copying from cells that contain formulas, you generally will be asked to state whether you want the cell references in the formulas to be

FIGURE 9-12

Graphical interfaces in the leading spreadsheet packages. The current trend in spreadsheets is toward graphical user interfaces (GUIs), which provide multiple windows and pull-down menus, allow presentation graphics to appear onscreen simultaneously with worksheet data, and provide WYSIWYG features for styling worksheets for presentations.

(a) Lotus Development's 1-2-3

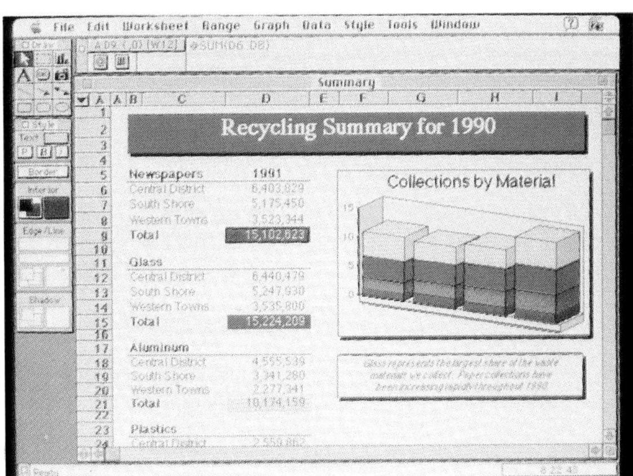

(b) Borland International's Quattro Pro

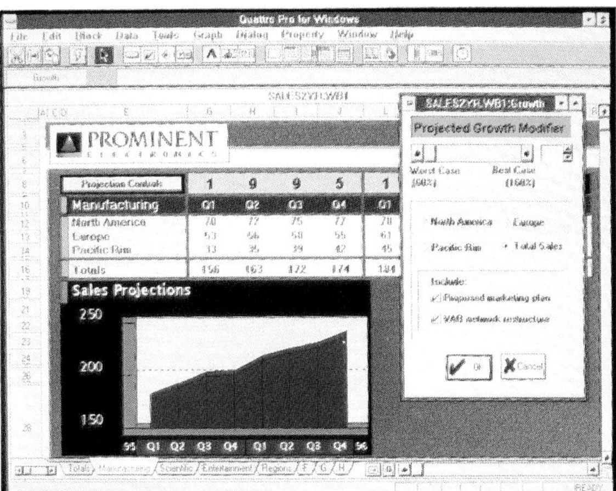

(c) Microsoft's Excel

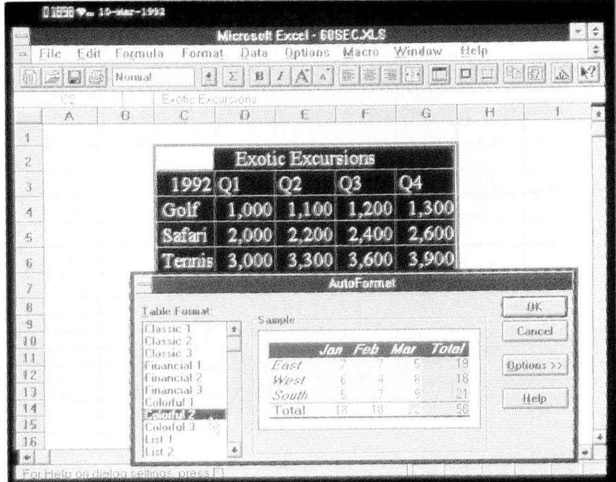

FIGURE 9-13

Entering and editing operations.

(a) **Inserting a row.** Both inserting and deleting involve moving the cell pointer to the appropriate position in the worksheet and issuing the proper command.

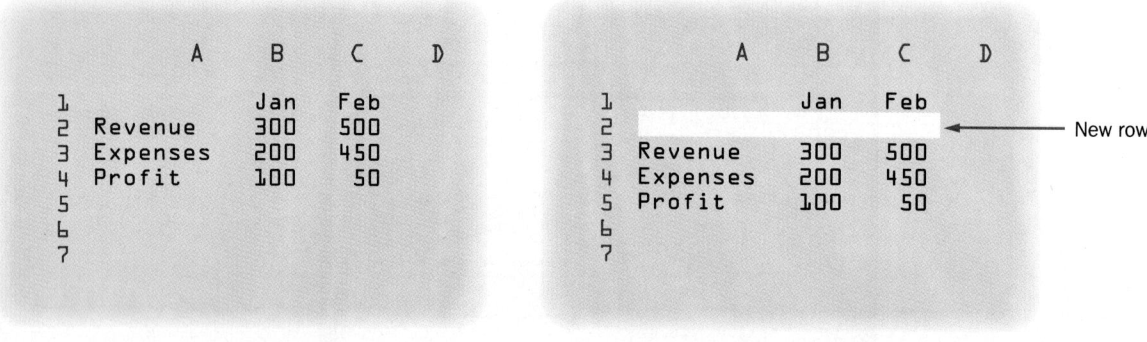

Before insertion

After insertion

(b) **Copying by relative replication.** In most spreadsheet packages, relative replication is the default copy operation.

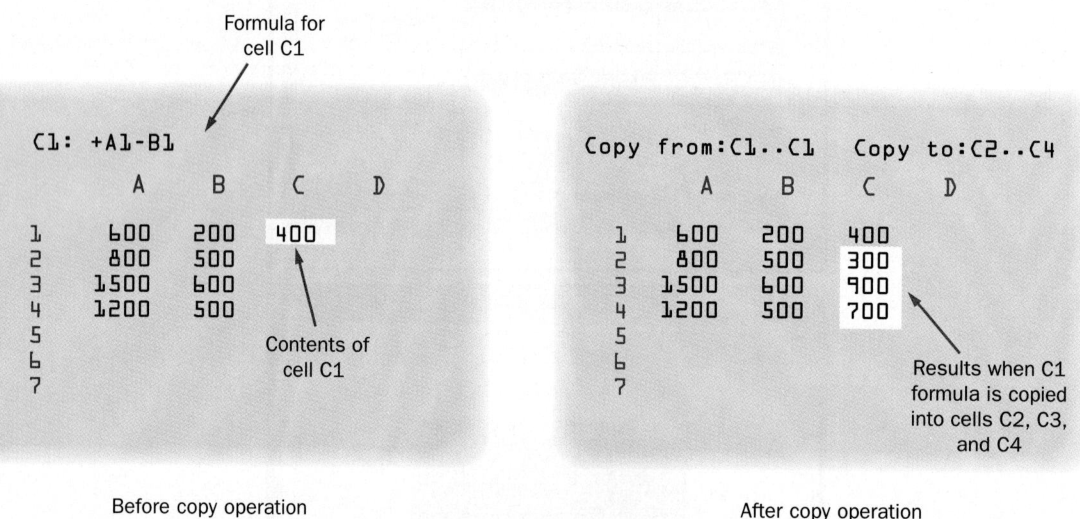

Before copy operation

After copy operation

Relative replication. Copying formulas in a source range of cells into a target range of cells relative to the row and column coordinates of the cells in the target range.

"relative," "absolute," or "mixed." These three methods of copying are illustrated in Figures 9-13b, 9-13c, and 9-13d, respectively.

■ RELATIVE REPLICATION **Relative replication** allows you to copy the contents of a range of cells relative to the row and column coordinates of the destination range. For example, in Figure 9-13b, say that you want the

(c) **Copying by absolute replication.** Copying by absolute replication involves marking each column and row reference in the cell address with a dollar ($) sign.

Formula for cell C1

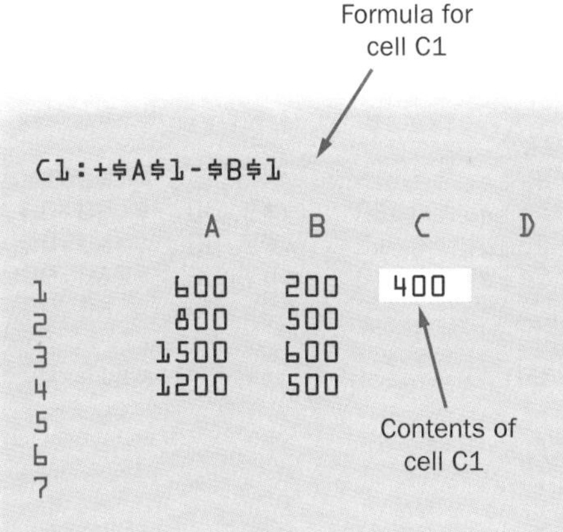

Contents of cell C1

Before copy operation

```
Copy from:C1..C1   Copy to:C2..C4
        A     B     C     D
1     600   200   400
2     800   500   400
3    1500   600   400
4    1200   500   400
5
6
7
```

Results when C1 formula is copied into cells C2, C3, and C4

After copy operation

(d) **Copying by mixed replication.** Mixed replication involves putting a dollar ($) sign in front of each column or row we wish to fix in place.

Formula for cell B4

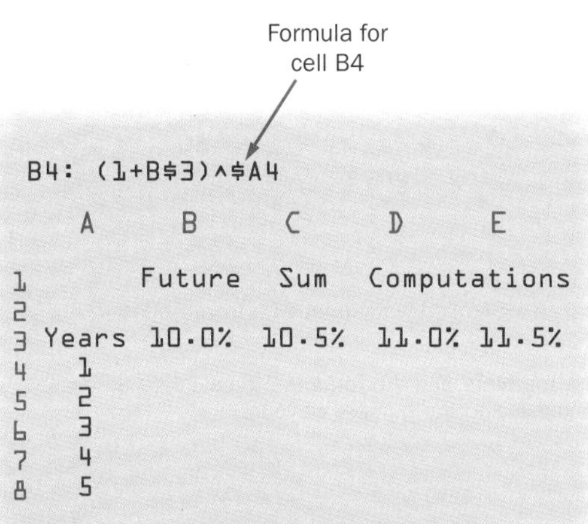

Before copy operation

Results when B4 formula is copied into RANGE B4..E8

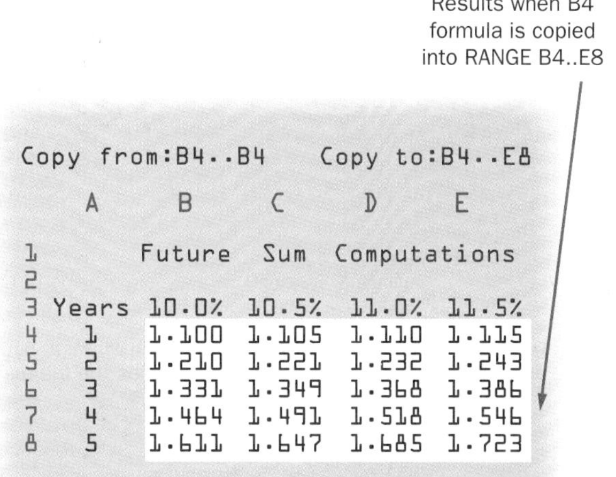

After copy operation

continued

value of each cell in column C to equal the corresponding column A entry minus the corresponding column B entry. In other words, you want

C1 = A1 − B1
C2 = A2 − B2
C3 = A3 − B3
C4 = A4 − B4

Figure 9-13 continued

(e) **Moving a row.** When the contents of a block (range) of cells are moved, they are "cut" out of one area of the worksheet and "pasted" into another of identical size.

	A	B	C	D
1	Name	Hours	Rate	Pay
2	Jones	10	$6.00	$ 60.00
3	Smith	40	$7.00	$280.00
4	Zimmer	20	$4.00	$ 80.00
5	Able	30	$3.00	$ 90.00
6				
7	Total			$510.00

Before move operation

	A	B	C	D
1	Name	Hours	Rate	Pay
2	Able	30	$3.00	$ 90.00
3	Jones	10	$6.00	$ 60.00
4	Smith	40	$7.00	$280.00
5	Zimmer	20	$4.00	$ 80.00
6				
7	Total			$510.00

After move operation

(f) **Freezing titles.** Freezing titles allows you to keep certain columns or rows of the worksheet in place while you are scrolling to other parts of it.

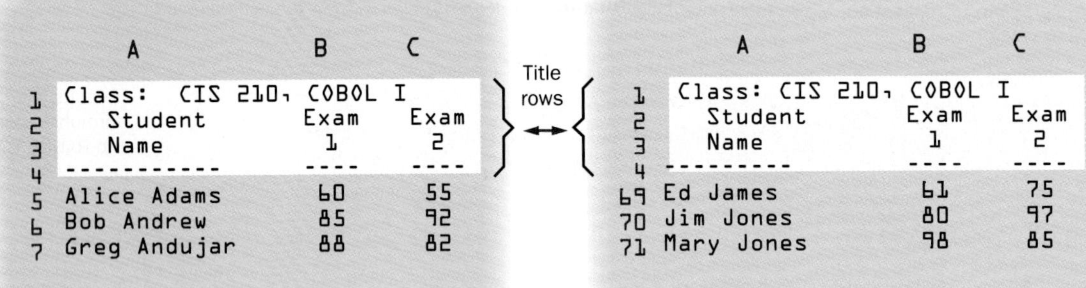

	A	B	C
1	Class: CIS 210, COBOL I		
2	Student	Exam	Exam
3	Name	1	2
4	-----------	----	----
5	Alice Adams	60	55
6	Bob Andrew	85	92
7	Greg Andujar	88	82

	A	B	C
1	Class: CIS 210, COBOL I		
2	Student	Exam	Exam
3	Name	1	2
4	---------	----	----
69	Ed James	61	75
70	Jim Jones	80	97
71	Mary Jones	98	85

Original window

Scrolled worksheet with frozen titles

(g) **Using templates.** The worksheet at the left contains both the blank template and the formulas to calculate the table amounts at the right (once the user supplies the interest rate, principal, and the number of years).

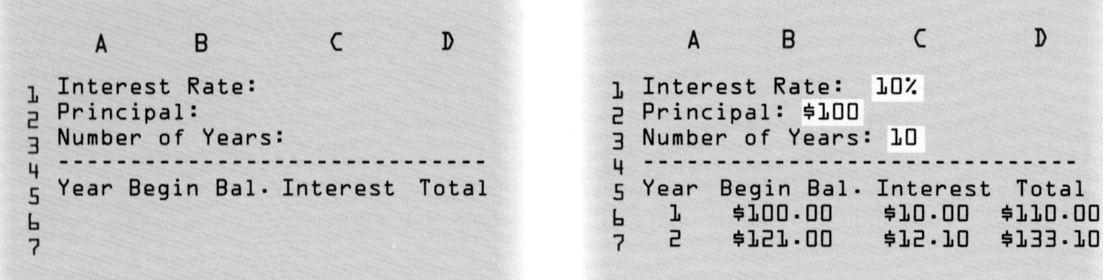

	A	B	C	D
1	Interest Rate:			
2	Principal:			
3	Number of Years:			
4	------	------	------	------
5	Year	Begin Bal.	Interest	Total
6				
7				

	A	B	C	D
1	Interest Rate: 10%			
2	Principal: $100			
3	Number of Years: 10			
4	------	------	------	------
5	Year	Begin Bal.	Interest	Total
6	1	$100.00	$10.00	$110.00
7	2	$121.00	$12.10	$133.10

Blank template

Filled-in template

Generally you can do this by placing the cell pointer at C1 and typing +A1 − B1. Then you can copy this formula into cells C2..C4 in the manner illustrated in the figure by specifying relative replication. In many packages, relative replication is the default when you copy.

- **Absolute Replication** In the previous example, had you asked instead for **absolute replication,** the spreadsheet package would have copied the formula verbatim into all four cells so that each contained the expression +A1 − B1 (see Figure 9-13c). Absolute replication is ideal when a computation yields a constant value that is to repeat in a range of cells.

  The steps taken to perform absolute replication are exactly like those to perform relative replication in most spreadsheet packages, except for one difference: The formula in the source cell must be written in the form

  ```
  +$A$1-$B$1
  ```

  In other words, dollar signs must be placed before each row and column being referenced.

Absolute replication. Copying verbatim the contents in one range of cells into another range of cells.

- **Mixed Replication** Many spreadsheet packages also allow **mixed replication**—a combination of absolute and relative replication—in which a row value can be kept constant while a column value is allowed to vary (or vice versa). Mixed replication is especially useful when handling formulas in which two parameters change. As the first parameter varies across columns (while the second stays constant), the second parameter varies across rows (while the first stays constant).

  Figure 9-13d shows mixed replication for compounding interest. Note that interest rate and years are the two parameters in cell B4. For each column, we want to keep the interest rate (in row 3) fixed as we vary the year from 1 to 5. For each row, we want to keep the year (in column A) fixed as we vary the interest rate from 10 to 11.5 percent. To allow us to mix addresses, we put a $ sign in front of the coordinate that we want to fix; thus, the formula in the source cell must be written as

  ```
  (1+B$3)^$A4
  ```

Mixed replication. Copying formulas in one range of cells into another range, while varying some cell references and leaving others constant.

Moving "Cutting and pasting" often is just as important in developing worksheets as it is in creating word-processed documents. Almost all spreadsheet packages enable you to move any row or column into another row or column position on the worksheet. As with the Copy command, you will need to specify a source range (the range you've moving from) and a destination range (the range you're moving to).

For example, suppose you decide to move row 5 into the row 2 position, as in Figure 9-13e. When moving, the software automatically makes all cell references point to the new worksheet locations. If your spreadsheet package also lets you cut and paste larger areas, as most do, you will be able to move, say, a contiguous 20-by-40 block of cells from one part of the worksheet to another.

Formatting Values Because spreadsheets are particularly useful for preparing financial schedules, it follows that many of the worksheet cells will contain values that represent monetary amounts. Most packages enable you to quickly put dollar signs, commas, and decimal points into these values (for example, to change 90000 to $90,000.00). Generally, all you have to do is identify the range of cells that you want edited and select a Currency option that automatically inserts the proper symbols in the proper places. Adding percent signs (%) usually is an equally straightforward process.

Selecting Column Widths Most packages allow you to change the width of columns on the worksheet. You can assign widths to each column individually, or you can select a single, global width that applies to all columns. Many spreadsheet packages have a spillover feature, which permits particularly long labels to spill over into adjacent columns to the right, provided that those cells are empty.

Freezing Titles Most spreadsheet packages have a Titles feature that allows you to keep a portion of the worksheet frozen in place on the screen when you are scrolling the rest of the worksheet. For example, if we used the Titles feature to freeze the first four rows of Figure 9-13f, we could use the down arrow key or PgDn key to scroll through data in the worksheet while the titles remained on the screen. When you freeze rows, you are working with a horizontally split screen. You can also freeze columns, resulting in a vertically split screen. You usually also have the option of freezing certain rows and certain columns at the same time.

Template.
A prelabeled onscreen form that requires only that the operator fill in a limited number of input values.

Using Templates A **template** is a worksheet in which rows and columns are prelabeled and many cells already contain formulas. Only the data are missing. Thus, the work involved in setting up the worksheet has already been done, leaving you more time to enter and analyze data. A template is shown in Figure 9-13g. In many spreadsheet packages, it is also possible to protect cells, such as those that contain the template's labels and formulas.

Advanced Features

In addition to the basic operations we've just covered, many of the leading spreadsheet packages offer a rich variety of advanced features. Four features that advanced spreadsheet users find useful are data management, macro facilities, multidimensional spreadsheets, and presentation graphics. Here we discuss the first three features and defer discussing presentation graphics until the last section of the chapter.

Data Management Most spreadsheets contain a facility for managing data. Two popular features in most spreadsheet programs' data management toolkits are sorting and searching (information retrieval).

- **Sorting** The ability to sort is a handy feature in almost any type of business software package. With a word processor, sorting enables you to prepare alphabetical listings of names as well as indexes, directories, and glossaries. With a spreadsheet package, you might find a sort facility handy for preparing phone and office directories, ordered listings of overdue accounts, and reports identifying fast-moving or high-selling products. Most spreadsheet packages allow you to sort on more than one field.

Many teachers use the spreadsheet's sort feature to keep grade books on students. Such a grade book can be maintained throughout the term in alphabetical order by student name, and at the end of the term, student records can be sorted according to final averages. Many spreadsheet packages also contain a *data distribution facility* so that a teacher can, among other things, quickly find the number of students with averages between 90–100, 80–89, 70–79, and so on.

- **Searching** Often each row in a worksheet represents some type of record. For example, if the worksheet stores company records, each row might contain a company name, a complete mailing address, a phone number, an employee record (see Figure 9-13e), and so on. If the worksheet is large (many can store thousands of records), it's handy to have a feature that will automatically extract records for you based on search criteria that you specify. For instance, you may wish to get a list of companies in Philadelphia, the address of Kane Publications, or a list of top employees. A search facility will enable you to gather this information rapidly and accurately.

Macro Facility One of the things you'll appreciate about spreadsheet packages is that they let you do a great deal of information processing without having to know how to program. However, if you do have the talent to write programs and if the spreadsheet package you are using has a macro facility, you can really put your worksheets into high gear.

A macro facility enables you to write programs within your worksheet. Each **macro** is, in fact, a program. It is identified by a name and consists of a series of keystrokes that the spreadsheet package executes every time you invoke the macro. In 1-2-3 and a number of other spreadsheet packages, for example, the macro shown in Figure 9-14 lets you automatically set column widths to 20 characters.

Macro.
A predetermined series of keystrokes or commands that can be invoked by a single keystroke or command.

When you depress the Alt key followed by the name of the macro (C), seven keystrokes (/WCS20~) are automatically made for you. Roughly translated, these keystrokes mean invoke the command menu (/), pick the worksheet command off of this menu (W), select the column-width option (C), choose the set option (S), set the column width to 20 characters (20), and hit the Enter key (~).

Macros often are written in contiguous worksheet cells, as Figure 9-14 shows. Frequently the macro is written in a remote set of cells so it does not interfere

FIGURE 9-14

Macro facility. This 1-2-3 macro, named C, lets you set a column width to 20 characters by merely depressing the Alt key and hitting the C key.

	AA	AB	AC
100	Name	Macro	Description
101	\C	/WCS20~	Widens columns

with worksheet labels and values that will be output later. Also, you will want to place the macro far away from the main part of the worksheet so that it doesn't get erased when you are deleting rows or columns. It's a good idea to document the macro, as shown in cell AC101, so you can remember later what it is supposed to do.

If you are really skilled at writing macros, you can write long programs and even programs that loop. Macros can also be used to accept inputs by the operator of the spreadsheet package and to summon menu screens.

Multidimensional Spreadsheets In many cases, it is easier and more practical to create several interrelated worksheets than to cram all of your data into a single worksheet or to develop several independent worksheets. For instance, suppose you have four worksheets with sales data, each one pertaining to a different quarter of the year. Rather than have one busy worksheet or four independent worksheets, it is often easier to integrate the worksheets into a single system, as shown in Figure 9-15.

In the figure, the worksheet for first-quarter sales is referred to as worksheet A, the worksheet for second-quarter sales as worksheet B, and so on. In this

FIGURE 9-15

Multidimensional spreadsheet capability. Each worksheet in a multidimensional system is identified by the letter identifier in its upper left-hand corner. Cell references must include this identifier when several worksheets are being interrelated, as they are here, to arrive at the sum in worksheet E.

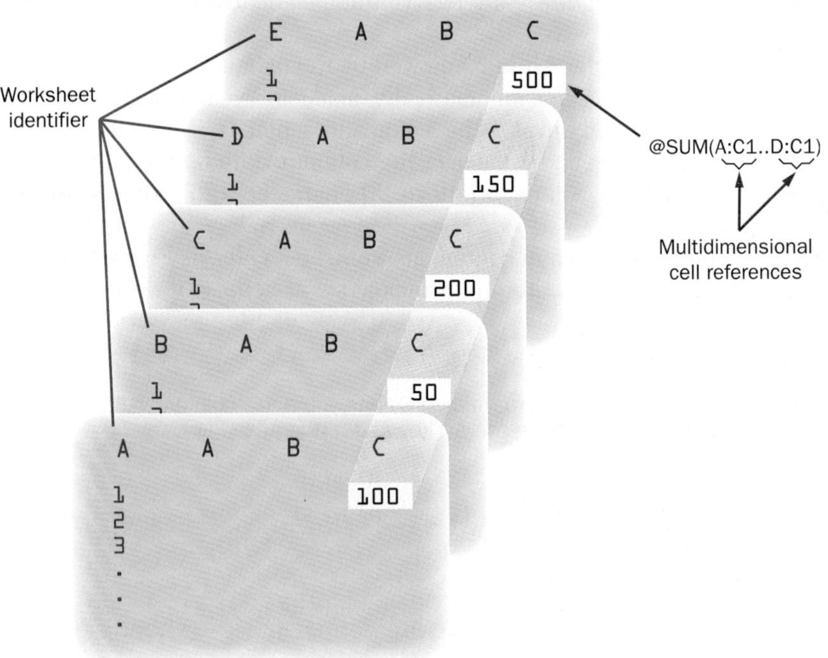

three-dimensional (3-D) application, each cell in each worksheet has three coordinates. For instance, the cell in column A, row 1 of the fourth worksheet is referred to as cell D:A1 (because D is the fourth letter of the alphabet).

When worksheets are represented in a systematic way, as illustrated in Figure 9-15, users can easily specify both the relationships that apply among rows and columns of a single worksheet and the relationships that apply over the set of worksheets. So, for instance, you could create a fifth worksheet (representing a summary for the year) and specify that the cells in this worksheet are to be calculated by summing respective cells in worksheets A through D (representing the four quarters), as shown in the figure. You could even go so far as to create additional worksheets, such as one that computed a trend from the first four worksheets and reported the results.

Spreadsheet packages that allow you to develop a system of worksheets in this way, with each worksheet having more than two coordinates to each cell, are often referred to as **multidimensional spreadsheets.** Most of the leading spreadsheet packages now have a multidimensionality feature. Such a feature allows a set of worksheets to be read like an "electronic book," with each page (worksheet) capable of providing additional information, finer detail, or a consolidated summary of those worksheets that precede it.

Multidimensional spreadsheet.
A program package that allows the construction of worksheets in which cells are referenced by more than two coordinates.

Multidimensionality is the major feature that distinguishes Lotus Development's 1-2-3 Version 3 line of spreadsheet products from its Version 2 line. Recently, spreadsheets such as Lotus' Improv (see Figure 9-16) have taken multidimensionality a step further. Improv contains drag-and-drop mouse tools that enable decision makers to quickly create multiple views of the same data to easily spot trends. Also, formulas are expressed in plain English rather than with cell references.

Presentation Graphics

There's an old saying that a picture is worth a thousand words. If you try to explain to others what you look like, for instance, it may take several minutes. Show them a color photograph, on the other hand, and you can convey the same or better information about yourself within seconds.

Pictures are also extremely useful in business. A person can often spot trends or make comparisons much more quickly by looking at a visual image than by reading text-only or number-only output containing the same information. Furthermore, a point can often be made far more dramatically and effectively.

Forms of Presentation Graphics

A **presentation graphic**—sometimes called a *presentation visual* or *chart*—is an image that visually enhances the impact of information communicated to other people. Presentation graphics can take many different forms, a number of which are illustrated in Figure 9-17. With the right types of software and hardware, the creation of presentation graphics is limited only by one's imagination.

Presentation graphic.
A visual image, such as a bar chart or pie chart, that is used to present data in a highly meaningful form.

There are several compelling reasons to use presentation graphics in business. Trends can be spotted or comparisons made much more quickly when data are

FIGURE 9-16

Dynamic view creation. People at meetings often have a need to inspect data from multiple viewpoints. For instance, the president might want to see data broken down by region (view *a*) while the sales manager might want to see line totals on each product (view *b*). Lotus' Improv spreadsheet, pictured here, enables data views to be changed in seconds simply by dragging and dropping row or column titles with a mouse.

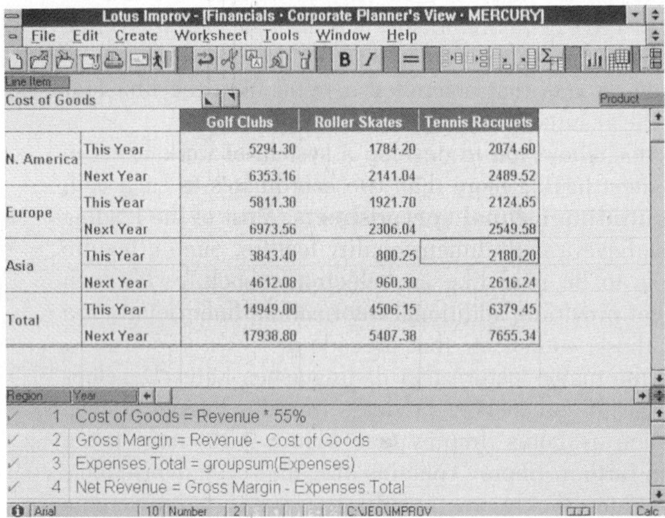

		Golf Clubs	Roller Skates	Tennis Racquets
N. America	This Year	5294.30	1784.20	2074.60
	Next Year	6353.16	2141.04	2489.52
Europe	This Year	5811.30	1921.70	2124.65
	Next Year	6973.56	2306.04	2549.58
Asia	This Year	3843.40	800.25	2180.20
	Next Year	4612.08	960.30	2616.24
Total	This Year	14949.00	4506.15	6379.45
	Next Year	17938.80	5407.38	7655.34

(a)

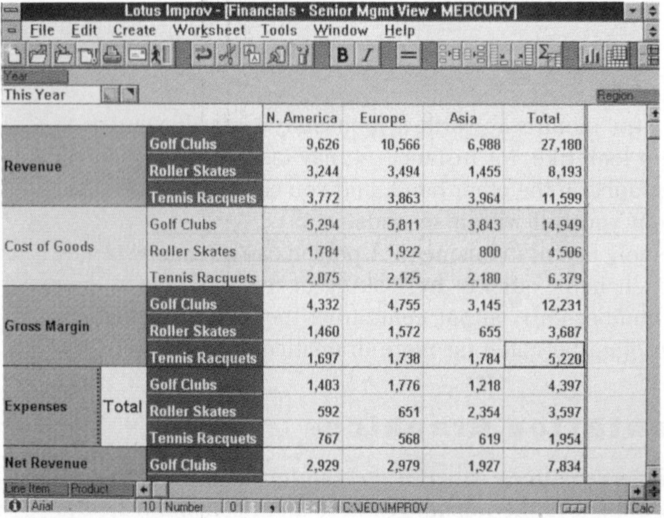

			N. America	Europe	Asia	Total
Revenue		Golf Clubs	9,626	10,566	6,988	27,180
		Roller Skates	3,244	3,494	1,455	8,193
		Tennis Racquets	3,772	3,863	3,964	11,599
Cost of Goods		Golf Clubs	5,294	5,811	3,843	14,949
		Roller Skates	1,784	1,922	800	4,506
		Tennis Racquets	2,075	2,125	2,180	6,379
Gross Margin		Golf Clubs	4,332	4,755	3,145	12,231
		Roller Skates	1,460	1,572	655	3,687
		Tennis Racquets	1,697	1,738	1,784	5,220
Expenses	Total	Golf Clubs	1,403	1,776	1,218	4,397
		Roller Skates	592	651	2,354	3,597
		Tennis Racquets	767	568	619	1,954
Net Revenue		Golf Clubs	2,929	2,979	1,927	7,834

(b)

FIGURE 9-17

Types of presentation graphics. Any type of graphical image that enhances the impact of information as it is shown to people is a presentation graphic. Although packages vary with respect to the number and type of presentation graphics they produce, most allow you to create simple bar, pie, and line charts.

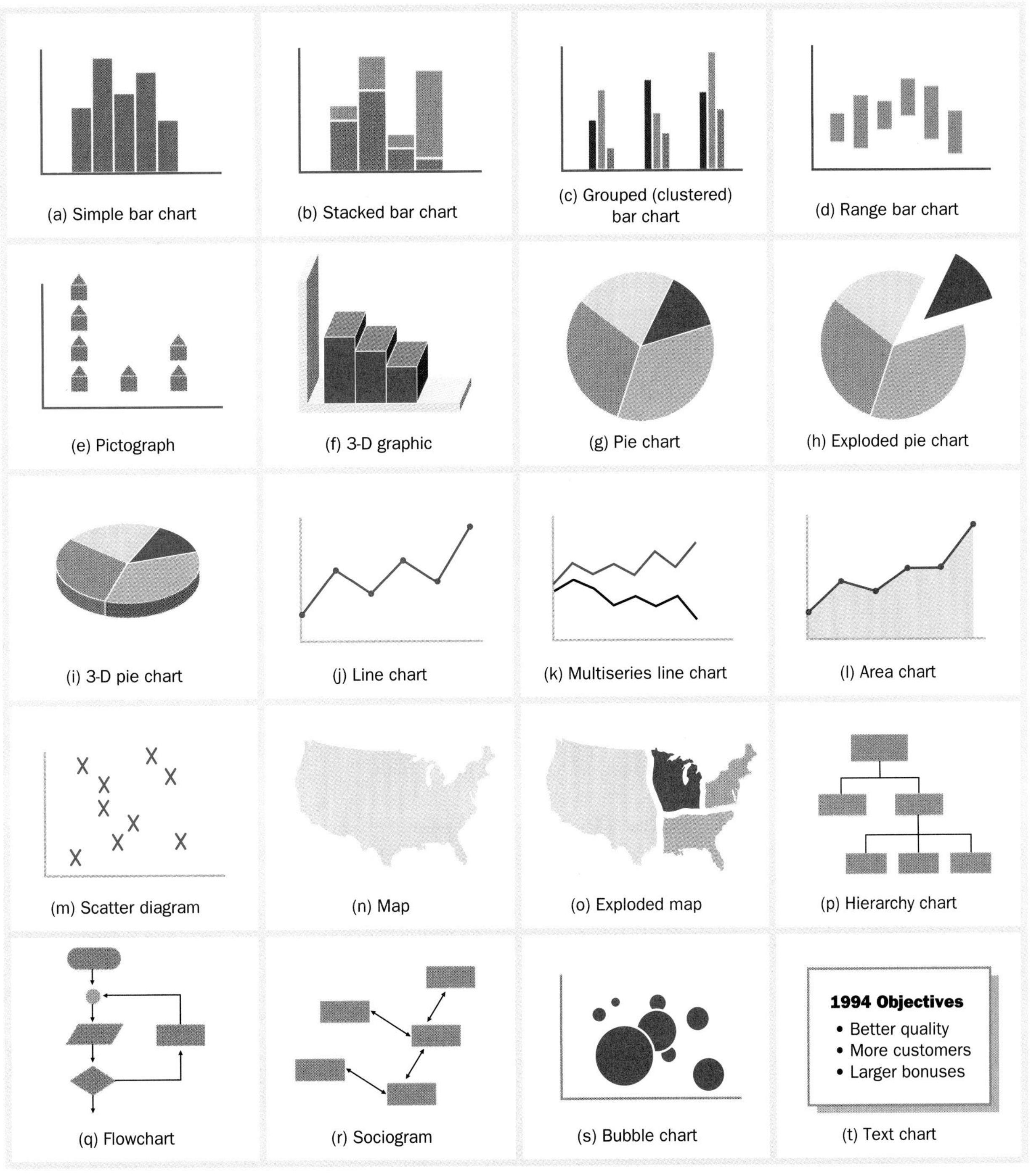

(a) Simple bar chart
(b) Stacked bar chart
(c) Grouped (clustered) bar chart
(d) Range bar chart
(e) Pictograph
(f) 3-D graphic
(g) Pie chart
(h) Exploded pie chart
(i) 3-D pie chart
(j) Line chart
(k) Multiseries line chart
(l) Area chart
(m) Scatter diagram
(n) Map
(o) Exploded map
(p) Hierarchy chart
(q) Flowchart
(r) Sociogram
(s) Bubble chart
(t) Text chart

in chart form. Presentation graphics can also be used to make a point much more convincingly or dramatically than plain text can. Recent studies have found that presentation graphics also make the presenter look more professional in the eyes of others.

Here, we'll discuss in detail three of the most widely used presentation graphics—bar charts, pie charts, and line charts. We'll also look at a number of ways in which these charts vary and examine where each is most appropriate. The best graphic in any given situation depends on the point you are trying to make.

Bar chart.
A presentation graphic that uses side-by-side columns as the principal charting element.

Bar Charts **Bar charts** are especially useful for comparing relative magnitudes of items and for showing the frequency with which events occur. They can also be used to illustrate changes in a single item over time.

In a typical bar chart, one axis represents a categorical or *qualitative* phenomenon; the other represents a numeric or *quantitative* one. For instance, in Figure 9-18a, the horizontal axis (x-axis) represents months, the qualitative phenomenon, whereas the vertical axis (y-axis) represents price, the quantitative one.

A number of different types of bar charts are available, including the simple bar chart, stacked bar chart, grouped (clustered) bar chart, range chart, pictograph, and 3-D bar chart (see Figures 9-17a through 9-17f, respectively).

Each type of bar chart has strengths and weaknesses relative to prospective applications. A *range chart,* for instance, would be most useful for showing daily highs and lows of a particular stock in the stock market (see Figure 9-18a). A *grouped (clustered) bar chart,* on the other hand, would be more useful for showing something such as overall income comparisons for this year and last year by quarter (see Figure 9-18b). Grouped bar charts are especially effective when you want to emphasize a difference between two items over time. When one set of bars is consistently bigger than another set of bars, as is the case here, a *stacked bar chart* can also effectively show the differences between the two sets of bars (see Figure 9-18c). A *Gantt chart,* shown in Figure 9-18d, is particularly handy for showing when events in schedules begin and end.

When designing bar charts, it's a good idea to keep the total number of categories on the x-axis to a half dozen or less. Any more than this may be too much information to cram into a single visual.

Pie chart.
A presentation graphic in which the principal charting element is a pie-shaped image that is divided into slices, each of which represents a share of the whole.

Pie Charts **Pie charts** are commonly used to show how parts of something relate to a whole (see Figure 9-17g to 9-17i). Each slice of the "pie," or circle, represents a percentage of share of the total. One of the major advantages of the pie chart is that it is extremely easy to understand.

Most presentation graphics packages enable you to "explode" a pie chart to emphasize one or more of the slices, as shown in Figure 9-19. The way a pie slice can be exploded varies from one software package to another. Some packages pull the slice out a fixed, predefined distance. Others enable you to specify how far you would like to pull the slice out by using a mouse to select the slice on the screen and drag it to the place where you want it. Virtually all packages allow you to color or texture each of the pie slices as well, as is illustrated in the figure.

Pie charts should not have more than a half dozen or so slices. The more slices there are, the harder it is to recognize relative sizes of the shares they

FIGURE 9-18

Four bar charts. Bar charts are especially useful for comparing the relative magnitudes of items and for showing the frequency with which events occur.

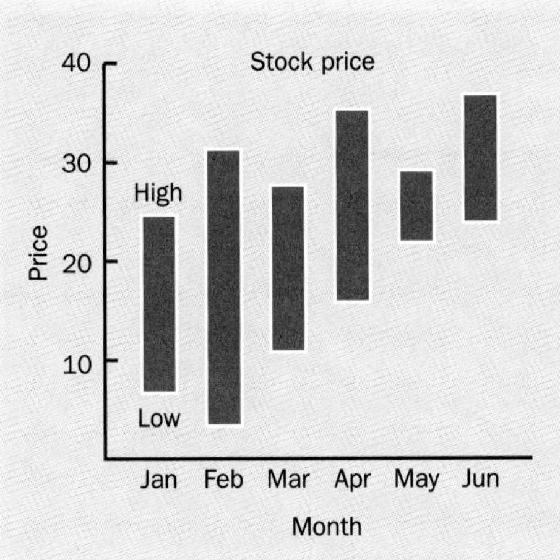

(a) Range chart

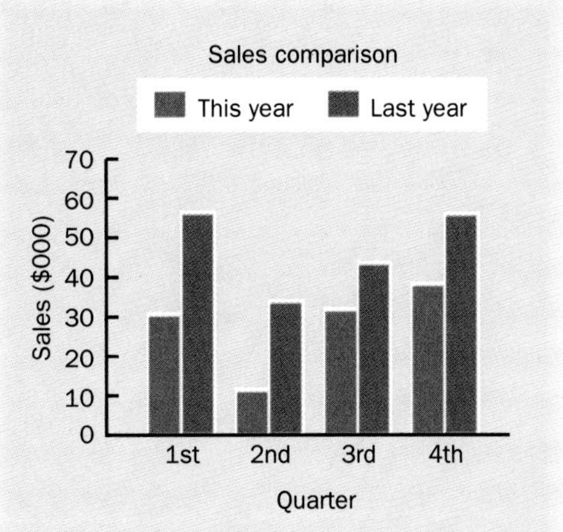

(b) Grouped bar chart

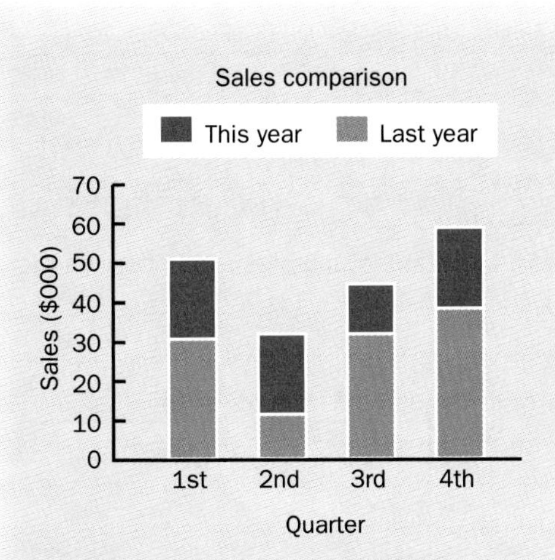

(c) Stacked bar chart

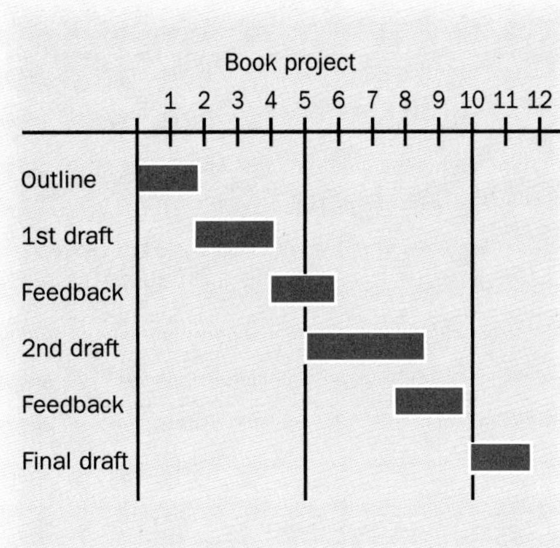

(d) Gantt chart

represent. When the number of slices in a pie chart becomes large, the smallest slices should be combined into an "other" slice.

Line Charts **Line charts** (see Figures 9-17j to 9-17l) are somewhat similar to bar charts. One major difference, however, is that line charts are used in cases where *both* axes represent quantitative phenomena. A second major difference is that, because the line in the chart is unbroken, the effect on the eye can be much more dramatic.

Line chart.
A presentation graphic in which the principal charting element is an unbroken line.

FIGURE 9-19

Exploded pie chart. In an exploded pie chart, a single pie slice is moved slightly from the rest of the pie to call attention to it.

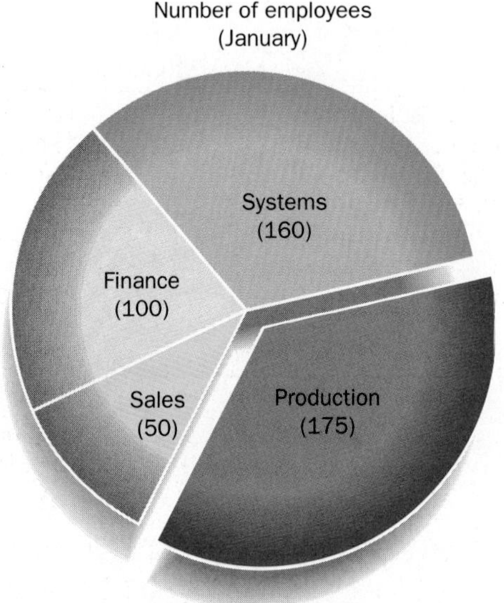

FIGURE 9-20

Line charts. Because the line in a line chart is unbroken, the effect on the eye can be dramatic.

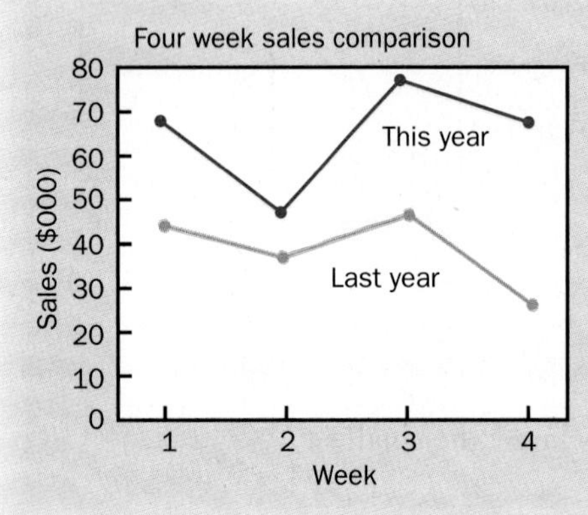

(a) Multiseries line chart

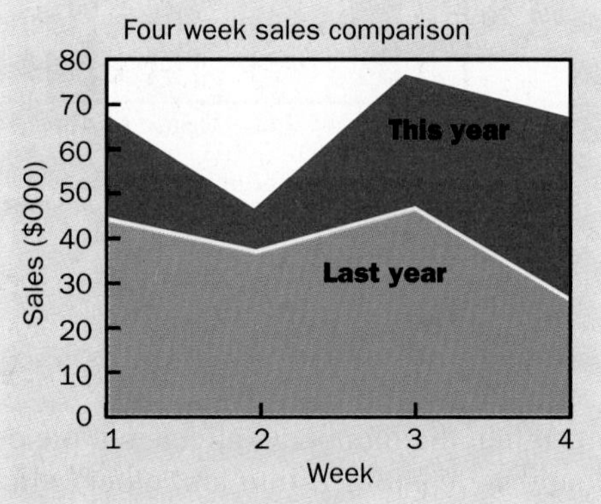

(b) Area chart

As with bar charts, there is a rich variety of line charts. Two examples are shown in Figure 9-20. And as with bar and pie charts, a line chart should not contain too many graphed lines. Lines often cross one another, adding a complexity you don't find in a bar or pie chart. Any more than four or five lines will probably make the visual look confusing.

Types of Packages

Presentation graphics software enables you to draw bar charts, pie charts, and similar graphics (see Figure 9-21). A variety of presentation graphics packages exist in the marketplace. Most of them fall into one of two classes: dedicated presentation graphics packages and presentation graphics packages that are bundled (integrated) with spreadsheet software.

Presentation graphics software.
A program package used to prepare line charts, bar charts, pie charts, and other information-intensive images.

Dedicated Packages Dedicated packages provide the most powerful types of graphics features—for instance, a wider selection of legend fonts, graph types, and device drivers. Many also come with clip art libraries and with painting/drawing software routines to dress up the graphs you create. In short, if your presentation graphics needs are extensive, a dedicated package is more

FIGURE 9-21

Creating a visual with presentation graphics software. Presentation graphics packages enable you to create graphs by simply selecting the type of graph you want from a menu and pointing to the data to be graphed. Other features are available that allow you to title and color graphs and that provide emphasis to graph elements.

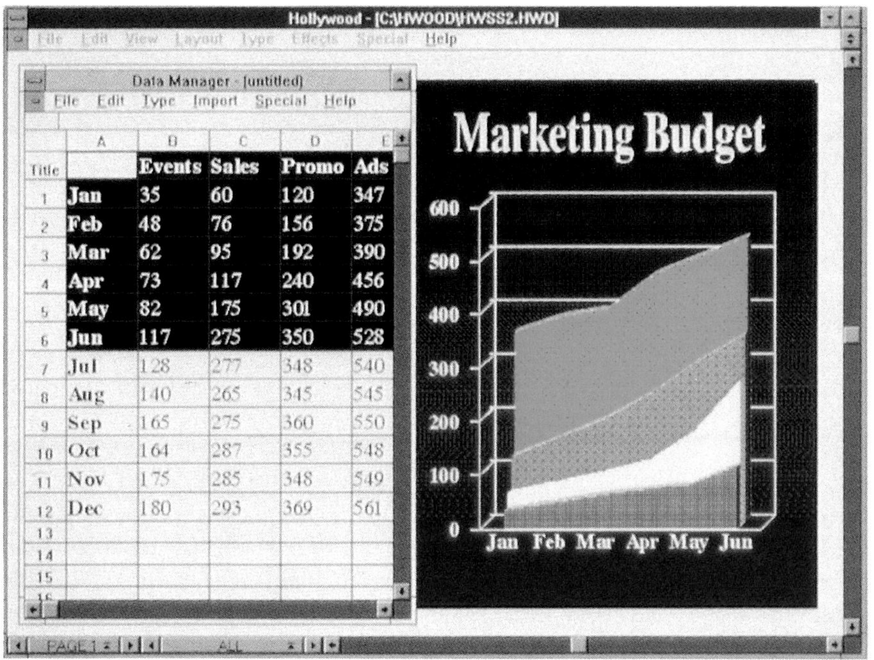

T O M O R R O W

Intelligent Spreadsheets and Graphics

Automating Decision Support for Managers

Is it possible for computers to make decision support any easier than they already have?

Absolutely. Developers of spreadsheets and presentation graphics will be adding a variety of "intelligent enhancements" to their packages over the next several years. The enhancements are designed to help managers interpret the meaning of information, to perform for managers routine tasks that are time consuming, and to provide general support for decision environments.

Some of these enhancements are beginning to trickle into the market already. But by the turn of the century, it's possible that many of them may be standard fare in packages. Following is a list of three important enhancements we are likely to see.

Automatic Updates Often, managers need the same type of information every month. For instance, a presentation the manager makes in February might feature several worksheets and bar charts based on January data. In March, the worksheets and bar charts in the presentation would instead reflect what took place in February, and so on. An intelligent updating feature automatically updates each monthly worksheet and its associated presentation visuals as soon as new monthly data are entered into the computer system. Users on a network will be able to view new worksheets and graphs at their workstations as soon as data have changed.

Smart Files A smart file is a worksheet or presentation graphic that's not only "aware" of its own content, but has the ability to act on this content to make routine decisions. Here's how a smart file might work. A worksheet that you pull from your computer system shows that sales were dramatically low last month. But because you are now using a smart file, this month you get more than just a standard worksheet. The low figures automatically trigger the spreadsheet program to prepare a special report, complete with bar and pie charts that compare activity for the last several months. The program may even do analysis and provide an explanation. The report is then automatically routed to the electronic mailboxes of coworkers over your company's computer network. Also, since not everyone may be authorized to see the full set of data, the smart file customizes the report for each person.

Automatic Chart Selection and Styling With all of the graphics options available today, creating effective presentation visuals can become a mind-boggling challenge.

First, consider *selection.* Many users of presentation graphics packages are not skilled at choosing the most appropriate type of visual to present

likely to contain the types of features you require. Some examples of dedicated packages are Harvard Graphics, Freelance Graphics, Persuasion, Pixie, and Hollywood.

Spreadsheet Packages Unfortunately, dedicated packages often lack some of the calculation and data-modeling features available with spreadsheets. Consequently, you either have to type data directly into them or import data to them from a spreadsheet package. Spreadsheet packages overcome this limitation by integrating both spreadsheeting and graphics functions into a single product. Spreadsheet packages are ideal for users who require a strong data manipulation capability and whose presentation graphics needs are relatively modest.

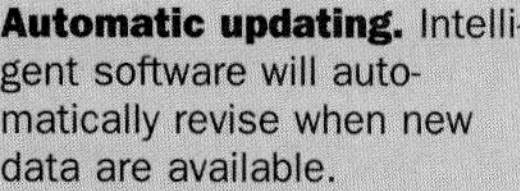

Automatic updating. Intelligent software will automatically revise when new data are available.

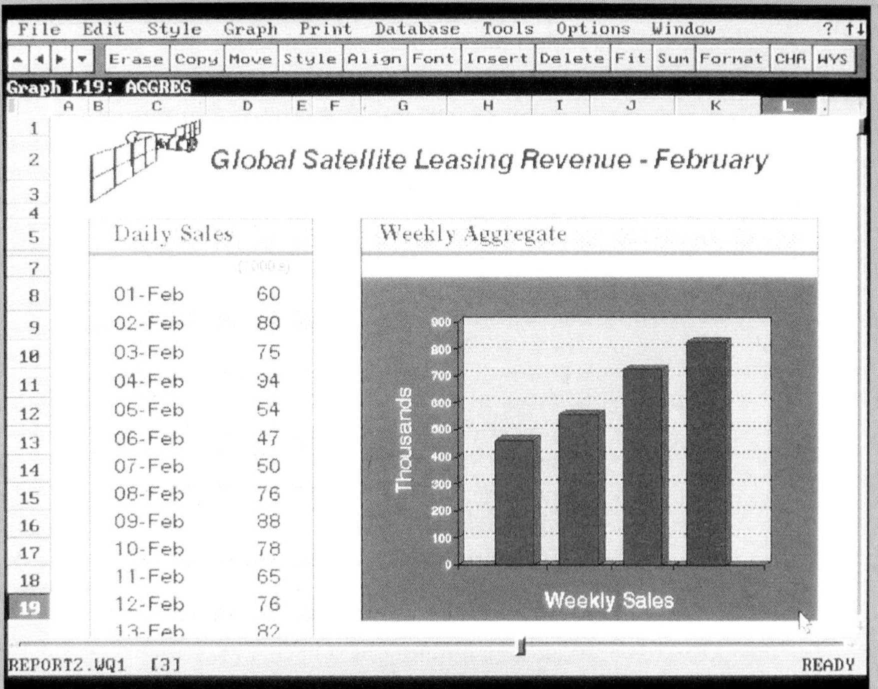

data. An intelligent graphics package will ask the user questions about the target audience and the data to be graphed. With these details out of the way, it will then automatically create the type of presentation visual that best depicts the data under consideration. The package will also have a modification feature that lets users point to any graph elements they want changed and correct them manually.

Now take *styling*. Styling involves such things as choosing colors, selecting fonts for titles and legends, balancing graphic elements visually, and scaling the axes and elements appropriately. A graphics artist may have the wherewithal to decide which colors out of a palette of 256,000 are most appropriate, but the average user does not. An intelligent graphics package will automatically choose effective, compatible colors for visuals. It will also be programmed to avoid "rookie" design mistakes such as putting too many colors into a visual or making too many pie slices in a pie chart.

One of the features that probably will be incorporated into future spreadsheet and presentation graphics packages—as the chapter Tomorrow box explains—is intelligence. Among other things, this feature will assist users who are not skilled in design matters to create professional-looking presentations, and it will enable documents to analyze themselves and create other documents when appropriate.

Summary and Key Terms

Two useful types of program packages for summarizing data so that they make sense to others are spreadsheets and presentation graphics software.

Spreadsheets An **electronic spreadsheet** package produces computerized counterparts to the ruled, ledger-style worksheets with which accountants frequently work. Spreadsheets first came to public notice in the late 1970s when a product named VisiCalc was developed. VisiCalc quickly convinced businesspeople of the usefulness of personal computers.

In electronic spreadsheets, the display screen is viewed as a *window* looking in on a big grid, called a **worksheet.** The worksheet consists of *rows* and *columns* that intersect to form **cells,** each of which can be accessed through a **cell address.** Columns are labeled by letters, and rows are labeled by numbers, so, for instance, cell (cell address) B3 is located at the intersection of the second column and third row.

Spreadsheet software often divides the screen into two principal areas. The worksheet itself is displayed in the **worksheet area,** or **window area.** The **control panel** is the area of the screen where users perform tasks such as preparing text (called *labels*) or numbers (called *values*) that are to be placed in the worksheet cells. A **label** is a cell entry that cannot be manipulated mathematically, whereas a **value** is an entry that can. The control panel also shows you the cell to which you are currently pointing, called the **current cell.** It is also the area used to display commands.

Most spreadsheet packages offer two pointing mechanisms: a cursor and a cell pointer (or highlight). The **cursor** is associated with the control panel, pointing to the place in that area where the next character typed in by the user will appear. The **cell pointer** (or **highlight**) is associated with the worksheet area, pointing to the current cell.

Spreadsheet packages are particularly valuable because they provide a **recalculation feature**—that is, they can perform recalculations in seconds that would require several hours to do manually or by writing a program in a regular programming language. It's this recalculation feature, and the **what-if analysis** it makes possible, that makes spreadsheets so popular.

A contiguous, rectangular block of cells is called a **range.** A range can be typed in explicitly or pointed to on the screen.

Most spreadsheet packages use a hierarchical series of menus from which users can select commands. The *main menu* (or *command menu*) shows the principal command set, while *submenus* prompt users for finer and finer levels of detail.

Spreadsheet packages have numerous features to aid in entering and editing data. Some of the basic entering and editing operations include inserting and deleting rows or columns, moving or copying the contents of cells from one part of the worksheet to another (through **relative replication, absolute replication,** or **mixed replication**), formatting dollar amounts and other values, selecting column widths, and freezing titles. Also, many packages have a **template** feature that permits the creation, saving, and protection of worksheets that have all of their rows and columns prelabeled, so that only the data need to be filled in.

A *data management* feature provides users with a variety of file-handling capabilities, including the ability to *search* for records with specific characteristics and to *sort* records on one or more fields.

A macro facility enables you to write programs within your worksheet. Each **macro** is, in fact, a program. It consists of a series of keystrokes that the spreadsheet package executes every time you invoke the macro.

Spreadsheet packages that allow you to develop worksheets with more than two cell dimensions are called **multidimensional spreadsheets.** A multidimensional feature allows a set of worksheets to be read like an "electronic book," with each page (worksheet) capable of adding detail to the one that precedes it.

Presentation Graphics A **presentation graphic**—sometimes called a *presentation visual* or *chart*—is an image that visually enhances in some way the impact of information communicated to other people. A presentation graphic can take a large number of forms.

Probably the three most common types of charts used for presentations are bar charts, pie charts, and line charts. **Bar charts** are especially useful for comparing relative magnitudes of items and for showing the frequency with which events occur. Some common forms of bar charts are range charts, grouped (clustered) bar charts, stacked bar charts, and Gantt charts. **Pie charts** are commonly used to show how parts of something relate to a whole. **Line charts** are used to represent graph data in which both axes are used to represent quantitative phenomena. Also, because the line in the chart is unbroken, the effect on the eye can be far more dramatic than that of a bar chart.

Presentation graphics software lets you draw bar charts, pie charts, and the like. Presentation graphics packages are either dedicated or integrated into a spreadsheet package. *Dedicated* packages provide the most sophisticated types of graphing capabilities, whereas *spreadsheet* packages consist of modest graphics features.

Review Exercises

Fill-in Questions

1. The principle behind electronic spreadsheets involves viewing the display screen as a(n) ______________ looking in on a big grid, called a(n) ______________.
2. Most spreadsheet packages provide two pointing mechanisms: a(n) ______________ and a(n) ______________.
3. Worksheet entries are created and edited in the ______________.
4. Three types of copying operations available in many spreadsheet packages are ______________, ______________, and ______________ replication.
5. A worksheet in which all rows and columns are prelabeled and formulas are supplied is called a(n) ______________.
6. The spreadsheet feature that allows users to embed small programs in a worksheet is called a(n) ______________ facility.
7. ______________ spreadsheet packages link together several interrelated worksheets.
8. Most presentation graphics packages fall into one of two categories: ______________ packages and ______________ packages.

Matching Questions

Match each term with the description that fits best.

a. +B1-B2*C2	d. JOHN SMITH
b. @SUM	e. 200
c. D4	f. F18..F28

____1. A label.

____2. A range.

____3. A numeric constant.

____4. A formula.

____5. A cell address.

____6. A function.

Discussion Questions

1. What purposes are served by electronic spreadsheets?
2. What is the difference between a label and a value?
3. What purpose does a range serve?
4. What are the differences between relative, absolute, and mixed replication?
5. Of what use is a template to users of spreadsheet software?
6. What does a spreadsheet's macro facility allow you to do?
7. What types of graphical images can you construct with presentation graphics software?
8. What is the difference between a dedicated presentation graphics package and a spreadsheet package with graphics capabilities?

Critical Thinking Questions

1. Is the average spreadsheet user actually "programming" when preparing a worksheet? Defend your response.
2. You need a plotter for your microcomputer system and want to spend no more than $500. You will use the plotter to prepare simple color graphs of bar charts, pie charts, and line charts. Some calls to local computer stores reveal that you can get about five or six product demonstrations. What questions should you get answered during these demonstrations?
3. Spreadsheets, oddly enough, evolved from word processors. What similarities are there between these two types of software packages?
4. Comment on this statement: "Nobody should graduate from a business school today without learning how to use a spreadsheet package."

Pegasus Design Window - dlgEditEmployee
Project
Dictionary
Screen
View
Object
SQL
Settings
Window
Help
New...
Edit...
Manage...
Staff...
Standards
Check out...
Check in...
Archive...
Build...
Reports...
Exit...
Contents
Maintain Clients
First Name:
Last Name:
K Jackson
New
Insert
Update
Delete
Close
Pushbutton
Pushbutton
Pushbutton
Editable Data Field used for input.
Tools
Standard
Edit Field
Lookup Edit Field
Display Only
SQL Link
Catalog...
SYSADM.EMPLOYEE
Link
Help...
None
COMPANYCODE
FIRST
SURNAME
SALUTATION
TITLE
EMPLOYEE_AREACODE
EMPLOYEE_PHONE
EMPLOYEE_FAX

Database Management

10

How do computers keep track of the thousands of facts needed to maintain business records? Often, it's through the use of database management software, which you'll be reading about in this chapter. In recent years, the electronic storage of picture and video data has revolutionized the database management function.

OUTLINE

Overview
Database Management Systems
  Database Management on Microcomputers
  Database Management on Large Computer Systems
  Advantages and Disadvantages of Database Management
Multimedia Data Management

LEARNING OBJECTIVES

After completing this chapter, you will be able to:

1. Explain what database management systems are and how they work.
2. Identify some of the strategies used for database management on both large and small computer systems.
3. Identify the advantages and disadvantages of database management.
4. Appreciate the emerging importance of multimedia data management.

Overview

People often need to summon large amounts of data rapidly. An airline agent on the phone to a client may need to search through mounds of data quickly to find the lowest-cost flight path from Tucson to Toronto two weeks hence. The registrar of a university may have to swiftly scan student records to find the grade point averages of all students who will graduate in June. An engineer may need to test several structural design alternatives against volumes of complicated safety and feasibility criteria before proceeding with a design strategy.

In this chapter, we'll cover database management systems, the type of software used specifically for such tasks. Database management systems are rapidly replacing the thick, hard-copy manuals that people have had to wade through to find the information their jobs require. We'll also consider the topic of multimedia data management, in which voice, graphics, and video data are combined into applications with the most traditional type of data—text.

Database Management Systems

Database management system (DBMS).
A software package designed to integrate data and provide easy access to them.

Database.
An integrated collection of data.

A **database management system (DBMS)** is a software system that integrates data in storage and provides easy access to them. The data themselves are placed on disk in a **database,** which can be thought of as an integrated collection of related files. The three files shown in Figure 10-1, which we will discuss in detail in the next subsection, collectively form a database.

While not all databases are organized identically, many of them are composed of files, records, and fields, as shown in the figure. There are three *files* in Figure 10-1—one for product, another for stock descriptions on hand, and another for open orders. Each file consists of several *records*. For instance, in the product description file there are five records—one each for skis, boots, poles, bindings, and wax. Finally, each record consists of distinct types of data called *fields*. The product description file shown here has four fields—product name, product number, supplier, and price.

The example shown in Figure 10-1 is a simplified one. "Real world" databases often consist of dozens of files, each containing thousands of records. Database management software enables queries and reports to be prepared by extracting information from one file at a time, and, as we will shortly see, from several files concurrently.

Database Management on Microcomputers

Relational database management system.
A database management system that links data in related files through common fields.

The best way to understand how a microcomputer-based database management system works is by reference to example. Many different database management systems are commercially available. Not all of them work the same way nor are they all equally easy to comprehend. In the example that follows we'll look at **relational database management systems**—the type found on most microcomputers and probably the easiest type to understand.

A Simple Example Imagine that you're a sales manager at a ski-equipment warehouse, and an order comes in for 160 pairs of ski boots. You first need to find out if the order can be filled from stock in inventory. If it can't, you next

FIGURE 10-1

Using a relational database management system. Data in various files can be pulled together quickly by their common fields (shaded here).

(a) Product description file

Product name	Product number	Supplier	Price
Skis	A-202	Ellis Ski Co.	90.00
Boots	A-211	Ajax Bros.	60.00
Poles	A-220	Bent Corp.	25.00
Bindings	A-240	Acme Co.	15.00
Wax	A-351	Candle Industries	3.00

(b) Inventory file

Product number	Uncommitted stock	On order?
A-202	15	Yes
A-211	90	Yes
A-220	30	Yes
A-240	25	Yes
A-351	80	No

(c) Order file

Shipment date	Product number	Amount
1/8	A-202	30
1/8	A-240	15
1/9	A-211	50
1/9	A-202	40
1/10	A-220	35
1/12	A-211	60

(d) Information screen

Product number	Product name	Date	Total stock
A-211	Boots	TODAY	90
		1/9	140
		1/12	200

need to know how long it will be before enough stock is available. You have an impatient client on the phone and require an immediate response.

This type of task is especially suited to a database management system. In Figure 10-1 an *inventory file* is used to store current stock levels, an *order file* is used to keep track of future shipments from vendors, and a *product description file* is used to store the product descriptions. The very notion of files is often transparent to the database end user, who knows only that the information is "in the database system" and usually has no idea from where the system is extracting it.

The following scenario would be ideal for you. At the microcomputer workstation on your desk, you key in the product description, "Boots." The computer system responds with a screen that shows the status of this product, including the current level of uncommitted stock, future delivery dates, and future delivery amounts (see Figure 10-1d). Within seconds, you are able to pull together the information necessary to satisfy the client's request and place the order.

Data from several files are pulled together quickly by a relational database management system through the fields (columns) that the files have in common. Relational database management systems are so named because they *relate* data in different files by common fields in those files. In the example we just covered, data from the three files were pulled together through a common product-number field (the highlighted column in Figure 10-1).

You should observe that a system that interrelates the files is critical for the type of information-retrieval task just described. Without an ability to interrelate files, you'd have to successively do the following: (1) access the product description file to get the product number; (2) check the inventory file to see if the order can be filled from current stock; and (3) if current stock is inadequate, look in the order file to see when there will be enough stock to fill the order. Because this serial, "file-conscious" process would be slower than having the files integrated in a manner transparent to the user, both service to clients and efficiency would suffer. DBMS-like packages that do not automatically interrelate files are sometimes called *file managers*.

Interacting with the DBMS Users interact with the database management system through either an easy-to-use retrieval/update facility that accompanies the database package or an applications program written in a programming language.

Usually the *retrieval/update facility* contains a graphical, menu-driven interface that lets users select choices onscreen and an easy-to-use language interface that allows commands to be typed in. Such a facility is designed primarily to satisfy the database needs of ordinary users. Among the most critical of these needs are creating the database, updating database data, and retrieving information from the database (making queries).

The *programming language facility* allows users to create complete computer programs. It often is targeted to more sophisticated users who want to design custom menus or screens or to create applications that go well beyond the standard ones offered with the database package. Most microcomputer-oriented DBMSs come equipped with their own proprietary programming language. A few also support applications developed in such public-domain programming languages as C, BASIC, and COBOL.

A database processing environment for a typical microcomputer system is illustrated in Figure 10-2. The DBMS serves as an interface between the user at one end and the data and programs at the other. As users develop programs and database data at their workstations, DBMS *utility programs* such as the data dictionary (to be discussed shortly) ensure that the data are properly prepared before storing them on disk. Other utility programs, such as a help facility, can be summoned quickly when the user needs assistance with executing a command or troubleshooting an error condition.

Users of microcomputer-based DBMSs must be able to do at least two principal tasks: (1) set up databases (an activity called *data definition*) and (2) create and use databases (an activity called *data manipulation*). Usually, database packages come with a single, proprietary language that can handle both these activities. Typically, this language can also be used to develop applications programs.

Data definition. The process of describing the characteristics of data that are to be handled by a database management system.

Template. A prelabeled onscreen form that requires only that the operator fill in a limited number of entries.

Data Definition Setting up the database, or **data definition,** mainly involves creating a screen form, or *template*, for each file in the database. The **template** is used for entering data. Each file that needs to be created will have its own distinctive template.

FIGURE 10-2

Database environment. The DBMS serves as an interface between users at one end and data and programs at the other.

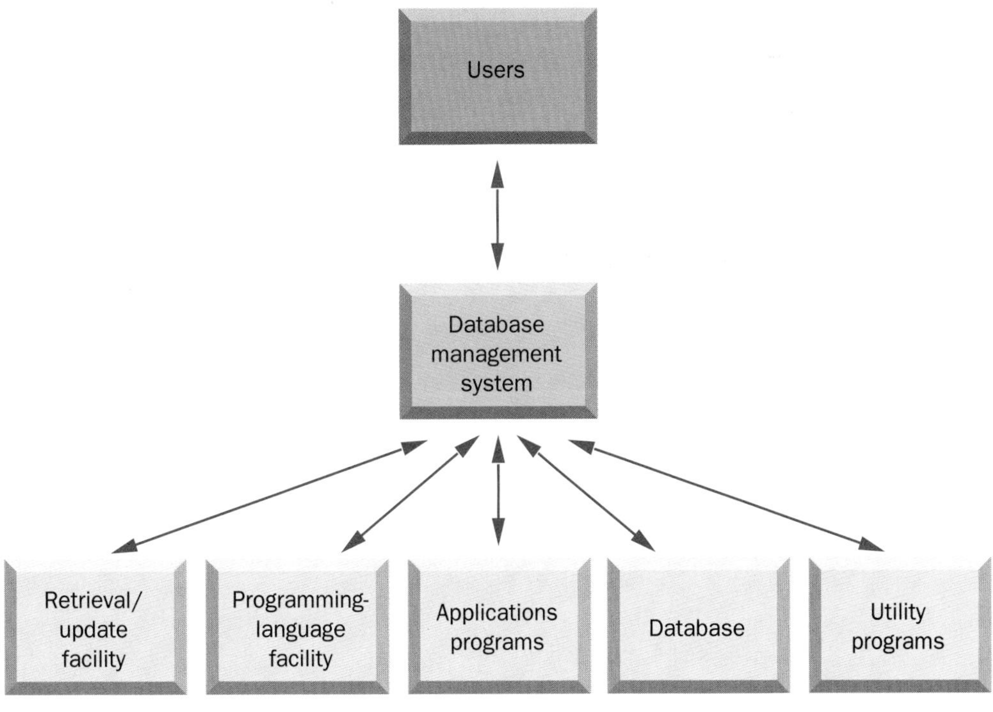

As you place data into the records of a file, you start with an unfilled template for each record to be keyed in. Then you repeatedly fill the template images at the keyboard and save the records onto disk. At any later point, you can modify or delete records from the file and add new ones. Templates for the database shown in Figure 10–1 are given in Figure 10–3.

Usually, each template will ask for the following types of information about the file:

- The name of each field.
- The maximum length of each field.
- The type of data (say, character or numeric) that is to go into each field.

FIGURE 10-3

Data definition. Data definition requires developing a file structure, or template, for each database file. The template (shown to the right of each file) contains such data as field names, field widths, and field types.

(a) Product description file

Product name	Product number	Supplier	Price
Skis	A-202	Ellis Ski Co.	90.00
Boots	A-211	Ajax Bros.	60.00
Poles	A-220	Bent Corp.	25.00
Bindings	A-240	Acme Co.	15.00
Wax	A-351	Candle Industries	3.00

PRODUCT
PRODUCT-NAME
PRODUCT-NUMBER -
SUPPLIER
PRICE

(b) Inventory file

Product number	Uncommitted stock	On order?
A-202	15	T
A-211	90	T
A-220	30	T
A-240	25	T
A-351	80	F

INVENTORY
PRODUCT-NUMBER -
UNCOMMITTED-STOCK
ON-ORDER?

Shipment date	Product number	Amount
1/8	A-202	30
1/8	A-240	15
1/9	A-211	50
1/9	A-202	40
1/10	A-220	35
1/12	A-211	60

ORDER
SHIPMENT-DATE / /
PRODUCT-NUMBER -
AMOUNT .

(c) Order file

This information is commonly referred to as a **file structure.** For example, suppose you've informed your microcomputer's relational database package that you want to create a file called INVENTORY (see Figure 10-3b). The package will ask you to describe each data field of the records that will go into the file. You might respond as follows:

File structure.
A collection of information about the records of a file, including the name, lengths, and types of the fields.

Field Name	Field Type	Width	Decimals
PRODUCT-NUMBER	Character	5	N/A
UNCOMMITTED-STOCK	Numeric	5	0
ON-ORDER?	Logical	1	N/A

Roughly translated, this structure declares that there will be three fields in the INVENTORY file—PRODUCT-NUMBER, UNCOMMITTED-STOCK, and ON-ORDER?. The PRODUCT-NUMBER field is composed of text, or *character*, data. The width of 5 means that product numbers will be five or fewer characters. The UNCOMMITTED-STOCK will consist of *numeric* data that will have a maximum width of five characters. Because stock is counted in units of product, there will be no decimal places. ON-ORDER? will be a *logical* field. A logical field contains either the value T (for true, or yes) or F (for false, or no). For instance, a product that was on order would typically be given the value T; a product not on order would receive the value F.

In most DBMSs, arithmetic computations can be performed on data that have been declared as numeric but not on data declared as character or logical. The "character," "numeric," and "logical" designations are commonly called **field descriptors.** Many database packages have these three descriptors as well as ones for *date* and *memo* fields (see Figure 10-4).

Field descriptor.
A code used to describe the type of data—say, numeric, character, logical—that occupy a given field in a data record.

File structures and other characteristics of the file are used by the DBMS to construct a **data dictionary** for the application. On most microcomputers, the data dictionary is kept *active* to the application. This means that when data are placed into the template and later used, the data dictionary monitors the applications environment and ensures that no data are entered or used in any conflicting way. So, for instance, you couldn't enter a seven-character product number if the dictionary expected all product numbers to be five characters long. Nor would the dictionary let you add a character field and a numeric field.

Data dictionary.
A facility that manages characteristics of data and programs in a database environment.

In many database systems, the data dictionary is also used to protect certain data from unauthorized use or alteration. Sensitive data such as salaries can be hidden so that only certain users of the database, furnished with the proper password, are authorized to retrieve them. Also, only users with access to another password would be allowed to update these data.

Data Manipulation The process of using the database in some hands-on fashion is called **data manipulation.** There are generally two ways to manipulate data in a microcomputer-oriented DBMS—through the retrieval/update facility that is provided with the DBMS and through an applications program developed with the programming-language facility.

Data manipulation.
The process of using program commands to add, delete, modify, or retrieve data in a file or database.

Data manipulation encompasses a variety of activities. Here we briefly cover some of the most important of them.

- **Creation of Database Data** This task consists of developing records for the database. Each template in the database is successively brought to

FIGURE 10-4

Field descriptors. Most business applications require use of five field descriptors—character, numeric, logical, date, and memo.

Field Type	Description
Character	*Character* fields store data that cannot be manipulated arithmetically. You can, however, sort, index, or compare on these fields.
Numeric	*Numeric* fields, which store integer numbers and numbers that contain decimal points, are those that can be arithmetically manipulated. Numbers on which you do not need to do arithmetic—such as employee identification numbers and product identification numbers—should be stored in character rather than numeric fields.
Logical	*Logical* fields store a single character of data—a "T" (for "true") or an "F" (for "false") or, alternatively, a "Y" (for "yes") and an "N" (for "no"). Tests on logical fields can be used to select records from a file, as can tests on character, numeric, and date fields.
Date	*Date* fields store dates, provided that they are in the format MM/DD/YY (such as 12/31/94). You can sort or index on date fields, and you can also subtract them to calculate the number of days elapsing between two dates.
Memo	*Memo* fields are used to store text information. They cannot be arithmetically manipulated or compared, but they can be edited and output, as can any other field.

the screen and filled with the records that pertain to it. In Figure 10-3, for example, you might first summon the template for the product-description file. Then you would type in the first record in that file and enter it. After you did this, a fresh template would appear on the screen. You would type in the second record, and so forth. When you had finished entering all the records for the product-description file, you would do the same thing for the next file—say, the inventory file.

- **File Maintenance** File maintenance consists primarily of updating records. This involves adding new records from time to time, deleting records that are no longer needed, and making modifications to records. Modifications are necessary because data such as prices and delivery schedules can change and also because errors are sometimes made in entering data.
- **Information Retrieval (Query)** The information on the screen in Figure 10-1d, where we needed to find out amounts and delivery dates of uncommitted stock, is an example of information retrieval, or query. *Query* is the ability to extract information from a database without having to write a program. Database queries can be simple or very complex. Figure 10-5 illustrates several queries from the database data described in Figures 10-1 and 10-3. Also provided are the DBMS's responses to those queries. One important fact you should keep in mind is that if you can *manually* pull together the data you need, you should be able to get your database management system to pull these same data together *automatically*—and a lot faster, too.

Structured Query Language (SQL). A popular language standard for information retrieval in relational databases.

Every database management system has its own way of letting users query the database for information. The style shown in Figure 10-5 is based largely on **SQL** (for **Structured Query Language**), which is recognized

FIGURE 10-5

Examples of database queries. The queries given here can be directed to the database data described in Figures 10-1 and 10-3. Each of the queries conforms to SQL, the de facto standard for information retrieval from relational databases.

Query

```
SELECT   PRODUCT-NUMBER, PRODUCT-NAME
FROM     PRODUCT
WHERE    PRICE < 20.00
```

Selects all records in the product file that have a price of less than $20.00; outputs only the product number and product name on each selected record. That is,

Response

```
A-240  Bindings
A-351  Wax
```

Query

```
SELECT   PRODUCT-NUMBER, UNCOMMITTED-STOCK, ON-ORDER?
FROM     INVENTORY
WHERE    UNCOMMITTED-STOCK > 20   AND   ON-ORDER? = T
```

Selects all records in the inventory file that have an uncommitted stock level of over 20 and that are on order (i.e., the value of ON-ORDER is "T," for true); outputs all fields of each selected record. That is,

Response

```
A-211  90  T
A-220  30  T
A-240  25  T
```

Query

```
SELECT  SHIPMENT-DATE, PRODUCT-NUMBER
FROM    ORDER
WHERE   SHIPMENT-DATE >= 1/9 OR AMOUNT >= 30
```

Selects all records in the order file where the shipment date is 1/9 or beyond, amount is 30 or more units, or both. Outputs only dates and product numbers. That is,

Response

```
1/8   A-202
1/9   A-211
1/9   A-202
1/10  A-220
1/12  A-211
```

Query

```
SELECT   PRODUCT-NAME, ON-ORDER?
FROM     PRODUCT, INVENTORY
WHERE    PRODUCT.PRODUCT-NUMBER = INVENTORY.PRODUCT-NUMBER
```

Creates new records by linking the product and inventory files through their common field, PRODUCT-NUMBER. The new records show the name of each product and whether or not it is on order. That is,

Response

```
Skis      T
Boots     T
Poles     T
Bindings  T
Wax       F
```

as today's de facto standard for information retrieval in relational databases. Recently, a number of tools have become available from both database vendors and vendors of add-on packages to make it easy for users to construct database queries without having to remember language syntax (see Figure 10-6).

Increasingly, database management systems are enabling storage and retrieval of information other than text, as shown in Figure 10-7.

FIGURE 10–6

Simplifying SQL with GUIs. The trend in database software today is toward graphical user interfaces (GUIs) that make it easier for ordinary users to construct SQL commands. Shown here are three different GUI approaches to the language interface illustrated in Figure 10–5.

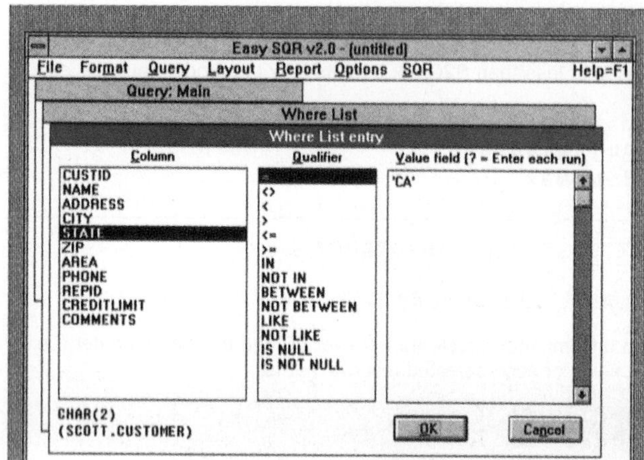

(a) Easy SQR lets users compose queries by placing search fields, search operators, and search criteria in separate windows.

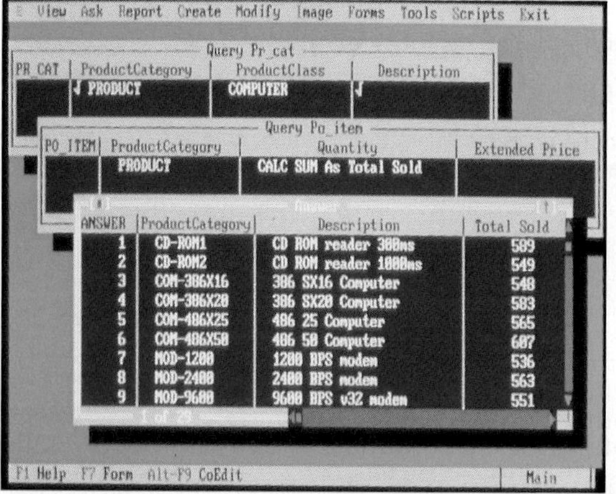

(b) In Paradox's "Query By Example" feature, users simply check fields and include example elements to perform queries across multiple tables.

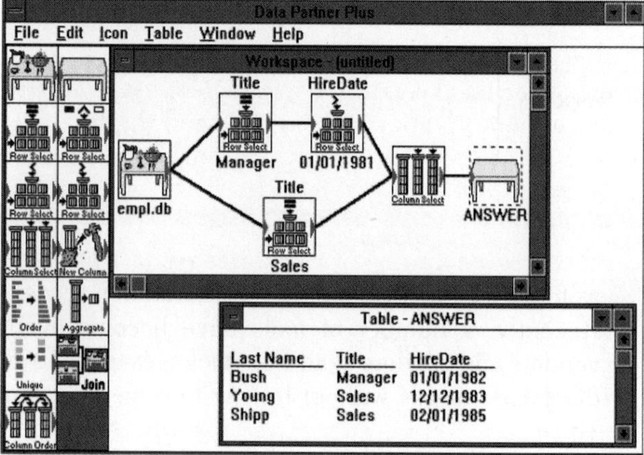

(c) Data Partner enables users to construct queries by connecting icons that symbolize access routines.

FIGURE 10-7

Graphics data. Database management packages are increasingly being used for storage and retrieval of graphics-oriented data. Here, photographic data are included along with regular text data in an electronic insurance record.

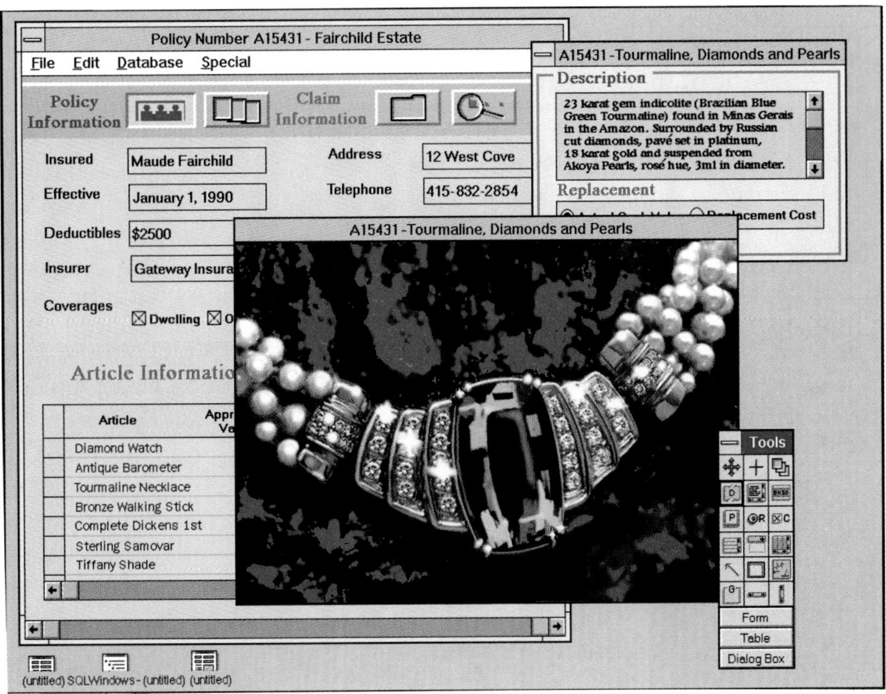

- **Reporting** Reporting is the process of arranging the information you need in a formal report. Most database management systems require that you produce a *report form* for each type of report you need. The report form specifies what the report will look like when it is output—how the report title and column headings will look, which fields will be placed into which columns, the criteria used to select records for the report, how records are to be arranged in the report, and the like. Typically, a series of easy-to-use menus will guide users through report preparation (see Figure 10-8).
- **Sorting** Sorting is the process of arranging records in some order. Most database management systems are equipped with the necessary tools to help you arrange records in virtually any sequence you desire. As with spreadsheets, you can choose several sort keys to do sorts within sorts.
- **Calculations** Often it is necessary to compute sums for columns, take averages, count records, and so forth. Although spreadsheet software is especially suited to these particular applications, database management systems include such math features, too.

Feature 10-1

Geographic Information Systems (GISs)

Data management with maps

For hundreds of years, when information had to be recorded on a map, it was drawn right on the map surface. Transparency overlays, introduced later, were a more sophisticated development, allowing different types of data to be layered on a single map. Sometimes the overlays were used jointly, but use of two or more overlays could make the maps confusing. Then, in the late 1980s, GISs were created.

Geographic information systems (GISs) are computerized display maps that are backed by powerful database systems. Advances in database technology, large-capacity storage (optical disk) devices, and improved computer graphics techniques have made GISs possible. Stored in the database are map images and useful geographic data such as demographic breakdowns, sales data, store and warehouse locations, trends, and market research data. Anything you can put on a map—including data on animal populations, land use, foliage growth, traffic patterns, mineral deposits, or pollution—is fair game for a GIS database.

GISs are a promising new area within the computing field. Following is a sampling of their wide range of applications.

- Oil companies such as Texaco, Shell, and Amoco use GISs to store exploration maps and data such as land-leasing arrangements, oil strikes, and terrain features. The systems have reduced the time needed to find promising places to drill and have made the process of locating drilling sites more accurate. GISs are also used by oil companies to locate profitable sites for gas stations.
- GISs have helped environmentalists in their attempt to control the 1989 *Exxon Valdez* oil spill at Prince William Sound in Alaska. A desktop mapping program called GeoREF has been used to collect environmental data, display it, and plan a cleanup strategy. Moreover, the maps have provided a useful electronic journal of the disaster so that its long-term impact can be more accurately assessed.
- Arby's uses GISs to assess the performance of its franchises and to select new sites. One of the key types of data it uses to select sites is traffic patterns. A spokesperson for the firm reports that GISs have dramatically reduced the number of bad decisions.

Database Management on Large Computer Systems

On large computer systems—say, a mainframe or a large network of microcomputers—DBMSs perform exactly the same sorts of roles as they do on standalone microcomputer systems. However, they are necessarily more sophisticated, for several reasons. First, data are often organized or distributed in a more complex way to provide faster access. Second, DBMSs on large systems must deal with the problem of several users trying to access the database, perhaps simultaneously. Third, because database technology began evolving at a time when many organizations had thousands of dollars already invested in programs written in traditional programming languages, DBMS vendors had to design their products to interface with these languages.

Hierarchical and Network Data Models The relational database model is particularly useful in managerial (decision-support) retrieval situations in

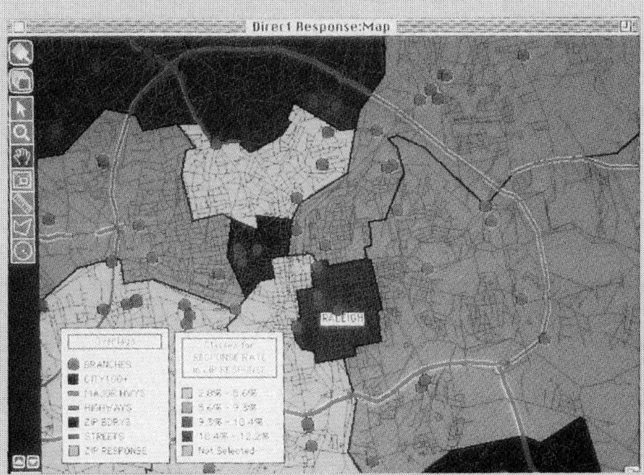

GIS applications. Using technology to determine areas of maximum market penetration (left) and to reduce emergency response time (right).

- The U.S. Geographical Survey (USGS) is planning to computerize its large collection of maps showing every town, river, lake, and highway in the country. These maps will be used for governmental planning purposes and also made available to GIS users in the private sector.
- A feed company in Minnesota uses a GIS to estimate the amount of feed it can sell in a 12-state area. Data on animal populations and average consumption by each species by county are used to estimate demand.
- A growing roster of companies—including Coca-Cola, UPS, and Federal Express—uses GIS techniques to route trucks along the fastest routes. The city of Albuquerque, New Mexico, uses small display screens in ambulances that help drivers navigate to their destinations. Shaving minutes off driving time can be critical in emergency situations.
- The city of Tacoma, Washington, is a leader in using GISs. The police department uses a GIS to track crimes, the fire department uses a GIS to cut response time in getting to a fire, city planners use a GIS to keep track of properties for tax assessment, and the water company uses a GIS to locate meters and valves.

which users are free to pose almost any sort of query to the database. In other situations, however, the types of queries that users need to make are highly predictable and limited. For instance, in banking, tellers usually have access only to the facts they need to perform their jobs, such as information on current customer account balances, deposits, and withdrawals. In these transaction processing environments, hierarchical and network database models are found more commonly than relational ones. Relational databases store data in tables, whereas hierarchical databases store data in trees and network databases store data in networks (see Figure 10-9). These models are explained below:

- *Hierarchical databases* store data in the form of a tree, where the relationship between data elements is one-to-many. Note that each professor in Figure 10-9a is assigned to one and only one department. If Professor Schwartz were a member of two departments—say, marketing and MIS—she would have to be represented twice in the database to maintain the hierarchical structure, once under marketing and once under MIS. The database system

FIGURE 10-8

Developing a report form. Many database packages require you to use a series of menus to develop onscreen a mockup of what a report will look like in print. Here, in this Paradox screen, the mockup appears on the top half of the screen; the report is on the bottom.

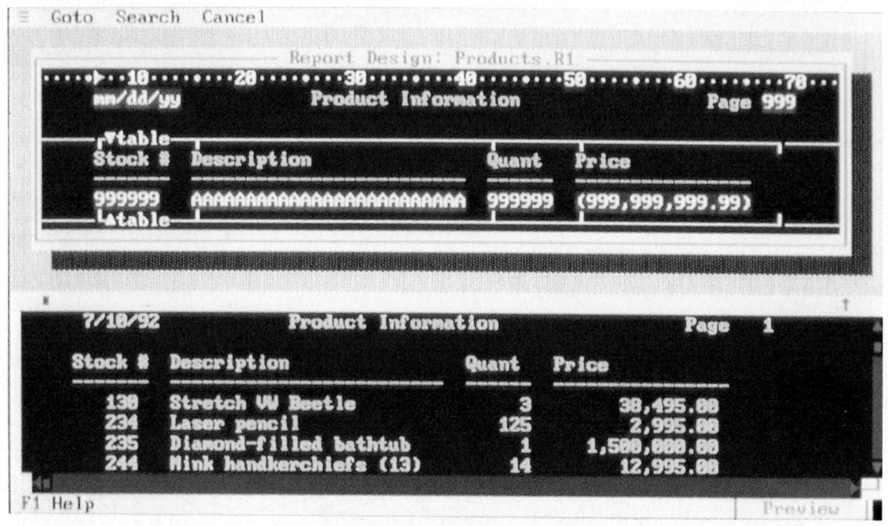

would then treat Professor Schwartz as two distinct individuals. She might even get two separate graduation invitations from the school's computer. Such an inefficiency can be tolerated, however, if it's relatively rare.

- In *network databases,* the relationship between data elements can be either many-to-one (*simple* networks) or many-to-many (*complex* networks). The solid lines in Figure 10-9b depict many-to-one relationships; many courses can be handled by one professor and by one grader. The dotted lines, on the other hand, represent many-to-many relationships, where classes can be cotaught by two or more professors or have multiple graders. Complex networks are usually harder to deal with, but they can always be decomposed into simple networks. Sometimes this is done when, like in the earlier case of Professor Schwartz, some minor duplication can be tolerated.
- In *relational databases,* as explained earlier, related data are placed into tables (see Figure 10-9c). Since the tables are independent, they can be dynamically linked by the user at program-execution time. This is in contrast to hierarchical and network databases, where data are prelinked.

Although further explanation of how hierarchical and network models work goes beyond the scope of this book, suffice it to say that these models store data in a way that makes access faster for predefined types of queries. Hierarchical and network databases have been around longer, too, so the security on these types of database systems is better than security on relational systems. Because hierarchical and network databases are harder to set up and use, professionals known as *database administrators (DBAs)* are commonly hired to assist.

FIGURE 10-9

Database models. Most commercial databases are of the hierarchical, network, or relational type.

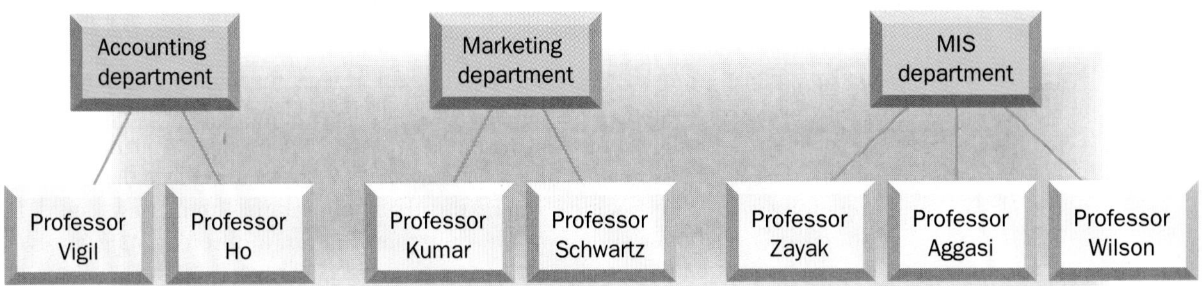

(a) Hierarchical

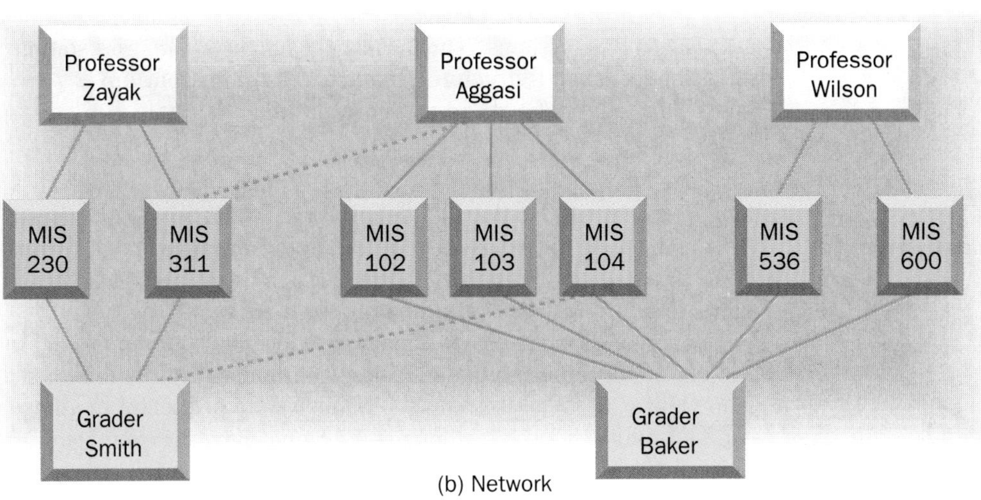

(b) Network

Course	Professor
MIS 230	Zayak
MIS 311	Zayak
MIS 102	Aggasi
MIS 103	Aggasi
MIS 104	Aggasi
MIS 536	Wilson
MIS 600	Wilson

Course	Grader
MIS 230	Smith
MIS 311	Smith
MIS 102	Baker
MIS 103	Baker
MIS 104	Baker
MIS 536	Baker
MIS 600	Baker

Professor	Department
Zayak	MIS
Aggasi	MIS
Wilson	MIS

(c) Relational

Distributed Client-Server Systems Increasingly, DBMSs on large computer systems are becoming distributed. The concept of a *distributed database* is relatively simple. Instead of a single database existing on a large, centralized mainframe—currently still the most widespread practice—the database is divided among several smaller computers that are hooked up in a client-server form of network.

In a distributed DBMS, data are divided among the member databases so as to optimize system performance measures such as communications cost, response time, and storage cost. Moreover, data can be placed at the sites at which they are most needed and best managed. A user calling into the database generally will have no idea where the data are coming from; they could be stored in a computer system in the same building, in a different state, or even in a different country.

When the user makes a request to a distributed DBMS, it is up to the DBMS to determine how to best get the data; how it will do this should be transparent to the user. Theoretically, users should be able to work under the illusion that all the data are stored locally. Ideally, there is a common, seamless interface among member systems. Thus, the user at any *client* workstation need learn only one command structure to get information from any *server* workstation hooked into the network, resulting in minimal delays.

Data definition language (DDL).
A language used to create, store, and manage data in a database environment.

Setting Up the Database Large DBMS packages usually have a special language dedicated to the data definition function. Such languages have generically come to be known as **data definition languages (DDLs).** Besides simply defining data, a major function of the DDL in these large packages is security—protecting the database from unauthorized use.

Because a large database management system in a firm is used by numerous people, the accompanying database is particularly vulnerable to security problems. For example, unscrupulous employees may attempt to alter payroll data, access privileged salary or financial account data, or even steal or erase data. To avoid these possibilities, the DBA may assign passwords when setting up the data dictionary, to determine which users access which data. This practice gives users only restricted views of the full database. For example, users working on a mailing list application that accesses an employee database will be locked out of access to data on employee salaries. Also, the DBA can allow some users to modify certain data and give other users of those data only retrieval privileges. For example, in an airline's passenger reservation database, a regular clerk or agent may not be allowed to rebook a special-rate passenger on an alternate flight, but a high-level supervisor, who knows the password, may be able to.

Processing Data DBMSs targeted to larger computer systems often contain separate language packages to handle retrieval/update and programming tasks. Both sets pose their own array of problems that the typical microcomputer DBMS user doesn't encounter.

For example, on large computer systems (or microcomputer systems linked by a network), users often need to access the same data at more or less the same time. This can cause several problems. For example:

- Only one seat is available on a flight. Two agents seize it at the same moment and sell it to different customers.

- A program is tallying a series of customer balances in a database. When it is halfway finished, another program controlled by someone else transfers $5,000 from account 001 (which the first program already has tallied) to account 999 (which it hasn't). Thus, the first program will "double count" the $5,000 and obtain erroneous results.

To prevent such problems, most database systems allow access users to place a temporary "lock" on certain blocks of data to ensure that no other modifications to these data will be made during their processing.

Another problem unique to DBMSs on large computer systems relates to the need of these DBMSs to tie into programs coded in widely-used programming languages. An interfacing feature known as a **data manipulation language (DML)** solves this problem, however. The DML is simply a set of commands that enables the language the programmer normally works with to function in a database environment. For example, if the programmer writes programs in COBOL, a COBOL DML must be used. The DML may consist of 30 or so commands, which the programmer uses to interact with data in the database.

Thus a COBOL program in a database environment consists of a mixture of standard COBOL statements and COBOL DML statements. The program containing this mixture of statements is then fed to the DBMS's COBOL **precompiler,** which translates this program into a standard COBOL program. This program then can be executed with the regular COBOL compiler available on the system.

High-level languages supported by their own DMLs are called **host languages.** Several host languages may be available on any particular system. Languages that a DBMS commonly employs as hosts are COBOL, C, PL/1, and BASIC.

Data manipulation language (DML). A language used by programmers to supplement some high-level language supported in a database environment.

Precompiler. A computer program that translates an extended set of programming language commands into standard commands of the language.

Host language. A programming language used to code database applications.

Advantages and Disadvantages of Database Management

A DBMS can offer several advantages over filing systems in which data appearing in independent files are not centrally managed and concurrently accessed. Several of these follow.

- **Better Information** Because many more data are integrated in a database environment than in a traditional file environment, information that otherwise might be difficult or impossible to pull together can be collected easily.
- **Faster Response Time** Data that would otherwise require several independent files are integrated into a single database, so complex requests can be handled much more quickly.
- **Lower Operating Costs** Because response time is faster, more work can be done by users in less time.
- **Fewer Storage Requirements** In a database system, integration often means that the same data need not appear over and over again in different files, thereby saving valuable disk space.
- **Better Data Integrity** In a database system, integration often means that a data update need be made in only one place to be automatically reflected throughout the system, thereby avoiding the error that is often introduced when the same update has to be made manually in several independent files.

- **Better Data Management** Since more data are centrally stored in a database than in independent files there is better control over such matters as the data dictionary, security, and standards.

However, there is a downside to database processing that an organization or individual should consider. The major problem is *cost.* Significant expenses are normally incurred in the following areas:

- **Database Software** Relative to other types of software, a DBMS is expensive. On large computer systems, database packages can cost several thousand dollars.
- **New Hardware** A DBMS often requires a great deal of memory and secondary storage, and accessing records can be time consuming. Thus, some users find it necessary to upgrade to a bigger, more powerful computer system after acquiring a DBMS.
- **Training** Microcomputer-based database management systems are often considerably more difficult to master than file managers, spreadsheets, and word processors. Relating data in different files can be tricky at times. Also, if you want to custom design your own applications with the programming-language facility, prepare for a substantial investment in learning time.
- **Conversion Effort** Moving from a traditional filing system to a database management system can entail considerable conversion expense. Data must be reorganized and programs rewritten. Fortunately, this is a one-time expense.

Cost is not the only problem. Database processing can increase a system's vulnerability to failure. Because the data in the database are highly integrated, a problem with a key element might render the whole system inactive. Despite the disadvantages, however, DBMSs have become immensely popular with both organizations and individuals.

Multimedia Data Management

Multimedia.
A type of computing in which text, graphics, voice, and video are intermixed in applications.

So far in this chapter we've concentrated on data management applications that involve text data. But, as you saw in Figure 10-7, graphic data such as drawings and photographs also need to be managed systematically. Carrying this thought further, there is no reason why voice and video data couldn't be included within a data management application. Applications in which several types of data intermingle in "object-oriented" files or databases are known as **multimedia** data management, or *multimedia,* applications (see the Tomorrow box). Currently, this is still a very new applications area for computers.

The marriage by computer of text, graphics, sound, and video data in a single application is among the most exciting new technological frontiers we will explore in the 1990s. As many of the major hardware and software vendors jockey to position their products in what appears will soon be a multibillion-dollar market, one question remains unanswered: In which applications areas will multimedia take off?

A variety of applications are now being reported in the press. Three of these are discussed in the following paragraphs and several others in Window 6.

TOMORROW

Managing Unstructured Data

A Look at Object-Oriented Databases

Traditionally, data management software has predominantly handled "structured" types of data, that is, those that fall neatly into rows and columns of text. Structured data are the type you've mostly been reading about in this chapter or working with in your computer lab. But new user needs and new trends in technology are creating other, more powerful possibilities that are putting an entirely new face on the data management function.

More types of data are being needed in applications today than ever before. In addition to text, the computer is now being widely used to store diagrams, still photographs, moving images, and voices. These multiple data types and the need to combine them into a multimedia format for applications have given rise to the possibility of *object-oriented databases.*

Here's how object-oriented databases and the objects they store work. In everyday life, various types of data naturally intermingle. A speech, for instance, consists of two types of data: a voice and a moving image of someone talking. Thus, we can consider the entire speech to be an "object," consisting of some voice and some moving-image data.

You can also combine other objects with the speech. If the speech is on the environment, for example, data such as pollution statistics and photographs of defoliated areas may also be useful to tack on to it. Each related batch of statistics and each related group of photographs may also be designated as objects. And, like the speech, any of these objects can be stored by the computer and given a name. All of these objects pertaining to the environment can then be assembled into an object-oriented database.

Just as with other types of databases, objects can be retrieved and cut and pasted as desired. This would enable you to create a customized presentation about the environment. Other people using the database would be able to prepare different presentations, targeted to different audiences.

Object-oriented databases. Storing data as they exist in real life—intermingled.

Note that object-oriented databases go far afield of traditional text databases. The data they deal with are "unstructured" objects, which can be virtually anything—a moving image with people talking, a photograph with a narrative, text with music, and so on. Unlike the conventional text-only database in which each record has a similar format, little similarity may exist between the objects in this format.

Several companies are now in the process of developing their own object-oriented databases. Texas Instruments, for instance, is working on a database that computer manufacturers and other customers can access electronically. The objects contain several types of data on product designs—designs that are now published in catalogs sent to customers. Because the information will be stored on the computer instead of in printed-page form, the online catalog can also have voice and video segments that make it even more useful.

Education and Training Multimedia is increasingly being used as an educational and training tool. Figure 10-10 features a multimedia application at Rensselaer Polytechnic Institute in Troy, New York, in which engineering students have access to a system that shows with text and video clips how plumbing hardware works. A student can "click" (select with a mouse) on a designated icon to pull up windows of related topics or fetch a glossary by clicking on specific words embedded within the text. Education is seen today as a prime area for multimedia product development. Some people have gone so far as to say that multimedia will completely change the way most people learn. Several companies have already started using multimedia to train their employees.

Entertainment Entertainment is another area where multimedia is almost guaranteed to be a success. As computer technology enables more and more types of information to be presented in new ways, a new breed of consumer product has evolved—one that combines some of the best features of a TV show and a book. Say, for instance, you wanted to learn about a subject like the Amazon. You might go to a store, where you would buy an optical disk containing all sorts of text, voice, and picture information about this endangered area. You could take a tour of the river, learn about the wildlife there, or watch a show about the risks posed by the cutting down of forests. The disk also might allow you to temporarily halt any of these shows to pull up statistical data about the things you were viewing or even maps of the area. Such "multimedia books" are now becoming widely available. What's more, microcomputers that cater to

FIGURE 10-10

Multimedia in education and training. Multimedia is increasingly being used as an education and training tool. In the application featured here, college engineering students are provided access to a desktop multimedia system that shows with text and video clips how plumbing hardware works.

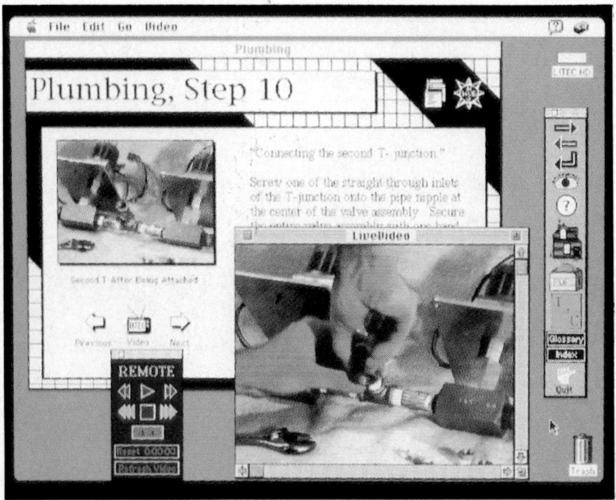

such multimedia applications, called *multimedia PCs*, are also beginning to sell briskly in both the business and consumer marketplaces (see Figure 10-11).

Live television is also likely to be packaged with a multimedia component in the future. Imagine watching a football game and being able to access football trivia or even another game in a window that you could blow up to any size. Multimedia may thus bring us to an age of "intelligent television."

Presentations Organizations are increasingly turning to multimedia to make presentations to important clients and hot business prospects. Knowing that business leaders are used to slick presentations, the city of Aurora, Colorado, recently turned to such an approach to woo new businesses to its area (see User Solution 10-1). Another popular use of multimedia as a presentation tool is in the design of self-guided tours. Texas A&M opted for this approach when it set up a new visitor center. The center features a multimedia presentation that lets visitors use mice at kiosk stations to get information about the school.

Summary and Key Terms

Database management software is widely used to manage large banks of data.

Database Management Systems A **database management system (DBMS)** is a software system that integrates data in storage and provides easy

FIGURE 10-11

Multimedia PCs. Multimedia PCs are microcomputer systems, accompanied by powerful CPU chips, that are configured with special features such as an optical disk unit, speakers, a microphone, and video and sound boards. Both desktop and laptop systems are currently available.

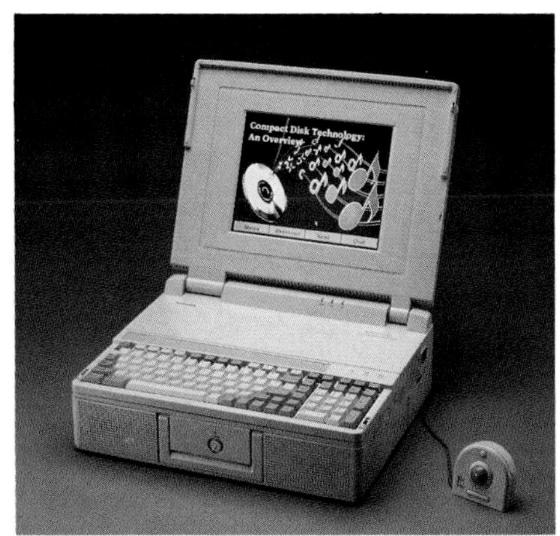

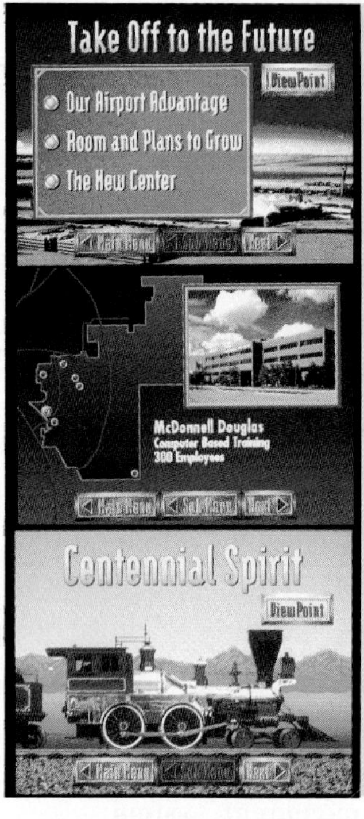

User Solution 10-1

Wooing Execs With Multimedia

Aurora, Colorado, has chosen the high-tech route to marketing its strengths to new businesses. A suburb of Denver—a city in the process of building the world's largest airport—Aurora is expected to benefit enormously by its strategic location. Realizing that business executives react positively to professional-looking presentations by the cities that are courting their companies, Aurora's Economic Development Council used a multimedia approach to showcase its offerings. The menu-driven system contains text, voice, photographs, and videotaped testimonials from business and civic leaders. Information on the area's vital statistics, nearby colleges, and airport and growth plans is also available (see photos). The interactive nature of the presentation allows it to be customized to the specific needs of each audience.

access to them. DBMSs enable concurrent access to data that could conceivably span several files.

The data in a DBMS are placed on disk in a **database,** which is an integrated collection of data.

Database management systems come in several types. **Relational database management systems** are the most common type found on microcomputer systems. These systems are so named because they relate data in various database files by common fields in those files.

Users gain access to the data they need through an easy-to-use *retrieval/update facility* that accompanies the DBMS or through an applications program written with a *programming language facility*. DBMSs also contain *utility programs* such as a data dictionary and a help facility.

One task performed by anyone setting up a database is **data definition**—the process of describing data to the DBMS prior to entering them. The descriptions of these data are used to create **file structures** and a **data dictionary** for the application. Both the file structure and data dictionary contain a **field descriptor** for each field of data in the database.

The process of using the database in some hands-on fashion is called **data manipulation.** Data manipulation encompasses a variety of activities, including the creation of database data, file maintenance, information retrieval (query), reporting, sorting, and calculating. **SQL** (for **Structured Query Language**) is today's de facto standard for information retrieval in relational databases. Database systems are generally one of three common types: relational, hierarchical, and network.

Many microcomputer-oriented DBMSs come with only a single proprietary language that has commands for data definition, retrieval/update, reporting, and programming functions. Large computer systems that use sophisticated DBMSs usually have a special language dedicated to each of these tasks. For example, a **data definition language (DDL)** handles data definition chores, placing key data for applications development and security purposes into a *data dictionary.* A **data manipulation language (DML)** extends the language the programmer normally works with into a database environment. Languages supported by their own DMLs are called **host languages.** A program called a **precompiler** translates DML commands into host-language commands, which in turn can be executed on the regular compilers available at the computer site.

On large computer systems, DBMS packages must also often deal with the data being *distributed* among several sites and with the problem of several users trying to access the database at the same time. To prevent problems associated with conflicting uses, most database systems allow users to place a temporary "lock" on certain blocks of data to ensure that no other modifications to these data will be made during their processing.

A DBMS can offer several advantages over filing systems in which data appearing in independent files cannot be centrally managed and concurrently accessed. Among these advantages are better information, faster response time, lower operating costs, fewer data storage requirements, better data integrity, and better data management. The biggest disadvantage is cost. Costs are normally incurred in the areas of new hardware and software, training, and conversion. Still another disadvantage is greater vulnerability to failure, because database data are integrated and a problem with any key element can render the whole system inactive.

Multimedia Data Management **Multimedia** data management refers to data management in which a combination of text, graphics, voice, and video data are involved in a computing application. Three promising applications areas for multimedia data management are education and training, entertainment, and presentations.

Review Exercises

Fill-in Questions

1. Each database record consists of distinct types of data called ____________.
2. The onscreen form used to create records in a database management environment is often called a(n) ____________.
3. An integrated collection of data is called a(n) ____________.
4. ____________ database management systems are the type of DBMSs typically found on microcomputers.
5. On hierarchical and network database management systems, a knowledgeable professional known as a(n) ____________ often is called on to set up the database for users.

6. The facility that manages characteristics of data and programs in a database environment is called a data ______________.
7. SQL is an acronym for ______________.
8. Applications in which several types of data are intermingled are known as ______________ data management.

Matching Questions

Match each term with the description that fits best.

a. precompiler
b. data definition language (DDL)
c. data manipulation
d. retrieval/update language
e. host language
f. data definition

___ 1. A language used to describe database data.

___ 2. A language supported by a DML (data manipulation language).

___ 3. A translator used to translate DML commands into commands that can be input to a regular language translator.

___ 4. A database software product that permits programmers and nonprogrammers to easily retrieve, add, delete, or modify database data with simple, Englishlike commands.

___ 5. Organizing data in the database so that programmers and users have good access to them, data are stored as efficiently as possible, and the database's security is maintained.

___ 6. A task that can be performed through either a retrieval/update language or a programming language.

Discussion Questions

1. What is the difference between a file and a database?
2. What is a database management system?
3. How do relational database management systems work?
4. What types of data are found in a file structure?
5. What is the difference between data description and data manipulation?
6. How do large database management systems solve the problem of one user trying to use data that are in the process of being updated by someone else?
7. Identify the advantages and disadvantages of database management systems.
8. What is multimedia data management?

Critical Thinking Questions

1. An owner of a small personnel agency is about to purcase a well-known database package to manage a growing client list on a microcomputer system. One of her employees is a computer whiz and has suggested writing the database package himself, to make it better fit the agency's needs. What should the owner do in this situation—say yes, say no, or gather more information?
2. Many people believe that, to the average business, the choice of a particular database management system is much more important than the choice of a particular word processor or a spreadsheet package. What do you think?
3. In the multimedia world of the future, might it be difficult to differentiate a book from a movie? Comment.

WINDOW 6

Multimedia Computing

It May Revolutionize the Way We Deal with Information

Multimedia computing is a technology that might make an orchestra conductor envious of the ordinary user. Press a button, and screens full of information appear on a computer monitor. Press another, and related video images arise from an onscreen window. Press yet another, and related talk or music emerges out of an attached sound system. The possibilities of such a technology, which got started in earnest only in 1987, are almost endless and range from business to entertainment. In this window, we look at some of the environments in which multimedia is currently being applied.

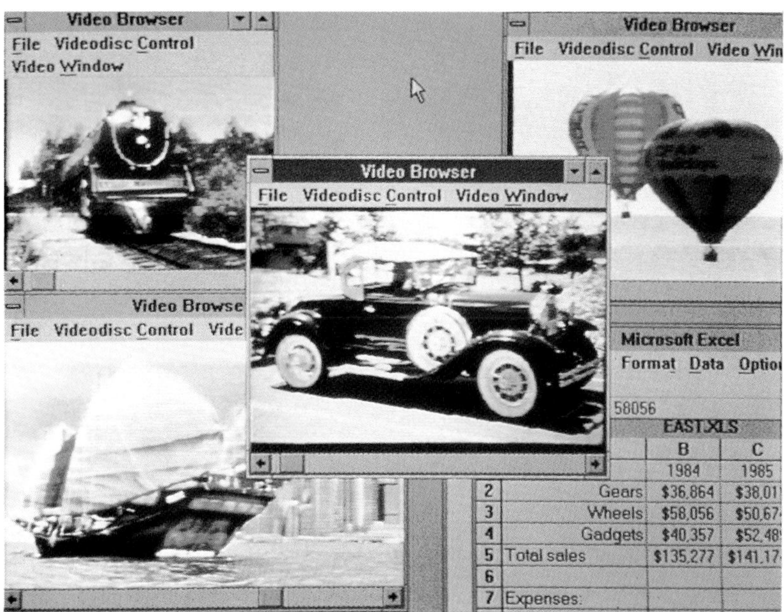

1. Multimedia products enable developers and users to combine the four principal types of data—full-video images, still images, text, and voice—into a single application or use.

Authoring Software

Developers typically begin creating multimedia products with *authoring software*—a special program package designed to put presentations and other multimedia products together quickly.

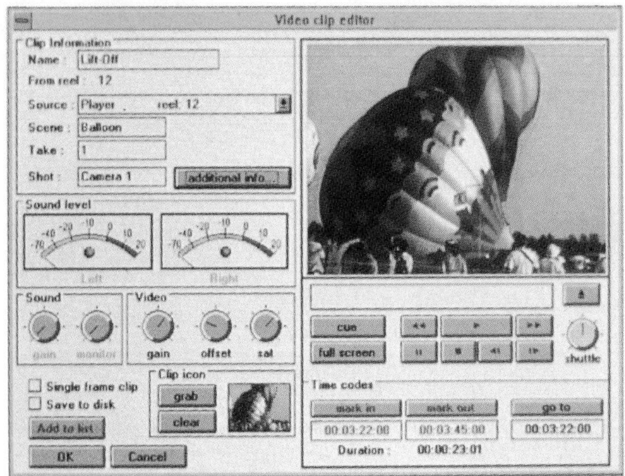

2

2. Authoring software often contains control panels, like the one featured here, to enable developers to adjust settings as they interweave different types of data.

3

3–5. Authoring software is frequently employed by in-house computer professionals—and even end users—to develop important business presentations. Unlike conventional slide shows, multimedia presentations can be customized in real time, enabling the presenter to field questions and explore audience interest areas.

4

5

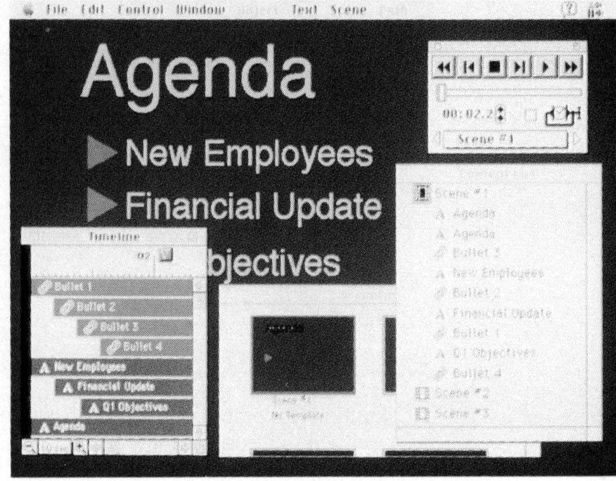

Authoring Application

At Ben & Jerry's, the Vermont ice-cream maker, authoring software was used to prepare a presentation for an interactive, touch-screen kiosk, used by people who come to tour the plant facilities.

6–7. An early step in the kiosk-presentation development was the *storyboard,* which dictates the order in which images are to be run in a full-video sequence. Individual images can be chosen from a window and dragged to the storyboard with a mouse.

6

7

8. Special effects can be added to provide a smooth transition when a new scene sequence replaces another. In the photo here, the developer can choose between a crossfade, wipe, and a zoom.

8

9

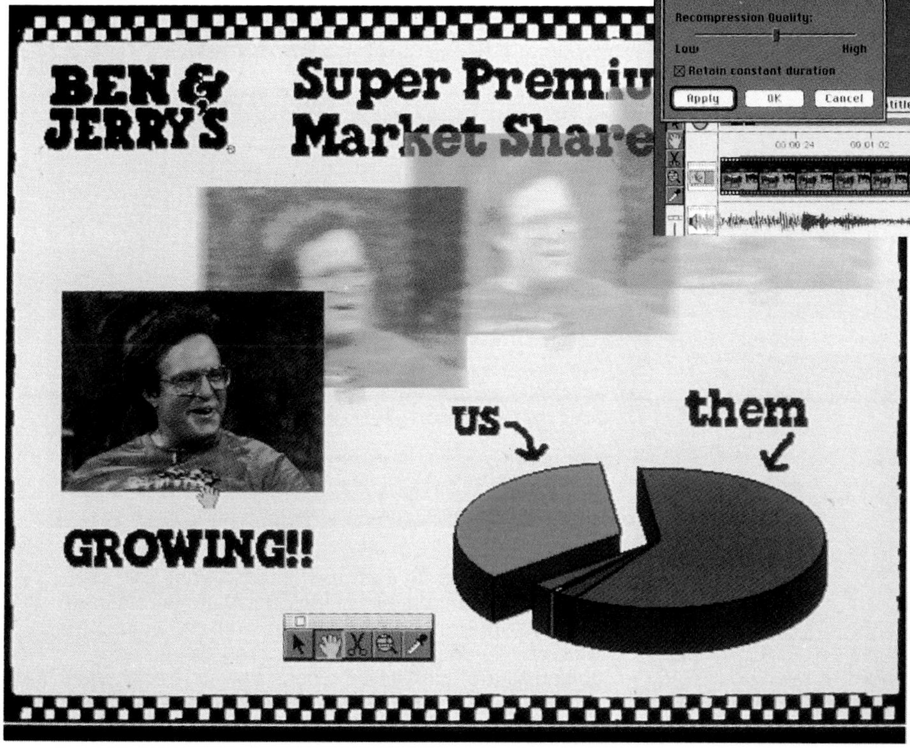

9. This still photo from the final product features a sequence with an interactive video window. At the bottom center of the screen are choices that anyone taking the Ben & Jerry's tour can make during the multimedia presentation.

Books and Magazines

In the entertainment field, compact discs aren't just for music anymore. Now—if your computer has an optical-disk drive—you can read, watch, and listen to books and magazines on it.

Creation Stories

SPIDER WOMAN, PEA-POD MAN, CHAMELEON'S CATCH —AND 90 OTHER TALES TOLD TO EXPLAIN HOW THE WORLD BEGAN AND WHAT HAPPENED NEXT

CD-ROM

MPC

10

10–11. *Creation Stories* is an optical-disk product that uses words and pictures to explain, from a variety of perspectives, how the world was created and how it evolved. In most CD-ROM books and magazines you can access much more than just text and still photos—short audio and video clips kick in when you select certain screen buttons.

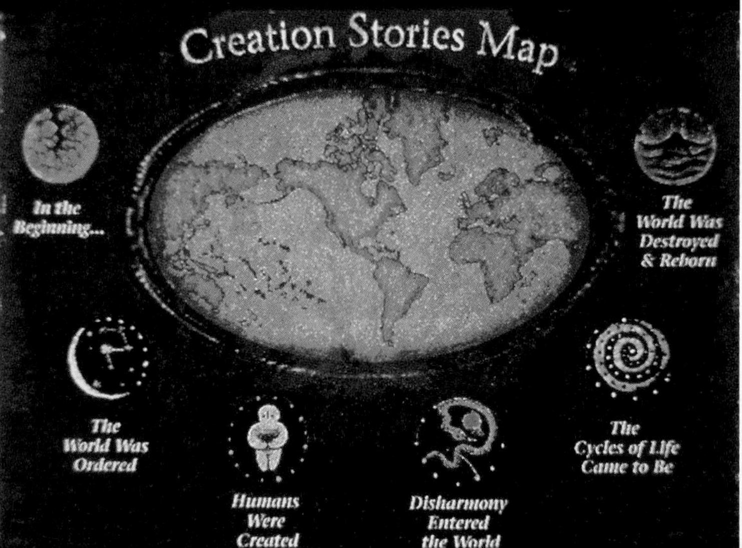

11

13

AT MARS AND JUPITER

A Pattern Unfolds SUBCHAPTERS

In the wake of the Voyager encounters, scientists intent on tracing the evolution of Jupiter's major moons had to return to the drawing boards. Plainly, Kuiper and the theorists who followed in his path had identified only a few of the variables in the cosmic equation that produced the Galileans and other regular satellite systems. As NASA's Bradford Smith put it, the Voyager data "shattered the dogma that the worlds of the outer solar system had been shaped by similar, predictable, and rather uninteresting processes." Yet the new picture was

MENU ECLIPSE MOON GLOSSARY 87 of 97

12

AT MARS AND JUPITER

A Pattern Unfolds SUBCHAPTERS

MENU ECLIPSE MOON GLOSSARY 87 of 97

12–13. Shown here are two images from *The View From Earth*, an optical-disk product that contains the contents of three books from the *Voyage Through the Universe* hardbound-book series. You can go on a guided tour of planets or access specific information through menus, a glossary, and an index.

14

15

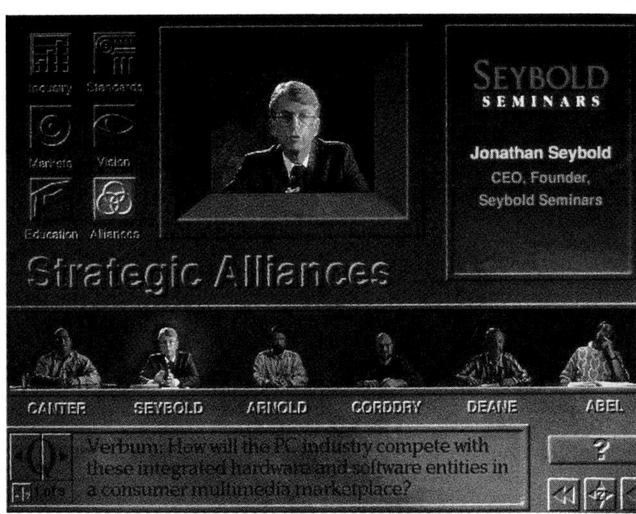

14–15. *Verbum* magazine is a CD-ROM product targeted to people interested in computer technology. Users can read about specific technologies, listen to roundtable discussions featuring industry authorities, pull up computer-generated art and animated features, listen to computer-generated music, and preview demonstration programs of major software products.

16

Travel and Tourism

In industries such as travel and real estate, multimedia computing provides potential clients the ability to take tours without ever leaving the host computer system.

16. Users can tour the Caribbean by selecting video, audio, and text segments.

Music

For several years, stereo buffs have enjoyed the benefits of compact-disc technology. The most recent crop of computer-based CD-ROM products goes a step further—you can both listen to music and read about it at the same time.

17

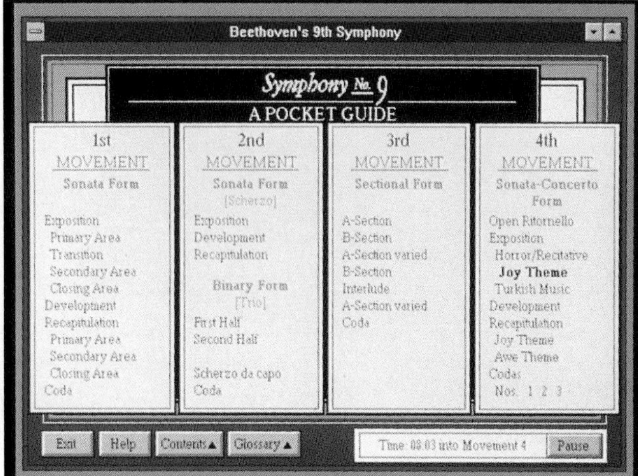

18

17–19. Microsoft's *Multimedia Beethoven* is a CD-ROM product featuring Beethoven's Ninth Symphony, as performed by the Vienna Philharmonic. Users can also listen to commentary and take a historical journey into Beethoven's life and times.

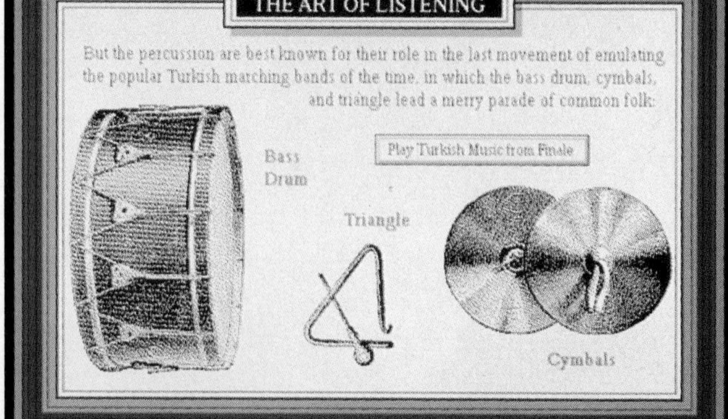

19

20

20–22. An online training application refers auto technicians to a set of manuals and lets them pull up video segments showing how certain types of repairs are done.

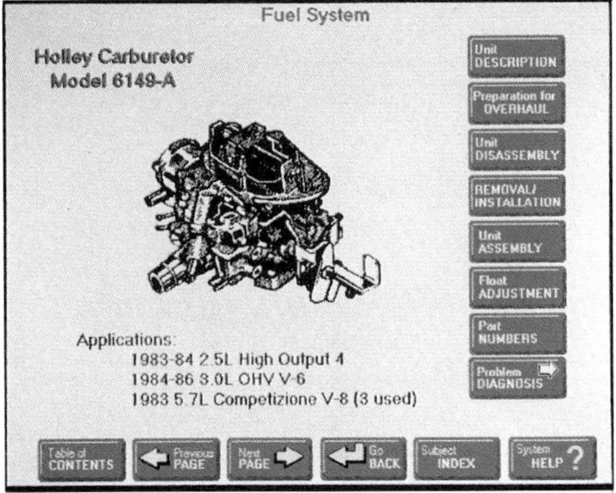

21

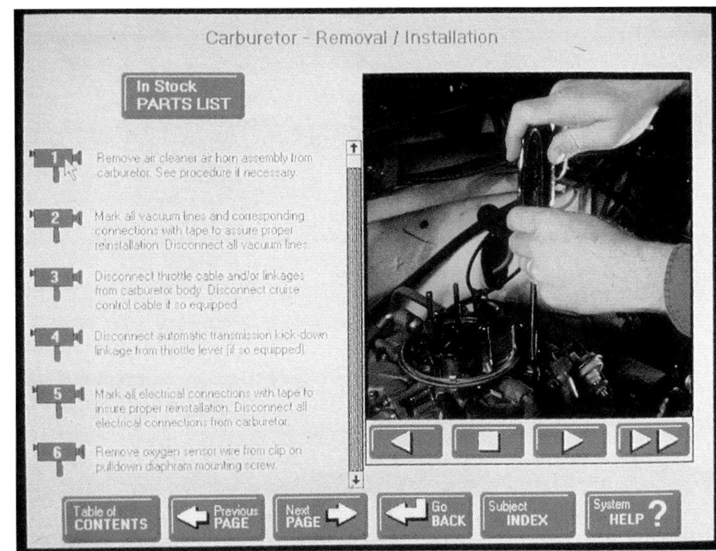

22

Education and Training

Multimedia computing is expected to make major inroads in the fields of education and training during the next several years. Someday soon, many of the books students use in school may also come with multimedia disk products.

23. Many companies are now turning to multimedia technology as a training and orientation tool for new hires, as is shown in this multimedia training application for employees of Marriott Corporation.

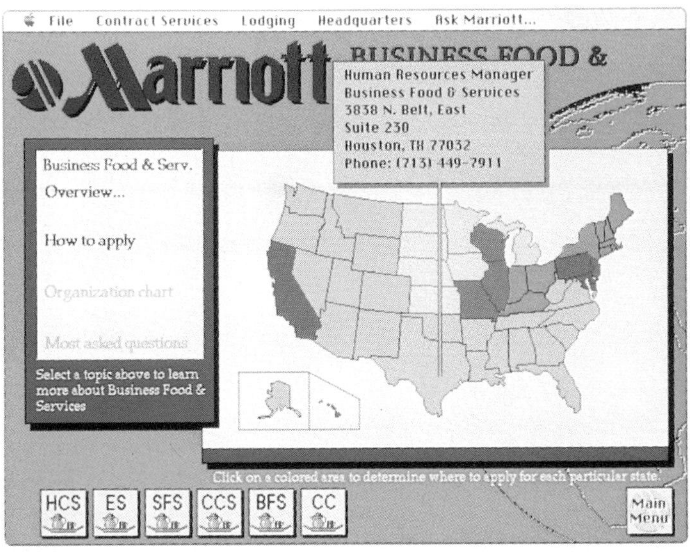

23

M O D U L E **E**

Information Systems

This module integrates several concepts from earlier chapters, tying together the parts of a computer system that involve hardware, software, data, people, and procedures.

Chapters 11 and 12 cover systems development and program development in organizations, respectively. In Chapter 11, we'll address types of systems, the various ways in which organizations build systems, and the sorts of activities performed and kinds of people involved in system building. In Chapter 12, we'll look in depth at applications software development and programming languages. Here, you'll learn about some of the tools used by computer professionals to design and code computer programs as well as the variety of languages commercially available.

Chapter 13 covers many of the things you should know about microcomputer systems if you decide to acquire one for your own use. Today, unprecedented numbers of people are purchasing their own microcomputer systems or being assigned to use one, making knowledge in this area essential for virtually everyone.

Developing Business Systems

11

How do organizations set up computer systems for use in their factories and offices? As Chapter 11 will explain, it's through a process called systems development, in which computer professionals, end users, and management collaborate to methodically weigh alternatives.

OUTLINE

Overview
On Systems
Business Systems
- Transaction Processing Systems
- Information Systems
- Office Systems
- Design and Manufacturing Systems
- Artificial Intelligence

Responsibility for Systems Development
- The Information Systems Department
- Outsourcing

The Systems Development Life Cycle
- The Preliminary Investigation
- Systems Analysis
- System Design
- System Acquisition
- System Implementation

Approaches to Systems Development
- The Traditional Approach
- Prototyping
- End-User Development

LEARNING OBJECTIVES

After completing this chapter, you will be able to:

1. Explain what a system is.
2. Describe several types of computer systems commonly found in business.
3. Define the roles of various people and information-systems areas involved in the systems development process.
4. Identify and describe the components of the systems development life cycle (SDLC).
5. Describe several approaches used to develop systems.

Overview

In previous chapters we considered primarily hardware and software. Here we turn to the process of putting together these elements into complete computer systems.

All organizations have various sorts of systems—for example, systems that attend to accounting activities such as sending out bills and processing payrolls; systems that provide information to help managers make decisions; systems for word processing and electronic-mail tasks; systems that help run factories efficiently; and so on. Such systems require considerable effort to design, build, and maintain. The process that includes planning and implementing systems is called *systems development*.

Unfortunately, since no two situations are exactly alike, there is no surefire formula for successful systems development. A procedure that works well in one situation may fail in another. These facts notwithstanding, there is a set of general principles that, if understood, will enhance the likelihood of the system's success. Those principles are the subject of this chapter.

The chapter opens with a general discussion of systems and systems development. Then we cover the types of systems commonly found in business. From there we turn to the computer professionals who are hired to develop systems in organizations and consider some of their primary responsibilities. Then we look at the systems development life cycle—the set of activities that are at the heart of every serious systems-building effort. Chapter 11 concludes with a discussion of the major approaches to systems development.

On Systems

System.
A collection of elements and procedures that interact to accomplish a goal.

A **system** is a collection of elements and procedures that interact to accomplish a goal. A football game, for example, is played according to a system. It consists of a collection of elements (two teams, a playing field, referees) and procedures (the rules of the game) that interact to determine which team is the winner. A transit system is a collection of people, machines, work rules, fares, and schedules that get people from one place to another. Similarly, a computer system is a collection of people, hardware, software, data, and procedures that interact to perform information processing tasks.

The function of many systems, whether manual or computerized, is to keep an organization well managed and running smoothly. Systems are created and altered in response to changing needs within an organization and shifting conditions in its surrounding environment. When problems arise in an existing system or a new system is needed, systems development comes into play. **Systems development** is a process that consists of analyzing an applications environment, designing a new system or making modifications to an old one, acquiring needed hardware and software, and getting the new or modified system to work (see the Tomorrow box).

Systems development.
The ongoing process of improving ways of doing work.

Systems development may be required for any of a number of reasons. New laws may call for the collection of data never before assembled; for example, the government may require new data on health-care benefits. The introduction of new technology, especially new computer technology, may prompt wholesale revision of a system. Or, as is the trend today, a company may decide to convert

TOMORROW

Re-Engineering

The High-Tech Equivalent of Putting the Horse before the Cart

In many ways, re-engineering is just old wine in a new bottle. But it's catching businesses and the information processing community by storm. And, who knows? It might become one of the big buzzwords of the 1990s.

Re-engineering is so simple it should have been obvious long ago. Here's the idea behind it: Instead of using computers to automate the way a process has always been performed, with re-engineering you first change the process to the way it really should work, applying computing power to the new system, if appropriate. In other words, rather than blindly going out and buying a new batch of hardware and software to help manufacture widgets faster on an assembly line, consider first that maybe you should be building widgets another way. That or be in the widget-design business instead.

Banc One Mortgage is one company that decided to re-engineer the way it performed its work before applying technology. In the 1980s, Banc One followed the traditional, assembly-line approach to processing loans. A loan application would move from one desk to another, then another, and so on, in a serial fashion. As the bank's mortgage business grew, the loan processing began to take longer and longer. But instead of hiring more people and bringing in more desks and computers, the bank began a team approach to process the loans instead. Today, groups of about 17 employees using networked computers convene electronically to process all aspects of a particular application at once. The bank says that not only is the job done faster, but workers also become cross-trained in each others' jobs.

Re-engineering. The art of rethinking what you're doing before acquiring technology to do it faster.

On a larger scale, many companies have re-engineered across the board to deal with the new economics of the 1990s. IBM, which began restructuring in the late 1980s, is a prime example. The computer giant went to a "flatter" organization by cutting out layer upon layer of middle management. The move eliminated a lot of expensive bureaucracy and provided IBM with an ability to respond much more quickly to customers and to changes in the business climate.

It's hard to call re-engineering a trend. Ideally, it should be the first step in every system-building process. No matter how you slice it, looking at re-engineering possibilities up front is the textbook way to think about systems development. Tomorrow's information system is not going to get you very far if you're trying to improve yesterday's process. Put another way, just running a race faster is not going to make you victorious if you're in the wrong race.

certain applications into a global, networked environment. These and other kinds of pressure often can bring about major changes in the systems by which work is done in an organization.

Business Systems

Undoubtedly, you've already encountered many types of business systems. When you go into the supermarket, you generally see in use electronic cash registers and various hand-held or laser scanning devices that are obviously a part of some supermarket system. Or, when you've registered for classes, perhaps you've observed someone at a display device checking to see whether a certain class you want to take is still open or whether you've paid all your bills—apparently as part of a registration system.

While there are hundreds of "types" of computer systems in existence today, many of those in business and most other organizations fall into one or more of four categories: transaction processing systems, information systems, office systems, and design and manufacturing systems. Here we'll look more closely at each of these. We will also explore the area of artificial intelligence, which can impart to a system certain characteristics that one would normally attribute to humans.

Transaction Processing Systems

Virtually every business must support a number of routine operations, most of which involve some form of tedious recordkeeping. These operations, such as payroll and accounts receivable, were some of the earliest commercial applications of computers in organizations and are still among the most important. Because these systems heavily involve processing of business transactions—such as paying employees, recording customer purchases and payments, and recording vendor receipts and payments—they are called **transaction processing systems** (see Figure 11-1).

Transaction processing system. A system that handles an organization's business transactions.

FIGURE 11-1

Transaction processing. Transaction processing systems are the backbone of most businesses. They track goods being sold, record payments made for cash or credit, and monitor inventory levels and orders of stock.

Some of the functions that one commonly finds as part of a transaction processing system are discussed below.

Payroll *Payroll programs* compute deductions, subtract them from gross earnings, and write paychecks to employees for the remainder. These programs also contain routines that prepare reports for management and for taxing agencies of the federal, state, and local governments.

Accounts Receivable The term *accounts receivable* refers to the amounts owed by customers who have made purchases on credit. Accounts receivable programs are charged with keeping track of customers' purchases, payments, and account balances. They also calculate and print customer statements and provide information to management. Other output includes sales analyses, which describe changing patterns of products and sales, as well as detailed or summary reports on current and past-due accounts.

Accounts Payable The term *accounts payable* refers to the money a company owes to other companies for the goods and services it has received. Accounts payable programs keep track of bills and often generate checks to pay them. They record who gets paid and when, handle cash disbursements, and advise managers whether they should accept discounts offered by vendors in return for early payment.

Order Entry Many businesses handle some type of order processing on a daily basis. Customers either call in orders by phone, send in written orders by ordinary mail or by computer, or place orders in person. The programs that record and help manage such transactions are called *order-entry software*.

Inventory Control The units of products that a company has in stock to sell at a given moment are called its inventory. *Inventory control programs* closely monitor the number of units of each product in inventory and ensure that reasonable quantities of products are maintained.

General Ledger *General ledger (G/L) programs* keep track of all financial summaries, including those originating from payroll, accounts receivable, accounts payable, and other sources (see Figure 11-2). They also ensure that the company's books balance properly. G/L programs also produce accounting reports such as income statements, balance sheets, and general ledger balances.

Information Systems

During the early days of commercial computing, businesses purchased computers almost exclusively to perform routine transaction processing tasks. Used in this way, the computer could cut clerical expenses considerably. However, as time passed, it became apparent that the computer could do much more than replace clerks. It could also provide information to assist management in its decision-making role.

A system that generates information for use by decision makers is called an **information system.** With an information system, management can incorporate much more information into decisions and spend less time gathering it. As a

Information system. A system designed to provide information to managers to enable them to make decisions.

FIGURE 11-2

The relationship among transaction processing systems.

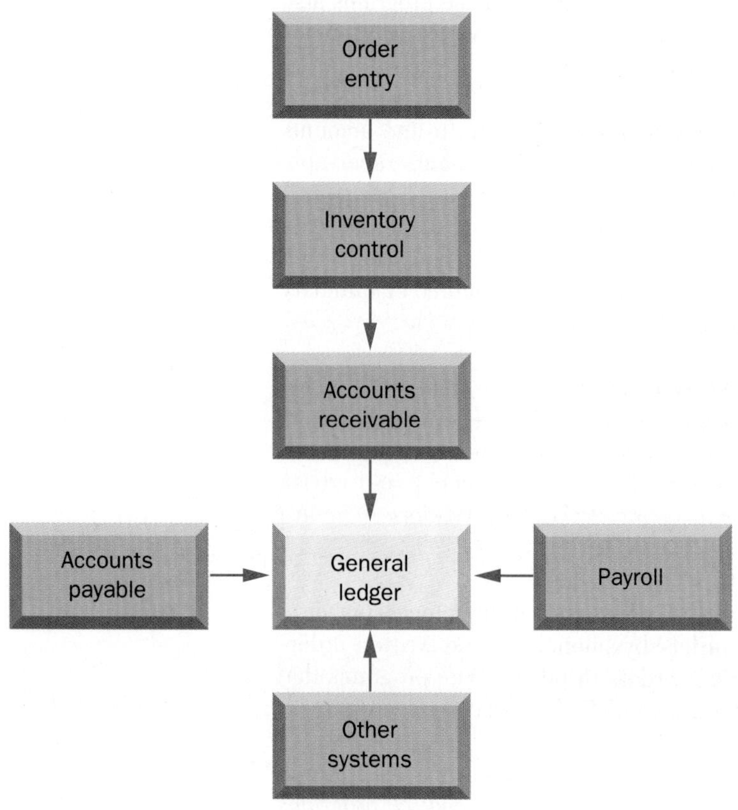

result, managers have more time to do the things they do best—think creatively and interact with people.

Two major types of information systems are information reporting systems and decision support systems. Here, we discuss both, along with two special types of decision support systems—those targeted to worker groups and those aimed at executives.

Information reporting system.
An information system whose principal outputs are preformatted reports.

Information Reporting Systems **Information reporting systems** were the first type of information system and are still widely used. They provide management with preselected types of information, generally in the form of computer-generated reports. The types of information that some managers receive are preplanned, just like the information you see on your monthly checking account statements. The individual *values* on your statements, such as check numbers and amounts, may change from month to month, but the *types* of information you receive remain the same. Also, you and every other person mailed checking account statements by your bank receive exactly the same type of information.

Many information reporting systems provide managers with information that is a by-product of the data generated through transaction processing.

Decision Support Systems During the 1970s, many companies began to call for systems that could field questions from managers. Such systems were expected to be particularly useful to top-level managers, whose requirements for information are somewhat unpredictable and unstructured. In response, the computer industry developed the decision support system.

A **decision support system (DSS)** helps people organize and analyze their own decision-making information. Thus, a "sales support system" is the name typically given to a DSS aimed at the special decision-making needs of salespeople or marketing personnel. A "fire-suppression support system" might be a DSS targeted to helping the director of a forest area develop specific strategies for fighting forest fires.

Decision support system (DSS).
A system that provides tools and capabilities to managers to help them satisfy their own information needs.

Let's put DSSs into perspective with an example. To assist with making product pricing decisions, a sales manager uses a DSS that has been set up on a microcomputer system. At the keyboard, the manager first requests the price of an item. Then he or she decides to ask for the average price of several other items, and then for the inventory turnover of yet a different item. A model may be used to predict the sales volume of items five years into the future. The manager can pose questions as the need evolves and receive answers at once. At the end of the interactive session, the manager uses the DSS to prepare a summary of important findings and some bar charts for a meeting. The next time the manager uses the DSS, other types of information may be collected and analyzed.

Generally, the DSS is built from a number of other productivity software tools that we have covered in this text. For instance, the sales manager might acquire a spreadsheet package or a database management system to build the sales support system just described. Figure 11-3 illustrates a decision support system at work.

Group Decision Support Systems A relatively recent development in the DSS area has been the emergence of the **group decision support system (GDSS).** A GDSS is a decision support system in which several people routinely interact through a computer network in order to solve common problems. In fields such as newspaper publishing, architectural design, insurance, and banking, a GDSS allows workers to share ideas and collaborate on decisions through computer and communications technology. Workers can electronically route their outputs to other workers in the chain and even meet electronically when there is a bottleneck of some sort. An example of this computer-age phenomenon is described in User Solution 11-1. The GDSS is sometimes referred to by the term **workgroup computing.**

Group decision support system (GDSS).
A decision support system in which several people routinely interact through a computer network to solve common problems. Also sometimes called **workgroup computing.**

Executive Information Systems **Executive information systems (EISs)** are DSSs customized to meet the special needs of individual executives—those people at the highest organizational level. As some executives see it, the business world today is so competitive and fast paced that they need instant

Executive information system (EIS).
A decision support system that is tailored to the needs of a specific, top-level individual in an organization.

FIGURE 11-3

Decision support systems (DSSs). DSSs help managers analyze business data and prepare presentation materials for meetings at their own desktop workstations.

access to fresh information. Among executives' favorite applications are using database management systems to access corporate and financial data, using electronic mail systems to streamline contact with subordinates, and using customized spreadsheet programs to display important ratios and trends in a graphical format. Because many executives can't type, many of them require easy-to-learn, easy-to-use graphical interfaces (see Figure 11-4). With the right type of a system, it simply takes some pointing and, perhaps, a few keystrokes or mouse clicks to get what they want in exactly the form they require.

Office Systems

Office automation (OA). The use of computer-based, office-oriented technologies such as word processing, desktop publishing, electronic mail, video teleconferencing, and the like.

In recent years, computer technology has been applied to the task of increasing productivity in the office. The term **office automation (OA)** has been coined to describe this trend. Automating the office can be done through a wide variety of technologies and processing techniques, several of which are discussed below.

Document Processing *Document processing* refers to the use of computer technology in the preparation of text-intensive documents such as letters, manuscripts, legal documents, articles, books, restaurant menus, reports, and the like. Two principal document-processing tools—word processing and desktop publishing—were covered extensively in Chapter 8.

Electronic mail. A facility that enables users to send letters, memos, documents, and the like from one hardware device to another.

Electronic Mail **Electronic mail** (or E-mail) makes it possible to send informative messages and documents from one terminal or computer system to another. Two familiar examples of electronic mail are the *fax (facsimile) machine*,

U s e r   S o l u t i o n   1 1 – 1

A GDSS Helps Insurers

In the insurance field, several photos and forms are often needed to process an accident claim. An adjuster may take a picture of a damaged car and prepare an adjustment form. An estimate and a claim form will also have to be filled out and filed. Gradually, a dossier on each accident will be developed. Many large insurance firms have turned to group decision support systems to make this complex process much simpler. All of these initial documents are read into the computer system with an image scanner and put into a form that can be annotated, processed, and shared electronically by people working over a network in the claims department. The claims-department employees can each in turn call up the file, sign off on certain documents, and add other documents. They can also "meet," using their workstations, to make joint decisions on particular cases. Processing claims in this way can be done faster and more cost effectively, with minimal chance of documents being lost, and with better service to the policyholder, too.

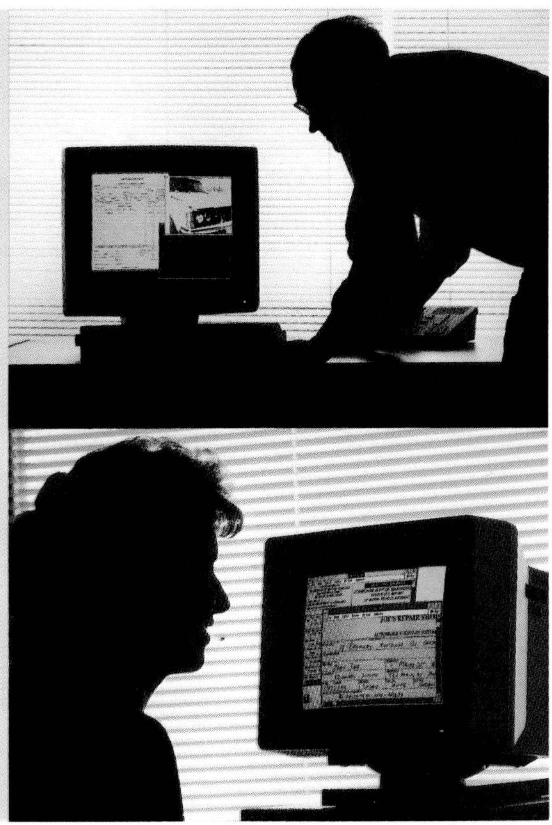

F I G U R E   11 - 4

Executive information systems (EISs). EISs are DSSs customized to meet the needs of executives, many of whom are not technologically sophisticated. Consequently, EISs are usually characterized by (a) easy-to-use graphic interfaces and (b) simplified procedures for making database queries.

(a)

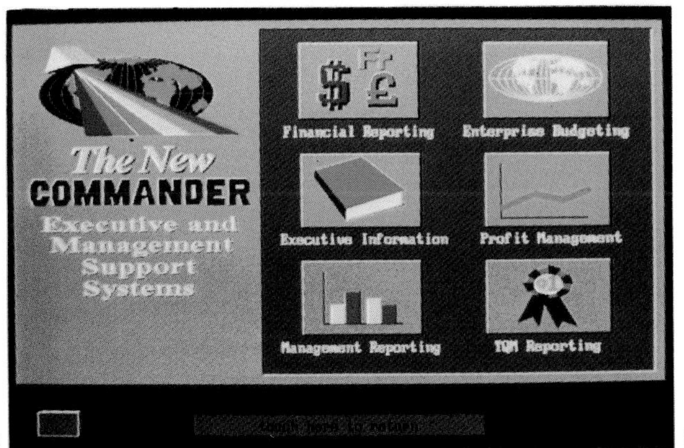

(b)

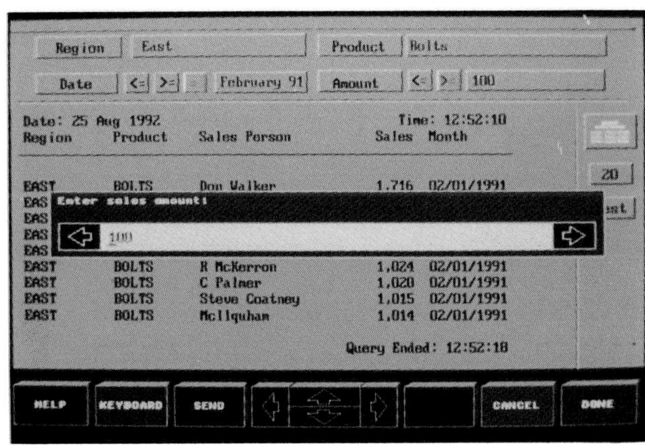

(such as the one pictured in Figure 6-4), which is used to transmit images of hard-copy documents over the phone wires, and *electronic mailboxes*, which are computer files that are set up to store any transmitted message that can be created in or converted to electronic form.

Desk Accessories *Desk accessories*, or *desktop organizers*, are packages that provide the electronic equivalent of features commonly found on an office desktop. Desk accessory software varies from vendor to vendor, but many of them offer such features as a calendar (see Figure 11-5), clock, calculator, and Rolodex-type file. Often, the feature is implemented in a window, which appears when a specific sequence of keys is activated.

Decision Support Tools Since many decisions are made by white-collar workers, in the office, it's understandable that many decision support systems are found in the office. Among the tools that are useful in such a setting are spreadsheets, presentation graphics, plotters and laser printers, color monitors, and relational database systems. All of these software and hardware tools have been discussed earlier in the book and have contributed to streamlining life at the office.

FIGURE 11-5

Desk accessory. Lotus Development Corporation's Organizer package is a desk accessory that incorporates a calendar, a to-do list, a planner, an address book, and electronic-mail capability.

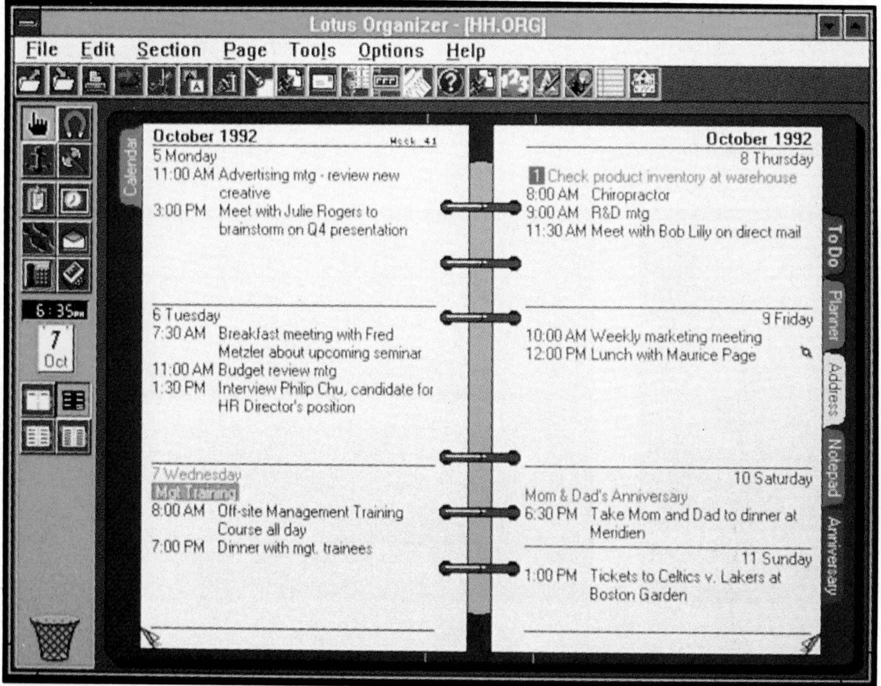

Teleconferencing **Teleconferencing** makes it possible for a group of people to meet electronically, thereby avoiding the time and expense they would incur if they were to physically get together in one spot (see Figure 11-6). *Audio teleconferencing*—also known as the conference phone call—allows a meeting to take place between several people on a phone system. *Video teleconferencing* systems, on the other hand, permit participants to see each other on video screens as well as to hear each other. *Computer teleconferencing*, which takes place at computer workstations, allows a conference to develop through messages sent to electronic mailboxes.

Teleconferencing. Using computer and communications technology to carry out a meeting in which not all the participants need be present at the same place or time.

Today, many teleconferencing sessions involve a combination of audio, video, and computer components. Desktop tools have also recently become available that enable teleconferencing participants to flip to images and point to parts of them or annotate them in real time (see Figure 11-7). Travel savings notwithstanding, the biggest benefit to teleconferencing is something most technology experts never anticipated—the ability to quickly bring together company expertise to solve problems.

Electronic Document Handling *Electronic document handling*, sometimes called *image processing*, refers to the use of computer systems to store and manipulate electronic copies of form documents and the like. User Solution 11-1, which describes electronic images of insurance forms being accessed in an office environment, is an excellent example of this technology in use. Relative to paper copies of documents, electronic documents are cheaper to handle, capable of being instantaneously transmitted, and far less likely to get misplaced or be mismanaged. Also, several people in different locations can access the same documents simultaneously.

FIGURE 11-6

Teleconferencing. Teleconferencing is available for (a) large groups in specially equipped conference rooms and (b) individuals and smaller groups at the desktop level. The biggest benefit to teleconferencing is its ability to bring problem-solving expertise together quickly.

(a)

(b)

FIGURE 11-7

Desktop teleconferencing tools. Sophisticated electronic packages are available that let conference users work with images in real time, using pointing and annotating tools.

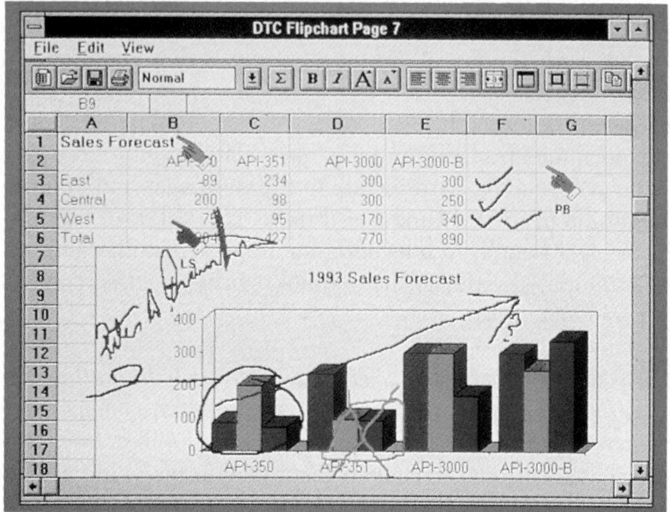

Telecommuting.
Working at home and being connected by means of electronic devices to other workers at remote locations.

Telecommuting **Telecommuting** is the term used to describe people working at home and linking up to their employers through a desktop workstation, laptop computer, fax machine, and/or another type of computer-age tool. Many typists and computer programmers, for example, telecommute to their jobs, perhaps because they prefer to do so or because they are more productive at home. Telecommuting can save workers both the time and expense involved in traveling to work. It can also save businesses the expense of maintaining office and parking space. For instance, at many consulting firms, where several employees can be expected to be on the road at any given time, regular offices aren't assigned; instead, employees book office space like hotel rooms. On the negative side, telecommuting limits the interpersonal contact that often makes working in an office lively and productive.

Design and Manufacturing Systems

Computers are widely used in business to improve productivity both at the design stage—through computer-aided design (CAD)—and at the manufacturing stage—through computer-aided manufacturing (CAM). With technology becoming ever more sophisticated, serious attempts have been made recently to more closely integrate design, manufacturing, and other business functions—a concept known as computer-integrated manufacturing (CIM).

Computer-aided design (CAD).
A general term applied to the use of computer technology to automate design functions.

Computer-Aided Design (CAD) Using **computer-aided design (CAD)**, product designers can dramatically reduce the time they spend at the drawing board." For example, using light pens and specialized graphics workstations (see Figure 11-8), engineers can sketch ideas directly into the computer system, which can then be instructed to analyze the proposed design in terms of how well it meets a number of design criteria. Taking into account the subsequent output of the computer, the designer can modify the drawings until a desirable design is achieved. Before the arrival of CAD, the designer had to produce by hand preliminary sketches and then advanced designs, representing refinements on the sketches. After models were built and tested, the designer had to prepare production drawings, which were used to build the equipment needed to manufacture the new product, whether it was a truck or a new toaster. Today, computer-aided assistance with all of these tasks is fairly common. CAD is especially helpful in the design of products such as automobiles, aircraft, ships, buildings, electrical circuits (including computer chips), and even running shoes. Window 7 provides several examples that provide insight into how CAD is implemented in design environments.

Computer-Aided Manufacturing (CAM) Computer applications are not limited to only the design phases of product development. In fact, computers were used on the factory floor well before engineers used them interactively for design. With each passing day, more and more of the actual process of production on the factory floor is becoming computerized.

Computer-aided manufacturing (CAM) includes the use of computers to help manage manufacturing operations and to control machinery used in manufacturing processes. One example is a system that observes production in an oil refinery, performs calculations, and opens and shuts appropriate valves

Computer-aided manufacturing (CAM). A general term applied to the use of computer technology to automate manufacturing functions.

FIGURE 11-8

Computer-aided design (CAD). Perhaps no field has been altered more by CAD than architecture. Using computers, any type of building can be (a) automatically designed and tested for safety and (b) rendered with realistic aesthetic effects.

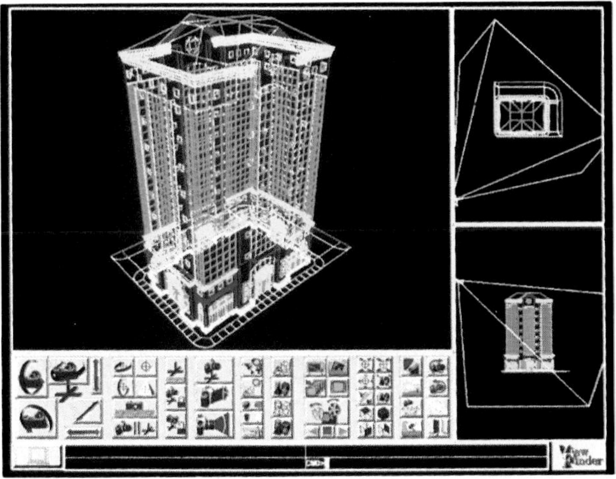

(a)

(b)

when necessary. Another system, commonly used in the steel industry, works from preprogrammed specifications to automatically perform the shaping and assembly of steel parts. Increasingly, robots are used to carry out processes once solely in the human domain (see Figure 11-9). CAM is also widely employed to build cars and ships, monitor power plants, manufacture food and chemicals, and perform a number of other functions.

Computer-integrated manufacturing (CIM). The use of technology to tie together CAD, CAM, and other business systems.

Computer-Integrated Manufacturing (CIM) Over the last few years serious efforts have been afoot to implement **computer-integrated manufacturing (CIM)** systems. The idea behind CIM is to tie together CAD, CAM, and other business activities (see Figure 11-10).

Here's how CIM might work: A large auto distributorship calls an auto manufacturer to check out the feasibility of changing a styling detail on 500 cars that are to be produced next month. The CAD part of the integrated system checks out the design change to see if it can be done and, also, what types of assembly-line changes are necessary. The CAD subsystem then automatically routes the information it has come up with to computers on the factory floor—which determine if the assembly line can make the shift and if new parts can be made available on time. To find out about the availability of the new parts, the factory computers may have to call up the computers of parts suppliers, which are also integrated into the system. Finally, all of the information is forwarded to accounting-department computers, which calculate the cost impact of the change.

In the CIM system just described, the distributor has the required information within a short period. Without CIM, such a request may take days or weeks

FIGURE 11-9

Robots at work. Robots take on jobs that are too physically demanding, time consuming, monotonous, dangerous, or expensive for humans to perform. (a) A robot helping to assemble a laptop computer at an IBM plant. (b) A robotic arm selecting a tape cartridge.

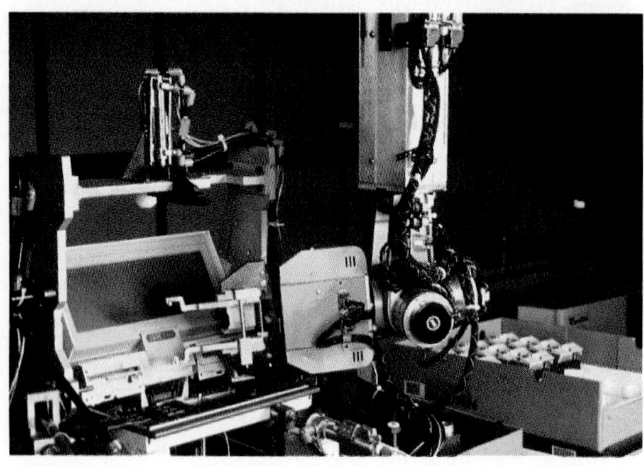

(a)

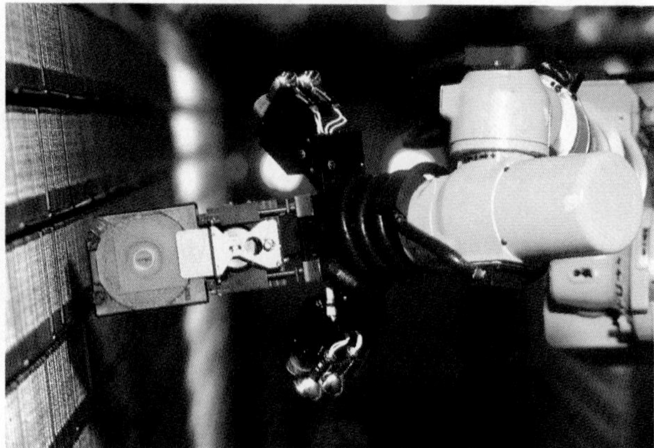

(b)

FIGURE 11-10

Computer-integrated manufacturing (CIM). CIM enables CAD, CAM, and other business activities to be tied together by computers. In the auto industry, CIM makes it possible to quickly check the effect of a design change on parts inventories, production schedules, and costs.

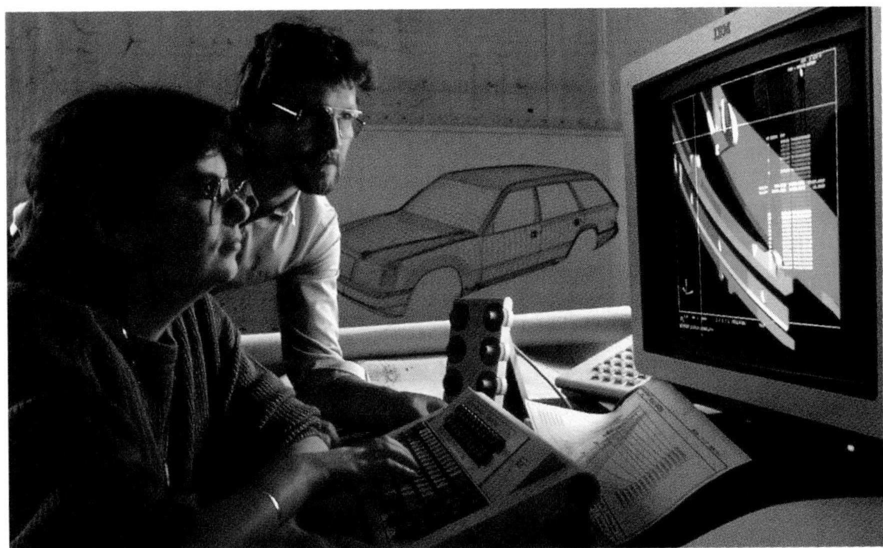

for a human to answer. Human labor is expensive and carries with it a greater chance of error. Today, with many organizations having thousands of computers and there being so many ways to tie together information from these computers usefully, some level of integration is a necessity.

Artificial Intelligence

A computer is a device that, given some instructions, can perform work at extremely fast speeds, drawing upon a large memory. It can also be programmed with a set of rules or guidelines—enabling it to draw certain types of conclusions based on the input it receives. A good deal of human mental activity involves these very processes. For this reason, the ability of computer systems to perform in ways that would be considered intelligent if observed in humans is commonly referred to as **artificial intelligence (AI).**

Today, the four main areas of AI are expert systems, natural languages, vision systems, and robotics.

Artificial intelligence (AI). The ability of a machine to perform actions that are characteristic of human intelligence, such as reasoning and learning.

Expert system. A program or computer system that provides the type of advice that would be expected of a human expert.

Expert Systems **Expert systems** are programs that provide the type of advice that would normally be expected from a human expert. In medicine, for instance, an expert system might be used to incorporate the thinking patterns of some of the world's leading doctors. For example, the system might be given a configuration of symptoms exhibited by a patient. If these symptoms might lead to the diagnosis of a disease the program knows something about, the program might ask the attending physician for further information about specfic details. Ultimately, through questioning and checking the patient's condition against a large database of successfully diagnosed cases, the program might draw conclusions that the attending physician may never have otherwise reached—and very quickly, no less.

Expert systems have enormous applications potential in business, where they can be used to capture the knowledge of expert business professionals into an active form and subsequently can be used to improve decision making within the firm or to train individuals. Today, the application of expert systems to the solution of business problems is just beginning to be felt. Figure 11-11 shows a number of present and proposed applications for expert systems in business. Feature 11-1 describes an expert-system technology called neural networks.

Natural Languages One of the greatest challenges currently facing scientists in the field of AI is to equip computer systems with the ability to communicate in *natural languages*—English, Spanish, French, Japanese, and so forth. Unfortunately, this challenge is not easily met. People have personalized ways of communicating, and the meaning of words varies with the context in which they are used. Also, the rules people employ to reach an understanding of what others are saying are highly complex and still not well understood by language

FIGURE 11-11

Business examples of expert systems. Within the coming decade, say industry analysts, expert system routines will become standard items in many software products.

Business Area	Application
Tax accounting	Assisting tax accountants by providing advice on the best tax treatment for an individual or corporation
Repair	Assisting machine repairpeople by providing expert diagnosis of malfunctions
Insurance sales	Helping an insurance agent tailor an insurance package to a client, given the client's insurance, investment, financial planning, and tax needs
Portfolio planning	Determining the best securities portfolio for a client, given the client's growth and equity objectives
Manufacturing	Finding the best way to design, produce, stock, and ship a product
System design	Determining the optimal hardware and software configuration to meet a set of user requirements
Multinational planning	Providing expert advice on whether a given business strategy will work in different countries, each with its own laws and customs
Government tax auditing	Using a complex set of criteria and a knowledge base of past audit cases to decide which individuals and companies to audit to maximize overall return
Credit authorization	Deciding whether to grant credit to individuals and companies based on both their past histories and other similar credit cases
Training	Putting newly hired employees into computer-simulated situations in which their performance is aided by or compared with experts

researchers. These hurdles notwithstanding, researchers have made some big strides in the direction of getting computers to listen to and respond in natural languages.

Vision Systems *Vision systems* enable computer-controlled devices to "see." A vision system might work as follows: Parts produced in a manufacturing process are sent along an assembly line for inspection. A vision system located at a station along the line takes a digital photograph of each part as it is going past the station. The photo is decomposed into vital data that are electronically compared to other data, showing how the part would compare if it were correctly produced. The vision system uses a set of rules to determine whether the part is correctly made or flawed. If the part is flawed, the vision system also identifies the nature of the flaw and the corrective action that should be taken.

Robotics **Robotics** refers to the study of the design, building, and use of robots. Robots are machines that, with the help of a computer, can mimic a number of human motor activities in order to perform jobs that are too monotonous or dangerous for their flesh-and-blood counterparts. Although it may seem like many of these robots are "dumb," they are often aided by a number of artificial intelligence techniques so that they may identify objects and states in their environments and so that they may act accordingly. Some robots can even "see" by means of imbedded cameras and "feel" with sensors that permit them to assess the hardness, temperature, and other qualities of objects. Robots can represent a substantial savings to a corporation, since they don't go on strike, don't need vacations, and don't get sick.

Robotics. The field devoted to the study of robot technology.

Responsibility for Systems Development

In large organizations—with thousands of employees and thousands of operational details to keep track of—there are usually thousands of systems, ranging from personal systems to systems that operate at an enterprisewide level. Deciding which systems best support the direction of the enterprise, and how much attention to give each one, is essentially where systems responsibility begins. In the typical business organization, a number of computer professionals share responsibility for the development of all but the very smallest of systems.

The *chief information officer (CIO)* holds primary responsibility for systems development. Often this position is at the level of vice-president. One of the CIO's duties is to develop a corporate strategy that defines the role of information processing within the organization. Another is to oversee the formulation of a five-year plan that maps out which systems are to be studied and possibly revamped during that period.

Because information processing affects not only the accounting functions in most firms but also other departments, including marketing, manufacturing, and personnel, a *steering committee* composed of top-level executives normally approves the plan. This committee also sets broad guidelines for performing computer-related activities. However, it does not become highly involved with technical details or the administration of particular projects, which are the responsibility of the information systems department.

Feature 11-1

Neural-Net Computing

Using artificial intelligence to recognize patterns

Most computing today is preprogrammed number crunching. Whether you are reformatting a document, doing spreadsheet computations, searching through a database, compiling a program, or coloring or rotating graphics images, you are simply executing a predetermined procedure at a high speed. Conventional computers are good at this type of thing. But if you ask them to recognize a handwritten letter, that's a different matter.

This is where neural nets come in. *Neural-net computing* refers to an artificial-intelligence technology in which the human brain's pattern-recognition process is emulated by a computer system. Neural-net systems aren't preprogrammed to provide predictable responses like conventional algorithms. Instead, they are designed to learn by observation.

Neural nets are usually software programs that work on conventional computers. Some research institutions have gone a step further, however, and have developed hardware-based neural nets—that is, computers with circuitry especially designed to solve pattern-recognition problems. This circuitry is often of analog design, in contrast to the digital (binary) circuitry that underlies conventional computers.

Technology taking a bite out of crime. Neural-nets are expected to help.

Neural-net computers translate pattern-recognition processes into small blocks of code that are processed in parallel. These computers simulate a network of hundreds or thousands of interconnected nodes, spanning several layers, that rapidly pass data among each other.

Although neural-net computing is largely a technology of tomorrow, several applications involving neural nets have already begun in earnest. These applications involve handwriting, speech, and image recognition; credit-risk assessment; crime analysis; and stock analysis.

Handwriting, Speech, and Image Recognition Recognition of a person's signature, voice, or face happens so quickly that you scarcely notice how the underlying process works. Neural

The Information Systems Department

Information systems department. The area in an organization that consists of computer professionals.

The **information systems department** varies widely in structure from one company to another. In one form the department is divided into three parts, as shown in Figure 11-12. The *data processing area* has primary responsibility for the development of large transaction processing systems—that is, those systems costing over $100,000 or so and affecting the entire organization. The *information center* normally is involved with smaller projects, say, those that help individual end users or end-user departments select microcomputer resources for their own, local use. The *office automation (OA) area* is in charge of ensuring that the organization takes full advantage of technologies such as word processing, desktop publishing, electronic mail, and the like.

nets attempt to emulate this process. Consider character recognition, for instance. The lower levels of the neural net may recognize that a character is composed of curves and straight lines. This information is passed to the next layer, which may attempt to determine the number of curves and lines and how they fit together. Finally, conclusions are passed to a third level, which may recognize the character as a capital "B." If the character can't be recognized, the neural net attempts to learn from the mistake. One financial-services institution is already using such an algorithm to recognize handwritten numerals on checks.

Credit-Risk Assessment Subtle patterns also exist in conventional text data, such as those found at financial institutions. If you were very sharp and studied the records of thousands of people who were granted and denied credit, you might eventually be able to discern which types of people were good credit risks and which types of people were poor ones. Of course, computers can work much faster than humans and can notice patterns that are hardly discernible. Neural nets are currently being applied to solve credit-risk assessment problems at American Express and other companies. Perhaps in the future, use of neural nets will help to avert catastrophes such as the recent U.S. savings and loan crisis.

Crime Analysis Neural nets are expected to offer some assistance in solving crimes. Many crimes, of course, display a pattern, and often this pattern is too subtle to be picked up without computer assistance. New York's Chase Manhattan Bank is currently using neural nets to examine hundreds of thousands of transactions daily and to look for fraudulent ones.

Stock Analysis One exciting neural-net application is a program that examines stock-market data for patterns and helps determine strategies for buying and selling stocks. At Boston-based Fidelity Investments, Brad Lewis—who manages the Disciplined Equity mutual fund—has outperformed the market consistently with a neural-net based computer model he began developing in business school. The model evaluates 180,000 pieces of data nightly to learn how the market is pricing stocks. It then reviews about a dozen characteristics of 2,000 target stocks to detect subtle patterns that are in line with current market valuations. Stocks are then selected by an "attractiveness rating."

Other applications for neural nets in the future abound. In medicine, neural nets may examine detailed records of patients having a specific disease and attempt to uncover an underlying pattern. In quality control, thousands of parts could be studied to uncover subtle structural problems. And, perhaps, the optimal mixture of glue, pulp, and water required to make top-quality paper can be determined with neural nets. Wherever there's a pattern to study, a neural-net application may be useful.

Data Processing Area The **data processing area** predates all other areas within the information systems department and is still considered by many to be the most important. After all, if their computers stopped processing high-volume business transactions, most large organizations would have to shut down.

Within the data processing area, the *systems analysis and design group* analyzes, designs, and implements new software and hardware systems. The *programming group* codes computer programs from program design specifications. The *operations group* manages day-to-day processing once a system has become operational.

The person most involved with systems development is the **systems analyst.** Generally speaking, the systems analyst's job in the data processing area is to

Data processing area. The group of computer professionals charged with building transaction processing systems.

Systems analyst. A person who studies systems in an organization in order to determine what actions need to be taken and how these actions may best be achieved with computer resources.

FIGURE 11-12

A possible organizational structure for an information systems department. Many information systems departments consist of three principal areas: data processing, an information center, and office automation.

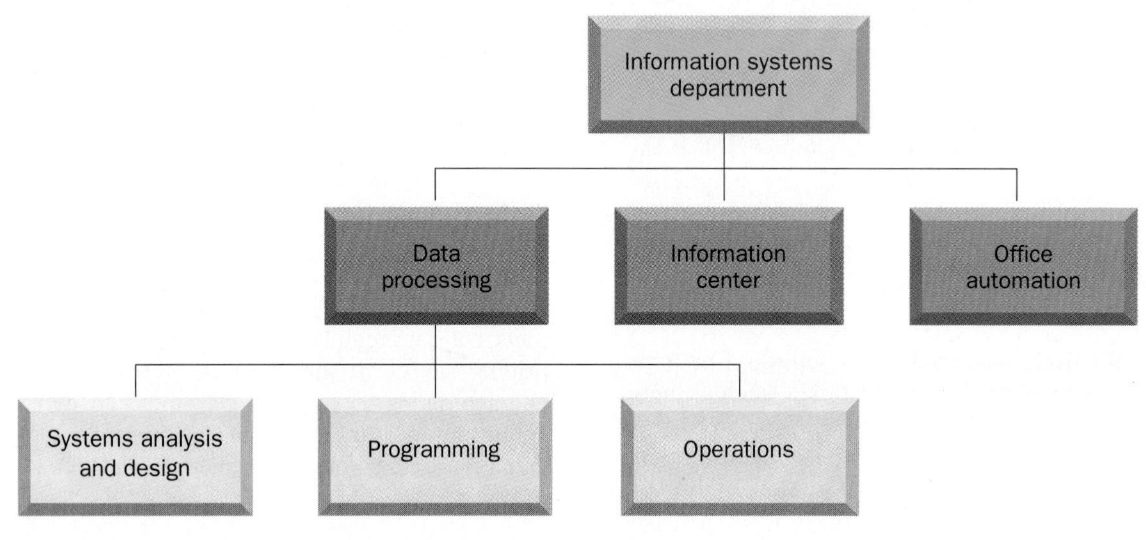

both plan and implement large systems that will use the computers the organization has or will acquire. When such a system is needed, the systems analyst interacts with current and potential end users to produce a solution. The analyst generally is involved in all stages of the development process, from beginning to end.

In most large projects, a team of people will be involved. A systems analyst will probably be appointed as a **project manager** to head up the team. Other people on the team might include users, programmers, an outside consultant, a cost accountant, and an auditor.

Project manager. A systems analyst who is put in charge of a team that is building a large system.

Information center. A facility in an organization charged with developing small systems.

Information Center The **information center** (IC) was originally conceived to help the individual end users in the organization make intelligent choices about the microcomputer hardware and software they need to better perform their jobs, as well as to promote an orderly acquisition of microcomputing resources within the organization as a whole. Many ICs are staffed primarily with *information center consultants* (systems analysts having special skills in the microcomputing area) and with *trainers*.

ICs often are set up similarly to a typical microcomputer store. A user walks in and talks to a consultant about specific microcomputing needs. Perhaps the user is a sales manager who needs a small decision support system to keep track of a field sales force. The manager and consultant sit down at one or two machines and experiment with some appropriate, off-the-shelf software. Eventually, through trial and error, they put together a small system.

Office Automation (OA) Area In many organizations, the **office automation (OA) area** is both the newest and the smallest group within the information systems department. The OA area is responsible for developing a cost-efficient, integrated approach to using office technologies such as electronic document processing and electronic mail. Typical duties, which resemble those of the IC, are arranging product demonstrations and helping end users and end-user departments select systems.

Office automation (OA) area.
The group of computer professionals charged with managing office-related computer activities within the organization.

Outsourcing

When an organization doesn't have the staff on hand to build or operate a system it needs, an outsourcing option is often chosen. **Outsourcing** involves turning over certain information systems functions to an outside vendor (see Figure 11-13). For instance, many banks outsource their check-processing operations—it is simply just too expensive to do such work in house. The equipment doing the sorting and routing of checks is owned and operated by a third-party company skilled at this sort of job.

Outsourcing.
The practice by which one company hires another company to do some or all of its information processing activities.

FIGURE 11-13

Outsourcing. At Electronic Data Systems (EDS), a leading outsourcer, building information systems is Job One. Shown here is EDS' Information Technology Center in Plano, Texas.

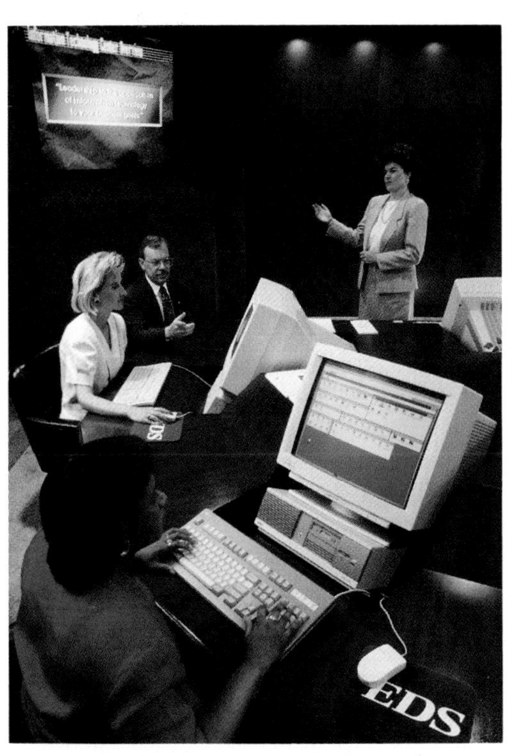

Why do companies outsource? A small firm might find it too expensive to keep in-house information systems personnel on hand, given its current work volume. Or a large company might not have the capacity or capital to expand its operations in house, so it may outsource some of them temporarily. And many firms have found it easier to outsource operations in areas in which it's too hard to find or too expensive to hire new personnel. Many firms also turn to an outsourcer when they think that the outsourcer could do the job better or cheaper than they.

Outsourcing may exist in a variety of different forms. In some cases, the outsourcer has its own computer center and supplies terminals and a network to the client. In other cases, the client firm has its own equipment and, needing someone to operate it, turns to the outsourcer to supply personnel. Virtually any conceivable support arrangement is available through outsourcing.

Along with the benefits to outsourcing come some serious drawbacks. Some firms simply hand over their work to an outsourcer then expect miracles. Leadership needs to come from the client, not from the outsourcing firm. Also, when in-house personnel have to mix with personnel of the outsourcer, conflicts sometimes arise. The in-house personnel may feel that their jobs are threatened by the outsourcer's personnel, or, perhaps, they may disagree about who is in charge. Finally, there are the matters of control and security. Although an outsourcer provides certain levels of assistance in these areas, the most control and best security are achieved when the client company does its own work at its own site. When work goes outside, anything can happen.

Despite the drawbacks, with both technology and business arrangements becoming more complex, outsourcing appears to be an unstoppable trend.

The Systems Development Life Cycle

Systems development often is subdivided into five steps, or phases:

- Phase 1: Preliminary investigation
- Phase 2: Systems analysis
- Phase 3: System design
- Phase 4: System acquisition
- Phase 5: System implementation

Systems development life cycle (SDLC). The process consisting of the five phases of system development: preliminary investigation, systems analysis, system design, system acquisition, and system implementation.

Collectively, these phases often are referred to as the **systems development life cycle (SDLC),** because they describe a system from the time it is first studied until the time it is put into use. When a new business pressure necessitates a change in a system, the steps of the cycle begin anew. The five steps of the SDLC apply in principle both to the large, multimillion-dollar information systems that run large corporations and to the $3,000 microcomputer systems that sit on many desktops in homes.

The five steps of the systems development life cycle do not always follow in a predetermined sequence. Frequently, analysis and design are interleaved. For instance, to look at an example from everyday life, when people develop a seven-day vacation plan, they don't usually completely design the plan as the first step and execute it, without modification as the second step. They might design a plan for day 1 and, when the day is over, analyze what has happened and use their experiences to design a plan for day 2. After day 2, further analysis is done to design day 3. And so on. Many systems are designed this way, "on the fly" as it were, as well.

The Preliminary Investigation

One of the first things to do when it is suggested that a new system is necessary is to conduct a **preliminary investigation,** or *feasibility study.* The purpose of this investigation is to quickly define and evaluate the problem at hand, to see if it is worthy of further study, and to suggest some possible courses of action. Accordingly, the investigation should examine such issues as the nature of the problem, the scope of the work involved with handling the problem, possible solution alternatives, and the approximate costs and benefits of the alternatives.

Preliminary investigation. A brief study of a problem area to assess whether or not a full-scale project should be undertaken. Also called a *feasibility study.*

Systems Analysis

Systems analysis is the phase of systems development in which the problem area is studied in depth and the needs of system users are assessed. The main activities conducted during systems analysis are fact collection and fact analysis.

Systems analysis. The phase of the systems development life cycle in which a problem area is thoroughly examined to determine what should be done.

Fact Collection The goal of fact collection is to gather information about the type of work being performed in the application under study and to ascertain what resources end users need. Later in this phase, the collection of facts should suggest some possible solutions. Deciding which facts to collect depends largely on the problem being studied. Four sources of information on the applications area and end-user needs are (1) written documents showing how the application under study is supposed to work, (2) questionnaires sent to users, (3) interviews of users, and (4) the personal observations of the systems analyst.

If the system being built crosses national borders, the analyst should also realize that additional risks will be involved and that facts should be collected about these risks (see Feature 11-2).

Fact Analysis As information is gathered about the application, it must be analyzed to reach some conclusions. Two useful tools for performing analysis are diagrams and checklists.

Data flow diagrams provide a visual representation of data movement in an organization. They show the relationship between activities that are part of a system as well as the data or information flowing into and out of each of the activities. Figure 11-14 shows a data flow diagram for the order-entry operation of a mail-order firm.

Data flow diagram. A graphically oriented systems development tool that enables a systems analyst to logically represent the flow of data through a system.

Checklists are often developed for such important matters as the goals of the system and the information needs of key people in the system. For example, an accounts receivable system should have such goals as getting bills out quickly, rapidly informing customers about late payments, and cutting losses due to bad debts. On the other hand, a decision support system that helps teachers advise students should increase the quality of information and decrease the time it takes to develop suitable curricula for students.

Common sense eventually must dictate which type of checklist or diagram is most appropriate for the situation at hand. The principal purpose of these

Feature 11–2

Developing International Systems

Risks to consider along with the incentives

It's no secret that commerce today is becoming an increasingly global affair. If a business is large, it's almost certain to have international branches, affiliates, or partners. And even if an organization is not directly involved in foreign trade, it's likely to somehow be impacted by events taking place in other countries.

Many incentives exist today for engaging in global trade. A company must look beyond national borders to invest its capital in the best markets, to manufacture goods at the lowest cost, and to sell goods and services where the demand or profits are strongest.

But along with the potential benefits an organization may realize with international expansion, a number of extra risks are introduced. Among those systems developers should be aware of are the following:

- **Language Barriers** In countries where the native language is not English, English-speaking personnel may have difficulty intermingling with foreign nationals who cannot speak English. Fortunately, due to early computing developments in the United States and England in the 1950s and 1960s, English has become the de facto standard language in the global computing community.
- **Culture** The importance of cultural differences between users and developers cannot be overestimated. People in different parts of the world often react differently to the same set of events. For instance, a system that depends on pinpoint timing and that works in a country with a sense of time urgency may not work in a slower-paced culture where immediacy is not a priority.
- **Political Climate** In countries where the political environment isn't stable, security issues such as backup and disaster recovery must assume greater importance in the development of systems. Also to be taken into account is the possibility that the entire investment can be lost if a hostile government takes over.
- **Hardware Availability** Some countries have very little hardware in place and the communications systems are poor. These are two reasons why systems development in the former Soviet Union and Eastern Bloc will probably creep along much slower than many people would initially expect.
- **Standards** Communications standards vary considerably from one country to another as does the availability and support of specific hardware and software products. When a system spans several countries, it may have to consist of a variety of incompatible products with different replacement cycles.
- **Laws and Customs** Virtually no two countries have the same sets of laws or customs. An especially knotty problem occurs when a country has laws regulating the flow of data that passes over its borders. For instance, in some countries laws require banks doing business within its borders to also process records locally.
- **Nationalism** Citizens in many countries resent it when foreign companies bring in their own people to manage local facilities or

tools is to help the analyst organize thoughts so that conclusions can be drawn about what the system under study should be doing.

System design. The phase of the systems development life cycle in which the parts of a new system and the relationships among them are formally established.

System Design

System design focuses on specifying what the system will look like. The system design phase normally consists of developing a model of the new system and performing a detailed analysis of benefits and costs.

Workday differences. Time zones can pose a challenge to global systems in the financial-services sector.

key decisions are made from a headquarters that may be continents away. In one case, a South American country forbade a U.S. firm to bring in its own computers because the computers were not manufactured locally.

- **Economic Differences** In some countries, a dollar will buy less than it does in others. Also, because exchange rates fluctuate, what seems like a good investment one year may come off as a bad one a year later. Communications costs can also vary widely from country to country.
- **Staffing** Not every country has a ready pool of skilled computer professionals available to press into service. The Middle East and many Third World countries have a shortage of such professionals. Europe, Australia, India, and the former Soviet Union, however, maintain a healthy supply.
- **Workday Differences** Many countries do not work on a 9-to-5 schedule or look at overtime work in the same way people do in North America. Also, time-zone differences can pose a challenge. In industries such as financial services, informations systems technology can be especially useful for monitoring worldwide operations and alerting people to events that have taken place while they were out of the office or asleep.

Development of a Model of the New System Once the analyst understands the nature of the design problem, it is usually helpful to draw a number of diagrams of the new system. The data flow diagrams discussed earlier, for instance, can show how data will flow through the new system.

When designing a system, the analyst must take into account output requirements; input requirements; data access, organization, and storage; processing;

FIGURE 11 – 14

A data flow diagram for a mail-order firm. An order triggers the processes of verification and assembly of the goods ordered, and payment is recorded by accounts receivable.

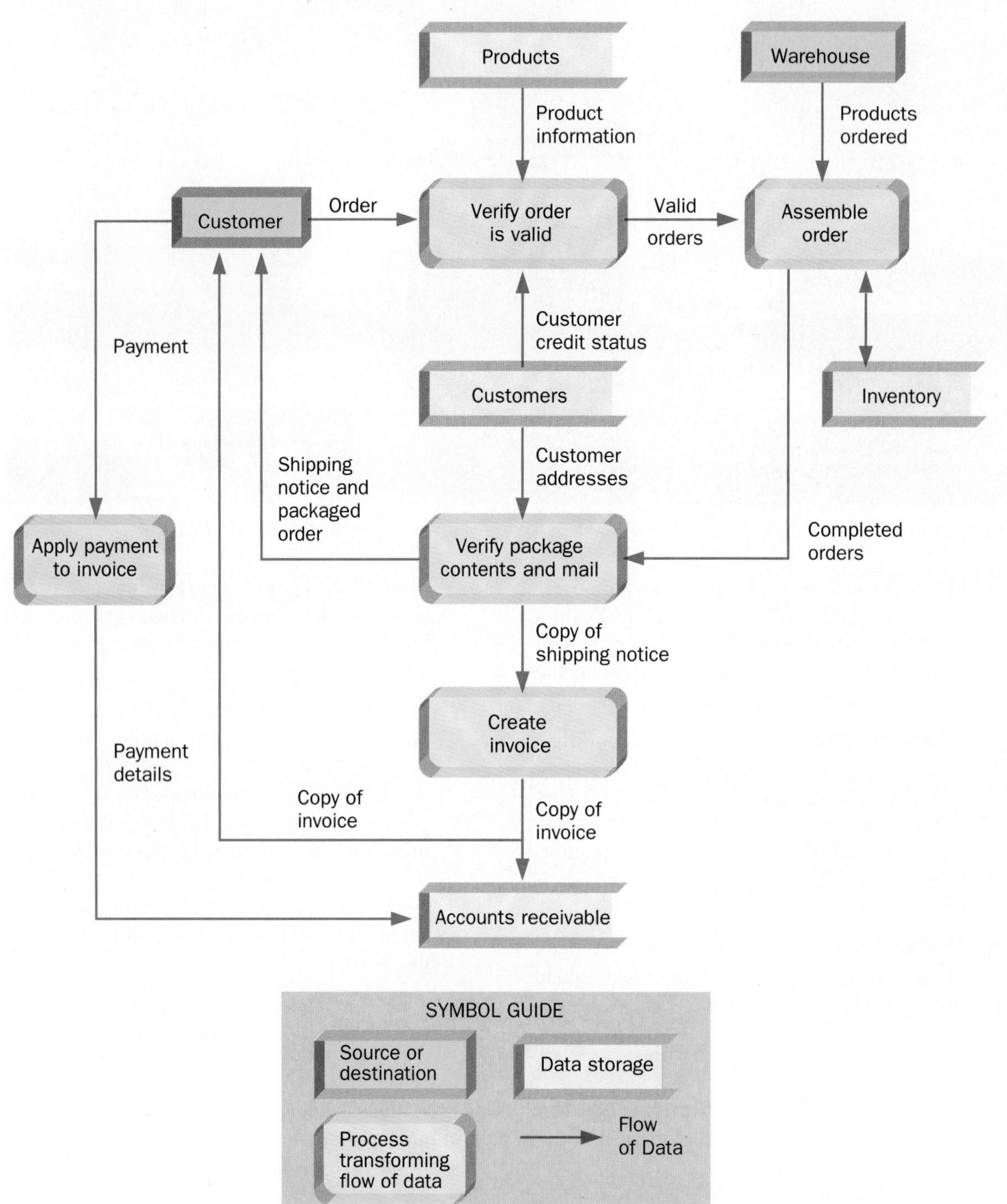

system controls; and personnel and procedure specifications. Figure 11-15 covers some of the issues that must be addressed in the design specification.

Analysis Benefits and Costs Most organizations are acutely sensitive to costs, including computer system costs. Costs include both the initial investment in hardware and software and ongoing costs such as personnel and maintenance.

FIGURE 11-15

Issues to cover during the system design specification. System design ultimately addresses all major elements of a computer system—hardware, software, data, people, and procedures.

Output Considerations

- What types of information do users need?
- How often is this information needed? Annually? Monthly? Daily? On demand?
- What output devices and media are necessary to provide the required information?
- How should output be formatted or arranged so that it can easily be understood by users?

Input Considerations

- What data need to be gathered?
- How often do data need to be gathered?
- What input devices and media are required for data collection and input?

Storage Considerations

- How will data be accessed and therefore organized?
- What storage capacity is required?
- How fast must data be accessed?
- What storage devices are appropriate?

Processing Considerations

- What type of functionality is required in the software?
- What type of processing power is required? A mainframe? A minicomputer? A microcomputer?
- What special processing environments must be considered? A communications network? A database processing environment?

System Controls

- What measures must be taken to ensure that data are secure from unauthorized use, theft, and natural disasters?
- What measures must be taken to ensure the accuracy and integrity of data going in and information going out?
- What measures must be taken to ensure the privacy of individuals represented by the data?

Personnel and Procedures

- What personnel are needed to run the system?
- What procedures should be followed on the job?

Some benefits can be computed easily by calculating the amount of labor saved, the reduction in paperwork, and so on. These are called *tangible benefits,* because they are easy to quantify in dollars.

Other benefits, such as better service to customers or improved information for decision makers, are more difficult to convert into dollar amounts. These are called *intangible benefits.* Clearly, the existence of intangible benefits makes it more difficult for management to reach firm decisions. On projects with a large number of such benefits, management must ask questions such as "Are the new services that we can offer to customers worth the $100,000 it will cost us?"

System Acquisition

Once a system has been designed and the required types of software and hardware have been specified, the analyst must decide from which vendors to buy the necessary components. This decision lies at the heart of the **system acquisition** phase.

System acquisition. The phase of the systems development life cycle in which equipment, software, or services are acquired from vendors.

RFPs and RFQs Many organizations formulate their buying or leasing needs by preparing a document called a **request for proposal (RFP).** This document contains a list of technical specifications for equipment and software, determined during the system design phase. An RFP is sent to all vendors who might satisfy the organization's needs. In the proposal they send back to the initiating organization, vendors recommend a hardware and/or software solution to solve the problem at hand and quote a price.

Request for proposal (RFP). A document containing a general description of a system that an organization wishes to acquire.

In some cases, an organization knows exactly which hardware and software resources it needs from vendors and is interested only in a quote on a specific list of items. In this case, it sends vendors a document called a **request for quotation (RFQ),** which names those items and asks only for a quote. Thus, whereas an RFP gives a vendor some leeway in making system suggestions, an RFQ does not.

Request for quotation (RFQ). A document containing a list of specific hardware, software, and services that an organization wishes to acquire.

Evaluating Bids Once vendors have submitted their bids or quotes in response to the RFP or RFQ, the buyer organization must decide which bid to accept. Two useful tools for making this choice are vendor rating systems and a benchmark test.

In a **vendor rating system**, such as the one in Figure 11-16, important criteria for selecting computer system resources are identified and each is given a weight. For example, in the figure, the "60" for hardware and "30" for documentation may be loosely interpreted to mean that hardware is twice as important as documentation to this organization. Each vendor submitting an acceptable bid is rated on each criterion, with the associated weight representing the maximum possible score. The buyer then totals the scores and chooses—possibly—the vendor with the highest total. Such a rating tool does not guarantee that the best vendor will always have the highest point total, but it does have the advantage of being objective and simple to apply. If several people are involved in the selection decision, individual biases tend to be "averaged out."

Vendor rating system. A point-scoring procedure for evaluating competing vendors of computer products or services.

Some organizations, after tentatively selecting a vendor, make their choice conditional on the successful completion of a "test drive," or **benchmark test.**

Benchmark test. A test used to measure computer system performance under typical use conditions prior to purchase.

FIGURE 11-16

A point-scoring approach for evaluating vendors' bids. Often, but not always, the vendor with the highest point total is the one selected.

Criterion	Weight (Maximum Score)	Vendor 1 Score	Vendor 2 Score
Hardware	60	60	40
Software	80	70	70
Cost	70	50	65
Ease of use	80	70	50
Modularity	50	30	30
Vendor support	50	50	50
Documentation	30	30	20
		(360)	325

Vendor 1 has highest total score

Such a test normally consists of running a pilot version of the new system on the hardware and software of the vendor under consideration. To do this, the acquiring organization generally visits the benchmark testing center of the vendor and attempts to determine how well the hardware/software configuration will work if installed. Benchmark tests are expensive and far from foolproof. It's very possible that the pilot system will perform admirably at the benchmark site but the real system, when eventually installed at the site of the acquiring organization, will not.

System Implementation

Once arrangements for delivery of computer resources have been made with one or more vendors, the **system implementation** phase begins. This phase includes all the remaining tasks necessary to make the system operational and successful.

System implementation. The phase of systems development that encompasses activities related to making the computer system operational and successful once it is delivered by the vendor.

To ensure that the system will be working by a certain date, the analyst must prepare a timetable. One tool for helping with this task is *project management software*, illustrated in Figure 11-17. This software shows how implementation activities are related, shows when activities must start and finish, and pinpoints critical activities.

Implementation consists of converting programs and data files from the old system to the new one, debugging converted and new applications programs, training and establishing ongoing support (see User Solution 11-2), and appraising the new system's performance. If the system has been designed well, it should be flexible enough to accommodate changes over a reasonable period of time with minimal disruption. However, if at some point a major change becomes necessary, another system will be needed to replace the current one. At this point, the systems development life cycle—from the preliminary investigation to implementation—will begin all over again.

FIGURE 11-17

Project management. Large projects are often managed with the assistance of project management software, or "project managers." Many project managers, like the one featured here, provide a project timetable and graphs showing project costs and how pieces of the project fit together.

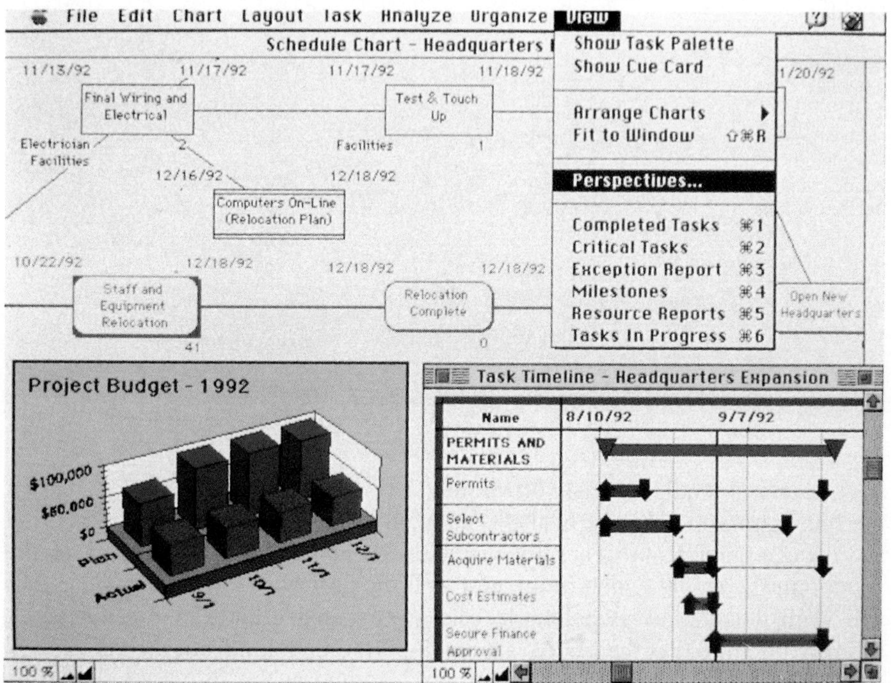

Approaches to Systems Development

In this section, we'll closely examine three approaches to systems development: the traditional approach, prototyping, and end-user development.

The Traditional Approach

Traditional approach. An approach to systems development whereby the five phases of the systems development life cycle are carried out in a predetermined sequence.

In the **traditional approach,** the phases of systems development are carried out in a predetermined order: (1) preliminary investigation, (2) systems analysis, (3) system design, (4) system acquisition, and (5) implementation. Each phase is begun only when the one before it is completed. Often, the traditional approach is reserved for the development of large transaction processing systems. Because the traditional approach is usually expensive and extensive, it normally is carried out by knowledgeable professionals—that is, by systems analysts.

Traditional systems development requires system users to consider proposed system plans by looking at detailed diagrams, descriptive reports, and specifications of the proposed new system. The entire system is specified and built before

User Solution 11–2

An Automated Help Desk That Really Helps

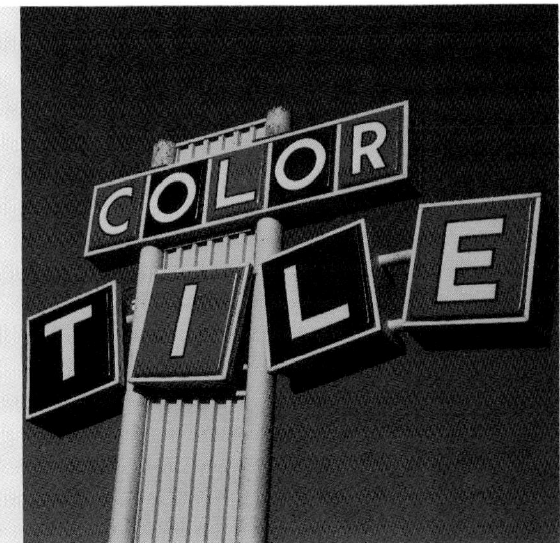

Color Tile, Inc., which sells tiles and related flooring products through hundreds of stores scattered geographically, is typical of many franchisers. Store personnel are constantly calling in to a centralized "help desk" asking for information about products, for example, "Can a certain type of cleaner be used on a certain type of tile?" Only a couple of years ago, callers spent an average of 15 minutes on the phone waiting for a technician to thumb through a variety of manuals, brochures, and handwritten documents for answers. And often there were no answers—only monster phone bills. But times have changed. The company now uses an automated expert system in which operators have their own computers and access to a problem-solving database. Today, 80 percent of the questions coming in from the field are answered on the first call—and they are answered faster and with fewer operators, too.

anyone gets to use it. As each phase of development is completed, users "sign off" on the recommendations presented to them by the analyst, indicating their acceptance.

In many organizations, the traditional approach to systems development has recently fallen into disfavor for many systems projects. First, systems often take too long to analyze, design, and implement under the traditional approach. By the time a system is finally put into operation, important new needs that were not part of the original plan may have surfaced. Second, the system being developed often is the wrong one. Managers almost always have difficulty expressing their information needs, and it is not until they begin to use a system that they discover what it is they really need.

Prototyping

To avoid the potentially expensive disaster that could result from completing every phase of systems development before users ever lay their hands on a system, many analysts have advocated prototyping as a means of systems development. In **prototyping,** the focus is on developing a small model, or *prototype,* of the overall system. Users work with the prototype and suggest modifications. The prototype is then modified, resulting in an improved prototype. As soon as the prototype is refined to the point where higher management feels confident that a larger version of the system will succeed, either the prototype can be gradually expanded or the organization can go "full steam ahead" with the remaining steps of systems development.

Prototyping.
A systems development alternative whereby a small model, or *prototype,* of the system is built before a full-scale systems development effort is undertaken.

In prototyping, analysis and design generally proceed together, in small steps that finally result in a completed system. The idea behind the prototyping process is virtually identical to the one described on pages 388–389 for developing vacation plans. Prototyping is illustrated in Figure 11-18.

End-User Development

End-user development. Systems development carried out by the end user.

End-user development is a relatively new form of systems development—one that has evolved from the microcomputing revolution. It is defined as a systems development effort in which the end user is primarily responsible for the development of the system. This is in contrast to other types of development, in which a qualified computer professional, such as a systems analyst, takes charge of the systems development process.

As you might guess, end-user development is feasible only in cases where the system being acquired is relatively inexpensive. A good example is the situation in which an end user purchases a microcomputer system and develops applications on his or her own. In developing the system, the end user might follow a prototyping approach or a method similar to traditional development.

FIGURE 11-18

Prototyping. Prototyping is an iterative process; after each prototype is built, the user and analyst try it out together and attempt to improve on it. Eventually, the prototype evolves into a finished system.

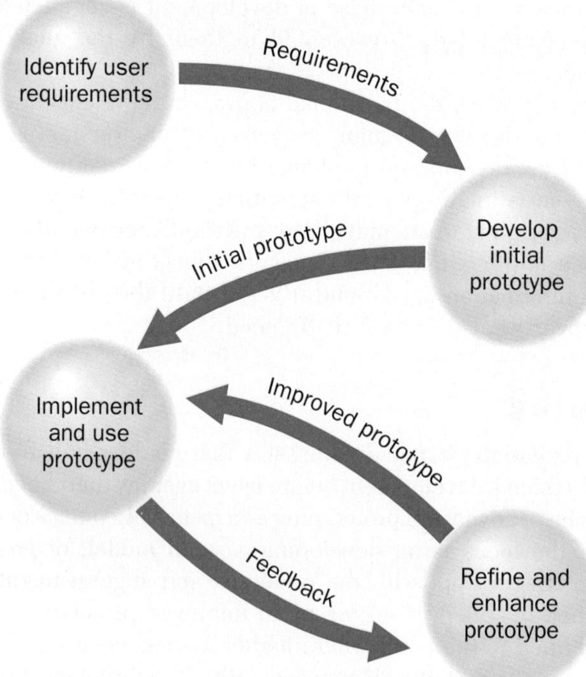

Summary and Key Terms

Types of systems and how organizations build them are the principal subjects of this chapter.

On Systems A **system** is a collection of elements and procedures that interact to accomplish a goal. The function of many systems, whether manual or computerized, is to keep an organization well managed and running smoothly.

Systems development is a process that consists of analyzing a system, designing a new system or making modifications to the old one, acquiring the needed hardware and software, and getting the new or modified system to work. Systems development may be required for any number of reasons; for example, changes in government regulations, new computer technology, and so forth.

Business Systems There are many types of systems used in business.

Transaction processing systems generally perform tasks that involve the tedious recordkeeping that organizations handle regularly.

Information systems, which fall into two classes—**information reporting systems** and **decision support systems (DSSs)**—provide decision makers access to needed information and to tools that generate information. **Group decision support systems (GDSSs)**—or **workgroup computing**—refers to DSSs in which several people routinely interact through a computer network in order to solve common problems. **Executive information systems (EISs)** are DSSs customized to meet the special needs of individual executives.

The term **office automation (OA)** refers to a wide range of systems, including those involving document processing, **electronic mail,** desk accessories, decision support tools, **teleconferencing,** electronic document handling, and **telecommuting.**

Computers are also widely used to improve productivity both at the design stage—through **computer-aided design (CAD)**—and the manufacturing stage—through **computer-aided manufacturing (CAM).** The use of technology to tie together CAD and CAM with other business sytems is called **computer-integrated manufacturing (CIM).**

The ability of some computer systems to perform in ways that would be considered intelligent if observed in humans is called **artificial intelligence (AI)**. The four main applications areas of AI are **expert systems,** natural languages, vision systems, and **robotics.**

Responsibility for Systems Development The *chief information officer (CIO)*, or someone with a similar title, holds primary responsibility for the overall direction of systems development. The technical details are the responsibility of individual areas—the **data processing area,** the **information center,** and the **office automation (OA) area**—within the **information systems department. Systems analysts** are the people involved most closely with the development of systems from beginning to end. Often, a systems analyst is the **project manager** on the team assigned to the systems project. When a company lacks the in-house expertise, time, or money to do its own information processing, it often turns to an **outsourcing** company to provide system services.

The Systems Development Life Cycle Systems development is often divided into five phases: preliminary investigation, systems analysis, system design, system acquisition, and system implementation. These phases are often collectively referred to as the **systems development life cycle (SDLC),** since they describe a system from the time it is first studied until the time it is put into use. When a new business pressure necessitates a change in the system, the steps of the cycle begin anew.

The first thing the systems analyst does when confronted with a new project assignment is to conduct a **preliminary investigation**, or *feasibility study*. This investigation addresses the nature of the problem under study, the potential scope of the systems development project, the possible solutions, and the costs and benefits of these solutions.

Next, the **systems analysis** phase begins. During this phase, the main objectives are to study the application in depth (to find out what work is being done), to assess the needs of users, and to prepare a list of specific requirements the new system must meet. These objectives are accomplished through fact collection and analysis.A number of tools can help with fact analysis, including **data flow diagrams** and *checklists*.

The **system design** phase of systems development consists of developing a model of the new system and performing a detailed analysis of benefits and costs.

Once a system has been designed and the required types of software and hardware have been specified, the analyst must decide from which vendors to buy the necessary components. This decision lies at the heart of the **system acquisition** phase. Many buying organizations notify vendors of an intention to acquire a system by submitting to the vendor a **request for proposal (RFP)** or **request for quotation (RFQ).** Vendors submitting bids are then commonly evaluated through a **vendor rating system** and then, possibly, a **benchmark test.**

Once arrangements have been made with one or more vendors for delivery of computer resources, the **system implementation** phase begins. This phase includes all the remaining tasks that are necessary to make the system operational and successful, including converting files, debugging, training, and performance appraisal.

Approaches to Systems Development In the **traditional approach** to systems development, the phases of the SDLC are carried out in a predetermined order—preliminary investigation, analysis, design, acquisition, and implementation. The focus in **prototyping** is on developing small models—or *prototypes*—of the target system in a series of graduated steps. **End-user development** is a systems development approach in which the user is primarily responsible for building the system. This is in contrast to other types of development, in which a qualified computer professional—such as a systems analyst—takes charge of the systems development process.

Review Exercises

Fill-in Questions

1. The term ______________ refers to money owed to a company by customers who have made purchases on credit.
2. CAD is an acronym for ______________.
3. The term ______________ refers to computer systems that perform human-like tasks.
4. The study of the design, building, and use of robots comprises the field of ______________.
5. A(n) ______________ committee composed of executives in key departments and other members of top management normally approves a plan for systems development.
6. ______________ refers to systems development in which users are primarily responsible for the development effort.
7. Benefits that are easy to quantify in dollars are called ______________ benefits.
8. A(n) ______________ consists of running a pilot version of a new system on the hardware and/or software of a vendor whose products are being considered for purchase or lease.

Matching Questions

Match each term with the description that best fits.

a. transaction processing system
b. CAM
c. expert system
d. DSS
e. CAD
f. prototyping

____1. A system possessing artificial intelligence.

____2. Pertains to the recordkeeping tasks that organizations handle on a day-to-day basis.

____3. A type of systems development.

____4. Refers to the use of computers in design.

____5. Pertains to the use of interactive computer systems for decision support.

____6. Refers to the use of computers in manufacturing.

Discussion Questions

1. What is systems development?
2. What are the main duties of the systems analyst?
3. Identify the five phases of the systems development life cycle.
4. What is computer-integrated manufacturing (CIM)?
5. Name several functions performed by transaction processing systems.
6. What is the difference between an information reporting system and a decision support system?
7. What are the advantages and disadvantages to outsourcing?
8. What is meant by artificial intelligence?

Critical Thinking Questions

1. There is a great deal of confusion with regard to computer terminology. For instance, many people refer to almost every computer system as an "information system." Also, the term "artificial intelligence" is widely applied to systems that save people a great deal of work—even when such systems do not use techniques that mimic human intelligence. Why, do you think, is there such confusion?
2. Whereas robots can perform many jobs adequately, there are a number of other jobs for which robots may never be used. What are three such jobs?
3. What two devices in Chapter 5 does a fax machine most resemble? Identify any similarities.
4. What are several reasons why an organization using a vendor rating system may choose to buy from a vendor other than the most highly rated one?
5. Can the prototyping approach to development be useful in situations in which computer systems are not involved? If you think so, provide an example.
6. Many observers of the computing scene have pointed out that some of the biggest problems in getting a system to work properly are people-related. Provide several examples that show how people problems can make a system fail.

7. Companies everywhere are increasingly outsourcing jobs to foreign countries. Today there is concern in the United States and Canada that manufacturing jobs will be lost to low-wage countries such as Mexico and to countries offshore, such as the Philippines or Taiwan. In nearby Mexico, blue-collar work can often be done for about one sixth the price of the same work in the United States—perhaps even with better quality. How has information technology contributed to the trend to move jobs off native soil? State reasons why this trend may have both positive and negative aspects.

W I N D O W 7

The World of Computer Graphics

Techniques and Applications

As you've seen in some of the other windows, computer systems are capable of producing some rather spectacular images. How are these images created? Here, we will look at several of the techniques used to produce computer graphics as well as how these graphics are being used in fields such as decision support, advertising, architecture, and animation.

1. Computer graphics techniques are increasingly being used to create the impossible photograph. Here, in some high-tech plastic surgery, a face is reshaped to fit a box—giving new meaning to the phrase "being a square."

Techniques

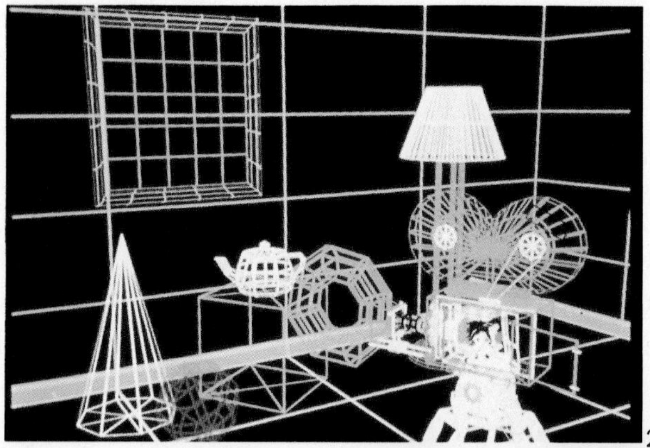
2

3

2–3. Three-dimensional computer graphics often start as wireframe models depicting geometrical shapes. These shapes are then rendered with color and shaded. Because the shapes are mathematically defined, they can easily be resized and rotated into different positions.

4

4. Computer graphics users frequently employ light sources that apply shadows and reflections to models.

5

5. Graphics artists often use the computer to impart special effects. Here, a balloon image is solarized.

6

7

8

9

6–9. Morphing is a technique in which two images are fed to the computer and other images are interpolated between them. Here, a car is morphed into a tiger for an Exxon ad. The opening image in this window is also a morph—between a face and a box—as was the villain-to-mummy sequence in photos 7–9 in Window 1.

Decision Support

10

11

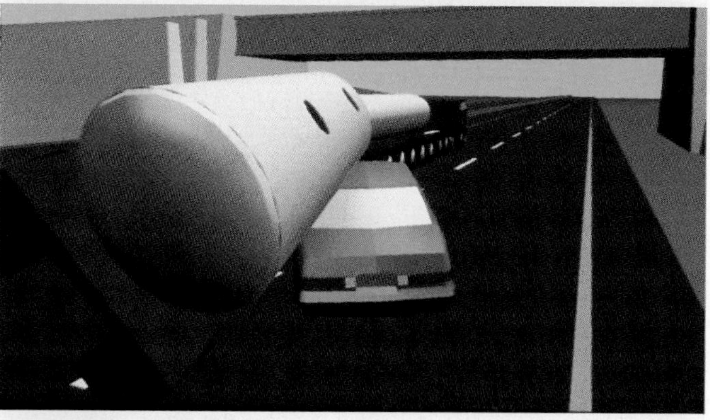

12

13

10–13. Computer graphics techniques are increasingly being brought into the courtroom to recreate accidents and help decide who was at fault.

14

14–16. Mapping software is often used to help businesses make decisions. Here, maps are employed to assess the potential impact of two banks merging (photo 14), market penetration in salesperson territories (photo 15), and customer distributions by region (photo 16).

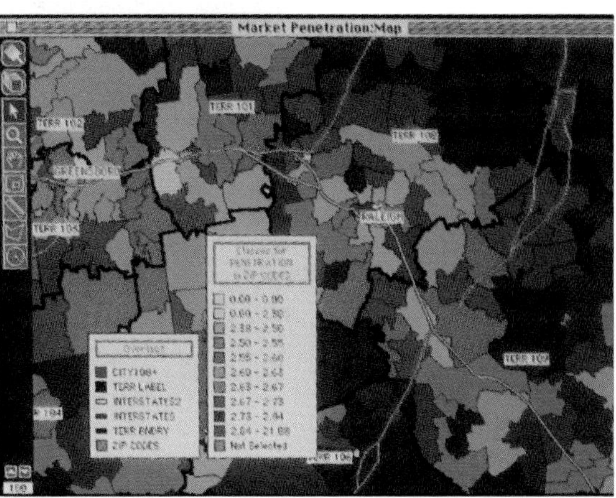

15

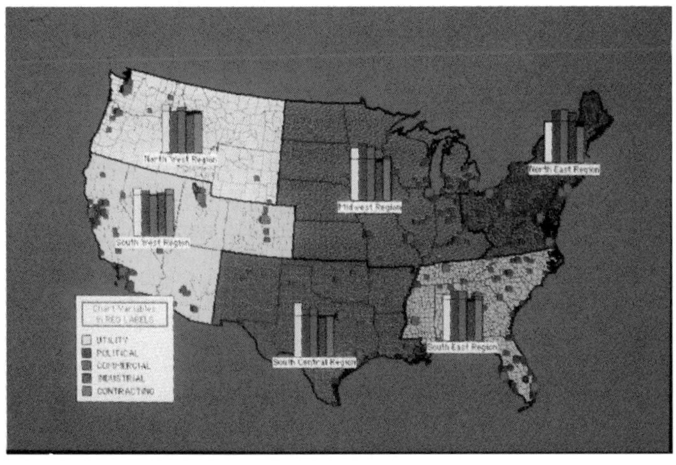

16

Architecture

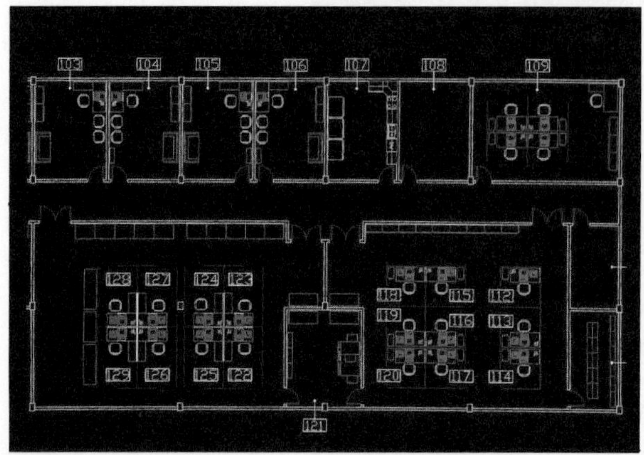

17

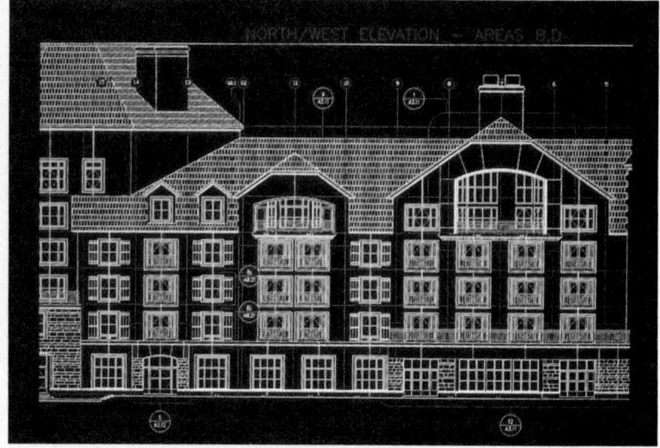

18

17–18. Simple, two-dimensional graphics can be employed for constructing floor plans and elevation drawings.

19

20

19–20. Site-visualization software enables clients of architectural firms to imagine what an undeveloped site will look like with the structure of their choice on it.

21

21–22. Because not only a building but also the sun and individual light bulbs can be modeled in three dimensions, architectural clients can see what their proposed home will look like in sunlight or at night—and even in fog or after a snowfall, for that matter.

22

23

23. Interior modeling, with realistic lighting effects, is a growing area of computer graphics applications. It is also an area where virtual reality is expected to make a big impact soon (see related story in the Tomorrow box in Chapter 2).

Computer Animation

24

24. Three-dimensional computer logos that are "toured" in an imaginary space are a familiar sight to anyone watching football or basketball games.

25. Computers have become a popular, cost-effective tool for creating cartoon animations.

25

26

26–27. This computer-generated commercial for Quaker Oats shows how, through the "magic" of technology, cartoon characters can be photorealistically brought into lifelike settings.

27

28

28–30. Karl Sims' *Panspermia* is a computer animation that is halfway between science fiction and science. A computer model is used to cause intergalactic plants to move in natural ways and to grow and cull themselves based on evolutionary principles.

29

30

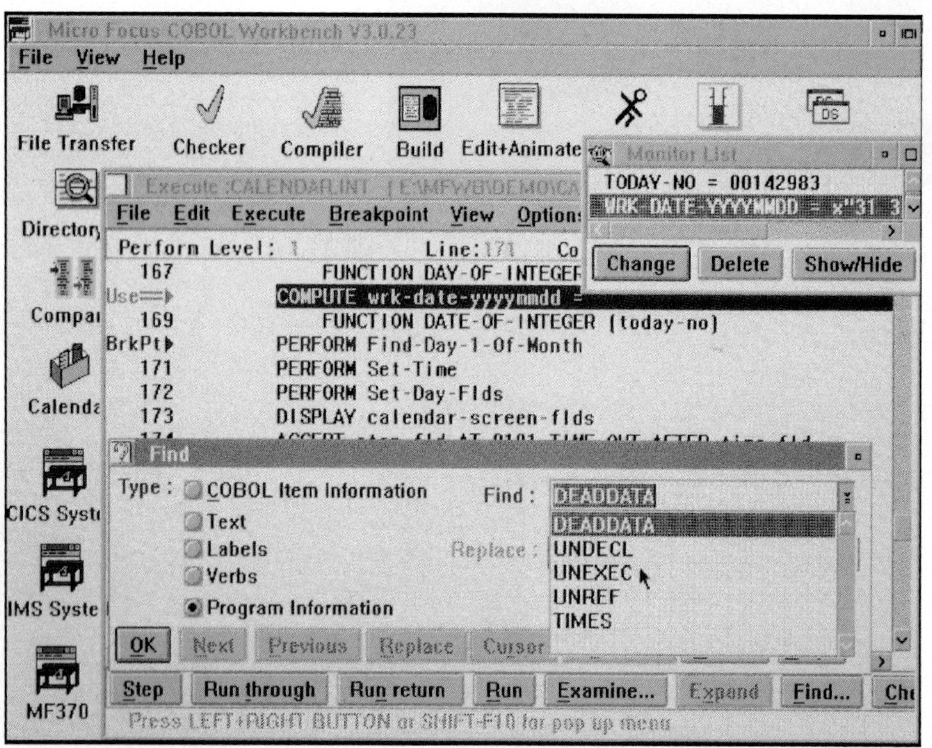

Micro Focus COBOL Workbench V3.0.23
File View Help
File Transfer
Checker
Compiler
Build
Edit+Animate
Directory
Calendar
CICS System
IMS System
MF370
Monitor List
TODAY-NO = 00142983
WRK-DATE-YYYYMMDD = x"31 3
Change
Delete
Show/Hide
Execute :CALENDAR.INT
File Edit Execute Breakpoint View Options
Perform Level: 1
Line:171
167 FUNCTION DAY-OF-INTEGER
Use COMPUTE wrk-date-yyyymmdd =
169 FUNCTION DATE-OF-INTEGER (today-no)
BrkPt PERFORM Find-Day-1-Of-Month
171 PERFORM Set-Time
172 PERFORM Set-Day-Flds
173 DISPLAY calendar-screen-flds
Find
Type : COBOL Item Information
Text
Labels
Verbs
Program Information
Find : DEADDATA
Replace :
DEADDATA
UNDECL
UNEXEC
UNREF
TIMES
OK
Next
Previous
Replace
Cursor
Step
Run through
Run return
Run
Examine...
Expand
Find...
Press LEFT+RIGHT BUTTON or SHIFT-F10 for pop up menu

Program Development and Programming Languages

12

What practices do organizations follow in developing programs? As discussed in this chapter, just like building a house involves much more than pounding nails into boards, creating good programs involves a lot of preplanning before a single line of code is ever written.

OUTLINE

Overview
Program Development Activities
The Make-or-Buy Decision
Program Design
- Program Design Tools
- Program Flowcharts
- Pseudocode
- Structure Charts

Programming Languages
- Low-Level Languages
- High-Level Languages
- Fourth-Generation Languages (4GLs)
- Natural Languages

Program Coding
Debugging and Testing Programs
Program Maintenance
Program Documentation
Quality Assurance
Computer-Aided Software Engineering (CASE)

LEARNING OBJECTIVES

After completing this chapter, you will be able to:

1. Identify and describe the activities involved with program development.
2. Recognize why it may be more advantageous to buy software in many instances than to develop it in-house.
3. Identify several of the language options available to code programs.
4. Describe a number of design and productivity tools used by computer professionals to develop software.
5. Explain some of the activities involved with debugging, maintaining, documenting, and ensuring quality among programs.
6. Explain the role played by CASE tools.

Overview

If you wanted to build a house, you'd probably begin with some research and planning. You might speak to various people about home design, draw up some floor plans, estimate the cost of materials, and so on. In other words, you wouldn't start digging a hole and pouring concrete on the very first day. Creating a successful applications program also requires considerable planning.

Computer professionals and advanced users need to develop their own software from time to time. Applications software development involves using a programming language or similar tool to code new applications programs from scratch. In Chapter 12 we will spend a great deal of time studying useful practices for developing applications programs. As you read this chapter, keep in mind that it is never enough just to write a program that works. Good programs must also be easy to understand and to maintain. A well-planned program may take slightly longer to write initially, but the subsequent savings in maintenance costs usually will make the effort well worthwhile.

The chapter opens by covering the sorts of activities that need to be considered when new applications software is required. From there, we turn to the make-or-buy decision, which deals with choosing either to develop applications software from scratch or to buy it prepackaged. Next we address three of the chapter's most important topics: program design, programming languages, and program coding. Then we turn to discussions of program debugging and testing, maintenance, documentation, and quality assurance. The chapter closes with a brief introduction to one of the hottest new software-development technologies—computer-aided software engineering (CASE).

Program Development Activities

There are two principal ways in which you can acquire applications programs: developing them from scratch and buying them in prepackaged form from an outside source. The method chosen generally depends on factors such as the quality of software available in the marketplace, the nature and importance of the application, the availability and capability of programmers, and cost. The developer of the software—whether it be you, a colleague, or an outside vendor—should follow certain steps to ensure that the software does its job.

Applications software development. The process of designing, coding, debugging and testing, maintaining, and documenting applications software.

The steps associated with creating applications programs are collectively referred to as **applications software development.** Applications software development normally begins with the program specifications that are developed during the systems analysis and system design phases of the systems development life cycle (SDLC), which we discussed in detail in Chapter 11. Program specifications cover program outputs, the processing to take place, storage requirements, and program inputs. Applications software development consists of the four following activities or steps:

- **Program Design** Planning the specific software solution to meet the program specifications.
- **Program Coding** Writing the program.
- **Program Debugging and Testing** Finding and eliminating errors in the program.
- **Program Maintenance** Making changes to the program over time.

While each of these critical development activities is taking place, there should be ongoing documentation. *Documentation* is the process of "writing up" the details about what the program does and how it works.

In a typical organization, the responsibility for successful program development is the job of systems analysts and programmers. **Systems analysts,** or simply *analysts,* specify the requirements that the applications software must meet. They work with end users to assess applications needs and translate those needs into a plan. Then they determine the specific resources required to implement the plan. For every program, the analysts create a set of technical specifications outlining what the program must do, the timetable for completing the program, which programming language to use, how the program will be tested before being put into use, and what documentation is required. **Programmers** then use these specifications to design a software solution. Later they translate that design into code—a series of statements in a programming language. *Maintenance programmers* monitor the finished program on an ongoing basis, correcting errors and altering the program as technology or business conditions change.

Systems analyst. A person who studies systems in an organization in order to determine what actions need to be taken and how these actions may best be achieved with computer resources.

Programmer. A person whose job is to write, maintain, and test computer programs.

The Make-or-Buy Decision

Once an individual or organization has established a set of technical requirements for a software solution to a problem, it must be decided whether the programs should be created in house or acquired from a software vendor. This consideration is frequently called the *make-or-buy decision.*

During the last several years, prewritten applications programs for such tasks as payroll, general-ledger accounting, financial planning, manufacturing control, and project scheduling have become more widely available from specialized vendors. These programs, called **applications packages,** normally consist of an integrated set of programs, documentation (usually of fairly high quality), and possibly training. Because they often provide immediate results at a reasonable cost, applications packages are becoming increasingly popular.

Applications package. A fourth-generation-language product that, when the user sets a few parameters, becomes a finished applications program ready to meet specific end-user needs.

But although applications packages offer many compelling advantages, they are not always appropriate. If a package was originally developed for a business that works differently from the one it's being sold to and the vendor has made only superficial attempts to adapt it for general use, it may prove to be more trouble than it's worth. Also, for some applications, little or no appropriate packaged software exists. In such cases, developing the software itself may be the organization's only alternative.

Today, most applications packages are developed by firms in the United States and made available in foreign-language versions. In the future, as explained in the Tomorrow box, U.S. software dominance may be challenged by events ranging from the breakup of the former Soviet Union to the increasing availability of technology resources worldwide.

Program Design

In the design stage of applications software development, the program specifications developed by the systems analyst are used to spell out as precisely as possible the nature of the required programming solution. The design, or plan,

TOMORROW

The Coming Threat to U.S. Software Dominance

Will the Software Industry Go the Way of Detroit?

It's a story about the U.S. auto industry that's been told many times. The usual spin it takes is that the carmakers got fat, happy, and uncompetitive. And then Japan ate their lunch. But a less well-known fact is that the same type of fate might be awaiting the U.S. software industry.

Consider the following facts. About 70 percent of the software now used worldwide is produced in the United States. The software industry is still growing by leaps and bounds. Programmers in North America often make five to ten times what programmers with equivalent skills—and an excellent knowledge of English—make in some foreign countries. However, improved communications and the tumbling of international barriers are making it easier than ever for countries outside of the United States to develop strong software industries.

According to some observers, including Edward Yourdon, a famous pioneer in the field of structured programming, the main problems facing the U.S. software industry are that programs are produced at a very high cost, with relatively low productivity, and with very low levels of quality.

Edward Yourdon. Structured-programming pioneer has reservations about the future of the U.S. software industry.

A good part of the blame for productivity may fall on management's shoulders. The software in-

derived from these specifications must address all the tasks that programs must do as well as how to organize or sequence these tasks when coding programs. Only when the design is complete does the next stage—the actual program coding—begin.

Program Design Tools

Program design tools are essentially planning tools. They consist of various kinds of diagrams, charts, and tables that outline either the organization of program tasks or the steps the program will follow. Once a program has been coded and implemented, program design tools serve as excellent documentation.

Program Flowcharts

Program flowchart. A visual design tool showing step by step how a computer program will process data.

Program flowcharts use *geometric symbols,* such as those in Figure 12-1, and familiar *relational symbols,* such as those in Figure 12-2, to graphically portray the sequence of steps involved in a program. The steps in a flowchart occur in dustry tends to promote from within the technical ranks. So people who become managers often have only technical backgrounds and very few management skills. Says Yourdon, "Managing people wasn't such a big problem when, for example, Apple's software was being written by one guy in a garage. But if you look at Apple's System 7 [operating system], which consisted of some 200 people working together, you face the same kind of management challenge that Boeing does when managing a team of 200 engineers that are building a 747."*

One might also point a finger at management as regards the quality issue. The United States puts a premium on getting products out the door quickly and generating a steady stream of profits in the short term. Consequently, products are often knowingly released with a large number of bugs—bugs that perhaps should have been ironed out.

The greatest threat to U.S. software dominance may come from countries like India, the Philippines, and the Arab nations—places where salaries are comparatively low, where English is widely spoken, and where the potential for networking is strong. While countries in the former Soviet Union have excellent technicians, they have a shortage of hardware and the communications systems are poor. That makes it difficult to set up the LANs and WANs needed to become a software powerhouse. Also, the notions of business competition and capitalism are still relatively new in that part of the world.

All of these observations pose several interesting possibilities for the future. Will other countries grab the software mantle from the U.S.? Will domestic firms increasingly develop branches in foreign countries to write their software, taking even more jobs away from home?

Not to worry, say some skeptics. They claim that since the United States is still by far the dominant user of the world's software, it is unlikely that such an important resource will be ported overseas. Managers have suffered so many disappointments from software promises in the past, say some, that the idea that software can be developed more successfully thousands of miles away is too much to swallow. Others point out cultural differences and the enormous distances between users and foreign programmers as being insurmountable barriers. They argue it requires a giant leap of faith to assume, for instance, that a programmer in New Delhi will be able to respond effectively to system requests from a wholesaler in Des Moines.

What scenario will eventually evolve? Stay tuned to the year 2010.

*From an interview with Edward Yourdon reported in *Computer News Link*, Summer, 1992.

the same logical sequence that their corresponding program statements follow in the program. To help you understand what these symbols mean and see how to use them, let's consider an example.

Scanning a File for Employees with Certain Characteristics A common activity in information processing is scanning an employee file for people with certain characteristics. Suppose, for example, a company's personnel department wants a printed list of all employees with computer experience and at least five years of company service. A flowchart that shows how to accomplish this task and also totals the number of employees who meet these criteria is shown in Figure 12-3.

This particular flowchart uses five symbols: start/stop, processing, decision, connector, and input/output. The lines with arrows that link the symbols are called *flowlines;* they indicate the flow of logic in the flowchart.

Every flowchart begins and ends with an oval-shaped *start/stop symbol.* The first of these symbols in the program contains the word *Start,* and the last contains the word *Stop.* The diamond-shaped *decision symbol* always indicates

FIGURE 12-1

ANSI program flowchart symbols.

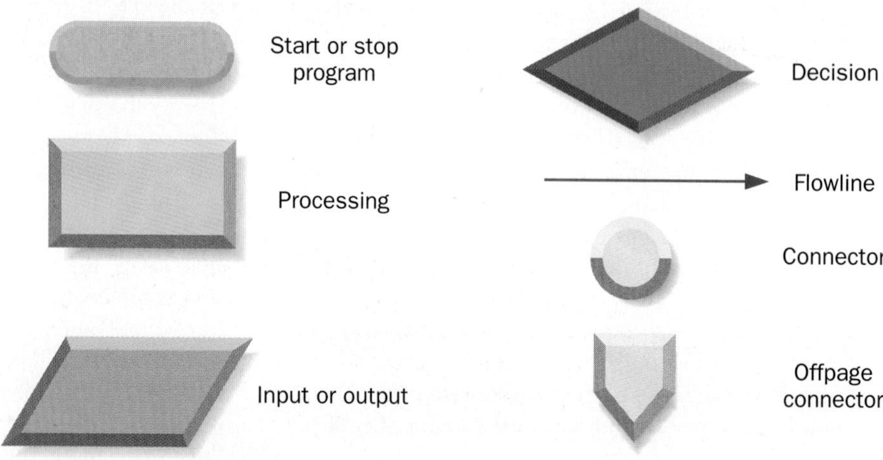

a question, which generally will have only two possible answers—yes or no (true or false). Decision symbols should always have one flowline entering and two flowlines (representing the two possible outcomes) exiting.

The rectangular *processing symbol* contains an action that needs to be taken—for example, "Set counter to 0" and "Add 1 to counter." The *connector symbol* provides a logical meeting point for several flowlines. The *input/output symbol* enables the logical process depicted in the flowchart to either accept data or output them.

The flowchart in Figure 12-3 involves a looping operation. We "read" a record, inspect it, and take an action; then read another record, inspect it, and take another action; and so on until the file is exhausted. When the computer reads a record, as indicated by the input/output symbol, it brings it into its memory and stores its contents (or field values). If a record meets both search criteria, we increment a counter by 1. After the last record is read and processed, we print, before ending the program, the value of the counter.

FIGURE 12-2

Relational symbols used in flowcharts.

Symbol	Meaning
<	Less than
≤	Less than or equal to
>	Greater than
≥	Greater than or equal to
=	Equal to
<>	Not equal to

FIGURE 12-3

Scanning an employee file. The situation that the flowchart represents is as follows: Print the names of all people in an employee file who have computer experience and at least five years of company service. Also, count the number of such people and print out this count.

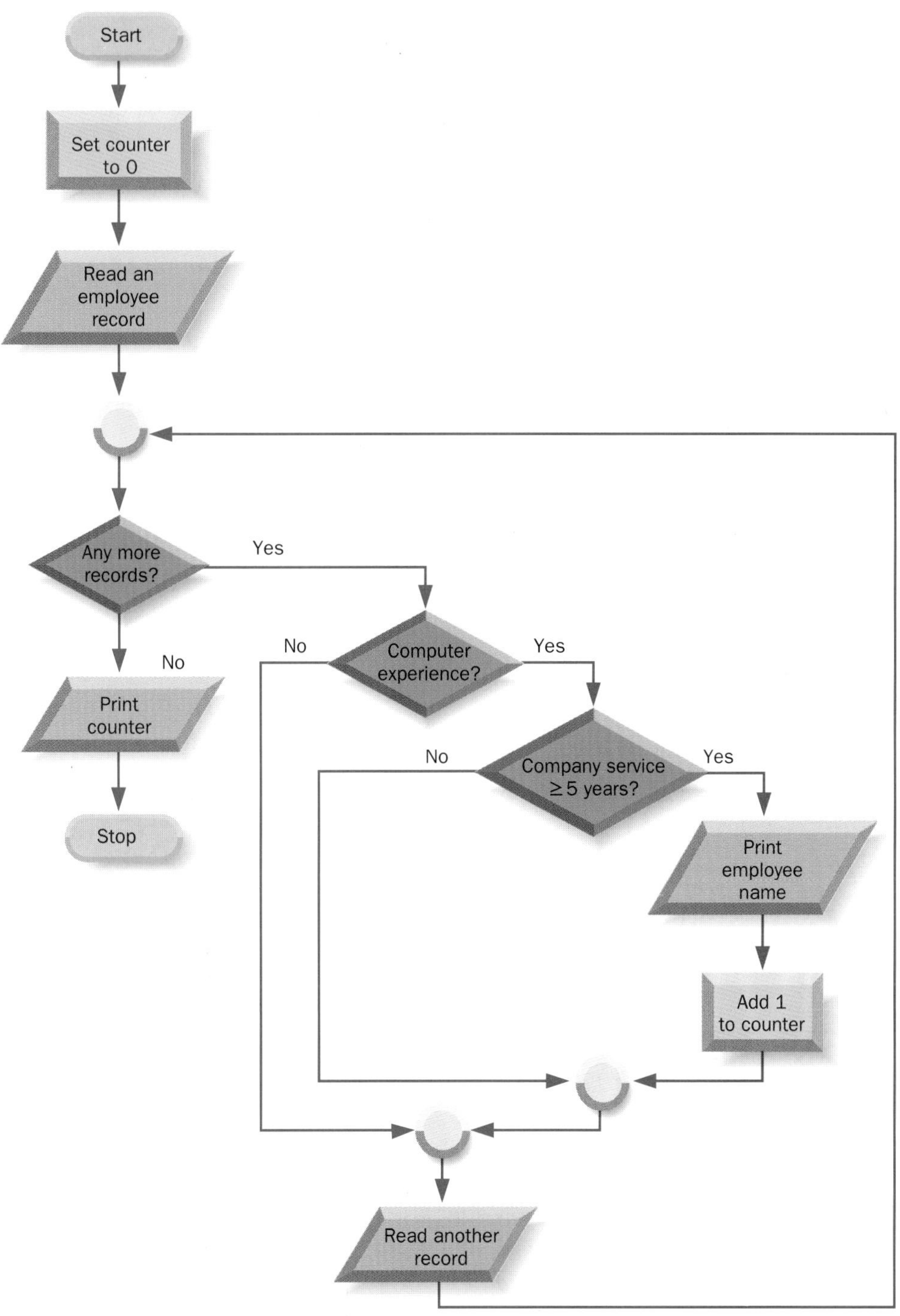

FIGURE 12-4

The three fundamental control structures of structured programming. Note that each structure has one entry point and one exit point.

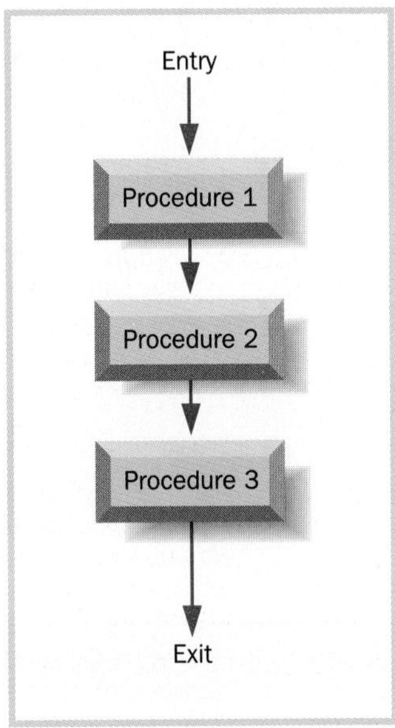

Sequence

Entry
True (Yes)
? condition
False (No)
Procedure 1
Procedure 2
Exit

Selection (If-Then- Else)

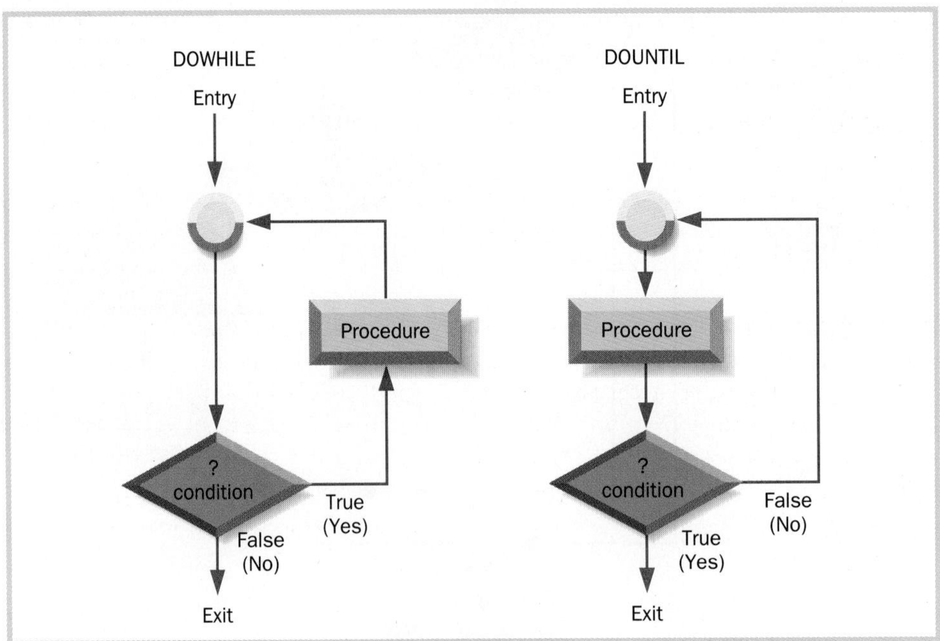

Looping (Iteration)

The Three Basic Control Structures Beginning in the 1960s, a number of researchers began to stress program design (planning) and the merits of separating the design process from the actual program coding. Many of their proposed ideas caught on, and over the last few decades a group of methods has evolved that has made program design more systematic and the programs themselves easier to understand and maintain. These methods usually are grouped together under the term **structured programming.**

Advocates of structured programming have shown that any program can be constructed out of three fundamental **control structures:** sequence, selection, and looping. Figure 12-4 illustrates these structures using flowchart symbols.

A **sequence control structure** is simply a series of procedures that follow one another. A **selection** (or **if-then-else**) **control structure** involves a choice: *If* a certain condition is true, *then* follow one procedure; *else,* if false, follow another. A *loop* is an operation that repeats until a certain condition is met. As Figure 12-4 shows, a **looping** (or **iteration**) **control structure** can take one of two forms: DOWHILE or DOUNTIL.

With **DOWHILE,** a loop is executed as long as a certain condition is true ("do *while* true"). With **DOUNTIL,** a loop continues as long as a certain condition is false ("do *until* true"). You should also note another major difference between these two forms of looping. With DOUNTIL, the loop procedure will always be executed at least once, because the procedure appears before any test is made about whether to exit the loop. With DOWHILE, the procedure may not be executed at all, because the loop-exit test appears before the procedure.

The three basic control structures are the major building blocks for structured program flowcharts and pseudocode. We discuss pseudocode later in the chapter.

The Case Structure By nesting two or more if-then-else's, you can build a fourth structure known as the **case control structure.** For example, in Figure 12-3, the two individual choices—"Computer experience?" and "Company service ≥ 5 years?"—result in the following four possibilities, or cases:

Case I: No computer experience, company service < 5 years
Case II: No computer experience, company service ≥ 5 years
Case III: Computer experience, company service < 5 years
Case IV: Computer experience, company service ≥ 5 years

One Entry Point, One Exit Point An extremely important characteristic of the control structures discussed so far is that each permits only one entry point into and one exit point out of any structure. This property is sometimes called the **one-entry-point/one-exit-point rule.** Observe the marked entry and exit points in Figure 12-4. The one-entry-point/one-exit-point convention encourages a modular, building-block programming approach that makes programs more readable and easier to maintain.

Pseudocode

An alternative to the flowchart that has become extremely popular in recent years is **pseudocode.** This structured technique uses Englishlike statements in place of the flowchart's graphic symbols. An example of pseudocode is shown in Figure 12-5.

Structured programming. An approach to program design that makes program code more systematic and maintainable.

Control structure. A pattern for controlling the flow of logic in a computer program.

Sequence control structure. The control structure used to represent operations that take place sequentially.

Selection (if-then-else) control structure. The control structure used to represent a decision operation.

Looping (iteration) control structure. The control structure used to represent a looping operation.

DOWHILE control structure. A looping control structure in which the looping continues as long as a certain condition is true (i.e., "do while true").

DOUNTIL control structure. A looping control structure in which the looping continues as long as a certain condition is false (i.e., "do until true").

Case control structure. A control structure that can be formed by nesting two or more selection control structures.

One-entry-point/one-exit-point rule. A rule stating that each program control structure will have only one entry point into it and one exit point out of it.

Pseudocode. A technique for structured program design that uses Englishlike statements to outline the logic of a program.

FIGURE 12-5

Pseudocode for solving the employee file problem of Figure 12-3. The problem requires printing the names of all people in an employee file with computer experience and at least five years of company service. A count of the number of such people is also required as output.

```
Start
Counter = 0
Read a record
DOWHILE there are more records to process
   IF computer experience
        IF company service ≥ 5 years
           Print employee name
           Increment Counter
        ELSE
           Next statement
        END IF
   ELSE
        Next statement
   END IF
   Read another record
END DO
Print Counter
Stop
```

FIGURE 12-6

Some rules for pseudocode. In addition to the rules shown here governing program control structures, pseudocode often begins with the keyword *Start* and ends with the keyword *Stop.*

Sequence Control Structure

```
BEGIN processing task
  Processing steps
END processing task
```

The steps in the sequence structure are normally written in lowercase letters. If the steps make up a well-defined block of code, they should be preceded by the keywords BEGIN and END.

Selection Control Structure

```
IF condition
  Processing steps
ELSE
  Processing steps
END IF
```

The keywords IF, ELSE, and END IF are always capitalized and tiered. The condition and processing steps normally are written in lowercase letters. The processing steps are indented from the keywords in the manner illustrated.

Looping (DOWHILE and DOUNTIL) Control Structures

```
DOWHILE condition          DOUNTIL condition
  Processing steps           Processing steps
END DO                     END DO
```

The keywords DOWHILE (or DOUNTIL) and END DO are always capitalized and tiered. The condition and processing steps follow the same lowercase convention and indentation rules as the selection control structure.

Pseudocode looks more like a program than a flowchart. In fact, it's often easier to code a program from pseudocode than from a flowchart, because the former provides a codelike outline of the processing to take place. As a result, the program designer has more control over the end product—the program itself. Also unlike a flowchart, pseudocode is relatively easy to modify and can be embedded into the program as comments. However, flowcharts, being visual, are sometimes better than pseudocode for designing logically complex problems.

There are no standard rules for writing pseudocode, but Figure 12-6 describes one set of rules that has a wide following. Note that all words relating to the three control structures of structural programming are capitalized and form a "sandwich" around other processing steps, which are indented. As Figure 12-5 shows, indentation is also used for readability. The keywords *Start* and *Stop* are often used to begin and end pseudocode, respectively.

Action Diagrams Pseudocode is now being widely employed in the creation of **action diagrams,** a tool used to develop applications programs rapidly while online to the CPU. Action diagrams are composed of brackets into which pseudocodelike statements are written (see Figure 12-7). These statements,

Action diagram. A programming tool that helps programmers code structured programs.

FIGURE 12-7

An action diagram. Action diagrams, which are created and modified with a special editor, are used to design and code pseudocodelike programs that are capable of being executed.

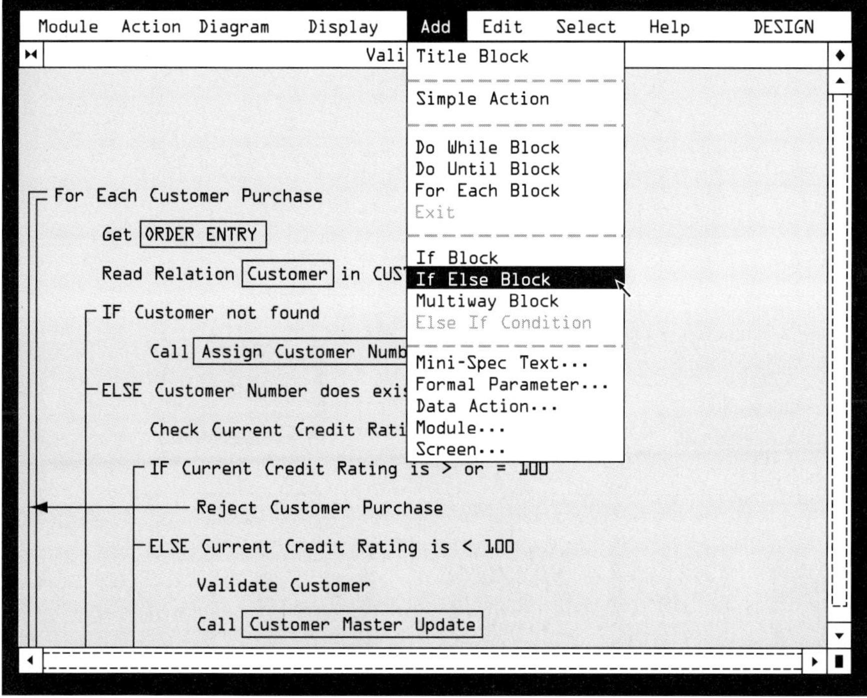

from which the computer is automatically able to develop executable code, are usually created with an *action-diagram editor.* Each control structure used in the diagram—sequence, selection, looping, or case—has its own set of brackets.

When the programmer signals that a particular control structure is to be used, the action-diagram editor creates both the appropriate pseudocode keywords and brackets. As programmers provide various conditions or field names at certain places within the brackets, the editor checks to see that the code is both valid and consistent with the existing code for the application. It does the latter by referring to the appropriate entries in the application's active data dictionary. If there is a problem, the editor will issue a warning or error message. Once an action diagram has been completed, it is automatically translated into executable code with a *code generator.* Action diagrams are an example of CASE tools, which are covered at the end of the chapter.

Structure Charts

Structure chart. A program design tool that shows the hierarchical relationship between program modules.

Structure charts, unlike flowcharts and pseudocode, depict the overall organization of a program but not the specific, step-by-step processing logic. They show how the individual program segments, or modules, are defined and how they relate to one another. Each module may consist of one or more fundamental control structures.

FIGURE 12-8

Structure charts. This program-design technique subdivides a program into individual modules, each of which represents a well-defined processing task. The modules are then arranged hierarchically in a top-down fashion, as illustrated here for a payroll application.

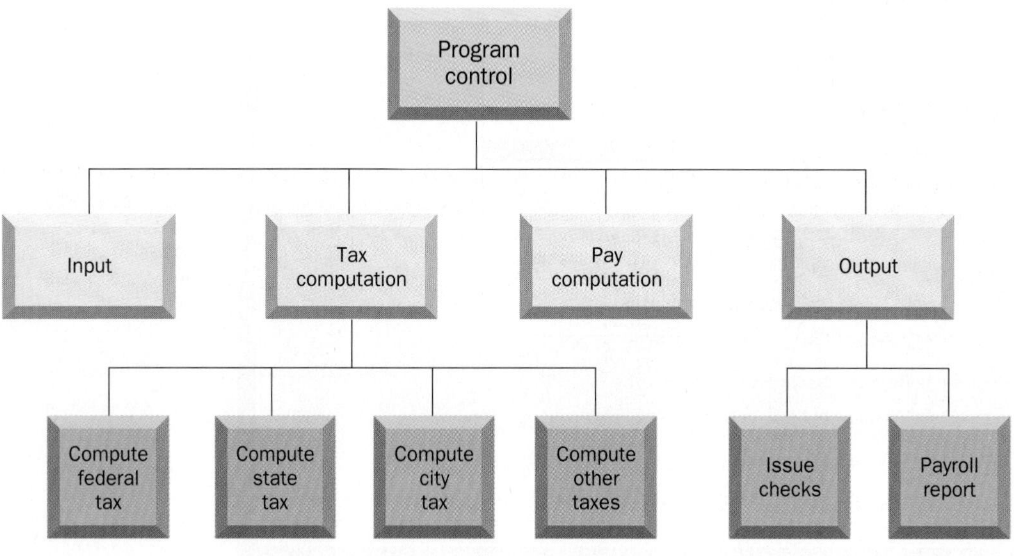

A typical structure chart, with its several rows of boxes connected by lines, looks like a corporate organization chart. Each box represents a program *module*—that is, a set of logically related operations that perform a well-defined task. The modules in the upper rows serve control functions, directing the program to process modules under them as appropriate. The modules in the lower boxes serve specific processing functions. These modules do all the program "work." The lines connecting the boxes indicate the relationship between higher-level and lower-level modules. Figure 12-8 is a structure chart for a payroll application.

Structure charts commonly embody a top-down design. **Top-down design** indicates that modules are conceptualized first at the highest levels of the hierarchy and then at progressively lower levels.

Top-down design. A structured design philosophy whereby a program or system is subdivided into well-defined modules and organized into a hierarchy.

Programming Languages

An important decision that must be made during the development of a program is the selection of a programming language. A **programming language** is a set of rules used to write instructions to the computer. Many users and organizations code the bulk of their applications in one or two prespecified languages, so this decision normally is very straightforward.

Programming language. A set of rules used to write computer programs.

Programming languages are commonly divided into three classes: low-level, high-level, and very-high-level (fourth-generation) languages.

Low-Level Languages

The earliest programming languages—machine and assembly languages—are called **low-level languages** because programmers who code in them must write instructions at the finest level of detail: the base level of the machine. In both machine languages and assembly languages each line of code corresponds to a single action of the computer system.

Low-level language. A highly detailed, machine-dependent programming language.

Virtually no one writes machine-language programs anymore, which consist of strings of 0s and 1s. Nonetheless, all programs must automatically be translated into machine language (by, say, a compiler or interpreter) before they are executed.

Assembly languages were developed to replace the 0s and 1s of machine language with symbols that are easier to understand and remember. The big advantage of assembly-language programs is executional efficiency: they're fast and consume little storage compared with their higher-level counterparts. Unfortunately, assembly-language programs take longer to write and maintain than programs written in higher-level languages.

Assembly language. A low-level programming language that uses mnemonic codes in place of the 0s and 1s of machine language.

High-Level Languages

High-level languages differ from their low-level predecessors in that they require less coding detail and make programs easier to write. Included in this class are what have come to be known as "third-generation" programming languages—BASIC, COBOL, Pascal, C, FORTRAN, PL/1, APL, and many others. A number of high-level languages that one commonly finds in computing environments are briefly discussed next.

High-level language. The class of programming languages that includes BASIC, COBOL, C, FORTRAN, and Pascal.

FIGURE 12-9

A sample BASIC program and its output. This program is designed to accept as input the name of a product, its unit selling price, and the number of units sold and to output this information along with the total dollar value of sales.

(a) BASIC program

```
 10     REM PROGRAM TO COMPUTE SALES
 20     REM AUTHOR - C.S. PARKER
 30     PRINT "    DESCRIPTION            PRICE        UNITS        TOTAL VALUE"
 40     A$="\                     \    $###.##        #,###         $###,###"
 50     READ ITEM$, PRICE, UNITS
 60     WHILE ITEM$ < > "LAST RECORD"
 70        VALUE = PRICE * UNITS
 80        PRINT USING A$; ITEM$, PRICE, UNITS, VALUE
 90        READ ITEM$, PRICE, UNITS
100     WEND
110     DATA "SMALL WIDGETS",150,100
120     DATA "LARGE SKY HOOKS",200,50
130     DATA "BLIVETS",100,3000
140     DATA "LAST RECORD",0,0
150     END
```

(b) Output from the program

```
DESCRIPTION                PRICE        UNITS           TOTAL VALUE
SMALL WIDGETS            $150.00          100             $ 15,000
LARGE SKY HOOKS          $200.00           50             $ 10,000
BLIVETS                  $100.00        3,000             $300,000
```

BASIC.
An easy-to-learn, high-level programming language developed at Dartmouth College in the 1960s.

BASIC **BASIC** (Beginner's All-purpose Symbolic Instruction Code) was designed to meet the need for an easy-to-learn beginner's language that would work in a "friendly," nonfrustrating programming environment. Over the years, it has evolved into one of the most popular and widely available programming languages. Because it is easy to learn and use, and because the storage requirements for its language translator are small, BASIC works well on almost all microcomputers. A BASIC program is illustrated in Figure 12-9.

Some experts think that BASIC's chief strength—ease of learning and use—is also its major drawback. Because beginners can get started quickly, they sometimes start off on the wrong foot by sacrificing good programming habits for quick results. Many versions of BASIC support unstructured, trial-and-error coding, so it's easy to write confusing, poorly organized programs.

COBOL.
A high-level programming language developed for transaction processing applications.

COBOL **COBOL** (COmmon Business-Oriented Language) is the principal transaction processing language in use today. Currently, some 70 to 80 percent of transaction processing applications on mainframes in large organizations are coded in COBOL. Not too long ago, use of COBOL was restricted almost exclusively to large computer systems. Today, however, with many programmers developing mainframe-based applications on microcomputer workstations, microcomputer-based COBOL is a fast-growing trend. A COBOL program is shown in Figure 12-10. The use of a graphical user interface employed with microcomputer-based COBOL-program development is shown in Figure 12-11.

FIGURE 12-10

A sample COBOL program and its output. This program solves the same sales problem as the BASIC program in Figure 12–9.

(a) COBOL program

```
IDENTIFICATION DIVISION.
  PROGRAM-ID. SALES.
  AUTHOR. PARKER.

ENVIRONMENT DIVISION.
CONFIGURATION SECTION.
  SOURCE-COMPUTER. VS9.
  OBJECT-COMPUTER. VS9.
INPUT-OUTPUT SECTION.
  FILE-CONTROL.
    SELECT DISKFILE ASSIGN TO DISK-A1F2-V.
    SELECT PRINTFILE ASSIGN TO SYSLST.
DATA DIVISION.
FILE SECTION.
FD  DISKFILE
    LABEL RECORDS ARE STANDARD.
01  DISKREC.
    05 PART-DESCRIPTION-IN      PIC X(20).
    05 PRICE-IN                 PIC 999.
    05 UNITS-SOLD-IN            PIC 9(5).
FD  PRINTFILE
    LABEL RECORDS ARE OMITTED.
01  PRINTLINE                   PIC X(120).
WORKING-STORAGE SECTION.
01  FLAGS.
    05 WS-END-OF-FILE.          PIC X(3) VALUE 'NO'.
01  HEADING-LINE.
    05 FILLER                   PIC X(9)  VALUE SPACES.
    05 FILLER                   PIC X(11) VALUE 'DESCRIPTION'.
    05 FILLER                   PIC X(10) VALUE SPACES.
    05 FILLER                   PIC X(5)  VALUE 'PRICE'.
    05 FILLER                   PIC X(7)  VALUE SPACES.
    05 FILLER                   PIC X(5)  VALUE 'UNITS'.
    05 FILLER                   PIC X(4)  VALUE SPACES.
    05 FILLER                   PIC X(11) VALUE 'TOTAL VALUE'.
01  DETAIL-LINE.
    05 FILLER                   PIC X(5)  VALUE SPACES.
    05 PART-DESCRIPTION-OUT     PIC X(20).
    05 FILLER                   PIC X(4)  VALUE SPACES.
    05 PRICE-OUT                PIC $ZZ9.99.
    05 FILLER                   PIC X(5)  VALUE SPACES.
    05 UNITS-SOLD-OUT           PIC ZZ,ZZ9.
    05 FILLER                   PIC X(5)  VALUE SPACES.
    05 SALES-VALUE              PIC $ZZZ,ZZ9.

PROCEDURE DIVISION.
010-HOUSEKEEPING.
    OPEN INPUT DISKFILE
         OUTPUT PRINTFILE.
    READ DISKFILE
         AT END MOVE 'YES' TO WS-END-OF-FILE.
    PERFORM 020-HEADINGS.
    PERFORM 030-PROCESSIT
         UNTIL WS-END-OF-FILE = 'YES'.
    CLOSE DISKFILE
          PRINTFILE.
    STOP RUN.
020-HEADINGS.
    WRITE PRINTLINE FROM HEADING-LINE
         AFTER ADVANCING 1 LINE.
```

CONTINUED

FIGURE 12-10 (CONTINUED)

```
030-PROCESSIT.
    MULTIPLY     UNITS-SOLD-IN
         BY      PRICE-IN
         GIVING SALES-VALUE.
    MOVE PART-DESCRIPTION-IN TO PART-DESCRIPTION-OUT.
    MOVE PRICE-IN              TO PRICE-OUT.
    MOVE UNITS-SOLD-IN         TO UNITS-SOLD-OUT.
    WRITE PRINTLINE FROM DETAIL-LINE
         AFTER ADVANCING 1 LINE.
    READ DISKFILE
         AT END MOVE 'YES' TO WS-END-OF-FILE.
```

(b) Output from the program

```
    DESCRIPTION              PRICE      UNITS       TOTAL VALUE
SMALL WIDGETS              $150.00        100        $ 15,000
LARGE SKY HOOKS            $200.00         50        $ 10,000
BLIVETS                    $100.00      3,000        $300,000
```

Many features differentiate COBOL from other languages. Almost all of them—including machine independence, self-documentation, and detailed input/output specifications—relate to COBOL's business transaction processing focus. But because COBOL programs use long, Englishlike names and specify formats in fine detail, they tend to be lengthy. Since lengthy programs take time

FIGURE 12-11

Microcomputer-based COBOL. Because display terminals connected to mainframes often lack color and graphical user interfaces, many programmers prefer developing mainframe-based COBOL applications on microcomputer workstations.

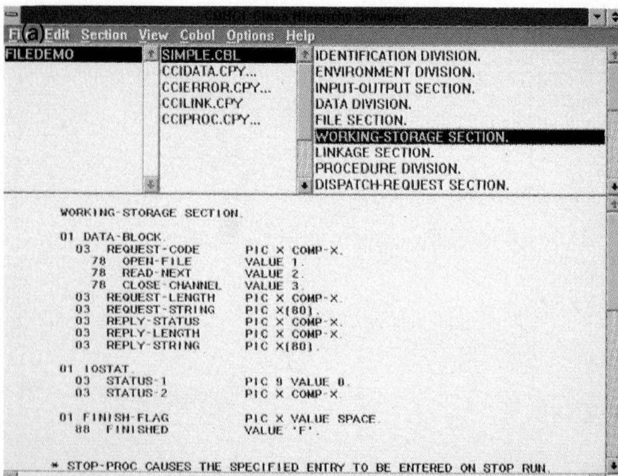

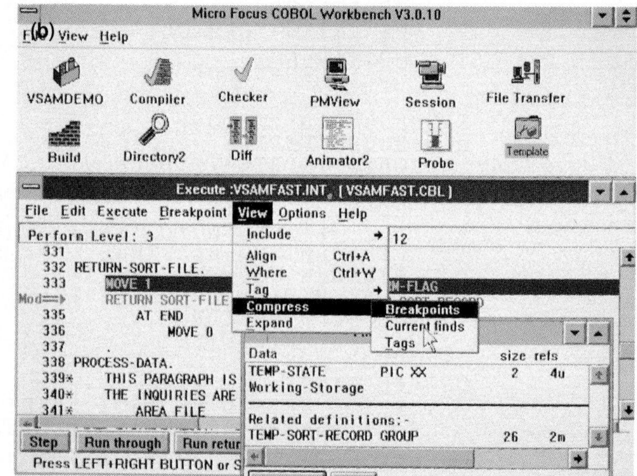

FIGURE 12-12

A sample Pascal program and its output. This program solves the same sales problem as the BASIC program in Figure 12–9.

(a) Pascal program

```
PROGRAM SALES (INPUT, OUTPUT);
(* PROGRAM TO COMPUTE SALES *)
(* AUTHOR -- C. S. PARKER *)

VAR  UNITS, INDEX          :INTEGER;
     PRICE, TOTAL          :REAL;
     PART                  :ARRAY [1..20] OF CHAR;

BEGIN
WRITELIN ('    DESCRIPTION          PRICE      UNITS      TOTAL VALUE ');
FOR INDEX := 1 TO 20 DO
  READ (PART[INDEX]);
  READLN (PRICE, UNITS);
WHILE NOT EOF DO
     BEGIN
     TOTAL := PRICE * UNITS;
     FOR INDEX := 1 TO 20 DO
       WRITE (PART[INDEX]);
       WRITELIN ('     $', PRICE:6:2, UNITS:11,'     $', TOTAL:9:2);
     FOR INDEX := 1 TO 20 DO
       READ (PART [INDEX]);
       READLN (PRICE, UNITS);
     END;
END.
```

(b) Output from the program

```
    DESCRIPTION          PRICE      UNITS      TOTAL VALUE
SMALL WIDGETS          $150.00       100        $ 15,000
LARGE SKY HOOKS        $200.00        50        $ 10,000
BLIVETS                $100.00     3,000        $300,000
```

to develop and maintain, COBOL is partly responsible for applications backlogs in many companies. In such firms, it often takes two to four years from the time an application is first approved until it is coded. (This has led some companies to adopt easier-to-code fourth-generation languages, which we'll discuss later in the chapter.) But with millions of dollars invested in COBOL programs and thousands of programmers versed in COBOL use, the language will likely endure for many more years. Despite the many complaints that COBOL is old-fashioned, cumbersome, and inelegant, if you're interested in making money as an applications programmer, COBOL is still clearly one of your best bets.

Pascal **Pascal,** named after the mathematician Blaise Pascal, was created primarily to fill the need for a teaching vehicle that would encourage structured programming. Today, Pascal is widely used in academia as a model for how a programming language should be designed. A Pascal program is shown in Figure 12-12.

Pascal.
A structured, high-level programming language that is often used to teach programming.

Although BASIC remains a strong favorite among beginners, Pascal is far superior to most versions of BASIC (and even COBOL) in its structured program-

FIGURE 12-13

A sample C program and its output. This program solves the same sales problem as the BASIC program in Figure 12–9.

(a) C program

```
/ *Program to compute sales* /
/ *Author -- C. S. Parker* /

#include <stdio.h>

main() {

  char *item[3] = {"SMALL WIDGETS   ", "LARGE SKY HOOKS", "BLIVETS        "};
  float price[3] = {150, 200, 100}, value[3];
  int units[3] = {100, 50, 3000};
  int i=0;

  while (i<3) {
     value[i] = price[i] * units[i];
     i++;
  };

  printf("    DESCRIPTION           PRICE        UNITS           TOTAL VALUE\n");
  for (i=0;i<3;i++){
    printf("%s\t\t$%5.2f\t\t%4d\t\t$%6.0f\n",
                                item[i], price[i], units[i], value[i]);
  };

}
```

(b) Output from the program

```
    DESCRIPTION           PRICE        UNITS           TOTAL VALUE
SMALL WIDGETS            $150.00        100             $ 15000
LARGE SKY HOOKS          $200.00         50             $ 10000
BLIVETS                  $100.00       3000             $300000
```

ming capability. To say that Pascal is a structured language means that, generally speaking, Pascal programs are made up of smaller subprograms, each of which is itself a structured program. This modular "building-block" approach makes it easier to develop large programs. In addition, most versions of Pascal contain a rich variety of control structures with which to manipulate program modules in a systematic fashion. Pascal also supports an abundance of data types and even lets you create new ones.

C.
A programming language that has the portability of a high-level language and the executional efficiency of an assembly language.

C C combines the best features of a structured, high-level language and an assembly language—that is, it's relatively easy to code and uses computer resources efficiently. Currently, it's one of the hottest languages for programmers to learn, largely because of its role in commercial software development. Many software vendors use C to code their products. A C program is shown in Figure 12-13.

C is used primarily by computer professionals. Although it resembles Pascal in many ways, it is not a language for beginners. Because it is a rich and sophisticated language, even experienced C programmers can get lost following a long C program.

FIGURE 12-14

A sample FORTRAN program and its output. This program solves the same sales problem as the BASIC program in Figure 12–9.

(a) FORTRAN program

```
C THIS PROGRAM COMPUTES SALES
C AUTHOR - C.S. PARKER

        CHARACTER PART*20
        INTEGER COUNT, RECORDS, UNITS

        READ (5, 100) RECORDS
        WRITE (6, 200)

        DO 999 COUNT = 1, RECORDS
        READ (5, 110) PART, PRICE, UNITS
        TOTAL = PRICE * UNITS
        WRITE (6, 210) PART, PRICE, UNITS, TOTAL
999     CONTINUE

100     FORMAT (I4)
110     FORMAT (A20,F6.2,I4)
200     FORMAT (5X,'DESCRIPTION',12X,'PRICE',7X,'UNITS',5X,'TOTAL VALUE')
210     FORMAT (1X, A,'        $',F6.2,I11,'      $',F9.2)

        STOP
        END
```

(b) Output from the program

```
    DESCRIPTION              PRICE       UNITS          TOTAL VALUE
 SMALL WIDGETS              $150.00        100           $ 15000.00
 LARGE SKY HOOKS            $200.00         50           $ 10000.00
 BLIVETS                    $100.00      3,000           $300000.00
```

Recently, a new version of C called C++ has been developed to encourage better design and programming practices. C++ is an *object-oriented* version of C (see photo on page 432). C++ is also a superset of C, making all C programs readable by C++ compilers. On the downside, C++ is still rapidly evolving as a language; consequently, few programmers are proficient in it, and many tools designed to work with C lack C++ interfaces.

FORTRAN FORTRAN (FORmula TRANslator), which dates back to 1954, is the oldest surviving high-level language still in wide use. It was designed by scientists and is oriented toward scientific, mathematical, and engineering problem solving. A FORTRAN program is shown in Figure 12-14.

FORTRAN. A high-level programming language used for mathematical, scientific, and engineering applications.

A key feature of FORTRAN is its ability to express sophisticated formulas easily. Complicated algebraic expressions are written in FORTRAN in nearly the same way as they are in conventional mathematical notation. Although BASIC, which was created as a simplified version of FORTRAN, is competitive in this area, many people consider FORTRAN superior because of its faster program execution. Since scientific and engineering programs are characterized

Feature 12-1

Visual Programming

What impact will OOP make?

Probably few would argue today that the latest rage on the programming-language scene is object-oriented programming (OOP). The basic idea behind OOP is to make writing program code more intuitive. That, OOP advocates hope, will widen the scope of applications development to include the ordinary user and make professionally prepared programs easier to develop and maintain.

Perhaps the key feature of OOP is *encapsulation*—bundling data and program instructions into modules called "objects." Here's an example of how it works. At Dunkin' Donuts—where OOP is being implemented to help franchisees better manage inventory, operations, and finances—objects are used to represent business functions. By selecting the "sales" object (icon) on the screen, a manager at a Dunkin' Donuts outlet can access sales figures and pull up a growth chart based on those figures. Other objects may come in the form of scrollable windows or an interrelated hierarchy of windows.

Many industry observers feel that the encapsulation feature of OOP is the natural tool for making the transition to complex applications in which speech and moving images are integrated with

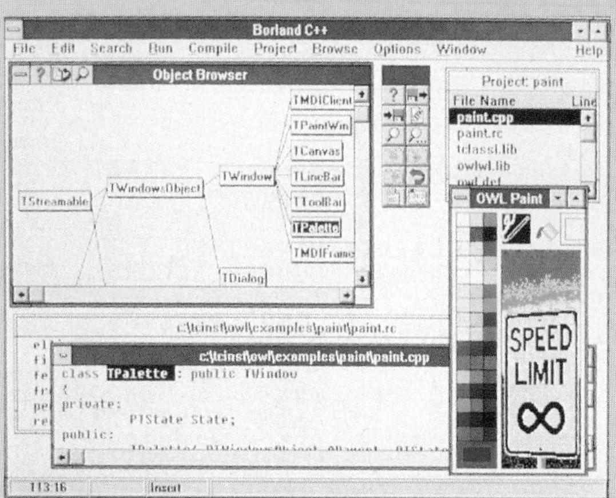

Borland's C++. Only a handful of languages today have object-oriented interfaces.

by numerous computations and frequent looping, execution speed is a primary concern. Most FORTRAN compilers are so effective at "number crunching" that they are even superior in this respect to the compilers of most modern languages. The reasons for this date back to the 1950s. When FORTRAN was first developed, it had to compete with assembly languages for execution efficiency, and this quality has remained an important factor in its design.

PL/1 *PL/1* (Programming Language/1) was introduced in the mid-1960s by IBM as a general-purpose language; that is, it was designed for both scientific and transaction processing applications. It's an extremely powerful language and has strong capabilities for structured programming.

APL *APL* (A Programming Language) was developed in the early 1960s to enable programmers to code rapidly. It is an extremely compact language, with conventions that are quite different than those of other programming languages. APL requires a special keyboard.

Ada *Ada,* a superset of Pascal, is a relatively new structured language initiated by the U.S. Department of Defense. As a superset of Pascal, it shares many of Pascal's properties. It is still too early, however, to guess how successful it will be in the business and academic worlds.

text and graphics. With moving images and voice built into the objects themselves, program developers avoid the sticky problem of deciding how each separate type of data is to be integrated and synchronized into a working whole.

A second key feature of OOP is *inheritance.* This allows OOP developers to define one set of objects, say "Employees at the Dearborn plant," and a specific instance of this object, say, "Welders." Thus, if employees at the Dearborn plant are eligible for a specific benefits package, welders automatically qualify for the package. If welder John Smith is later relocated from Dearborn to Birmingham, Alabama, where a different benefits package is available, there will be no problem. An icon representing John Smith—such as John Smith's face—can be selected on the screen and dragged with a mouse to the icon representing the Birmingham plant. He then automatically "inherits" the Birmingham benefit package.

The combination of encapsulation and inheritance leads to two major benefits: code reusability and the ability to make changes rapidly.

Reusable code means that new programs can easily be cut-and-pasted together from old programs. All one has to do is access a library of objects and stitch them into a working whole. Code reusability is critical in programming because it eliminates the need to write code from scratch and then debug it. Thus, reusability makes both program development and program maintenance faster by an order of magnitude or more. Such productivity gains can be influential to the corporate bottom line; recent studies show that about 80 percent of commercial programmer time is spent keeping existing programs up to date.

While OOP has gotten rave reviews so far, it's still too early to tell what its full impact will be. To date, many languages still lack object-oriented interfaces. Not only that, many traditional programmers find object-oriented programming "counterintuitive" to the way they've been trained for years to think about development. Also, object-oriented tools for users are still too new to reliably predict what their eventual effect might be. Although impressed so far, the corporate world is wary of jumping in feet first where new tools are concerned.

Logo *Logo* is a programming language that also represents a philosophy of learning. It was developed in the 1970s by Seymour Papert of MIT, who incorporated into its specification some of the learning theories of Swiss psychologist Jean Piaget. Logo has been very popular with children, many of whom find it both easy to learn and exciting.

RPG *RPG* (Report Program Generator) was developed by IBM in the early 1960s to produce reports quickly on small computers. Programmers provide facts on special coding forms about what a report should look like, and, after the forms are machine coded, the RPG package determines how the job will be done and creates (generates) a computer program that will produce the desired report.

Smalltalk *Smalltalk,* pioneered at the University of Utah in the late 1960s, represents a significant departure from conventional programming languages. Specifically, Smalltalk is an **object-oriented programming language;** that is, it works with *objects* and *messages* that encapsulate both instructions and data rather than with a set of instructions and a separate set of data, as in traditional languages. Some experts think that at some point in the future, object-oriented languages will dominate the programming language landscape (see Feature 12-1).

Object-oriented programming language. A language that works with objects and messages rather than with separate instructions and data.

LISP and Prolog *LISP* (LISt Processor) and *Prolog* are used to develop applications in the field of artificial intelligence, a topic we covered in Chapter 11. LISP, a programming language that is nearly as old as FORTRAN, is often implemented on a special, dedicated computer system. Prolog, created about 1970, is designed to run on an ordinary computer.

Fourth-Generation Languages (4GLs)

Fourth-generation language (4GL). An easy-to-learn, easy-to-use language that enables users or programmers to code applications much more quickly than they could with third-generation languages.

Machine language and assembly language characterized the first and second generations of computing, respectively. During the third generation, languages such as FORTRAN, BASIC, and COBOL became dominant. Today, in the so-called fourth generation of the computer age, a new breed of languages has arrived. These *very-high-level languages* are appropriately called **fourth-generation languages (4GLs).** In contrast to lower-level languages, they are much easier to use and, consequently, they result in increased on-the-job productivity.

The 4GLs found in the market are diverse and serve a wide range of application areas. Some are targeted to users, some to programmers, and some to both. Six types of 4GLs commonly found in commercial software products are described in the following list and summarized in Figure 12-15. Many of these language functions overlap in a single product. For instance, Lotus Development Corporation's 1-2-3 is a decision support system tool with facilities for report generation, retrieval and update, and graphics generation.

Report Generators A *report generator* is a tool that enables you to prepare reports quickly and easily. For instance, report generators packaged with database management systems allow you to create reports by declaring which data fields are to be represented as report columns and which report columns are to be used to sort data. The report is then generated automatically.

Retrieval and Update Languages As more and more busy people learned to use computers to search through large files and databases, it became increasingly important to develop language products that would make this process as painless as possible. *Retrieval and update 4GLs* allow you to retrieve or update

FIGURE 12-15

Types of fourth-generation languages (4GLs). 4GLs have evolved to make both end users and programmers more productive.

Report generators Used to generate reports quickly

Retrieval and update languages Used to retrieve information from files or databases and to add, delete, or modify data

Decision support system tools Used to create financial schedules, budgets, models of decision environments, and the like

Graphics generators Used to quickly prepare presentation graphics

Applications packages Prewritten programs for applications such as word processing, payroll, and various accounting tasks

Applications generators Used to quickly prepare applications programs, without having to resort to programming in a third-generation language in large files or databases without having to spend weeks learning a complicated programming syntax to do so.

Decision Support System Tools *Decision support system tools* provide computing capabilities that help people make decisions. Perhaps the most familiar of such tools is the spreadsheet package, which we covered in Chapter 9. Other examples are modeling packages, which allow you to create complex mathematical models, and statistical packages, which facilitate statistical analysis.

Graphics Generators *Graphics generators*, often called presentation graphics routines, are tools that help you to prepare business graphs. When you invoke the graphics generator, it will ask you a number of questions about your graph—what type it is, where the data are to create the graph, what colors and titles you want, and so on. After you satisfactorily respond to all of the questions, the graph is automatically created. We covered presentation graphics in some detail in Chapter 9.

Applications Packages An *applications package* is a "canned" program designed to perform some common business application, such as payroll, accounts receivable, invoicing, or word processing. Like a graphics generator, an applications package usually asks the user a number of questions. The responses are subsequently used to assign values to parameters within the package, to customize it to specific needs.

Applications Generators An *applications generator* is a package that enables you to quickly code applications software. These packages work in a variety of ways. For instance, some are primarily *code generators*— that is, they contain routines that allow shorthand code or pseudocode to be automatically translated (generated) into a third-generation language such as COBOL (refer back to Figure 12-7). Others, such as Microsoft's *Visual BASIC*, are designed expressly to create graphical-user-interface (GUI) environments such as new Microsoft Windows programs (see Figure 12-16). Visual BASIC is also the standard language used to develop applications in the Microsoft Office suite of application programs.

One of the newest types of applications generators is *authoring software*, used to develop multimedia applications. These 4GL tools enable text, graphics, voice, and video data to be combined and synchronized to form an applications environment such as a training or presentation device for the user. Apple's HyperCard was one of the first authoring programs to become commercially successful. While a detailed discussion of authoring software is beyond the scope of this text, Window 6 illustrates a few of its features.

Natural Languages

Software that uses a **natural-language interface** enables humans to communicate with the computer system in their native language—whether it be English, Spanish, Japanese, or any other tongue. The user of a natural-language interface does not have to learn the rules, or syntax, of a particular computer language. Instead, requests are typed out at a keyboard as if one were writing a memo or instructions to a human assistant.

Natural-language interface. Software that allows users to communicate with the computer in a conversational language such as English, Spanish, and Japanese.

FIGURE 12-16

Visual BASIC. This Windows-oriented applications generator includes programming tools for adding messaging, pen computing, and video and voice components to applications. It can also be used to access databases on PCs, minicomputers, and mainframes.

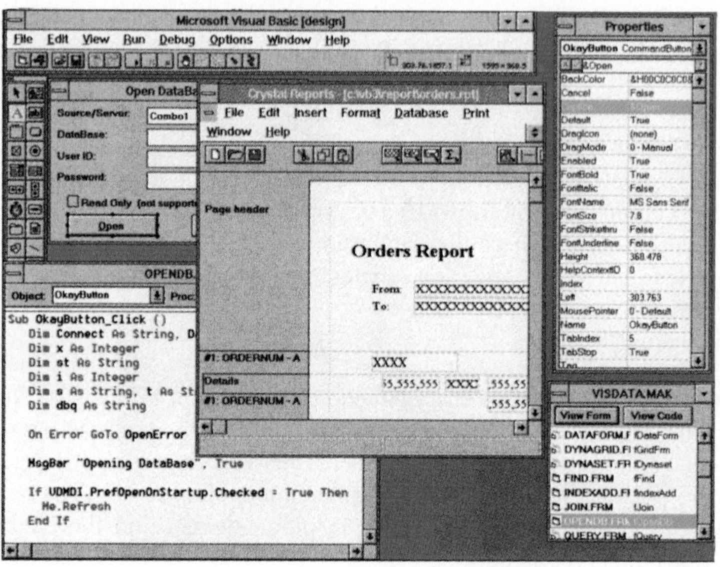

Natural-language processing is still in its infancy. It is most frequently employed as a "front end" in file or database management packages, handling situations in which users need to retrieve information or generate simple reports. Users type the information request in a natural language. As each request is typed in, the natural-language system builds a command that can be processed by the file or database management package in use. Then the system hands over the request to the package for execution. Theoretically, the same natural-language front end can be used on any software package, so the user can conceivably work with hundreds of different programs without having to know a conventional programming language.

A typical natural-language dialogue between the user and computer is shown in Figure 12-17. Today, most natural-language systems work with typed-in requests similar to the one shown in the figure. As voice input and output systems improve, it is likely that the preferred interface for most natural-language applications will not be typed-in text but voice. Someday you might find a friendly talking head on the screen whose lips are in sync with the computer voice chip and who can personalize the entire interaction for you.

As in human conversation, it is expected that users of natural-language systems will converse using everyday words, whole sentences and sentence fragments, and ambiguous phrases. The user may misspell words, misuse words, or use slang or words with multiple meanings. The natural-language system must contain advanced software that attempts to determine what the user means

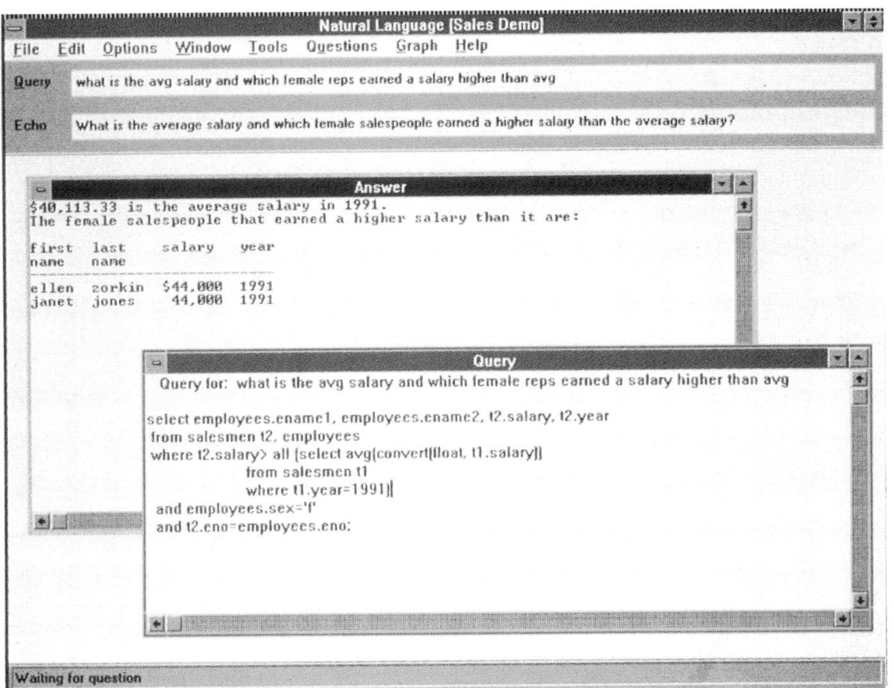

FIGURE 12-17

Natural language. A good natural language provides users considerable latitude in composing query instructions and echoes back, for verification purposes, how the computer system is interpreting the instructions.

by looking for key words, making assumptions, and drawing conclusions from earlier dialogue. A good natural-language system interacts heavily with the user to try to clarify each request so that it can take the right action. As you can see in the dialogue in the figure, the natural-language system echoes back to the operator any assumptions that it is making as a result of an input.

Program Coding

Once the program design is complete and the development language has been chosen, the next step is to code the program. **Coding** is the actual process of writing the program in a programming language.

Coding.
The writing of programming-language instructions.

During the coding, computer professionals often take advantage of a number of special tools and methods that help make them more productive. The purpose of these techniques is to ensure that programmers produce code rapidly while creating programs that are both easy to maintain and as error-free as possible. Four techniques that are useful in many programming environments are coding standards, fourth-generation languages, reusable code, and data dictionaries.

Coding Standards Many organizations and individuals follow a set of *coding standards,* which are essentially a list of rules designed to standardize programming style. These rules may cover items such as acceptable program structures, field-naming conventions, and comment conventions. Rules such as these help make programs readable and easy to maintain. If programs consistently use the same set of conventions, anyone making changes to the program knows what to expect.

Fourth-Generation Languages In the last section we covered *fourth-generation languages*—languages that simplify using computers. Although many products using these languages—such as word processors and spreadsheets—are targeted primarily to the needs of end users, others have been created specifically to streamline the applications development process for professional programmers. For instance, applications generators enable programmers to quickly develop applications without having to deal directly with a traditional third-generation programming language such as COBOL or BASIC. Applications packages such as accounting programs provide an easy, off-the-shelf solution to many applications development problems.

Reusable Code Related programs often use the same blocks of code. Take, for example, payroll programs. A company may have a dozen or more of them—programs that cut checks to employees; report every check issued by the treasurer's office; report payments to the city, state, or federal government; and so on. Rather than have programmers code each of these programs from scratch, most organizations keep libraries of reusable code available. **Reusable code,** as you might guess, refers to "generic" code segments that can be used over and over again by several programs. Thus, reusable code enables programs to be "cut and pasted" quickly from pretested, error-free code segments.

Reusable code. Program segments that can be reused several times in constructing applications programs.

Data Dictionaries A **data dictionary** is similar to an ordinary dictionary in that it contains rules of usage for an alphabetical list of words. The words are those encountered in the company's information processing environment. Among them would be, for example, names of fields, records, files, and programs.

Data dictionary. A facility that informs users and programmers about characteristics of data and programs in a database or a computer system.

Data dictionaries can be active or passive. An *active* data dictionary is online to an application as a programmer is developing it. If, say, a programmer attempts to use a field name improperly or inconsistently, the active data dictionary will immediately warn the programmer, and it may prohibit the alleged infraction from being part of the finished software product. A data dictionary that is not online during application development is *passive.*

Debugging and Testing Programs

Debugging is the process of ensuring that a program is free of errors, or "bugs." Debugging is usually a lengthy process, sometimes amounting to over 50 percent of a program's development time.

Debugging. The process of detecting and correcting errors in computer programs or in the computer system itself.

Preliminary Debugging The debugging process often begins after the program is initially entered into the computer system. Rarely is any program error-free the first time the programmer attempts to execute it. A very long program may have well over a hundred errors of one sort or another—and maybe even thousands—at the outset. The computer's systems software usually provides the programmer with a list of informative "error messages" indicating the source of many of the bugs. At this point, the programmer again checks the code to see what's wrong, makes the necessary corrections, and reexecutes the program. This "execute, check, and correct" process will probably be repeated several more times before the program is free of bugs.

Testing At some point in the debugging process, the program will appear to be correct. At this point, the original programmer—or, preferably, someone else—runs the program with extensive *test data.* Good test data will subject the program to all the conditions it might conceivably encounter when it is finally implemented. The test data should also check for likely sources of coding omissions. For example, will the program issue a check or a bill in the amount of $0.00? Does the program provide for leap years when dating reports? Although rigorous testing significantly decreases the chance of malfunctioning when a program is implemented, there is no foolproof guarantee that the completed program will be bug-free.

Proper debugging is vital, because an error that costs only a few dollars to fix at this stage in the development process may cost many thousands of dollars to correct after the program is implemented. Feature 12-2 covers some of the procedures used by commercial software developers to debug and test programs.

Program Maintenance

Virtually every program, if it is to last a long time, requires ongoing maintenance. Program **maintenance** is the process of updating software so that it continues to be useful. For instance, if new types of data are added to a database and existing programs must be modified to use these data, program maintenance is necessary. Program maintenance is also commonly triggered by new software releases, new equipment announcements, and changes in the way business is conducted.

Maintenance. The process of making upgrades and minor modifications to systems or software over time.

Program maintenance is costly to organizations. It has been estimated that many organizations spend well over half of their programming time just maintaining existing applications programs. One of the major reasons why such tools as coding standards, fourth-generation languages, reusable code, and data dictionaries are so popular today is because these tools can result in lower maintenance costs.

Program Documentation

Program **documentation** includes manuals that enable users, maintenance programmers, and operators to interact successfully with a program. If you've ever had the frustration of trying to get something to work from poorly written instructions, you can appreciate how valuable good documentation can be.

Documentation. A detailed written description of a program, procedure, or system.

User documentation normally consists of a user's manual. This manual should provide instructions for running the program, a description of language commands, several examples of situations the end user is likely to encounter, and a troubleshooting guide to help with difficulties.

Feature 12–2

Beta Testing

How commercial developers get users into the act

Before the PC became a regular fixture, developing commercial software was a relatively simple process. A software vendor wrote a program, tested it internally, and then released it for general use. But times have changed.

In recent years, with the possible configurations of equipment numbering in the thousands, it is impossible to fully test software in house. So software developers have turned to the actual product users to serve as guinea pigs through a process commonly known as *beta testing.* To test Windows 3.1 and OS/2 Version 2.0, for instance, Microsoft and IBM each sent out preliminary copies of their respective software—called "beta versions"—to over 25,000 users.

Beta testing is usually done in waves. The first beta version may go to only a few dozen hard-

Usability lab. Observing users firsthand, before the software gets out the door.

Programmer documentation usually consists of any tools that will simplify maintenance of the program. These might include a program narrative, design tools such as flowcharts and structure charts, a listing of the program, and a description of inputs and outputs. There should also be a set of procedures to help programmers test the program.

Operator documentation includes manuals that assist machine operators in setting up hardware devices, learning the ins and outs of successful hardware operation, and diagnosing machine malfunctions. Operator documentation is machine-dependent, and, unless you have a good grounding in computer fundamentals, it can be difficult to read through.

Quality Assurance

Quality assurance. The process of making sure quality programs are written in a quality way.

Quality assurance, as regards applications development, refers to the process of making sure quality programs are written in a quality way. The quality assurance function in many firms is carried out by a staff that's charged with making an independent, unbiased audit of program-development operations.

A major focus in quality assurance is on the outputs produced by programs. Not only are outputs checked for accuracy, but also for completeness, timeliness, relevance, and understandability. Furthermore, outputs are compared against original user requests to make sure programs are doing exactly what they are supposed to do—serving key user needs. System messages to the user are also evaluated to ensure programs are easy to use.

core users, the subsequent version may go to a couple of hundred users, and so on. Several thousand users may test the last version, since that's the one the developer goes with before making final adjustments to the product.

Beta testing serves a variety of purposes. First and foremost it samples the software over the numerous hardware platforms collectively owned by the user base. Beta testing can also save time and money when the final release is shipped, because the developer picks up valuable knowledge on how to inform users of upgrades. And—although few vendors would "fess up" to the fact—beta testing is a good vehicle for marketing a new product to consumers and for getting them excited about it prior to shipment.

Unfortunately for you interested testers out there, the compensation is small for beta testing while the expectations are large. Often, testers receive a free copy of the package when it's released and maybe some promotional items, such as a T-shirt and mug. The vendor, on the other hand, usually expects some type of reporting on a regular basis.

Beta testing is not in any way a substitute for in-house testing. Users are often busy people who have regular jobs. Understandably, they typically won't have the time to give the beta test their best shot. According to one industry consultant who specializes in new information technology, it is not unusual for only ten percent of the beta testers to actually load and use the programs they are sent.

Many companies will also test software long before the beta test. Some of the largest software developers have usability labs that first put the software through a "reality check," to see if users understand the package (see photo). The lab may contain one-way mirrors as well as experienced trainers and pyschologists that can recognize user confusion when they see it. Often, even programmers are invited in to see how users react to their work. Usually monitored are such indicators as the amount of time it takes to do a task, the number of keystrokes and errors made, the types of keystrokes and errors made, and if and how the user employed a mouse.

Program development activities are another major target in the quality-assurance effort. Here, it is important to ascertain that programs have been developed using acceptable design and coding standards and that they have been properly tested and documented.

Quality-assurance specialists also look closely at program and system security. It is critical that programs and their data be secure from tampering and unauthorized use and that proper program controls be in place to safeguard against errors.

Computer-Aided Software Engineering (CASE)

Software development has never been an easy process. In fact, a partner at Arthur Andersen & Co. recently estimated that the average business applications program takes some 32,000 hours to develop from start to finish—an effort worthy of a team of three dozen programmers working for almost three years. And that represents only the programs that get finished! No wonder managers are looking for a better way to get programs developed.

In the last dozen years, a number of solutions have surfaced. Among the most promising are **CASE (computer-aided software engineering)** tools. The objective of CASE tools is automating one or more stages of applications

Computer-aided software engineering (CASE). Program products that automate systems and program development activities.

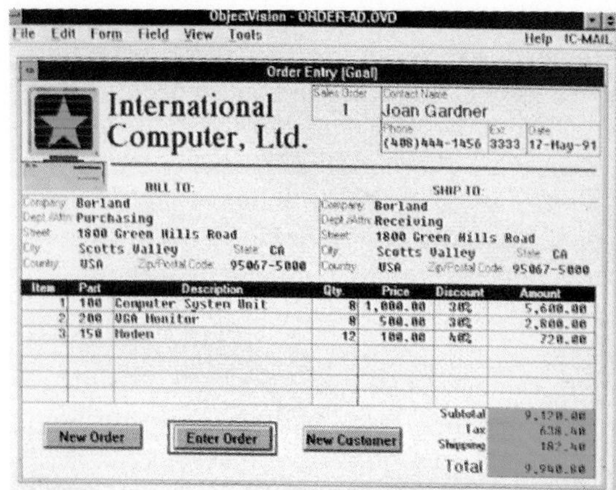

User Solution 12-1

Developing A Small System in Record Time

To help its clients get an understanding of how quality is defined around the world, Ernst & Young, a New York-based accounting and consulting firm, sent hundreds of people a questionnaire to be filled out by hand. When the surveys were completed and returned, the firm outsourced the work of keying the data into the computer and summarizing it. The outsourcer used Borland International's ObjectVision—a CASE product that has both a forms generator and a database—to quickly develop a screen form that looked like the ones that were mailed out and to report results. The form made it easy for the hefty task of inputting data to be done by temporary workers. ObjectVision can also be used to fill out forms directly on the computer, bypassing the need to rekey data and forcing survey participants to answer all survey questions.

software development. Although CASE is in its infancy now and has numerous bugs to be worked out, many people believe that most commercial software will be developed through a CASE-type approach at a not-too-distant future point.

Many of the CASE products now offered in the marketplace are called *software engineering workbenches.* Like a carpenter's workbench, which comprises a number of the tools of the carpentry trade—hammers, saws, chisels, drill bits, and the like—software engineering workbenches contain a number of design, programming, and maintenance tools that get software products developed faster. For instance, such a workbench might consist of an action-diagram editor, a fourth-generation language, a code generator, a feature that facilitates the development of reusable code libraries, an active data dictionary, and tools that help turn unstructured programs into structured ones (see Figure 12-18). The specific tools included in the workbench vary from one vendor to another.

No company has yet developed an everything-but-the-kitchen-sink CASE package, the panacea that will cure every company's applications software development headaches. Consequently, an organization may have to shop around for several CASE products that will meet its needs collectively. This is easier said than done; many CASE tools are incompatible with one another and may not interface well with other proprietary software products that the organization is using. Fortunately, CASE vendors realize this and currently are attempting to forge alliances with other vendors to establish standards that will increase CASE applicability. Currently the most successful product in the CASE marketplace is Index Technology Corporation's Excelerator, a PC-based workbench product targeted primarily to systems analysis and design and to documentation. User Solution 12-1 describes one company's choice of Borland International's ObjectVision CASE tool to meet the needs of a particular application.

FIGURE 12-18

A CASE package. CASE products make it possible to develop applications software faster, with fewer coding mistakes.

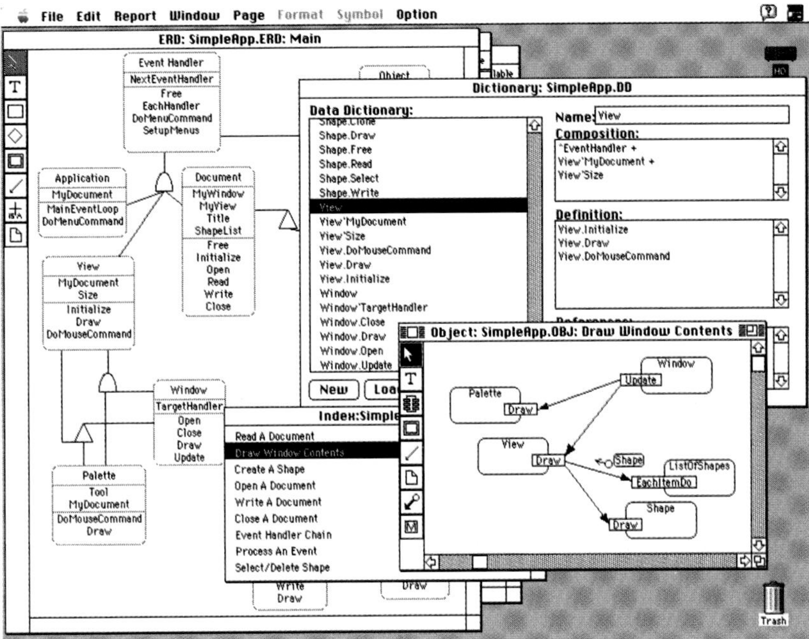

Summary and Key Terms

Like building a house, creating a successful applications program requires considerable planning.

Program Development Activities The steps associated with creating successful applications programs are called **applications software development.**

In most large organizations, the development of applications software is the job of systems analysts and programmers. **Systems analysts** are the people who work with users to assess needs, translate those needs into a list of technical requirements, and design the necessary software specifications. The design is then handed to a **programmer,** who codes the program from it. Maintenance programmers monitor the software on an ongoing basis, correcting errors and altering the software as applications needs change.

The Make-or-Buy Decision Many organizations choose to buy their software in the form of prewritten **applications packages** rather than creating it in house. The consideration to create software or acquire it from a vendor, which often takes place after the analysis and design stages of systems development, is frequently called the *make-or-buy decision.*

Program Design Many tools are available to help the analyst design programs, including program flowcharts, pseudocode, and structure charts.

Program flowcharts use geometric symbols and familiar logical symbols to provide a graphic display of the sequence of steps involved in a program. The steps in a flowchart follow each other in the same logical sequence as their corresponding statements will follow in a program.

A group of techniques has evolved that has made program design more systematic and programs themselves easier to understand and maintain. These techniques are often grouped together under the term **structured programming.** Advocates of structured programming have shown that any program can be constructed out of three fundamental **control structures**—sequence, selection, and looping.

A **sequence control structure** is simply a series of procedures that follow one another. The **selection** (or **if-then-else**) **control structure** involves a choice: *If* a certain condition is true, *then* follow one procedure; *else,* if false, follow another. A **looping** (or **iteration**) **control structure** repeats until a certain condition is met. A *loop* can take two forms: **DOWHILE** and **DOUNTIL.** By nesting two or more if-then-else's, you can build a fourth control structure, known as a **case control structure.** All of these control structures follow the **one-entry point/one-exit-point rule**—that is, a structure can have only one way into it and one way out of it.

Pseudocode is a structured technique that uses Englishlike statements in place of the graphic symbols of the flowchart. Pseudocode is commonly employed in the creation of **action diagrams.**

Structure charts, unlike flowcharts and pseudocode, depict the overall, hierarchical organization of program modules and not the specific, step-by-step process logic involved. **Top-down design** indicates that modules are defined first at the highest levels of the hierarchy and then at successively lower levels.

Programming Languages An important decision that must be made during the design phase is the selection of a **programming language.** Programming languages are either **low-level languages,** such as machine and **assembly languages; high-level languages,** such as **BASIC, Pascal, COBOL, C, FORTRAN,** PL/1, APL, Ada, Logo, RPG, Smalltalk (an **object-oriented language**), LISP, and Prolog; or *very-high-level* languages, which are also called **fourth-generation languages (4GLs).** Six types of 4GLs commonly used are report generators, retrieval and update languages, decision support system tools, graphics generators, applications packages, and applications generators. Interfaces that use **natural languages** are also available; they enable humans to communicate with the computer system in their own native language—whether it be English, Spanish, or Japanese.

Program Coding Once analysts have finished the program design for an application, the next stage is to code the program. **Coding,** which is the job of programmers, is the process of writing a program from scratch from a set of design specifications. Among the techniques that have been developed to increase programmer productivity are coding standards, fourth-generation languages, **reusable code,** and **data dictionaries.**

Debugging And Testing Programs **Debugging** is the process of making sure that a program is free of errors, or "bugs." Debugging is usually a lengthy process, sometimes amounting to over 50 percent of the total development time for an in-house program. Once preliminary debugging is complete, programs will also have to be *tested.* Good test data will subject the program to all the conditions it might conceivably encounter when finally implemented.

Program Maintenance Program **maintenance** is the process of updating software so that it continues to be useful. Program maintenance is costly; it has been estimated that some organizations spend well over half of their programming time just maintaining existing applications.

Program Documentation Program **documentation** includes manuals that enable users, maintenance programmers, and operators to interact successfully with a program. Although noted as the final stage of the program development cycle, documentation is an ongoing process that must be addressed throughout the life of the project.

Quality Assurance **Quality assurance,** as it regards applications development, refers to the process of making sure quality programs are written in a quality way. Closely checked for quality are the outputs produced by programs, the program development process itself, and security.

Computer-Aided Software Engineering (CASE) **Computer-aided software engineering (CASE)** refers to computer programs that assist in the development of other software. CASE packages differ widely, and no one vendor has produced a product that will cure every applications development headache.

Review Exercises

Fill-in Questions

1. ______________ define the requirements that applications software must meet to satisfy users' needs.
2. ______________ refers to the writing of computer programs.
3. The process of detecting and correcting errors in computer programs is called ______________.
4. A program ______________ uses geometric symbols and familiar relational symbols to provide a graphic display of the steps involved in a program.
5. ______________ is a program design tool that uses Englishlike statements.
6. ______________ is the principal transaction processing language in use today.
7. Report generators, retrieval and update languages, applications packages, and applications generators are all examples of ______________ languages.
8. Program pieces designed to be "cut and pasted" into several programs are called ______________.

Matching Questions

Match each term with the description that fits best.

a. Visual BASIC	e. flowchart
b. sequence	f. pseudocode
c. debugging	g. Pascal
d. documentation	h. program design tool

____ 1. A structure chart, for example.

____ 2. The process of ridding a program of errors.

____ 3. A graphical design tool with boxes and arrows showing step by step how a computer will process data.

____ 4. A program control structure.

____ 5. A technique for designing programs that uses Englishlike statements resembling actual program statements to show the step-by-step processing a program will follow.

____ 6. A high-level programming language named after a mathematician.

____ 7. A written description of a program, such as a manual.

____ 8. An applications generator.

Discussion Questions

1. What is done during applications software development?
2. What is an applications package? Provide two examples.
3. Name some advantages and disadvantages of applications packages relative to in-house systems development.
4. Why have structured techniques evolved as a major strategy in program design?
5. Name three fundamental control structures of structured programming and provide an example of each.
6. What is the difference between the DOWHILE and DOUNTIL control structures?
7. What is the difference between a flowchart and a structure chart?
8. What need is met by each of the following programming languages: BASIC, COBOL, FORTRAN, C, Pascal?
9. Identify several types of fourth-generation languages and the principal purpose each one serves.
10. Identify some ways to increase programmer productivity.
11. What is the purpose of program maintenance?
12. Why is program documentation important?

Critical Thinking Questions

1. Most end users and programmers within organizations would prefer to work with a widely used applications package than a comparable software product developed in-house. Why is this so, and what benefits and/or problems does the widely used applications package present to the organization?
2. Computer programs have been created that distinguish people who are good credit risks from those who are not. How, would you suppose, do computer programs make this distinction?
3. With so many programming languages around today, why are new ones constantly being developed? Do any of these new programming languages really have a chance at wide acceptance, given the number of languages now is use?
4. Chapter 12 discusses the use of CASE tools in software development. If you had to justify the purchase of a $10,000 CASE package to your busy boss—who doesn't have even the vaguest notion of what CASE is—what would you say in that all-important first 60 seconds of your pitch?
5. India has recently become a major source of programmers to the world. How have both information technology and nontechnology-related conditions within India made it easier for programmers in that nation to compete in the global marketplace?

Becoming a Microcomputer Owner or User

13

How do you go about acquiring a microcomputer system and keeping it up to date? Read Chapter 13 to find out. As people increasingly rely on microcomputers for their own use, it is becoming ever more important to be knowledgeable about them.

OUTLINE

Overview
The Microcomputer Marketplace
- Microcomputer Products
- Sales and Distribution

Selecting a Computer System
- Analyzing Needs
- Listing Alternatives
- Evaluating Alternatives
- Choosing a System

Operating a Computer System
- Backup
- Proper Maintenance of Resources
- Troubleshooting and Repairs

Upgrading
- Functional versus Technological Obsolescence

Learning More about Microcomputers

LEARNING OBJECTIVES

After completing this chapter, you will be able to:

1. Identify some of the leading companies in critical market segments of the microcomputer industry, as well as the key sales and distribution alternatives for microcomputing products.
2. Explain how to select a microcomputer system for home or office use.
3. Name some practices designed to protect software, hardware, and data resources from damage, and list some important guidelines that you should follow when troubleshooting problems and having equipment repaired.
4. Describe some of the ways in which a computer system can be upgraded, and explain under what conditions an upgrade should take place.
5. Name several sources for learning more about microcomputer systems.

Overview

It is becoming more common for a person to own a microcomputer or to use one at work. Consequently, more people than ever before are acquiring their own microcomputer resources, taking care of their systems, deciding when to call for outside help, upgrading their systems on their own, and so on. The purpose of this chapter is to make you aware of the many ins and outs connected with being an owner or a user of a microcomputer system.

Chapter 13 opens with a discussion of the vendors in the microcomputer marketplace and the distribution channels they use to sell their products at the retail level. Then we look at some of the things you should know when acquiring a microcomputer system for home or work. From there we turn to several operation and maintenance issues. Next, upgrading a computer system is covered. Finally, we discuss some of the sources that are at your disposal for learning more about microcomputers.

The Microcomputer Marketplace

The microcomputer marketplace comprises a wide variety of firms that make hardware and software products. Because many hardware and software manufacturers do not sell directly to the public, several companies are in business solely for sales and distribution purposes.

Microcomputer Products

Only about a decade ago, many of the companies that make today's most familiar microcomputer products didn't even exist. Today, several of them earn more than a billion dollars a year in revenues. Almost overnight, the microcomputer industry has become both the fastest-growing and the largest segment of the computer industry.

Some of the big names in each of the major market segments of the microcomputer industry are covered in the following paragraphs.

System Units IBM, Apple, and Compaq are the big three in the desktop microcomputer marketplace. There are other companies—such as Dell, AST, and Gateway—who, like Compaq, have become highly successful largely by producing IBM-compatible microcomputers. **IBM-compatible microcomputers** (or *DOS-compatible microcomputers*) are microcomputers that can run the same software as that targeted to DOS-based IBM microcomputers. Most IBM-compatible machines made today will run virtually any major applications software product designed to work on DOS-based IBM microcomputers.

IBM-compatible microcomputer. A microcomputer that can run the same software as DOS-based IBM microcomputers run.

Laptop computers are currently the fastest-growing segment within the microcomputer marketplace. User Solution 13-1 addresses *docking stations*, which extend the usefulness of laptops in an office environment.

Software Among the largest independent software producers (and their leading products) are Microsoft Corporation (MS-DOS, Windows, and Windows NT operating-system software; language translators; Word; Excel; Access; and Works), Lotus Development Corporation (1-2-3 and Notes), Borland Interna-

User Solution 13–1

Docking Stations

Need to change a laptop computer into a desktop computer? Then consider a docking station (photo). A laptop is to a docking station as a Winnebago is to an RV park—you just hook it up and a variety of new resources are instantly at your disposal. Docking stations are useful for companies that have laptop-equipped workers who need the facilities of a more powerful, desktop system every so often. By fitting the laptop unit into the docking station, users can tap into such equipment as a laser printer, an image scanner or film recorder, or an SVGA monitor.

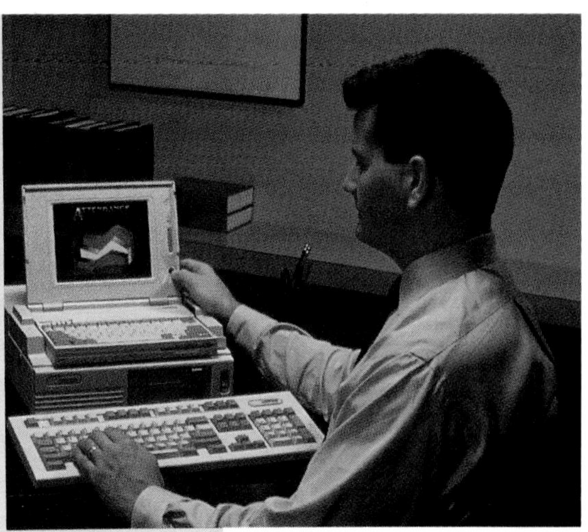

tional (Quattro, Paradox, and dBASE), and WordPerfect Corporation (WordPerfect). At one time, many of these companies could have been characterized as single-product firms. Today, the leaders in this segment are in a period of aggressive diversification, internally developing new products and acquiring and partnering with other companies that have related product lines. Many program packages are sold as *software suites*, in which several full-featured software packages are bundled together and sold at a reduced price.

Monitors and Printers With the exception of a few U.S. companies such as IBM and Hewlett-Packard, these two segments are dominated by the Japanese. Some of the major players are Epson, Toshiba, Amdek, Brother, Fujitsu, Canon, NEC, Okidata, and C. Itoh.

Computer and Memory Chips The chip markets are ruled by Intel, Motorola, and Japanese companies. Intel makes CPU chips for most of the leading IBM and IBM-compatible system units, whereas Motorola makes chips for the Apple Macintosh line of computers. There are also a number of manufacturers such as Cyrix and Advanced Micro Devices (AMD) that produce Intel-compatible chips. Recently, IBM, Motorola, and Apple have teamed up to produce the PowerPC computer chip, which competes head-to-head against Intel chips.

Disk Systems Some of the more familiar firms in the marketplace for diskette drives and hard-disk drives are Conner, Control Data, IBM, Seagate, and Tandon. In the optical-disk-drive marketplace, Canon and Philips are big names. Such companies as Iomega have done well with disk cartridges.

Diskettes The competition in the diskette segment is among the fiercest imaginable, because there are not many important ways to differentiate diskettes. If the diskette "works" (that is, the quality level is sufficiently high—which is usually the case if you purchase a familiar brand), price is the only factor on which to compete. Most diskettes are sold by companies that don't make diskettes; instead they buy them from someone else and put their own labels on them.

A roster of some of the most familiar companies in the microcomputer marketplace appears in Figure 13-1, along with a description of the major product offerings that have made these companies famous. The popularity of U.S. packaged software in Japan is covered in Feature 13-1.

Sales and Distribution

Hardware and software microcomputing products are most often acquired from retail computer stores, mail-order houses, discount and department stores, and manufacturers.

Retail Computer Stores Organizations that need strong local support often turn to retail computer stores such as Computerland, Circuit City, and Egghead

FIGURE 13-1

Who's who in the microcomputer marketplace. This list shows the products or product lines for which several leading companies are most famous.

Company	Principal Product(s)
Adobe	Assorted desktop publishing software products
Apple	Microcomputer systems
AST	A wide variety of hardware products
Autodesk	AutoCAD design software
Borland	A wide variety of software products
Canon	Printers and related products
Commodore	Amiga microcomputer system
Compaq	Microcomputer systems
Computer Associates	A wide variety of software products
Dell	Microcomputer systems
Gateway	Microcomputer systems
Hayes	Modems
Hewlett-Packard	Microcomputer systems and laser printers
IBM	A wide variety of microcomputing products
Index Technology	Excelerator, a CASE product
Intel	Chips for IBM and IBM-compatible computers
Lotus Development	1-2-3 spreadsheet package
Microsoft	A wide variety of software products
Motorola	Chips for Apple computers; communications products
NEC	A wide variety of hardware products
Novell	NetWare operating system
Packard Bell	Microcomputer systems
Quadram	A wide variety of hardware products
Qume	Printers
Seagate	Hard disks
Software Publishing	Harvard Graphics presentation software
Symantec	A wide variety of software products
Toshiba	A wide variety of hardware products
WordPerfect	WordPerfect word processing package
Zeos	Microcomputer systems

Feature 13-1

Selling Technology to Japan

The future outlook for PC software is strictly positive

For the past several years, a major complaint directed at Japan has been that it has created stiff trade barriers for foreign companies that want to do business within its borders. One industry, however—based largely outside Japan—has thrived under Japanese foreign policy. It is the microcomputer software industry, which consists mostly of packaged products made by companies in the United States.

Among the leading packaged applications-software products in Japan today are Lotus Development's 1-2-3, Microsoft's Excel and Works, Borland's dBASE and Paradox, and Autodesk's AutoCAD. To put Japan's reliance on foreign packaged software in better perspective, consider that U.S.-based Microsoft Corporation is over 30 times the size of Japan's biggest packaged-software company.

Outside venders currently control about half of Japan's packaged-software market. For a variety of reasons, some experts believe that this market could increase more than tenfold in size during the next decade. Why? For one, packaged software is increasing in popularity—by leaps and bounds—virtually everywhere in the world. Also, most software created in Japan is still custom made, and only recently has packaged software started to become popular there. By some estimates, per-capita packaged software use in Japan is only a fifth of that in the United States.

Ironically, many industry observers feel that Japan's protectionist trade barriers are exactly the issue that has given foreign packaged-software vendors an edge. Barriers made it possible for Japanese companies to charge high prices for their products. This inevitably made those companies and products less competitive. Also, while the rest of the world was developing applications software that would run with widely used standard interfaces—such as Microsoft's Windows—Japanese companies were developing nonstandard products that were inherently more difficult to interconnect and use. Now these companies are far behind and playing catch-up.

Microsoft. Over 30 times larger than nearest Japanese rival.

Foreign versions of packaged software have to be carefully customized to meet the language restrictions in each user country. For example, Japanese versions of software rely on thousands of characters not found in the English alphabet. Also, foreign versions of software often must contain special features that appeal to local users. As a case in point, when Lotus Development Corporation first went to Japan, it customized 1-2-3 so that the Japanese version included on-screen grid lines in graphs.

Software (see Figure 13-2). Generally, the salespeople at these stores are relatively knowledgeable about computers and help buyers try out hardware and software before making a commitment. If a purchased item does not work as advertised, some stores take great pains to resolve any problems. Typically, retail computer stores also offer consulting, repair, and other support services to users.

FIGURE 13-2

Retail computer stores. Today, computer stores are a fixture at shopping malls everywhere. Some stores, like Egghead Software (pictured here), specialize in software, while others concentrate on hardware and repair services.

FIGURE 13-3

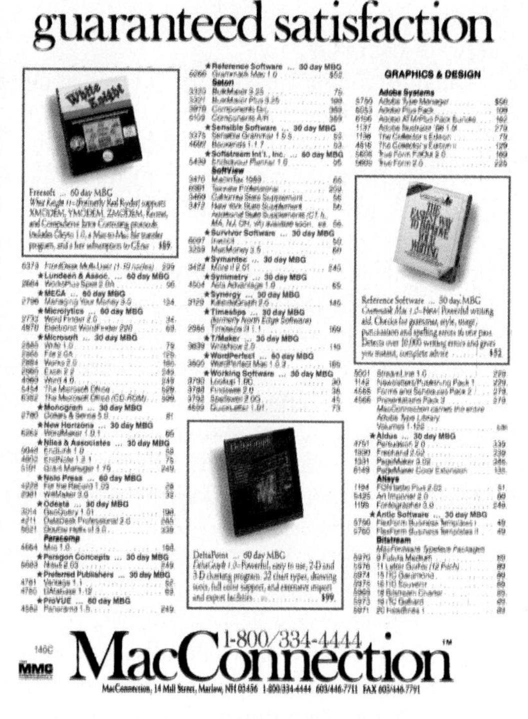

Mail-order houses. Mail-order houses like MacConnection (featured here) and PC Connection, which respectively specialize in Apple Macintosh products and IBM-compatible microcomputing products, regularly advertise their prices in the leading microcomputer journals.

Other Retail Stores During the last few years, microcomputer hardware and software have become so popular that many other types of retail stores have added such items on their showroom floors. Today, you can buy hardware and software at discount stores (such as Wal-Mart), department stores (such as Sears), office supply stores (such as Office Depot), and bookstores (such as Waldenbooks). As a general rule, these types of stores have better prices than computer stores, but there is sometimes less of a selection available and many have little or no support.

Mail-Order Firms Another source of computer products is mail-order firms. These companies regularly publish price lists in microcomputer journals and can ship products within 24 hours of a request (see Figure 13-3). Because these companies don't have to pay for a showroom and a large staff of knowledgeable salespeople, their prices are usually much lower than those of retail computer stores and competitive with discount stores. Also, many mail-order firms have access to an enormous stock of goods and can get almost any item to buyers quickly via UPS or Federal Express. A disadvantage of mail-order shopping is that buyers need to know exactly what they want, because most mail-order firms don't maintain showrooms or a large technical staff.

Manufacturers A fourth alternative for buying hardware and software is going directly to the manufacturer, although this is not always possible. Many manufacturers have exclusive selling arrangements with certain wholesalers and with buying consortiums such as schools and large computer clubs. Also, when manufacturers do sell directly to the general public, they sometimes sell only in large quantities—perhaps only *very* large quantities. Buying directly from the manufacturer usually means lower prices but often does not include ongoing support. Such support, if needed, must be purchased from another firm.

When buying a computer system, don't overlook used equipment. Ads for used equipment can usually be found in the classified section of local newspapers. If you take this route, ask to try out the equipment before you buy it. If the equipment functions properly during the trial period, it will probably work fine. Be especially careful to check how the monitor works over a period of a couple of hours, and evaluate the output quality of the printer as well. You should pay considerably less for a used system than you would for a new one.

Selecting a Computer System

Chances are good that at some point in your life you will need to select a microcomputer system to better perform your job. Selecting a microcomputer system for home or for business use must begin with the all-important question: "What do I want the system to do?" Once you've determined the purposes to which the system will be put, you must choose among the software and hardware alternatives available. Finally, you need a method to evaluate the alternatives and to select a system.

Analyzing Needs

With regard to computer systems, a *need* refers to a requirement that the computer system must be capable of meeting. For instance, at a videotape rental store, a computer system must be able to enter bar codes automatically from tapes being checked in and out, identify customers with overdue tapes, manage tape inventories, and do routine accounting operations. All four of these uses are needs.

A person owning a computer system will find dozens of ways to use it, but he or she may often justify the acquisition of a microcomputer system on the basis of only one or two needs. For example, many managers do so much financial planning that a spreadsheeting capability alone is enough to justify the entire computer-system cost. Many writers find word processing so indispensable to their livelihoods that it matters little what else the computer system can do. And sales personnel working out of the office can often justify a laptop computer simply on the basis of its usefulness as an account-closing tool at client sites. Figure 13-4 provides a list of potential needs that are met by microcomputer systems.

If you're not really sure what you want a system to do, you should think twice about buying one. Because computer systems that are specially configured to serve certain applications (say, games) are often poor at others (such as word processing), you can easily make some expensive mistakes if you're uncertain.

As part of the needs analysis, you should look closely at budgetary constraints. Every user has many needs, but it is their affordability that separates the real needs from the pipe dreams.

Listing Alternatives

Once a set of needs has been established, the next step is to list some alternative systems that might satisfy those needs. You should almost always consider applications software first, then the computer and systems-software "platform" that best meet your applications-software requirements.

Platform.
A set of computer-system architecture and systems-software choices that limit the user to work in a certain way.

A **platform** is a set of computer-system architecture and system-software choices that limit the user to work in a certain way. For instance, an IBM-compatible 80486 system unit running under Microsoft Windows 3.1 is an example of a platform. With such a base, the user would be able to buy any software that could run under DOS 6.2 or Windows 3.1 (or earlier versions and releases of these products).

Applications software is selected first because it most closely relates to needs. For instance, if you want a computer system to perform desktop publishing, it would be wise to first look at the various desktop publishing packages available. It makes no sense to choose a system platform first and then find out that it doesn't support the type of desktop publishing package you prefer.

Often, in the world of microcomputers, decisions are highly interrelated, so that software and hardware must be selected jointly. A software product may work only with a specific set of hardware. For instance, a certain word processor might be available only for an Apple Macintosh computer system, and it might also require a laser printer to work most effectively. An illustration software package may function optimally only if a specific type of graphics interface hardware is used—say, a digitizing tablet and a cursor movement device. Also, most illustration packages require a capacious hard disk, because graphics images require large amounts of storage. Because of the interrelated nature of many software and hardware products, it sometimes helps to make a list of

FIGURE 13-4

Microcomputer needs. Most users buy a microcomputer system on the basis of one or two of the needs listed here.

Word Processing

Word processing is the most common microcomputer application; many people have a need to create memos, letters, manuscripts, and other documents.

Spreadsheets

Business users find microcomputers handy for preparing budgets and other financial schedules and for analyzing information to improve decision making.

Organizing, Scheduling, Mailing, and Networking

Microcomputers are commonly being used as electronic desktops to coordinate office activities and to provide an environment in which people can communicate more effectively.

Desktop Publishing

Microcomputer systems are useful for preparing books and articles whose quality is comparable to that of products done on a professional printer's press.

Preparing Slides and Presentation Materials

35mm slides, automated slide shows, overhead transparencies, multimedia presentations, and handout materials are frequently produced on a microcomputer.

Retrieving Information from Local or Remote Databases

Users of all types find the microcomputer a handy device for looking up information.

Transaction Processing

Many database services let people use their microcomputer systems to shop, bank, and buy and sell stocks from the home—and businesses use microcomputers, too, to process these and other transactions.

Learning

An abundance of microcomputer software—some of it in multimedia form—is available today to provide instruction on virtually any subject.

Software Development

By using microcomputer systems with CASE tools and object-oriented interfaces, programmers are developing software for all sizes of computers.

Design

Artists and designers find the microcomputer indispensable for creating products that would be impossible or too expensive to do manually.

Games and Entertainment

Electronic games have always been popular on microcomputer systems; today, devices such as televisions, VCRs, and music synthesizers are teaming up with microcomputers to take entertainment potential further.

system alternatives, in which each alternative listed consists of the principal platform and other hardware and software elements that can be added to it—both now and over time.

You can get a list of software and hardware products from the leading microcomputer journals. (We'll discuss some of these journals later in the chapter.) Many of these journals also periodically describe the best and worst features of products and give each product an overall rating (see Figure 13-5). The ratings can be used as input for evaluating products, your next step in acquiring a microcomputer system.

Evaluating Alternatives

Alternative products are best examined by "test driving" them. You must keep in mind that when observing the performance of a software package, you are viewing its performance on a given configuration of hardware. A software package that runs smoothly on a Dell 80486-based computer system won't necessarily run as well on a Compaq 80386 system, which uses a slightly different architecture and a less powerful chip. Also, the look, feel, and performance of a software package on a computer in the Apple Macintosh line will be notably different

FIGURE 13-5

Product ratings. Software evaluations are a regular feature in *Infoworld,* a popular microcomputer journal. One week, six word processors might be compared; the next week, ten database management systems may be reviewed. Each multipage comparison is summed up in a "report card" (shown here for four workgroup scheduling packages) that provides an overall rating for each product evaluated.

REPORT CARD INFO WORLD

Workgroup Scheduler/Mail Packages

	(InfoWorld weighting)	(Your weighting)	**The Coordinator II** Version 2.1	**Office Works** Version 2.0	**Right Hand Man** Version 5.1	**Word Perfect Office** Version 3.0
List price			$1,800 (10-user)	$495 (six-user)	$1,169 (10-user)	$495 (five-user)
Performance						
Scheduling	(125)	( )	Good	Good	Excellent	Good
Messaging features	(150)	( )	Excellent	Good	Very Good	Very Good
Archiving	(50)	( )	Excellent	Good	Good	Good
Printing/ word processing	(50)	( )	Good	Poor	Good	Very Good
Gateways	(125)	( )	Very Good	Satisfactory	Very Good	Excellent
Documentation	(50)	( )	Very Good	Good	Good	Excellent
Ease of administration	(75)	( )	Very Good	Satisfactory	Very Good	Satisfactory
Ease of learning	(50)	( )	Good	Very Good	Very Good	Satisfactory
Ease of use	(100)	( )	Good	Good	Good	Good
Error handling	(50)	( )	Very Good	Very Good	Good	Very Good
Support						
Support policies	(25)	( )	Satisfactory	Good	Good	Excellent
Technical support	(25)	( )	Satisfactory	Very Good	Very Good	Very Good
Value	(125)	( )	Good	Good	Very Good	Very Good
Final scores			**7.3**	**5.9**	**7.4**	**7.3**
Use your own weightings to calculate your score						

GUIDE TO REPORT CARD SCORES

InfoWorld reviews only finished, production versions of products, never beta test versions.

Products receive ratings ranging from unacceptable to excellent in various categories. Scores are derived by multiplying the weighting (in parentheses) of each criterion by its rating, where:

Excellent = 1.0 — Outstanding in all areas.
Very Good = 0.75 — Meets all essential criteria and offers significant advantages.
Good = 0.625 — Meets essential criteria and includes some special features.
Satisfactory = 0.5 — Meets essential criteria.
Poor = 0.25 — Falls short in essential areas.
Unacceptable or N/A = 0.0 — Fails to meet minimum standards or lacks this feature.

Scores are summed, divided by 100, and rounded down to one decimal place to yield the final score out of a maximum possible score of 10 (plus bonus). Products rated within 0.2 points of one another differ little. Weightings represent average relative importance to *InfoWorld* readers involved in purchasing and using that product category. You can customize the report card to your company's needs by using your own weightings to calculate the final score.

than they are on an IBM or IBM-compatible machine. Sometimes it's quite difficult, when selecting a configuration of hardware and software, to see the entire system together, but it's certainly advisable to do this whenever possible.

Selection Criteria In evaluating software and hardware products, a number of criteria will help you make your final selection.

The most important selection criterion is usually *functionality*—the type of work the product does. For many people, ease of learning and ease of use follow closely behind. Also, most people prefer widely used products rather than unknown ones, because the large user base with the popular products ensures that vendor support will be around for a long time. In addition, if you are considering using a microcomputer system in an office environment dominated by, say, Apple Macintoshes, choosing that type of computer would probably be more convenient from the standpoint of having local expertise available for support. Good written documentation showing how to use the hardware or software is also important; when a helping hand isn't readily available, documentation is often the best alternative for answering a tough question.

A list of important criteria for selecting a microcomputer system is provided in Figure 13-6. The increasingly important issue of getting good support tomorrow from the vendor you choose today is the subject of the Tomorrow box.

Software and Hardware Specifics Before looking over software or hardware, you should make a checklist of properties that the software or hardware should possess—and be sure to watch for these during the test drive. A rehearsed presentation made by a salesperson is likely to point out only the strengths of a product, not its weaknesses.

For instance, in examining word processors, you should consider the type of text they output (e.g., do they allow proportionally spaced characters, half lines, subscripts and superscripts, and so on?), see how easy it is to execute standard commands (such as moving the cursor, centering, moving and copying text, indenting, reformatting, or footnoting), check the quality of the spelling checker and thesaurus features, and find out what advanced features the word processors possess (e.g., graphics and desktop publishing features). Again, consider the entire system. For example, if you are planning to buy an inexpensive dot-matrix printer that can't handle proportional spacing, certain types of graphics, or subscripts and superscripts, it may make little difference that a

FIGURE 13-6

Important selection criteria. Buyers generally select computer systems on the basis of some combination of these criteria.

- Product functionality
- Ease of learning and use
- Cost
- Vendor reputation
- Support
- Expandability
- Meets industry standards
- Speed
- Favorable reviews
- Delivery
- Documentation

T O M O R R O W

Software Support

Tomorrow's Concern about Today's Purchase

Computer instructors and trainers often try to teach their students an economic lesson that sounds simple on the surface but frequently doesn't sink in. It goes something like this: If software product A costs $5 and software product B costs $300, and both software products serve essentially the same needs, which should you buy? Assume that your time is worth $100 per hour and that you will spend 20 extra hours figuring out how software product A works because the user manual that came with it isn't worth a darn.

If you understand that time is money and you've answered "software product B," congratulate yourself on a correct response. But if you're like a lot of people, you'll miss the underlying lesson here and wind up learning it the hard way later on, when you discover the true value of support. In other words, saving pennies today can cost you a bundle tomorrow.

OS/2 help desk. A major support issue is having vendor assistance only a phone call away.

There are two main sources of support: vendors and other users.

Vendor support can come in a lot of ways. Probably the most visible is the documentation you get when you buy a product. Good documentation should include a comprehensive hard-copy reference manual, a context-sensitive online-help

word processor supports these features. Some of the items that you should watch for particularly when buying specific types of software packages are enumerated in Feature 13-2.

Hardware items that usually will need to be considered when buying a microcomputer system are the system unit and RAM, diskette and hard-disk units, a monitor, a keyboard, and a printer. Some of the questions that need to be addressed when buying these types of hardware are shown in Feature 13-3.

Choosing a System

After you have considered the alternatives, it's time to choose a system and purchase it.

People choose between system alternatives in a number of ways. For instance, some people make a formal list of selection criteria (such as those shown in Figure 13-6) and quantitatively rate each alternative on each of these criteria. They then select the alternative that scores the highest. This method was discussed in Chapter 11 (see Figure 11-16).

Others prefer to make their choices less formally. After thinking about needs and the criteria that they will use to evaluate alternatives, they select a computer feature, and a learning module that gets you started using the software. Needless to say, the manual should be clearly written. Unfortunately, many of the people who write documentation for software products are technical folks without sufficient writing and organizational skills, which mean you may end up wasting valuable time trying to figure out how the product works.

Another major source of support is the vendor hotline. Many vendors provide 800-area-code phone numbers for users to call to get help with problems—often free of charge. When evaluating a software package it is important to check out how easy it is to reach the hotline and the quality of service provided.

Many vendors also provide their own in-house electronic bulletin boards. These make it possible for the vendor to announce new hardware drivers and product information and to post useful macros. Users making contact with the bulletin board can download information to their local computer systems, where it is immediately available for use. Many vendors also regularly supply CD-ROM optical disks to their commercial users—disks that have the same knowledge base to which their own support representatives have access.

The microcomputer journals periodically publish statistics about user satisfaction as regards vendor support. Some vendors may also be willing to send you the results of independent support-department audits.

As far as *user support* is concerned, usually Rule One is to buy into a package that's widely used. This way, when you have problems, there's a large base of people to tap into if you don't want to turn to the vendor. Help might just be a scream away if you are working in an office where several other people are using the package.

Also, many users post problems on public bulletin boards. The message you post might be read by literally hundreds of other users, and there's a good possibility that someone out there has encountered and solved the problem you are now wrestling with. If the problem is knotty enough, you might get a satisfactory answer much faster than by going through the vendor hotline.

With the more widely used packages, you will also find formal user groups. User groups enable you to meet other users in person and to talk about common problems and creative ways to use the software. Many large user groups even publish their own newsletters.

system as soon as it "feels right." In fact, several researchers have found that a large number of microcomputers are acquired in small quantities and that very little formal analysis, if any, is undertaken before the purchase. Although such an acquisition process could be criticized for lack of thoroughness, many managers claim that they are too busy to spend the time researching choices with greater care. There is, of course, a negative side to rushed selections. Just as a car owner can go through years of torture driving around in the wrong type of car, so too can a computer buyer wind up with years of headaches resulting from a poor computer-system choice. The expense of a computer-system mistake may be much greater, however.

Operating a Computer System

Once you've acquired a computer system, it is important that you develop a set of practices to protect your software, hardware, and data from damage and from costly mistakes. Three important areas in this regard are backup of programs and data, proper maintenance of hardware and I/O media, and troubleshooting and repairs. A fourth area, securing the data on your computer system, is covered in Chapter 14.

Feature 13–2

Buying Software

Some important questions to ask

When buying applications software such as word processors, spreadsheets, and database management systems, be sure to get answers to the following questions:

Word Processing

Does the package contain all the features that you want? Make a list of features and check a reference manual, trade book, or product review to see what the package has or lacks.

Will the package work on your hardware configuration? Keep in mind that printing attractive fonts, proportionally spaced text, and graphics usually requires a laser printer. If the package lets you preview and edit graphics outputs, you will need a graphics-oriented monitor. GUI-oriented word processors require the power of an 80486 computer with lots of storage.

Will the package fit on your system? Look closely at the RAM and hard-disk requirements of the package to see if it fits.

Does the package implement word processing features in a way you find compatible with your work style? The best way to answer this question is to try out the system at a store, in school, or at a friend's house. Of course, don't forget to check that the package exists in a version that will work on your system.

Buying software. Because of the need for long-term support, business users often favor familiar product names.

Spreadsheets

Does the package contain all the features that you want, and does it implement them in a way that is comfortable with your work style? Most major spreadsheet packages are remarkably alike. They contain virtually the same types of commands

Backup

Virtually everyone who has logged months or years of his or her life on a computer system will swear to you that, sooner or later, you will lose some critical files. Maybe lightning will strike nearby, zapping your RAM. Or maybe a small brownout will cause the heads on your hard disk to drop out of orbit and crash onto the disk surface, carving a miniature canyon through the electronic version of a 45-page term paper that's due tomorrow. Computer veterans will also tell you that these file losses always seem to happen at the worst possible times.

and closely follow the gridlike user interface of Lotus Development Corporation's 1-2-3. Today, most spreadsheet products differ in regard to their graphics features and their ability to present data in creative ways.

Will the package fit on your system? Consider the RAM and hard-disk requirements of the package.

Will the package work on your hardware configuration? Check the graphics requirements of the package. If you are going to be using a great deal of presentation graphics, you will probably want a fast CPU and a laser printer. Of course, check that the package exists in a version that will work on your system.

Database Management Systems

Do you have plenty of storage? Compared to other types of productivity software, database management systems are very data-intensive. If you need to relate files so that the contents of several files are available simultaneously, you will almost certainly need lots of RAM and hard disk.

Does the package contain all of the features that you want and implement them in a way that you find comfortable with your work style? Database management systems are like word processors, in that both a software package's features and its look and feel can vary tremendously from vendor to vendor. Before buying a package, make a checklist of the features that you need and see how each feature is implemented in the packages you are considering purchasing.

Will the package work on your hardware configuration? Check that the package exists in a version that will work on your system.

How easy is the package to learn and use? Data management is generally harder to master than word processing or spreadsheets. Some packages, in fact, are targeted more toward programmers than toward ordinary users. Make sure that the package you want to buy comes with documentation, demo disks, or learning manuals that you are able to read and understand. If the vendor learning and documentation tools are mediocre, look for some good trade books to help you get started.

How fast is the package? Because data management packages are data-intensive, the speed with which the package can retrieve information is extremely critical. It will probably be difficult for you to design a benchmark test to test speed yourself before you buy, so to judge the package under consideration, read closely the results of the comparative product tests published regularly in the computer journals.

What type of backup procedures do you plan to use? One of the worst of all computer nightmares is having a large database destroyed when a hard disk malfunctions and there is no backup. When considering buying a database management system, you should consider what backup options are available to you. A backup tape unit is most convenient for large databases but will add to the cost of having database management in your applications portfolio.

Fortunately, there is a solution to most of these problems—backup. Creating **backup** means making a duplicate version of any file that you can't afford to lose so that, when the fickle finger of fate causes inadvertent erasure, you're confronted with only a minor irritant rather than an outright catastrophe. Theoretically, you can back up any file on your computer system. The backups you create—through, say, a file-copy, disk-copy, or backup command—can be on diskette, hard disk, optical disk, streaming tape, or virtually any other secondary storage medium.

Backup.
A procedure that produces duplicate copies of programs or data.

One common form of backup is making a duplicate of a long file that is being developed in RAM. For instance, suppose you are word processing a

Feature 13–3

Buying Hardware

Some important questions to ask

When buying a system unit, storage, a monitor, a keyboard, or a printer, be sure to get answers to the following questions:

System Unit

What brand of system is best for your needs? Buy a system that runs the type of software with which you wish to work and that is widely supported. Buying a bargain-basement system could leave you completely on your own, and it could cost you more in the long run than you save on the purchase price.

Does the system unit have enough power to meet current and future applications needs? Most computers sold today are 32-bit machines and run at speeds of from 20 to 100 MHz or more. You should buy a system that will last for several years.

RAM

How much memory does your most memory-intensive application require? If you are planning to move up to OS/2 or Windows NT at some point in the future, for instance, applications will require several megabytes of RAM. Other sophisticated operating systems and operating environments can also be memory intensive.

Can memory be expanded later if you need more? Determine in what increments and to what maximum it can be extended. As an example, many machines allow memory expansion in 1-MB or 2-MB increments.

Secondary Storage

Will you need one or two diskette drives? What disk diameter and capacity will you need? Recall from Chapter 4 that drives accommodate either 3½-inch or 5¼-inch disks and that disk capacities usually run from 360 KB to 2.88 MB. Many people today use systems that have one 1.44 MB 3½-inch diskette drive and one 1.2 MB 5¼-inch diskette drive.

Buying hardware. Make sure the equipment you select meets both your present and continuing needs.

Will you need a hard disk? Most business software requires a hard disk to run. Recall from Chapter 4 that hard disks today range from 20 to a few hundred megabytes in capacity, and most use either an IDE, ESDI, or SCSI format. Computer professionals often advise that you figure out the minimum amount of storage you will need and at least double or triple that figure in order to meet future needs.

Monitor

Do you need a color or monochrome monitor? Most business software made today is optimized for use on desktop, CRT-type color monitors. Monochrome monitors are very popular on laptop computers and may display in either green, amber, or blue foregrounds.

How readable is the screen? Always inspect the output of the monitor you are considering before making a purchase. Monitors often work in several different display modes, some suitable for text and others for graphics. You only have one pair of eyes, so, if you're going to be spending many hours at a monitor screen each day, a monitor choice can be extremely important.

Which graphics standards (for example, VGA and SVGA) does the monitor support? If you are working in a graphical environment, consider an SVGA display or, alternatively, a larger-than-normal screen size. If the work you do requires especially fine resolutions, make sure that you evaluate how well the monitor produces such outputs.

Does the monitor have adjustable features? Especially important are an adjustable base, which helps ward off glare, and brightness and contrast controls.

Keyboard

Does the keyboard feel comfortable as you type on it? If possible, type on the keyboard before buying; notice especially the key spacing and how the keys feel to your touch.

Does the keyboard have an assortment of special keys and features? Many people like light indicators showing if certain keys are active.

Are the keys placed in an arrangement that you prefer? Even though most people use the QWERTY key arrangement, several other keyboard layouts are available. Also, make sure that the special keys are conveniently located.

Does the keyboard have adjustable features? It is especially important that the keyboard is detachable, enabling you to move it about to suit your comfort, and that it has an adjustable slope.

Printer

What type of printer (for example, impact dot matrix, laser, color thermal transfer) is best for your needs? For most people, the choice will be between an impact dot-matrix printer and a laser printer. If you are selecting a more exotic type of printer, make sure that the software you are planning to buy supports it.

How fast is the printer? Impact dot-matrix printers typically are rated at several hundred characters per second (cps), whereas most microcomputer-oriented laser printers print anywhere from two to eight pages per minute.

What types of outputs can the printer produce (e.g., text or both text and graphics)? Be sure to examine closely both the range and the quality of outputs. Some laser printers, for instance, will print large-point-size text with jagged contours and others limit the size of the text. You should never buy a printer unless you first see its outputs—and as wide a range of outputs as possible.

Can the printer be run in several modes? Impact dot-matrix printers should be capable of being run in a fast, draft-quality mode and a slow, letter-quality mode. Many laser printers have an adjustment for darkness that enables you to get lighter copies for drafts, which extends the life of the toner cartridge. Check the output quality in each of the available modes.

Other Hardware

If you are buying other hardware, make sure that your system has enough ports and expansion slots to accommodate it.

If you are buying a modem, decide whether you want it to be internal or external, how fast it must be, and whether or not it meets the communications standards prescribed by the application for which you intend it.

If you are thinking about buying a mouse, which is useful in a GUI environment, consider the alternative of getting a trackball. Many people dislike using a mouse because it must moved around a desktop; trackballs, in contrast, are stationary.

Optical disk units have decreased so much in price that you might consider getting one even if you don't need it immediately. Not only will it allow you to play music CDs on your computer system, but also it will enable you to become immediately familiar with one of the fastest-growing areas in technology.

paper for a class. About every half hour or hour, you should make sure that you save the current version of the document file onto disk. That way, if the power goes out on your system, you will have lost only what you have typed in since the last save command. Many commercial packages provide certain types of automatic backup of files, but unless you know for sure what is being backed up and when, it's safer to do it yourself.

Full backup.
A procedure that produces a duplicate copy of all files onto a secondary storage medium.

There are many different strategies for backing up files on a hard disk or a diskette. One is to perform a **full backup,** in which you back up all of the files on disk several times throughout the day or at the end of a day or a session. The advantage to a full backup is that it is relatively straightforward, and, since it employs a "shotgun" approach to backup, it sometimes saves "treasures" that you neglected to copy previously. On the down side, a full backup takes longer than a backup in which selected files are targeted for copying. Also, you need more storage space to contain the copied files.

Partial backup.
A procedure that produces a duplicate copy of selected files onto a secondary storage medium.

An alternative to the full backup is a **partial backup,** in which only files created or altered since the last backup are copied. Many people who have hard disks will perform a partial backup daily and a full backup weekly.

Whenever you make backup copies on a disk, make sure that the backup files are not stored on the same disk as the originals. In theory, they shouldn't even be in the same room or building. Then, if a serious accident such as a fire or flood occurs at one location, the files at the other location will be safe. A variety of accidents that can destroy programs and data—accidents that are all good reasons to do disk backup—are listed in Figure 13-7.

FIGURE 13-7

Good reasons for backing up files. Taking a few extra minutes to make duplicate copies of important files can avert a potential disaster.

Why back up?

- A disk sector goes bad, destroying part of a file.
- A file that you thought you no longer had a need for and erased turns out to be important.
- You modify a file in an undesirable way, and the damage done is irreversible.
- You accidentally reformat a disk.
- The disk suffers a head crash.
- A power brownout or failure at the time of saving a file causes "garbage" to be saved.
- You save a file to the wrong subdirectory, overwriting a different file that has the same name.
- While rushing your work, you make a mistake that causes the wrong files to be erased.
- You unwittingly destroy a file while working on it—say, by deleting parts of it erroneously and then saving the file.
- Malfunctioning hardware or software causes files to be erased.
- A computer virus enters your system and destroys files.
- Your disk is physically destroyed—for instance, a diskette is left in the sun or the hard disk is given a jolt. Alternatively, a fire or flood may destroy the disk.
- Someone steals your diskette or hard disk.

Proper Maintenance of Resources

Microcomputer systems consist of sensitive electronic devices, so they must be treated with appropriate care. In this section we discuss protecting your computer system with a surge suppressor; caring for disks; protecting your computer system from dust, heat, and static; and protecting printers and monitors.

Surge Suppression One of the best devices to have on your computer system to minimize the chance of unexpected damage is a surge suppressor. A **surge suppressor,** which is installed between your system unit and the electrical outlet providing the power, is a hardware device that prevents random electrical power spikes from causing damage to your system (see Figure 13-8).

Surge suppressor. A device that protects a computer system from random electrical power spikes.

The power going into most homes is uneven. Power spikes, such as those caused from electrical storms, and power brownouts caused by drops in power can damage data or your system. Probably the most common problem caused by a spike or brownout is loss of data in RAM. Cases have also been reported, however, of loss of data in secondary storage and destruction of equipment.

A surge suppressor cannot guarantee complete protection. If lightning strikes your house, even a top-of-the-line surge suppressor will probably fail to protect your equipment. If you live in an area prone to severe lightning storms, the best thing that you can do if you are working on your computer system when a storm hits is save to disk what you've been working on, turn off your system,

FIGURE 13-8

Surge suppressor. The system unit and its support devices feed into the surge suppressor, which is plugged into a standard wall outlet. This permits you to turn on all of your equipment, as well as a nearby lamp or two, with the flick of a single switch.

and unplug the surge suppressor. Lightning can cause damage to electrical equipment—whether it's turned on or off—if it is plugged in.

Disk Care Precautions taken with diskettes and hard disks will safeguard any data stored on them.

Diskettes may look like inert slabs of plastic, but they are extremely sensitive items and must be cared for accordingly. Never touch the exposed diskette surface or bend the diskette in any way. Also, keep the diskette away from magnetic objects, motors, stereo speakers, and extreme temperatures. Of course, never insert a warped disk into a drive.

With a hard disk, the most important precaution to take is ensuring that the disk is in a place where it is not likely to be bumped.

Dust, Heat, and Static Each of the tiny processor and memory chips in your hardware units are packed tightly with thousands or millions of circuits. Dust particles circulating in the air can settle on a chip, causing a short circuit. Many people buy dust covers that fit snugly over each of their hardware devices to prevent foreign particles in the air from causing hardware failure.

System units that support add-in boards require cooling fans. These boards generate heat, and too much heat inside the system unit can cause all sorts of problems. When inserting add-in boards, you should place them as far apart as possible to avoid heat buildup. Also, most boards draw power off the system's main power unit (as do many internal hard disks), so be particularly careful about overtaxing the power unit.

Static electricity is especially dangerous because it can damage chips, destroy programs and data in memory, or disable your keyboard. So that those nasty little electrical discharges from your fingertips don't wreak havoc, you might consider buying an antistatic mat for under your workstation chair or an antistatic spray for your keyboard. Static electricity is more likely in dry areas and in the wintertime, when there's less humidity in the air.

Other Concerns CRT-type monitors have a phosphorescent surface that is "lit up" by an electronic gun. If you keep your monitor at a high brightness level and abandon it for an hour or two, the phosphorescent surface will be "torched" rather than merely lit up. This means that ghosty character images will be permanently etched on the screen, making it harder to read. Software packages called **screen savers** are available that either dim your monitor or create random patterns on the screen when the display remains unchanged for a given number of minutes.

Screen saver. A software product designed to protect the phosphor coating on the inside of a display screen from damage when the display is turned on but is not used for an extended period.

Printers are particularly prone to failure because they are electromechanical devices. If you have an impact dot-matrix printer, the most vulnerable mechanism in the unit is the print head. Like typewriter keys, these print heads will wear down over time. Still, you can take precautions to prevent rapid wear, such as making sure that the head is cleaned periodically, not using the printer excessively for graphics (which wear the head more rapidly), and making sure that the head is not adjusted for carbon copies (which makes the head strike harder) if you want only single copies.

Naturally, as with other electronic devices, you shouldn't switch hardware units on and off excessively.

Troubleshooting and Repairs

If you work with computers for any length of time, at some point you will probably have an experience when your hardware or software does not work properly. You may turn on your computer system one day and get no response. Perhaps your monitor screen will begin flickering badly every few seconds. Or maybe you will issue a familiar command in a software package that you work with regularly and the keyboard will lock up or the command will remain unexecuted. When such an event takes place, you will need to troubleshoot to isolate the underlying problem. If the problem is serious enough, repairs may be necessary.

Troubleshooting *Troubleshooting* refers to any actions taken to diagnose or solve a problem. Unfortunately, many problems are unique to specific types of hardware and software, so there's no simple troubleshooting remedy that works all of the time. Nonetheless, the following are some simple steps and guidelines that will help you out in a surprising number of instances.

- Try again. An unusual number of procedures work when you try a second or third time. You may have pressed the wrong keys the first time, or not pressed the keys hard enough. If the problem persists, attempt to save your work, restart (reboot) your computer system, and try again.
- Check to see that all of the equipment is plugged in and turned on and that none of the cables are detached or loose.
- Recall exactly what happened between the time the system was operating properly and the time you began to encounter problems. There might have been an electrical storm outside, and your system was plugged in and damaged by lightning. Or perhaps you installed new systems software during your last session, and these changes are affecting the way your current application works.
- Be observant. If strange noises came out of the disk drives when you unsuccessfully tried to boot the system up, those noises might be important. Even though solving the problem may be beyond your capabilities, you may be able to supply important facts to the people repairing your system. The faster the repair technicians can diagnose and fix your system, the less money you will spend in repair costs.

You should weigh the time that it takes to solve a problem yourself against the cost of outside repair. It's not a disgrace to have to give up if the problem is more than you can handle. It is simply an admission that your time is valuable and that you are wise enough to know when to call in a professional for assistance.

Repairs In some cases, a problem is simple enough that no repair is necessary or you can do repairs yourself. However, when the repair is beyond the scope of your capabilities, you will need to seek professional help. Likely sources of professional help are the party that sold you the defective hardware or software, retail computer stores in your area, and computer repair technicians listed in the Yellow Pages of your local phone book (see Figure 13-9).

FIGURE 13-9

Repair. As technicians repair computer systems, many of them also field calls from users about problems.

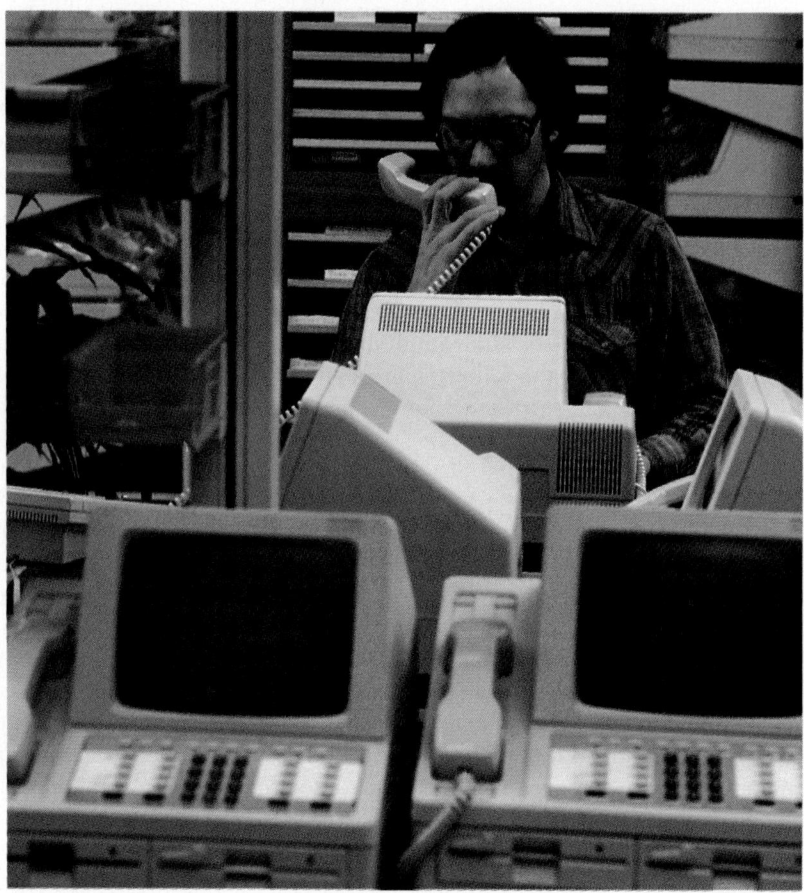

Keep the following considerations in mind when thinking about having someone else diagnose or repair your system:

- Is it better to repair old equipment or to buy new equipment? For instance, if the equipment to be repaired costs less than \$100, it may be cheaper to buy new equipment.
- Will the repair work be done under warranty? Most new equipment is sold with a **warranty** stating that the manufacturer will pay for certain repairs if the equipment fails within a given number of days or months after purchase. If the warranty hasn't expired, the repair may cost you nothing. Be aware that many manufacturers state in their warranty that the warranty becomes void if you attempt to repair the equipment yourself or if a repair is attempted by an unauthorized person or shop. Most equipment manufacturers publish a list of authorized repair shops.

Warranty.
A conditional pledge made by a manufacturer to protect consumers from losses due to defective units of a product.

- Can you get an estimate before proceeding with the work? In many cases, repair technicians can provide a free estimate of what the repair will cost. If they can't, you might want them to diagnose the problem first and to call you when they are able to provide an estimate. You never, ever want to put yourself in a situation in which you are presented with an unexpected, outrageously expensive repair bill.
- Is priority service available? People who use their computers as part of their jobs often need repairs immediately. Many repair shops realize this and will provide same-day or next-day turnaround for an extra fee.

When you buy a computer system, you often will have the option of buying an extended maintenance contract with it to cover certain types of repairs beyond those stated in the warranty. Figure 13-10 lists a number of the points covered by both warranties and maintenance contracts.

Upgrading

Hardware and software generally need to be upgraded over time. **Upgrading** a computer system means buying new hardware or software components that will extend the life of your current system. The question you must ask when considering a costly upgrade is the same one that you would ask when considering costly repairs to a car: Should I be spending this money on my current system or start fresh and buy a completely new system?

Upgrading. The process of buying new hardware or software in order to extend the life of a computer system.

FIGURE 13-10

Contracts. A good warranty or maintenance contract should cover the clauses listed here.

Coverage

The contract should state clearly if both parts and labor are covered.

Contract Period

Many contracts cover a period of one or two years. Some vendors provide a "lifetime" guarantee on certain types of parts.

Repair Procedure

A procedure should spell out clearly what steps will be taken when a problem occurs. Often, the vendor will first try to diagnose the problem over the phone. If this fails, either you will have to bring or send the unit to an authorized repair center or a technician will be dispatched to your home or office within a certain number of hours or days. If you can't afford to be without your computer system for an appreciable period, this part of the contract may be the most critical. Some contracts will provide you with a "loaner" system while yours is being repaired.

Hotline

Many companies provide a hotline for you to call when you have a question or problem. Sometimes you can call toll free, and sometimes you won't be billed for the vendor's time. It's a good idea to check how easy it is to reach the hotline; some of them are so understaffed that it takes days for calls to be returned.

Other Clauses

Most contracts will be void if you attempt to repair the equipment yourself or let someone who's not an authorized repairperson do it.

When you acquire a microcomputer system initially, it is extremely important to have an upgrade strategy. Ideally, you should buy a microcomputer system that adheres to a well-supported standard and that is flexible enough and powerful enough to be upgraded to meet reasonable future needs over the course of its lifetime. Of course, it is not possible to anticipate all of those needs, but not putting any thinking into system growth can invite disaster.

Hardware Some common types of hardware upgrades include adding more RAM to a system, adding boards to increase the speed of the CPU or to provide new types of functionality, and adding new input or output equipment such as an image scanner or a pen plotter.

Unless your system is powerful enough to handle growth, many upgrades will not be possible. For instance, if you have an Intel 80286-based processor, intensive software upgrades—such as those requiring a Windows-based environment—usually cannot be accommodated. The CPU is not powerful enough. Also, it's important to check both the number of expansion slots used for add-in boards. If new peripherals require add-in boards, and all of the expansion slots that allow such boards to communicate with the CPU are used up, upgrading is not possible.

Today, some microcomputer systems sold in the marketplace are touted as *upgradable PCs* (see Figure 13-11). These devices are designed with upgrading in mind, making it possible to swap out components—like the CPU chip or the internal hard disk—as more powerful ones become available. Upgradable PCs are not without their limits; they may not be able to take advantage of future technology that the PC designers didn't anticipate.

FIGURE 13-11

Upgradable PC. The 4000/XE Dell Server Series is a family of 486-based upgradable PCs. The machines are built to accommodate several upgrading paths, one of them being the Intel Pentium processor.

Software Software vendors typically enhance their products in some major way every year or so. Each of these upgrades—which are called **versions**—is assigned a number, such as 1.0, 2.0, 3.0, and so on. The higher the number, the more recent and more powerful the version. Minor versions, called **releases,** are typically numbered in increments of 0.1—say, 1.1, 1.2, 1.3, and so on.

Version.
A major upgrade of a software product.

Release.
A minor upgrade of a software product.

Each version of a software product is almost guaranteed to be more sophisticated and more complex and to require more RAM than its predecessors. For example, it's not unusual for a package that five years ago fit on one or two diskettes and worked with 256 KB to fit on eight or nine diskettes and require one or more megabytes of RAM today. The technical documentation accompanying the software is much more extensive than it was a few years ago and harder for the average person to understand. Fortunately, however, the quality of user training has increased dramatically and is geared to people at various levels of expertise.

Most software products tend to be *upward compatible.* This means that applications developed on earlier releases of the software will work on later releases of the software. Downward compatibility is generally rare.

Functional versus Technological Obsolescence

Many microcomputer products serve needs for several years before they must be replaced. A product is said to be **functionally obsolete** when it no longer meets the needs of an individual or business. However, improvements to hardware and software products are continuous, and often a product is replaced on store shelves with a newer version or release before it is functionally obsolete. A product in this latter class is said to be **technologically obsolete.**

Functionally obsolete.
Refers to a product that no longer meets the needs of an individual or business.

Technologically obsolete.
Refers to a product that, although superseded by a newer version or release, still meets the needs of an individual or business.

In upgrading, a common problem is that users believe the product they are using is functionally obsolete when it is merely technologically obsolete. Because of the rapid pace of technology, virtually anyone buying a computer system today will have at least one technologically obsolete component within a matter of months. Consequently, it's often not feasible to keep current with versions or releases of products as soon as they become available. The most valid reasons for switching from a technologically obsolete product to a newer version are that the older product is also functionally obsolete, the older product results in considerably higher operating costs than the newer one, or support is no longer available for the older product.

Learning More about Microcomputers

A wealth of resources is available to those who want to learn more about microcomputer systems and their uses. Classes, computer clubs, computer shows, magazines, newspapers, newsletters, books, and electronic media are all sources of information about microcomputers.

Classes A good way to learn any subject is to take an appropriate class. Many colleges, universities, and community colleges offer microcomputer-oriented courses for undergraduate and continuing-education students. Probably the fastest way to find out about such courses is to phone a local college and ask to speak to the registrar or to someone in a computer-related academic department.

Clubs Computer clubs are another effective way to get an informal education in computers. They are also a good place to get an unbiased and knowledgeable viewpoint about a particular product or vendor. Generally clubs are organized by region, product line, or common interests. Apple computer enthusiasts join clubs such as Apple-Holics (Alaska), Apple Pie (Illinois), or Apple Core (California). Clubs such as The Boston Computer Society serve the needs of a more diverse group of microcomputer buffs. Many clubs also function as buying groups, obtaining software or hardware at reduced rates. Computer clubs range in size from two or three members to several thousand.

Shows Computer shows give you a firsthand look at leading-edge hardware and software products. Such shows typically feature numerous vendor exhibits as well as seminars on various aspects of computing. The annual West Coast Computer Faire, held in the San Francisco area, is one event specifically oriented toward smaller computers.

Periodicals Periodicals are another good source of information about microcomputers. Magazines such as *Byte, Popular Computing, PC,* and *MacWorld* (see Figure 13-12) focus on microcomputers. Computer magazines vary tremendously in reading level. You'll probably find and be able to browse through these publications and more at your local bookstore or computer store.

Books One of the best ways to learn about any aspect of personal computing is to read a book on the subject. A host of softcover and hardcover books are available, covering topics ranging from the simple to the highly sophisticated. Included are "how-to" books on subjects such as operating popular microcomputer systems or productivity software packages, programming in microcomputer-based languages, and the technical fundamentals of microcomputers. You can find such books in your local library, computer stores, and bookstores.

Electronic Media One easy way to learn a subject in our electronic age is to pick up a training disk or view a videotape or television show devoted to the subject. Today many microcomputer-oriented software packages are sold with training diskettes that provide screen-oriented tutorials, showing you which keys to press and the results. Interactive CD-ROM with full-motion video, as well as other types of professionally prepared "courseware," may also be available. Videotapes are sometimes available for standard videocassette players, so you can see how something works simply by watching your television. Television shows such as PBS's "The Computer Chronicles," which may feature a program on optical disks one week and a program on bus architectures the next, are specifically targeted to microcomputer users.

Summary and Key Terms

Chapter 14 covers such activities as users acquiring their own computer resources, using and taking care of their own systems, and upgrading systems on their own.

The Microcomputer Marketplace The microcomputer marketplace comprises a wide variety of firms that make hardware and software products. One important market segment, composed of microcomputer system units, is dominated primarily by IBM, Apple, and **IBM-compatible microcomputers.**

Hardware and software microcomputing products are most often acquired by users from retail stores, mail-order houses, and manufacturers.

Selecting a Computer System When selecting a computer system, the steps include analyzing needs, listing system alternatives, evaluating alternatives, and choosing a system. Although applications software is normally selected before a computer and systems-software **platform,** software and hardware choices for microcomputers are often interrelated so that you must consider them jointly.

Operating a Computer System **Backup** refers to making a duplicate copy of valuable files. Two types of backup are **full backup** and **partial backup.** Microcomputer systems contain sensitive electronic devices, so they must be treated with care and protected from damage. A **surge suppressor** will prevent

FIGURE 13-12

Microcomputer periodicals. One of the largest reader audiences consists of users who want information about specific types of hardware platforms. *PC Week, PC World,* and *PC Magazine* are targeted largely to users of IBM and IBM-compatible microcomputers, whereas *MacWorld* and *MacWeek* are for users of the Apple Macintosh. *Infoworld* caters to both IBM and Macintosh environments.

most random electrical spikes from entering your system and causing damage. Precautions taken with diskettes and hard disks will safeguard any data stored on them. Other practices can protect your system from dust, heat, and static. Software called **screen savers** can protect your monitor. Printer life can often be extended by taking precautions with the print head.

Although no two problems with a computer system are ever totally alike, some useful guidelines can be followed when troubleshooting problems and when having equipment repaired. For instance, just trying a procedure out a second time often solves a problem. When considering a repair, you should check first to see what protection is granted under **warranty.**

Upgrading **Upgrading** a computer system means buying new hardware or software components that will extend the life of your current system. When considering a hardware upgrade, you must consider such things as your current system's storage capacity, the number of expansion slots, and the power of the system unit. Software upgrades are often accomplished by acquiring a new **release** or **version** of the program that you are currently using. You need to ask yourself whether upgrading is better than starting fresh and buying a new computer system. You also must consider whether you are planning to replace a product that's only **technologically obsolete** instead of **functionally obsolete.**

Learning More about Microcomputers A wealth of resources is available to those who want to learn more about microcomputer systems and their uses. Classes, computer clubs, computer shows, magazines, newspapers, newsletters, books, and electronic media are all sources of information about microcomputers.

Review Exercises

Fill-in Questions

1. A(n) ______________ microcomputer runs the same software as that targeted to DOS-based IBM microcomputers.
2. With a(n) ______________ PC, you may be able to swap out an 80486 chip for a Pentium chip.
3. A minor upgrade of a software package is called a(n) ______________.
4. The most important selection criterion is ______________, which refers to the type of work a hardware or software product does.
5. ______________ refers to making, for security purposes, a duplicate copy of a file.
6. A(n) ______________ is a hardware device designed to stop power spikes from damaging a computer system.
7. A(n) ______________ usually states that a product manufacturer will pay for defective software or hardware for a given period of time under certain conditions.
8. A product that no longer meets the needs of a user is said to be ______________ obsolete.

Matching Questions

Match each term with the description that fits best.

a. Compaq
b. Toshiba
c. Intel
d. Microsoft
e. Cyrix
f. Motorola
g. Seagate
h. Lotus Development

___ 1. Makes CPU chips for the Apple Macintosh line of computers.

___ 2. A large U.S.-based maker of IBM-compatible microcomputers.

___ 3. Produces primarily disk products.

___ 4. Famous for Windows and MS-DOS, as well as a wide variety of other software products.

___ 5. Makes most CPU chips for IBM and IBM-compatible microcomputers.

___ 6. Mostly known for its popular spreadsheet.

___ 7. Produces Intel-compatible CPU chips.

___ 8. A famous foreign-based maker of printers.

Discussion Questions

1. In the world of microcomputers, what is an IBM-compatible microcomputer?
2. Who are the three leading manufacturers of desktop system units?
3. Name four places that users often turn to for buying microcomputer products.
4. Name several criteria that are important to consider when evaluating alternative computer systems for purchase.
5. Provide several examples that show why it is important to back up files.
6. Give several guidelines that are useful when troubleshooting a problem with your computer system.
7. What is the difference between a version and a release of a software package?
8. What is the difference between technological obsolescence and functional obsolescence?

Critical Thinking Questions

1. Almost every other year, a major new microprocessor chip is introduced, and it leads to the development of a new "family" of faster, more capable computer systems. What problems does this pose for a typical corporation?
2. A number of newer microcomputer systems have multiuser capabilities, allowing several users to share the system at once. For instance, a single system unit, hard disk, and printer might be shared by four people, each with his or her own monitor and keyboard. But despite the multiuser capabilities of such systems, they are often bought for a single individual and are not shared. Why do you think this is so?
3. Four nations that have recently become a force on the microcomputing scene are Korea, Hong Kong, Singapore, and Taiwan. What are these nations doing well to have become such an important factor in the microcomputer industry?

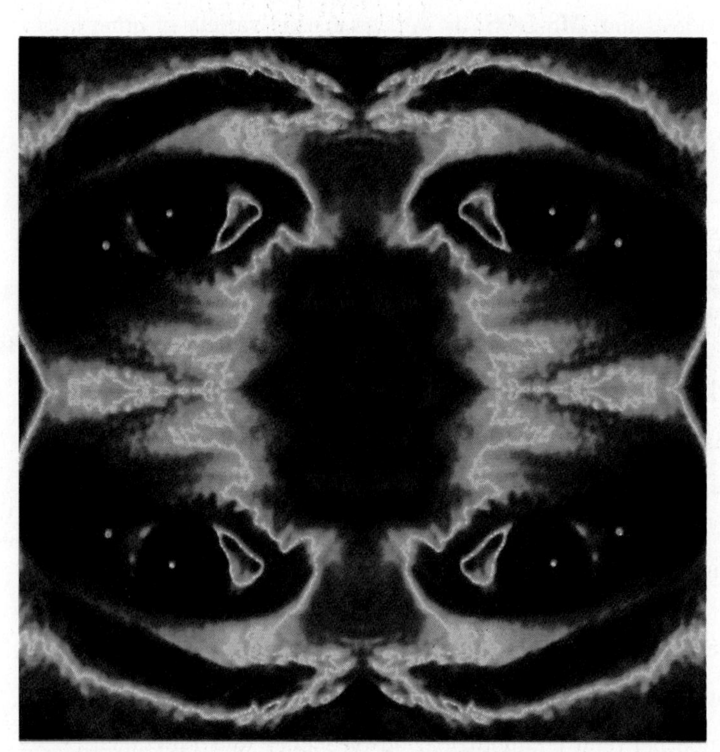

M O D U L E F

Computers in Society

No study of computers is complete without a look at the impact these devices have had on the very fabric of our society. In the workplace, computers have created many jobs and careers but also have made others obsolete. Likewise, in society as a whole, they have created both opportunities and problems. Many people praise computers as a major source of progress. Others wonder if we are indeed any better off today than we were before the age of computerization.

Chapter 14 discusses many of the opportunities and problems created by the proliferation of computers. Window 8, which accompanies the chapter, looks retrospectively at the history of computers.

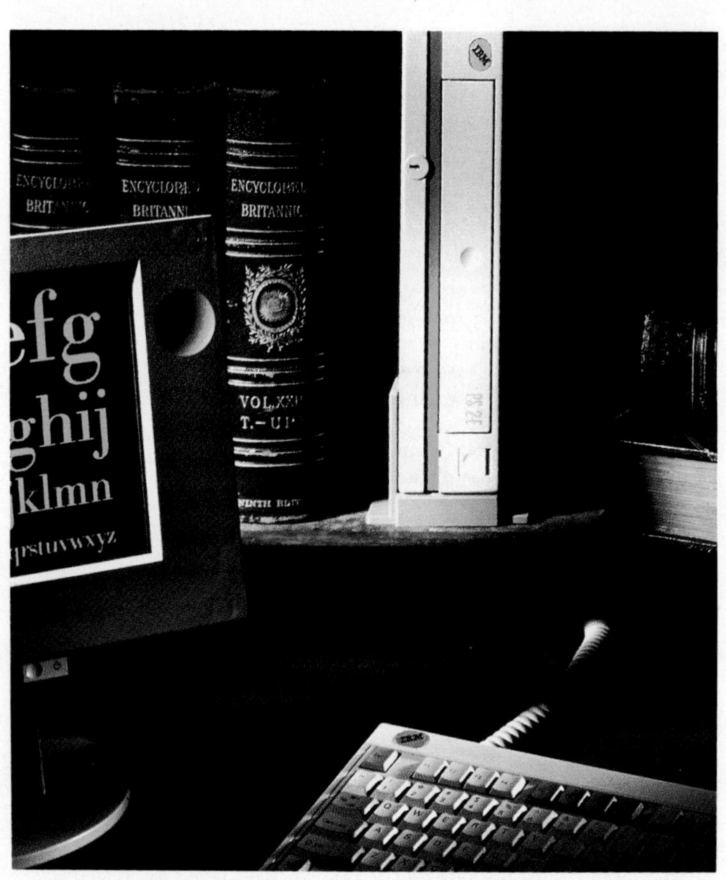
IBM
efg
ghij
jklmn
qrstuvwxyz

Computers in Our Lives: The Costs and the Benefits

14

How are computers impacting people outside the workplace? Perhaps in more ways than you would initially guess. In this chapter we'll look at the costs and benefits of living in the computer age.

OUTLINE

Overview

Computers, Work, and Health
- Stress-related Concerns
- Ergonomics-related Concerns
- Environment-related Concerns
- Other Areas of Concern

Computer Crime
- Types of Computer Crime
- Preventing Computer Crime

Computers and Privacy
- Privacy Legislation
- Privacy and Electronic Mail
- Caller Identification

Ethical Issues Regarding Computers

Computers in Our Lives: Today and Tomorrow
- Computers for Home and Personal Use
- Computers in Education
- Computers in Entertainment and Leisure Activities
- Computers in Science and Medicine

LEARNING OBJECTIVES

After completing this chapter, you will be able to:

1. Describe some health-related concerns that people have regarding computers.
2. Explain what computer crime is, give several examples of it, and describe how computer crime can be prevented.
3. Appreciate how computer technology can encroach on people's privacy and describe some of the legislation enacted to prevent such abuses.
4. Explain what is meant by "ethics," and provide several examples of ethical misbehavior as regards computer-related matters.
5. Describe several applications in which computers affect the day-to-day life of the average person.

Overview

Since the early 1950s, when the era of commercial computing began, computers have rapidly woven their way into the fabric of modern society. In the process, they've created both opportunities and problems. Consequently, they've been both cursed and applauded—and for good reason.

So far in this book, we've focused on the opportunities. We've examined the impact computers have had in organizations and on the people who work there. Through the text and windows, we've seen how these devices have been put to work on routine transaction processing tasks, used to provide managers with better information for decision making, and employed to design and manufacture better products. In this chapter, we'll examine some of the effect that computer technology has had or is likely to have on our lives outside the workplace.

Before we look at these social benefits, let's examine some of the problems computers have created. Although the computer "revolution" has brought undeniable benefits to society, it has also produced some troubling side effects. Like any fast-paced revolution, it has been disruptive in many ways. Some jobs have been created, others lost, and still others threatened. In addition, an increasing variety of health-related concerns affecting people's working with computer-related technologies have surfaced. Computers have also immensely increased access to information, creating new possibilities for crime—even at the international level—and threatening personal privacy. Clearly some controls to limit the dangers that these awesome devices pose will always be needed. In this chapter, we highlight four important problem areas: computers and health in the workplace, computer crime, computers and privacy, and ethical uses of technology.

Perhaps one of the biggest problems posed by technological progress is that computers have evolved quickly and unpredictably, in relatively little time, into the very core of most of our lives (see Window 8).

Computers, Work, and Health

Computers have been said to pose a threat to our mental and physical well-being. Although the body of scientific evidence supporting this claim is far from conclusive, and is likely to be that way for many more years, we should all be aware of the major concerns raised about the possible effects of computers on our health.

Stress-related Concerns

Emotional problems such as financial worries, feelings of incompetence, and disorientation often produce emotional *stress*. This stress, in turn, may have been triggered by layoff or reassignment, fear of falling behind, or job burnout.

Layoff or Reassignment One of the first criticisms leveled at computers upon their entry into the workplace was that their very presence resulted in job-related stress. When computers came in, many people were laid off and had to find new jobs. Clerical workers especially worried about job security.

Many feared the full potential of computers in the office, never knowing when machines might replace them. These fears are still widespread today.

Even people who were not laid off found that their jobs had changed significantly and that they had no choice but to retrain. Airline agents, for example, had to learn how to manipulate a database language and to work with display terminals. Secretaries were pressured into learning word processing (and perhaps electronic spreadsheets, electronic data management, and electronic mail) to keep in tune with state-of-the-art office work. Many workers never made the transition successfully.

A growing fact of life is that because of computers, fewer people are needed to do many types of work today. Computers are also regularly changing the way work is done—often, in ways that are difficult to predict. Even modern computer networks are posing a new threat to workers in that companies no longer have to physically staff each location as heavily with local expertise as in the past. Networks also mean that work can be transferred overseas more easily (see Feature 14-1).

Fear of Falling Behind The microcomputing boom has placed computing power of awesome dimensions at almost everyone's fingertips. Some researchers perceive a widespread fear that failure to learn how to use these machines will make one "fall behind." One example is the numerous noncomputer-oriented executives, managers, and educators who see themselves being upstaged by their computer-knowledgeable colleagues. The surge of interest in microcomputers has even made many programmers who work in mainframe environments feel that they are somehow falling behind.

Burnout Burnout is caused not by fear of computers (*cyberphobia*) but by overuse of them (*cyberphelia*). The infusion of microcomputers into home and office has raised new concerns about what will happen to children who withdraw into their computer systems, to computer-bound managers who have inadvertently been swept into the tide of the computer revolution, or to couples or families whose intimacy may be threatened by computer overuse in their homes.

To date, little research has been done on computer burnout. What makes this area so controversial is the compelling flip-side argument that most victims of computer burnout would burn out on something else if computers didn't exist.

Ergonomics-related Concerns

Ergonomics is the field that addresses such issues as making products and work areas comfortable and safe to use. With respect to technology, ergonomics covers the effects on workers of things such as display devices, keyboards, and workspaces. Let's consider some of the major fronts of ergonomic research.

Ergonomics. The field that studies the effects of things such as computer hardware, software, and workspaces on employees' comfort and health.

Dangers Posed by Display Devices For nearly a decade, large numbers of data-entry operators have reported a variety of physical and mental problems stemming from their interaction with display devices. The complaints have centered on visual, muscular, and emotional disorders resulting from long hours of continuous display device use. These include blurred eyesight, eyestrain, acute fatigue, headaches, and backaches. In response to these problems, several

Feature 14–1

Toward a National Technology Policy

When does government intervention help or hinder?

When people discuss the key industries that will determine the global competitiveness of nations in the next decade, technology is always a visible force. Widely regarded as being among the most critical industries as we move into the 21st century are computer systems and software, communications, microelectronics, robotics and machine tools, and biotechnology and new materials.

All the talk about key industries raises an important question: Should government protect these industries through legislation or should it let them compete on their own steam, letting the chips fall where they may? As with most issues regarding government intervention, there is both a "for" side and an "against" side. Below we will consider each of these in turn.

The "For" Argument Advocates for government intervention point to the case of Japan. In Japan, government and industry have collaborated during the last couple of decades in such industries as automobiles, consumer electronics, robotics, and microelectronics. Working together, they have fashioned one of the economic miracles of the century.

Which jobs should be kept home? The role played by government is a hotly debated item.

Government can be a big help to getting new industries launched in the United States, too, say the advocates. After all, had not the U.S. government been the first (and, for a long time, the only) consumer of the products of the U.S.

states and cities (such as San Francisco) have passed laws that curb display device abuse. In addition, vendors of these devices have redesigned their products with features such as tiltable screens and detachable keyboards to make them more comfortable to use.

Dangers Posed by Keyboards Years ago, computer keyboards frequently were built into display units, making it difficult for operators to move them about as freely as they could if the keyboards had been detached. Most claims that a computer keyboard could result in injury seemed to be put to rest after most keyboard manufacturers started making detachable keyboards—that is, until recently. Today, some people are experiencing a condition known as *carpal tunnel syndrome*, a painful and crippling complex of symptoms affecting the computer industry in the 1940s and 1950s, the industry would not be where it is today. Who knows, maybe England would have been the world's information-technology powerhouse instead? Or Nazi Germany?

One area in which the government might be able to play an important role now is fiber-optic cable transmission. As covered in Chapter 6, a fiber-optic superhighway in the United States could bring unprecedented amounts of computing power within reach of almost every U.S. resident and business. Japan intends to be "all-fiber optic" by the year 2015.

The "Against" Argument Those opposed to the government taking an active role in the technology race point out that government is ill suited to pick winners and losers in the private sector. When the government gets involved, they say, things often turn out worse. Governments are notoriously slow and inefficient, and their decision patterns are often harder for companies to predict than free-market forces.

Take the inexpensive flat-panel display screens that Japanese manufacturers were "dumping" on the U.S. market a few years ago. Most flat-panel screens are used to build laptop computers, and the Japanese companies were selling these screens to U.S. laptop companies at prices that were allegedly below their cost.

Manufacturers of flat-screen devices in the United States were up in arms, claiming that Japanese firms were trying to put them out of business. Worse yet, they claimed, the predatory pricing would kill off the flat-panel-screen industry within the United States. If the United States lost its competitiveness in flat-screen technology, foreign powers could conrol pricing on U.S. products that use flat screens.

But, laptop makers countered, by putting import tariffs on screens—thereby artificially making screens more expensive—the U.S. government would cause laptops to be that much more expensive to the U.S. consumer. (Almost half the cost of many laptops is in the price of the screen.) They also claim that tariffs on Japanese screens would cause them, the U.S. laptop makers, to have to set up their own laptop manufacturing plants overseas in order to continue to give U.S. customers low prices. That would mean creating more jobs overseas—and losing more at home.

Those against government technology policy also argue that the United States does not have to be and cannot be the world leader in every single technology. Being a pioneer doesn't always translate into being the biggest winner. As a case in point, IBM let Apple and other companies be the pioneers in microcomputer systems, forcing them to pay the price of making learning mistakes. Finally, when the market ripened to an irresistable size and there was less risk to entry, IBM came out with its IBM PC—and walked away with the biggest share of the industry revenues. Of course, don't forget the VCR. While it was invented in the United States, it was the Japanese who made it into a successful consumer product.

hand and wrist that has been traced to the repetitive finger movements routinely made when using a keyboard. The condition, which may not strike everyone who puts in long hours on a keyboard, and which can disappear in some cases, makes it difficult to use a keyboard, drive long distances, and even hold up a book to read, among other things. Physicians recommend that to minimize the chance of such an injury, you take breaks every hour or so and relax your arms and hands so that blood flows freely throughout your body. Recently, a number of innovatively designed keyboards have come to the fore that attempt to reduce stress in the hands and wrists (see Figure 14-1).

Workspace Design Display devices and keyboards are not the only things that can torture people at workstations. For example, the furniture may be nonadjustable, forcing the terminal user into awkward postures that are guaranteed to produce body kinks. Or the lighting may be so bright that it causes a headache-producing glare on the display screen. There may even be disconcerting noise levels present due to poorly designed office equipment or acoustics. Ergonomics researchers are constantly studying such problems, and the results of their efforts are becoming apparent in the consumer products now being offered to the ergonomics-conscious buyer. Figure 14-2 illustrates some principles of good workspace design.

Environment-related Concerns

The surge in microcomputer use during the last several years has caused a variety of environmental concerns.

Take power use. The U.S. Environmental Protection Agency (EPA) has estimated that home and office microcomputer systems now annually consume about $2 billion worth of electricity. This indirectly has resulted in the discharge of tons of pollutants into the atmosphere. The microcomputer industry has responded by adding a variety of energy-saving devices into computer hardware. Among these devices are power-management software that puts the CPU, hard-disk unit, and display into a "sleep mode" when they are not being used, low-power-consumptive chips and boards, and flat-panel displays. Of course, users can help, too. EPA statistics suggest that most of the time a microcomputer system is turned on, it is not in use.

FIGURE 14-1

Stress-reducing keyboard. Standard keyboards are often criticized for straining the tendons that run through the wrist and connect the fingers to the forearm muscles. To reduce such stress, the Kinesis keyboard shown here places keys in two curved wells, shoulder distance apart.

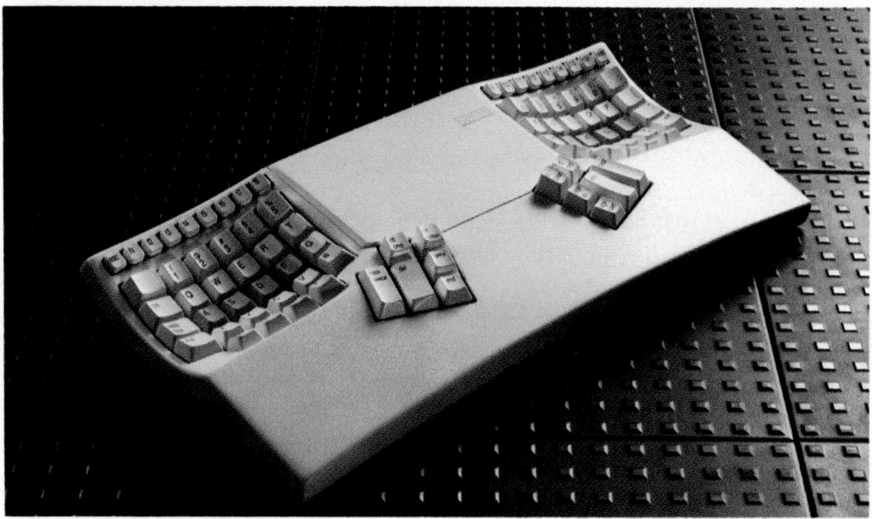

FIGURE 14-2

Workplace Design. Features such as detachable keyboards, tilt capabilities on both keyboards and display devices, and adjustable furniture have contributed to making life more pleasant for display device users.

The pollution problem goes much deeper than just the higher electrical use. Other major concerns include the following:

- Many laptop-computer batteries used today are of the nickel cadmium (nicad) type. Cadmium is a highly toxic material that requires special disposal procedures. The trend today is toward batteries with less toxicity.
- Toner cartridges for laser printers and personal copiers are getting to be a common sight at landfills. While such cartridges can be refilled or recycled—the environmentally best things to do—relatively few are.
- The so-called "paperless office" that many visionaries predicted for the computer age has become a myth. Because computer outputs are so easy to produce, more paper than ever is now being consumed. It is estimated that U.S. businesses generate almost 800 billion pages a year—an amount that would stack 50,000 miles high! Recycling and cutting down on paper use are two solutions.

Other Areas of Concern

Besides the aforementioned concerns, there are many other social-related worries regarding computers. One is whether we are coming to rely on them too much. Dr. Joseph Weizenbaum of MIT, a luminary in the field of artificial intelligence, has voiced another concern: Will future generations rely on computers so much that they lose sight of the fundamental thought processes that computers are intended to model? Many teachers complain that some children who own pocket calculators can't do arithmetic by hand.

There is no question, of course, that computers have altered the structure of work and play just as mechanized farm machinery changed the nature of agriculture and airplanes and automobiles changed the nature of travel. Many people have accepted these disruptions as the price of "progress."

Computer Crime

Computer crime. The use of computers to commit unauthorized acts.

Computer crime is loosely defined as the use of computers to commit unauthorized acts. The law is spotty on computer crime. The federal government, through the Computer Fraud and Abuse Act of 1986, has made it a felony to knowingly and fraudulently access confidential programs or data in federal-level computers. Most states also have laws that address some aspect of computer crime. But such laws notwithstanding, computer crime is hard to pin down.

One reason is that it is often difficult to decide when an unauthorized act is really a crime. No one would doubt that a bank employee who uses a computer system to embezzle funds from customers' accounts is committing a crime. But what about an employee who "steals time" on a company computer to balance a personal checkbook for a home or business? Or someone who uses the same computer to word process a personal letter to a friend? Aren't those acts also unauthorized? Where does one draw the line?

Another problem in pinning down computer crime is that judges and juries often are bewildered by the technical issues involved in such cases. Also, companies that discover computer criminals among their employees frequently are reluctant to press charges because they fear adverse publicity.

Types of Computer Crime

Computer crime has many forms. Some cases involve the use of a computer for theft of financial assets, such as money or equipment. Others concern the copying of information-processing resources such as programs or data to the owner's detriment. Still other cases involve manipulation of data such as grades for personal advantage. By far, the majority of computer crimes are committed by insiders.

The cost of computer crime to individuals and organizations is estimated at billions of dollars annually. No one knows for sure what the exact figure is, because so many incidents are either undetected or unreported.

As in many fields, a specialized jargon has evolved in the area of computer-related crime. Following is a sampling of some of the specific forms computer crime can take.

Data Diddling *Data diddling* is one of the most common ways to perform a computer crime. It involves altering key production data on the computer system in some unauthorized way. Data diddlers often are found changing grades in university files, falsifying input records on bank transactions, and the like.

The Trojan Horse The *Trojan horse* is a procedure for adding concealed instructions to a computer program so that it will still work but will also perform unauthorized duties. For example, a bank worker can subtly alter a program that contains thousands of lines of code by adding a small "patch" that instructs the program not to withdraw money from a certain account.

Salami Shaving *Salami shaving* involves manipulating programs or data so that many small dollar amounts—say, a few cents' worth of interest payments—are shaved from a large number of transactions or accounts and accumulated elsewhere. The victims of a salami-shaving scheme generally are unaware that their funds have been tapped, because the amount taken from each individual is trivial. The recipient of the salami shaving, however, benefits from the aggregation of these small amounts, often substantially. Some of the earliest frauds were perpetrated by unscrupulous programmers working on their own behalf in banks. Recently, several supermarkets have been accused of salami shaving at the checkout counter by not conscientiously updating computer-stored prices to reflect lower shelf prices.

Superzapping *Superzapping* is a technique made possible by a special program available on most computer systems—a program that bypasses all system controls when the computer "crashes" and cannot be restarted with normal recovery procedures. This program, in effect, is a "master key" that can provide access to any part of the system. The superzap program is a highly privileged "disaster aid" that very few computer professionals are authorized to use. In the wrong hands, it can be used to perform almost any unauthorized task.

Trapdoors *Trapdoors* are diagnostic tools, used in the development of systems programs, that enable programmers to gain access to various parts of the computer system. Before the programs are marketed, these tools are supposed to be removed. Occasionally, however, some blocks of diagnostic code are overlooked. Thus, a person using the associated systems program may be provided unauthorized views of other parts of the computer system.

Logic Bombs and Computer Viruses *Logic bombs* are programs or short code segments designed to be executed at random or at specific times to perform unauthorized acts. In one documented case, a programmer inserted into a system a logic bomb that would destroy the company's entire personnel file if his name was removed from it. Sometimes the term **computer virus** is used to describe a logic bomb in which a piece of unauthorized code is transmitted from program to program during a copy operation and destroys data or crashes the computer system as soon as it is unwittingly executed (see Feature 14-2).

Computer virus.
A small block of unauthorized code, transmitted from program to program by a copy operation, that performs destructive acts when executed.

Scavenging As its name implies, *scavenging* involves searching through trash cans, offices, and the like for information that will permit unauthorized access to a computer system. Students, for example, will sometimes look through discarded listings at the mainframe computer site for an identification number that will open to them the resources of others' accounts. Many organizations use document shredders to deter scavengers.

Feature 14–2

Virus Protection

What to do when your computer system catches a "cold"

If your computer system comes down with nVir-a, nVir-f, INIT 29, ANTI, WDEF A or B, Michelangelo, Stoned, or Jerusalem, reach for your electronic medicine chest. It's got a computer virus.

A *computer virus* is a small block of code, often hidden inside a larger program, that is designed to create malicious damage or pull a harmless prank. Malicious damage includes such things as destroying programs and data or gumming up your computer system so that it's difficult or impossible to continue working. Pranks include such things as flashing messages on your display screen from time to time to let you know that your computer system has been invaded by someone who delights in this sort of practical joke.

Viruses often work by copying code onto programs or data on a disk or in memory. Many may even replicate themselves onto other disks, thereby spreading infection. The virus also contains a mechanism that at a specific time or moment (say, on a specific day or when an infected program performs a certain operation) destroys data or pulls pranks.

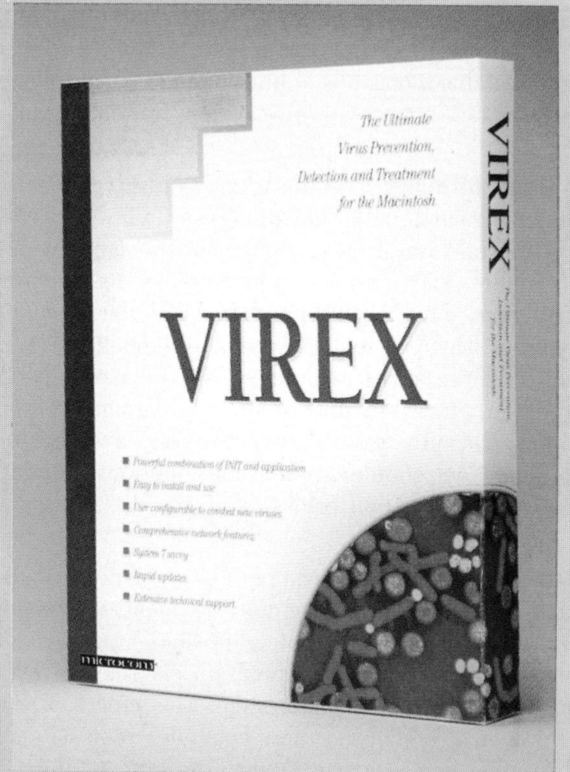

Vaccine software. An ounce of prevention is worth a pound of cure.

In November 1988, a virus implanted in a computer system disabled thousands of computers that were hooked into Arpanet, a nationwide network connecting dozens of colleges,

Data Leakage Some pieces of data generated by organizations are highly confidential and not intended for outsiders' eyes. Generally these organizations carefully control any computer output that leaves their premises. In *data leakage,* however, confidential data are coded in sophisticated ways so that they can be removed undetected. For example, sensitive data can be transformed through a coding process called *encryption* (discussed shortly) into useless nonsense. Then, after they leave the premises unnoticed, these data are decoded into their original form and used for unauthorized purposes.

Wiretapping There are many documented cases of people who have wiretapped computer systems to obtain information illegally. Some transmission facilities, such as satellites, are highly susceptible to *wiretapping* (as evidenced by those "illegal" rooftop dishes that intercept cable TV). Others, such as fiber optic cable, are extremely difficult to penetrate.

universities, and research labs. When any computer system in the network read a program containing the predator code, the virus filled up the memory of that computer system with garbage, effectively choking out legitimate applications and grinding the system to a halt.

The Michelangelo virus, named for the sixteenth-century Italian artist, has been devised to detonate any time the clock of an infected computer strikes March 6, the artist's birthday. On hard-disk systems, Michelangelo attaches itself to routines that *boot,* or start up, the computer, causing them to be moved to hard-to-find locations and causing vital directory data on the disk to be overwritten with random characters. Any diskettes inserted into a drive of an infected system are themselves infected, and data destroyed, during read/write operations.

Your system is vulnerable to viruses virtually any time you use it. At especially high risk are people who work on networks, people who use software that comes from unknown origins, and people who let others use their system. If you are concerned about viruses, you can protect yourself by (1) avoiding high-risk situations, (2) never using any new software unless all of the software and data that you can't afford to lose are backed up on offline diskettes, (3) locking up disks (a virus, for instance, can't write to a diskette when the latter has been made "read only" through the write-protect notch), (4) keeping high-risk software away from your hard disk, and (5) using some type of *vaccine program.*

To date, a number of vaccine programs have surfaced to combat computer viruses. Three of the most widely used are Symantec's SAM, Mainstay's AntiToxin, and Datawatch's Virex. Vaccine programs are priced at about $100 and are accompanied by a list of the specific strains of viruses that they can protect your system from.

Vaccine programs scrutinize code for suspicious patterns. If something looks strange, they often can intercept an activity before it takes place and apprise you of what's going on. Many are also designed to repair damaged files in the event that a virus it is able to recognize has infected some programs or data. Some can even prevent a program or data with a recognized virus from ever executing.

Many vaccine programs are designed to check for virus activity upon system log-in, during system use, and upon log-off. Some packages provide a log of all virus alerts, which lets you keep tabs on suspicious activity over a period of time.

Unfortunately, no vaccine program is foolproof. New viruses are being discovered all the time, so vaccine programs need to be updated constantly. Updates may cost anywhere from $10 to $25 annually.

Software Piracy **Software piracy,** the unauthorized copying or use of a computer program, is often a crime. A person who makes an unauthorized copy of a program can be guilty of breaking copyright laws. It is definitely a crime to copy a program and then attempt to sell it for profit. The law is generally more lenient if one just uses an unauthorized copy that was made by someone else, but this use may constitute a crime as well.

Software piracy. The unauthorized copying or use of computer programs.

Hacking **Hacking** is a computer term referring to the activities of people who "get their kicks" out of using computers or terminals to crack the security of some computer system. Many people engage in hacking purely for the challenge of cracking codes; others do it to steal computer time or to peek at confidential information. Intentions aside, hacking often is considered a breaking-and-entering crime similar to forced entry into someone's car or home.

Hacking. Using a microcomputer system or terminal to penetrate the security of a large computer system.

Counterfeiting Hard as it is to believe, microcomputer-based color copier technology is so sophisticated today that it has opened the door to a brand new type of computer crime—counterfeiting. The U.S. Secret Service recently arrested a person who made over $1 million worth of photocopied money and traveler's checks. In another case that involved counterfeit rail tickets on a commuter line, an official of the railroad conceded that the fake, copier-produced tickets looked better than the real ones. But would-be counterfeiters, beware: many of the new color copiers print "invisible" codes on outputs, making counterfeit money easier to spot. Also, laws are being introduced that will make it easier to identify the owner of a machine from its output.

Preventing Computer Crime

Organizations can combat computer crime in many ways.

Hire Trustworthy People Employers should carefully investigate the background of anyone being considered for sensitive computer work. Some people falsify résumés to get jobs. Others may have criminal records. Despite the publicity given to groups such as hackers, studies have consistently shown that most computer crimes are committed by insiders.

Beware of Malcontents The type of employee who is most likely to commit a computer crime is one who has recently been terminated or passed over for a promotion, or one who has some reason to "get even" with the organization. In cases in which an employee has been terminated and potential for computer crime exists, records should be updated immediately to indicate that the person involved is no longer an employee.

Separate Employee Functions An employee with many related responsibilities can commit a crime more easily than one with a single responsibility. For example, the person who authorizes adding new vendors to a file should not be the same one who authorizes payments to those vendors.

Restrict System Use People who use a computer system should have access only to the things they need to do their jobs. A computer operator, for example, should be told only how to execute a program and not what the program does. People who need only to retrieve information should not also be given updating privileges.

Password.
A word or number used to permit selected individuals access to a system.

Access card.
A plastic card that, when inserted into a machine and combined with a password, permits access to a system.

Biometric security device.
A device that, upon recognition of some physiological or learned characteristic that is unique to a person, allows that person to have access to a system.

Limit Access to Programs and Data On many systems, users can restrict access to programs and data with **passwords.** For example, a user might specify that anyone wanting access to a program named AR-148 must first enter the password FRED. Users can change passwords frequently and also can protect particularly sensitive files with several passwords. Today many organizations use measures such as *access cards* and sophisticated *biometric security devices* in place of or in combination with passwords. **Access cards,** such as those used in automatic teller machines at banks, activate a transaction when they are used in combination with a password or number. **Biometric security devices** activate a transaction by recognizing some unique physiological characteristic of a person—such as a fingerprint or handprint—or some unique learned characteristic—such as a voice or signature (see Figure 14-3).

Use Site Licensing Software vendors often protect their products from unauthorized copying with site licenses. A **site license** allows organizations buying a software product to make copies of it and to distribute the copies among employees for internal use.

Site license. A right purchased by an organization that enables employees to freely use or copy software for specific, authorized purposes.

Disguise Programs or Data through Encryption Some users and vendors encrypt data or programs to protect them. **Encryption** is the process of disguising data and programs by using some coding method. The encrypting procedure must provide for both coding and decoding. As with passwords, the encryption method should be changed regularly if it is to protect particularly sensitive

Encryption. A method of disguising data or programs so that they are unrecognizable to unauthorized users.

FIGURE 14-3

Biometric security. Biometric security devices activate a transaction by recognizing some unique physiological characteristic of a person—such as a fingerprint or handprint—or some unique learned characteristic—such as a voice or signature.

Physiological Characteristic

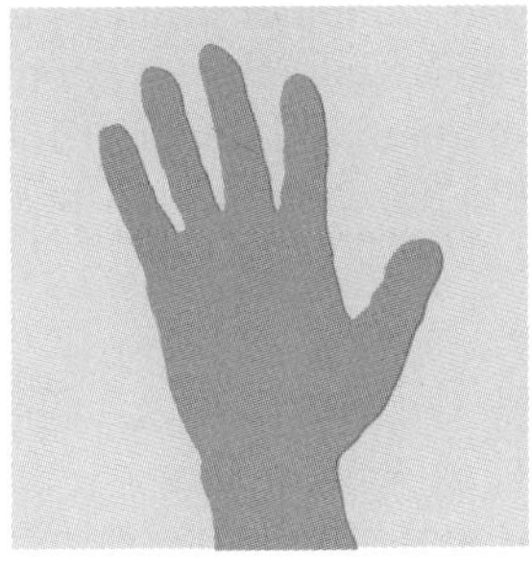

Handprint

Fingerprint

Retina pattern in eye

Learned Characteristic

Signature

Voice

Keystroking pattern

materials. Some software packages, such as Microsoft's Excel, have built-in encryption routines.

Devise Staff Controls Overtime work should be carefully scrutinized, because computer crimes often occur at times when the criminal is unlikely to be interrupted. Sensitive documents that are no longer needed should be shredded. Access to the computer room or program/data library should be strictly limited to authorized personnel. **Callback devices,** which hang up on and call back people phoning in from remote locations, should be used in communications systems to deter hacking and virus implantation.

Callback device.
A device on the receiving end of a communications network that verifies the authenticity of the sender by calling the sender back.

Monitor Important System Transactions The systems software should include a program for maintaining a log of every person gaining or attempting to gain access to the system. The log should contain information on the terminal used, the data files and programs used, and the time at which the work began and ended. Such a log allows management to isolate unauthorized system use.

Conduct Regular Audits Unfortunately, many crimes are discovered by accident. Key elements of the system should be subjected to regular **audits**—inspections that certify that the system is working as expected—to ensure that there is no foul play.

Audit.
An inspection used to determine if a system or procedure is working as it should or if claimed amounts are correct.

Educate Employees One of the best ways to prevent computer crime is to educate employees about security matters. People should be told about various types of computer crime and the conditions that foster them, informed of the seriousness of computer crime, and instructed on what to do when they suspect a computer crime is taking place or is about to occur.

Computers and Privacy

Almost all of us have some aspects of our lives that we prefer to keep private. These may include a sorry incident from the past, sensitive medical or financial facts, or certain tastes or opinions. Yet we can appreciate that sometimes selected people or organizations have a legitimate need for some of this information. A doctor needs accurate medical histories of patients. Financial information must be disclosed to credit card companies and college scholarship committees. A company or the government may need to probe into the lives of people applying for unusually sensitive jobs.

No matter how legitimate the need, however, once personal information has been made available to others, there is always the danger that it will be misused. Some of the stored facts may be wrong. Facts may get to the wrong people. Facts may be taken out of context and used to draw distorted conclusions. Facts may be collected and disseminated without one's knowledge or consent. People who are victimized may be denied access to incorrect or sensitive data. As it applies to information processing, **privacy** refers to how information about individuals is used and by whom.

Privacy.
In a computer processing context, refers to how information about individuals is used and by whom.

The problem of how to protect privacy and ensure that personal information is not misused was with us long before electronic computers existed. But modern computer systems, with their ability to store and manipulate unprecedented quantities of data and to make those data available to many locations, have added a new dimension to the privacy issue. The greater the ability to collect, store, use, and disseminate information, the greater the potential for abuse of that information (see Feature 14-3).

Privacy Legislation

Since the early 1970s, the federal government has sought to protect citizens' rights by passing legislation to limit the abuse of computer data banks. Some important laws enacted for this purpose are the Fair Credit Reporting Act, the Freedom of Information Act, the Education Privacy Act, and the Privacy Act.

The *Fair Credit Reporting Act (1970)* is designed to prevent private organizations from unfairly denying credit to individuals. It stipulates that people must have the right to inspect their credit records. If a reasonable objection about the integrity of the data is raised, the credit reporting agency is required by law to investigate the matter.

The *Freedom of Information Act (1970)* gives individuals the right to inspect data concerning them that are stored by the federal government. The law also makes certain data about the operation of federal agencies available for public scrutiny.

The *Education Privacy Act (1974)* protects an individual's right to privacy in both private and public schools that receive any federal funding. It stipulates that an individual has the right to keep matters such as course grades and evaluations of behavior private. Also, individuals must have the opportunity to inspect and challenge their own records.

The *Privacy Act (1974)* primarily protects the public against abuses by the federal government. It stipulates that collection of data by federal agencies must have a legitimate purpose. It also states that individuals must be allowed to learn what information is being stored about them and how it's being used and that individuals must have the opportunity to correct or remove erroneous or trivial data.

Most privacy legislation, as you can see, relates to the conduct of the federal government and the organizations to which it supplies aid. Some state governments have enacted similar legislation to protect individuals from abuses by state agencies. The federal government currently is developing private-sector privacy guidelines similar to those of federal and state agencies.

Privacy and Electronic Mail

The recent case involving Lieutenant Colonel Oliver North and the hearings on arms sales to Iran, in which electronic-mail messages between White House staffers were sought as evidence, raised a new issue concerning technology and right to privacy. Some people believe that the objective of electronic mail is to promote a free-flowing dialogue between workers—that is, to increase the effectiveness of organizational communication. They claim that electronic mail should be viewed as the modern-day version of informal chatting around the water cooler, and that electronic mail messages should not in any way be confused with official company records. Others claim that the law applies to hard-copy and soft-copy data in the same way, and that any business document created on the premises of an organization is not the property of the individual

Feature 14 – 3

How Do They Know I Ski?

How Far Will Marketing Databases Go?

Advocates have called them necessary and effective. Detractors have called them dangerous and diabolical. They're marketing databases, and what you've seen of them today is probably only the beginning.

Marketing databases contain information about the consuming public. These databases record where people live, what they are inclined to do, and what they buy. Using this information, marketers attempt to determine the best way to promote specific products to specific people. Virtually any time you leave traceable information about yourself anywhere, there's a good chance that it will eventually find its way into somebody's marketing database.

When you buy a house, for example, your name, address, and the sales price are recorded in a county courthouse. These records are available to the public, including micromarketers. *Micromarketers* are companies that specialize in creating marketing databases and selling them to companies that produce consumer goods and services. The micromarketer typically breaks down the neighborhoods in a region into several dozen categories. Consumers are placed into one of these categories according to their address. For instance, a "Blueblood Estates" category might be a neighborhood in which the very wealthy live. A "Shotguns and Pickups" category, by contrast, might refer to a rural area where

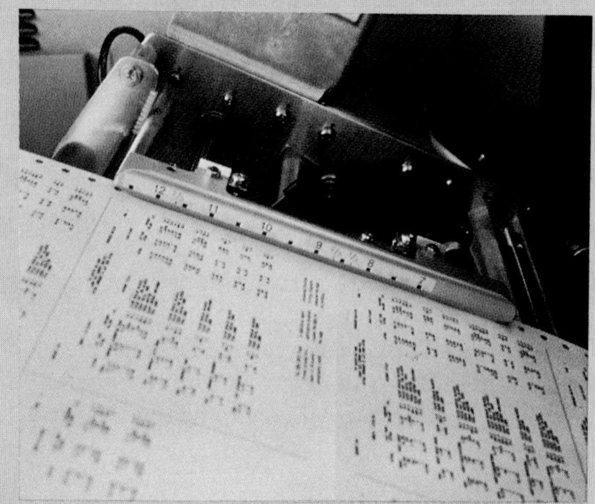

Micromarketing. Is your name on someone's list?

but of the organization. Currently under consideration is the *Communications Privacy Act,* which addresses such issues, as well as the key matter of when it's appropriate to destroy government electronic-mail backups. Recently, a law professor at a leading university recommended that companies in the private sector should not keep backups on file longer than ten days.

Caller Identification

Caller identification. Refers to the use of a telephone or answering device that displays the phone numbers of incoming calls.

Caller identification refers to a relatively new technology in which a telephone contains a microprocessor and a tiny display that will output the phone number of any incoming call. Thus, the party receiving the call can identify the caller before picking up the phone. Many people have praised caller identification systems as a good way of screening or cutting down on unwanted calls. Others have been less enthusiastic, seeing these systems as a potential invasion of privacy. For instance, a person living in an apartment or house in a dangerous neighborhood might be afraid to report a crime taking place outside, fearing that his or her identity could be leaked out and cause the criminal to take revenge at some point in the future.

trailers are the likely abode. There are also categories for urban professionals, the elderly, and so on.

Each category is correlated in the micromarketer's computer system with certain buying preferences, a technique known as *geodemographics.* "Blueblood Estates" types are likely to buy expensive cars and take trips to places such as Aspen, St. Thomas, and Patagonia. Those of the "Shotguns and Pickups" sort are more likely to be interested in fishing equipment, chainsaws, and Elvis collectables. This information helps the micromarketer customize a direct mail (unaffectionately called "junk mail") campaign to consumers' specific tastes.

In addition to geodemographic data, micromarketers also collect data showing consumers' past purchasing behavior. Every time you make a computerized purchase, valuable data can be gathered about your purchasing tastes and entered into a computer system. Records kept by stores, credit card companies, banks, the companies whose magazines you subscribe to, and other organizations are sold to the micromarketer. Even the government sells information.

A shift in marketing trends has necessitated micromarketing. Not long ago, consumer-products companies produced a small line of products that had little variation. If you wanted a pair of jeans, for instance, you'd better have liked the blue denim variety; it was the only type there was. Today, you can get your jeans in different colors, in different styles, in different fabrics, prewashed, stone-washed, regular or boot cut, with or without rivets, ad nauseum. You've probably noticed that other products seem to come in endless variations. Mass marketing is out; niche marketing, or micromarketing, is in.

Micromarketing, in order to work optimally, requires, in the words of the late Arthur Miller, a "womb-to-tomb dossier" on every consumer. As more and more transactions and records become computerized, it will be easier for the micromarketer to know how much you earn, the names and ages of your children, and where you went and what you did last week. And consider this: In the future, as cars and televisions become more computerized, electronic data may be gathered about exactly where you go, what you are watching, and how much time you spend doing things. How much will you be willing to let the micromarketer know?

Some companies have designed phone systems that connect caller identification systems to customer and vendor databases. Thus, for each incoming call, the recipient immediately knows the name of the caller or the company at the other end of the line. At the same time, the system can pull up and display certain types of information related to the transaction about to take place.

Ethical Issues Regarding Computers

Ethics.
A term that refers to standards of moral conduct.

Ethics refers to standards of moral conduct. For example, telling the truth is a matter of ethics. An unethical act isn't always illegal, but sometimes it is. For example, purposely lying to a friend is unethical but normally is lawful, but perjuring onself as a courtroom witness is a crime. Whether or not criminal behavior is involved, ethics play an important role in shaping the law and in determining how well we get along with other people. Some questions to ask when considering an action that might be ethically questionable are provided inFigure 14-4.

FIGURE 14-4

Ethical guidelines. When considering an action that bothers you from an ethical viewpoint, ask yourself these questions. Answering "yes" to certain key questions might be a tipoff that something you are considering doing is wrong. The propriety of an act must ultimately be a matter resolved in your own conscience.

- Will you benefit in any way from the questionable action you are considering taking?
- Are you not disclosing certain facts to others because you are afraid they will disapprove of the action?
- Are you purposely coloring facts to portray a situation as being better or worse than it actually is to bias someone in a certain way?
- If the same action that you are considering was instead done to you, would you feel taken advantage of, used, lied to, disrespected, or abused in any way?
- Could anyone possibly object to the action as being unfair?
- Will anyone be harmed by the action?
- Do you feel yourself rationalizing your behavior in some way?
- Could the action ultimately result in the evolution of a destructive practice or socially undesirable trend?

Today, there are a number of ethical concerns in the computer area. Several examples of these are listed below:

- People tend to use computer resources casually in ways that, although not criminal, are ethically questionable. For instance, some people regularly use a software package that they don't own for personal purposes, claiming they are doing so just to "get the feel of it." Although most vendors encourage limited experimentation with their products, they frown on someone who hasn't bought the package using it regularly.
- A student may casually eavesdrop on a university mainframe system on data not intended for his or her use. This may entail neither a prosecutable crime nor a major security threat, but that makes the act no less ethically reprehensible.
- A computer professional working for one software company leaves and takes a job for a competing company. During the first few days with the new employer, the professional divulges product-development secrets that were entrusted in confidence by the former employer, putting the new employer at a distinct competitive advantage.
- A medical programmer is assigned to quickly code a software routine that is to be part of a system that monitors the heart rate of hospital patients. Before the program can be fully tested, the programmer is ordered to hand it over, so that the system can meet its promised deadline. The programmer tells the project supervisor that the code may contain serious bugs. The supervisor responds, "It's not our fault if the program fails because the deadline is too tight."
- A large software company, hearing that a small competitor is coming out with a new product, spreads a rumor that it is working on a similar product. While the large company never provides a formal release date for its product,

User Solution 14-1

Was It Wrong?

Here we have yet another case of a computer solving an old problem in a new way. But now we raise an issue of a different sort: Is the type of solution described ethical?

Photos are commonly manipulated and/or retouched to emphasize certain characteristics. However, when *National Geographic* used a computer to move pyramids closer on the cover of its February 1982 issue, it raised several eyebrows. Was it a breach of public trust in the magazine's reputation for accurate reporting of fact to do such a thing? *National Geographic* has taken static on the matter for over a decade—just like *TV Guide* did when they put Oprah Winfrey's face on Ann-Margret's body on a 1989 cover. Some posit that, while it's okay to doctor advertisements or illustrations in a way that makes it obvious that retouching has been done, it's another matter to alter an image and then pass it off as accurate. Others counter that no harm has been done, since technology has changed the standards by which people evaluate photographic information and many people read magazines like *National Geographic* strictly for entertainment purposes.

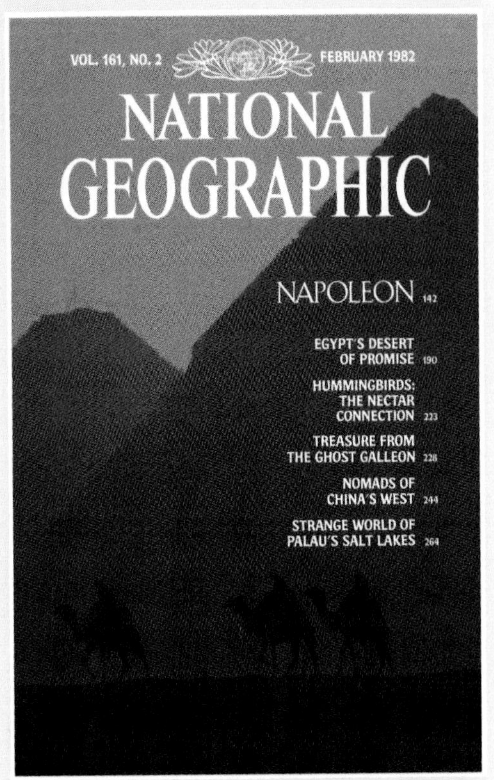

it leaves potential users with the fear that they will be taking a major risk by adopting the small-competitor's product. (Incidently, software that exists more in people's imaginations than in actuality is sometimes referred to as **vaporware.**)

Vaporware. Software that exists more in people's imaginations then in actuality.

- A magazine that you subscribe to sells your name to a company that develops marketing databases (see Tomorrow box). Soon, your mailbox is flooded with pesky junk mail and you are regularly getting calls at dinnertime from companies trying to sell you something you don't need or want.

Ethics has taken on more significance in recent years because the workplace has become increasingly multicultural and diverse. Different cultures have different values—what might seem ethically problematic to a person in the United States might be a normal way of doing business in Mexico or Japan. And vice versa. Such phenomena as increasing divorce rates and changing family structures have tended to broaden ethical norms within cultures over time.

Deciding whether or not an issue warrants a debate about ethical concerns is not always easy. An interesting issue that falls into this category involves using computers to manipulate photographs. As User Solution 14-1 asks, is the public being hoodwinked when images that are intended to disseminate fact are doctored for aesthetic emphasis?

Many scholars think that educating people about ethical matters is being pushed aside today in the rush to achieve measurable results. A movement is afoot to change this, however. Several professional computer organizations—such as the Data Processing Management Association (DPMA) and the Association for Computing Machinery (ACM)—have established codes of ethics for computer professionals. Also, ethics is frequently a topic in computer journals and at professional conferences today.

Computers in Our Lives: Today and Tomorrow

The number of uses to which computers have been put is so large and heterogeneous that it almost defies classification. As you've seen, computers are valuable, on-the-job tools whether you are a company executive, a manager, an engineer, a marketing research analyst, an accountant, a financial analyst, a lawyer, a doctor, a dentist, a real estate broker, an architect, or even a farmer or rancher. And although it may be hard to believe, the impact of the computer on those occupations and others is just beginning.

Outside the workplace, computers have also asserted their presence into our lives. Let's see how.

Computers for Home and Personal Use

When inexpensive microcomputer systems first became widely available in the late 1970s, many people predicted that soon there would be a computer system in every home. After all, computers are useful tools, and think about what happened in the case of other great inventions, such as the car, phone, and television. We are still far from being a society in which every home has a desktop personal computer system. However, those "brainy" little microcomputers and memory chips that are used to make desktop computers are finding their way into scores of other products purchased for personal use. Following are several examples.

Electrical Gadgets Today almost everybody in this country uses a variety of electrical gadgets—television sets, stereo systems, videocassette recorders (VCRs), washing machines, cameras, phones, kitchen appliances, and so on. Increasingly these products are coming packaged with built-in microprocessors and solid-state memories that provide a variety of special functions. The electronic components in your VCR, for instance, enable you to "program" the VCR to record television programs while you are away. Built-in components on your stereo system provide features such as "quartz tuning" and let you save your favorite radio stations in memory for easy access through push buttons. Electronic processors and memories in kitchen appliances can accept instructions, store them, and perform them according to a designated timetable. Recently, there has been a lot of interest in the building of an *information superhighway*—especially as regards the marriage of television technology with high-speed communications (see the Tomorrow box).

TOMORROW

Interactive Television

Looking Down the Information Superhighway

Picture this. It's the year 2005 and you suddenly have an urge to watch some old reruns of *Beavis and Butthead*. You go to a touch-tone phone or a keyboard that's attached to your television, make selections off a few menus, and presto. Within seconds, you're sitting on the couch with a bag of potato chips, in tube heaven.

Sound unbelievable? It's actually the way many people feel that future television will be delivered. Soon, basically any product that has ever been in either celluloid or printed form will theoretically be available on your screen. That includes movies and television shows, concerts and sporting events, newspapers and books, shopping guides and catalogs. The list is virtually endless.

What's more, interactive TV will give you a much greater choice of channels—maybe 500 says the cable-TV industry. What will people do with all of those choices? Plenty. Pet owners might be able to tune into The Pet Channel; Elvis fans, The Elvis Channel; the rod-and-reel set, The Fishing Channel. Some observers have even speculated that certain channels will become electronic malls, enabling you to shop for products by computer. If, say, you wanted to buy a scanner for your computer, you could flip to The Computer Shopping Channel, choose "scanners" off a menu, and watch a video clip showing specific products available.

Eventually, channels will also be interleaved. For instance, if there are 50 basketball games going on in a single night, a sports superchannel might give you the option of watching any ten of them. You can hop from one game to another or watch a few onscreen simultaneously, in separate screen windows.

Many people feel that computer technology will be the driving force behind interactive TV. After all, digital computer screens can now display crisper video images than conventional analog TV, and what else but computers can store and manipulate at high speed all the data that will be required in such a massive delivery system? The coming electronic superhighway, which will use fiber optic cable and microwave transmission to bring us such services, is expected to be in place sometime around the turn of the century.

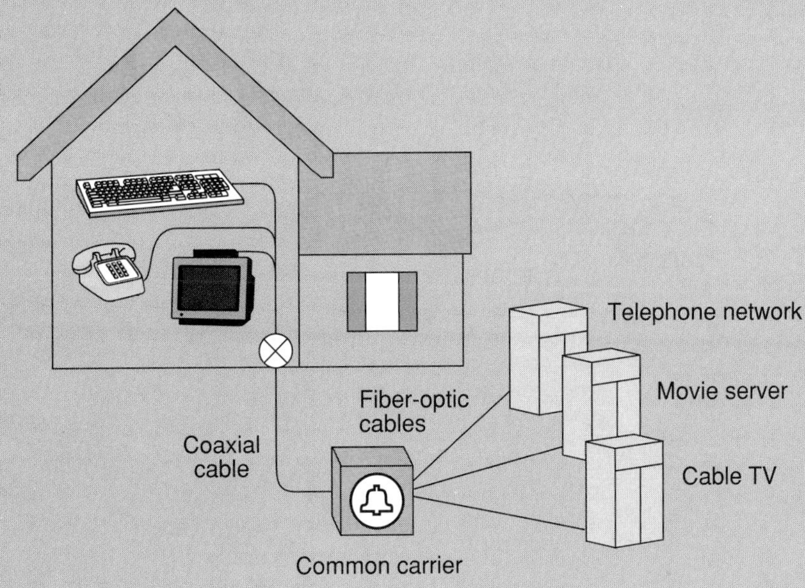

Computerized Cars The car is one product that has been enhanced in a variety of ways through built-in microprocessors and memories (see Figure 14-5). Some of the earliest microprocessors were employed as control mechanisms—for instance, as regulators in electronic ignition systems. Lately they have been employed in more "exotic" applications—such as climate and cruise control—and it is not unusual for a car to have dozens of electronic chips of one form or another. In fact, creative use of microcomputing gadgets within cars is becoming a major selling point of cars themselves.

Computerized Homes Homes all over the world are being built today with computer-controlled devices that provide security, greet and identify visitors, monitor and water the lawn while the owners are away, and automatically regulate the temperature in the home. Although the potential for this type of microcomputer application seems far-reaching, it is limited by the reality that many people want their homes to reflect an ambience in which computers play little or no part.

Home Banking and Shopping Electronic funds transfer (EFT) systems have long existed. The earliest systems enabled funds to be wired between banks. Later came the automatic teller machine. Most recent to the scene are home-computer-based communications packages and services that enable you to make transactions at banks, brokerage houses, travel agencies, and retail stores. The promise of home banking and shopping is yet to be fulfilled, although some industry observers see both of these applications as future giants.

FIGURE 14-5

Smart cars. Today, it's not unusual for a car to have dozens of processor chips of one sort or another.

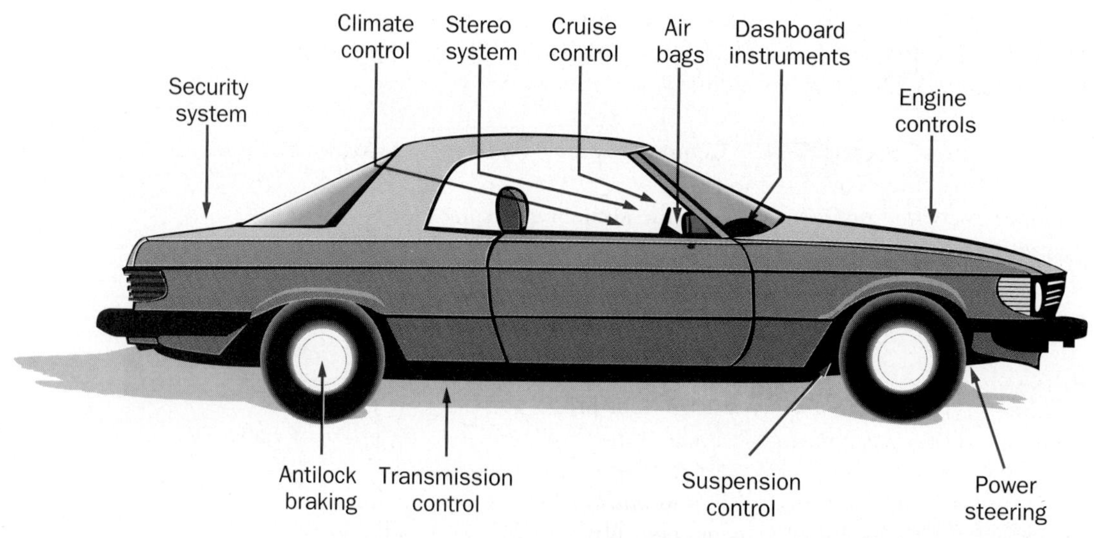

Cottage Industries We are living in an age in which information—the very thing that computers are best at producing—has become a highly salable commodity. As business-related computing products continue to drop in price, it is likely that many more of them will be used to create or enhance home-based businesses, or *cottage industries.* To some extent, this phenomenon has been observed with the availability of powerful desktop microcomputer systems. The feasibility of home-based businesses has also been fueled by technologies such as desktop publishing, personal copiers, inexpensive facsimile machines, modems, laptop computers, and satellite dishes.

Computers in Education

Some of the earliest electronic computers were installed in academic institutions in the 1940s and 1950s, where they were either studied as a curiosity in their own right or used to perform calculations rapidly. Thus, one of computers' earliest applications in education involved the training of engineers, who had to know how to build computers.

As computers found their way into businesses, data processing and information systems courses evolved in business schools. Some academic visionaries, such as John Kemeny at Dartmouth College in the 1960s, realized early on that computers would be useful for performing work in an ever wider variety of disciplines. And so BASIC was developed and rapidly became part of every student's life at Dartmouth.

Today computers and education are combined in many different ways.

Learning about Computers Learning about computers involves taking courses that teach you general computer principles or hands-on use of a specific software package. As with other disciplines, learning about computers can be approached from several perspectives. For example, *computer science* (a technically oriented perspective), *computer information systems* (a business perspective), and *computer operations* (a hands-on, operational perspective). In a large university, it's common to see 50 or more courses collectively devoted to covering such multiple emphases. Many large businesses and independent training firms also provide computer courses.

Computer-Enhanced Instruction Computers are also widely used to assist in the process of teaching (see Figure 14-6).

With *computer-assisted instruction (CAI),* the student and computer take part in an interactive dialog. For example, a high-school algebra student using a CAI package may be given a problem on the screen to solve. If the answer given is correct, the package poses another problem, perhaps one that's more advanced. If the answer is wrong, the package may go into a "remedial mode" in which it either gives hints, shows how to solve the problem, or provides another problem on the same level. Each student progresses at his or her own pace. At the end of the session, the student is graded. A "progress report" may also be provided.

New technologies such as *optical disk* and *multimedia* are just beginning to be used to assist in the educational process (see Window 6). These technologies enable students to access books and video clips on their computer systems. Of

FIGURE 14-6

Education. Computers are widely used today to teach all types of courses at all levels of the educational system.

course, no computer-enhanced instructional tool has ever been recognized as a solution that will meet every teaching need. In many situations the computer may never seriously challenge the purely human, personal approach to education.

Problem Solving One of the first applications of computers in education was for solving difficult problems. Today, students in diverse disciplines use computers to produce cash flow statements, develop business strategies through what-if scenarios, simulate product designs, plan facilities, test decision alternatives, compute mathematical curves, and produce course papers. The list is almost endless. Also, virtually every professor involved in research uses computers in one form or another to discover and organize new scientific facts or just to become more efficient at getting work done.

Computers in Entertainment and Leisure Activities

There are so many entertainment and leisure activities that support computer use that these applications are almost impossible to enumerate. Let's consider a few selected applications of general interest—sports, movies and television, music, and art.

Sports Among the earliest applications of computers in sports were highly simplified computerized baseball games. The user would select opposing lineups and then issue a RUN command at the terminal. Subsequently the computer would use random numbers to simulate a ballgame and, within seconds, print out a box score. This may not seem very interesting, perhaps, but better things were to come. Today there are sophisticated products that enable users to "participate" in sports such as baseball, football, auto racing, and flying without ever leaving the comfort of their living rooms.

In televised sports broadcasting, the computer has added dazzle. Take those flashy graphics, for instance. There are attractive screens of scores and statistics, possibly a digitized freeze-frame of tennis or racing-car action that you saw live just seconds before, and sequences of fantasy flights over a basketball court or football field. Computer graphics and animation have made all of this possible.

In sports such as baseball, football, tennis, hockey, and basketball, as well as in Olympic competitions, coaches and managers are trusting computers to analyze player performances and game plans. What else but a computer could quickly determine that Kirby Puckett batted .314 against right-handers last month and .289 against left-handers? Some ballplayers even have their own laptop computers and personal databases to help them develop playing strategies.

Combine all of these applications with electronic scoreboards, computer-controlled ticketing, and all of the other computerized activities performed by any profit-making enterprise and you have an idea of the impressive array of computing power in the sports industry today (see Figure 14-7).

Movies and Films Robots were among the earliest computer technologies to be worthy subjects of moviemaking. Then, with the 1950s and the ominous

FIGURE 14-7

Computers in sports. Today, computers are used in sports in a variety of ways. Two prominent applications are (a) to assist athletes preparing for the Olympic Games and (b) to help broadcasters keep track of vital statistics for professional sporting events.

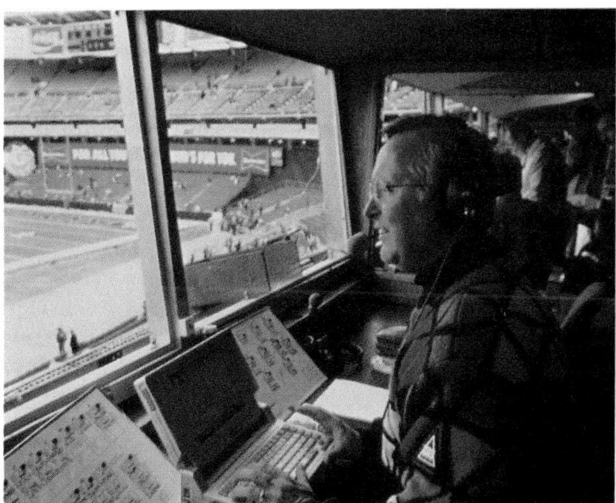

presence of the Cold War and atomic weapons, movies began to portray the computer as an infallible, Big Brother-type device that insensitive powermongers would use to rule the world. A major emphasis in movies today, of course, is the notion that computer systems are indeed fallible and that a human software oversight could cause some global disaster.

In the last several years, computers have figured prominently in the actual creation of movies and films (see Figure 14-8). For example, movies such as *Terminator 2: Judgment Day* would have been impossible without computers to keep track of and integrate the numerous special effects involved. Many scenes in that film used computers to combine live images, drawings, and dynamic electronic models. The colorized versions of old classics such as *The Maltese Falcon* and *Yankee Doodle Dandy* would not have been possible without computers, nor would the restored versions of many old color films whose original prints have faded. At the 1989 Academy Awards, the computer virtually won an Oscar in its own right when the computer-generated film *Tin Toy* was the top vote getter in the animated short film category. Some people believe that the day is now in sight when the motion-picture industry will be able to release films that can be customized by viewers.

Music Although creating music may be an art, sound is a matter of physics. Musicians frequently use computers called *electronic synthesizers* to store sounds, recall them from memory to have them played, and distort them in new and unusual ways. The use of computer technology in creating music is widespread today, and artists ranging from Stevie Wonder (popular music) to Herbie Hancock

FIGURE 14-8

Computers in film. Computers often assist in the creation of (a) cartoons and (b) special effects.

(a)

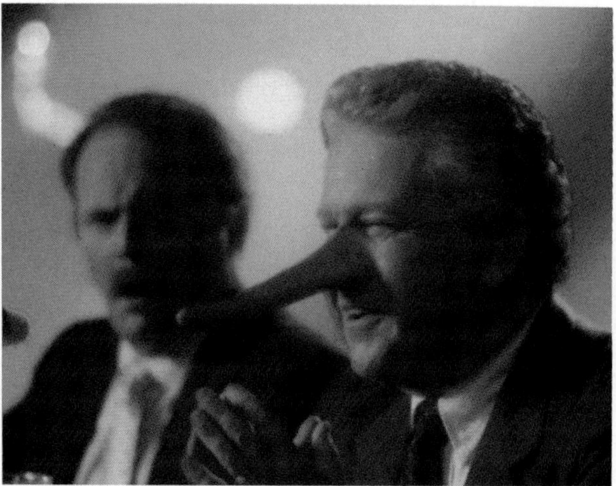

(b)

(jazz) to Pierre Boulez (classical music) have accepted technology as an important force in the creation of their works. Musicians use the computer as writers use a word processor, but instead of words, they store, edit, cut, and paste sounds. Today many musical pieces are so rich with electronically produced sounds that it's difficult for a nonexpert to tell what came directly from an acoustic instrument and what was electronically enhanced.

The computer plays many other important roles in the music industry today. For example, DJs and their staffs use computer-controlled equipment to edit and organize music for their radio shows. Also, written musical scores are prepared with desktop publishing systems that use specialized fonts, document preparation software, and laser printers.

Art At one time the only way an artistic image could be created was for someone to paint, draw, weave, or sculpt it completely by hand. Then the Gutenberg press arrived, and images could be mass produced. Although that event probably created panic among people contemplating a calligraphy career, the would-be Renoirs and Van Goghs had little to worry about.

The industrial revolution gave rise to the so-called industrial arts, and machines such as the Jacquard loom, which could weave under program control, appeared. When photography was invented in the mid-1800s, it threatened the painters of the day, but it later evolved into an art form of its own, with a different set of standards.

Now that the computer has arrived, there are new perceived threats to artists on all levels—but there are also great opportunities. With a computer, images of virtually any shape can be created, colored in any of thousands of colors, enlarged, rotated, blended, combined with other images, illuminated by one or more shadow-casting light sources, and so forth. Also, colors, positions, and shapes of objects can be changed at electronically fast speeds to create new images. For example, a computer was used to generate the images in Figure 14-9 as well as the stunning images in Windows 2 and 7. A computer enables the artist to see a variety of images and store the most promising of them, all in a span of time that would be impossible with only canvas and brush.

Nonetheless, painters are still far from being replaced. Like photography, computer art has evolved into an art form in its own right. So, too, has computer-enhanced photography (see Figure 14-10).

Computers in Science and Medicine

Science and medicine account for a myriad of computer applications. In this section, we'll look specifically at how computers are used for weather forecasting, environmental simulations, patient diagnosis, life-support systems, and to assist handicapped people.

Science One of the earliest applications of computer power in a scientific field was weather forecasting. To predict the weather accurately, data on current weather conditions must be input to the computer, which then analyzes mounds of data on past conditions. Because predicting weather is often a round-the-clock chore that requires supercomputer-sized computational and storage capacity, it is usually done at a national level at places such as the National Center for Atmospheric Research (NCAR) in Boulder, Colorado.

FIGURE 14-9

Computer art. The computer is a useful tool for artists of all types—most of whom are not computer professionals. Computer art has rapidly evolved into a form in its own right, with its own shows and contests.

Today, computer applications in the field of science virtually defy enumeration. Computers are used to control scientific experiments, uncover significant trends or properties in data, and perform various types of research functions. One popular tool is simulation. *Simulation* involves building a mathematical model of a real-life object or situation and thoroughly testing it with "dummy" data before the object is built or the situation encountered. A car may be modeled on a computer screen. Then, before the car is actually built, the computer simulates real-life events such as accidents and stresses. Simulation is also useful to governments and businesses for predicting economic changes in society, the environmental impact of new policies, and consumer reaction to the effects of price changes.

Medicine It is indeed comforting to know that computers are hard at work helping health-care professionals ensure that you remain healthy and live longer (see Figure 14-11).

Computer-assisted diagnosis refers to a number of hardware or software technologies that assist physicians in diagnosing patients' conditions. One example is inputting data about a patient's condition to a software program that compares the condition to previously diagnosed ones in a large patient database. The program then outputs relevant statistics to help the attending physicians diagnose the ailment. Many of these programs are expert systems; they employ artifical intelligence techniques that enable them to actually draw some conclusions for the physician.

FIGURE 14-10

Computers and photography. Computers are widely used to both (a) enhance photographic images and (b) produce photorealistic art. Today, most publishers convert photographs into digital form for printing purposes.

Computer-assisted tomography, sometimes referred to as CAT or PET scanning, is another computer-assisted diagnosis technique. It employs X-ray hardware and computer technology to provide physicians with three-dimensional pictures of the organs in a person's body. Thus, the physicians have more information on which to base a diagnosis than they would from a traditional two-dimensional X-ray.

Computerized life-support systems provide nursing support, although they usually bear no resemblance to their human counterparts. These systems monitor bedridden patients, freeing human nurses from the need for uninterrupted observation. A system might continuously monitor signs such as heart rate, temperature, and blood pressure and activate a silent alarm if something goes outside an acceptable range.

Today computers are being used in many ways to help the handicapped (see Figure 14-12). Computer-aided instruction (CAI), for example, has been used successfully to provide assistance to people with special learning needs. Computers have been used to artifically simulate the human voice, enabling cerebral palsy victims to "speak." The United States recently passed into law the Americans with Disabilities Act (1990), which requires U.S. organizations as of 1992 to make "reasonable accommodations" for handicapped workers. Although the law is vague, accommodations would likely include such aids as visual interfaces

FIGURE 14-11

Computers in medicine. Computers are used in the health-care industry today for virtually everything from patient management to assisting with the diagnosis of illnesses.

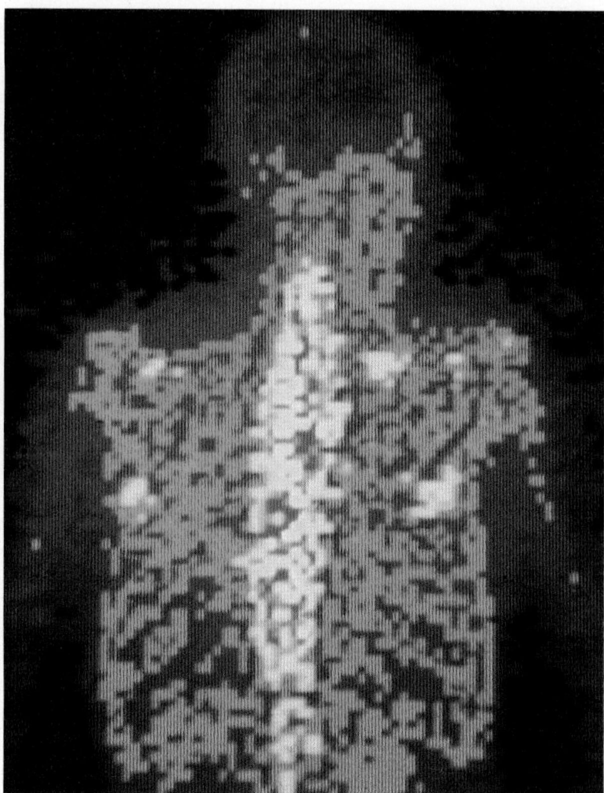

for the deaf and audio interfaces for the blind. Workers who feel that their employers are adopting a take-me-to-court attitude can file a civil lawsuit or a complaint with the Equal Employment Opportunity Commission.

Summary and Key Terms

Since the early 1950s, when the era of commercial computing began, computers have rapidly woven their way into the fabric of modern society. In the process, they have created both opportunities and problems.

Computers, Work, and Health One of the first criticisms leveled at the entry of computers into the workplace was that their presence resulted in stress. Stress-related concerns triggered by the so-called computer revolution include fear of layoff or reassignment, fear of falling behind, and job burnout. In addition

FIGURE 14 - 12

Technology and the handicapped worker. Most assistive technologies fall into one or more of the categories given here.

Category	Examples
Magnified output	Large-screen displays that make reading easier
Audio/Voice output	Hardware and software that can read words aloud and provide audio rather than visual outputs
Alternative input	Voice-input devices, oversized-key keyboards, and devices that can accept input from mouth-held wands or from eye movements
Environmental control	Devices that activate appliances, change television channels, and turn lights on and off
Word aids	Tools that can anticipate words or commands, thereby making expression easier
Instructional aids	Software that provides special accommodations for the learning impaired

to these problems, other concerns related to **ergonomics**-related issues, such as display device usage and workspace design, have surfaced. Many people also worry about environment-related issues and about our society's apparent overreliance on computers.

Computer Crime **Computer crime** is loosely defined as the use of computers to commit unauthorized acts. Some states have laws that address computer crime directly; others do not. In practice, however, computer crime is hard to pin down even in states that have such laws. It is hard to decide when an unauthorized act is really a crime, judges and juries often are bewildered by the technical issues involved, and companies frequently are reluctant to press charges.

Computer crime may take many forms. Types of computer crime include data diddling, the Trojan horse technique, salami-shaving methods, unauthorized use of superzap and trapdoor programs, logic bombs, **computer viruses,** scavenging, data leakage, wiretapping, **software piracy, hacking,** and counterfeiting.

Organizations can combat computer crimes in many ways: hiring trustworthy people; taking precautions with malcontents; separating employee functions; restricting system use; limiting access to programs and data with **passwords, access cards,** and **biometric security devices; site licensing;** devising staff controls; disguising particularly sensitive programs and data through **encryption;** using **callback devices;** monitoring important system transactions; conducting regular **audits;** and educating employees.

Computers and Privacy Most people want some control over the kinds of facts that are collected about them, how those facts are collected and their accuracy, who uses them, and how they are used. Modern computer systems, with their ability to store and manipulate unprecedented quantities of data and make those data available to many locations, have added a new dimension to the personal **privacy** issue. Recently, two relatively new technologies—electronic mail and **caller identification** phone systems—have created further concerns about invasion of privacy.

Ethical Issues Regarding Computers **Ethics** refers to standards of moral conduct. Today one of the most important concerns in the ethics area as regards computers is using someone else's property in an unauthorized way. Another is leading people to believe something that's more fiction than fact when it works to one's advantage—such as the case with **vaporware.**

Computers in Our Lives: Today and Tomorrow Today the number of uses to which computers have been put is so large and heterogeneous that it almost defies classification. Most of this text has examined the uses of computers in the ordinary business workplace. Outside this workplace, computers of some sort are found in the home, in educational institutions, in entertainment and leisure activities, and in science and medicine.

Review Exercises

Fill-in Questions

1. Fear of computers is known as ______________.
2. ______________ is the field that covers the effects of factors such as equipment and computer workspaces on employees' productivity and health.
3. ______________ refers to standards of moral conduct.
4. The unauthorized copying or use of computer programs is known as software ______________.
5. The ______________ Act was designed to prevent private organizations from unfairly denying credit to individuals.
6. ______________ refers to phone systems that can display the phone numbers corresponding to incoming calls.

Matching Questions

Match each term with the description that fits best.

a. computer virus
b. data diddling
c. salami shaving
d. hacking
e. trapdoor
f. superzap

___ 1. The deduction of small amounts from a large number of randomly selected accounts.

___ 2. Refers to a program that can bypass all system controls.

____3. Is transmitted through a copy operation.

____4. A diagnostic tool that allows viewing of computer storage.

____5. The altering of an organization's production data.

____6. Using a terminal or microcomputer system to illegally break into a larger computer system.

Discussion Questions

1. Identify some specific problems caused by the rapid spread of computer use in society.
2. Describe some ways in which computers may affect our health or well-being.
3. Why is computer crime so difficult to pin down?
4. Name some of the forms computer crime can take.
5. How does a computer virus work?
6. Provide some examples demonstrating unethical behavior related to the use of computers.
7. Name some rights of individuals that computer privacy laws have tried to protect.
8. Identify some ways in which computers affect our daily lives.

Critical Thinking Questions

1. A clerk in a steel company uses a company-owned mainframe computer, on company time, to handicap horses for a local racetrack. Is a crime being committed? From a privacy standpoint, how do you feel about the steel company randomly checking the contents of files on its mainframe, from time to time, to ensure that employees are using the computer for work-related tasks?
2. A defense lawyer gets a computer researcher to electronically enhance photographs taken at the scene of an accident to prove that her client wasn't completely at fault. The enhanced photographs appear to show that there was some prior damage to the plaintiff's car, which, if true, would contradict statements made by the plaintiff. What problem might the lawyer have in presenting the case?
3. In a recent editorial in *Computerworld,* a software consultant touched off a flood of fiery protest by remarking that software piracy is overblown as an issue. He argued that:
   a. Most people who pirate software wouldn't have bought the software in the first place, so pirated software doesn't necessarily represent lost revenue.
   b. Pirates who like a product often buy future releases of it to access new features, so pirating often has a positive effect on future sales.
   c. The estimate of the value of stolen software—which ranges from $170 million to $4 billion a year—overstates the real drain on profits because it multiplies the number of illegal copies times sales price.

   Please comment.

4. A software developer creates a program to protect against computer viruses. To finance the advertising campaign for this product, the developer decides to call several computer executives at large firms and try to get them to put up $5,000 each. This, the developer believes, will both produce the funds needed and make the executives more likely to buy the product. Does this strategy seem sound to you from both a business and an ethical standpoint?

5. As hinted in Feature 14-3, there is considerable fear that marketing databases can be used to invade a person's privacy. What important issue areas do you feel should be addressed by the government to ensure that the privacy of individuals isn't invaded by micromarketers? For instance, one critical issue area concerns *access*; that is, who will have access to the marketing data and under what circumstances will access be granted?

6. United States Labor Secretary Robert B. Reich once pointed out that it is difficult these days to tell whether some businesses are domestic or foreign. For instance, say that Company A is headquartered in your country and virtually all its owners and directors are fellow citizens. However, most of its employees and all of its manufacturing facilities are located on foreign soil. Company B is just the opposite; while most of its employees and plants are in your country, virtually all of its owners and directors are foreign based. Which company would you say is domestic and which is foreign? Which company should your country's economic policy favor?

WINDOW 8

The History of Computers

A Picture Essay of the People and Devices That Pioneered the Computer Revolution

Electronic computers as we know them were invented a little over 50 years ago. However, the history of computers actually goes back much further than that. Since the beginning of civilization, merchants and government officials have used computing devices to help them with calculations and recordkeeping.

1. Even long before modern computers came along, many large organizations were beginning to drown in a sea of paperwork. This turn-of-the-century photo, of Prudential's New Jersey headquarters, illustrates the earliest benefit computers provided—replacing armies of clerks with machines that were cheaper, faster, and more accurate.

Early History

Most computers prior to 1900 were predominantly *mechanical* machines, working with gears and levers. Operation was completely manual. Throughout the 1930s and 1940s, computers came to depend more and more on electricity for power, giving rise to *electromechanical* devices. By 1950, the era of solid-state *electronics* began to mature, ushering in the modern computer age we know today.

2. This crank-driven *difference engine*, built by Charles Babbage in England in the 1830s, was one of the forerunners to today's modern computers. Babbage's attempts to build machines that were more sophisticated were thwarted because the parts he needed could not be produced.

3. A milestone on the way to the modern computer was passed during the 1890 U.S. Census. Herman Hollerith, a federal employee who is pictured here, created an electromechanical device that collapsed the tabulation of census figures from a decade to only three years.

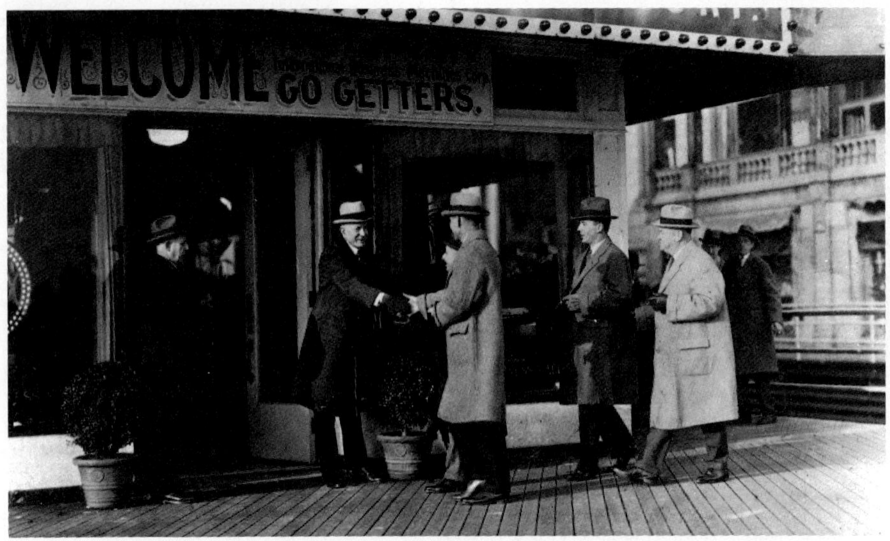

4. Throughout the 1930s, IBM was the leader of punched-card tabulating equipment. IBM president and founder, Tom Watson, is shown here greeting some of the stars of his sales force. Watson pioneered the role of marketing computer systems—selling business solutions rather than just electronic boxes.

5. The age of electromechanical devices reached its zenith in the early 1940s with the development of the Mark I. Despite its sleek, futuristic look, the Mark I was technologically obsolete almost upon completion. The age of electronics was about to dawn.

6. The ABC—for Atanasoff-Berry Computer—is today widely acknowledged as the world's first electronic computer. Built by John Atanasoff and Clifford Berry of Iowa State University around 1940, the ABC helped graduate students solve simultaneous linear equations.

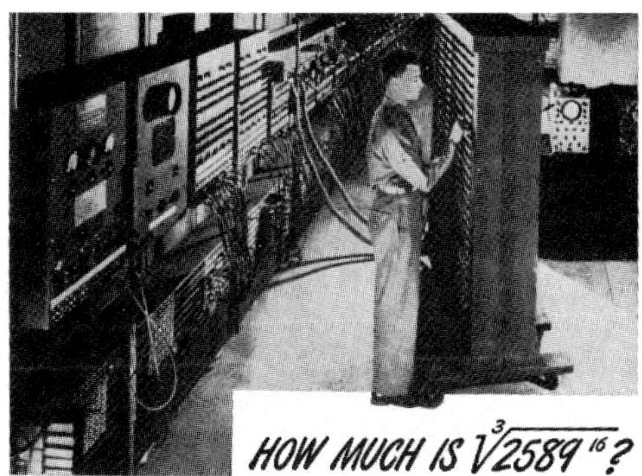

The Army's ENIAC can give you the answer in a fraction of a second!

Think that's a stumper? You should see *some* of the ENIAC's problems! Brain twisters that if put to paper would run off this page and feet beyond . . . addition, subtraction, multiplication, division—square root, cube root, any root. Solved by an incredibly complex system of circuits operating 18,000 electronic tubes and tipping the scales at 30 tons!

The ENIAC is symbolic of many amazing Army devices with a brilliant future for you! The new Regular Army needs men with aptitude for scientific work, and as one of the first trained in the post-war era, you stand to get in on the ground floor of important jobs which have never before existed. You'll find that an Army career pays off.

The most attractive fields are filling quickly. Get into the swim while the getting's good! 1½, 2 and 3 year enlistments are open in the Regular Army to ambitious young men 18 to 34 (17 with parents' consent) who are otherwise qualified. If you enlist for 3 years, you may choose your own branch of the service, of those still open. Get full details at your nearest Army Recruiting Station.

YOUR REGULAR ARMY SERVES THE NATION AND MANKIND IN WAR AND PEACE

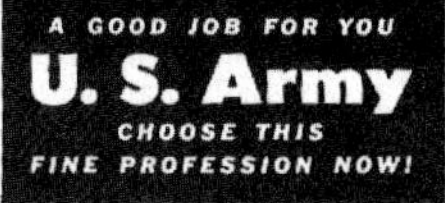

A GOOD JOB FOR YOU
U. S. Army
CHOOSE THIS
FINE PROFESSION NOW!

7. ENIAC, the world's first large-scale, general-purpose electronic computer, was unveiled in 1946. Built by two former professors at the University of Pennsylvania, ENIAC (for Electronic Numerical Integrator and Calculator) used 18,000 vacuum tubes—like the ones seen on old radios—and was said to dim the lights of Philadelphia when it ran.

The First Generation (1951–1958)

The history of the commercial-age computers is often discusssed in terms of its generations. First-generation computers used vacuum tubes (similar to those in ENIAC) as their principal logic element. Though tubes enabled computers to run faster than electromechanical machines, they were large and bulky, generated excessive heat, and were prone to failure.

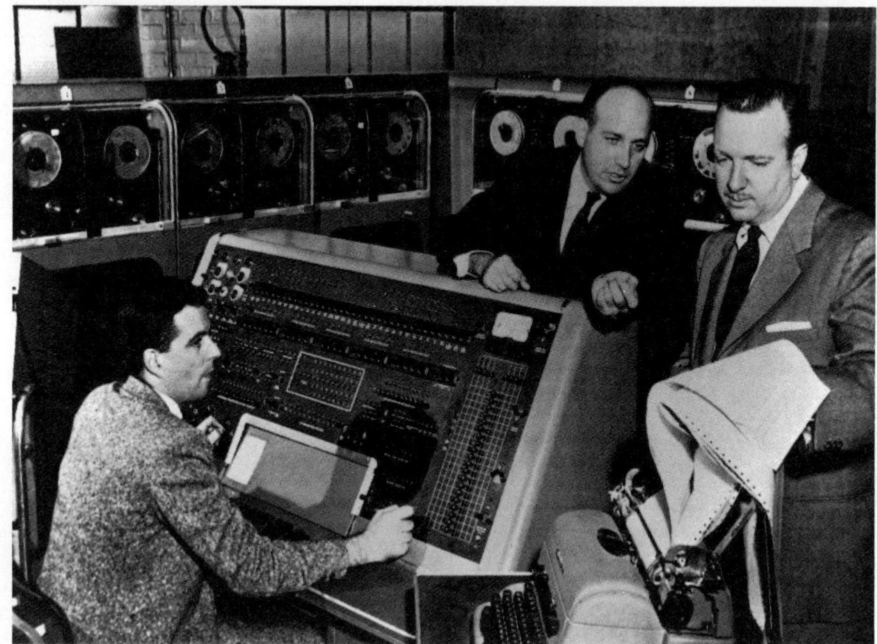

8. The UNIVAC I, circa 1951, was the first computer to be mass produced for general use. It was also the first computer used to tabulate returns in a U.S. presidential election. In 1952, it declared Dwight Eisenhower the victor over Adlai Stevenson only 45 minutes after the polls closed.

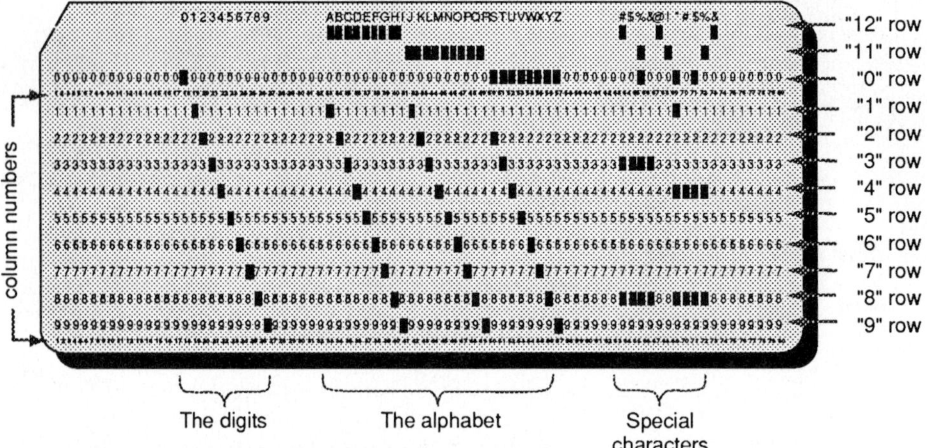

9. Most computers of the first and second generations relied heavily on punched-card input. Each standard punched card held 80 characters of data, with holes in the card representing characters. Today's high-capacity diskette, which can fit in a shirt pocket, can store the data equivalent of tens of thousands of punched cards.

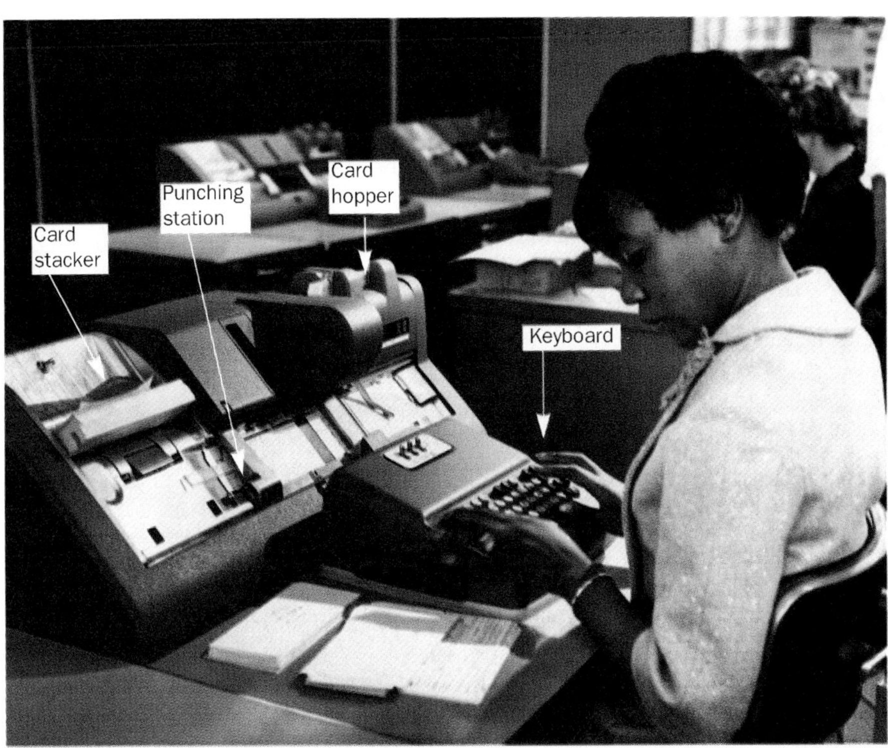

10. An operator at a keypunch machine is shown preparing punched cards for processing. Blank cards were manually stacked in a hopper at the top right of the machine. As each blank card was fetched, it passed through a station that punched holes corresponding to keys struck by the operator. Finished cards were automatically routed to the output stacker at the top left.

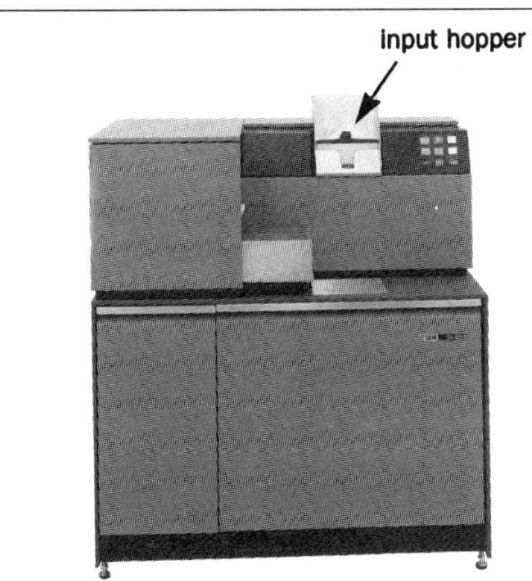

11. Once a keypunch-machine operator finished punching a stack of cards, the cards were manually placed in the input hopper of a card reader—the device used to communicate the contents of the cards to the CPU.

12. Computer professionals often relied on sorting machines, such as those shown here, to arrange cards in a certain order prior to processing. The machines could only sort on one card column at a time.

The Second Generation (1959–1964)

In second-generation computers, transistors replaced vacuum tubes as the main logic element. Other noteworthy innovations of the second generation included more reliance on tape and disk storage, magnetic-core memory, replaceable boards, and high-level programming languages.

13. A second-generation transistor (left) is compared in size to the first-generation vacuum tube it replaced. Transistors performed the same function as tubes but made computers faster, smaller, and more reliable.

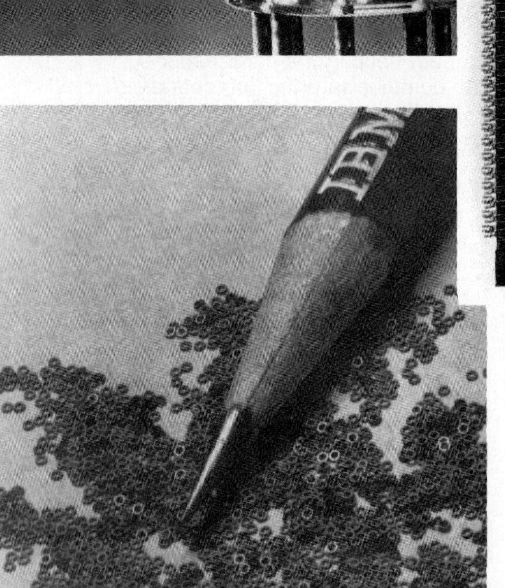

14–15. Small, doughnut-shaped magnetic cores (left), which were strung on tiered racks (top) within the system unit, became the standard for second-generation computer memory. Each tiny core could hold a computer bit, and data were created by magnetizing each core clockwise or counterclockwise.

16. The U.S. Navy's Grace Hopper developed the first assembly language in 1952 and was one of the principal figures in the development of the COBOL language in 1960.

The Third Generation (1965–1970)

The third generation of computers evolved when small integrated circuits—"computer chips" as we know them today—began replacing conventional transistors. Other noteworthy developments of the third generation were the rise of operating systems, minicomputers, and word processing technology.

17. One of the most important developments of the third generation was the IBM System/360. Unlike previous computers, System/360 constituted a full line of compatible computers, making upgrading much easier. Many of today's mainframes are designed much like the popular 360 line.

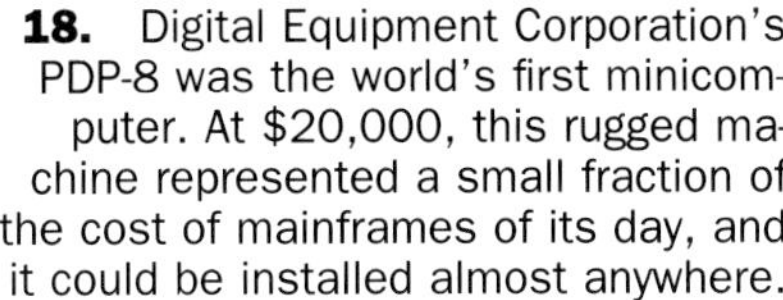

18. Digital Equipment Corporation's PDP-8 was the world's first minicomputer. At $20,000, this rugged machine represented a small fraction of the cost of mainframes of its day, and it could be installed almost anywhere.

19–20. Kenneth Olsen and An Wang were two of the early pioneers in the development of minicomputers. Olsen (left) founded Digital Equipment Corporation (DEC) in an old Massachusetts wool mill. Wang (right) founded Wang Corporation, which became an early leader in word processing technology.

The Fourth Generation (1971 to Present)

The fourth generation of computers is probably best known for the dawning of the age of the microcomputer. Improved manufacturing techniques enabled more and more circuitry to be squeezed onto a chip.

21–22. Today, it is possible to manufacture tiny chips that have over a million circuits in an area that can fit through the eye of a needle (top). As electronic components shrunk, smaller computer systems followed and, also, computerized consumer devices such as this early spelling toy (right).

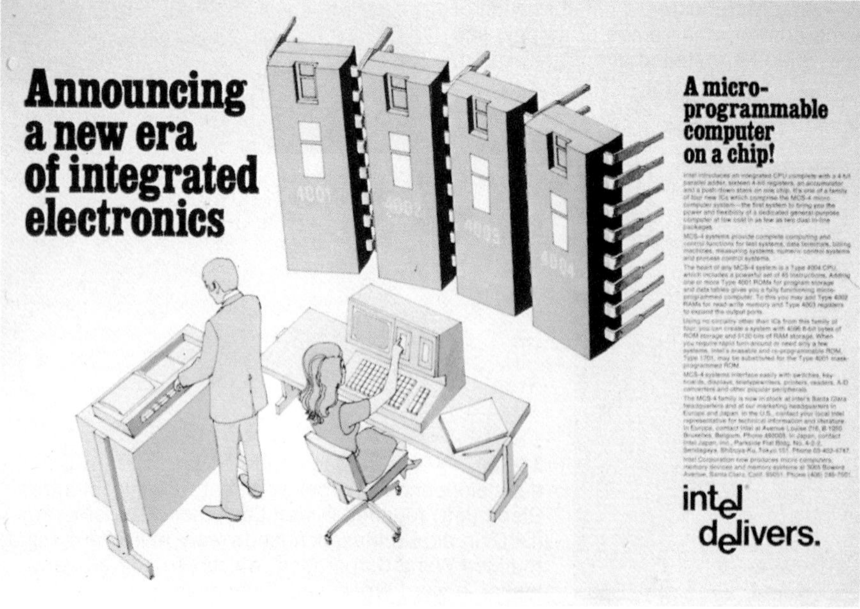

23. The first computer on a chip was the Intel 4004. On November 15, 1971, *Electronic News* carried the first advertisement for this breakthrough product. With only 2,250 transistors—which is less than 1 percent of the elements on most of today's microprocessors—the 4004 was an adequate processor for simple electronic devices such as calculators and cash registers.

24–25. The first fully assembled microcomputer system unit was the Altair 8800. Although the company that developed the Altair went bankrupt, the BASIC language translator for this computer was written by Bill Gates (right), who went on to found Microsoft Corporation and became a billionaire.

26–27. The first commercially successful microcomputer company was Apple. Below are Steve Wozniak and Steve Jobs, Apple's founders, holding the system board for the Apple I—their first computer (left). Although less powerful than the Altair 8800, the Apple I was cheaper and less complicated.

28. One of the early pioneers in the development of productivity software was Mitch Kapor, creator of the 1-2-3 spreadsheet program and founder of Lotus Development Corporation.

NUMBERING SYSTEMS

A

OUTLINE

Numbering Systems
The Decimal Numbering System
The Binary Numbering System
The Hexadecimal Numbering System
Computer Arithmetic

LEARNING OBJECTIVES

After completing this appendix, you will be able to:

1. Describe how the decimal, binary, and hexadecimal numbering systems work.
2. Convert values in one numbering system to those of another.
3. Add and subtract with the binary and hexadecimal numbering systems.

In Chapter 3, you learned that fixed-length codes such as ASCII and EBCDIC are often used to represent numbers, letters of the alphabet, and special characters. Although these codes are handy for storing data and transporting them around a computer system, they are not designed to do arithmetic operations. For this type of use, numbers must be stored in a "true" binary form that can be manipulated quickly by the computer.

This appendix covers several fundamentals of numbering systems. The two primary systems discussed are the decimal numbering system (used by people) and the binary numbering system (used by computers). Also discussed is the hexadecimal numbering system, which is a shorthand way of representing long strings of binary numbers so that they are more understandable to people. The appendix also covers conversions between numbering systems and principles of computer arithmetic.

Numbering Systems

A *numbering system* is a way of representing numbers. The system we most commonly use is called the *decimal,* or base ten, system (the word *decimal* comes from the Latin word for *ten*). It is called *base 10* because it uses ten symbols—the digits 0, 1, 2, 3, 4, 5, 6, 7, 8, 9—to represent all possible numbers. Numbers greater than nine are represented by a combination of these symbols.

Because we are so familiar with the decimal system, it may never have occurred to most of us that we could represent numbers in any other way. In fact, however, nothing says that a numbering system has to have ten possible symbols. Many other numbers would do as a base.

We saw in Chapter 3 that the *binary,* or base 2, system is used extensively by computers to represent numbers and other characters. Computer systems can perform computations and transmit data thousands of times faster in binary form than they can using decimal representations. Thus, it's important for anyone studying computers to know how the binary system works. Anyone contemplating a professional career in computers should also understand the *hexadecimal* (base 16) system. Before we examine some of the numbering systems used in computing—and learn how to convert numbers from one system into another—let's look more closely at the decimal numbering system. Insight into how the decimal system works will help us understand more about the other numbering systems.

The Decimal Numbering System

Decimal.
A numbering system with ten symbols—0, 1, 2, 3, 4, 5, 6, 7, 8, and 9.

All numbering systems, including the decimal system with which we work in our everyday lives, represent numbers as a combination of ordered symbols. As stated earlier, the **decimal*** (or base 10) system has ten acceptable symbols—the digits 0, 1, 2, . . . , 9. The positioning of the symbols in a decimal number is important. For example, 891 is a different number than 918 (with the same symbols occupying different positions).

The position of each symbol in any decimal number represents the number 10 (the base number) raised to a power, or exponent, that is based on that

*Boldfaced terms used in this appendix can be found in the Glossary at the end of the book.

FIGURE A-1

How the decimal (base ten) system works.

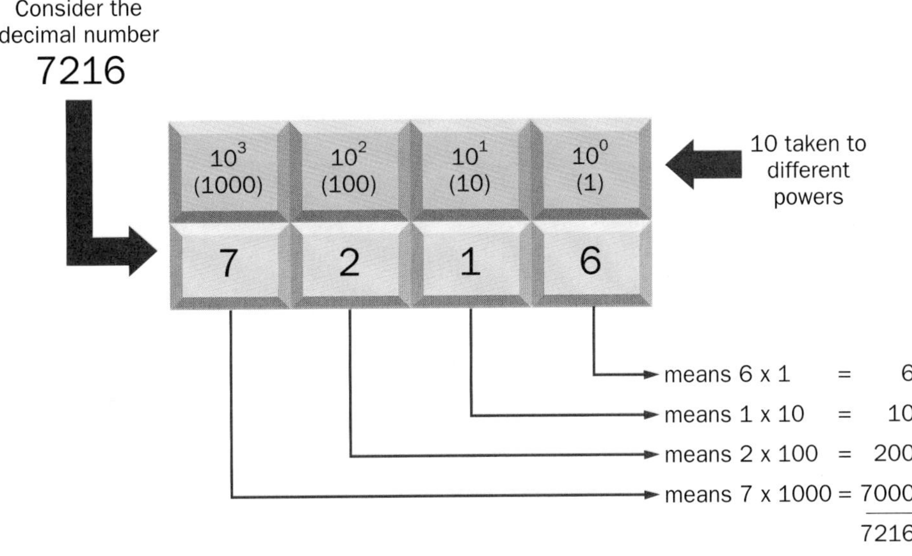

position. Going from right to left, the first position represents 10^0, or 1; the second position represents 10^1, or 10; the third position represents 10^2, or 100; and so forth. Thus, as Figure A-1 shows, a decimal number like 7,216 is understood as $7 \times 10^3 + 2 \times 10^2 + 1 \times 10^1 + 6 \times 10^0$.

The Binary Numbering System

The **binary,** or base 2, system works in a manner similar to the decimal system. One major difference is that the binary system has only two symbols—0 and 1—instead of ten. A second major difference is that the position of each digit in a binary number represents the number 2 (the base number) raised to an exponent based on that position. Thus, the binary number 11100 represents

Binary.
A numbering system with two possible states—0 and 1.

$$1 \times 2^4 + 1 \times 2^3 + 1 \times 2^2 + 0 \times 2^1 + 0 \times 2^0$$

which, translated into the decimal system, is 28. Another example of a binary-to-decimal conversion is provided in Figure A-2.

Converting in the reverse direction—from decimal to binary—is also rather easy. A popular approach for doing this is the *remainder method.* This procedure employs successive divisions by the base number of the system to which we are converting. Use of the remainder method to convert a decimal to a binary number is illustrated in Figure A-3.

To avoid confusion when different number bases are being used, it is common to use the base as a subscript. So, referring to Figures A-2 and A-3, for example, we could write

$$89_{10} = 1011001_2$$

FIGURE A-2

Binary-to-decimal conversion. To convert any binary number to its decimal counterpart, take the rightmost digit and multiply it by 2^0 (or 1), the next-to-rightmost digit and multiply it by 2^1 (or 2), and so on, as illustrated here. Then add up all the products so formed.

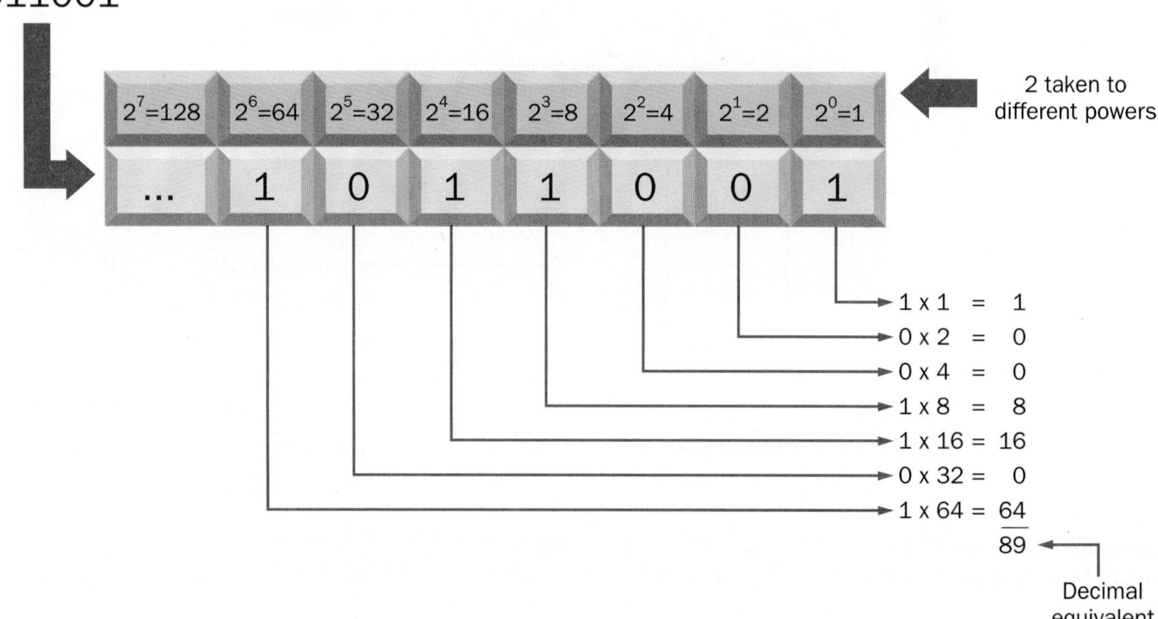

In addition, when we are using numbering systems other than the decimal system, it is customary to pronounce each symbol individually. For example, 101_2 is pronounced "one-zero-one" rather than "one hundred one." This convention is also used with other nondecimal systems.

The binary system described here is sometimes referred to as *true-binary representation.* True-binary representation does not use a fixed number of bits, as do ASCII and EBCDIC, nor is it used to represent letters or special characters.

The Hexadecimal Numbering System

Often diagnostic and memory-management messages are output to programmers and technically oriented users in hexadecimal (or *hex*) notation (see Figure A-4). Hex is a shorthand method for representing the binary digits that are stored in the computer system. Because large binary numbers—for example, $1101010001001110 1_2$—can easily be misread by programmers, binary digits are grouped into units of four that, in turn, are represented by other symbols.

FIGURE A-3

Decimal-to-binary conversion using the remainder method. In this approach, we start by using the decimal number to be converted (89) as the initial dividend. Each successive dividend is the quotient of the previous division. We keep dividing until we've reached a zero quotient, whereupon the converted number is formed by the remainders taken in reverse order.

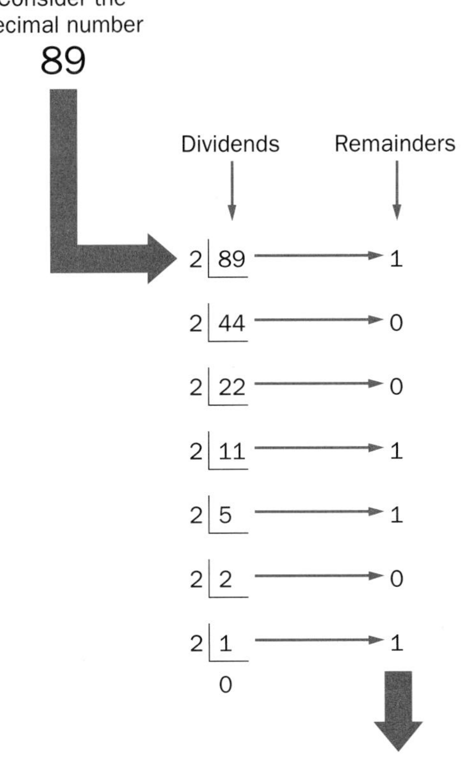

Collecting the remainders backwards we get the binary number 1011001.

Hexadecimal. Pertaining to the numbering system with 16 symbols: 0, 1, 2, 3, 4, 5, 6, 7, 8, 9, A, B, C, D, E, and F.

Hexadecimal means base 16, implying that there are 16 different symbols in this numbering system. Since we have only ten possible digits to work with, letters are used instead of numbers for the extra six symbols. The 16 hexadecimal symbols and their decimal and binary counterparts are shown in Figure A-5.

Hexadecimal is not itself a code that the computer uses to perform computations or to communicate with other machines. It does, however, have a special relationship to the 8-bit bytes of ASCII-8 and EBCDIC that makes it ideal for displaying messages quickly. As you can see in Figure A-5, each hex character has a 4-binary-bit counterpart, so any combination of 8 bits can be represented by exactly two hexadecimal characters. Thus, the letter *A* (represented in EBCDIC by 11000001) has a hex representation of C1.

Let's look at an example to see how to convert from hex to decimal. Suppose you receive the following message on your display screen:

```
PROGRAM LOADED AT LOCATION 4F6A
```

This message tells you the precise location in memory of the first byte in your program. To determine the decimal equivalent of a hexadecimal number such

FIGURE A-4

Hexadecimal display. Programmers often rely on the hexadecimal numbering system to give them information about where programs and data are stored in memory. Here, Quarterdeck's Manifest—a diagnostics and resources-management software package—tells how the first megabyte of memory is allocated by the DOS operating system.

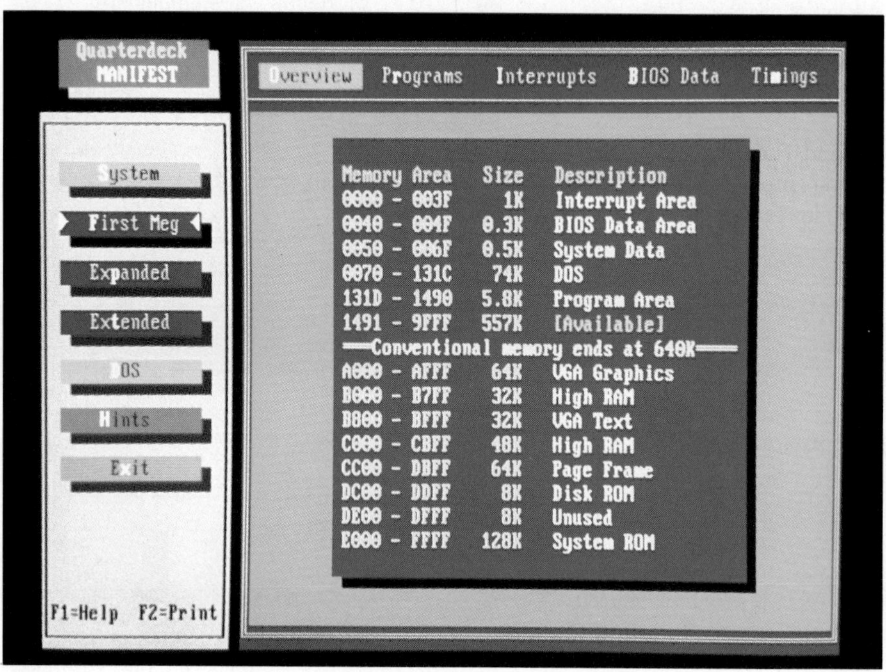

FIGURE A-5

Hexadecimal characters and their decimal and binary equivalents.

Hexadecimal Character	Decimal Equivalent	Binary Equivalent
0	0	0000
1	1	0001
2	2	0010
3	3	0011
4	4	0100
5	5	0101
6	6	0110
7	7	0111
8	8	1000
9	9	1001
A	10	1010
B	11	1011
C	12	1100
D	13	1101
E	14	1110
F	15	1111

as 4F6A, you can use a procedure similar to the binary-to-decimal conversion shown in Figure A-2 (refer to Figure A-6).

To convert the other way—from decimal to hex—we again can use the remainder method, this time dividing by 16. A decimal-to-hex conversion using the remainder method is illustrated in Figure A-7.

To convert from base 16 to base 2, we convert each hex digit separately to four binary digits (using the table in Figure A-5). For example, to convert F6A9 to base 2, we get

F	6	A	9
1111	0110	1010	1001

or 1111011010101001_2. To convert from base 2 to base 16, we go through the reverse process. If the number of digits in the binary number is not divisible by 4, we add leading zeros to the binary number to force an even division. So, for example, to convert 1101101010011_2 to base 16, we get

0001	1011	0101	0011
1	B	5	3

or $1B53_{16}$. Note that three leading zeros were added to make this conversion.

One final word before we close. In Chapter 3 we mentioned that 32-bit computer chips, such as the Intel 80386 and 80486, are capable of addressing

FIGURE A-6

Hexadecimal-to-decimal conversion. To convert any hexadecimal number to its decimal counterpart, take the rightmost digit and multiply it by 16^0 (or 1), the next-to-rightmost digit and multiply it by 16^1 (or 16), and so on, as illustrated here. Then add up all the products so formed.

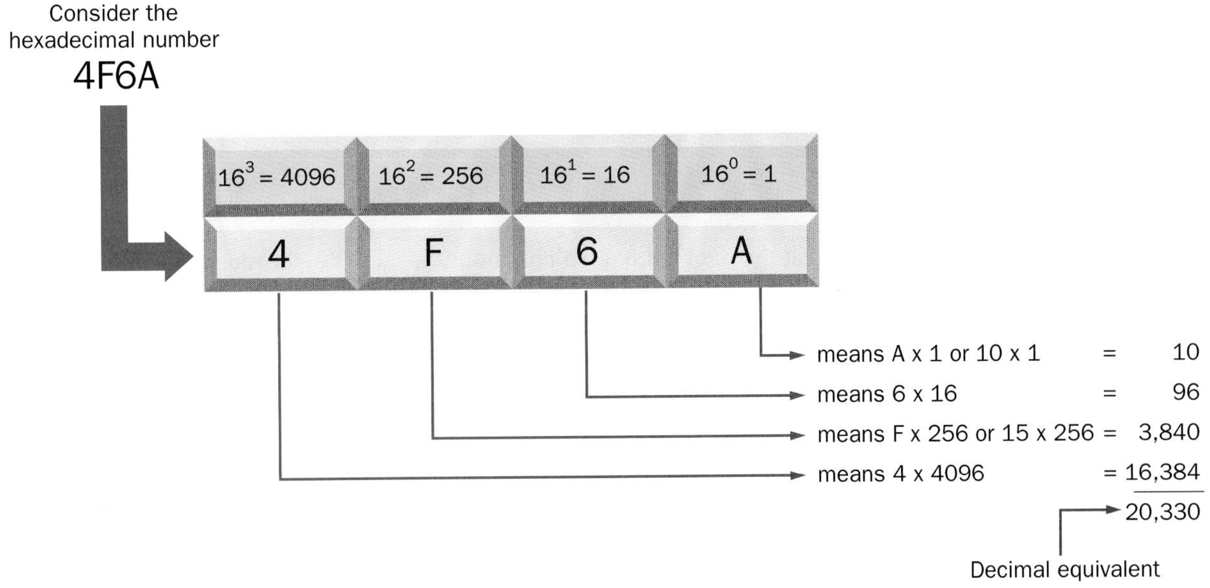

Consider the hexadecimal number
4F6A

$16^3 = 4096$	$16^2 = 256$	$16^1 = 16$	$16^0 = 1$
4	F	6	A

means A x 1 or 10 x 1 = 10
means 6 x 16 = 96
means F x 256 or 15 x 256 = 3,840
means 4 x 4096 = 16,384
20,330
Decimal equivalent

FIGURE A-7

Decimal-to-hexadecimal conversion using the remainder method. To convert 20330_{10} to a hexadecimal number, we start our successive divisions by 16 using 20330 as the initial dividend. Each successive dividend is the quotient of the previous division. As in Figure A–3, we divide until we've reached a zero quotient and form the converted number by taking the remainders in reverse order.

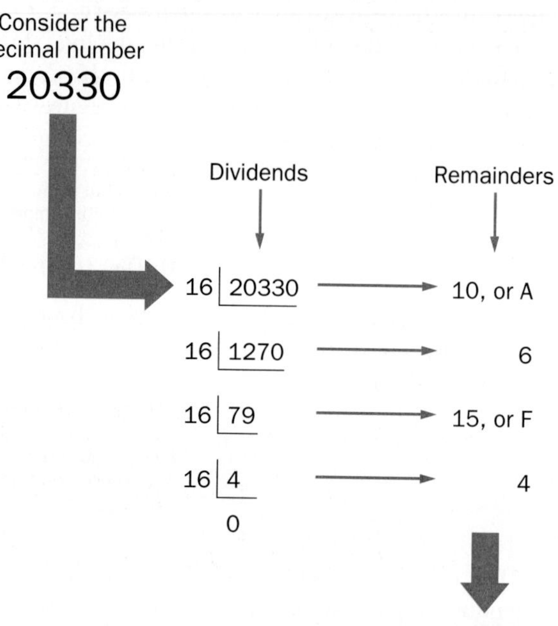

about 4 billion bytes (4 gigabytes) of memory. You may have then wondered at that time, "Why 4 billion bytes?" Note that the maximum address in a 32-bit computer is a string of 32 1-bits, or

```
11111111111111111111111111111111
```

which, expressed in hex, is

```
FFFFFFFF
```

Note that the decimal equivalent is 4,294,967,296—or roughly 4 billion bytes.

A table summarizing all of the conversions covered in this appendix is provided in Figure A-8.

Computer Arithmetic

To most of us, decimal arithmetic is second nature. Addition and subtraction have been part of our education since kindergarten or first grade. Addition and subtraction using binary and hexadecimal numbers is not much harder than the same operations with decimal numbers. Practically the only difference is in the number of symbols used in each system.

Figure A-9 provides an example of addition and subtraction with decimal, binary, and hexadecimal numbers. Note that, as in decimal arithmetic, you carry to and borrow from adjacent positions as you move from right to left.

FIGURE A-8

Summary of conversions.

From Base	To Base 2	To Base 10	To Base 16
2		Starting at rightmost digit, multiply binary digits by 2^0, 2^1, 2^2, etc., respectively. Then add products.	Starting at rightmost digit, convert each group of four binary digits to a hex digit.
10	Divide repeatedly by 2; then collect remainders in reverse order.		Divide repeatedly by 16; then collect remainders in reverse order.
16	Convert each hex digit to four binary digits.	Starting at rightmost digit, multiply hex digits by 16^0, 16^1, 16^2, etc., respectively. Then add products.	

Instead of carrying or borrowing 10, however—as you would in the decimal system—you carry or borrow 2 (binary) or 16 (hexadecimal).

Summary and Key Terms

This appendix covers several fundamentals of numbering systems.

Numbering Systems A *numbering system* is a way of representing numbers.

The Decimal Numbering System The number system we most commonly use is called the **decimal,** or base 10, system. It is called base 10 because it uses ten symbols—the digits 0, 1, 2, 3, 4, 5, 6, 7, 8, 9—to represent all possible numbers. The position of each symbol in any decimal number represents the number 10 (the base number) raised to a power, or exponent, which is based on that position.

FIGURE A-9

Adding and subtracting with the decimal, binary, and hexadecimal numbering systems.

	Decimal	Binary	Hexadecimal
Addition	142 +47 189	10001110 +101111 10111101	8E +2F BD
Subtraction	142 −47 95	10001110 −101111 1011111	8E −2F 5F

The Binary Numbering System The **binary,** or base 2, system works in a manner similar to the decimal system. One major difference is that the binary system has only two symbols—0 and 1—instead of ten. A second major difference is that the position of each digit in a binary number represents the number 2 (the base number) raised to an exponent based on that position.

The Hexadecimal Numbering System Because large binary numbers can easily be misread by programmers, binary digits often are grouped and represented by other symbols. The **hexadecimal,** or base 16, system is used to represent a grouping of four binary digits. There are 16 different symbols in this system. Since we have only ten possible digits to work with, the letters A–F are used instead of numbers for the extra six symbols. The position of each digit in a hexadecimal number represents the number 16 raised to an exponent based on that position.

Computer Arithmetic It is a relatively straightforward process to convert any value in one numbering system into a value in another system and to perform computer arithmetic on these values.

Exercises

1. Convert the following binary numbers to decimal numbers:
   a. 1011_2 ____________
   b. 101110_2 ____________
   c. 1010011_2 ____________
2. Convert the following decimal numbers to binary numbers:
   a. 51_{10} ____________
   b. 260_{10} ____________
   c. 500_{10} ____________
3. Convert the following binary numbers to hexadecimal numbers:
   a. 101_2 ____________
   b. 11010_2 ____________
   c. 111101000010_2 ____________
4. Convert the following hexadecimal numbers to binary numbers:
   a. $F2_{16}$ ____________
   b. $1A8_{16}$ ____________
   c. $39EB_{16}$ ____________
5. Convert the following hexadecimal numbers to decimal numbers:
   a. $B6_{16}$ ____________
   b. $5E9_{16}$ ____________
   c. $CAFF_{16}$ ____________

6. Drawing on techniques you've learned in this appendix, provide an expression to convert the base 6 (yes, six) number 451_6 to a decimal number: ______________.
7. Adding the binary numbers 11011001 and 1011101 yields ______________.
8. Adding the hexadecimal numbers 8E and 5D yields ______________.
9. Subtracting the binary number 1011 from 101110 yields ______________.
10. Subtracting the hexadecimal number B6 from F2 yields ______________.

GLOSSARY

The terms shown in boldface are presented in the text as key terms. The number(s) in parentheses at the end of the definition of each term indicates the page (or pages) on which the term is boldfaced in the text. The terms shown in boldface italic are other commonly used and important words often encountered in information processing environments. The italic number in parentheses after the definition of each term indicates the page on which the term is first mentioned.

Absolute replication
In spreadsheets, copying verbatim the contents in one range of cells into another range of cells. (313)

Access card.
A plastic card that, when inserted into a machine and combined with a password, permits access to a system. (492)

Access mechanism.
A mechanical device in the disk pack or disk unit that positions the read/write heads on the proper tracks. (102)

Accumulator.
A register that stores the result of an arithmetic or logical operation. (70)

Action diagram.
A programming tool that helps programmers code structured programs. (423)

Ada.
A structured programming language developed by the Department of Defense and named after Ada Augusta Byron, the world's first programmer. *(432)*

Add-in board.
A board that may be inserted into the computer's system unit to perform one or more functions. (81)

Add-on package.
A software package that supplements the activities of a larger software package, either by providing new functions or improving on already existing functions. (275)

Address.
An identifiable location in storage where data are kept. Primary storage and direct-access secondary storage devices such as disk are addressable. *(68)*

Address register.
A register containing the memory location of data to be used. (69)

AI.
See Artificial intelligence. (381)

ALU.
See Arithmetic/logic unit. (67)

American National Standards Institute (ANSI).
An organization that acts as a national clearinghouse for standards in the United States. *(75)*

Analog transmission.
The transmission of data as continuous-wave patterns. (190)

Analysis.
In program and systems development, the process of studying a problem area to determine what should be done. *(389)*

ANSI.
See American National Standards Institute. *(75)*

API.
See Applications programming interface. (231)

APL.
An acronym for A Programming Language. APL is a highly compact programming language popular for problem-solving applications. *(432)*

Applications generator.
A fourth-generation-language product that can be used to quickly create applications software. *(435)*

Applications package.
A fourth-generation-language product that, when the user sets a few parameters, becomes a finished applications program ready to meet specific end-user needs. (415)

Applications programming interface (API).
A set of functions that are part of one software package and available to other packages. (231)

Applications software.
Programs that do the useful work—such as payroll, inventory control, and accounting tasks—for end users of a computer system. Contrasts with systems software. (48)

Applications software development.
The process of designing, coding, debugging and testing, maintaining, and documenting applications software. (414)

Arithmetic/logic unit (ALU).
The part of the computer that contains the circuitry to perform addition, subtraction, multiplication, division, and comparison operations. (67)

Architecture.
The underlying design of a computer system. Architecture is largely a function of the CPU and bus in use. (83)

Artificial intelligence (AI).
The ability of a machine to perform actions that are characteristic of human intelligence, such as reasoning and learning. (381)

ASCII.
An acronym for American Standard Code for Information Interchange. ASCII is a fixed-length, binary-based code widely used to represent data for processing and communications. (74)

Assembler.
A computer program that takes assembly-language instructions and converts them to machine language. (239)

Assembly language.
A low-level programming language that uses mnemonic codes in place of the 0s and 1s of machine language. (425)

Asynchronous transmission.
The transmission of data over a line one character at a time. Each character is preceded by a "start bit" and followed by a "stop bit." Contrasts with synchronous transmission. (194)

Audit.
An inspection used to determine if a system or procedure is working as it should or if claimed amounts are correct. (494)

Authoring software.
Programming packages used to develop multimedia applications. (*435*)

Back-end processor.
A computer that relieves the main computer of processing tasks for selected large banks of data. (208)

Backup.
Making duplicate copies of programs or data. (463)

Bar chart.
A presentation graphic that uses side-by-side columns as the principal charting element. (320)

Bar code.
A machine-readable code consisting of sets of bars of varying widths. The codes are prominently displayed on the packaging of many retail goods and are commonly read with special reading equipment. (150)

BASIC.
An acronym for Beginner's All-Purpose Symbolic Instruction Code. BASIC is an easy-to-learn, high-level programming language developed at Dartmouth College in the 1960s. (426)

Batch processing.
Processing transactions or other data in groups at periodic intervals. Contrasts with realtime processing. (53)

Benchmark test.
A test used to measure computer system performance under typical use conditions prior to purchase. The test is analogous to a rigorous "test drive" taken with a car before buying it. (394)

Binary.
A number system with two possible states. The binary system is fundamental to computers because electronic devices often function in two possible states—for example "on" or "off," "current present" or "current not present," "clockwise" or "counterclockwise," and so forth. (71, A-3)

Biometric security device.
A device that, upon recognition of some physiological or learned characteristic that is unique to a person, allows that person access to a system. (492)

Bit.
A binary digit, such as 0 or 1. The 0- or 1-states are used by computer systems to take advantage of the binary nature of electronics. Bits often are assembled into bytes and words when manipulated or stored. (72)

Bit mapping.
A term, used with certain display devices and printers, that means that each of the dots in the output image may be individually operator-controlled. (136)

Bits per second (bps).
A measure of the speed of a communications device. (190)

Board.
A hardware device into which processor chips and memory chips are fitted, along with related circuitry. *(77)*

Bps.
See Bits per second. (190)

Bridge.
An interface that enables two similar networks to communicate. Contrasts with gateway. (203)

Bug.
An error in a program or system. *(438)*

Bus.
A set of wires that acts as a data highway between the CPU and other devices. (82)

Bus network.
A telecommunications network consisting of a line and several devices that are tapped into the line. The network is so named because data are picked up and dropped off at devices similarly to the way in which passengers are picked up and dropped off at bus stops. (204)

Byte.
A configuration of seven or eight bits used to represent a single character of data. (75)

C.
A programming language that has the portability of a high-level language and the executional efficiency of an assembly language. (430)

Cache disk.
A disk management scheme whereby more data than necessary are read from a disk during each time-consuming disk fetch and are stored in memory to minimize the number of fetches. (108)

CAD.
See Computer-aided design. (378)

CAD/CAM.
An acronym for *computer-aided design/ computer-aided manufacturing.* CAD/ CAM is a general term applied to the use of computer technology to automate design and manufacturing operations in industry. *(378)*

CAI.
See Computer-assisted instruction. *(503)*

Callback device.
A device on the receiving end of a communications network that verifies the authenticity of the sender by calling the sender back. (494)

Caller identification.
A term that refers to a telephone or answering device that displays the phone numbers of incoming calls. (496)

CAM.
See Computer-aided manufacturing. (379)

Cartridge disk.
Magnetic disk in which a single disk platter is contained in a sealed plastic case, which in turn is mounted onto a disk unit when data are to be read from or written to the disk inside. (107)

Cartridge tape.
Magnetic tape in which the supply and take-up reels are contained in a small plastic case, which in turn is mounted onto a tape unit when data are to be read from or written to the tape inside. (112)

CASE.
See Computer-aided software engineering. (441)

Case control structure.
A control structure that can be formed by nesting two or more selection control structures. (421)

Cathode-ray tube (CRT).
A display device that contains a long-necked display-tube mechanism similar to that used in television sets. (134)

Cell.
In spreadsheet software, an area of the worksheet that holds a single label or value. (297)

Cell address.
The column-row combination that uniquely identifies a spreadsheet cell. (297)

Cell pointer.
In spreadsheet software, a cursorlike mechanism used to point to cells on the display screen. (301)

Cellular phone.
A mobile phone that uses special stations called cells to communicate over the regular phone system. (183)

Central processing unit (CPU).
The piece of hardware, also known as the *computer*, that interprets and executes program instructions and communicates with input, output, and storage devices. (8, 40)

Chief information officer (CIO).
The person in an organization who oversees routine transaction processing and information systems activities as well as other computer-related areas. (*383*)

CIM.
See Computer-integrated manufacturing. (380)

CIO.
See Chief information officer. (*383*)

Client.
A device designated to receive service in a client-server network. (198)

Client-server LAN.
A LAN that is comprised of *client* devices, which receive service, and *server* devices, which provide service. (198)

Clip art.
Prepackaged artwork designed to be imported into text documents or charts, by desktop publishing or presentation graphics software. (283)

Coaxial cable.
A transmission line developed for sending data at high speeds. (186)

COBOL.
An acronym for Common Business-Oriented Language. COBOL is a high-level programming language developed for transaction processing applications. (426)

Coding.
The writing of instructions, in a programming language, that will cause the computer system to perform a specific set of operations. (437)

COM.
See Computer output microfilm. (161)

Command language.
A programming language used to communicate with the operating system. (223)

Command-language translator.
Systems software that translates instructions written in a command language into machine-language instructions. (223)

Common carrier.
A government-regulated private organization that provides communications services to the public. (195)

Communications medium.
The intervening substance, such as a telephone wire or cable, that connects two physically distant hardware devices. (185)

Communications satellite.
An earth-orbiting device that relays communications signals over long distances. (188)

Compiler.
A computer program that translates a source program written by a user or programmer in a high-level or very-high-level programming language into machine language. The entire translation takes place before the program is executed. Contrasts with interpreter. (238)

Computer.
See Central processing unit. (8, 40)

Computer-aided design (CAD).
A general term applied to the use of computer technology to automate design functions in industry. (378)

Computer-aided manufacturing (CAM).
A general term applied to the use of computer technology to automate manufacturing functions in industry. (379)

Computer-aided software engineering (CASE).
Program products that automate systems and program development activities. (441)

Computer-assisted instruction (CAI).
The use of computers to supplement personalized teaching instruction by providing the student with sequences of instruction under program control. The progression through the instructional materials in such a system enables students to learn at their own rate. *(503)*

Computer crime.
The use of computers to commit unauthorized acts. (488)

Computer-integrated manufacturing (CIM).
The use of technology to tie together CAD, CAM, and other business systems. (380)

Computer output microfilm (COM).
A term referring to equipment and media that reduce computer output to microscopic form and put it on photosensitive film. (161)

Computer system.
When applied to buying a "computer system," the term generally refers to the equipment and programs being sold. When applied to a computer-based operation in an organization, it is commonly defined as all the equipment, programs, data, procedures, and personnel supporting that operation. (8)

Computer virus.
A small block of unauthorized code, transmitted from program to program by a copy operation, that performs destructive acts when executed. (489)

Concentrator.
A communications device that combines control and multiplexing. Concentrators have a store-and-forward capability that enables them to store messages from several low-speed devices before forwarding them at high speeds to another device. (207)

Control-break reporting.
A term that refers to "breaks" in the normal flow of information in a computer report that periodically occur for subtotals and totals. *(52)*

Control panel.
In spreadsheet software, the portion of the screen display that is used for issuing commands and observing what is being typed into the computer system. (300)

Control structure.
A pattern for controlling the flow of logic in a computer program. The three basic control structures are sequence, selection (if-then-else), and looping (iteration). (421)

Control unit.
The part of the CPU that coordinates the execution of program instructions. (68)

Coprocessor.
A dedicated processor chip that is summoned by the CPU to perform specialized types of processing. *(80)*

CPU.
See Central processing unit. (8, 40)

Crosshair cursor.
A digitizing device that is often moved over hard-copy images of maps and drawings to enter those images into the computer system. (156)

CRT.
See Cathode-ray tube. (134)

Current cell.
In spreadsheet software, the worksheet cell at which the highlight is currently positioned. (300)

Cursor.
A highlighting symbol that appears on a display screen to indicate the position where the next character (or group of characters) typed in will appear. (133, 300)

Daisywheel printer.
A low-speed printer with a solid-font printing mechanism consisting of a spoked wheel of embossed characters. Daisywheel printers are capable of producing letter-quality output. *(138)*

Data.
A collection of raw, unorganized facts. (8)

Data access.
Fetching data from a device either sequentially or directly. (116)

Database.
An integrated collection of data stored on a direct-access storage device. (47, 332)

Database administrator (DBA).
The person or group of people in

charge of designing, implementing, and managing the ongoing operation of a database. *(344)*

Database management system (DBMS).
A software package designed to integrate data and provide easy access to them. (332)

Data definition.
The process of describing the characteristics of data that are to be handled by a database management system. (335)

Data definition language (DDL).
A language used by a database administrator to create, store, and manage data in a database environment. (346)

Data dictionary.
A facility that informs users and programmers about characteristics of data and programs in a database or a computer system. (337, 438)

Data flow diagram.
A graphically oriented systems development tool that enables a systems analyst to logically represent the flow of data through a system. (389)

Data manipulation.
The process of using language commands to add, delete, modify, or retrieve data in a file or database. (337)

Data manipulation language (DML).
A language used by programmers to supplement some high-level language supported in a database environment. (347)

Data organization.
The process of establishing a data file so that it may subsequently be accessed in some desired way. Three common methods of organizing data are sequential organization, indexed-sequential organization, and direct organization. (116)

Data processing area.
The group of computer professionals within the information systems department who are charged with building transaction processing systems. (385)

Data processing system.
See Transaction processing system. *(370)*

DBA.
See Database administrator. *(344)*

DBMS.
See Database management system. (332)

DDL.
See Data definition language. (346)

Debugging.
The process of detecting and correcting errors in computer programs or in the computer system itself. (438)

Decimal.
A number system with ten symbols—0, 1, 2, 3, 4, 5, 6, 7, 8, and 9. (A-2)

Decision support system (DSS).
A system that provides tools and capabilities to managers to enable them to satisfy their own information needs. (373)

Default.
The assumption that a computer program makes when no specific choice is indicated by the user or programmer. (223)

Design.
The process of planning a program or system. Design is normally undertaken after a problem has been thoroughly analyzed and a set of specifications for the solution established. *(390, 415)*

Desk accessory.
A software package that provides the electronic counterpart of tools commonly found on a desktop—a clock, calendar, notepad, and rolodex file, for instance. Also called a *desktop organizer. (376)*

Desktop computer.
A microcomputer system that can fit on a desktop. Some familiar examples are computers in the IBM PS/2 and Apple Macintosh II lines. *(15)*

Desktop publishing.
A microcomputer-based publishing system that can fit on a desktop. (277)

Detachable-reel tape.
Magnetic tape that is wound onto a single reel, which in turn is mounted onto a tape unit with an empty take-up reel when data are to be read from or written to the tape. (111)

Device driver.
A utility program that enables an applications program to function with a specific hardware device. (245)

Digital transmission.
The transmission of data as discrete impulses. (190)

Digitizer.
An input device that converts a measurement into a digital value. (153)

Digitizing tablet.
A digitizer that consists of a flat board and also a device that traces over the board, storing the traced pattern in computer memory. (156)

Direct access.
Reading or writing data in storage so that the access time involved is relatively independent of the location of the data. (95)

Direct organization.
A method of organizing data on a device so that they can be accessed directly (randomly). (123)

Disk access time.
The time taken to locate and read (or position and write) data on a disk device. (104)

Disk cylinder.
All tracks on a disk pack that are accessible with a single movement of the access mechanism. (103)

Disk drive.
A mechanism within the disk storage unit on which disk packs, diskettes, or disk cartridges are placed to be accessed. *(22)*

Diskette.
A small, removable disk made of a tough, flexible plastic and coated with a magnetizable substance. (96)

Disk pack.
A group of tiered hard disks that are mounted on a shaft and treated as a unit. A disk pack must be placed on a disk unit in order to be accessed. (101)

Disk unit.
A direct-access secondary storage device that uses magnetic or optical disk as the principal I/O medium. (100)

Disk utility.
A program that assists with such disk-related tasks as backup, data compression, space allocation, and recovering from accidental data destruction. (241)

Display device.
A peripheral device that contains a viewing screen. (132)

Display terminal.
A communications workstation that consists of a display device and a keyboard. (132)

DML.
See Data manipulation language. (347)

Documentation.
A detailed written description of a program, procedure, or system. (439)

Dot-matrix character.
A character composed from a rectangular matrix of dots. *(139)*

DOUNTIL control structure.
A looping control structure in which the looping continues as long as a certain condition is false (i.e., "do until true"). (421)

DOWHILE control structure.
A looping control structure in which the looping continues as long as a certain condition is true (i.e., "do while true"). (421)

Downloading.
The process of transferring data or information from a large computer system to a smaller one. Contrasts with uploading. (202)

Drum plotter.
An output device that draws on paper that is rolled along a cylindrically shaped drum. *(159)*

DSS.
See Decision support system. (373)

EBCDIC.
An acronym for Extended Binary-Coded Decimal Interchange Code. EBCDIC is a fixed-length, binary-based code widely used to represent data on IBM mainframes. (74)

E-cycle.
The part of the machine cycle in which data are located, an instruction is executed, and the results are stored. (70)

EDI.
See Electronic data interchange. (180)

EFT.
See Electronic funds transfer. *(502)*

Electronic bulletin board.
A computer file that is shared by several people, enabling them to post or broadcast messages. (181)

Electronic data interchange (EDI).
A computer procedure that enables standard business documents, such as purchase orders and invoices, to be exchanged from one company's computer system to the computer system of another company. (180)

Electronic document handling.
The use of computer systems to store and manipulate electronic copies of form documents. *(377)*

Electronic funds transfer (EFT).
Pertains to systems that transfer funds by computer from one account to another, without the use of written checks. *(502)*

Electronic mail.
A facility that enables users to send letters, memos, documents, and the like from one hardware device to another. (374)

Electronic mailbox.
A storage area used to hold a recipient's electronic mail. (181, 376)

Electronic spreadsheet.
A productivity software package that enables operators to create tables and financial schedules quickly by entering labels and values into cells on a display-screen grid. (297)

Encryption.
A method of disguising data or programs so that they are unrecognizable to unauthorized users. (493)

End user.
A person who needs computer-produced results in his or her job. (13)

End-user development.
Systems development activities carried out by the end user. (398)

Ergonomics.
The field that studies the effects of things such as computer hardware, software, and workspaces on employees' comfort and health. (483)

Ethics.
A term that refers to standards of moral conduct. (497)

Executive information system (EIS).
A decision support system that is tailored to the needs of a specific, top-level individual in an organization. (373)

Expert system.
A program or computer system providing the type of advice that would be expected of a human expert. (381)

Expert system shell.
A prepackaged expert system that lacks only a knowledge base. (381)

External disk.
A disk unit that is not housed within the computer's system unit. Contrasts with internal disk. *(102)*

External storage.
See Secondary storage. (11)

Facsimile (fax) machine.
A device that can transmit or receive hard-copy images of text, pictures, maps, diagrams, and the like over the phone lines. (182, 374)

Fiber optic cable.
A cable composed of thousands of hair-thin, transparent fibers along which data are passed from lasers as light waves. (186)

Field.
A collection of related characters. (46)

Field descriptor.
A code used to describe the type of data—say, numeric, character, or logical—that occupy a given field in a data record. (337)

File.
A collection of related records. (46)

File directory.
A directory on an input/output medium that provides data such as name, length, and starting address for each file on the medium. (100)

File structure.
A collection of information about the fields of a file, including the names, lengths, and types of the fields. (337)

Film recorder.
A cameralike device that captures computer output on film. (161)

Firmware.
Software instructions that are written onto a hardware module. (81)

Flatbed plotter.
An output device that draws on paper that is mounted on a flat drawing table. *(159)*

Flat-panel display.
A slim-profile display device. (134)

Floppy disk.
See Diskette. *(97)*

Floptical disk
A cartridge disk that relies on a combination of magnetic and optical technology. (107)

Flowchart.
See Program flowchart. *(416)*

Font.
A typeface in a particular point size—for instance, 12-point Helvetica. (265)

FORTRAN.
An acronym for FORmula TRANslator. FORTRAN is a high-level programming language used for mathematical, scientific, and engineering applications. (431)

Fourth-generation language (4GL).
An easy-to-learn, easy-to-use language that enables users or programmers to code applications much more quickly than they could with third-generation languages such as BASIC, FORTRAN, and COBOL. (434)

Front-end processor.
A computer that is positioned in a network to screen messages sent to the main computer and that also relieves the main computer of certain computational chores. (207)

Full backup.
A procedure that produces a duplicate copy of all files onto a secondary storage medium. (466)

Full-duplex transmission.
A type of transmission in which messages may be sent in two directions simultaneously along a communications path. (190)

Functionally obsolete.
Refers to a product that no longer meets the needs of an individual or business. (473)

Function key.
A special keyboard key that executes a preprogrammed routine when depressed. *(131)*

Gateway.
An interface that enables two dissimilar networks to communicate. Contrasts with bridge. (203)

GB.
See Gigabyte. (75)

GDSS.
See Group decision support system. (373)

General-purpose computer.
A computer capable of being programmed to solve a wide range of problems. *(9)*

Gigabyte (GB).
Approximately 1 billion bytes. (75)

Graphical user interface (GUI).
Refers to the use of computer graphics screens that make it easier for users to interact with software. (223)

Group decision support system (GDSS).
A decision support system in which several people routinely interact through a computer network to solve common problems. (373)

Hacking.
A term that, when used with computers, often relates to using a microcomputer system or terminal to break into the security of a large computer system. (491)

Half-duplex transmission.
Any type of transmission in which messages may be sent in two directions—but only one way at a time—along a communications path. (190)

Handwriting recognition device.
A device that can identify handwritten characters. (158)

Hard copy.
A permanent form of usable output; for example, output on paper or film. Contrasts with soft copy. (130)

Hard disk.
A rigid platter coated with a magnetizable substance. (96)

Hard return.
In word processing, the use of the Enter key to provide line spacing. Contrasts with soft return. (261)

Hardware.
Physical equipment in a computing environment, such as the computer and its support devices. (12)

Hashing.
A key-to-disk mathematical transformation in which the key field on each record determines where the record is stored. *(123)*

Hexadecimal.
Pertaining to the number system with 16 symbols: 0, 1, 2, 3, 4, 5, 6, 7, 8, 9, A, B, C, D, E, and F. (A-5)

Hierarchical local network.
A star-shaped local network in which a relatively powerful CPU is at the top of the hierarchy and communications terminals or less-powerful CPUs are at the bottom. (202)

High-level language.
See High-level programming language. (425)

High-level programming language.
The class of programming languages used by most professional programmers to solve a wide range of problems. Some examples are BASIC, COBOL, FORTRAN, and Pascal. (425)

Highlight.
See Cell pointer. (301)

Host computer.
In telecommunications, a computer that is used to control a communications network. *(198)*

Host language.
A programming language used to code applications within a specific software system, such as a database environment. (347)

IBM-compatible microcomputer.
A microcomputer that can run the same software as DOS-based IBM microcomputers run. (450)

Icon.
A graphical image on a display screen that invokes a particular program action when selected by the operator. (153)

I-cycle.
The part of the machine cycle in which the control unit fetches an instruction from memory and prepares it for subsequent processing. (70)

If-then-else (selection) control structure.
See Selection control structure. (421)

Illustration software package.
A program package that enables users to paint or draw. (283)

Image scanner.
A device that can "read" into digital memory a hard-copy image such as a text page, photograph, map, or drawing. (150)

Impact dot-matrix mechanism.
A print head that forms dot-matrix characters through impact printing. (139)

Impact dot-matrix printer.
A printer whose print head is an impact dot-matrix mechanism. *(139)*

Impact printing.
The information of characters by causing a metal hammer to strike a ribbon into paper or paper into a ribbon. Contrasts with nonimpact printing. (139)

Indexed-sequential organization.
A method of organizing data on a direct-access medium so that it can be accessed directly (through an index) or sequentially. (120)

Information.
Data that have been processed into a meaningful form. (9)

Information center.
A facility in an organization that develops small systems. (386)

Information processing.
Pertains to computer operations that transform data into meaningful information. (9)

Information reporting system.
An information system whose principal outputs are preformatted, hard-copy reports. (372)

Information retrieval.
Online inquiry, through a display terminal or microcomputer workstation, to computer files or databases. (52)

Information system.
A system designed to provide information to managers to enable them to make decisions. (371)

Information systems department.
The area in an organization that consists of computer professionals—managers, analysts, programmers, operations personnel, trainers, specialists, and the like. (384)

Input.
Anything supplied to a computer or computer-system process or involved with the beginning of such a process, such as the data to be keyed in. Contrasts with output. (7)

Input device.
A machine used to supply data to the computer. Contrasts with output device. (7, 42)

Input/output (I/O) media.
Objects used to store data or information before or after processing. Examples include magnetic disk, magnetic tape, and paper. (8, 45, 130)

Instruction register.
The register that holds the part of the instruction indicating what the computer is to do next. (69)

Integrated software package.
A software package that bundles two or more major software functions into a single package. *(298)*

Internal disk.
A disk unit that is housed inside the computer's system unit. Contrasts with external disk. *(102)*

Internal storage.
See Primary storage. (10)

Interpreter.
A computer program that translates a source program written by a user or programmer in a high-level or very-high-level language into machine language. The translation takes place on a line-by-line basis as each statement is executed. Contrasts with compiler. (239)

I/O media.
See Input/output media. (8)

Issuance.
The use of computers to produce transaction processing documents such as paychecks, bills, and customer reminder notices. (52)

Iteration control structure.
See Looping control structure. (421)

Joystick.
An input device, resembling a car's stick shift, that often is used for computer games and computer-aided design (CAD) work. (155)

KB.
See Kilobyte. (75)

Keyboard.
An input device composed of various typewriterlike keys, arranged in a configuration similar to that of a typewriter. Computer keyboards also have a number of special keys that initiate preprogrammed routines when activated. (131)

Key field.
A field used to identify a record. (114)

Kilobyte (KB).
Approximately 1,000 (1,024, to be exact) bytes. (75)

Label.
In spreadsheet software, a cell entry that cannot be manipulated mathematically. (301)

LAN.
See Local area network. (198)

Language translator.
A systems program that converts an applications program into machine language. (238)

Laptop computer.
A portable computer light enough to be operated while it rests on one's lap. *(7, 16)*

Laser printer.
A nonimpact printer that works on a principle similar to that for a photocopier. *(143)*

Light pen.
An electrical device, resembling an ordinary pen, used to enter input by pointing to a display screen. (153)

Line chart.
A presentation graphic in which the principal charting element is an unbroken line. (321)

Line printer.
A high-speed printer that produces output one line at a time. (141)

Linkage editor.
A systems program that binds together related object-module program segments so that they may be run as a unit. (239)

LISP.
A language widely used for artificial intelligence applications. *(434)*

Load module.
A complete machine-language program that is ready to be executed by the computer. Also called a *load program.* (239)

Local area network (LAN).
A local network, without a host computer, that usually consists entirely of microcomputer workstations and shared peripherals. (198)

Local network.
A privately run communications network of several machines located within a mile or so of one another. (198)

Logo.
A programming language often used to teach children how to program. *(433)*

Looping (iteration) control structure.
The control structure used to represent a looping operation. Also see DOUNTIL control structure and DOWHILE control structure. (421)

Low-level language.
A highly detailed, machine-dependent programming language. Included in the class of low-level languages are machine and assembly languages. (425)

Machine cycle.
The series of operations involved in the execution of a single machine-language instruction. (70)

Machine language.
A binary-based programming language that the computer can execute directly. (77)

Machine-readable.
Any form in which data are represented so that they can be read by a machine. (8)

Macintosh System Software.
The operating system that's used primarily on Apple's Macintosh line of computer systems. (231)

Macro.
A predetermined series of keystrokes or commands that can be invoked by a single keystroke or command. (315)

Magnetic disk.
A secondary storage medium consisting of platters made of rigid metal (hard disk) or flexible plastic (diskette). (96)

Magnetic ink character recognition (MICR).
A technology, confined almost exclusively to the banking industry, that involves the processing of checks inscribed with special characters set in a special magnetic ink. (151)

Magnetic tape.
A plastic tape with a magnetic surface for storing data as a series of magnetic spots. (111)

Mailing list program.
A program used to generate mailing labels. (271)

Mail merge program.
A program specifically designed to produce form letters. (271)

Mainframe.
A large, transaction-processing-oriented computer capable of supporting powerful peripheral devices. (19)

Main memory.
The computer system's primary bank of memory; contrasts with memory products such as ROM and flash memory. *(10)*

Maintenance.
A term that refers to making minor modifications and upgrades to systems or software over time to ensure that they continue to meet the needs of an organization. (439)

Maintenance programmer.
A programmer involved with keeping an organization's existing programs in proper working order. *(412)*

Master file.
A file containing relatively permanent data, such as customer names and addresses. (47)

MB.
See Megabyte. (75)

Megabyte (MB).
Approximately 1 million bytes. (75)

Memory.
See Primary storage. (68)

Menu.
A set of options, provided at a display device, from which the operator makes a selection. *(24)*

MICR.
See Magnetic ink character recognition. (151)

Microcode.
Instructions that are built into the CPU to control the operation of its circuitry. (70)

Microcomputer.
See Microcomputer system. (15)

Microcomputer system.
The smallest and least expensive type of computer system. Also called a *personal computer system.* (15)

Microfiche.
A sheet of film, often 4 by 6 inches, on which computer output images are stored. *(161)*

Microprocessor.
A CPU on a silicon chip. *(15)*

Microsecond.
One millionth of a second. (70)

Microspacing.
A technique used by some printers and software packages to insert fractional spaces between characters to give text a typeset look. (269)

Microwave.
An electromagnetic wave in the high-frequency range. (187)

Millisecond.
One thousandth of a second. (70)

Minicomputer.
An intermediate-size and medium-priced type of computer. (17)

Mixed replication.
In spreadsheets, copying formulas in one range of cells into another range while varying some cell references and leaving others constant. (313)

Modem.
A contraction of the words MOdulation and DEModulation. A communications device that enables computers and their support devices to communicate over ordinary telephone lines. (191)

Monitor.
(1) A video display. (2) The supervisor program of an operating system. (132)

Monochrome.
A term used to refer to a display device that operates in a single foreground color. *(134)*

Monospacing.
A printing feature that allocates the same amount of space on a line to each character. Contrasts with proportional spacing. (269)

Mouse.
A device used to rapidly move a cursor around a display screen. (153)

MS-DOS.
An operating system widely used by microcomputer systems similar to those made by IBM. (229)

Multidimensional spreadsheet.
A program package that allows the construction of worksheets in which cells are referenced by more than two coordinates. (317)

Multimedia.
A type of computing in which text, graphics, voice, and video are intermixed in applications. (348)

Multiplexer.
A communications device that interleaves the messages of several low-speed devices and sends them along a single, high-speed transmission path. (206)

Multiprocessing.
The *simultaneous* execution of two or more program sequences by multiple computers operating under common control. (227)

Multiprogramming.
The execution of two or more programs, possibly being run by different users, *concurrently* on the same computer. (225)

Multitasking.
The ability of a single-user operating system to enable two or more programs or program tasks to execute concurrently. (225)

Nanosecond.
One-billionth of a second. (71)

Narrowband transmission.
Low-speed transmission, characterized by telegraph transmission. (190)

Natural language.
Refers to languages such as English, Spanish, and Japanese that are used by people in everyday conversation. (435)

NetWare.
The most widely used operating system on local area networks (LANs). (236)

Network.
A system of machines that communicate with one another. *(195)*

Nonimpact printing.
The formation of characters on a surface by means of heat, lasers, photography, or ink jets. Contrasts with impact printing. (141)

Nonvolatile storage.
Storage that retains its contents when the power is shut off. Contrasts with volatile storage. (94)

OA.
See Office automation. (374)

Object module.
The machine-language program that is the output from a language translator. Also called an *object program.* (239)

Object-oriented programming language.
A language that works with objects and messages rather than with separate instructions and data. (433)

OCR.
See Optical character recognition. (146)

Office automation (OA).
The use of computer-based, office-oriented technologies such as word processing, desktop publishing, electronic mail, video teleconferencing, and the like. (374)

Office automation (OA) area.
The group of computer professionals within the information systems department that is charged with managing office-related computer activities within the organization. (387)

Offline.
Anything not in or prepared for communication with the CPU. Contrasts with online. (46)

One-entry-point/one-exit-point rule.
A rule stating that each program control structure will have only one entry point into it and one exit point out of it. (421)

Online.
Anything ready for or in communication with the CPU. Contrasts with offline. (46)

Operating environment.
A term that refers to a graphical interface or the combination of an operating system and graphical interface—for instance, MS-DOS running under Microsoft Windows. (223)

Operating system.
The main collection of systems software that enables the computer system to manage the resources under its control. (218)

Optical character recognition (OCR).
The use of light reflectivity to identify marks, characters, or codes and the subsequent conversion of such symbols into a form suitable for computer processing. (146)

Optical disk.
A disk read by laser beams rather than by magnetic means. (115)

Orphan.
The first line of a paragraph when it is separated from the rest of the paragraph by a page or column break. Contrasts with widow. (274)

OS/2.
An operating system designed by IBM for high-end IBM and IBM-compatible microcomputers. (233)

Output.
Anything resulting from a computer or computer-system process or involved with the end result of such a process, such as information. Contrasts with input. (7)

Output device.
A machine used to output computer-processed data, or information. (7, 42, 130)

Outsourcing.
Refers to a company hiring another company to do some or all of its information processing activities. (387)

Page description language (PDL).
A language used to communicate instructions to a laser printer. (280)

Page-makeup software.
Programs used to compose page layouts in a desktop publishing system. (282)

Page printer.
A high-speed printer that delivers output one page at a time. (145)

Parallel processing.
A computer system that operates with two or more CPUs, which share work and process pieces of this work simultaneously. (86)

Parallel transmission.
Data transmission in which each bit in a byte has its own path and all of the bits in a byte are transmitted simultaneously. Contrasts with serial transmission. (193)

Parity bit.
An extra bit added to the byte representation of a character to ensure that there is always either an odd or an even number of 1-bits transmitted with every character. (76)

Partial backup.
A procedure that produces a duplicate copy of selected files onto a secondary storage medium. (466)

Pascal.
A structured high-level programming language that is often used to teach programming. (429)

Password.
A word or number used to provide selected individuals access to a system. (492)

PBX.
See Private branch exchange. (201)

PC-DOS.
The operating system most widely used on IBM microcomputers. (229)

PDL.
See Page description language. (280)

Peer-to-peer LAN.
A LAN in which all of the user workstations and shared peripherals in the network operate on the same level. (199)

Peripheral equipment.
All the machines that make it possible to get data and programs into the CPU, get processed information out, and store data and programs for ready access to the CPU. (7, 40)

Personal computer.
See Microcomputer system. (15)

Personal computer system.
See Microcomputer system. *(15)*

Picosecond.
A trillionth of a second. (71)

Pie chart.
A presentation graphic in which the principal charting element is a pie-shaped image that is divided into slices, each of which represents a share of the whole. (320)

Pixel.
On a display screen, a single dot used to compose dot-matrix characters and other images. (135)

Platform.
A set of computer-system architecture and systems-software choices that limit you to work in a certain way. (456)

Plotter.
An output device used for drawing graphs and diagrams. (159)

PL/1.
An acronym for Programming Language/1. PL/1 is a structured, general-purpose, high-level programming language that can be used for scientific, engineering, and business applications. *(432)*

Point-of-sale (POS) system.
A computer system, commonly found in department stores and supermarkets, that uses electronic cash register terminals to process and record sales transactions. (147)

Point size.
A measurement used in the scaling of typefaces. (265)

Port.
An outlet on the computer's system unit through which a peripheral device may communicate. (81)

Portable computer.
A microcomputer system that is compact enough to be carried about easily. *(15)*

POS system.
See Point-of-sale system. (147)

Precompiler.
A computer program that translates an extended set of programming language commands into standard commands of the language. (347)

Preliminary investigation.
In systems development, a brief study of a problem area to assess whether or not a full-scale systems project should be undertaken. Also called a *feasibility study*. (389)

Presentation graphic.
A visual image, such as a bar chart or pie chart, that is used to present data in a highly meaningful form. (317)

Presentation graphics software.
A program package used to prepare line charts, bar charts, pie charts, and other information-intensive images. (323)

Primary storage.
Also known as *memory* and *internal storage*, a section of the computer system that temporarily holds data and program instructions awaiting processing, intermediate results, and output produced from processing. (10)

Printer.
A device that places computer output onto paper. (139)

Privacy.
In a computer processing context, refers to how information about individuals is used and by whom. (494)

Private branch exchange (PBX).
A call-switching station that an organization acquires for its own use. (201)

Private wide area network.
A wide area network that is built by an organization for its own use. (197)

Processing.
See Information processing. (7)

Productivity software.
Program packages—such as word processors, spreadsheets, presentation-graphics packages, and database management systems—designed to make workers more productive at their jobs. (48)

Program.
A set of instructions that causes the computer system to perform specific actions. (8)

Program flowchart.
A visual design tool showing step by step how a computer program will process data. (416)

Programmer.
A person whose job is to write, maintain, and test computer programs. (13, 415)

Programming language.
A set of rules used to write computer programs. (9, 425)

Project manager.
(a) A systems analyst who is put in charge of a team that is building a large system. (b) A software package that is used to manage projects. (386)

Prolog.
A language widely used for artificial intelligence applications. *(434)*

Proportional spacing.
A printing feature that allocates more horizontal space on a line to some characters than to others. (269)

Protocol.
A set of conventions used by machines to establish communication with one another in a telecommunications environment. (205)

Prototyping.
A systems development alternative whereby a small model, or *prototype,* of the system is built before a full-scale systems development effort is undertaken. (397)

Pseudocode.
A technique for structured program design that uses Englishlike statements to outline the logic of a program. Pseudocode statements closely resemble actual programming code. (421)

Public access network.
A network, such as the phone system, that is designed to be used by the general public. (195)

Quality assurance.
The process of making sure quality programs are written in a quality way. (440)

Queue.
A group of items awaiting computer processing. *(244)*

RAM.
See Random access memory. (80)

RAM disk.
A disk management system in which a portion of RAM is set up to function as disk. (108)

Random access.
See Direct access. (95)

Random access memory (RAM).
The computer system's primary storage. (80)

Range.
In spreadsheets, a set of contiguous cells. (303)

Read-only memory (ROM).
A software-in-hardware module that can be read but not written on. (81)

Read/write head.
A magnetic station on a disk access mechanism or tape unit that reads or writes data. (94)

Realtime processing.
Updating data immediately in a master file as transactions take place. Contrasts with batch processing. (54)

Recalculation feature.
The ability of spreadsheet software to quickly and automatically recalculate the contents of several cells based on new operator inputs. (302)

Record.
A collection of related fields. (46)

Redlining.
A word processing facility that provides the electronic equivalent of the editor's red pen. (274)

Reduced instruction set computing (RISC).
A term referring to a computer system that gets by with a fewer number of instructions than conventional computer systems, thereby reducing system overhead and, in many cases, decreasing the time needed to process programs. (86)

Register.
A high-speed staging area within the computer that temporarily stores data during processing. (68)

Relational database management system.
A database management system that supports relational databases—that is, databases in which data records are placed into files and the files can be interrelated by common fields (columns). (332)

Relative replication.
In spreadsheets, copying formulas in a source range of cells into a target range of cells relative to the row and column coordinates of the cells in the target range. (310)

Release.
A minor upgrade of a software product. (473)

Report Program Generator (RPG).
A report-generation language popular with small businesses. *(433)*

Request for proposal (RFP).
A document containing a general description of a system that an organization wishes to acquire. The RFP is submitted to vendors, who subsequently recommend specific systems based on the resources they are able to supply. (394)

Request for quotation (RFQ).
A document containing a list of specific hardware, software, and services that an organization wishes to acquire. The RFQ is submitted to vendors, who subsequently prepare bids based on the resources they are able to supply. (394)

Resolution.
A term referring to the sharpness of the images on an output medium. *(135)*

Retrieval/update language.
A fourth-generation language specifically tailored to information retrieval and updating operations. *(334)*

Reusable code.
Program segments that can be reused several times in constructing applications programs. (438)

RFP.
See Request for proposal. (394)

RFQ.
See Request for quotation. (394)

Ring network.
A telecommunications network in which machines are connected serially in a closed loop. (204)

RISC.
See Reduced instruction set computing. (86)

Robotics.
The field devoted to the study of robot technology. (383)

ROM.
See Read-only memory. (81)

RPG.
See Report Program Generator. (433)

Screen saver.
A software product designed to protect the phosphor coating on the inside of a display screen from damage when the display is turned on but is not used for an extended period. (468)

Secondary storage.
Storage, provided by technologies such as disk and tape, that supplements memory. Also called *external storage.* (11)

Secondary storage device.
A machine, such as a tape unit or disk unit, capable of providing storage to supplement memory. (42)

Sector.
A pie-shaped area on a disk. Many disks are addressed through sectors. (98)

Selection.
The process of going through a set of data and picking out only those data elements that meet certain criteria. (52)

Selection (if-then-else) control structure.
The control structure used to represent a decision operation. (421)

Sequence control structure.
The control structure used to represent operations that take place sequentially. (421)

Sequential access.
Fetching records in storage ascendingly or descendingly by the key field on which they are physically ordered. (95)

Sequential organization.
Arranging data on a physical medium either ascendingly or descendingly by some key field. (118)

Serial transmission.
Data transmission in which every bit in a byte must travel down the same path in succession. Contrasts with parallel transmission. (193)

Server.
A computer that manages shared devices, such as laser printers or high-capacity hard disks, on a local area network (LAN). (198)

Simplex transmission.
Any type of transmission in which a message can be sent along a path in only a single prespecified direction. (190)

Simulation.
A technique whereby a model of a real-life object or situation is built and tested prior to constructing the object or encountering the situation. *(508)*

Site license.
A right purchased by an organization that enables employees to freely use or copy software for specific, authorized purposes. (493)

Smalltalk.
An object-oriented programming language. *(433)*

Smart card.
A credit-card-sized piece of plastic that contains a microprocessor and storage. (158)

Soft copy.
A nonpermanent form of usable output—for example, display output. Contrasts with hard copy. (130)

Soft return.
In word processing, an automatic line return carried out by the software when a typed word exceeds the rightmost margin. Contrasts with hard return. (261)

Software.
Computer programs. (12)

Software piracy.
The unauthorized copying or use of computer programs. (491)

Software suite.
A set of compatible, full-featured software packages sold at a price less than the sum of the component packages. *(297)*

Solid-font mechanism.
The printing element on a printer, such as a daisywheel printer, that produces solid characters. Contrasts with dot-matrix mechanism. (139)

Sorting.
The process of arranging data in a specified order. (52)

Source-data automation.
Making data available in machine-readable form at the time they are collected. (146)

Source module.
The original form in which a program is entered into an input device by a user or programmer prior to its being translated into machine language. Also called a *source program.* (239)

Spelling checker.
A program often used adjunctively with a word processor to check for misspelled words. (269)

Spooling program.
A program that temporarily stores input or output in secondary storage to expedite processing. (243)

SQL.
See Structured Query Language. (338)

Star network.
A network consisting of a host device connected directly to several other devices. (203)

Storage.
Pertains to areas that hold programs and data in machine-readable form. (7)

Storage register.
A register that temporarily stores data that have been retrieved from memory prior to processing. (70)

Streaming tape.
A cartridge tape used exclusively for backup purposes. *(112)*

Structure chart.
A program design tool that shows the hierarchical relationship among program modules. A structure chart closely resembles the common organization chart. (424)

Structured programming.
An approach to program design that uses a restricted set of program control structures, the principles of top-down design, and numerous other design methodologies. (421)

Structured Query Language (SQL).
A popular language standard for information retrieval in relational databases. (338)

Style sheet.
A collection of font and formatting specifications that can be saved as a file and later used to format documents in a particular way. (275)

Summarizing.
The process of reducing a mass of data to a manageable form. (52)

Supercomputer.
The fastest type of computer. Typically, supercomputers are found in engineering or scientific research environments. (20)

Supervisor.
The central program in an operating system. The supervisor has the ability to invoke other operating system programs to perform various system tasks. (221)

Surge suppressor.
A device that protects a computer system from random electrical power spikes. (467)

Synchronous transmission.
The transmission of data over a line, one block of characters at a time. Contrasts with asynchronous transmission. (195)

System.
A collection of elements and procedures that interact to accomplish a goal. (368)

System acquisition.
The phase of the systems development life cycle in which equipment, software, or services are acquired from vendors. (394)

System board.
A board that contains the computer. Sometimes called a *motherboard.* (77)

System clock.
The timing mechanism within the computer that governs the transmission of instructions and data through the circuitry. (70)

System design.
The phase of the systems development life cycle in which the parts of a new system and the relationships among them are formally established. (390)

System implementation.
The phase of systems development that encompasses activities related to making the computer system operational and successful once delivered by the vendor. (395)

System unit.
The hardware unit that houses the computer and its memory, as well as a number of other devices, such as add-in boards and related circuitry. (40, 77)

Systems analysis.
The phase of the systems development life cycle in which a problem area is thoroughly examined to determine what should be done. (389)

Systems analyst.
A person who studies systems in an organization to determine what actions need to be taken and how these actions may best be achieved with computer resources. (385, 415)

Systems development.
The process of studying a problem or opportunity area, designing a system solution for it, acquiring the resources necessary to support the solution, and implementing the solution. (368)

Systems development life cycle (SDLC).
The process consisting of the five phases of system development: preliminary investigation, systems analysis, system design, system acquisition, and system implementation. (388)

Systems software.
Computer programs, such as the operating system, language translators, and utility programs, that enable application programs to run on a given set of hardware. Contrasts with applications software. (48, 218)

Tape unit.
A secondary storage device on which magnetic tapes are mounted. (113)

Technologically obsolete.
Refers to a product that, although superseded by a newer version or release, still meets the needs of an individual or business. (473)

Telecommunications.
A term that refers to transmitting data over a distance—over the phone lines, via privately owned cable, or by satellite, for instance. (178)

Telecommuting.
The substitution of working at home, and being connected through electronic devices to other workers at remote locations, for the commute to work. (378)

Teleconferencing.
Using computer and communications technology to carry out a meeting in which the participants need not all be present at the same site. (377)

Template.
A prelabeled onscreen form that requires only that the operator fill in a limited number of input values. (335)

Terabyte.
Approximately 1 trillion bytes. (75)

Terminal.
Technically speaking, any device that is not a host device. *(43)*

Terrestrial microwave station.
A ground station that receives microwave signals, amplifies them, and passes them on. (187)

Thesaurus feature.
A routine, often accompanying a word processor, that enables electronic lookup of word synonyms. (270)

Time-sharing.
Interactive processing in which the computer is shared by several users at more or less the same time. The computer system interleaves the processing of the programs so that it appears to each user that he or she has exclusive use of the computer. (226)

Top-down design.
A structured design philosophy whereby a program or system is subdivided into well-defined modules, organized in a hierarchy, which are developed from the top of the hierarchy down to the lowest level. (425)

Touch-screen device.
A display device that can be activated by touching a finger to the screen. (155)

Track.
A path on an input/output medium on which data are recorded. (97)

Trackball.
A cursor-movement device that consists of a sphere, with only the top of the sphere exposed outside its case. (153)

Traditional approach.
An approach to systems development whereby the five phases of the systems development life cycle are carried out in a predetermined sequence. (396)

Transaction file.
A file of occurrences, such as customer payments and purchases, that have taken place over a period of time. (47)

Transaction processing system.
A system that processes an organization's business transactions. Operations falling into the transaction processing category include payroll, order entry, accounts receivable, accounts payable, inventory, and general ledger. (370)

Twisted-pair wires.
A communications medium consisting of pairs of wires twisted together and bound into a cable. The public-access telephone system consists mainly of twisted-wire cabling. (186)

Typeface.
A collection of printed characters that share a common design. (265)

UNIX.
A multiuser, multitasking operating system. (232)

Universal product code (UPC).
The bar code that is prominently displayed on the packaging of almost all supermarket goods, identifying the product and manufacturer. A variety of optical scanning devices may be used to read the codes. *(150)*

UPC.
See Universal product code. *(150)*

Updating.
The process of bringing something up to date by making corrections, adding new data, and so forth. (53)

Upgrading.
The process of buying new hardware or software to extend the life of a computer system. Contrasts with replacement. (471)

Uploading.
The process of sending data from a small computer system to a larger computer system for storage or processing purposes. Contrasts with downloading. (202)

Utility program.
A program used to perform some frequently encountered operation in a computer system. (241)

Value.
In spreadsheet programs, a cell entry that can be manipulated mathematically. Contrasts with label. (301)

Value-added network (VAN).
A term that most commonly refers to a service offered over the public-access phone network by a firm other than the phone company, thereby adding value to the network. (195)

VAN.
See Value-added network. (195)

Vaporware.
Software that exists more in people's imaginations than in actuality. (499)

Vendor rating system.
An objective point-scoring procedure for evaluating competing vendors of computer products or services. (394)

Version.
A major upgrade of a software product. (473)

Very-high-level language.
A problem-specific language that is generally much easier to learn and use than conventional high-level languages such as BASIC, FORTRAN, COBOL, and Pascal. *(434)*

Virtual memory.
An area on disk in which programs are "cut up" into manageable pieces and staged as they are processed. While the computer is processing a program, it fetches the pieces that are needed from virtual memory and places them into conventional memory. (227)

Voice-grade transmission.
Medium-speed transmission characterized by the rates of speed available over ordinary telephone lines. (190)

Voice-input device.
A device capable of recognizing the human voice. (157)

Voice mail.
An electronic mail system in which spoken phone messages are digitally recorded and stored in an electronic mailbox. (181)

Voice-output device.
A device that enables the computer system to produce spoken output. (160)

Volatile storage.
Storage that loses its contents when the power is shut off. Contrasts with nonvolatile storage. (94)

WAN.
See Wide area network. (195)

Warranty.
A conditional pledge made by a manufacturer to protect the consumer from losses due to defective units of a product. (470)

What-if analysis.
An approach to problem solving in which the decision maker repeatedly commands the computer system to recalculate a set of figures based on alternative inputs. (302)

Wide area network (WAN).
A network that covers a wide geographical area. (195)

Wideband transmission.
High-speed transmission characterized by the rates of speed available over coaxial cable, fiber optic cable, and microwave. (190)

Widow.
The last line of a paragraph when it is separated from the rest of the paragraph by a page or column break. (274)

Winchester disk.
A sealed data module that contains a disk, access arms, and read/write heads. *(101)*

Window.
Refers to either (1) using the display screen as a "peek hole" to inspect contiguous portions of a large worksheet or (2) a box of information overlaid on a screen display. (230, 255)

Window area.
In spreadsheet software, the portion of the screen that contains the window onto the worksheet. Also called the *worksheet area.* (300)

Windows.
A graphical operating environment created by Microsoft Corporation. (229)

Windows NT.
A multitasking, multiprocessing operating system designed by Microsoft Corporation for 32-bit microcomputers. (235)

Word.
A group of bits or characters that are treated by the computer system as a unit. (80)

Word processing.
The use of computer technology to create, manipulate, and print text material such as letters, legal contracts, and manuscripts. (260)

Wordwrap.
In word processing, the feature that automatically produces soft returns. (261)

Workgroup computing.
A computer application in which a group of workers interdependently use the same set of software and data on a network. (373)

Worksheet.
In spreadsheet software, the grid that contains the actual labels and values. (297)

Worksheet area.
See Window area. (300)

WYSIWYG.
An acronym for "What You See Is What You Get," WYSIWYG shows on the display screen an output image identical or very close to the desired, final hard-copy image. (266)

ANSWERS TO FILL-IN AND MATCHING REVIEW EXERCISES

Chapter 1

Fill-in Questions

1. processing
2. primary or internal
3. information
4. software
5. secondary or external
6. hardware
7. program
8. computer system

Matching Questions

1. e 2. f 3. a 4. c
5. b 6. d

Chapter 2

Fill-in Questions

1. input/output medium
2. master
3. online
4. Applications
5. Systems
6. field
7. Batch
8. realtime

Matching Questions

1. b 2. f 3. c 4. e
5. a 6. d

Chapter 3

Fill-in Questions

1. accumulator
2. thousandth
3. terabyte
4. read-only memory
5. parity
6. reduced instruction set computing
7. parallel

Matching Questions

1. b 2. d 3. g 4. e
5. h 6. a 7. f 8. c

Chapter 4

Fill-in Questions

1. volatile
2. disk pack
3. cylinder
4. optical
5. small computer system interface
6. tracks
7. hashing
8. write once read many

Matching Questions

1. d 2. a 3. c 4. f
5. e 6. b

Chapter 5

Fill-in Questions

1. hard copy
2. pixels
3. cursor
4. monochrome
5. near-letter-quality
6. thermal-transfer
7. ink-jet
8. flatbed, drum
9. bit-mapped
10. film recorder

Matching Questions

1. e 2. f 3. g 4. b
5. d 6. a 7. h 8. c

Chapter 6

Fill-in Questions

1. Electronic data interchange
2. facsimile (fax)
3. Coaxial cable
4. digital
5. Fiber optic cable
6. modem
7. Synchronous
8. Common carriers
9. Asynchronous
10. star

Matching Questions

1. d 2. e 3. b 4. a
5. f 6. c

Chapter 7

Fill-in Questions

1. Systems
2. operating system
3. multiprogramming
4. Time-sharing
5. Multiprocessing
6. NetWare
7. language translator
8. Utility

Matching Questions

1. e 2. d 3. a 4. c
5. f 6. b

Chapter 8

Fill-in Questions

1. wordwrap
2. Proportional spacing
3. mailing list
4. dedicated
5. what you see is what you get
6. orphan
7. page-description language
8. clip art

Matching Questions

1. e 2. b 3. a 4. f
5. c 6. d

Chapter 9

Fill-in Questions

1. window, worksheet
2. cursor, cell pointer (highlight)
3. control panel
4. absolute, relative, mixed

5. template
6. macro
7. Multidimensional
8. dedicated, integrated

Matching Questions

1. d 2. f 3. e 4. a
5. c 6. b

Chapter 10

Fill-in Questions

1. fields
2. template
3. database
4. Relational
5. database administrator
6. dictionary
7. Structured Query Language
8. multimedia

Matching Questions

1. b 2. e 3. a 4. d
5. f 6. c

Chapter 11

Fill-in Questions

1. accounts receivable
2. computer-aided design
3. artificial intelligence
4. robotics
5. steering
6. End-user development
7. tangible
8. benchmark test

Matching Questions

1. c 2. a 3. f 4. e
5. d 6. b

Chapter 12

Fill-in Questions

1. Systems analysts
2. Coding
3. debugging
4. flowchart
5. Pseudocode
6. COBOL
7. fourth-generation
8. reusable code

Matching Questions

1. h 2. c 3. e 4. b
5. f 6. g 7. d 8. a

Chapter 13

Fill-in Questions

1. IBM-compatible
2. upgradeable
3. release
4. functionality
5. Backup
6. surge suppressor
7. warranty
8. functionally

Matching Questions

1. f 2. a 3. g 4. d
5. c 6. h 7. e 8. b

Chapter 14

Fill-in Questions

1. cyberphobia
2. Ergonomics
3. Ethics
4. piracy
5. Fair Credit Reporting
6. Caller identification

Matching Questions

1. c 2. f 3. a 4. e
5. b 6. d

Appendix A

1. a. 11
   b. 46
   c. 83
2. a. 110011
   b. 100000100
   c. 111110100
3. a. 5
   b. 1A
   c. F42
4. a. 11110010
   b. 000110101001
   c. 0011100111101011
5. a. 182
   b. 1513
   c. 51967
6. $(4 \times 6^2) + (5 \times 6^1)$
   $+ (1 \times 6^0) = 175$
7. 100110110
8. EB
9. 100011
10. 3C

CREDITS

Module A opening photo © 1991 Karl Sims, Thinking Machines Corp.

Chapter 1 opening photo Courtesy of International Business Machines Corporation.

Figure 1–1A Courtesy of International Business Machines Corporation.

Figure 1–1B Courtesy of GRID Systems.

Figure 1–1C Courtesy of International Business Machines Corporation.

Figure 1–3 WordPerfect v.5.1 package shots reprinted under authorization from WordPerfect Corporation. All rights reserved.

Figure 1–4A Courtesy of International Business Machines Corporation.

Figure 1–4B Courtesy of Compaq Computers.

Figure 1–4C Courtesy of Sharp Electronics Corp.

Figure 1–5, 1–6 Courtesy of International Business Machines Corporation.

Figure 1–7 Photo by Paul Shambroom, Courtesy of Cray Research, Inc.

User Solution 1–1 Reprinted with permission of Compaq Computer Corporation. All rights reserved.

Feature 1–1 Courtesy of International Business Machines Corporation.

Feature 1–2 Courtesy of Apple Computers, Inc. Photo by Dave Martinez.

User Solution 1–2 Created using the Arts & Letters Graphics Editor by Computer Support Corp.

Tomorrow Box 1A Courtesy of Apple Computers, Inc. Photo by John Greenleigh.

Tomorrow Box 1B Courtesy of Skytel.

Window 1–1 Courtesy Time Arts Inc.

Window 1–2 Courtesy of International Business Machines Corporation.

Window 1–3 Courtesy of Compaq Computers.

Window 1–4 Photo courtesy of Hewlett-Packard Company.

Window 1–5 Courtesy of International Business Machines Corporation.

Window 1–6 Courtesy of W. Industries and Rock, Kitchen, Harris, Leicester, England.

Window 1–7, 1–8, 1–9 © 1989 Lucasfilm Ltd. Paramount Pictures Inc. All rights reserved. Courtesy of Industrial Light & Magic.

Window 1–10 Created by Marialine Prieur of Voire (Lyon, France) using TDI software.

Window 1–11 Image courtesy MK-Ferguson Company. "Brew Master" image of complex piping assembly. Rendered with ModelView.

Window 1–12 Courtesy of Package Design of America.

Window 1–13 Created by Renault (Paris, France) using TDI software.

Window 1–14 Pixar/Colossal Pictures 1991.

Window 1–15 Courtesy of Pixar.

Window 1–16 Perry Woodworth, created with CorelDraw. Courtesy of Corel Corp.

Window 1–17, 1–18, 1–19 Courtesy of International Business Machines Corporation.

Window 1–20, 1–21 Courtesy of Evans & Sutherland Computer Corporation.

Window 1–22 Images by Richard Podolsky using GAIA Software on a Macintosh Computer.

Window 1–23 Courtesy of Rockwell International/ David Perry.

Window 1–24 Courtesy of International Business Machines Corporation.

Window 1–25 Courtesy of Ford Motor Company.

Chapter 2 opening photo Image courtesy of Colgate-Palmolive, J. Crawford, "Irish Spring Deodorant."

Figure 2–1 Images supplied by Logitech, Inc.

Figure 2–2A Courtesy of NEC Technologies, Inc.

Figure 2–2B Photo courtesy of Hewlett-Packard Company.

Figure 2–3A Courtesy of International Business Machines Corporation.

Figure 2–3B Photo courtesy of Hewlett-Packard Company.

Figure 2–3C Courtesy of International Business Machines Corporation.

Figure 2–3D Courtesy of Iomega Corp.

Figure 2–4A Courtesy of Nashua Computer Products.

Figure 2–4B Photo courtesy of Memory Media Products.

Figure 2–9A Photo courtesy of American Airlines.

Figure 2–9B, 2–11 Courtesy of International Business Machines Corporation.

User Solution 2–1 Courtesy of Pier I Imports.

User Solution 2–2 Photograph courtesy of Norand Corporation, Cedar Rapids, Iowa.

Tomorrow Box 2 "The Lawnmower Man" image courtesy Allied Vision Lane Pringle Productions, © 1992. CyberJobe animation by Angel Studios, California.

Module B opening photo © 1991 Karl Sims, Thinking Machines Corp.

Chapter 3 opening photo Courtesy of AT&T Archives.

Figure 3–8A, 3–8B Courtesy Intel Corporation.

Figure 3–9 Courtesy of Motorola.

User Solution 3–1 Courtesy of Nimrod International Sales, Inc.

Feature 3–1 Courtesy Intel Corporation.

Tomorrow Box 3 Courtesy of International Business Machines Corporation.

Feature 3–2 Courtesy Intel Corporation.

Chapter 4 opening photo Courtesy of International Business Machines Corporation.

Figure 4–2 Courtesy of Maxell Corporation of America.

Figure 4–11 Photo courtesy of Iomega Corporation.

Figure 4–12 Photo courtesy of Iomega Corporation.

Figure 4–13A Courtesy of International Business Machines Corporation.

Figure 4–13B Photo courtesy of BASF.

Figure 4–14 Courtesy of International Business Machines Corporation.

Figure 4–15 Courtesy of StorageTek.

Figure 4–16 Photo courtesy of Memory Media Products.

Figure 4–17 Courtesy of Everex.

Figure 4–18 Photo courtesy of BASF.

Figure 4–20A Courtesy of International Business Machines Corporation.

Figure 4–20B Courtesy of Pioneer Communications of America.

Figure 4–21A Courtesy of International Business Machines Corporation.

Figure 4–21B Maps from DeLorme Street Atlas USA™, Freeport, Maine.

User Solution 4–1 Courtesy of James Dowlen Artworks.

User Solution 4–2 Courtesy of Whirlpool Corporation.

Tomorrow Box 4 Courtesy of PhotoDisc, Inc.

Chapter 5 opening photo Images supplied by Logitech, Inc.

Figure 5–2A Courtesy of International Business Machines Corporation.

Figure 5–2B Courtesy of Compaq Computers.

Figure 5–2C Reprinted with permission of Compaq Computer Corporation. All rights reserved.

Figure 5–4A Courtesy Autodesk, Inc.

Figure 5–4B Screen captures from Harvard Graphics®, including text material, are used with the permission of Software Publishing Corporation, which owns the copyright to such product. Harvard Graphics® is a registered trademark of Software Publishing Corporation. The Harvard Graphics® program is a product of Software Publishing Corporation and has no connection with Harvard University. Windows is a trademark of Microsoft Corporation.

Figure 5–4C Courtesy of Cornerstone Technology 1993.

Figure 5–5A, 5–5B Reprinted from PC Computing, October 1991. Copyright © 1991, Ziff Communications Company.

Figure 5–7 Courtesy of Dataproducts Corporation.

Figure 5–10 Courtesy of OKIDATA, Microline® 320.

Figure 5–11A Courtesy of Citizen America Corporation.

Figure 5–11B Courtesy of Seiko Instruments USA.

Figure 5–12A Photo courtesy of Hewlett-Packard Company.

Figure 5–14, 5–15 Courtesy of International Business Machines Corporation.

Figure 5–19A Photo courtesy of NCR Corp.

Figure 5–19B Courtesy of International Business Machines Corporation.

Figure 5–19C Photo courtesy of Intermec Corporation.

Figure 5–20A Courtesy of International Business Machines Corporation.

Figure 5–20B Images supplied by Logitech, Inc.

Figure 5–21A Charles S. Parker.

Figure 5–21B Courtesy of International Business Machines Corporation.

Figure 5–23A Photo courtesy of Hewlett-Packard Company.

Figure 5–23B Courtesy of International Business Machines Corporation.

Figure 5–24A, 5–24B Images supplied by Logitech, Inc.

Figure 5–24C Courtesy of CalComp.

Figure 5–25 Courtesy of Toshiba America.

Figure 5–26A Courtesy of Summagraphics Corporation.

Figure 5–26B Courtesy of CalComp.

User Solution 5–1 Courtesy of In-Flight Phone Corporation.

Tomorrow Box 5A Courtesy of International Business Machines Corporation.

Tomorrow Box 5B Courtesy of VideOcart, Inc.

Feature 5–1 Courtesy of GRID Systems.

User Solution 5–2 Courtesy of US Postal Service, Oklahoma City, OK.

Window 2–1 Courtesy of Time Arts, Inc.

Window 2–2 Courtesy of Computer Associates ®

Window 2–3 Courtesy of AXA Corporation.

Window 2–4 Courtesy of Computer Associates ®

Window 2–5 Courtesy of Quantel USA.

Window 2–6 Jody Vergil, created with CorelDraw. Courtesy of Corel Corp.

Window 2–7, 2–8 Steve Arscott, created with CorelDraw. Courtesy of Corel Corp.

Window 2–9, 2–10, 2–11 Courtesy of Clifford Pickover, *Mazes for the Mind* (St. Martin's Press, NY, 1992).

Window 2–12, 2–13, 2–14 © 1991 Karl Sims, Thinking Machines Corp.

Window 2–15, 2–16 Jon Watson, Strata Vision 3d. Courtesy of Strata, Inc.

Window 2–17 © 1989 ARC—All rights reserved. Courtesy of Pixar.

Window 2–18 Courtesy of Light Source Computer Images, Inc.

Window 2–19 "Happy Holidays" by Juliette Beckstrand, courtesy of Wasatch Computer Technology.

Window 2–20 Steve Green, created with CorelDraw. Courtesy of Corel Corp.

Window 2–21 Eric Lindstrom, created with CorelDraw. Courtesy of Corel Corp.

Window 2–22, 2–23 Courtesy of Time Arts, Inc.

Module C opening photo M. Tolson of XAOS-Computer Animation and Design. Courtesy of Silicon Graphics.

Chapter 6 opening photo Courtesy of McCaw Cellular Communications, Inc.

Figure 6–2 Courtesy of International Business Machines Corporation.

Figure 6–3 Screen shot 1992 Lotus Development Corporation. Used with permission of Lotus Development Corporation. cc: Mail is a trademark of Lotus Development Corporation.

Figure 6–5A, B, C, D, E, F Courtesy of Prodigy Services Company.

Figure 6–6 Courtesy of McCaw Cellular Communications, Inc.

Figure 6–8 Courtesy of Corning Incorporated.

Figure 6–9 Courtesy of Harris Corporation.

User Solution 6–1 Reprinted with permission of Compaq Computer Corporation. All rights reserved.

Tomorrow Box 6 Courtesy of Panasonic Co.

User Solution 6–2 Reprinted with permission of Compaq Computer Corporation. All rights reserved.

Feature 6–2 Photo courtesy of Intermec Corporation.

Window 3 (all) Courtesy of Prodigy Services Company.

Chapter 7 opening photo Reprinted with permission from Microsoft Corporation.

Figure 7–4 Courtesy of Microsoft, Inc.

Figure 7–6 Courtesy of Hauppauge Computer Works, Inc.

Figure 7–7, 7–8 Courtesy of Apple Computer, Inc. Photographers: Will Mosgrove and John Greenleigh.

Figure 7–9 Courtesy of International Business Machines Corporation.

Figure 7–14 Courtesy of Symantec Corporation.

Tomorrow Box 7 Courtesy of Intel Corporation.

Feature 7–1 © Robbie McLaran/Outline.

User Solution 7–1 © 1985 Jeff Smith.

User Solution 7–2 Photo courtesy of Fidelity Investments.

Feature 7–2 Screen shot 1992 Lotus Development Corporation. Used with permission of Lotus Development Corporation. Lotus Magellan is a registered trademark of Lotus Development Corporation.

Window 4–1 Screen shot 1992 Lotus Development Corporation. Used with permission of Lotus Development Corporation. Lotus Notes is a trademark of Lotus Development Corporation.

Window 4–2, 4–3 Courtesy of International Business Machines Corporation.

Window 4–4 Screen shot 1994 Lotus Development Corporation. Used with permission of Lotus Development Corporation. WordPerfect is a registered trademark of Lotus Development Corporation.

Window 4–5 Courtesy of Fifth Generation Systems, Inc.

Window 4–8 Courtesy of International Business Machines Corporation.

Module D opening photo © 1991 Karl Sims, Thinking Machines Corp.

Chapter 8 opening photo Courtesy of International Business Machines Corporation.

Figure 8–5, 8–9 © Adobe Systems Incorporated. All rights reserved.

Figure 8–8A Courtesy of WordPerfect Corp.

Figure 8–8B Courtesy of Microsoft, Inc.

Figure 8–13 Reprinted with permission from Microsoft Corporation.

Figure 8–15 © 1991 Adobe Systems Incorporated. This illustration was produced using the Adobe Photoshop and Adobe Illustrator™ software programs. All rights reserved.

Figure 8–17 Courtesy of Cornerstone Technology.

Figure 8–18 Aldus Pagemaker 4.2 © Aldus Corporation 1992. Used with the express permission of Aldus Corporation. Aldus, PageMaker and FreeHand are registered trademarks of Aldus Corporation. All rights reserved.

Figure 8–20 Courtesy of Gold Disk, Inc.

Figure 8–21 Courtesy of Fractal Design.

Tomorrow Box 8 Screen shot 1992 Lotus Development Corporation. Used with permission of Lotus Development Corporation. Ami Pro is a trademark of Lotus Development Corporation.

Window 5–1 Aldus PageMaker 4.2 © Aldus Corporation 1992. Used with the express permission of Aldus Corporation. Aldus, PageMaker and FreeHand are registered trademarks of Aldus Corporation. All rights reserved.

Window 5–3, 5–4 Aldus Guide to Basic Design © Aldus Corporation 1988. Used with the express permission of Aldus Corporation. Aldus, PageMaker and FreeHand are registered trademarks of Aldus Corporation. All rights reserved.

Window 5–5 © Adobe Systems Incorporated. All rights reserved.

Window 5–6 © 1991 Adobe Systems Incorporated. All rights reserved.

Window 5–7 © Adobe Systems Incorporated. All rights reserved. This illustration was produced using the Adobe Smart Art™ software program.

Window 5–9 Courtesy of Computer Associates.®

Window 5–10 Courtesy of Quantel U.S.A.

Window 5–11, 5–12 Courtesy of Computer Associates.®

Window 5–13, 5–14 Courtesy of Micrografx.

Window 5–15 EdPage, editorial pagination product of Atex Publishing Systems Corporation, Bedford, MA.

Chapter 9 opening photo Quattro Pro is a registered trademark of Borland International, Inc.

Figure 9–12A Screen shot 1992 Lotus Development Corporation. Used with permission of Lotus Development Corporation. Lotus and 1-2-3 are registered trademarks of Lotus Development Corporation.

Figure 9–12B Quattro Pro for Windows is a registered trademark of Borland International, Inc.

Figure 9–12C Reprinted with permission from Microsoft Corporation.

Figure 9–16A, 9–16B Photo © 1994 Lotus Development Corporation. Used with permission of Lotus Development Corporation. Improv is a registered trademark of Lotus Development Corporation.

Figure 9–21 Courtesy of Claris Corporation.

Feature 9–1A Reprinted with permission from Microsoft Corporation.

Feature 9–1B Photo © 1994 Lotus Development Corporation. Used with permission of Lotus Development Corporation. Lotus SmartSuite is a registered trademark of Lotus Development Corporation.

User Solution 9–1 Courtesy of Old Town Builders.

User Solution 9–2 Robert Fletcher, created with CorelDraw. Courtesy of Corel Corp.

Tomorrow Box 9 Quattro Pro is a registered trademark of Borland International, Inc.

Chapter 10 opening photo Reprinted by permission of Gupta Technologies, Inc.

Figure 10–6A Courtesy of Sybase, Inc.

Figure 10–6B Paradox 5.0 is a registered trademark of Borland International, Inc.

Figure 10–6C Courtesy of Icons International.

Figure 10–7 Reprinted by permission of Gupta Technologies, Inc.

Figure 10–8 Paradox 5.0 is a registered trademark of Borland International, Inc.

Figure 10–10 Courtesy of Rensselaer Polytechnic Institute.

Figure 10–11A Courtesy of International Business Machines Corporation.

Figure 10–11B Courtesy of Toshiba, Inc.

Feature 10–1A Courtesy of International Business Machines Corporation.

Feature 10–1B Courtesy of Tactics International, Limited.

Tomorrow Box 10 Courtesy of International Business Machines Corporation.

User Solution 10–1A, 10–1B, 10–1C Multimedia Presentation by Cimarron International.

Window 6–1 Courtesy of International Business Machines Corporation.

Window 6–2 Courtesy of Matrox.

Window 6–3, 6–4, 6–5 Permission granted by Macromedia, 1992.

Window 6–6 through 6–9 Image is copyright of Ben & Jerry's Homemade Ice Cream, Inc., 1992.

Window 6–10 through 6–13 Courtesy of Warner New Media.

Window 6–14, 6–15 Courtesy of Verbum Journal of Personal Computer Aesthetics.

Window 6–16 Courtesy of International Business Machines Corporation.

Window 6–17, 6–18, 6–19 Reprinted with permission from Microsoft Corporation.

Window 6–20, 6–21, 6–22 Courtesy of Owl International.

Window 6–23 Permission granted by Macromedia, 1992.

Module E opening photo Clifford A. Pickover, *Mazes for the Mind* (St. Martin's Press, NY, 1992).

Chapter 11 opening photo Courtesy of International Business Machines Corporation.

Figure 11–1A, 11–1B, 11–3 Courtesy of International Business Machines Corporation.

Figure 11–4A, 11–4B Courtesy of Comshare, Inc.

Figure 11–5 Screen shot 1992 Lotus Development Corporation. Used with permission of Lotus Development Corporation. Lotus Organizer is a trademark of Lotus Development Corporation.

Figure 11–6A Photo courtesy of Hewlett-Packard Company.

Figure 11–6B Courtesy of TEL Corp.

Figure 11–7 DeskTop Conferencing screen image provided by Fujitsu Networks Industry, Inc. USA.

Figure 11–8A Courtesy of Intergraph Corporation. ModelView Viewfinders Menu with wire frame microstation model and solid I/EMS Model.

Figure 11–8B Courtesy of The Callison Partnership.

Figure 11–9A, 11–9B, 11–10, 11–16 Courtesy of International Business Machines Corporation.

Figure 11–13 Photo courtesy of EDS.

Figure 11–17 Courtesy of Claris Corporation.

User Solution 11–1A, 11–1B Courtesy of Wang Laboratories.

User Solution 11–2 Charles S. Parker

Tomorrow Box 11 Courtesy of International Business Machines Corporation.

Feature 11–1 Reprinted with permission of Compaq Computer Corporation. All rights reserved.

Feature 11–2 Photo courtesy of Hewlett-Packard Company.

Window 7–1 Courtesy of Pacific Data Images and J. Walter Thompson, NY.

Window 7–2, 7–3 Copyright © 1990, Pixar. All rights reserved. Rendered by Thomas Williams and H.B. Siegel using Pixar's PhotoRealistic RenderMan™ software.

Window 7–4 Courtesy of Electric Image, Inc.

Window 7–5 Courtesy of Matrox.

Window 7–6, 7–7, 7–8, 7–9 Courtesy of Pacific Data Images and McCann-Erickson (Houston).

Window 7–10, 7–11, 7–12, 7–13 Courtesy of Forensic Technologies International Corporation.

Window 7–14, 7–15, 7–16 Courtesy of Tactics International Limited.

Window 7–17, 7–18 Courtesy of Autodesk, Inc.

Window 7–19, 7–20 Copyright 1990 New World Graphics. Produced by Tom Welsh.

Window 7–21, 7–22 Courtesy of The Callison Partnership.

Window 7–23 Image courtesy of Kohn Pedersen Fox International.

Window 7–24 Courtesy of Pacific Data Images and ABC.

Window 7–25 Created by Ex Machina (Paris, France) using TDI Software. Courtesy of Cramblitt & Company.

Window 7–26, 7–27 Courtesy of Pacific Data Images and Quaker Oats Company.

Window 7–28, 7–29, 7–30 © 1990 Karl Sims, Thinking Machines Corp.

Chapter 12 opening photo Courtesy of Micro Focus.

Figure 12–11A, 12–11B Courtesy of Micro Focus.

Figure 12–16 Courtesy of Microsoft, Inc.

Figure 12–17 Courtesy Natural Language, Inc., Berkeley, California, Copyright, 1992.

Figure 12–18 Courtesy of Excel Software (515) 752–5359.

Tomorrow Box 12 Courtesy of American Programmer, Inc.

Feature 12–1 Borland C++ is a registered trademark of Borland International, Inc.

Feature 12–2 Photo courtesy of Hewlett-Packard Company.

User Solution 12–1 ObjectVision for Windows is a registered trademark of Borland International, Inc.

Chapter 13 opening photo Courtesy of Compaq Computers.

Figure 13–2 Photo courtesy of Egghead Software, North America's leading reseller of personal computer software.

Figure 13–3 MacConnection.

Figure 13–8 Courtesy of Curtis Manufacturing Co. Inc.

Figure 13–9 Courtesy of International Business Machines Corporation.

Figure 13–11 Courtesy of Dell Computers.

Tomorrow Box 13 Courtesy of International Business Machines Corporation.

Feature 13–1 Reprinted with permission from Microsoft Corporation.

Feature 13–2 Photo courtesy of Egghead Software, North America's leading reseller of personal software.

Feature 13–3 Courtesy of International Business Machines Corporation.

User Solution 13–1 Courtesy of Compaq Computers.

Module F opening photo Clifford A. Pickover, *Mazes for the Mind* (St. Martin's Press, NY, 1992).

Chapter 14 opening photo Courtesy of International Business Machines Corporation.

Figure 14–1 Courtesy of Kinesis Corporation.

Figure 14–6A, 14–6B Courtesy of International Business Machines Corporation.

Figure 14–7A Courtesy of U.S. Olympic Committee Photo Library.

Figure 14–7B Reprinted with permission of Compaq Computer Corporation. All rights reserved.

Figure 14–8A Courtesy of Time Arts, Inc.

Figure 14–8B Courtesy of Pacific Data Images and Bruce Dorn Films.

Figure 14–9A, 14–9B Courtesy of Truevision and the 1992 Truevision International Videographics Competition.

Figure 14–10A Aldus Photostyler 1.0 © Aldus Corporation 1991. Used with the express permission of Aldus Corporation. Aldus Photostyler are registered trademarks of Aldus Corporation. All rights reserved.

Figure 14–10B Courtesy of Electric Image, Inc.

Figure 14–11A, 14–11B Courtesy of International Business Machines Corporation.

Feature 14–1 Photo courtesy of Hewlett-Packard Company.

Feature 14–2 Courtesy of Datawatch Corporation.

Feature 14–3 Courtesy International Business Machines Corporation.

Window 8–1 Photo courtesy Prudential Insurance Company.

Window 8–2 through 8–5 Courtesy of International Business Machines Corporation.

Window 8–6 Courtesy Iowa State University.

Window 8–7 U.S. Army.

Window 8–8, 8–10, 8–11, 8–12 Courtesy of International Business Machines Corporation.

Window 8–13 Courtesy of AT&T Archives.

Window 8–14, 8–15 Courtesy of International Business Machines Corporation.

Window 8–16 Courtesy of U.S. Navy.

Window 8–17 Courtesy of International Business Machines Corporation.

Window 8–18, 8–19 Photos courtesy of Digital Equipment Corp.

Window 8–20 Photo courtesy of Wang Labs.

Window 8–21 Courtesy of International Business Machines Corporation.

Window 8–22 Photo courtesy of Texas Instruments.

Window 8–23 Intel Corporation

Window 8–24 Courtesy of Microsoft, Inc.

Window 8–25 Reprinted with permission from Microsoft Corporation.

Window 8–26, 8– 27 Courtesy of Apple Computer, Inc.

Window 8–28 Courtesy of Kapor Enterprises, Inc. © Seth Resnick.

Appendix A-4 Quarterdeck Office Systems is a leader in developing multitasking and memory management software that enhances the performance for DOS-based computers. Courtesy of Quarterdeck Office Systems.

INDEX

Page numbers in *italics* refer to illustrations, photos, and other figures.

ABC (Atanasoff-Berry Computer), *517*
Absolute replication, in spreadsheets, *311*, 313
Accelerator board, 82
Access, 95, 116
Access (Microsoft), 450
Access cards, 492
Access mechanism, *102*, 102–103
Access rights, 237
Accounting applications, 382
Accounts payable systems, 371, *372*
Accounts receivable systems, 371, *372*
Accumulator, 69, 70
Acquisition. *See* System acquisition
Action diagrams, *423*, 423
Active window, 254
Ada, 432
Add-in boards, 81, 82
Add-on packages, for word processing, 275–276
Address
  cell, 297
  definition of, 68
  disk, 96
Address register, 69–70
Adobe, 452
Adobe Illustrator, 285
Adobe Postscript, 280
Advanced Micro Devices (AMD), 451
AI. *See* Artificial intelligence (AI)
Aldus Freehand, 285
Aldus PageMaker, 279, *281*, 281, 282, *289*
Algorithmic art, 170–171
Altair 8800, 230, *523*
ALU. *See* Arithmetic/logic unit (ALU)
American Express, 385
America Online, 183, 195
Ami Pro, 260, 270, *271*, 298
Amoco Corporation, 342
Analog transmission, 190, *191*
Animation, *410–411*, *506*, 506
AntiToxin, 491
APL, 432
Apple Computer Corporation, 18, 297, 417
Apple computers, 15, *16*, 18, 80, 81–82, 83, 106, 137, 194, 223, 231, 241, 251, 450–452, 456, 458
Apple Core, 474
Apple-Holics, 474
Apple Newton, 19
Apple Pie, 474
Applications
  accounting, 382
  advertising, *35*, *405*, *410*
  airline industry, *53*
  architecture, *379*, *408–409*
  art, *31*, *35*, 167–173, *410–411*, 505–507, *506*, *508*, *509*
  automotive industry, 381, *502*, 502
  banking, *53*
  business, *32*, *382*
  construction, 200
  customer support, 118
  decision support, 373–374, *406–407*
  design, *34*
  desktop publishing, 279
  education, *36*, 503–504
  engineering, *136*
  entertainment, *33*, *360–362*, 504–507, *505*, *506*
  environment, 14, *37*
  geographic, *117*, 342–343
  government, 11, *37*
  home and personal use, 500–502, *501*
  hotel industry, 20–25, *363*
  insurance, 375
  law, *406*
  leisure activities, 504–507, *505*, *506*
  mapping, 342–343, *343*, 407
  medical, 11, *37*, 507–510, *510*, 511
  movie and film, *505*, 505–506
  music, 506–507
  personnel, 49–55, *50–51*
  photography, 41, 119, *172*, 507, *509*
  publishing, 277–279
  real estate, 54–55
  sales, 6, *32*, 148–149, 307
  science, 507–508
  sports, 504–505, *505*
  stock market, *184*, 228, 385
  telecommunications, *178*, 179–185
  teledemocracy, 26
  travel and tourism, *361*
Applications generators, 434
Applications package, 415, 434
Applications programming interface (API), 231
Applications software, 48
Applications software development, 414. *See also* Program development
Arby's, 342
Architecture applications, *379*, *408–409*
Arithmetic/logic unit (ALU), *66*, 67–68
Arithmetic operations, 67
Art applications, *31*, *35*, 167–173, *410–411*, 505–507, *506*, *508*, *509*
Artificial intelligence (AI)
  definition of, 381
  expert systems, *384*, 384–385
  natural languages, 382–383
  neural-net computing, *384*, 384–385
  robotics, *380*, 383
  vision systems, 383
Artisoft, 199
Ascender, *280*, 280
ASCII, *74*, 74–75
Assemblers, 239
Assembly languages, 425
Association for Computing Machinery (ACM), 500
Associations, computer industry, 500
AST, 452
Asynchronous transmission, *194*, 194–195
AT&T, 195
Atanasoff, John, 517
Atanasoff-Berry Computer (ABC), *517*, 517
ATMs (automatic teller machines), 10
Audits, 494
Authoring software, *358–359*
Autodesk, 452
Automated help desk, 397
Automatic teller machines (ATMs), 10
Automotive industry applications, *381*, *502*, 502

Babbage, Charles, 516
Back-end processor, 207

Backup
definition of, 463
full, 466
partial, 466
reasons for, 466
and removability of secondary storage systems, 95
strategies for, 466
utilities, 241, 242, *243*
Banc One Mortgage, 369
Bar charts, *319,* 320, *321*
Bar code, *150,* 150–151
Baseband networks, 200
Baseline, *280,* 280
BASIC, 230, 238, 334, 347, 425–426, *426, 436,* 438
Batch processing, 53–54
Benchmark test, 394–395
Berry, Clifford, 517
Beta testing, *441,* 441–442
Bibliographic databases, 275
Bidirectional printing, 144
Binary, definition of, 71, A3
Binary-based code, 74–75
Binary numbering system, 71–74, *72, 73,* A2, A3–A4
Binary-to-decimal conversion, A3, *A4,* A9
Biometric security devices, 492–493, *493*
Biotechnology, 85
Bit, 72
Bit-mapped fonts, 282, *284*
Bit mapping, 136–137
Bits per second (bps), 190
Block marking, 262, *263*
Body-copy typeface, 280
Books, for education and training, 474
Bookshelf (Microsoft), *275,* 275
Border, 254
Borland International, *432,* 442, 450–453
Boston Computer Society, 474
Bps (bits per second), 190
Bricklin, Dan, 297
Bridges, 203
Broadband networks, 200
Brother, 451
Buffer, 195
Bulletin boards. *See* Electronic bulletin boards
Burnout, 483
Bus, 82–83, *83*
Business applications, *32*
Business systems
artificial intelligence, *384*
information systems, *386*
transaction processing systems, *370, 372*
Bus networks, *204,* 204
Buying
microcomputer hardware, *464,* 464–465
microcomputer software, *462,* 462–463
Byte, 75
Byte, 474

C (language), 334, 347, *430,* 430–431
C + +, 431, *432*
Cache card, 82
Cache disk, 108–109
CAD systems. *See* Computer-aided design (CAD)
Calculations, in DBMS, 341
Callback devices, 494
CAM. *See* Computer-aided manufacturing (CAM)
Canon, 451, 452
Carpal tunnel syndrome, 484–485
Cars, computerized, *502,* 502
Cartridge disks, *106,* 107
Cartridge tapes, *112,* 112, *113*
CASE. *See* Computer-aided software engineering (CASE)
Case control structure, 421
Cathode-ray tube (CRT), *133,* 134
CBXs (computerized branch exchanges), 202
CD-ROM (Compact Disk/Read-Only Memory), 115, 474
CDs. *See* Compact disks (CDs)
Cell, 297
Cell address, 297
Cell pointer, 301
Cell stations, 185
Cellular phones, 183–184, *185,* 185
Census, 516
Centering, in word processing, 265
Central processing unit (CPU)
add-in boards, 81, 82
arithmetic/logic unit (ALU) in, *66,* 67–68
ASCII and, 74–75
binary systems and, 71–74, *72, 73*
chips, 77–80, *79,* 84–85
circuits in, 84–85
components of, *66,* 67–71
control unit in, 68
data and program representation in, 71–77
definition of, 8, 40
EBCDIC and, 74–75
I/O bus, 82–83, *83*
functions of, *66,* 67–71
machine cycles of, 70–71, *71*
machine language and, 77
memory and, 68
and parallel processing, 86
parity bit and, 75–76
ports, 81–82
RAM, 80–81
reduced instruction set computing (RISC), 85–86
registers and, 68–70
ROM (read-only memory), 81
specialized processor chips, 80
speed of, increasing, 84–86
system unit, 77–83, *78, 79*
Centronics interface, 194
CGA (Color Graphics Adapter), 137
Champion Products, 6
Character addressable, 136
Characters per second, 145
Charts. *See* Presentation graphics
Chase Manhattan Bank, 385
Check box, *253,* 254
Checklists, 389
Chief information officer (CIO), 383
Chips. *See* CPU chips
CIM. *See* Computer-integrated manufacturing (CIM)
CIO (chief information officer), 383
Circuit City, 452
Claris, 285
Classes, 473–474. *See also* Education and training
Click, 254
Client, definition of, 198
Client-server LANs, 198
Clip art, 283, *284*
Clip-art libraries, *284*
Clipboard, 254
Clock, 376
system clock, 70
Close box, 254
Clubs, 474
Clustered bar chart, 319, 320
Coaxial cable, 186
COBOL, 230, 238, 334, 347, 426–429, *427–428,* 438, 520
Coca-Cola, 343
Code generators, 424
Coding, 437
standards, 438
Color display devices, *133,* 134
Color Graphics Adapter (CGA), 137
Color Tile, Inc., *397,* 397
COM (computer output microfilm), 161
Command buttons, *252,* 254
Command language, 223
Command-language translator, 223
Commodore, 452
Common carriers, 195

Communications interface, 25
Communications management devices, *206*, 206–207
Communications media, 185–189, *187*, *188*. *See also* Telecommunications
  definition of, 185
Communications satellites, *188*, 188
Communications software, 49
Communications systems, 7, 177–207
Compact disks (CDs), 7, 95–96
  photo, *119*
Compaq computers, 16, 452, 458
Compilers, 238, *240*
CompuServe, 26, 183, 195, 196–197
Computer-aided design (CAD)
  definition of, 378
  examples of, *34*, *136*, 136, *379*
  in 1990s workplace, 7
  purpose of, 49, 378–379
Computer-aided manufacturing (CAM), 379–380
Computer-aided software engineering (CASE), 49, 441–442, *443*
Computer animation, *410–411*, *506*, 506
Computer applications. *See* Applications
Computer arithmetic, A8–A9
Computer art, 167–173. *See also* Art applications
Computer-assisted diagnosis, 508, *510*
Computer-assisted tomography, 509
Computer Associates, 452
Computer chips. *See* CPU chips
"Computer Chronicles, The," 474
Computer conferencing, 182, *378*
Computer crime
  definition of, 488
  prevention of, 492–494, *493*
  types of, 488–492
Computer graphics. *See* Graphics
Computer-integrated manufacturing (CIM), 380–381, *381*
Computerized branch exchanges (CBXs), 202
Computerized life-support systems, 509
Computerland, 452
Computer operations personnel, 13, *22*
Computer output microfilm (COM), 161
Computer storage, 10–12
Computer stores, 452–455, *454*
Computer systems
  definition of, 8
  maintenance of, 467–486
  in microcomputer marketplace, 450–455
  operation of, 461–466
  repairs, 469–471, *470*
  selection of, 455–465
  and surge suppression, *467*, 467–468
  troubleshooting, 469
  types of, 15–20
  upgrading of, 471–473
Computer teleconferencing, 377, *378*
Computer virus, 489, 490–491
Computers. *See also* Applications; Computer systems; Hardware; Microcomputers; Peripheral equipment; Software
  benefits of, 14
  components and basic functions of, 7–13
  definition of, 8, 40
  effectiveness of, 14
  efficiency of, 14
  ergonomics-related concerns, 483–486, *486*, *487*
  and ethical issues, 497–500
  and health, 482–488
  history of, 515–523
  mainframes, 19–20, *20*
  microcomputers, 15–17, *16*
  minicomputers, *17*, 17–18
  in 1990s workplace, 4–7
  and privacy, 494–497
  reduced instruction set computing (RISC), 85–86
  selection of, 455–465
  size categories of, 15–20
  and societal issues, 25–26
  speeds of, 70–71, 84–86
  and stress-related concerns, 482–483
  supercomputers, 20, *21*, *87*, 87
Concentrators, 207
Concurrent-processor board, 82
Conferencing. *See* Computer conferencing; Teleconferencing
Connector symbol, *418*, 418, *419*, *420*
Conner, 451
Context-sensitive help, 254
Control-break reporting, 52
Control Data, 451
Control-menu icon, 254
Control panel, 254, *300*, 300
Control structures, in program flowcharts, 421
Control unit, 68
Conversion to and from binary-based forms, A3–A4, *A4*
Coprocessing, 80, 228
Coprocessor board, 82
Copying
  in spreadsheets, 308–313, *310–311*
  in word processing, 262
Corel Draw!, 285
Corner, definition of, 254
Cottage industries, 503
Counterfeiting, 492
Courier typeface, *266*
CPU. *See* Central processing unit (CPU)
CPU chips, 22, 77–80, *79*, 84–85, 451, 521–522, *522*
Cray supercomputer, *21*, 86
Credit-risk assessment, 385
Crime. *See* Computer crime
Crime analysis, *384*, 385
Crosshair cursor, *156*, 156
CRT (cathode-ray tube), 134, 468
CSMA/CD, 205
Current cell, 300
Cursor, 133, 300
Cursor movement, 261
Customer support applications, 118
Cylinder concept, 104
Cyrix, 451

Daisywheel printers, *138*, 138, 143
DAs. *See* Desk accessories (DAs)
Data
  definition of, 8–9
  organizing, 46–48
  representation of, 71–77
Data access, 116
Database administrators (DBAs), 344
Database environment, *335*
Database management system (DBMS)
  advantages and disadvantages of, 347–348
  calculations in, 341
  conversion effort for, 348
  creation of data in, 337–338
  data definition in, 335, *336*
  data manipulation in, 335, 337–341
  definition of, 6, 23, 332
  examples of, 332–334, *333*
  file maintenance in, 338
  and geographic information systems, 342–343, *343*
  hardware for, 348
  and hierarchical databases, 342–344, *345*
  information retrieval in, 338–339, *339*
  interacting with, 334–335, *335*
  on large computers, 342–347
  on microcomputers, 23–24, 332–341
  and network databases, 342–344, *345*
  in 1990s workplace, 6
  processing data on, 346–347
  programming language facility of, 334, 335
  purpose of, 49

Database management system *continued*
and relational DBMS, *333, 345*
reporting in, 341, *344*
retrieval/update facility of, 334, *335*
selection criteria for, 463
setting up, 346
software for, 348
sorting in, 341
Structured Query Language in, 338–339, *340*
training, 348
utility programs of, *335*, 335
Databases
bibliographic, 275
definition of, 47, 332
object-oriented, *349*, 349
relational, 332, *333*
Data compression programs, 241
Data definition, in DBMS, 335, *336*
Data definition languages (DDLs), 346
Data dictionaries, 337, 438
Data diddling, 488
Data distribution facility, in spreadsheets, 315
Data flow diagram, 389, *392*
Data leakage, 490
Data management, in spreadsheets, 314–315. *See also* Database management system (DBMS); Multimedia data management
Data manipulation, in DBMS, 335, 337–341
Data manipulation language (DML), 347
Data movement time, 104
Data organization
definition of, 116
direct, 123
indexed-sequential, 120–123, *122*
overview of, 46–48, *47, 48*
in secondary storage, 118, 120–124
sequential, *120–121*, 120, 123
Data processing area, 385, *386*
Data Processing Management Association (DPMA), 500
Data storage, 114–115
DBAs (database administrators), 344
dBASE, 238, 451, 453
DBMS. *See* Database management system (DBMS)
DDLs (data definition languages), 346
Debugging, 438–439
DEC (Digital Equipment Corporation), 521
Decimal-hexadecimal conversion, A7, *A8, A9*
Decimal numbering system, A2, *A3*
Decimal-to-binary conversion, A7, *A8, A9*
Decision support system (DSS)
definition of, 373
example of, *374, 406*
and executive information system, 373–374, *375*
fourth-generation languages in, 434
and group decision support system, 373, 375
tools, 376, 435
Decision symbol, 417, *418, 419, 420*
Dedicated packages, for presentation graphics, *323*, 323
Defaults, 223
Deleting
in spreadsheets, 308
in word processing, 261–262
Dell, 452, 458
DeLorme Mapping, 115–116, *117*
Demodulation, 191
Density, of diskettes, 98
Descender, *280*, 280
Design. *See* Computer-aided design (CAD); Program design
Desk accessories (DAs), 49, 241, 254, *376*, 376
Desktop (GUI applications), *224*, 254
Desktop computers, 15, *16*, 71
Desktop organizers, *376*, 376
Desktop publishing
applications for, 279
clip-art libraries for, 283, *284*
compared with word processing, 277–278
components of, 278–285
definition of, 7, 277–278, *278*
fonts available for, 282, *284*
graphics-oriented monitor for, 281, *282*
hardware for, 278–282
high-end microcomputer for, 278–279, *285*
illustration software for, 283–285, *285*, 292
laser printer for, 279–280
in 1990s workplace, 7
page layout in, *290*
page-makeup software for, 282, *283*
photographs used in, *293*
purpose of, 49, 260
software for, 282–285
step-by-step approach to, *289–293*
typefaces used in, *291*
Desktop teleconferencing tools, 378
Detachable-reel tapes, *45*, 45, 111, *113*
Device drivers, 242, 245–246
Dialog box, *253*, 254
Difference engine, *516*
Digital Equipment Corporation (DEC), 521
Digital transmission, 190–191, *191*, 192–193
Digitizers, 133, 153–156, *156*
Digitizing tablet, *156*, 156
Direct access, 95
Direct Access Storage Subsystem (IBM), 109
Direct organization, 123
Disk access time, 103–104
Disk
address, 96
controller, 106
controller card, 82
cylinders, 103, *104*
drive, 22, *100*, 100, 101
drive doors, *101*
emulation, 108
optimizers, 241, 242
pack, 101
systems, 451
toolkits, 241, 242
units, *44*, 44, 100
utilities, 241–242
Diskettes
care of, 100, 468
definition of, 22–23, 96, 97
formatting of, 98, *99*, 100
inserting into drive, *100*, 100
maintenance of, 468
product information on, 451–452
sectoring on, 98, *99*, 100
size of, 97–98, *98, 99*
storage capacities of, 98
surface of, *97*, 97
types of, *45*, 45, 97–98, *98, 99*
using, *100*, 100
write-protect notch on, 98, *99*
Diskette units, *22*, 22–23, *44*, 44
Display adapter board, 81, 82
Display devices. *See also* Monitors
and bit mapping, 136–137
CRT (cathode-ray tube), *133*, 134
definition of, 132
and ergonomics-related concerns, 483–484
flat-panel, *133*, 134, 135
graphics standards for, 137–138
of microcomputer systems, *22*
monochrome versus color, *133*, 134
as output device, *43*, 43, 132–133
resolution of, 135
text versus graphics in, 135–138
types of, 132–138
Display terminal, *43*, 43, 132
Display typeface, 280
Distributed transaction processing, *178*, 179–180
DML (data manipulation language), 347
Docking stations, 450, *451*, 451

Documentation, 439–440
Document-management utilities, 242, 244
DOS, 229, 450, 456
DOS commands, *231*
Dot-matrix characters, *135, 138, 139, 140*
Dot-matrix mechanisms, *138–140,* 139–141
Double-density diskettes, 98
DOUNTIL control structure, 421, 422
DOWHILE control structure, 421, 422
Dow Jones News/Retrieval, 183, 203
Downloading, 202
Draft-quality printing, 141
Drawing packages, 284
Drive. *See* Disk
Drop-down list box, 255
Drum plotters, 159, *160*
DSS. *See* Decision support system (DSS)
Dun & Bradstreet, 183
Dunkin' Donuts, 432
Duplexing, 196–197
Dupont, 181
Dvorak keyboard, 132

EBCDIC, *74,* 74–75, *114*
E-cycle, 70, *71*
EDI. *See* Electronic data interchange (EDI)
E-disk, 108
Editing
  in spreadsheets, 308–314, *310–312*
  in word processors, 260–263
Education and training. *See also* End-user development
  applications, *36*
  books for, 474
  classes, 473–474
  clubs, 474
  computers in, 504
  curricula, 503
  electronic media, 474
  for end users, 473–474
  multimedia data management in, *350, 363*
  periodicals, 474, *475*
  shows, 474
Education applications, *36,* 503–504
Education Privacy Act (1974), 495
Effectiveness, 14
Efficiency, 14
EFT (electronic funds transfer), 502
EGA (Enhanced Graphics Adapter), 137
Egghead Software, 452–453, *454*

EIS. *See* Executive information system (EIS)
EISA (Enhanced Industry Standard Architecture), 83
Electrical gadgets, 500
Electromechanical machines, 516
Electronic bulletin boards, 26, 181–182
Electronic data interchange (EDI), *180,* 180–181
Electronic disk, 108
Electronic document handling, *136,* 136–137, 377
Electronic funds transfer (EFT), 502
Electronic mail (E-mail), 58, *199,* 201, 374, 495
Electronic mailboxes, *181,* 181, 376
Electronic spreadsheets, *296,* 297. *See also* Spreadsheets
Electronic synthesizers, 506–507
Electrostatic plotters, 159, *160*
Electrothermal printing, 141, 143
E-mail. *See* Electronic mail (E-mail)
Embedded formatting codes, *267,* 267
Embedded typesetting codes, 275
Emulator board, 82
Encryption, 493–494
End user
  definition of, 13
  profile of, 22–25
End-user development
  and backups, 462–463, 466
  definition of, 398
  and disk care, 468
  education and training, 473–474
  and maintenance of resources, 467–468
  and microcomputer marketplace, 450–455
  and operating a computer system, 461–471
  and repairs, 469–471, *470*
  and selection of computer system, 455–465
  and surge suppression, *467,* 467–468
  and troubleshooting, 469
  and upgrading, 471–473
Fnhanced Graphics Adapter (EGA), 137
Enhanced Industry Standard Architecture (EISA), 83
Enhanced small device interface (ESDI) standard, 106
ENIAC, 517, 518
Entertainment applications, *33, 360–362,* 504–507, *505, 506*
Environmental applications, 14, *37*

Environment-related concerns, 486–487
EPROM (erasable programmable read-only memory), 81
Epson, 451
Ergonomics, 483–486, *486, 487*
Ernst & Young, 442
ESDI (enhanced small device interface) standard, 106
Ethernet, 200
Ethics, 497–500
Even-parity systems, 76
Excel (Microsoft), 297, 453
Executive, 235
Executive information system (EIS), 373–374, *375*
Expansion slots, 81
Expert systems, 381–382, 397
Exploded pie charts, *319,* 320, *322*
Extended VGA (XVGA), 137
Extender utilities, 242
External commands, 241
External hard-disk system, 102
External storage. *See* Secondary (external) storage
Extra-density diskettes, 98
Exxon Valdez oil spill, *37,* 342

Facsimile (fax) machines, *182,* 182–183, 374
Fair Credit Reporting Act (1970), 495
Fault-tolerant computing, 228
Fax board, 81, 82, 183
Fax machines, *182,* 182–183, 374
Fax servers, 198
Feasibility study, 389
Federal Express, 343, 455
Fiber optic cable, *186,* 186–187, 193
Fidelity Investments, 232, 385
Field, definition of, 46, *47*
Field descriptor, 337, 338
File
  definition of, 46, *47*
  directory, 100
  maintenance, in DBMS, 338
  managers, 334
  servers, 198
  structure, in DBMS, 337
  transfer utilities, 242
Film recorders, 161
Films. *See* Movies
Firmware, 81
First generation of computers, 518–520
Fixed-media secondary storage systems, 95
Flash memory, 68, 69
Flatbed plotters, 159, *160*

Flat-panel display, *133,* 134, 135
FlightLink, 135
Floppy disks, 22–23, 97–100
Floptical disk, *107,* 107
Flowcharts, 416–421, *418–420*
Flowlines, 417, *418, 419*
Folio, 280
Font libraries, 276
Font manager, 255
Fonts, 144, 265, *266,* 280, 282, *284,* 284
Footers, in word processing, 265
Footnoting, in word processing, 269
Ford Motor Company, 154
Formatting codes, embedded, 267
Formatting diskettes, 98–100, *99*
Formulas, in spreadsheets, 302, 305
FORTRAN, 230, *431,* 431–432
Fourth generation of computers, 522–523
Fourth-generation languages (4GLs) 434–435, 438
Freedom of Information Act (1970), 495
Freehand, 285
Freelance Graphics, 324
Front-end processors, 207
Fujitsu, 451
Full backup, 466
Full-duplex transmission, 190
Full justification, 264
Functionality, 459
Functionally obsolete, 473
Function keys, 131–132
Functions, in spreadsheets, 305, 306

GaAs (gallium arsenide) chips, *84,* 84–85
Gantt chart, 320, *321*
Gates, Bill, 230, *523*
Gateway Computers, 452
Gateways, 203
GB. *See* Gigabyte (GB)
G-byte. *See* Gigabyte (GB)
GDSS. *See* Group decision support system (GDSS)
General ledger (G/L) systems, 371, *372*
General Motors, 181
General-purpose word processing packages, 260
GEnie, 183, 195
Geodemographics, 497
Geographic information systems (GISs), 342–343, *343*
Geometric symbols, in program flowcharts, 416, *418*
GeoREF, 342
Geosynchronous orbit, 188
Gigabyte (GB), 75, 115
GISs. *See* Geographic information systems (GISs)
Global positioning systems (GPSs), 188, 189
G/L systems. *See* General ledger (G/L) systems
Go (execution) stage, 239, *240*
Government applications, 11, *37*
GPSs. *See* Global positioning systems (GPSs)
Grammar checkers. *See* Style/grammar checkers
Graphical command interfaces, 270–271
Graphical user interfaces (GUIs), 223, 224, *251–253,* 262, 270–271
  in DBMS, *340*
  glossary, 254–255
  in spreadsheets, 308, *309*
Graphic coprocessor, 80
Graphics. *See also* Presentation graphics
  applications of, *136,* 136
  bit mapping and, 136–137
  in DBMS, *341*
  standards for, *137,* 137–138
  techniques and applications of, *403–411*
  versus text on display devices, 135–138
  in word processors, 270–271, *271,* 275
Graphics adapter board, 82
Graphics generators, 434, 435
Graphics-oriented monitor, 281, 282
Greeking, 280
GRiD, 476
Group decision support system (GDSS), 373, 375
Grouped bar chart, *319,* 320, *321*
GUIs. *See* Graphical user interfaces (GUIs)

Hacking, 491
Half-duplex transmission, 190
Halftoning, 281
Hand-held computers, *16,* 17, 18–19, *19*
Handicap, people and computers, 509–511
Handshaking, 205
Handwriting recognition device, 154, 158, 384–385
Hanging indent, 264
Hard copy, 130
Hard disks, *45*
  access mechanism for, *102,* 103–104
  and access time, 103–104
  cylinders, 103, *104*
  definition of, 96
  external system, 102
  internal system, 102
  for large computers, *45, 108, 109,* 109–111
  partitioning of, 105–106
  reading and writing data on, 102–103, *103, 104*
  sectoring of, 104
  for small computers, *45,* 101–106, *102*
  standards for, 106
  subdirectories on, 104–105, *105*
Hard disk units, *22,* 23, *44,* 44, *102*
Hard return, 261
Hardware. *See also* Central processing unit (CPU); Computers; Microcomputers
  communications management devices, 206–207
  definition of, 12
  for desktop publishing, 278–282
  peripheral equipment, 40, 42–46
  product information on, 450–455
  sales and distribution of, 452–455, *454*
  selection criteria for, 459–461, 462–463, *464,* 464–465
  upgrading of, 471
  used, 455
Harley-Davidson Inc., 307
Harvard Graphics, 324
Hashing algorithms, 123, *124*
Hayes, 452
Head crash, 103
Headers, snd word processing, 265
Health concerns, 482–488
Helical-scan recording, 112
Helvetica typeface, *266*
Hewlett-Packard, 280, 451, 452
Hexadecimal numbering systems, A4–A8, *A6–A8*
Hexadecimal-to-decimal conversion, A5, A7, *A7, A9*
Hierarchical databases, 342–344, *345*
Hierarchical local networks, 198, 202
High-density diskettes, 98
High-level languages, 425–434, *426–431*
Highlight, spreadsheet, 301
History of computers
  ABC (Atanasoff-Berry Computer), *517*
  Babbage, Charles and his engines, 516

ENIAC, *517*
first generation, *518,* 518, *519*
fourth generation, 522, *522–523*
Hollerith and the census, *516*
Jacquard loom, 507
microcomputers, *522–523*
punched cards, *518–519*
second generation, *520*
from 17th century to 1950s, 516, *516–517*
third generation, *521*
UNIVAC I, *518*
Hollerith, Herman, *516*
Home banking and shopping, 502
Homes, computerized, 502
Home uses of computers, 501–503
Hopper, Grace, *520*
Host languages, 347
Hotel industry applications, 20–25, 363

IBM-compatible computers, 80, 106, 251, 450, 456
IBM computers, 15, *16, 20,* 46, 80, 81, 83, 102, 104, 106, *109,* 112, *131,* 131, 137, 194, 221, 230, 233–234, 516
IBM Corporation, 198, 222, 230, 234, 241, 251, 369, 440, 450–453, *516*
IBM ES/9000 mainframe, *20*
IBM System/360, *521*
IC. *See* Information center (IC)
Iceberg 9200 Disk Array Subsystem, *109,* 110
Icons, 153, 255
I-cycle, 70, *71*
IDE (integrated drive electronics) standard, 106
Illustration software, 283, *285, 292*
Illustrator, (Adobe) 285
Image recognition, 384–385
Image scanners, 150–151, *151,* 282
Imagesetting, 277
Imaging applications, 41
Impact dot-matrix mechanism, *139,* 139–141, *140,* 143
Impact printing, 138–141, *143*
Improv (Lotus), 317, *318*
Indenting, in word processing, 264
Indexed-sequential organization, 120, *122,* 123
Index preparation, in word processing, 274
Index Technology, 452
Industry Standard Architecture (ISA), 83
Information, definition of, 9
Information center (IC), *386,* 386
Information center (IC) consultants, 386
Information processing, 49–58, *50–51*
definition of, 9
Information reporting system, 372
Information retrieval, *50–51,* 52–55
in DBMS, 338, *339,* 339
subscription-based services for, 183, *184*
Information superhighway, 501
Information systems, 372–374
definition of, 371–372
Information systems department, 384–387, *386*
Information utilities, 26, 183, *184*
Infoworld, 458, 475
Inheritance, 433
INITs (initializing utilities), 241
Ink-jet printers, 143
Input, 7, 12, 56
Input devices, 56, *58*
definition of, 7, 42, 130
digitizers, 153–156
handwriting recognition devices, 158
image scanners, 150–151, *151*
keyboards, *42,* 42, 131–132
magnetic ink character recognition (MICR), 151–152, *152*
mouse, *42,* 42–43
optical character recognition, 146–147, 150
scanners, 56, *58*
smart cards, *158,* 158–159
source data automation, 146–159
voice-input devices, 157
Input/output (I/O) media, 8, *45,* 94
Input/output symbol, *418,* 418, 419, 420
Input spooling area, 244
Inserting
in spreadsheets, 308, *310*
in word processing, 261–262
Instruction register, 69
Instruction set, 85–86
Insurance applications, 375
Intangible benefits, 394
Integrated drive electronics (IDE) standard, 106
Integrated services digital network (ISDN), 192
Integrated software packages, 297, 298
Intel, 451, 452, *522*
Intel chips, 78, *79,* 80, 198, 221, 222, 235, 279, 451, *522,* A7
Intelligent graphics, 324–325
Interleaved processing techniques, 224, 225–228
Internal hard-disk system, *102,* 102
Internal storage. *See* Memory; Primary (internal) storage
International systems, 390–391, *391*
Internet Access, 183
Inter-organizational systems (IOSs), 180
Interpreters, 239
Inventory control systems, 371, *372*
I/O bus, 82–83, *83*
I/O media. *See* Input/output (I/O) media
IOSs (inter-organizational systems), 180
ISA (Industry Standard Architecture), 83
ISDN (integrated services digital network), 192
Issuance, *50–51,* 52
Iteration (looping control structure), *420,* 421, 422

Jacquard loom, 507
Japan
national technology policy in, 484–485
U.S. software in, 453
Jobs, Steve, *523*
Job-control language (JCL), 223
Joystick, 155, *156*
Justifying, in word processing, 264

Kapor, Mitch, *523*
KB. *See* Kilobyte (KB)
K-byte. *See* Kilobyte (KB)
Kernel, 221
Kerning, 281
Keyboards
characteristics of, 131–132
definition of, 131
diagram of, *131*
and ergonomics-related concerns, 484–485, *486*
as input devices, *42,* 42
of microcomputer system, *22*
selection criteria for, 465
Keyboard utilities, 242
Key field, 114–115
Keypunch machine, *519*
Kilobyte (KB), 75
Kiosks, multimedia, *10,* 10–11, *36,* 148, *155*
Kodak, and photo CDs, 119

Label, in spreadsheets, 301, 304
Label-prefix characters, 304
Language interface, *224*

Languages. *See* Programming languages; names of specific programming languages
Language translators, *77,* 238
LANs. *See* Local area networks (LANs)
LANtastic, 199
Laptop computers, 6, 7, *16*
Laser printers, *142,* 143, 144, 279–280
LCD (liquid crystal display), 134
Leading, 281
Left justification, 264
Leisure applications, 504–507, *505, 506*
Letter-quality printers, 138
Lexis, 183
Light pen, 153–155
Line charts, *319,* 321, *322,* 323
Line printers, *144,* 145
Line return, in word processing, 261, *262*
Linesize box, 255
Line spacing, in word processing, 263
Linkage editor, 239, *240*
Liquid crystal display (LCD), 134
LISP, 434
List box, 255
L.L. Bean, and photo CDs, 119
Load module, 239
Local area networks (LANs), 198–203, *199,* 204
  wireless, 202–203
Logic bombs, 489
Logical operations, 67
Logic-seeking devices, for printers, 144
Logo, 433
Looping (iteration) control structure, *420,* 421, 422
Lotus 1-2-3, 297, 298, 317, 434, 450–453
Lotus Development Corporation, 244, 317, *376,* 434, 450, 452
Lotus products
  1-2-3, 297, *309*
  Improv, 317, *318*
  Magellan, *244*
  Notes, *251,* 450
  SmartSuite, *298,* 298
Low-density diskettes, 98
Low-level languages, 425

MacConnection, *454*
Machine cycles, 70–71, *71*
Machine language, 70, 77, 238
Machine-readable, 8
Macintosh computers. *See* Apple computers
Macintosh System Software, 231, *234*
Macros, 273
  in spreadsheets, *315,* 315–316
MacWorld, 474, *475*
Magellan (Lotus), 244
Magnetic cores, *520,* 520
Magnetic disks
  cache, 108–109
  cartridge, *106,* 107
  definition of, 96
  diskettes, 96, 97–100
  hard, 96
  for large computers, *108, 109,* 109–111
  RAM, 108
  removable-pack units, *108,* 109
  sealed-pack, *109,* 109
  for small computers, 101–106, *102*
Magnetic disk units, *44,* 44
Magnetic ink character recognition (MICR), 146, 151–152, *152*
Magnetic tape
  cartridge, *45,* 45, *112,* 112
  definition of, 111
  detachable-reel, 111
  and processing, *113,* 113–114
  storing data on, *114,* 114–115
  types of, *111,* 111–112, *112*
Magneto-optical (MO) disks, 115
Mail. *See* Electronic mail (E-mail)
Mailing list program, 271
Mail merge program, 271
Mail-order firms, *392, 454,* 455
Mail servers, 198
Mainframes, 19–22, *20*
Main memory, 68, 80
Main menu, in spreadsheets, 307, *308*
Mainstay, 491
Maintenance
  contracts, 471
  definition of, 439
  and disk care, 100, 468
  and dust, 468
  and heat, 468
  of microcomputer systems, 467–468
  of monitors, 468
  of printers, 468
  of programs, 439
  and static, 468
  and surge suppression, *467,* 467–468
Maintenance contracts, 471
Manufacturing. *See* Computer-aided manufacturing (CAM); Computer-integrated manufacturing (CIM)
Mapping applications, *117,* 342–343, *343, 407*
Mark I, *517,* 517
Marketing databases, 496–497
Marriott, *363*
Massively parallel processing (MPP), 87
Master file, 47, 120
Math coprocessor chip, 80
MB. *See* Megabyte (MB)
M-byte. *See* Megabyte (MB)
McDraw, 285
MCGA (Multi-color Graphics Array), 137
MCI, 195
McPaint, 285
MDA (Monochrome Display Adapter), 137
Mead Corporation, 183
Media, Communications, 183
Media mode, 190
Media signal, 190–193, *191, 192*
Media speed, 190
Medical applications, 11, *37,* 507–510, *510,* 511
Medis, 183
Megabyte (MB), 75
Megahertz (MHz), 71
Memory
  address, 68
  definition of, 10–11, 68
  erasable programmable read-only (EPROM), 81
  flash, 68, *69*
  main, 68
  programmable read-only (PROM), 81
  random access (RAM), 80–81
  read-only (ROM), 81
  size of, 68
  virtual, 227
Memory chips. *See* CPU chips
Memory expansion board, 82
Memory protection, 235
Menu bar, *253,* 255
Menus, *24*
Mervyn's, 87
Mflops, 71
MHz (megahertz), 71
Michelangelo virus, 490–491
MICR. *See* Magnetic ink character recognition (MICR)
Micro. *See* Microcomputers
Micro Channel Architecture, 83
Microcode, 70
Microcomputers
  add-in boards for, 81, *82,* 451
  buses for, 82–83
  buying hardware for, 464–465
  buying software for, 462–463
  cartridge tape for, *112,* 112
  computer and memory chips for, 77–81, 451
  definition of, 15
  diskettes for, 97–100

docking stations for, 450, *451*, 451
for desktop publishing, 278–279
end-user needs for, 461–471
hard disks for, 101–106, *102*
IBM-compatible, 450
LAN technology and, 198–201
mail-order firms for, *454*, 455
maintenance of, 467–468
manufacturers of, 452, 455
modems, for 191–192, 452
monitors for, 132–138, 451
operating systems for, 228–237
printers for, 138–144, 451
product information on, 450–455
retail stores for, 452–455, *454*
sales and distribution of, 452–455, *454*
secondary storage devices for, *44*
software producers and products, 450–451, 452
speeds of, 71
system units for, 77–83, 450
types of, 15–17, *16*
uses of, 22–25, *457*

Microcomputer systems
components of, *22*, 22–25
definition of, 15, *16*

Microfiche card, 161
Microfilm reel, 161
Micromarketers, 496–497
Microprocessor, 22
Microsecond, 70
Microsoft products
Access, 450
Bookshelf, 275, *276*
Excel, 297, 453
MS-DOS, 229
Multimedia Beethoven, *362*
Office, 298
Visual BASIC, 435, *436*
Windows, 222, *226*, 229, *233*, 235, 241, 251, 450, 453, 456
Windows NT, 221, 222, 229, 235–236, *237*
Word, 260, 282, 450
Word for Windows, 270
Works, 298, 450, 453

Microsoft Corporation, 229, 230, 440, 450, 452–453
Microspacing, 269, *272*
Microwaves, 187
Military applications, 189
Millisecond, 70
Minicomputers, *17*, 18
Mips, 71
Mixed replication, in spreadsheets, *311*, 313
Models, in spreadsheets, 305
Modem, *191*, 191, *192*, 196–197
Modem board, 82, *192*
Modem software, 196–197
Modulation, 191
Monitor (or supervisor), 221
Monitors. *See also* Display devices
definition of, 132
for desktop publishing, *282*, 282
for microcomputer system, *22*
multiscan, 138
as output devices, *43*, 43
screen savers for, 468
selection criteria for, 464–465

Monochrome Display Adapter (MDA), 137
Monochrome display devices, *133*, 134
Monospacing, 269
Morphing, *405*
Motherboard, 77–78, *79*
Motorola, 78, 80, 451, 452
Motorola chips, 222, 232, 279
Mouse, *22*, 24, *42*, 42–43, *153*, 153
Movies, computers and the 55, *505*, 505–506
Moving
in spreadsheets, *312*, 313
in word processing, 262

MPP (massively parallel processing), 87
MS-DOS, 229
Multi-color Graphics Array (MCGA), 137
Multidimensional spreadsheets, *316*, 316–317
Multifunction board, 82
Multimedia
definition of, 348
in education, *350*, 503
PCs, *351*

Multimedia Beethoven, *362*
Multimedia data management
and authoring software, 358
education and training uses of, *350*, *363*, 503
entertainment uses of, *360–362*
presentation uses of, *353*, *357–363*
travel and tourism uses of, *361*

Multimedia kiosks, *10*, 10–11, 148, *155*
Multiple-column formatting, in word processing, 268–269
Multiplexers, *206*, 206–207
Multiprocessing, 227–228
Multiprogramming, 225
Multiscan monitors, 138
Multisync monitors, 138
Multitasking, 225, *226*
Multiuser systems, 15
Music applications, *362*

Nanosecond, 71
Narrowband transmission, 190
National Center for Atmospheric Research (NCAR), 507
National Geographic, 499
National technology policy, 484–485
Natural-language interface, 435
Natural languages, 72–73, 382–383, 435–437, *437*
Near-letter-quality (NLQ) printing, 141
NEC, 139, 452
Need, computer, 455
NetWare, 236–237, *238*
NetWare Lite, 199
Network databases, 342–344, *345*
Networks
bus, 204
client-server, 198
local, 198–203
peer-to-peer, 199
ring, 204
star, 203–204
typologies of, 203–204, *204*
wide area, 195–198

Neural-net computing, *384*, 384–385
Newton, Apple 18–19
New Yorker Magazine, The, *279*
NLQ (near-letter-quality) printing, 141
Nonimpact printing, 141, *142*, 143
Nonvolatile storage, 94
Notebook computers. *See* Laptop computers
Notes (Lotus), *251*, 450
Novell, Inc., 199, 236, 452
NuBus, 83
Numbering systems
binary, 71–74, *72*, *73*, A2, A3–A4
computer arithmetic and, A8–A9
decimal, A2–A3
definition of, A2
hexadecimal, A4–A8, *A6–A8*

Numeric constants, in spreadsheets, 305
Numeric keypad, 132
Numeric (math) coprocessor, 80

Object module, 239
Object-oriented databases, *349*, 349
Object-oriented programming language, *432*, 432–433
ObjectVision, *442*
Obsolescence, functional versus technological, 473
OCR. *See* Optical character recognition (OCR)
Odd-parity systems, 76
Office (Microsoft), 298

Office automation (OA), 374
Office automation (OA) area, 384, *386*, 387
Office systems
  decision support tools, 376
  definition of office automation, 374
  desk accessories, *376*, 376
  desktop publishing, 374
  electronic mail, 374–376
  telecommuting, 378
  teleconferencing, *377*, 377, *378*
  word processing, 374
Offline, definition of, 46
Old Town Builders, 303
Olsen, Kenneth, *521*
One-entry-point/one-exit-point rule, 421
Online, definition of, 46
Online help, *253*, 255
Operating environment, 223
Operating systems
  assignment of resources by, 221, 223–224
  definition of, 49, 218
  descriptions of, 228–237
  differences among, 220–221
  functions of, 218–220, *219*, 221–225
  gateway role of, *219*, 219–220
  interleaved processing techniques, 225–228
  monitoring activities by, 224–225
  and partitioning hard disk, 106
  popular samples of, 220–221, 228–237
  scheduling resources and jobs by, 223–224
  32-bit, 222
Operations, computer, 385
Operator documentation, 440
Optical character recognition (OCR), 146–147, 150, 151
Optical characters, *147*, 147, 150
Optical codes, *150*, 150
Optical disks
  applications of, 115–116, *117*, 118
  CD-ROM, 115
  definition of, 115
  fully erasable, 115
  in education, 503
  as input/output media, *45*, 45
  storage capacity of, 115, *116*
  WORM (Write Once, Read Many) disks, 115
Optical disk units, *44*, 44, *116*
Optical jukeboxes, 115
Optical marks, 147
Optical processing, 85
Order-entry systems, 371, *372*
Orphans, in word processing, *274*, 274
OS/2, 221, *222*, 222, 233–235, *236*
Outline fonts, 282, *284*, 284
Output, 58–59. *See also* Graphics; Text
  definition of, 7
  developments in, *167–173*
  as hard copy, 130, 138
  as soft copy, 130
Output devices
  computer output microfilm (COM), 161
  definition of, 7, 42, 130
  display devices, *43*, 43, 132–138, *133*
  film recorders, 161
  plotters, 159, *160*
  printers, *43*, 43, 138–146
  voice-output devices, 159–160
Output spooling areas, 243
Outsourcing, *387*, 387
Overstriking, *140*, 140

PABXs (private automatic branch exchanges), 202
Pack, 101
Packard Bell, 452
Page description language (PDL), 280
Page layout
  in desktop publishing, *290*
  in word processing, 8, 26
PageMaker, 279, 282, *283*, 283, *289*
Page-makeup software, 282, *283*
Page printers, *145*, 145–146
Paginating, in word processing, 265
Paint program, 255, 284
Paintbrush, 285
Palette, 255
Palmtop computers, 17, *26*
Paradox, *344*, 451, 453
Parallel ports, 81–82
Parallel processing, 86, 87, 228
Parallel transmission, *193*, 193–194
Parity, 196–197
Parity bit, 75–76
Partial backup, 466
Partitioning, of hard disk, 105–106
Pascal (language), *429*, 429–430
Password, 492
Payroll systems, 371, *372*
PBXs. *See* Private branch exchanges (PBXs)
PC, 474
PC-DOS, 229
PCL (Printer Command Language), 280
PCs. *See* Personal computers (PCs)
PDAs. *See* Personal digital assistants (PDAs)
PDL (page description language), 280
Peer-to-peer LANs, 199
Pen computing, 154
Pen plotters, 159, *160*
Pentium chips, *79*, 198, 221, 222, 235
Performance monitors, 242
Periodicals, 474, *475*
Peripheral equipment. *See also* specific types of equipment
  classification of, 40
  definition of, 7, 40
  input devices, 42–43, 131–132, 146–159
  input/output (I/O) media, *45*, 45, 132
  online versus offline, 46
  output devices, 42, *43*, 43, 132–146, 159–161
  secondary storage devices, 42, 43–45, *44*, 94
  selection criteria for, 463
Personal computers (PCs). *See also* microcomputers
  definition of, 15
  flash memory for, 69
  multimedia and, *351*
  speeds of, 71
  upgradable, 472
Personal digital assistants (PDAs), 17, 18–19, *19*
Personnel applications, 49–55, *50–51*
Persuasion, 324
Philips, 451
Phone Home, *67*
Photo CDs, *119*, 119
Photographs, in desktop publishing, *293*
Photography applications, 41, 119, *172*, 507, *509*
Photorealism, 172
Phototypesetting, 281
Physical lines, for telecommunications, 185–187
Pica, 281
Picoseconds, 71
Pie charts, *319*, 320, *322*
Pier 1 Imports, and online processing, 46
Pixel, 135
Pixie, 324
PL/1, 347, 432
Platform, 456
Plotters, 159, *160*
Pointer, 24–25, 255, 301
Point-of-sale (POS) system, 147, 148
Point sizes, 265, *266*, *280*, 281
Popular Computing, 474
Portable computers, 15–16
Ports, 81–82
Postal Service, U.S., 157
PostScript, 280, 282

PowerPC, 221, 451
Precompiler, 347
Preliminary investigation, in systems development, 389
Presentation graphics
 bar charts, *319*, 320, *321*
 dedicated packages for, 323–324, *323*
 definition of, 317
 examples of, *136*, 136
 forms of, 317–323, *319*, *321–322*
 intelligent, 324–325
 line charts, *319*, 321, *322*, 323
 multimedia data management and, 351–352, *353*
 in 1990s workplace, 7
 pie charts, *319*, 320, *322*
 purpose of, 49, 317–320
 software for, *323*, 323–325
Presentation Manager, 233
Preview feature, *268*
Primary (internal) storage, 10–11, 68. *See also* Memory
Printer Command Language (PCL), 280
Printers
 comparison of, 143
 definition of, 138–139
 high-speed, 144–146
 impact, *138–140*, 138–141, 143
 for large computers, *144*, *145*, 145–146
 line, *144*, 145
 low-speed, 143–144, 145
 maintenance of, 468
 for microcomputers, 143–144
 nonimpact, 141, *142*, 143
 as output devices, *43*, 43
 page, *145*, 145–146
 selection criteria for, 465
 speed of, 143–146
Print-formatting operations, in word processing, 263–269
Print servers, 198
Print-thimble printers, 138–139, 143
Privacy
 and caller identification, 496–497
 definition of, 494
 and electronic mail, 495–496
 legislation on, 495
 marketing databases and, 496–497
Privacy Act (1974), 495
Private automatic branch exchanges (PABXs), 202
Private branch exchanges (PBXs), 198, 201, 204
Private wide area networks, 197–198
Processing, 56–58. *See also* Information processing
 definition of, 7
 relationship with other computer functions, *12*
Processing symbol, *418–420*, 418
Prodigy, 26, 183, *184*, 195, 196–197, 198, *213–215*
Productivity software, 48, 49, 257–363. *See also* Database management system (DBMS); Desktop publishing; Presentation graphics; Spreadsheets; Word processing
Program coding, 437–438
Program design
 action diagrams, *424*
 control structures in flowcharts, 422
 flowcharts for, *418–420*
 pseudocode, *422–423*, 422
 purpose of, 415–416
 structure charts, *424*
 symbols in flowcharts, *418*, 418
 tools for, 416
Program development
 activities in, 414–415
 and coding, 437–438
 debugging and testing programs, 438–439
 and design, 415–425
 and documentation, 439–440
 and maintenance, 439
 make-or-buy decision and, 415
 quality assurance in, 440–441
Program documentation, 439–440
Program flowcharts, 416, *418–420*
Programmable read-only memory (PROM), 81
Program maintenance, 439
Programmer documentation, 440
Programmers, 13, 22, 415
Programming group, in information systems area, 385
Programming language facility, of DBMS, 334, *335*
Programming languages. *See also* specific languages
 assembly, 425
 definition of, 9–10, 425
 fourth-generation, 434–435
 high-level, 425–434, *426–431*
 low-level, 425
 natural, 435–437, *437*
Programs
 definition of, 8, 9–10
 representation of, 71–77
Program tools, 416
Project management software, *396*
Project manager, 386
Prolog, 434
PROM (programmable read-only memory), 81
Proportional spacing, in word processing, 269
Protocols, 205
Prototyping, 397–398, *398*
Pseudocode, 421–423
Public-access networks, 195
Publishing applications, 277–279
Pull-down menus, *253*, 255
Punched cards, *518*, 518–519

Quadram, 452
Quality assurance, 440–441
Quark Inc., 282
Quark XPress, 282
Quattro, 297, 451
Query. *See also* Information retrieval
 in DBMS, 338–339, *339*
 definition of, 52–53
Queue, 244
Qume, 452
QWERTY keyboard, 132

Radio buttons, *253*, 255
RAID (redundant arrays of inexpensive disks), *109*, 110–111
RAM (random access memory), 80–81, 464
RAM disk, 108
Random access, 95
Random access memory (RAM), 80–81, 464
Range, *303*, 303
Range chart, *319*, 320, *321*
Range concept, in spreadsheets, *303*, 303–304
Read-only memory (ROM), 68, 81
Read/write head, 94, *102*, *103*
Realtime processing, *53*, 54–55
Recalculation feature, of spreadsheets, *301*, 302
Record, definition of, 46, *47*
Recording window, 100
Records, CD-type programming for, 96
Red-green-blue (RGB) types of display devices, 134
Redlining, 274
Reduced instruction set computing (RISC), 85–86
Redundant arrays of inexpensive disks. *See* RAID
Re-engineering, *369*, 369
Reference shelves, 275
Reformatting, in word processing, 265
Registers, 68–70
Relational database management system, 332, *345*

Relational databases, 332, *333*
Relational symbols, in program flowcharts, 416, 418
Relative replication, in spreadsheets, *310*, 310–313
Releases (software), 473
Remainder method, A3
Removable-media secondary storage systems, 95
Removable-pack disk units, *108*, 109
Rensselaer Polytechnic Institute, *350*, 350
Repairs, computer, 469–471, *470*
Replacing text, in word processing, 262–263, *264*
Report generators, 433–434
Reporting, in DBMS, 341, *344*
Request for proposal (RFP), 394
Request for quotation (RFQ), 394
Resolution, of display devices, *135*, 135
Retail computer stores, 452–453, *454*, 455
Retailing applications. *See* Sales applications
Retrieval/update facility, of DBMS, 334, *335*
Retrieval and update languages, 434–435
Reusable code, 433, 438
Reuters, 183
Reverse video, 134
RFP (request for proposal), 394
RFQ (request for quotation), 394
Ring networks, *204*, 204
RISC (reduced instruction set computing), 85–86
RLL (run length limited) standards, 106
Robotics, *380*, 383
ROM (read-only memory), 68, 81
Roman type, 281
Root directory, *105*, 105
Rotational delay, 104
RPG (Report Program Generator), 433
RS-232C (interface), 194
RS-422 (interface), 194
Rule, 281
Run length limited (RLL) standard, 106

SAA (Systems Applications Architecture), 234
Salami shaving, 489
Sales applications, 6, *32*, 148–149, 307
Sales and distribution, in microcomputer marketplace, 452–455, *454*
SAM, 491
Sans serif, 281
Satellites. *See* Communications satellites
Scanner, *58, 150, 151*
Scavenging, 489
Science applications, 507–508
Screen, 281
Screen capture programs, 242
Screen menu, *24*, 24
Screen saver, 242, 468
Script, 281
Scroll arrows, 255
Scroll bars, *253*, 255
Scrolling, 261, 301
SCSI (small computer system interface) standards, 106
SDLC (systems development life cycle), 388
Seagate, 451, 452
Sealed-pack disks, *109*, 109
Sears, 198, 455
Secondary (external) storage
  cache disk, 108–109
  cartridge disk, *106*, 107
  definition of, 11
  floptical disk, *107*, 107
  for large computers, *108, 109*, 109–111
  magnetic disk, 96–111
  magnetic tape, *111*, 111–115
  for microcomputers, *44*
  nonvolatile, 94
  optical disk, 115–116, *116–117*, 118
  physical parts of, 94
  properties of, 94–96
  RAID, *110*, 110–111
  RAM disk, 108
  relationship with other computer functions, *12*
  removable versus nonremovable media, 94–95
  selection criteria for, 464
  sequential versus direct access, 95–96
  for small computers, 101–109, *102*
Secondary storage device, 42, 43–44, *44*
Second generation of computers, 520
Sector, 98
Sectoring
  on diskettes, 98, *99*, 100
  of hard disks, 104
Security procedures, 95, 492–494
Seek time, 104
Selection, *50–51*, 52
Selection (if-then-else) control structure, *420*, 421, 422
Selection of a computer system, 460–461, 462
  criteria for, *458*, 459, 462–463
  alternatives in, 456–459
  needs analysis, 455–456, 457
  software and hardware specifics, 459–460
Sequence control structure, *420*, 421, 422
Sequential access, 95, 115
Sequential organization, 115–118, *120*, 120, 123
Sequential update, 120, *121*
Serial ports, 81–82
Serial transmission, *193*, 193–194
Serif, *280*, 281
Server, definition of, 198
Sharp Travel Organizer, *16*
Shell Oil, 342
Shopping, home, 148, 502
Shows, computer, 474
Silicon chips, 84, 85
Simple networks, 171
Simplex transmission, 190
Simulation, 508
Single in-line memory modules (SIMMs), 81
Single-user systems, 15
Site license, 493
Size box, 255
Size buttons, 255
SkyTel Message Card, *19*
"Slave chips," 80
Small computer system interface (SCSI) standard, 106
Smalltalk, 433
Smart cards, *158*, 158–159
Smart files, 324
SmartSuite (Lotus), *298*, 298
Soft copy, 130
Soft return, 261
Software. *See also* Database management system (DBMS); Desktop publishing; Presentation graphics; Spreadsheets; Word processing
  applications software, 48, 49
  buying, *462*, 462–463
  CPU chips and, 80
  definition of, 12, 48
  evaluations of, 458
  integrated packages, 298
  language translators, 218, 238–239
  major producers and products, 452
  operating systems, 49, 218–238
  package, 12, *13*
  piracy, 491
  productivity software, 48, 49
  programming languages, 425–437
  selection criteria for, *458*, 459

suites, 297, *298,* 298, 451
support, 460–461
systems software, 48–49, 218–246
upgrading of, 471–473
upward compatibility of, 473
utility programs, 218, 240–246
Software Publishing, 452
Solid-font characters, *138*
Solid-font mechanism, 138
Song Stalker, 96
Sony, 18
Sorting, *50–51,* 52
in DBMS, 341
machine, *519*
in spreadsheets, 314–315
in word processing, 274
Source data automation
definition of, 146
digitizers, 153–156
handwriting recognition devices, 158
image scanners, 150–151, *151*
magnetic ink character recognition (MICR), 151–152, *152*
optical character recognition, 146–147, 150
smart cards, *158,* 158–159
voice-input devices, 157
Source module, 239
Spacing, in word processing, *272*
Specialized carrier companies, 195
Specialized processor chips, 80
Speech recognition, 384–385
Spelling checker, 269, *272*
Spooling software, *242,* 242–245, *245*
Sports applications, 504–505, *506*
Spreadsheets
absolute replication in, *311,* 313
advanced features of, 314–317
anatomy of worksheet, 297, *300*
column widths in, 314
commands in, 306, 307
control panel for, *300,* 300
copying in, 308, *310–311*
data management in, 314–315
definition of, 6, 297
deleting in, 308
entering and editing operations, 308, 310–311, *310–312,* 313–314
formatting values in, 313–314
freezing titles in, *312,* 314
functions in, 305, 306
graphical user interfaces (GUIs) in, 308, *309*
inserting in, 308, *310*
as integrated software packages, 297, *298*
intelligent, 324, 325
labels and values in, 304–305
macro facility in, *315,* 315–316
manually prepared and electronic worksheets, *296*
menus in, 307, *308*
on microcomputer system, 23
mixed replication in, *311,* 313
moving in, *312,* 313
multidimensional, *316,* 316–317
in 1990s workplace, 6
principles of operation, 297–308
purpose of, 49
range concept in, *303,* 303–304
recalculation feature of, *301,* 302
relative replication in, *310,* 310–311
screens, *299,* 299–301, *300*
searching in, 315
selection criteria for, 457, 458, 462–463
sorting in, 314–315
templates, *312,* 314
worksheet, creating, 301–302
worksheet area, *300,* 300–301
SQL (Structured Query Language), 338–339, *340*
Stacked bar chart, *319,* 320, *321*
Star networks, 203, *204*
Start/stop symbol, 417, *418, 419*
Steering committee, 383
Stock market applications, 184, 228, 385
Storage, 59. *See also* Memory; Secondary (external) storage
of data on tape, *114*
definition of, 7
primary, 10–11, 68
relationship with other computer functions, *12*
secondary, 11, 42, 43–45, *44,* 94–124
Storage register, 69, 70
StorageTek, *109,* 110, 111
Streaming tapes, 112
Stress-reducing keyboard, 486
Stress-related concerns, 482–483
String search, 244
Structure charts, *424,* 424
Structured programming, *420,* 421
Structured Query Language (SQL), 338–339, *340*
Style (typography), 281
Style/grammar checkers, 270, 275–276, *277*
Style sheet, 275
Subdirectories, 104–105, *105*
Summarizing, *50–51,* 52
Supercomputers, 20, *21,* 87
Superconductors, 85
Superminicomputers, 18
SuperSmart Card, *158*
Super VGA (SVGA), *137,* 137–138
Supervisor program, 221
Superzapping, 489
Support, software, 460–461
Surge suppression, *467,* 467–468
SVGA. *See* Super VGA (SVGA)
Symantec, 452, 491
Synchronous transmission, *194,* 194–195
System. *See also* Computer systems
acquisition, 394
board, 77–78, *79*
clock, 70
definition of, 368, 412
design, in systems development, 390
implementation, in systems development, 395
System unit
definition of, 40, 77, *78*
of microcomputer system, *44,* 450
selection criteria for, 464
Systems analysis, 389
Systems analyst
definition of, 385, 415
role of, 13, 22
Systems Applications Architecture (SAA), 234
Systems development
approaches to, 396–398
definition of, 368
end-user, 398
and information systems department, 384–387
and outsourcing, 387–388
preliminary investigation in, 389
prototyping in, 397–398
responsibility for, 383–388
system acquisition in, 394–395
system analysis in, 389–390
system design in, 390–394
system implementation in, 395
traditional approach to, 396–397
Systems development life cycle (SDLC), 388–395
Systems software
definition of, 48–49, 218
and language translators, 218, 238–239
and operating system, 218–238
and utility programs, 218, 240–246

T1 multiplexers, 207
Table of contents preparation, in word processing, 274
Tandon, 451
Tangible benefits, 394
Tape cartridge, *111*
Tape reel, *111*

Tape units, *44,* 44–45, *112, 113,* 113–114
TB. *See* Terabyte (TB)
T-byte. *See* Terabyte (TB)
Technical workstations, 136
Technologically obsolete, 473
Technology policy, national, 484–485
Telecommunications
  applications in, 178, 179–185
  asynchronous versus synchronous transmission, *194,* 194–195
  cellular phones, 183, *185,* 185
  communications among devices, 205–207
  communications management devices, *206,* 206–207
  communications media, 185–195
  communications satellites, *188,* 188
  definition of, 178
  digital lines, 192–193
  distributed transaction processing, *178,* 179–180
  electronic bulletin boards, 181–182
  electronic mailboxes and voice mail, *181,* 181
  facsimile (fax) machines, *182,* 182–183
  global positioning, 188, 189
  information retrieval, 183
  local networks, 198–203, 199
  media mode, 190
  media signal, 190–193, *191, 192*
  media speed, 190
  microwaves, *187,* 187
  modems for, *191,* 191–192, *192*
  network typologies, 203–204, *204*
  parallel versus serial transmission, *193,* 193–194
  physical lines, 185–187
  protocols for, 205
  simple system, *185,* 185
  strategic alliances, 180–181
  wide area networks, 195–196
Telecommuting, 378
Teleconferencing, 182, *377,* 377, *378*
Teledemocracy, 26
Television, and computers, 501
Templates
  definition of, 314, 335
  in databases, 335–337
  in spreadsheets, *312,* 314
Terabyte (TB), 75
Teraflops computer, 87
Terrestrial microwave stations, *187,* 187
Testing programs, 440–441, 439
Texaco, 342
Text, 135–138
Text box, *253,* 255
Text editor, 242
Thermal-transfer printers, *141,* 141, 143
Thesaurus feature, 270, *273*
Third generation of computers, 521
Thumbnail, 281, 293
Time-sharing, 226–227
Times typeface, *266*
Title bar, 255
Titles, freezing of, in spreadsheets, *312,* 314
Toggle key, 262
Token passing, 205
Token ring, 204
Toolbox, 255
Top-down design, 425
Toshiba, 451, 452
Touch-screen device, *155,* 155
Touchtone Delta MPP supercomputer, 87
Tourism applications, 361
Trackball, *156,* 156
Tracks, 97
Trainers, 386
Training. *See* Education and training; Education applications; End-user development
Transaction file, 47, 120
Transaction processing systems, 370–372, *372*
  definition of, 370
Transistors, *520*
Trapdoors, 489
Travel applications, 361
Trojan horse, 489
Troubleshooting, 469
True-binary representation, 74, A4
TrueType, 282
TRW, 179, 230
TSR (terminate-and-stay-resident), 241
Turbo board, 82
Turner Construction Company, 200
Twisted-pair wires, 185, 186
Typefaces, 265, *266, 291*
Typeover mode, 262
Typesetting, 277
Typesetting codes, embedded, 275
Typography, terminology of, 280–281

UNIVAC I, *518*
Universal product code, (UPC), *150,* 150
UNIX, 221, 222, 232–233, *235*
Updating, *50–51,* 53–55
  automatic, 324, *325*
  sequential, 120, *121*
Upgradable PC, *472,* 472
Upgrade board, 82
Upgrading, 471–473
Uploading, 202
UPS, 343, 455
Used equipment, 455
User. *See* End user
User documentation, 439
User support, 461
U.S. Geographical Survey (USGS), 343
U.S. Postal Service, 157
US Sprint, 195
Utility programs
  of DBMS, *335,* 335
  definition of, 218, 241
  device drivers, 245–246
  disk utilities, 241–242
  spooling software, 242–245, *245*
  types of, 242

Vaccine program, 242, 490
Vacuum tube, 85
Value-added networks (VANs), 195–197
Values, in spreadsheets, 301, 304
Vaporware, 499
VCRs (videocassette recorders), 500
Vendor rating systems, 394, *395*
Vendor support, 460–461
Ventura Publisher, 282
Versions of software, 229, 473
Vertical justification, 281
VGA. *See* Video Graphics Array (VGA)
Video board, 82
Videocassette recorders (VCRs), 500
Video Graphics Array (VGA), *137,* 137–138
Video teleconferencing, *377,* 377
Virex, *490,* 491
Virtual memory, 227
Virtual reality, *33, 54,* 54–55, 149
Virus. *See* Computer virus
VisiCalc, 297
Vision systems, 383
Visual BASIC, 435, *436*
Voice-grade transmission, 190
Voice-input devices, 157
Voice mail, 181
Voice-output devices, 159–160
Voice recognition, 157
Volatile storage, 94
Volatility, of RAM, 81

Waldenbooks, 455
Wal-Mart, 455
Wang, An, *521*
Wang, 201

WANs. *See* Wide area networks (WANs)
Warning box, *252,* 255
Warranty, 470–471
Watson, Tom, *516*
Weather forecasting, 507
Weight (typography), *281,* 281
Weizenbaum, Joseph, 487–488
What-if analysis, 302, 303
Whirlpool, 118
Wide area networks (WANs), 195–198
Wideband transmission, 190
Widows, in word processing, *274,* 274
Winchester disks, 101
Window, 230, *252,* 255
Window area, on spreadsheets, *299,* 300–301
Windows (Microsoft), 222, *226,* 229, *233,* 241, 251, 450, 453, 456
Windows NT, 221, 222, 229, 235–236, *237*
Wireless LANs, 202–203
Wiretapping, 490
Wizzard, 18
Word (Microsoft), 260, 282, 450
Word for Windows, 270
WordPerfect, 260, 270, 282, 451–452
WordPerfect for Windows, 270
Word processing
- add-on packages, 275–276
- advanced operations on, 269–275
- basic procedures, 260–269
- bibliographic databases, 275
- centering in, 265
- compared with desktop publishing, 277–278
- copying in, 262
- definition of, 6, 260
- deleting in, 261–262
- embedded typesetting codes, 275
- entering and editing operations, 260–263
- font libraries, 276
- footnoting, 269
- general operations, 260
- general-purpose versus special-purpose, 260
- graphical, 270–271, *271*
- graphics feature, 275
- headers and footers, 265
- indenting in, 264
- index preparation in, 274
- inserting in, 261–262
- justifying in, 264–265
- learning to use, 260–275
- line return, 261, *262*
- line spacing, adjusting, 263
- macros, 273
- mail merge program, 271–272
- math feature, 272–273
- on microcomputer system, 23
- moving cursor, 261
- moving text, 262
- multiple-column formatting, 268–269
- in 1990s workplace, 6
- orphans and widows, *274,* 274
- page format, establishing, 265
- paginating, 265
- print-formatting operations, 263–269
- proportional spacing, 269, *272*
- purpose of, 49, 260
- redlining in, 274
- reference shelves, 275, *276*
- reformatting in, 265
- replacing in, 262–263, *264*
- scrolling in, 261
- searching in, 262–263, *264*
- selecting typefaces, 265, *266*
- selection criteria for, 457, 462–463
- software for desktop publishing, 282
- sorting in, 274
- spelling checker, 269–270, *272*
- style/grammar checkers, 275–276, *277*
- style sheet, 275
- tabbing, 265
- table of contents preparation, 274
- thesaurus feature, 270–271, *273*
- types of, 260
- WYSIWYG, 266–268, *267, 268,* 270–271

Words (byte multiples), 75, 80
Wordwrap, 261, *262*
Workgroup computing, 200
Workgroup utilities, 242
Workplace
- ergonomics-related concerns, 483–486
- handicapped workers and technology in, 511
- stress-related concerns, 482–483

Works (Microsoft), 298, 450, 453
Worksheet area, *300,* 300
Worksheets, *296, 299,* 301–302
Workspace, design of, 485–486, *487*
WORM (Write Once, Read Many), 115
Wozniak, Steve, *523*
Wright-Patterson Air Force Base, 202
Write-protect notch, 98, *99*
WYSIWYG, 266–268, *267, 268,* 270–271

Xerox Corporation, 19, 200, 282
X-height, *280,* 281
XVGA (extended VGA), 137

Yourdon, Edward, *416,* 416

Zeos, 452
Zoom box, 255
Z-Soft, 285